MUSIC AND SPIRITUALITY

Music and Spirituality

Theological Approaches, Empirical Methods, and Christian Worship

Edited by
George Corbett and Sarah Moerman

https://www.openbookpublishers.com

©2024 George Corbett and Sarah Moerman (eds). Copyright of individual chapters is maintained by the chapter's authors.

This work is licensed under an Attribution-NonCommercial 4.0 International (CC BY-NC 4.0). This license allows you to share, copy, distribute and transmit the text; to adapt the text for non-commercial purposes of the text providing attribution is made to the author (but not in any way that suggests that they endorse you or your use of the work). Attribution should include the following information:

George Corbett and Sarah Moerman (eds), *Music and Spirituality: Theological Approaches, Empirical Methods, and Christian Worship*. Cambridge, UK: Open Book Publishers, 2024, https://doi.org/10.11647/OBP.0403

Copyright and permissions for the reuse of many of the images included in this publication may differ from the above. This information is provided in the captions and in the list of illustrations. Every effort has been made to identify and contact copyright holders and any omission or error will be corrected if notification is made to the publisher.

Further details about CC BY-NC licenses are available at
https://creativecommons.org/licenses/by-nc/4.0/

All external links were active at the time of publication unless otherwise stated and have been archived via the Internet Archive Wayback Machine at https://archive.org/web

Updated digital material and resources associated with this volume are available at https://www.openbookpublishers.com/product/0403#resources

ISBN Paperback: 978-1-80511-302-7
ISBN Hardback: 978-1-80511-303-4
ISBN Digital (PDF): 978-1-80511-304-1
ISBN Digital eBook (EPUB): 978-1-80511-305-8
ISBN HTML: 978-1-80511-307-2

DOI: 10.11647/OBP.0403

Cover image: Hans Memling, *Christ with Singing and Music-Making Angels* (1483–1494), Royal Museum of Fine Arts Antwerp, Wikimedia, https://commons.wikimedia.org/wiki/File:Musicerende_engelen,_Hans_Memling,_(1483-1494),_Koninklijk_Museum_voor_Schone_Kunsten_Antwerpen,_779.jpg
Cover design: Jeevanjot Kaur Nagpa

Contents

Acknowledgments ix

Notes on Contributors xi

Introduction 1
George Corbett and Sarah Moerman

Foreword: A Composer's Perspective 13
James MacMillan

I. THEOLOGICAL APPROACHES 19

1. Encountering the Uncontrollable: Music's Resistance to Reductionism and Its Theological Ramifications 21
Jeremy Begbie

2. Cross and Consolation: Music's Empathic Spirituality 41
Peter C. Bouteneff

3. Music, Breath, and Spirit 55
Michael O'Connor

4. An Adorative Posture towards Music and Spiritual Realities 73
Férdia J. Stone-Davis

5. Religion, Science, and Music: An Augustinian Trinity 87
Bennett Zon

6. Dissonant Spirituality:
A Hermeneutical Aesthetics of Outlaw Country 109
C.M. Howell

II. EMPIRICAL METHODS 137

7. From the Sacred to the Ordinary through the Lens of
   Psychological Science 139
   Yeshaya David M. Greenberg

8. An Inquiry into Musical Trance 159
   Dilara Turan

9. An Ethnomusicology of Spiritual Realities 193
   Jeffers Engelhardt

10. The Concept of 'Atmosphere' as a Bridge between Music and
    Spirituality 209
    Bernard Łukasz Sawicki OSB

11. Spiritual Subjects: Musicking, Biography, *and* the Connections
    We Make 233
    Maeve Louise Heaney VDMF

12. The Impetus to Compose: Where is Fantasy Bred? 255
    Richard E. McGregor

III. CHRISTIAN WORSHIP 271

13. Music in Christian Services as a Means to Induce Religious
    Feelings 273
    Melanie Wald-Fuhrmann

14. Spiritual Cultures: Innovations in Choral and Classical Music 285
    Jonathan Arnold

15. Listening to the Lived Experiences of Worshippers:
    A Study of Post-Pandemic Mixed Ecology Worship 305
    Elspeth Manders

16. An Abductive Study of Digital Worship through the
    Lenses of Netnography and Digital Ecclesiology 327
    Tihomir Lazić

17. Choral Singers and Spiritual Realities: A Perspective from
    St Mary's Catholic Cathedral 355
    Michael Ferguson

18. Music and Spirituality in Communal Song: Methodists and
    Welsh Sporting Crowds   371
    Martin V. Clarke

Afterword: A Psychologist's Perspective   389
    John Sloboda

List of Figures and Tables   399

Bibliography   401

Index   451

Acknowledgments

Sarah and I would like to thank the Templeton Religion Trust for a project grant contributing to its research cluster *Art Seeking Understanding*. As part of our project, we sought to develop a three-way interdisciplinary conversation between theology, musicology, and psychology and neuroscience, which led to an international workshop on Music and Spiritual Realities, as well as, in due course, to this volume. We would like to thank Christopher Brewer and all the staff of TRT and the wider ASU 'community of practice' for their help and advice on our project.

Our project team in the University of St Andrews brought together colleagues from the Institute for Theology, Imagination and the Arts (ITIA) in the School of Divinity; the Music Centre; and the School of Psychology and Neuroscience. We would like to thank especially our two senior research collaborators—Michael Ferguson (musicology) and Ines Jentzsch (cognitive neuroscience)—as well as our advisors—David Brown, James MacMillan, Andrew Torrance, and Brendan Wolfe—who contributed invaluably at different stages of the project. We are also particularly grateful for their assistance, in different ways, to Christopher Bragg, Oliver Crisp, Kate Dove, Michael Downes, Tania Holland Williams, Claire Innes-Hopkins, Susan Millar, Lyndsay Mitchell, Elizabeth O'Keeffe, and Deborah Smith.

Our workshop formed part of the annual meeting of the European Academy of Religion at the University of St Andrews in June 2023, and we are grateful to the organisers, and especially Brendan Wolfe and Sterling Yates, for their collaboration. We would like to thank all the speakers at our workshop (and contributors to this volume), as well as the many workshop attendees who contributed to the rich intellectual conversations both inside and outside the scheduled sessions. We hope you will continue to be part of the ongoing scholarly conversation which this volume seeks to foster.

We were delighted to collaborate with Open Book Publishers on this project, and we are grateful to the OBP team for their support in developing this edited volume. Thank you, in particular, to Alessandra Tosi, Adèle Kreager, Jeevanjot Nagpal, and to the two anonymous peer reviewers. Finally, I would like to thank the School of Divinity's Deas Fund for funding a research assistant, and Rosemary Williams for her meticulous work in preparing the bibliography, as well as the University of St Andrews' Institutional Open Access Fund which co-funded, with TRT, the subvention grant.

Notes on Contributors

Jonathan Arnold is Executive Director of the Social Justice Network in the Diocese of Canterbury. Prior to this, he was Dean of Divinity and Fellow of Magdalen College at the University of Oxford, and, for many years, a member of the professional choir The Sixteen. His publications include *The Great Humanists* (2011), *Sacred Music in Secular Society* (2014), and *Music and Faith: Conversations in a Post-Secular Age* (2019).

Jeremy Begbie is Thomas A. Langford Distinguished Research Professor of Theology at Duke Divinity School, and the McDonald Agape Director of Duke Initiatives in Theology and the Arts (DITA). His publications include *Theology, Music and Time* (2000), *Resounding Truth: Christian Wisdom in the World of Music* (2007), and *Abundantly More: The Theological Promise of the Arts in a Reductionist World* (2023).

Peter C. Bouteneff is Professor of Systematic Theology and Kulik Professor of Sacred Arts at St Vladimir's Orthodox Theological Seminary, where he is also founding director of the Institute of Sacred Arts. His publications include *Sweeter than Honey: Orthodox Thinking on Dogma and Truth* (2006), *Arvo Pärt: Out of Silence* (2015), and *How to Be a Sinner: Finding Yourself in the Language of Repentance* (2018).

Martin V. Clarke is Senior Lecturer in Music at the Open University. He is the author of *British Methodist Hymnody: Theology, Heritage and Experience* (2018), editor of *Music and Theology in Nineteenth-Century Britain* (2012), and he co-edited, with Trevor Herbert and Helen Barlow, *A History of Welsh Music* (2022).

George Corbett is Professor of Theology at the University of St Andrews. His publications include *Dante and Epicurus* (2013), *Dante's Christian Ethics* (2020), and, as editor, *Annunciations: Sacred Music for the Twenty-First Century* (2019).

Michael O'Connor is Associate Professor at St Michael's College in the University of Toronto, and former Director of St Michael's Schola Cantorum. He is the author of *Cajetan's Biblical Commentaries: Motive and Method* (2017) and co-edited, with Hyun-Ah Kim and Christina Labriola, *Music, Theology, and Justice* (2017).

Jeffers Engelhardt is Professor of Music at Amherst College. He is the author of *Singing the Right Way: Orthodox Christians and Secular Enchantment in Estonia* (2015), and he co-edited, with Philip V. Bohlman, *Resounding Transcendence: Transitions in Music, Religion, and Ritual* (2016) and, with Andrew Mall and Monique Ingalls, *Studying Congregational Music: Key Issues, Methods, and Theoretical Perspectives* (2021).

Michael Ferguson is Lecturer and Coordinator of Academic Music at the University of St Andrews, and Director of Music at St Mary's Catholic Cathedral in Edinburgh.

Yeshaya David M. Greenberg is a psychologist and social neuroscientist. He is the founding director of CHIME (Center for Health Innovation, Music, and Education), and an honorary research associate at the Autism Research Centre at Cambridge University. He has published the largest studies to date on autism (*Proceedings of National Academy of Sciences*, 2018), on music and culture (*Journal of Personality & Social Psychology*, 2022), and on theory of mind (*Proceedings of the National Academy of Sciences*, 2022).

Maeve Louise Heaney VDMF is Associate Professor in the Faculty of Theology and Philosophy, and the Xavier Chair for Theological Formation, at Australian Catholic University. She is the author of *Music and Theology: What Music Says about the Word* (2012) and *Suspended God: Music and a Theology of Doubt* (2022).

C.M. Howell is a doctoral researcher at the University of St Andrews, where he is working on the theological aesthetics of Eberhard Jüngel.

Tihomir Lazić is Senior Lecturer in Systematic Theology at Newbold College of Higher Education, a musician and worship leader, and the author of *Towards an Adventist Version of Communio Ecclesiology: Remnant in Koinonia* (2019).

James MacMillan is one of today's most successful composers, whose works are performed and broadcast around the world, and he is also internationally active as a conductor. He is Professor of Theology and Music at the University of St Andrews, founder of The Cumnock Tryst, and was awarded a knighthood for his services to music in 2015.

Elspeth Manders is a doctoral student at the University of St Andrews. Prior to this she obtained an MLitt in Sacred Music from the University of St Andrews, and a BA (Honours) in Music from the University of Oxford.

Richard E. McGregor is Professor Emeritus of Music at the University of Cumbria, and he currently lectures at the Royal Conservatoire of Scotland. He edited *Perspectives on Peter Maxwell Davies* (2000), and he is the author, with Nicholas Jones, of *The Music of Peter Maxwell Davies* (2020).

Sarah Moerman is a Research Fellow in Theology and Music at the University of St Andrews. She also holds a research fellowship in social cognition from the University of Birmingham which provides psychology cross-training for theologians. Her research focuses on the various intersections between music, theology, and psychology.

Bernard Łukasz Sawicki OSB is Associate Professor in Theology at the Pontifical University of Saint Anselm in Rome. His publications include *The Concept of the Absurd and its Theological Reception in Christian Monasticism* (2005), *W chorale jest wszystko* [In Gregorian Chant Is All] (2014), and *The Music of Chopin and the Rule of Saint Benedict* (2014).

John Sloboda is Emeritus Professor at the University of Keele, where he founded and directed the Study of Musical Skill and Development, and at the Guildhall School of Music and Drama. His publications include *The Musical Mind: The Cognitive Psychology of Music* (1985), *Exploring the Musical Mind: Cognition, Emotion, Ability, Function* (2005) and, as co-editor with Patrik N. Juslin, *Handbook of Music and Emotion: Theory, Research, Applications* (2009).

Férdia J. Stone-Davis is Senior Scientist for the Austrian Science Fund (FWF) Research Project 'The Epistemic Power of Music', and Director of Research at the Margaret Beaufort Institute, Cambridge. She is the author of *Musical Beauty: Negotiating the Boundary between Subject and*

Object (2011), editor of *Music and Transcendence* (2015), and co-editor, with M. J. Grant, of *The Soundtrack of Conflict: The Role of Music in Radio Broadcasting in Wartime and in Conflict Situations* (2013).

Dilara Turan is a Research Assistant in the Department of Music, Istanbul Bilgi University, Turkey, where she also received her doctorate. Her current research focuses on the spirituality of music and the cultural study of avant-garde music practices.

Melanie Wald-Fuhrmann is Director of the Department of Music at the Max Planck Institute for Empirical Aesthetics (MPIEA) and Professor of Systematic Musicology at the Goethe University, Frankfurt/Main. Her publications include *Welterkenntnis aus Musik: Athanasius Kirchers 'Musurgia universalis' und die Universalwissenschaft im 17. Jahrhundert* [Knowledge of the World from Music. Athanasius Kircher's 'Musurgia universalis' and Universal Science in the Seventeenth Century] (2006), *'Ein Mittel wider sich selbst': Melancholie in der Instrumentalmusik um 1800* ['A Means Against Itself': Melancholy in Instrumental Music around 1800] (2010), and as co-editor, with Klaus-Peter Dannecker and Sven Boenneke, *Wirkungsästhetik der Liturgie: Transdisziplinäre Perspektiven* [Aesthetics of Liturgy: Transdisciplinary Perspectives] (2020).

Bennett Zon is Professor of Music at Durham University. He is Founding Director of the International Network for Music Theology and Inaugural President of the International Nineteenth-Century Studies Association. His publications include *Music and Metaphor in Nineteenth-Century Britain* (2000), *Representing Non-Western Music in Nineteenth-Century Britain* (2007), and *Evolution and Victorian Musical Culture* (2017).

Introduction

George Corbett and Sarah Moerman

The composer Sir James MacMillan has called music 'the most spiritual of the arts', and for many people, both religious and non-religious alike, this rings true.¹ But what do people mean by 'music' and 'spiritual' in this context, and what is the nature of their perceived relationship? Do certain kinds of music more readily afford spiritual experiences than others? What do psycho-physiological measures—such as heart and breathing activity, electrodermal activity, and saliva samples—reveal about perceived spiritual experiences? What are the practical implications of all this in the musical programming of Christian worship services? How has online Christian worship changed the dynamic between music and spiritual experience? These are just some of the questions that scholars explored at an interdisciplinary workshop on Music and Spiritual Realities co-hosted by the University of St Andrews' School of Divinity, Music Centre, and School of Psychology and Neuroscience in June 2023.² As co-organisers and editors, we issued all contributors with a core challenge, from which these further questions emerged:

---

1   James MacMillan, 'The Most Spiritual of the Arts: Music, Modernity, and the Search for the Sacred', in *Annunciations: Sacred Music for the Twenty-First Century*, ed. by George Corbett (Cambridge, UK: Open Book Publishers, 2019), pp. 9–16, https://doi.org/10.11647/OBP.0172

2   For an introduction to the research project, see the short film by Templeton Religion Trust, 'Music as a Bridge to Spirituality', online video recording, *YouTube*, 16 March 2023, https://www.youtube.com/watch?v=ei0mPuJBnUI&t=8s; for a short film about the workshop itself, see University of St Andrews, 'Music and Spiritual Realities: International Workshop', online video recording, *YouTube*, 16 November 2023, https://www.youtube.com/watch?v=uWfXQGYYPO0&t=10s. One of the speakers at the workshop (and author of Chapter 10 in this volume) wrote up his own reflections on the workshop: see Bernard Sawicki, 'Music and Spiritual Realities International Workshop (University of St Andrews, 19th-21st June

how would you, with your own area of expertise, your own research experience, and your own research methodologies, address or seek to demonstrate the commonly-perceived connection between music and spiritual realities? This volume, the fruit of that workshop, brings the interdisciplinary field of Christian theology and music into conversation with new musicology, ethnomusicology, and congregational music studies, as well as with psychology and neuroscience, in order to respond to this challenge.

Since its foundation in 2000, the Institute for Theology, Imagination, and the Arts (ITIA), in the University of St Andrews' School of Divinity, has pioneered research exploring the relationship between Christian theology and music.[3] The interdisciplinary field of Christian theology and music is now well-established with centres, graduate programmes, research networks, and publications, including a forthcoming *Oxford Handbook of Music and Christian Theology* in five volumes.[4] As this field first developed in Schools of Divinity and Faculties of Theology, rather than in Religious Studies programmes, this has affected its methodological approaches and areas of focus; thus, for example, Christian theologians have tended to have a pastoral concern for the music of their own immediate denomination and culture, whereas, in the field of religious studies, there has been more scholarly attention to world Christianities and to world religions.[5] While there have been invaluable contributions

---

2023) The Main Topics and Outlook: the Perspective of New Horizon of the Sacred Music', *Ecclesia orans*, 41 (2024), 155-77.

3   The scholarship of Jeremy Begbie—the Co-Founder, with Trevor Hart, of ITIA—has been especially influential on the field. See, for example, Jeremy Begbie, *Sounding the Depths: Theology through the Arts* (London: SCM Press, 2002); Idem, *Resounding Truth: Christian Wisdom in the World of Music* (London: SPCK, 2007); and Idem, *Music, Modernity, and God: Essays in Listening* (Oxford: Oxford University Press, 2013). See also, in particular, David Brown and Gavin Hopps, *The Extravagance of Music* (Cham: Palgrave MacMillan, 2018), and Corbett, ed., *Annunciations*.

4   See *Oxford Handbook of Music and Christian Theology*, ed. by Steve Guthrie and Bennett Zon (Oxford: Oxford University Press, forthcoming), 5 vols.

5   For an introduction to the study of music and world Christianities, see *The Oxford Handbook of Music and World Christianities*, ed. by Jonathan Dueck and Suzel Ana Reily (Oxford: Oxford University Press, 2013). To address the relative dearth of scholarship analysing the relationship between music and world religious traditions, Guy Beck has recently proposed a new interdisciplinary field—'musicology of religion'—to advance scholarship in this area (Guy Beck, *Musicology of Religion: Theories, Methods, and Directions* (New York: State University of New York Press, 2023)).

to the study of the relationship between Christian theology and music historically and in practice, as well as in relation to individual composers, there has heretofore been little engagement with empirical and scientific perspectives.[6]

Just as there has been a growing attention in Christian theology to the arts in general, and to music specifically, as a source of spiritual understanding, insight, and growth, so developments in musicology have made the field more open to an engagement with Christianity and with theological concerns. 'New' or 'critical' musicology shifts scholarly attention from a traditional focus on representing and reproducing a particular composer's intention embodied in the score, to a focus on how music is perceived or experienced. While leading proponents have typically excluded any possibility of transcendence or religious meaning in music,[7] more recent scholarship has challenged this 'illiberal exclusion', and shown how 'new musicology' does indeed open a productive space to explore the spiritual dimension of music.[8] In ethnomusicology, scholars have highlighted that music is ultimately something that is done—enacted and embodied—and that any search for meaning in music must necessarily take this into account. Christopher Small's widely-adopted neologism 'musicking' helpfully points to

---

[6] The scholarship in the field of Christian theology and music is now considerable. In addition to the forthcoming Oxford handbook, see, for just a few examples, *Creative Chords: Studies in Music, Theology and Christian Formation*, ed. by Jeff Astley et al. (Leominster: Gracewing, 2000); the expansive corpus by Jeremy Begbie including *Resonant Witness: Conversations between Music and Theology*, ed. by Jeremy Begbie and Steven Guthrie (Grand Rapids, MI: W. B. Eerdmans, 2011); Maeve Heaney, *Music as Theology: What Music has to say about the Word* (Eugene, OR: Pickwick Publications, 2012); and *Music and Transcendence*, ed. by Férdia J. Stone-Davis (Burlington: Ashgate, 2015). Heidi Epstein's *Melting the Venusburg: A Feminist Theology of Music* (New York: Continuum, 2005) continues to be the seminal feminist work in the field. The theology of composers, as diverse as Richard Wagner, Olivier Messiaen, and Arnold Schoenberg, has begun to receive significant scholarly attention (for examples, see, respectively, Richard Bell, *The Theology of Wagner's Ring Cycle: The Genesis and Development of the Tetralogy and the Appropriation of Sources, Artists, Philosophers, and Theologians* (Eugene, OR: Cascade, 2020); *Messiaen the Theologian*, ed. by Andrew Shenton (Abingdon: Routledge, 2010); and Julie Brown, *Schoenberg and Redemption* (Oxford: Oxford University Press, 2014)).

[7] See, for example, Lawrence Kramer, *Expression and Truth: On the Music of Knowledge* (Berkeley, CA: University of California Press, 2012).

[8] Brown and Hopps, *Extravagance*. See also Gavin Hopps, 'Music and Theology: Some Reflections on "the Listener's share"', in Corbett, ed., *Annunciations*, pp. 337–62.

music as an activity (a verb) rather than a static thing (a noun), whether practising, rehearsing, performing, listening, or otherwise participating in the social, cultural, and communal dimensions of music.[9] These ideas have been at the core of the emerging interdisciplinary field of Christian congregational music studies, which has sought to understand music as lived action in the specific realm of Christian religious practice.[10]

While psychologists and neuroscientists have conducted extensive research on music or musicking, they have tended not to explore music's relationship to spirituality, whether in explicitly Christian contexts or not.[11] The interdiscipline of cognitive musicology, for example, has begun to integrate psychological approaches to both musical production and consumption, exploring the neurological processes impacted by both music-making and music-listening. However, computational cognitive modelling of emotional and mental processes is limited to directly observable and quantifiable effects, and 'in-the-moment' experience, missing the depth of experience that may come in time; it has also not explored music's affordance for deeper understanding of spiritual realities. While psychologists have identified the need for an experiential, phenomenological approach to advance understanding that is more gradual, holistic, and embodied in nature—rather than the mere accumulation of factual or propositional knowledge—this, again, has rarely taken into account the relationship between music and spirituality. As Yeshaya David M. Greenberg remarks in this volume, 'when it comes to the realm of science, the terms "music" and "spirituality" are rarely uttered in the same breath and almost never appear together in any title or abstract in a peer-reviewed empirical study.' Likewise, John Sloboda commented at our workshop, 'the number of psychologists who are studying music and religion, you can count them on one hand', while 'something is happening here that is

---

9   See, especially, Christopher Small, *Musicking: The Meanings of Performing and Listening* (Middletown, CT: Wesleyan University Press, 1998); and Tia DeNora, *Music in Everyday Life* (Cambridge, UK: Cambridge University Press, 2000).

10 See, for example, *Christian Congregational Music: Performance, Identity and Experience*, ed. by Monique Ingalls et al. (Abingdon: Routledge, 2013) and *Studying Congregational Music: Key Issues, Methods, and Theoretical Perspectives*, ed. by Andrew Mall et al. (Abingdon: Routledge, 2021).

11 For helpful overviews, see, for example, *The Cognitive Neuroscience of Music*, ed. by Isabelle Peretz and Robert Zatorre (Oxford: Oxford University Press, 2003) and *The Oxford Handbook of Music Psychology*, ed. by Susan Hallam et al. (Oxford: Oxford University Press, 2008).

pushing forward the field in a way that I don't think has been pushed forward in any other arena that I know of'.[12]

Our workshop thus set these three broad fields in dialogue with each other, drawing together and evaluating existing methodologies, as well as suggesting and pioneering new ones. Contributors to Part II and Part III of this volume present new psychological and empirical research on music and spirituality, as well as providing their own constructive reviews of the extant scholarly literature in these areas. In opening up these interdisciplinary conversations, this volume does so predominantly in relation to Christian theological approaches to music (as in Part I), and to worship practices of music in Western Christianity (as in Part III). While there is a considerable diversity of denominational perspectives and contexts presented (including Catholic, Orthodox, Anglican, Methodist, and Pentecostal), the anchoring of the conversation in the Western Christian tradition allowed for some common points of reference and discussion, and provided a necessary focus to the volume. Nonetheless, as indicated by Greenberg's empirical study of the psychological effects of singing wordless sacred melodies called *nigunim* on a large group of Jewish participants (just one of his case studies involving participants from multiple religions and faith traditions in Chapter 7) or by Dilara Turan's empirical research on the musical trance scene of modern-day Turkey (Chapter 8), it would be beneficial, in a future workshop or volume, to anchor the interdisciplinary conversation in another religious tradition, or in relation to musical practices from other parts of the world. Likewise, while most contributors to our volume refer exclusively to a Western classical understanding of music, and are concerned with notated music, many of their conclusions and methodological approaches might be qualified, enriched, and advanced by an engagement with non-Western understandings, as well as with oral singing traditions or improvised traditions.[13]

---

12   See University of St Andrews, 'Music and Spiritual Realities: International Workshop'.

13   On spirituality and oral singing, see, for example, Nancy L. Graham, 'Spirituality by Heart', in *Living Song—Singing, Spirituality and Wellbeing,* ed. by June Boyce-Tillman et al. (Oxford: Peter Lang, 2021), pp. 67–82; on spirituality and improvisation, see, for example, Bruce E. Benson, *Liturgy as a Way of Life: Embodying the Arts in Christian Worship* (Grand Rapids, MI: Baker Academic, 2013).

While necessarily limited in scope, our volume contributes distinctively, indeed, to a much broader discussion of music and spirituality in contemporary scholarship, one which encompasses different religious and faith traditions, as well as secular forms of spirituality.[14] This scholarly and lay discussion has been a pre-eminent concern of June Boyce-Tillman, whose series 'Music and Spirituality' (numbering sixteen volumes since 2014) is especially valuable to research in the field, ensuring a range of experiences and voices are heard and represented, and decentring fields which otherwise typically centre particular doctrinal, ethnic, and musicological foci.[15] Two volumes in the series are particularly pertinent to our own. Noting that experiencing music is often considered 'the last remaining ubiquitous spiritual experience in Western culture', the second volume of her series—*Experiencing Music—Restoring the Spiritual*—takes a similar starting point.[16] In this monograph, Boyce-Tillman decouples 'religion' from 'spirituality', describing the 'development of a spirituality based on process rather than the dogmas and creeds of the defined world religions'; and she explores how music can be a 'trigger' for the spiritual, including outside the realm of explicitly religious or sacred music.[17] The ninth volume, *Enlivening Faith*, is more narrowly focused on music and spirituality in different Christian contexts, including prayer, liturgy, and education.[18] The series as a whole is notable for the breadth and range of religious and non-religious beliefs and practices, and of musical genres and styles, covered. Boyce-Tillman's series also programmatically critiques imbalances in the scholarly literature—as in relation to gender,[19]

---

14 See, for example, *Sacred Sound: Music in Religious Thought and Practice*, ed. by Joyce Irwin (Chico: Scholars Press, 1983); Guy L. Beck, *Sonic Theology: Hinduism and Sacred Sound* (Charleston, SC: University of South Carolina Press, 1993); Jacob Neusner, *Judaism's Theological Voice: The Melody of the Talmud* (Chicago, IL: University of Chicago Press, 1995); and *Experiencing Music in World Religions*, ed. by Guy. L. Beck (Ontario: Wilfrid Laurier University Press, 2006).

15 The series 'Music and Spirituality' is published by Peter Lang. In addition to being the overall editor of the series, June Boyce-Tillman is author or co-editor of twelve of the sixteen volumes published thus far.

16 June Boyce-Tillman, *Experiencing Music—Restoring the Spiritual: Music and Well-Being* (Oxford: Peter Lang, 2016), p. 7.

17 Ibid., p.4.

18 *Enlivening Faith: Music, Spirituality and Christian Theology*, ed. by June Boyce-Tillman et al. (Oxford: Peter Lang, 2019).

19 Thus the first volume of the series, *In Tune with Heaven or Not: Women in Christian Liturgical Music* (Oxford: Peter Lang, 2014) takes its title from a Church of England

sexuality,[20] and race[21]—as well as effectively addressing the complex capacities of music and spirituality for healing from abuse and trauma.[22] Our volume—with its thematic focus on Christian music in Western contexts—has somewhat conformed to type in some of these areas, and Boyce-Tillman's series is, in this respect, a useful point of contextual correlative and potential critique.[23] The question of positionality is, nonetheless, the central concern of Maeve Louise Heaney, in her discussion of our scholarly status as 'spiritual subjects' with our own partial lenses (Chapter 11), and this concern recurs in the volume, and is underlined by John Sloboda in his Afterword as well.

---

report on Church Music from 1992, and critiques the gendered perception of church leadership, questions the absence of women's voices from the 1992 report, and highlights women's contributions in Christian liturgical music from Hildegard to the present.

20 See, especially, volume 7 of the series, which brings together queer studies and discussions of music and spirituality: *Queering Freedom: Music, Identity and Spirituality (Anthology with Perspectives from Over Ten Countries)*, ed. by Karin Hendricks et al. (Oxford: Peter Lang, 2018).

21 See, for example, Nancy L. Graham, *They Bear Acquaintance: African American Spirituals and the Camp Meetings* (Oxford: Peter Lang, 2017); and *Ritualised Belonging: Musicking and Spirituality in the South African Context*, ed. by June Boyce-Tillman et al. (Oxford: Peter Lang, 2021). For an exploration of issues of gender expression, sexuality, and race in the specific context of Black Pentecostal congregations, see also Alisha Lola Jones, *Flaming? The Peculiar Theopolitics of Fire and Desire in Black Male Gospel Performance* (Oxford: Oxford University Press, 2020).

22 For example, well-being, abuse, and trauma are addressed in volumes 2, 3, 6, 11, 13, 14, and 16 of the series. Boyce-Tillman charts her own autobiographical account of music, abuse, and vocation to the Anglican priesthood in June Boyce-Tillman, *Freedom Song: Faith, Abuse, Music and Spirituality: A Lived Experience of Celebration* (Oxford: Peter Lang, 2018).

23 Thus, for example, although the editorship is gender balanced, the contributing authors are not. This is partly generational. We did, however, approach other female scholars who were unable to contribute, and, in our open call, we accepted all papers by female contributors, as well as inviting an early-career female postgraduate student to contribute. Although there are a series of initiatives seeking to address historical imbalances, there are wider gender and ethnicity imbalances in theology relative to other disciplines, and this has also been true of theology and music. On theology and gender, see, for example, Mathew Guest, Sony Sharma, and Robert Song, *Gender and Career Progression in Theology and Religious Studies* (Durham: Durham University, 2013), https://www.durham.ac.uk/media/durham-university/departments-/theology-amp-religion/GenderCareerProgressioninTRS-ProjectReport.pdf; on theology and race, see, for example, the initiatives within the Society for the Study of Theology at https://www.theologysociety.org.uk/initiatives/theology-and-race/.

As organisers and editors, we provided all contributors with a provisional definition of 'spiritual' as 'a perceived area of human experience beyond the material'. Thus, in the context of Christian theology, one might distinguish between spiritual realities (such as God, angels, the human soul), spirituality (which we might think of as a person's disposition or openness to the spiritual, as someone may identify as 'spiritual', or as having a 'spirituality'), and spiritual experience (a state of a person, as when someone experiences 'the presence of God' or being 'closer to God', or an altered state of consciousness). However, we left it to each contributor to interrogate this definition in their own way, or to work with another approach to spirituality, and we were intentionally open to a more 'thin, vague, and useful understanding of spirituality', as advocated by John Swinton, for example, in the practical context of medical care.[24] The first step, for us, was to name and recognise the lived reality of people's perceived spiritual experiences through music. Each scholar in this volume addresses this spiritual experience through music in different ways, and with different levels of conceptual precision. The volume's tripartite division—Theological Approaches, Empirical Methods, and Christian Worship—is likewise intended to be suggestive and indicative, rather than exclusionary. Thus, in terms of content, the first six chapters are more theological, and yet contain insights about methodology and worship practice, while many chapters in the other two sections have strong theological components. This division may also serve readers coming to the volume for the first time: a linear progression is but one way through: thus, for example, those readers concerned more with questions of method (especially empirical methods) might be advised to start with Part II, those with questions about the practice of music in Christian worship with Part III.

In the volume's first chapter, Jeremy Begbie underlines music's resistance to those reductionist habits of thought and language which

---

24 Medical practitioners are increasingly aware of patients' need for spiritual care, and of the reality of their spiritual concerns, and yet this spiritual exigency has historically been overlooked, in part due to an uncomfortableness with something so difficult to pin down precisely. See John Swinton, *Spirituality and Mental Health Care: Rediscovering a 'Forgotten' Dimension* (London: Jessica Kingsley Publishers, 2001); see also Ewan Bowlby, 'From Beaune to "Breaking Bad": Using the Arts to Meet Cancer Patients' Need and Desire for Spiritual Care' (unpublished doctoral thesis, University of St Andrews, 2022), https://doi.org/10.17630/sta/243

would pre-emptively exclude discussion of 'spiritual realities', before providing a renewed theological account of both music and language as vital means of 'sense making' which can direct our access to spiritual concerns. In Chapter 2, Peter C. Bouteneff similarly focuses on sacred music (with its balance of sacred text and music) as a productive site for considering music's 'empathetic spirituality', which he does with specific reference to the music of Arvo Pärt. Liturgical singing is also the focus of Michael O'Connor's chapter, which explores the spirituality of music—a spirituality which is *through, with and in*, the material and physical body and not *beyond* it—in light of the work of the Holy Spirit, and with particular attention to the theological-musical writings of Hildegard of Bingen. In Chapter 4, Férdia Stone-Davis argues that to grasp at religious knowledge or music, or religious knowledge through music, in a purely rational or demonstrative way is, ultimately, to avoid it; instead, she proposes an 'adorative posture' to both music and spiritual realities, where the affective and intellective powers are together necessary for our experience and understanding. While the first four chapters take predominantly emic perspectives, Bennett Zon tackles head on atheistic scepticism about God and spiritual realities per se, let alone their purported relationship with music. Zon argues, though, that music—considered as an 'experimental constant'—might help us to understand better the complex historical relationship between religion and science, with specific reference to Augustine's theo-psychological understanding of music, which leads us from *ordinary* music (which we compose and listen to) to *extraordinary* music (the harmony of the universe). In Chapter 6, C.M. Howell similarly addresses the question of secularity in the contemporary West, in which 'spirituality' can be radically reoriented to socio-cultural conditions within a closed 'immanent frame', with no reference to the transcendent or supernatural. Methodologically, Howell draws on German aesthetics to propose a holistic approach to the phenomenon of music reception, which allows the immaterial (and unquantifiable) to be appreciated alongside its material (and quantifiable) counterpart, taking as his case study 'outlaw country' music, a 'dissonant' form of American country music which emerged towards the end of the long 1960s.

    A core theme running through this volume is the strange lack of empirical research on spiritual experience through music, despite it being a widespread sociological phenomenon. In Chapter 7, the psychologist and social neuroscientist Yeshaya David M. Greenberg documents this lacuna before giving case studies of his own pioneering empirical research while, in Chapter 8, Dilara Turin analyses the neurological and cognitive processes involved when rhythmic units, pitch, tempo, and communal chanting induce altered states of consciousness in participants of the musical trance scene. In Chapter 9, Jeffers Engelhardt addresses critically the secular and positivist methodological presuppositions of ethnomusicology, and of the social sciences more broadly, according to which 'other-than-human' agency, or the position of a religious insider, have traditionally been framed out of the discipline; he also gives examples of new ethnomusicological methods which seek to include, or entangle, the emic perspective. While, in Chapter 10, Bernard Łukasz Sawicki argues for a methodological focus on 'atmosphere'—the reciprocal relationship with the environment, including its mood, presence, inhabitation, and landscape—as a necessary bridge to understand the relationship between music and spiritual experience, Maeve Louise Heaney, in Chapter 11, privileges attention on the spiritual subjects themselves, cautioning against the scholarly tendency to assume uncritically an 'objective' perspective. In Chapter 12, Richard E. McGregor describes his methodological attempts—as musicologist and composer—to understand 'what "happens" during the composition of a musical work', a happening commonly referred to in spiritual terms, as an 'inspiration'.

The third part of the volume turns specifically to the context of Christian practice and worship. While a core purpose of music in Christian services is to facilitate access to spiritual realities and to induce religious feelings—such as love of God, devotion, gratefulness, and contrition—there have been strikingly few empirical studies to investigate whether, in practice, worshippers experience such feelings through music and, if so, to what degree. In Chapter 13, Melanie Wald-Fuhrmann analyses the results of two empirical studies involving Catholic congregations in Germany as well as proposing new lines of inquiry, while, in Chapter 14, Jonathan Arnold, surveys the results of three empirical research projects in England and the Netherlands on the spiritual effects of Anglican Evensong. The COVID-19 pandemic, with its temporary restrictions on in-person Christian worship, has dramatically changed the profile of contemporary worship for good, with in-person, online, and mixed-ecology worship now the norm for many communities. In Chapter 15, Elspeth Manders charts the theological and musicological implications of these changes, and analyses the results from two local empirical studies in the Chelmsford diocese; in Chapter 16, Tihomir Lazić deploys netnography—ethnographic principles to study digital communities and the collection of data from online spaces—to explore the theological, ecclesiological, and moral implications of online worship. But what of the spiritual experience of singers themselves? In Chapter 17, Michael Ferguson draws on his perspective as Director of Music at St Mary's Catholic Cathedral in Edinburgh to explore the spiritual effects of bodily positioning in the liturgical space, clothing and robes, and the relationship of individual singer to the ensemble on the spiritual experiences of choral singers; in Chapter 18, Martin V. Clark examines comparatively the spiritual experiences of British Methodists and Welsh sporting (rugby and football) fans, in which music-making appears to give spiritual expression to the function or purpose of the communal gathering.

The volume opens with a Foreword by Sir James MacMillan, whose faith has been so central to his own compositional process, and closes with an Afterword by John Sloboda, who reflects on the progress, or its lack, in the study of music and religion since his seminal paper 'Music and Worship: A Psychologist's Perspective' of 1998.[25]

---

25 The paper is reprinted as John A. Sloboda, 'Music and Worship: A Psychologist's Perspective', in Astley, ed., *Creative Chords*, pp. 110–25.

Foreword:
A Composer's Perspective

James MacMillan

The inspiration for my third symphony, subtitled 'Silence', comes from the novel of the same name by one of Japan's greatest twentieth century writers, Shūsaku Endō, who died in 1996.[1] His book—made into a film by Martin Scorsese[2]—asks profound philosophical questions and resonates with one of the most anguished questions asked some 2,000 years ago 'My God, my God, why have you abandoned me?' It is a question that has been asked continuously since, right through Auschwitz and into our own time. Endo's 'silence' is the silence of God in the face of terrible events springing from the merciless nature of man: torture, genocide, holocaust. One of Endo's characters comments, 'I cannot bear the monotonous sound of the dark sea gnawing at the shore. Behind the depressing silence of this sea, the silence of God… the feeling that while men raise their voices in anguish, God remains with folded arms, silent'. For Endo—a Christian convert—this silence is not absence, however, but presence. Rather than 'nihil', it is the silence of accompaniment, as Christ accompanies us in our via dolorosa, through the valley of tears, suffering with us as one of us. But the notion of silence as presence—as mystical or metaphysical substance—is one that has many musical analogies. The emptiness and solitude of a composer's silence is pregnant with the promise of possibility and potency, and music itself grows out of silence.

---

1   James MacMillan, *Symphony No. 3: 'Silence'* (London: Boosey & Hawkes, 2002); Shūsaku Endō, *Silence*, trans. by William Johnston (London: Peter Owen, 1976).
2   *Silence*, dir. by Martin Scorsese (Paramount Pictures, 2016).

Descend into silence, indeed, and you become an extension of it. A composer should feel the silence adhering to him. And yet, we fill our worlds with everything that will challenge, contradict, and ultimately kill this precious silence. Music itself has been harnessed and co-opted as a weapon in this elemental war, transformed as it is into muzak—everywhere. Musicians should not collude with this. The war against silence is also a war against us, and against the interior life, from where spring our inspirations to create. In the early 1600s, the philosopher and boredom theorist Blaise Pascal wrote, 'All of humanity's problems stem from a man's inability to sit quietly in a room alone'. Since this is what composers do a lot of the time, in following our vocations as creators, we should ask, and we should be asked, 'why are we different? Are composers' problems different? Why are we able to sit quietly in a room alone? Are we more fortunate than everyone else? Are we the most fortunate of the fortunate?' On one level we are, but the descent into silence comes with a price. There is a deep fear of silence. And it is natural for composers to feel it too. This disquiet at being alone, at holding our tongues, at being starved of distraction has been with us, all of us, from the beginning—it is our natural state. More so today than ever. So we wage war on it. Silence is almost extinct.

Why do we resist going there? There is clearly a fear of nothingness—the abyss of non-being. That is completely natural. We avoid thinking about our own deaths, for example—the deep scandal of being irrelevant to this exciting, throbbing, living world. How dare they imagine going on without me? But what if there is something even more terrifying than nothing at the heart of this silence? What if Endo is right—that this silence is not absence? But presence? If it's not 'nihil' that is there, but 'accompaniment'? What are we being accompanied by? When stoics, mystics, saints, and composers dig deep into this silence searching for what is there, what if they meet that which searches in the opposite direction? Something that is searching for us? Coming back at us... I don't know if that is what John Cage had in mind when he devised his 4'33"—that is, 4 minutes and 33 seconds of silence—a kind of provocation to our listening sensibilities, or lack of them: a kind of goad to make us hear music and other things better, a kind of challenge perhaps to our 'Entertain me and entertain me now' culture. It may come as a surprise to some that his original title for this apparently jocular little slice of aesthetic naughtiness was 'Silent Prayer'.[3]

This silent 'place' is not necessarily a happy or contented 'place'. Sometimes the silence is dreadful and terrifying. No wonder Beethoven raged against his dying of the sound. What a frightening place to travel into, for anyone who has ever heard, never to emerge again. What an especially vile place for a musician and composer to go to and never return from. But go he did. A prison from where the condemned man will never exit. And the condemned man was Beethoven. Not just hell on earth, but hell in his own soul. And in that soundless, airless vacuum of nothing what did the composer meet? We will never know, of course, but we have messages from that deep impact, postcards from the other planet, air from this harrowed, empty place that now fills our planet with sound. His silence was pregnant. His nihil was accompanied. What became present in that ghastly absence of sound were some of the greatest masterpieces a human being has ever composed. If you want to know what is there, in that silence, what awaits, searching back at you, have a look and listen again to Beethoven's late string quartets.

I tell the young composers that I meet that this is the 'place' where we must go. Not deafness, not airlessness, not outer space. But silence. It calls us from its depth—deep calling on deep—like a monstrous ocean. It is imperative that we obey its command. It's as simple as that. Because when all the lessons are over, when you've completed your last counterpoint exercise, when you've learned all you can about how to orchestrate, when you've done modernism, postmodernism, minimalism, neo-complexity, and musica negativa until you can't think straight, there is only one other place to go. It is perfectly understandable if one chooses to get off the boat now. But for those who have to continue, how should we travel into this unexplored domain?

Have you ever gazed into the eyes of another person for a long time? I suppose husbands, wives, and partners do it. I suppose parents do it with their children. But otherwise it's weird, uncomfortable, unnatural. Twenty years ago, the psychologist Arthur Aron did an experiment.

---

3   See James Pritchett, *The Music of John Cage* (Cambridge, UK: Cambridge University Press, 1993), p. 59: '"Silent Prayer," as it was thus described in 1948, is clearly the first glimmer of an idea that, four years later, would become 4' 33"; while "Silent Prayer" is not 4' 33" itself, it is its ancestor'.

He was able to get complete strangers to fall in love in his laboratory. The participants sit and look into each other's eyes for four minutes (or maybe four minutes, thirty-three seconds!) without saying a word. Two of the subjects got married six months later. In this scenario, four minutes becomes a very long time—it is as though one is being pulled towards the other. Is this, perhaps, like staring into a religious icon? What actually is staring back at us? What does it see in our eyes, looking in? Gazing silently into the blind eyes on an icon is meant to let us see into the beauty of the divine presence. Icons are very important objects in the Greek and Russian Orthodox spiritual tradition. They are considered as windows into the soul of God. But God looks back. Silently. Some of the most powerful artistic representations of the nature of Heaven depict the Father staring into the eyes of the Son—for ever. Silently.

I've come to realise, then, that it is this ongoing encounter with silence that is the necessary state for a composer. Both eyes and ears turn to this empty place in an apparent and paradoxical search for sounds. Sounds which germinate in a place empty of sound. Sounds which are quickened into existence in a state of sonic vacuum—an apparent absence which brings forth presence. There is obviously a religious dimension to this but I'm keen to speak of it in ways that people and composers of very different worldviews and understandings can adapt to their own creative searches. For some, gazing at and listening for beauty is a matter of belief, but the composer's search for the numinous can take many forms—a deep, attentive looking and listening—and can be integrated into our lives as a spiritual practice, or perhaps simply as an imaginative discipline and search for the inner imagination, a search for the interior life.

My analogy with gazing at icons is intended to be helpful to my fellow composers. The composer John Tavener told me that in the Orthodox tradition icons are a form of prayer. He said to me, 'Jesus is the image (icon) of the invisible God'. When you look at an icon, it is meant to make you aware that you are in the presence of the divine. Icons, then, are not just art with a religious theme. Instead, they are sacred art because they bring the viewer into the presence of the holy. When one fixes one's undivided attention on these images over a substantial period, the images may come to life and enter into animated dialogue with the practitioner, or so the thinking goes. Painters and creators of icons say that the image being gazed at seems to look at you, coming nearer and nearer, even into your soul. Notice how prominent the eyes are in icons. The understanding is that heaven is looking back at you.

It is said that icons are designed to be doors between this world and another world. And my suggestion is that the musical analogy of this—which does not necessarily involve or need a specific image—brings the composer to an ambiguous hybrid place where his or her world comes into contact or communion with another state, and where the mysterious silent encounter sparks sonic life and compositional possibilities. The new music that we—as composers—are always seeking thereby arises from deep within our creative imaginations and, if you like, from deep within our souls. It is music that emerges when the silent composer descends into a deeper silence, an objective other place or state to which he or she adheres and of which he or she has become an extension. Silence listening to silence.

I. THEOLOGICAL APPROACHES

1. Encountering the Uncontrollable: Music's Resistance to Reductionism and Its Theological Ramifications

Jeremy Begbie

In this chapter, I explore the way in which the practices of music press against reductionism, and the theological resonances this provokes. I suggest that music is especially effective in countering reductionist habits: more than any other art form, it stubbornly refuses to be treated as an equivalent or merely an instance of something else, or as nothing but its component parts. Music makes sense, certainly, but in and through the distinctiveness of its own forms of life. I home in on one form of reductionism that I suspect lies behind many of the concerns of this volume—'naturalistic reductionism'—and on the paradigm of language that regularly attaches to it. I argue that music's challenge to the impulses that propel this reductive outlook (and its favoured language) pushes us in decidedly theological directions—although perhaps not in the ways that we might expect.

To begin with, however, a little throat-clearing. We have been asked to consider the ways in which music might connect with 'spiritual realities'. And we have been told that the term is to be taken as referring to 'a perceived area' or 'dimension of human experience *beyond the material*'.[1] I offer three comments on this.

---

1 George Corbett and Sarah Moerman, 'Call for Papers: Music and Spiritual Realities International Workshop: EuARe 19-21 June 2023 at St Andrews', *University of St*

First, if music is regarded in *this* sense as supremely spiritual ('the most spiritual of the arts', as some would say), the implication might be that music is uniquely able to lead us beyond the physical in such a way as to leave the physical behind. This clearly carries some difficulties. In recent years, the philosophy of music has seen what Julian Johnson has called a 'lurch' towards the body: a fresh recognition of music's bodily entailments, the physiological processes that make music possible, the ways our bodies interact musically with other bodies and the physical world at large.[2] Further, it hardly needs to be said that in many religious traditions, materiality is regarded as intrinsically valuable, with its own ineradicable goodness. If we are to attend to the 'spiritual' in our encounter with music, then care is needed over what 'beyond the material' may imply (even if inadvertently).

Second, though I am a musician, I come to this discussion primarily as a Christian theologian. This does not for a moment preclude the value of non-theological perspectives on our theme. Numerous disciplines are currently illuminating the links between music and what is spoken of as 'the spiritual.' But since it is far from obvious that 'the spiritual' is understood in anything like a univocal sense in contemporary discourse, it seems wise to have at least a measure of clarity about what we might be investing in the phrase. And here my own interests are unashamedly theological: they concern how talk of 'spiritual realities' might relate to the 'spiritual reality' of overriding concern to theology, namely God (as distinct from all that is not God).

Third, in exploring why it is that the language of 'spiritual' and 'spirituality' is so readily and widely used in relation to the world of music, we would do well not to jump to theological conclusions too quickly. So, for example, it may well be that we are aware of dimensions of musical experience that consistently resist exhaustive explanation

---

Andrews, https://music-spirituality.wp.st-andrews.ac.uk/call-for-papers/, my italics. See further George Corbett and Sarah Moerman, 'A Toolkit to Measure the Spiritual', *University of St Andrews*, https://music-spirituality.wp.st-andrews.ac.uk/a-toolkit-to-measure-the-spiritual/

2   Julian Johnson, *After Debussy: Music, Language, and the Margins of Philosophy* (Oxford: Oxford University Press, 2020), p. 16. See Carolyn Abbate, 'Music—Drastic or Gnostic?', *Critical Inquiry* 30.3 (2004), 505–36; Mickey Vallee, *Sounding Bodies Sounding Worlds: An Exploration of Embodiments in Sound* (Singapore: Palgrave Macmillan, 2019); Bettina Varwig, *Music in the Flesh: An Early Modern Musical Physiology* (Chicago, IL: Chicago University Press, 2023).

in terms of the natural sciences, or features of musical experience that radically exceed the expressive power and scope of language. And it may well be that many will draw on 'spiritual' language to speak of such intuitions. But to assume that music's inexplicability and ineffability can *straightforwardly* be aligned with, say, the Christian God, is questionable. For the cynic may well respond: these phenomena only show that the world is a lot more interesting and mysterious than we thought; they do not have to be intimating anything directly about God. After all, in the Jewish, Christian, and Muslim traditions, God is not 'another' reality within the created world alongside others—a spiritual reality, filling the gaps left by explicable physical things or the spaces that language cannot reach. Rather, God is the origin and sustainer of all things, of all that is not God, whether physical or non-physical, speakable or unspeakable. If we are to make fruitful theological connections between music and 'spiritual realities,' it is worthwhile being alert to this kind of category error.

I. Reductionism and Its Drives

With these caveats in mind, let me turn to a few comments about reductionism and its characteristic moves.[3] Reductionism is often signalled by the presence of words such as 'just', 'only', 'merely', 'really', and (especially) 'nothing but'. To say A reduces to B is to say that A is nothing over and above B, nothing but B. Much of the energy behind the work of the Templeton Foundation has been directed against what we might call naturalistic reductionism (NR), which I take to be characterised by at least three commitments. First, there is a denial of the reality of any non-physical entity or property, including, of course, God—a view sometimes known as 'physicalism'.[4] Second, there is a supreme confidence in the universal reach of the 'hard' or natural sciences—physics above all—to secure reliable knowledge. And third,

---

3   For a fuller discussion, see Jeremy Begbie, *Abundantly More: The Theological Promise of the Arts in a Reductionist World* (Grand Rapids, MI: Baker Academic, 2023).

4   Sometimes this goes by the name of 'materialism': the belief that there is only one sort of stuff, namely matter—the stuff pre-eminently studied by physics. Many prefer the term 'physicalism', given that physics has shown that what we call 'matter' is nothing as stuff-like as we might have supposed. And since we are here talking about realities studied by what many see as the supreme science (i.e., physics), it makes sense to speak of physicalism here.

NR will typically seek to account for complex wholes entirely in terms of their constituent parts: a rainbow is nothing but water droplets refracting light of different wavelengths, the mind is nothing but billions of neurons firing, and so on.[5]

In late modernity there are many signs that this outlook is waning. There is after all nothing in the natural sciences that requires any of these commitments (a repeated refrain in Templeton literature). And the resurgence of interest in 'spirituality' (broadly understood) is widely regarded as evidence of at least a general dissatisfaction with NR. But here I want to focus on the drives that propel NR rather than NR itself, drives which are arguably still pervasive across many domains of culture.[6] I highlight three of these. First, there is a drive toward ontological singularity—an aspiration to identify one class of existing entities that can be considered fully and properly real. In NR, the favoured ontological type will typically be some kind of microphysical particle, the basic unit of matter. Second, there is the drive toward favouring one type of language as the sole means to engage truthfully with the authentically real. In the case of NR, the assumption is that language at its purest takes the form of denotation and assertion, picking out things for attention and affirming things about them. These two drives are often harnessed to a third: a pressure toward control and mastery. One of the main attractions of reductionism, of whatever type, is that it purports to give us access to what is *really* the case, along with the language to identify and commandeer it. And this in turn—at least in principle—opens up immense possibilities for managing and manipulating anything we encounter, from sub-atomic particles to the person next door.

The potential negative consequences of such a drive toward mastery hardly need to be pointed out: they are epitomised in the late modern ethos of instrumentalisation, domination, and possession—something

---

5 For full treatments, see, for example, Lynne Rudder Baker, *Naturalism and the First-Person Perspective* (Oxford: Oxford University Press, 2013); Stewart Goetz and Charles Taliaferro, *Naturalism* (Grand Rapids, MI: Eerdmans, 2008); and Peter Harrison and Jon H. Roberts, *Science without God?: Rethinking the History of Scientific Naturalism* (Oxford: Oxford University Press, 2019).

6 Picking up a phrase from Rita Felski, reductionism is perhaps less a philosophy than a 'thought style', characterised by distinctive drives or ambitions. See Rita Felski, *The Limits of Critique* (Chicago, IL: University of Chicago Press, 2015), p. 2.

recently explored in an especially pointed way by the German sociologist, Hartmut Rosa.[7] All three of these drives (much simplified here) are closely associated with NR, but they can be found far beyond those who consciously seek to take their cues from the natural sciences. And, of course, all three make it exceedingly hard to talk of 'spiritual realities'. As far as ontological singularity is concerned, unless 'spiritual realities' are regarded as themselves the 'real' realities (as in some venerable philosophical traditions), they will likely be shoe-horned into accounts of entities that are regarded as properly real (in the case of NR, physical entities and properties). Further, 'spiritual realities' will almost certainly be seen as breaking out of the protocols of declarative-assertive language, and very likely as exceeding control and mastery. Further, these drives would seem to be foreign to what we have come to call 'the arts', especially the non-verbal arts. Many have claimed that the arts offer distinctive and potent counter-pressures to the singularising, one-language-fits-all, and controlling momentum of reductionism.[8] For rather than singularise, the arts typically open up multiple levels of meaning. They do not easily submit to the demands of straightforward depiction and assertion, and they certainly kick against being controlled (have you ever tried organising artists?).

II. Music, Language, and Reductionism

Our particular focus here, however, is on music. Music seems to pose an especially strong challenge to reductionist drives. Indeed, in modernity music has often been called upon to provide a counter-reductionist imagination of the world. A striking example is the exaltation of instrumental music we find in some of the German Romantics of the late eighteenth and early nineteenth centuries, against the background of what they saw as the closed and de-sacralising worldview associated with the ever-expanding natural sciences.[9] Wordless music becomes elevated to a quasi-divine status, in some instances furnishing an entire

---

7   Hartmut Rosa, *The Uncontrollability of the World*, trans. by James C. Wagner (Cambridge, UK: Polity Press, 2020).
8   See Begbie, *Abundantly More*, ch. 6.
9   For discussion, see Jeremy Begbie, *Music, Modernity, and God: Essays in Listening* (Oxford: Oxford University Press, 2013), ch. 5.

metaphysics of the infinite.[10] And since then there have been numerous attempts to advance theological or 'spiritual' agendas by harnessing music's potent anti-reductionist capacities. But what are these capacities? For the remainder of this chapter, I concentrate on one that many would see as key to music's resistance to reductive ambitions, and thus to its theological/spiritual potential. It concerns music's relation to language.

It is a truism to say that hearing a piece of music outweighs anything we could ever say about it. Music makes us acutely aware of the inadequacies of language. As George Steiner comments: 'In the face of music, the wonders of language are also its frustrations'.[11] Indeed, many would claim that language is not only inadequate in the presence of music but distorts and cramps music's possibilities through its tendency to tie down, foreclosing meaning.[12] How many liner notes or concert programmes have actually helped listeners to hear more, and to want to hear more? Here I shall argue that music does indeed resist wholesale assimilation to language (both in what music evokes and the ways it evokes it), and that this can indeed have theological ramifications. However, we need to avoid mistaken contrasts between language and music—especially those that trade on shrunken (reductive!) views of the former, and there needs to be due attention to the roles that language is called upon to play within specific theological traditions.

(a) A Pervasive Paradigm

The issue of music's relation to language is highly contested. But we can at least begin to open it up by expanding on the second of the reductive drives I highlighted above: the drive toward privileging one understanding—and thus one type—of language. At the risk of extreme generalisation, we can tease out some of the common assumptions about language that haunt discussions of the music–language relation in modernity. At the basic level, it is often assumed that truthful engagement with reality reaches its supreme and paradigmatic realisation in language, and moreover that language is so essential to the process of

---

10 See, for example, Mark Evan Bonds, *Absolute Music: The History of an Idea* (New York: Oxford University Press, 2014).
11 George Steiner, *Errata: An Examined Life* (London: Phoenix, 1997), p. 65.
12 So, for example, Susan Sontag, 'Against Interpretation', in Susan Sontag, *Against Interpretation and Other Essays* (Harmondsworth: Penguin, 2009), p. 8: 'Interpretation makes art manageable, conformable'.

understanding that there can be no 'sense-making' without it. With this often goes the belief that language can be truth-bearing only insofar as it conforms to (or can be reduced to) a particular *modus operandi*. Truth-bearing language entails the encoding of thoughts that correspond or 'refer' directly to entities (ideas, events, objects, or whatever), and such encoding takes the form of attaching specific terms to the mental act of referring, according to an ideal of one-to-one correspondence. Crucial to this are denotation and assertion: language enables us to pick out pre-existing things for attention (denotation), things about which we go on to say something (assertion). Denotative assertions are understood to be literal, third-person, dispassionate, body- and context-independent, with a clear subject–predicate structure and a singular meaning. With this often goes the belief that language's distinctive strength is—so to speak—its ability to get a fix on reality. This is where our third drive, the impulse to *control* is especially apparent. Through its power to specify and name, language possesses the ability to stabilise, command, and manipulate its subject-matter. The strength of language (its greatest strength?) is the way it functions as a technology of mastery, a means of commandeering the world-as-experienced.[13]

(b) A Place for Music?

Clearly, the musician is going to feel distinctly awkward in this environment, especially if she wants to claim that music is in some sense capable of bearing truth. Music does not generally operate through encoding thoughts that refer through one-to-one correspondence, or through denoting and asserting: we would struggle to say anything as basic as 'this is a chair' in music, or to sum up a piece of music in anything like that form.[14] And most music is not third-person, dispassionate, body- and context-independent, let alone in subject–predicate form

---

13 The literature on this paradigm, or something very like it, is vast. But, for an exceptionally lucid treatment and critique, see Charles Taylor, *The Language Animal: The Full Shape of the Human Linguistic Capacity* (Cambridge, MA: The Belknap Press of Harvard University Press, 2016).

14 This is not to deny that music operates with relatively stable 'codes' of reference within specific cultures—film composers would be lost without these. But although there may be correspondence here, there are no claims being made. To quote Taylor on a piece by Frédéric Chopin, 'A human possibility is articulated and disclosed ... but nothing at all is asserted' (*The Language Animal*, p. 236).

or singular in meaning. Nor does it seem to have powers of control comparable to those of language's power to identify and specify.

Faced with this, those with a theological interest in music are often tempted to take one of two paths. (I am simplifying drastically here.) (1) On the one hand, some will accept the basic paradigm just outlined, and insist we tie music as closely as possible to worded texts—as in song-settings, hymns, etc. In this way, music can do its own (primarily emotional) work, but wholly in service to the truth-bearing, referential power of texts. Such an outlook has a long and venerable history, and has been adopted by many theologians, Augustine and Calvin among them. It surfaces prominently in the Protestant Reformations, especially in the Reformed stream, where a strong concern for Scriptural authority is allied to a no-less-strong suspicion of non-verbal media. Words— above all the words of Scripture—are needed to keep music's emotional power properly directed and in check. Music should thus conform in every possible way to a text.[15]

(2) On the other hand, there are those who broadly accept our linguistic paradigm, but point to the radical disparities between music and language. If music is going to be allowed to do its own theological/'spiritual' work, it must be decoupled from language as far as possible. This is a common trope in modernity, especially since the nineteenth century. We have already mentioned the German Romantics' adulation of textless music. Recent years have seen a swathe of writing on music's ineffability, its vibrant refusal of any kind of linguistic capture or containment. According to the oft-quoted Vladimir Jankélévitch, music can *'express infinitely that which cannot be explained'*.[16] Jankélévitch distinguishes between the 'untellable'—what cannot be spoken about, and the 'ineffable'—what can be spoken about but in an infinite variety of ways. Music is ineffable in that there are 'infinite interminable things

---

15 For discussion, see Begbie, *Music, Modernity, and God*, pp. 180–83. It is worth mentioning a related strategy: to try to show that, in fact, at a basic level music does or can operate in language-like ways. In the eighteenth century, it was common to pinpoint devices or motifs within music that supposedly 'refer' to specific phenomena, the commonly cited phenomena being affective states. And there have been numerous attempts to demonstrate close structural similarities between music and language.

16 Vladimir Jankélévitch, *Music and the Ineffable*, trans. by Carolyn Abbate (Princeton, NJ: Princeton University Press, 2003), p. 71. Italics original.

to be said of it'.¹⁷ In making or encountering music we discover an excess, an abundance of life that inevitably invites speech but resists linguistic enclosure. When adopted by those with more overt theological agendas, these lines of thought lead some to hold that it is primarily music's indeterminacy that gives it its theological potency. Its freedom from the apparatus of reference and correspondence, from dependence on the concrete particular,¹⁸ from language's inevitably controlling tendencies, give it a remarkable capacity for serving as a vehicle of the infinite, for mediating a sense of 'transcendence', even offering—according to Russell Re Manning—a 'theology after writing'.¹⁹

Although I have sympathy with elements in both of these approaches, (1) and (2), I believe they are beset by significant weaknesses. Both tend to operate with a reductive view of language according to the paradigm I have described, with its associated ethos of control. The first approach will assume the paradigm and press music into its service; the second will assume the paradigm and insist on music's radical divergence from it. But what if we were to question the paradigm itself?

A further weakness of (2) in particular is that it can give the impression that the more music can be disentangled from language, the more it will be suited to mediate the divine. It is as if language as such is to be seen as inherently an obstacle to the infinite. But this sits uneasily alongside something basic to many faith traditions (including Christianity): that there are certain instantiations of language that are believed to play a normative and authoritative role in the mediation of God's presence and activity (sacred texts, for example). What if we were to relinquish the axiom that language per se is an impediment to the presence and activity of God?

---

17 Ibid., p. 72.
18 As in Friedrich Schleiermacher's *Christmas Eve: Dialogue on the Incarnation*, trans. by Terrence N. Tice (Lewiston, NY: John Knox Press, 1990). One of Schleiermacher's characters speaks of a singing piety 'which ascends most gloriously and directly to heaven' because '[n]othing peculiar or accidental restrains either [singing or piety] ... Never does music weep or laugh over particular circumstances, but always over life itself' (p. 47). This, she believes, also applies to an authentic religious sensibility.
19 See, for example, Russell Re Manning, 'Unwritten Theology: Notes Towards a Natural Theology of Music', in *Music and Transcendence*, ed. by Férdia J. Stone-Davis (Burlington: Ashgate, 2015), pp. 65–73.

(c) Music and Language: A Little Pre-History

All of this suggests we might need to re-think at least some of the common default ways of thinking about music's relation to language. One useful perspective to draw on here is a recent and growing current of writing on the evolutionary pre-history of both music and language, drawing on a panoply of disciplines (including evolutionary anthropology, archaeology, neuroscience, and the philosophy of language). I claim no special expertise in this field, and the jury is still out on many issues. But something of a consensus seems to be surfacing, and one that is highly illuminating for our purposes. According to this literature, our capacity for language and our capacity for 'musicking'[20] emerged together, alongside each other.[21] In his immensely thorough study, Gary Tomlinson speaks of the 'co-evolution' of music and language.[22] This cuts against accounts which have held that one sprung from the other (for example, Steven Pinker's famous thesis that music is evolutionary froth on the surface of language, a disposable pleasure stimulus).[23] It certainly questions the assumption that music's significance for us can be accounted for largely or wholly within a linguistic frame of reference. Further, many scholars have postulated the existence of some kind of precursor to what we now know as music and language, out of which both emerged: a 'protodiscourse'[24] consisting of emotionally charged vocalisations closely related to bodily gesture. (We might think here of infant-directed speech (IDS), the prattling language adults often use with babies.) According to the Oxford anthropologist Iain Morley,

---

20   Christopher Small, *Musicking: The Meanings of Performing and Listening* (Hanover, NH: University Press of New England, 1998).
21   Gary Tomlinson, *A Million Years of Music: The Emergence of Human Modernity* (New York: Zone Books, 2018), pp. 13–14, et passim.
22   Ibid.; Ian Cross, 'The Evolutionary Basis of Meaning in Music: Some Neurological and Neuroscientific Implications', in *The Neurology of Music*, ed. by Frank Clifford Rose (London: Imperial College Press, 2010), pp. 1–15; and Steve Brown, 'A Joint Prosodic Origin of Language and Music', *Frontiers in Psychology*, 8 (2017), 1894. For a semi-popular presentation, see Steven J. Mithen, *The Singing Neanderthals: The Origins of Music, Language, Mind and Body* (London: Phoenix, 2006).
23   Steven Pinker, *How the Mind Works* (New York: Norton, 2009), p. 528, puts it starkly: 'As far as biological cause and effect are concerned, music is useless'. He muses, further, 'I suspect that music is auditory cheesecake, an exquisite confection crafted to tickle the sensitive spots of at least six of our mental faculties' (p. 534).
24   Tomlinson, *A Million Years*, p. 108.

> It would seem that social-affective content was initially the most important component of vocal communication, one element of a system of gestural expression and comprehension of emotional state, and that this remains a very important component of our vocalization behaviours today ... This system of vocal and kinaesthetic communication of emotion constituted the foundation for vocal communication out of which later emerged culturally-shaped melodic, rhythmic musical behaviours and semantic, lexical linguistic capabilities.[25]

Further still, most scholars of this field of study hold that this protodiscourse (and thus musicking and language) was inherently social: it arose out of, and generated fruitful embodied relations with others—group cohesion, commonality of mood, a sense of shared purpose, etc.

What about the differences between musicking and language as they developed into the forms we know today? Again, the field is highly complex, but, according to Tomlinson, very early on, humans developed certain competencies which made possible what we now call music, and which musicking in turn encouraged and nourished. Among others, Tomlinson highlights the capacities of entrainment (co-ordination of bodily movement with an internally or externally generated pulse), discrete pitch perception, and hierarchical ordering.[26] In due course there appeared patterned rhythms, melodies, metre, and so forth—characteristics of music as we practice it today. Language, by contrast, though employing such devices as intonation, rhythm, and volume, does not rely on entrainment, discrete pitch-perception, or hierarchical ordering. But it clearly does involve the ability to single out objects for attention and predicate properties of them—a capacity not typically attempted by music.[27]

These findings would seem to put a large question mark against some of the key assumptions about language we have sketched above.

---

25 Iain Morley, *The Prehistory of Music: Human Evolution, Archaeology, and the Origins of Musicality* (Oxford: Oxford University Press, 2013), p. 321.
26 Tomlinson, *A Million Years*, pp. 76–83, 197–205, 161–62, 169.
27 Paraphrasing Tomlinson, Julian Johnson writes: 'the non-referential and musical aspects of protolanguage [protodiscourse] represents a very significant achievement of the human mind ... 'Musicking' ... embodied the achievement of a sophisticated non-referential communication' (*After Debussy*, p. 31). Of course, being able to distinguish and identify things with precision and consistency and assert things of them does not exhaust the powers of language.

First, they suggest that *both* music and language are means of 'sense-making'—that is to say, both are ways in which we interact appropriately with the world we inhabit, human and non-human, and 're-present' it truthfully. There is no need to privilege language in this respect and set it in a league of its own.

Second, the evidence concerning a 'protodiscourse' suggests that *both* language and music depend upon pre-articulate and pre-theoretical bodily know-how, affective or emotional dispositions, and embeddedness in communities of trust.[28] If music foregrounds these dimensions, it is only bringing to the surface things on which the use of language depends at every turn, even the most formal and technical languages. The psychiatrist and prolific writer Iain McGilchrist mounts a convincing case for claiming that many of the woes of modernity—including our social uprootedness and our tendency to instrumentalise others—arise from divorcing language from its bodily, social, and empathetic capacities. It is just here that music can, so to speak, remind language of its roots.[29]

Third, *both* language and music ought to be treated as intrinsically communal. Language no less than music began in 'functions that are related to empathy and common life, not competition and division; promoting togetherness'.[30] 'To be inducted into language', writes Charles

---

28   This links up with influential streams of philosophical writing, of which Michael Polanyi and Maurice Merleau-Ponty are among the prime representatives. See Begbie, *Abundantly More*, pp. 112–13.

29   Iain McGilchrist, *The Master and His Emissary: The Divided Brain and the Making of the Western World* (New Haven, CN: Yale University Press, 2012), ch. 3. Tomlinson writes: 'there can be little doubt that [language] retains in its pragmatic structure the rhythms and emotional flux of human protodiscourse. These ancient elements, however, are more evident still in musicking. For this reason *musicking should occupy a special place in the effort that has recently coalesced from several disciplines to analyse and describe the embodied aspects of all our modes of consciousness*. Musicking is a human activity unique in the degree to which it highlights somatic experience while structuring it according to complex, abstract, and relatively recent outgrowths of our cognition', my italics (Tomlinson, *A Million Years*, p. 289). Along similar lines, Hanne Appelqvist, 'Philosophy of Language,' in *The Oxford Handbook of Western Music and Philosophy*, ed. by Tomás McAuley, Nanette Nielsen, Jerrold Levinson, and Ariana Phillips-Hutton (Oxford: Oxford University Press, 2020), p. 365, contends that 'instead of using a particular account of linguistic meaning and understanding as a tool to explain music, we ought to look to music itself as a phenomenon that serves to illuminate the nature of linguistic meaning and understanding'.

30   McGilchrist, *The Master and His Emissary*, p. 119.

Taylor, 'is to be in a relation of potential communion with others'.[31] This would suggest that there is no particular need to posit an intrinsic link between language and harmful control. The development of referential language has undoubtedly made it possible for us to grasp things in the world:[32] to get a 'hold' of specific entities, objects, and ideas. But this process need not necessarily be damaging, or manipulative. Learning someone's name may of course be directed toward dominating them, but it can also bring to light their particularity and uniqueness—indeed, it can be a way of loving someone. The linguistic drive to manipulative containment is certainly a pathology, but not a necessity.

The supposed paradigm of truthful language use that we outlined above would thus seem to be woefully inadequate and potentially misleading. Doubtless, the kind of language celebrated by this model has led to immeasurable leaps in our understanding of the world. But as a wealth of studies have shown, it is akin to a small village in a large county. Not least, narrowly focusing on the denotative and assertive capacities of language can easily overlook the truth-bearing capacities of non-literal, figurative language (metaphor, simile, and so forth).

A fourth and fairly obvious consequence of these evolutionary observations is that music will be profoundly misunderstood if conceived as a system of signification that depends on depiction, on guiding our attention to extra-musical 'objects'. The point has been developed at some length by Rosa, in ways that are both fresh and suggestive. '[T]he peculiar quality of music', he writes, 'lies in its ability to produce a highly specific form of relating to the world',[33] Music has 'no content of its own,' nor does it provide a 'cognitive reference point'; rather, it modulates, or 'negotiates the quality of relation *itself*, whereas languages and sign systems can only ever thematize one particular relationship to or segment of the world at a time. ... Music is the rhythms, sounds, melodies, and tones *between* self and world, even if these of course have their source in the social world and the world of things'.[34]

---

31 Taylor, *The Language Animal*, p. 90.
32 McGilchrist, *The Master and His Emissary*, pp. 111–13.
33 Hartmut Rosa, *Resonance: A Sociology of the Relationship to the World* (Medford, MA: Polity Press, 2019), p. 94.
34 Ibid. Italics original.

III. Back to Theology (and 'the Spiritual'?)

It is time to return to our main topic—spiritual realities and music. Clearly, if 'spiritual realities' are understood to be realities within the space–time continuum that resist explanation according to the kind of crude and stark physicalism that informs NR, then our encounter with music presents a formidable challenge to such an austere creed. Indeed, NR's inability to provide compelling accounts of numerous phenomena of human experience that grate against the drives of NR, and on which the making and hearing of music appears to depend (e.g. first-person experience, intention, purpose, and so forth), should give the hard-line naturalist serious pause for thought. But, as I made clear at the start, my main interest here is in 'spiritual reality' understood theologically, as a way of speaking of the reality of God, and the Christian God in particular. And as far as music's resistance to reductionism is concerned, I have focused on the way it presses against reductionist accounts (and uses) of language. What are the *theological* implications of this resistance?

(a) Keeping Language Open without Leaving It Behind

I would suggest that among the most important ways in which music can evoke the active presence of the divine is through making us aware of the finitude, the limits of all language about and to God—and thus the inadequacy of all God-talk. Theological language finds its ultimate legitimation in a God whose life is not contained or bounded by finitude: words must always remain open to (or be opened up by) that which infinitely exceeds their grasp. Music is not of course infinite, but its refusal to be contained by language or to carry the specificity of which referential language is capable makes it well placed to gesture toward the uncontainability of God, countering the illusion that through speaking and writing we can in some manner grasp or circumscribe the divine. In the presence of, say, the words of the *Sanctus* in a eucharistic liturgy—'Holy, Holy, Holy'—music's capacity to evoke a sense of uncontainability may profoundly deepen a congregation's sense of the boundless inexhaustibility of divine holiness.[35] The music, that is,

---

35 For a fuller discussion of the interaction of music and texts, see Begbie, *Music, Modernity, and God*, chs 7 and 8.

may well bring worshippers a kind of awareness that the texts on their own do not provide. And textless music can play a similar role. It is not at all surprising that much of the instrumental music of Arvo Pärt, for example, induces for many a sense of the limitlessness of the divine Spirit, given the way his music, though never formless, undifferentiated, or inchoate, nevertheless studiously avoids the directional implications, gestures of closure, and referential dynamics of speech. There is thus a crucial current of truth in accounts which see in music's resistance to linguistic determination one of its strongest theological assets. George Steiner rightly observes that 'music puts our being as men and women in touch with that which *transcends the sayable,* which outstrips the analysable ... the meanings of music transcend'.[36] The German Romantics are indeed profoundly significant in this respect; as I have argued elsewhere, their witness to modes of sense-making outside the purely verbal are of perennial value to theology.[37]

Nonetheless, if we carry this line of thinking forward, it is worth registering a few cautions. First, there are many finite and this-worldly things that transcend the sayable, so if we want to make specifically theological claims about the power of music in this respect, or to justify a claim that something recognisably theological might actually be happening in a particular instance, we would need to say rather more about the *Theos* we might have in mind. The notions of 'beyondness', non-finitude, alterity, ineffability, transcendence, etc. on their own provide relatively meagre fare for making theologically informed judgements. If the Christian God is in view, for example, at some point reference will need to be made to the content of this God's self-disclosure.

Second, in the case of language about/to God, the danger of imagining we can in some sense contain God in speech is of course idolatrous, and has led to some of the most shameful horrors in history ('Thus says the Lord...' declares the religious tyrant). We have all met the kind of scripturalism that seeks to justify the value of something by measuring it against an explicit reference to the Bible; or a doctrinal rigidity that becomes fixated on propositions for their own sake, rather than on the living divine reality to which they bear witness and in whose life they

---

36   George Steiner, *Real Presences: Is There Anything in What We Say?* (London: Faber & Faber, 1989), 218, my italics.
37   Begbie, *Music, Modernity, and God*, ch. 5.

are meant to share. Despite all of this, however, I would suggest that the enemy here is not language per se, but, as we have indicated, specific types of language coupled with a narrow model of the way truthful language typically operates. Theology, as with scripture, is marked by a huge variety of language forms, and even those that take a subject–predicate, assertive structure will often be severely misunderstood if seen as driven primarily by the deleterious attempt to seize and contain, to stifle openness and mystery, to put God at our disposal. (And, we might add, valuable as music might be in setting off this danger, are we to assume that idolatry is *less* common among musicians than amongst speakers and writers?)

Third, we would do well to avoid the simply binary in which language is regarded as an opaque screen and music as transparent and direct. There is a grain of truth here, of course, in that music does depend to a very large degree on the immediacy of bodily, sensual, and affective awareness. In the absence of the apparatus of words and the possibilities of reference they enable, music relies on these modes of knowing to a heightened degree. However, even the most formal and abstract language would make no sense without its embeddedness in the bodily, sensual, and affective; and the fact that language employs terms that denote does not thereby cancel such embeddedness, nor does it restrict the capacity of language to be a vehicle of 'communion' between persons. Rita Felski can speak of language as 'more like an interface than a firewall, an array of devices that connect us to other things'.[38]

The need to offset these negative assumptions about language are especially important in the theological arena. To underline a point we touched upon earlier, in many faith traditions, we find the audacious claim that human speech has been assumed by God into God's purposeful interaction with the world, not negated or denigrated as such. For the Christian, language, in all its frailty and proneness to sin, is held to be part of the 'flesh' the Word came to assume and re-make in Jesus Christ. The church commits to the normativity of certain speech-acts—supremely Christ's own words, and Scripture as a whole—not because of some imported philosophy of language or

---

38 Rita Felski, *Hooked: Art and Attachment* (Chicago, IL: The University of Chicago Press, 2020), p. 70.

a fetish about words, but because our ability to speak belongs to the humanity God came to redeem and re-instate. In this outlook, although speaking to and about God is of course prone to destructive hubris, it need not be irredeemably stuck there. And the same goes for speech between persons. Language is not essentially a hurdle to be overcome, an impediment to communion with God and others. *'The design plan for language'*, Kevin Vanhoozer avers, *'is to serve as the medium of covenantal relations with God, with others, with the world'*.[39] Music may well free us *from* the illusion that we can get our linguistic fingers around God, but it can also free us *for* an engagement with language such that words can become a vehicle of communion rather than a tool of seizure or mastery.

Fourth, if these reflections are along the right lines, it would seem decidedly odd to turn to music in order to escape responsibility to language, to strive for a 'beyond' that is wholly and utterly unreachable by speech, out of the belief that this will somehow guarantee a superior and more veridical access to the divine. This is not to say that all music needs to be tied at every point to a text (or textual explanation) in order for it to have theological power or validity,[40] nor that music is incapable of bearing its own kind of witness to, and enacting in its own way, dimensions of a text's meanings that the text itself may be relatively impotent to express. Nor, is it to deny that music can be a godsend when destructive uses of language do need escaping. What I am questioning is treating language per se as something from which we need to be freed, and music as the liberator par excellence.[41]

39　Kevin J. Vanhoozer, *Is There a Meaning in This Text? The Bible, the Reader, and the Morality of Literary Knowledge* (Leicester: Apollos, 1998), p. 206. Italics original.

40　I have sometimes been criticised for holding this view, although in fact I have never held it. Being faithful to texts—which in the case of the church entails being oriented to theological truth by Scripture, and secondarily by the church's confessions and creeds—does not imply that an art like music is of value if and only if it directly 'illustrates' a biblical text or a theological doctrine. A far subtler approach to theological language is needed than this would imply. I have addressed these matters at length in *Music, Modernity, and God*, chs 7 and 8.

41　An observation by Rowan Williams on the negating impulse in theology is worth citing here: 'The risk of a negative theology in abstraction, the identification of the sacred with the void, is the purchase it gives to a depoliticized—or even anti-political—aesthetic, in which there is a subtle but unmistakable *suggestion that social and linguistic order (as opposed to this or that questionable order) is what we need to be delivered from, and that a particular kind of artistic praxis can so deliver'*. Rowan Williams, *Wrestling with Angels: Conversations in Modern Theology* (Grand Rapids, MI: Eerdmans, 2007), p. 31, my italics.

A fifth and final comment. Throughout this chapter, I have returned intermittently to the theme of control or containment—understood as a danger, a pathology—and I have spoken of music's distinctive resistance to this reductive impulse vis-à-vis language and the way this can gesture towards divine uncontainability. However, what I have said so far could give the impression that this uncontainability is a static affair, a function of a motionless, bare infinity. But there is a feature basic to all music (as far as we know) that can suggest something far livelier and more generative, and far more theologically fruitful—namely, repetition. It is well known that repetition is hard to sustain in language without inducing boredom. But it seems to be a kind of default or natural condition of music, not least in music we find interesting and compelling. Musicians cannot seem to get enough of saying the same thing over and over again (even if some degree of difference and variation is always present). There is a continual reaching for the next thing, for 'another', eliciting a sense of overflow, a habitual bias towards 'more ... and more'. The psychologist Elizabeth Hellmuth Margulis writes: 'music is the canonical domain of repetition, and when we reinterpret another domain to emphasize its repetitiveness, we are, in fact, examining a quasi-musical aspect of that domain'.[42] She continues:

> My claim is that part of what makes us feel that we're a musical subject rather than a musical object is that we are endlessly listening ahead, such that the sounds seem almost to execute our volition, after the fact. This sense of super-expressive voice ...... can be pleasurable in and of itself. It is the pleasure of *expansion, of movement beyond limits*, of increased power—all characteristic of strong experiences of music as chronicled by existing experimental work.[43]

Christian theology witnesses to a divine momentum or rhythm at work in the world that by its very nature is unlike the closing of a circle—the return of something to a starting point—but rather a movement that always 'exceeds,' surpasses any predictable limit. In theological terms, this is the momentum of the Holy Spirit (the 'spiritual reality' par excellence, we might even say)—an outward, outgoing dynamic,

---

42 Elizabeth Hellmuth Margulis, *On Repeat: How Music Plays the Mind* (New York: Oxford University Press, 2014), p. 4.
43 Ibid., p. 12, my italics.

so the Christian tradition maintains, which belongs to the very heart of God's own life. This may be another reason why music for many is so suggestive of the (uncontainable) divine—and the divine here conceived not as motionless infinity but as limitless life.

(b) Jubilant Uncontainability

I close by citing some extraordinary reflections by Augustine (354–430) that bring together many of the themes of this chapter.[44] They come in the light of reflecting on words from Psalm 33: 'Sing to him a new song; play skilfully on the strings, with loud shouts' (v. 3). What does it mean to exult 'with loud shouts'? Augustine answers:

> It is to realize that words cannot communicate the song of the heart. Just so singers in the harvest, or the vineyard, or at some other arduous toil express their rapture to begin with in songs set to words; then as if bursting with a joy so full that they cannot give vent to it in set syllables, they drop actual words and break into the free melody of jubilation [*et eum in sonum iubilationis*]. The jubilus is a melody which conveys that the heart is in travail over something it cannot bring forth in words. And to whom does that jubilation rightly ascend, if not to God the ineffable? Truly is he ineffable whom you cannot tell forth in speech, yet we ought not to remain silent, what else can you do but jubilate? In this way the heart rejoices without words and the boundless expanse of rapture is not circumscribed by syllables.[45]

In another place, Augustine writes,

> Consider, beloved ones, how people sing songs when they are making merry. ... You know how sometimes, in between songs with words, the singers seem to overflow with a joy that the tongue is inadequate to express verbally; you know how then they let out wild whoops to give utterance to a gladness of spirit, since they are unable to put into words what the heart has conceived.[46]

---

44 For a fuller version of what follows, see Begbie, *Abundantly More*, pp. 210–15.
45 Augustine, *St Augustine on the Psalms*, trans. by Scholastica Hebgin and Felicitas Corrigan, 2 vols (Westminster, MD: Newman Press, 1961), II, pp. 111–12.
46 Augustine *Enarrationes in Psalmos* 94.3, as translated in Carol Harrison, *On Music, Sense, Affect, and Voice* (New York: T&T Clark, 2019), p. 143.

By 'jubilation' ('whoops' in this translation; I am reminded of Nick Cave's phrase, 'spasms of delight'),[47] Augustine seems to intend an affectively charged flow of unconstrained and wordless praise that overspills the capacities of speech. And he believes this is especially apt as a mode of praise for a God who, although within reach of language, cannot be constrained by it. This jubilation is not everyday speech ('He most definitely has singing in mind'),[48] yet it is not an organised or regularly patterned melody. Might it be close to what Pentecostals call 'singing in the Spirit'?

In any case, this jubilation eludes any deadening will to control. The fact that it is a form of praise is no accident: in praise, God is being honoured (among other things) as humanly uncontrollable, by speech as much as anything else. This is a wordless witness to the impossibility of God being encompassed by spoken words. It 'arises from the struggle to articulate what is ineffable—and then, suddenly, we are set free: the *jubilus* escapes, explodes'.[49] And yet Augustine never suggests that jubilation releases us from all accountability to normative language (and certainly not from responsibility to the Psalms of scripture). There is no hint that he sees language per se as a necessary evil, as inherently 'containing' and idolatrous. In Isaac Harrison Louth's words, 'Augustine writes that singers in jubilation turn away from the syllables of words towards sound but notes that the very joy which motivates them springs in the first place from their exulting in the words of the songs ... There is a way in which jubilant sound burst[s] forth from the text and, at the same time, works itself free from the text'.[50] The *jubilus* arises from the uncircumscribable joy of reading or hearing the words of the Psalms. And of that joy, Augustine believes, there is no limit or end.

---

47 Rowan Williams, 'Nick Cave: My Son's Death Brought Me Back to Church', *The Times*, 4 March 2023, https://www.thetimes.co.uk/article/nick-cave-my-sons-death-brought-me-back-to-church-qdskjx277
48 Harrison, *On Music, Sense, Affect, and Voice*, p. 142.
49 Ibid., p. 145.
50 From an unpublished paper, quoted in Harrison, *On Music, Sense, Affect, and Voice*, p. 144, n. 89.

2. Cross and Consolation: Music's Empathic Spirituality

Peter C. Bouteneff

In Andrei Tarkovsky's stunning film of 1979, the eponymous Stalker philosophises as follows:

> You were speaking of the meaning of our life ... of the unselfishness of art ... Take music, for instance. ...If it is connected at all [to reality], this is just mechanics. It's not connected by way of ideas, only by sheer sound, devoid of any associations. And yet, music, as if by some miracle, gets through to our heart. What is it that resonates in us in response to noise brought to harmony, making it the source of the greatest delight which stuns us and brings us together?[1]

This somewhat tortured character is the most perspicacious of the film's core threesome and has the most important insights of them all. The others are stuck in a cold intellectualism. A liminal figure negotiating different planes of reality, the Stalker alone is capable of this perceptive observation about music and its unique power. Specifically, he speaks of its capacity to stun us, and to unite us to one another. Music acts in an elemental way that does not call attention to itself. It is 'unselfish'. So in the first instance this cinematic quotation calls us to reflect on the sheer power of music, to reach us, to stun us, and in some way to unite us.

---

1   *Stalker*, dir. by Andrei Tarkovsky (Goskino 1979).

I. Music's Power

When scientific studies compare the various senses and the directness and immediacy of their reach into our inner lives, the olfactory always wins. Our brain's anatomy has it that smell is the most direct way into our nervous system, and therefore into our sensory world. Yet, despite the prominence of incense in some of our religious rites and practices, there is not nearly as much to be done with it, in the sense of 'sacred art', as there is with music. So it would be more difficult to argue that perfume or incense are the most spiritual of the arts.[2] The auditory shares an interesting feature with the olfactory: we cannot readily shut it off. We have eyelids that allow us readily to close ourselves off from the visual. But we do not have earlids. The input of sound is constant, short of our conscious decision to plug our ears with our fingers, but even then, the power of sound—more so than light—is felt on the entire body. Music is sound, and sound is the movement of air which impresses itself on the totality of the human body—and in a special way, on the eardrum and the mechanisms which translate those vibrations to the brain. And it is impossible to switch all of that off, perhaps not even in a comatose state—where music has been known to reach people as nothing else could.

This power of sound, of music, can cut both ways. As Arvo Pärt observed in a memorable conversation with the Icelandic composer Björk Guðmundsdóttir, 'You can kill people with sound. And, if you can kill [with it] then maybe there is sound which is the opposite of killing'.[3] That is rather minimalistic praise of music, or of the potential of sound. In a moment, he turns his attention to music, but initially Pärt means to point us to the extraordinary potential of sound, one that can cut both ways. It can, perhaps, actually give life. He goes on 'The distance between these two points [sound that kills and sound that gives life] is very big. And you are free. You can choose'.

---

2   But see Susan Ashbrook Harvey's classic *Scenting Salvation: Ancient Christianity and the Olfactory Imagination,* Transformation of the Classical Heritage 42 (Berkeley, CA: University of California, 2006).

3   See 'Video: Björk Interviews Arvo Pärt', *Estonian World,* 16 July 2020, https://estonianworld.com/culture/video-bjork-interviews-arvo-part/

The suggestion here is that just as music is potentially the most vivifying of the arts, music, or at least sound more broadly, can likewise be the most potentially destructive. It was not rhetoric but song that the sirens used in order to lure the sailors of ancient myth to their destruction on the rocks. Religious puritans will always cavil at the appearance of any new form of music, from the Renaissance—where even the tritone, the 'devil's interval', sparked controversy—all the way up to the twentieth century, when jazz, blues, and rock were met with panic about the dangers of syncopation and infectious rhythm, not to mention the sexually provocative lyrics that often accompanied them.

Just as some people extol the spiritual potency of music, others live in fear of its power to deceive us into perdition. The point is that music is powerful stuff. Seeing music as somehow special, unique, and superlative in this regard is also not new. Identifying music with core principles, of mathematics, of the organisation of the universe, is a near perennial insight—at least as old as Pythagoras. Some of the earliest findings from prehistoric hominids 40,000 years ago include flutes made from bone, and we may suppose that vocalisation, and the rhythmic striking of things, long predated the sophistication of tooled wind instruments. In so far as the human being is a creative being, the human being is a musical entity.

What is the difference, then, between music's power, and its *spiritual* power? Or is there a difference?

II. Music's Spiritual Capacity

Sir James MacMillan's identification of music as 'the most spiritual of the arts' is a beautiful and bold assertion, naturally impossible to substantiate, and certain to be contested by proponents of poetry, the narrative arts, visual arts, cinema, dance, all of which are able to bring us to tears, as well as to our knees. Yet there really is something unique about music. In a fine essay published in the *Guardian*, MacMillan cites two contemporary churchmen to underscore his assertion.[4] One is the Scottish Jesuit John McDade, who says, 'Music may be the closest human

---

4 James MacMillan, 'Divine Accompaniment', *Guardian*, 18 July 2003, https://www.theguardian.com/music/2003/jul/19/classicalmusicandopera.artsfeatures

analogue to the mystery of the direct and effective communication of grace'. The other is Rowan Williams—someone well versed in poetry, fiction, theatre, and iconography, who observes that 'To listen seriously to music, and to perform it, are among our most potent ways of learning what it is to live with and before God'.[5] Williams thus expresses the power of music in explicitly spiritual, theological terms. But note that neither thinker speaks in terms as absolute as MacMillan. McDade says 'maybe'. Williams says music is '*among* our most potent ways' Godward. He goes on just a bit later in a similarly strong-but-qualified observation, 'The authority of music, what silences us and holds us, is, then, *one of the fullest* parables we have of the authority of God'.[6]

I can relate to this reluctance to apply superlatives; we are all too aware of the alternatives that have equal claim to power and loftiness. We must be honest: calling music 'the most spiritual of the arts' is an indefensible claim, and yet it is being made by one of the greatest living composers of sacred music. I cannot but imagine that it was made in the spirit of almost playful provocation, as well as a call to serious attention not only to its transcendent power, but the singular nature of that potency. Music's uniqueness has to do with a concatenation of factors, including the elemental way in which sound acts on us, the mathematical formulas which bring us the harmonic series, the way that our sensory radar picks up on that harmony, all of which allow a musician to skilfully interweave harmony and dissonance, the visceral power of rhythm which too becomes the substrate of play between regularity, syncopation, and disruption. Music is an interaction of the materiality of sound, harmony, and rhythm, the conscious deployment of silence, and in all of this, the flow of time.[7] But thus far I've still only managed to suggest some of the factors involved in its power in general, and its uniqueness, without even getting into the question of the spiritual.

And that is largely because the 'spiritual' is notoriously (or happily) difficult to define and quantify. In fact, the impossibility of nailing it down is one of its inherent characteristics, one of the things that

---

5 See Rowan Williams, 'Keeping in Time', in Rowan Williams, *Open to Judgment: Sermons and Addresses* (London: Darton, Longman & Todd, 1994), p. 249.
6 Ibid., p. 249, my italics.
7 Time, indeed, is the focus of Rowan Williams' essay cited above.

makes the spiritual spiritual. Some of the qualities people associate with spirituality are so broad and vast that we could simply equate the potential power of music with its potential spiritual power. In other words, the way that music can make us feel—inspired, wistful, insignificant, enveloped, self-forgetting, or even empowered—is akin to many definitions of spirituality, especially as some of these feelings can be related to transcendence. Music transports us, and for a great number of people that is largely what spirituality consists of: bringing us to awareness of and communion with a vaster, more capacious, perhaps more significant realm.

III. Sacred Music and Its Texts

The relationship between music and spirituality—including spirituality-as-transcendence—comes into one particular focus in what we call 'sacred music'. Some audiences apply the category of 'sacred' or 'spiritual' to any piece of music that they have found to be transporting, whether it is Johann Sebastian Bach's Mass in B Minor or Radiohead's 'Idioteque'. In such cases, spirituality is entirely subjective. Fair enough. But, technically speaking, 'sacred music', as a genre or category, is music that has been composed with an explicit intention of praising God. In this case, we can at least provisionally link 'sacred' to 'religious'. As spiritually affecting as people may find John Luther Adams' 'Become Ocean', or Sigur Rós's 'Svefn-g-englar', these are not technically 'sacred music.'

There are of course borderline cases, such as John Coltrane's album, *A Love Supreme*, composed 'in gratitude to God', with words whose syllables are at some points articulated by Coltrane's saxophone.[8] Apart from dedications that indicate an overall intention or orientation, the explicitness of the God-praising intention of a composition lies in the texts to which it is set. Whether it is sung or otherwise heard, or—in rarer

---

8   In the liner notes to the 1965 album, released by Impulse! Records, Coltrane writes, 'This album is a humble offering to Him. An attempt to say "THANK YOU GOD" through our work, even as we do in our hearts and with our tongues. May He help and strengthen all men in every good endeavor'. The words to the fourth part of the composition, entitled 'Psalm' are 'sung' by Coltrane's sax. For this last point I am indebted to Yeshaya David M. Greenberg, who shared with me some of his own unpublished writing on the subject.

instances—where it is otherwise conveyed through melody and rhythm in syllabic mimesis,[9] text constitutes a fixed and traceable indicator of the sacred function of a piece of music.

We will recall Plato's caution about textless music.[10] Plato insisted that music could yield insight into the world's mysteries. But if people were to be taught by it properly rather than simply carried away with its visceral effects, they needed the words. Only words could reliably guide the composition of the music; the music must follow their shape and rhythm.[11] Augustine (354–430) agreed with Plato (ca. 427–348 BC) both about music's 'hidden affinity' with the human spirit, and with his insistence on text—on the words that would shepherd the listener's reaction and response.[12] Music and word thus belong in symbiotic relationship. And so, musical settings of sacred text—especially when these are artful and perhaps even prayerful—are spiritually affecting in a clearer and more quantifiable way.

Otherwise, we are back to generalised observations simply about music's 'power to transport'. These are, by definition, unmeasurable and subjective, even as they are also undeniable. But to be frank, calling attention to music's transcendent power can be mundane if not banal. Of course music can be transporting and beautiful and affective and make us forget about ourselves. I focus here on another dimension of the spiritual power of music, one that may appear more immanent than transcendent. For I think that music exerts much of its spiritual power by being empathetic. By this I mean that the spiritual power of music rests to a considerable degree in its capacity to reflect—and therefore 'hear' or register—our lived experience of the world, one which is inevitably bittersweet, simultaneously sad and bright.

---

9   We have just seen how Coltrane does this. As for Arvo Pärt, to whom we will again turn shortly, see Peter Bouteneff, 'Tacit Texts: Considerations on Pärt's Settings of the Word', *Res Musica* 14 (2022), 76–81.

10 A helpful, concise summary of Plato on this subject can be found in Jeremy Begbie, *Resounding Truth: Christian Wisdom in the World of Music* (London: SPCK, 2008), pp. 80–82.

11 See Plato, *Republic* 3.398d. See Peter C. Bouteneff, *Arvo Pärt: Out of Silence* (Yonkers, NY: SVS Press, 2015), pp. 61–62.

12 'I feel that when the sacred words are chanted well, our souls are moved and are more religiously and with a warmer devotion kindled to piety than if they are not so sung' (Augustine, *Confessions* 10.33.50, cited in Begbie, *Resounding Truth*, p. 320, n. 36).

IV. Bright Sadness

The importance of empathy, and specifically the capacity of music to accompany and validate one's sadness, is likewise common in other art forms. The film *Inside Out* (2015), like many Pixar films, is ostensibly for children but carries its greatest and most profound pleasures for the adults in the room. *Inside Out* sets itself a goal that would be ambitious for any film, much less a work of children's animated fantasy: to alert us to the ways in which joy is not only inevitably tinged with sorrow, but even is enhanced, or 'thickened' by sorrow. One may argue that the film sees itself as a corrective of a particularly American obsession with happiness over everything else. Ironically, Pixar's parent corporation Disney used to call its theme park 'The Happiest Place on Earth', something that sounds to many of us like a nightmare. But *Inside Out* goes much further. One of the film's most important observations, one that assists its fundamental insight about the contribution that sadness makes to joy, is that those who are experiencing sorrow do not, in the first instance, want or need to be 'cheered up'. They need to be heard, listened to, accompanied, specifically in their desolation. Rather than chase away sorrow, we must give it its full due, trusting that when we do so it will only clarify for us what joy is in the first place.

One review of the film suggests that it asks and answers the question of what it means to 'be okay', in the sense of to be managing, to be doing alright.

> So what does it mean to be okay? It does not mean being happy. It has nothing to do with typical conceptions of success. ... Being okay is probably more akin to finding a sense of integrity in our actual disintegrated experiences.... It's about acknowledging the muck rather than escaping it. It's about working through unpleasantness rather than going around it or presuming that we will always arrive at the other side of it.
> To be okay is to be okay that we're not okay.[13]

Other films have made similar points—not only that happiness is not all it's cracked up to be, but that it is never unmitigated, unalloyed. In

---

13   Roberto Sirvent and Duncan Reyburn, 'Inside Out and Philosophy: What Does it Mean to be Okay?', *And Philosophy*, 7 November 2015, https://andphilosophy.com/2015/11/07/inside-out-and-philosophy-what-does-it-mean-to-be-okay

our cynical era, it is almost too easy to highlight the superficiality of happiness and brightness, such that to be happy is to be in denial. The films of David Lynch, as just one example, are characterised by that distrust of joy—even a kind of glorification of the ugly—and embody it disarmingly well. My intention in this chapter is simply to draw attention and give shape to the idea that the greatness and power of art may be proportional to the ways it reflects and puts us in touch with life's vicissitudes. Art is at its best when it is true to life, in its actual variegated complexity. We know that art can be powerful simply in making us feel something—anything—acutely. But great art will never be devoid of either joy or sadness. Rather it will artfully configure them together.

I am hopeful that these observations from cinema and art will amplify my point about music and its spirituality. Music is potentially expressive of the same range of human emotional experience, and of the range of feelings that inevitably describe our lives. Specifically, music is another medium for the artful configuration of joy and sadness. In certain misguided times and places, music that was seen as overly sad was suppressed—to wit the 'Picardy third', that final major-key triad ensuring that however 'sad' a composition was allowed to get, it could not end on that note, as it were. Not that major and minor tonalities are universally happy and sad respectively—there is a vast literature on that subject—but they are one of the more fundamental ways that Western music, at least, gives expression to these poles. And if the major is, for many, a 'happier' tonality, it is owing to the harmonic series, which makes the major third more inherently consonant than the minor third. So rather than obsess over major and minor as such, we can suggest that music reflects and moves us emotionally by a complex interweaving of consonance and dissonance. Whatever the mechanics, the positive and even spiritual power of music that allows itself to enter the realms of grief, dolour, loss, and sorrow is something that science, in fact, has begun to observe with interest and consistency.[14]

---

14   Three recent articles in the journal *Musicae Scientiae* are illustrative: Henna-Riikka Peltola and Tuomas Eerola, 'Fifty shades of blue: Classification of Music-Evoked Sadness', *Musicae Scientiae* 20 (2016), 84–102; Annemieke J. M. Van den Tol, Jane Edwards, and Nathan A. Heflick, 'Sad Music as a Means for Acceptance-Based Coping', *Musicae Scientiae* 20 (2016), 68–83. See also Olivia Ladinig, Charles

V. Arvo Pärt: A Case Study in Bright Sadness

Books and essays have been written about Arvo Pärt and the particular ways in which he configures loss and hope, desolation and consolation.[15] His compositional trajectory is by now well known. He began in the 1960s as a celebrated composer: first of twelve-tone music, then of collage compositions that jaggedly contrasted passages of alienating atonality with sublime harmony (often quoting Bach verbatim). Over an eight-year period during which he wrote little of significance, he immersed himself in the Franco-Flemish music of the fifteenth and sixteenth centuries and plainchant, seeking another, more pure mode of expression. This led to a decisive move away from serial atonality, away from cluttered complexity, into a new mode of composition. Beginning in 1976, after a series of untexted compositions (*Für Alina, Fratres, Spiegel im Spiegel, Cantus in Memoriam Benjamin Britten*, and *Tabula Rasa*, all of which are among his most enduring) his prolific oeuvre ever since has consisted almost exclusively in settings of sacred text. Plato would be relieved.

(a) The Role of Text

The choice to work with passages of scripture, liturgy, and hagiography bring Pärt's work decisively into what we categorised above as 'sacred music'. But text alone does not make the music spiritually affecting, and that fact is attested by an array of listeners from widely different locations of faith, age, and preferred musical genres. In fact, the explicitly religious texts of Pärt's compositions may if anything be seen as impediments to the spiritual power they exert on those listeners who are indifferent or even hostile to religion. That said, the text plays a critical role in Pärt's oeuvre in two ways. One is by shaping the music. Whether the text is actually sung—as it is in most cases—or 'played' a cappella, Pärt's music reflects every syllable of the text, for example by lengthening accented syllables relative to unaccented syllables, so that

---

Brooks, Niels Chr. Hansen, and Katelyn Horn David Huron, 'Enjoying Sad Music: A Test of the Prolactin Theory', *Musicae Scientiae* 25 (2021), 429–48.

15 See, for example, Peter C. Bouteneff, *Arvo Pärt: Out of Silence* (Yonkers, NY: SVS Press, 2015), esp. Part III: Bright Sadness.

the music can sound more or less as if the text is spoken. That method is adopted perhaps in the service of comprehensibility—which gives us one clue to the composer's priorities. In all, one can perceive a kind of obedience to the text, where the composer can say, 'The words shape my music', or 'My music is merely a translation of the words'. But that points us to another, more fundamental way in which the text shapes the music, and that is through the composer's love for it. Stemming in turn from his deeply-felt faith, we must remark upon the composer's fidelity (again, obedience) to what the words of scripture, or prayer, are actually saying. Even if the words and their meaning fall upon deaf ears, I would argue that it is that devotion to the text's sacred meaning, together with Pärt's compositional genius, that carries a spiritual force even to the non-religious listener.[16]

(b) The Way of Tintinnabuli

But there is another way in which Pärt's music reaches its listeners with a kind of mystical force. It is a quiet power, because his music tends toward softness and simplicity—more accurately associated with reduction than minimalism. But this is where I return to my thesis that much of the spiritual force of art comes from its empathic character. Again and again, we come across reviews of Pärt's music that highlight how it somehow manages to convey both brokenness and healing, loss and hope, desolation and consolation. We encounter this sentiment in the interview with Björk that I referred to earlier, in the seminal essays and interviews from the 1980s, and in Alex Ross's now iconic 2002 essay in the *New Yorker*.[17] Ross mentions how he keeps hearing stories from different people, about how Pärt's music accompanied their emotional suffering, their physical illness, their journey towards death: 'One or two such anecdotes seem sentimental; a series of them begins to suggest a slightly uncanny phenomenon', he writes. I have heard several of these

---

16 See my 'The Sound—and Hearing—of Arvo Pärt', in *Arvo Pärt: Sounding the Sacred*, ed. by Peter Bouteneff, Jeffers Engelhardt, and Robert Saler (New York: Fordham University Press, 2021), pp. 8–21, and my lecture 'Music as Translation: The Movement from Text to Reception in Arvo Pärt's Music', online video recording, *YouTube*, 26 March 2020, https://www.youtube.com/watch?v=xTLAvEWaR1M

17 Alex Ross, 'Consolations: Arvo Pärt', *The New Yorker*, 2 December 2002, https://www.therestisnoise.com/2004/04/arvo_prt_1.html

myself, from people who had never read a word about Pärt or been aware of this apparent phenomenon. Perhaps you have too. Somehow this music fulfils an inner need in those who hurt, grieve, suffer illness, or are near death.

As difficult as it may be to quantify or to explain how Pärt's music achieves that effect, there are some clear connections to be drawn between it and his compositional method. The technical method cannot explain everything, as if you could follow certain instructions and create music that accompanies the suffering, but it shows us that there is something more than just angel dust involved. I will not explain the tintinnabuli method at length, since this has been covered in numerous books and essays, beginning with Paul Hillier's 1987 monograph on Pärt.[18] But the idea lies with two voices that find expression within the music, usually simultaneously. These are, respectively, the melody or 'M' voice, that is drawn on the notes of the diatonic scale, and the triad or 'T' voice, that is constrained to the reigning triad of a given composition's key. Of course, much if not most Western tonal music consists in melodies and triads. It is a matter of how these are combined, and those compositions that follow the tintinnabuli rule strictly (*Für Alina, Missa syllabica, Passio Domini Nostri Jesu Christi secundum Joannem,* for example) allow us to trace each of these two voices very clearly, and see how these compositions both emulate and also transcend the classical Western musical tradition.

And the interesting thing that happens, when you combine these two voices, is the dynamic interplay between consonance and dissonance. Tension and resolution. Minor seconds and major seconds, minor sixths and perfect fifths, etc. Again, most Western tonal music will feature an interplay between consonance and dissonance—it is a matter of deployment. And perhaps the most distinct feature of Pärt's tintinnabuli works is the way in which the triad voice follows relatively jagged lines—fifths, thirds, octaves—where the classical tradition would have trained our ears to look for more stepped gradations between the notes. What we hear, with repeated listening, may be this jagged triad voice, or the stepwise melody voice, but mostly it is the alchemy between the

---

18 Paul Hillier, *Arvo Pärt* (Oxford: Oxford University Press, 1987). See also Leopold Brauneiss 'Musical Archetypes: The Basic Elements of the Tintinnabuli Style,' in *The Cambridge Companion to Arvo Pärt,* ed. by Andrew Shenton (Cambridge, UK: Cambridge University Press, 2012), p. 52f.

two that creates the eponymous 'little bell' sonority of tintinnabuli. Such that the two voices ultimately form an indissoluble unity. 1+1=1. This, simply put, is the mechanics behind the magic.

Naturally these formulae and their deployment will not reach everyone the same way—there has been no lack of unimpressed criticism of Pärt (partly in reaction to the rapturous reviews that proliferated during the 1980s). But there is a consensus among those who are drawn to his music that its effect is 'spiritual', that it speaks to barrenness and leaves it with some kind of hope.

The tintinnabuli method can be discerned in its germ form in a few works composed during Pärt's eight-year transition period between serial music and the 1976 breakthrough of *Für Alina*. But once it becomes fully ingrained in Pärt's oeuvre, its effect goes beyond a stylistic gimmick. It becomes subject to qualitative interpretation, by the composer himself, in ways confirmed by his listeners. The overall effect of 'bright sadness' is actually divided among the two voices: the melody is the sadness, the triad is the brightness. How odd this might sound, especially given Pärt's lopsided preference for the minor keys. How, you may ask, is the minor triad a stand-in for 'brightness'? Obviously, it is richer and more complicated than the outward effects of major and minor tonalities. The composer associates the triad and melody voices, respectively, in the following ways:[19]

Melody (M) voice	Triad (T) voice
Straying	Stability
Vulnerability	Solidity
Suffering	Consolation
My sins	Forgiveness of my sins
Human	Divine

By the time we reach the last of these pairings we see that the stakes are rather high. But we also perceive the inevitably Christian implications and foundations of this system. The application for formal Christology rests with the confluence of the human and divine, in one 'hypostasis',

---

19　These pairings derive from the composer's interviews and reflections across decades.

one concrete reality. To get fully Chalcedonian on the matter, the two are never separated or divided, nor are they confused or changed into one another.

But we need not get so theological to make this work. It is the elemental Christian dynamic that is at play, of death-and-resurrection, of redeemed suffering, expressed in Christ's own words, 'unless a grain of wheat falls into the earth and dies, it remains just a single grain; but if it dies, it bears much fruit' (John 12:24). It is the logic of the cross, about which we can sing, in some of our traditions, 'Lo, through the cross, joy has come into the world'. Christian faith is founded on that strange and painful paradox that ultimate gladness and brightness come by way of suffering and even death. In this way, then, the triad voice, even if it is an elemental minor-key triad, is the voice of the 'brightness' in the bright-sadness dynamic. We are not talking about the kind of joy evoked in Movement IV of Ludwig van Beethoven's Ninth Symphony. It is more often the subdued but pervasive assurance that death and suffering are not final. 'I have said this to you, so that in me you may have peace. In the world you face persecution. But take courage; I have overcome the world' (John 16:33). Christ has broken the world's cycle of pain and death.

Conclusions

By way of conclusion, let us return to Pärt's non-Christian hearers, who may be decidedly uninterested in being preached at with a Christian message. One may only surmise that what is reaching them is not, in any explicit manner, Jesus Christ, his death on the cross, his descent into Hades to harrow it, and his resurrection. Much as non-Christian readers appreciate the Chronicles of Narnia without a Christocentric reading of Aslan, what is reaching them, according to their own accounts, in Pärt's work is the reality of all this that rings true in so much human experience: life is full of pain, suffering, anguish, and evil. And yet, we persevere in the sure hope that this is not *all* there is to life, and perhaps even that goodness ultimately prevails. These intuitions and experiences are fundamentally human, such that in some way, shape, or form they inform all the world' major religious traditions and spiritual teachings. The Psalms are an especially potent example of texts whose spiritual power rests in their unflinching reflection of pain, suffering, and despair, combined with the ever-present conviction that God overcomes it and redeems it.

But even apart from the implied redemptive message, the music also operates purely at the level of the pain it reflects. For this is what the suffering need from each other, and from their art. Not to be cheered up. Not to be manipulated into happiness, or brought to numbness. But to be heard in their suffering. When we say that art 'reflects' our sorrow, it means that art somehow 'listens' to it. I realize this sounds implausible but it is so. And the best (which is to say the most attuned) art then goes one step further: hearing our pain, it reveals that pain does not have the last word. This, I would argue is so elemental a need, that addresses so fundamental a human reality, that to reflect and address such a need makes music nothing less than *spiritual*.

As clarified above, I have been operating on the supposition that spirituality does not rest primarily with the ethereal, much less with the magical or supernatural. Spirituality may indeed have to do with a 'higher power', with things bigger than ourselves. But if that higher power remains in the heavens, if it does not come down to us, it is of no use to anyone. If its only claim to greatness is its impenetrability, or its mystique, frankly it is not all that great. I find it unhelpful, even potentially damaging, to pit the 'supernatural' against the 'natural', as if our hope lies with escape from the daily stuff of the world. In fact, the best definition of the word 'mystical' does not have to do with esotericism or immateriality. It has to do with lived experience. What we find to be 'spiritual' is located in the deepest centre of our psychosomatic core, where grief and gladness meet. Something that we know deeply but not fully, something we feel but cannot completely explain, and perhaps especially, a gift that we receive that we know ourselves to be unworthy of. If that is what music conveys better than anything else—not in its otherworldliness but precisely in its visceral effect on us—then it is surely the most spiritual of the arts. And Arvo Pärt is one of the composers that shows this to be so.

3. Music, Breath, and Spirit

Michael O'Connor

In 1179, Hildegard of Bingen (ca. 1098–1179) was accused of contravening canon law by permitting the body of a man who had been excommunicated to be buried on her monastery's consecrated ground. The local ecclesiastical authorities, acting on behalf of the bishop of Mainz who was away in Rome, insisted that the body be disinterred. Hildegard refused. She asserted that the man had in fact been reconciled to the church before his death, his excommunication lifted. The authorities rejected this claim and instead placed the monastery under interdict: there would be no celebration of Mass, no reception of the Eucharist, and no singing of the Divine Office. The sisters' spiritual life must continue without the benefit of sacraments or singing. Eventually, witnesses were produced and the interdict was lifted. Hildegard died six months later. This 'last, bitter controversy' drew from Hildegard a remarkable letter to the Prelates of Mainz, in which she not only protests her innocence but reflects theologically on what it means for liturgical singing to be silenced.[1] It is this punishment, rather than the alleged offence, that takes up most of her attention: not only did absence make the heart grow fonder, it produced her most condensed and luminous theology of music. Prayer, worship, liturgy are more than words. For Hildegard, what had been taken away from her community was not merely an optional addition, but the essence of worship itself: the conjoining of heaven and earth. In the course of this theological reflection, she has much to say

---

1   The expression 'last, bitter controversy' is used as a chapter heading in *The Personal Correspondence of Hildegard of Bingen*, ed. by Joseph L. Baird (Oxford: Oxford University Press, 2006), pp. 155–66. The 'Letter to the Prelates of Mainz' (Letter 72), is found on pp. 156–61.

about the connection between singing and breathing, in which the link between respiration and spirituality is more than simply etymological.

More than 800 years later, public health measures enacted during the COVID-19 pandemic sent congregations home and gave rise to numerous experiments with remote and online worship. Christian communities were to conduct their spiritual lives without the benefit of sacraments or collective, in-person singing. And even when churches returned to in-person gatherings, congregational singing was silenced or heavily restricted. It is essential that we learn from what was implemented so suddenly, and with little preparation. However, this is not the only or even the most important musical consequence of the pandemic. 'We share the air' has for decades been the strapline for a campaign to raise awareness of allergies and sensitivities to scented products. COVID-19 adds a further layer of relevance to the slogan, helping to show both the positive and the negative dimensions of the interrelatedness of all things. One of the contested aspects of the pandemic was the way the virus transmits. The World Health Organization, among other public health bodies, was at first reluctant to declare the virus to be 'airborne'.[2] It is now incontestable that SARS-CoV-2 is an airborne pathogen— it hangs in the air like cigarette smoke (or incense) and spreads in crowded indoor spaces over distances far greater than two metres.[3] Like the experience endured by Hildegard and her sisters, pandemic safety measures and the ongoing experience of a respiratory virus should stimulate a renewed appreciation and understanding of sung worship.

In this chapter, I will approach these issues in the wider context of creation and incarnation, and, beyond that, I will be looking for a foundation in trinitarian theology that will offer a fruitful approach to breathing, music, and spirit. I will draw on a wide and diverse range of sources where attention has been paid to the respiratory dimension of theology, and in particular on the insights of medieval polymath Hildegard of Bingen who, as Margot Fassler has observed, 'is the only Doctor of the Roman Catholic Church from whom a large body of

---

2   Reasons for this are many but it seems that 'following the science' in pursuit of the common good was often waylaid by following the politics. This is nothing new— think tobacco, fossil fuels, and factory farming.

3   Trisha Greenhalgh et al., 'Ten Scientific Reasons in Support of Airborne Transmission of SARS-CoV-2', *The Lancet* 397.10285 (2021), 1603–05.

liturgical song survives'.⁴ My focus will be on liturgical singing, with a recurring emphasis on the pairing of word with breath/respiration. This seems opportune in an investigation of music and spiritual realities, for three reasons: first, because respiration is commonly aligned with 'spirit' (in God and humans);⁵ second, because of the important role of breathing in music-making; and third, because of the ways that COVID-19, a respiratory virus, has affected our consciousness about breathing and our relationship to the air.

From the point of view of scholars working on 'music and spiritual realities', the interdisciplinary field is ecumenical and pluralist. Every study has, at least implicitly, its own theological starting point and those starting points will be diverse and sometimes in tension (e.g., natural theology and Barthian neo-orthodoxy); it helps to make those starting points explicit, and open to critique and refinement. This paper offers a statement of one possible Roman Catholic approach. My methodological assumptions are largely pre-critical, following practices typical of patristic and medieval writers, enshrined not only in strictly theological works but also in liturgical texts and lectionaries and continued by hymn writers and poets.⁶ The aim is not to give the 'official' account (there isn't one); rather, I am attempting a thought experiment on music and worship, open to questions of spirit and spirituality. And I intend this chapter to be ecumenically open: while it draws on Catholic theology and liturgical experience, I hope its insights will be of interest beyond a Catholic readership.

I. On Spirit and Spirits

Two formulations of spirit have tended to characterise Christian thought on the topic. A predominant model, which we may oversimplify by labelling 'Neoplatonic', sees all things in a great chain of being. At the

---

4   Margot Fassler, 'Angels and Ideas: Hildegard's Musical Hermeneutic as Found in *Scivias* and Reflected in *O splendidissima gemma*', in *Unversehrt und Unverletzt: Hildegards von Bingen Menschenbild und Kirchenverständnis Heute*, ed. by Rainer Berndt SJ and Maura Zátonyi OSB (Münster: Aschendorff, 2015), pp. 189–212, at 202.
5   See Chapter 12 by Richard E. McGregor in this volume.
6   For a forthright defence of such an approach, see David C. Steinmetz, 'The Superiority of Pre-Critical Exegesis,' *Theology Today* 36 (1980), 27–38, reprinted in *The Theological Interpretation of Scripture*, ed. by Stephen E. Fowl (Oxford: Oxford University Press, 1997), pp. 26–38.

top of the chain is God, pure spirit. Next, the pure spiritual creatures, the angels. The human soul is next, then the human body, followed by the rest of material creation, animal, vegetable, and mineral. There is a great divide between spirit and matter, with human beings occupying the pivotal place as embodied souls, the whole in microcosm. When we speak of spirit and spirituality, therefore, we are alluding to this upper realm of souls, angels, and God. The problem with this model is that it encourages us to focus on the line at the midpoint, separating matter from spirit. And it encourages us to imagine two categories of existence: God, angels, and souls in one category (spirits), and all others in another (matter). In this way, it relativises other distinctions (e.g., between God and creatures, between bodies of rational beings and all other bodies, between living and non-living beings). These are not minor issues.

There is an alternative: for the Christian (indeed, for any classical theist), the most important dividing line is not that between the human body and the human soul, but that between God and creatures. The ontological difference here could not be greater; all other distinctions pale by comparison. The differences between angel and human, tree and stone, are not as great as that between any of these and God. The most fundamental thing we can say about human beings is that they are creatures.[7] The ensuing distinction between human body and soul no longer appears to be so pivotal; and while this distinction is too important and too deeply embedded in Christian tradition to be discarded, what remains is a softer (non-Cartesian) dualism.[8] As a result, the terminology of spirit and spirituality is complicated, ambiguous, polyvalent.[9] Some of our talk about music and spiritual realities will be about human knowing, loving, imagining, feeling, hoping. Some of it

---

7 Frank Senn, *Embodied Liturgy: Lessons in Christian Ritual* (Augsburg, MN: Fortress, 2016), p. xi.
8 Eleonore Stump, *Aquinas* (London: Routledge, 2003), pp. 191–216.
9 The Hebrew and Greek words normally translated as 'spirit' in biblical texts (*ruah* and *pneuma* respectively), are both also used for 'breath' and 'wind'—not to mention 'ghost'. (The same applies in the case of the Latin *spiritus*.) The tripping hazards extend to typography: for example, in Romans 1:4, the risen Jesus is said to be declared Son of God according to the 'the spirit of holiness/sanctification' (New Revised Standard Version; New American Bible Revised Edition, Douai–Rheims), or 'the Spirit of holiness' (King James Version, English Standard Version, Revised Standard Version, New International Version, Geneva). These typographical decisions have exegetical implications.

may be about theories of angelic music and the harmony of the spheres. Some of it may be about God. If both religious and non-religious people think of music as 'the most spiritual of the arts', then we have to ask: what are they thinking about? Are they looking for evidence (empirical or otherwise) of the same thing? It is a completely uncontroversial thing to say that 'music lifts my spirits', but more debatable to say that music is a 'vehicle for the Holy Spirit'. And while these claims may be compatible, they are not necessarily so; furthermore, while the former may be susceptible to direct empirical detection, the latter, in classical philosophical theology, is not.

Nevertheless, it may be impossible to achieve complete clarity and discretion, for several reasons. First, there may be a theological reason for the verbal slipperiness:

> ... *pneuma* means both the human spirit or the divine Spirit and the breath of either creaturely life or God, and indeed biblical theology tends to see the breath of life as indeed the breath or Spirit of God which is then also the source of human spirit.[10]

Second, with respect to the Son of God, he became a human being—a thinking, feeling, willing, loving animal—and, since the ascension, he is thoroughly at home in the divine sphere, filled with the Spirit, seated body and soul at the right hand of the Father (Acts 2:33).[11] And third, with respect to the church, the Second Vatican Council speaks of the Holy Spirit as the 'soul of the church', not implying a second incarnation, or a physical composition of divine and human, but rather aiming to capture the conviction that the same Spirit who is in Christ the head is also in the members which make up his body, the church.[12] In Christology and ecclesiology, divine and human 'spirit' are present and entangled and not always easy to distinguish. Furthermore, while the distinction between Creator and creatures holds for now, the

---

10 Robert Davis Hughes III, 'Catching the Divine Breath in the Paschal Mystery: An Essay on the (Im)passibility of God, in honor of Elizabeth Johnson', *Anglican Theological Review* 94.3 (2011), 527–39, at 535.

11 Thomas F. Torrance, 'The Mind of Christ in Worship: The Problem of Apollinarianism in the Liturgy', in Thomas F. Torrance, *Theology in Reconciliation: Essays towards Evangelical and Catholic Unity in East and West* (London: Geoffrey Chapman, 1975), pp. 139–214.

12 Yves Congar, *I Believe in the Holy Spirit II: Lord and Giver of Life* (London: Chapman, 1983), p. 19.

mind-boggling Christian claim is that, if the divine plan of deification (divinisation, *theosis*) is accomplished (2 Pet 1:4; 2 Cor 3:18), then even that distinction may cease to be meaningful.

II. The Eternal Now

What we know about God is far less than what we do not know about God.[13] Trinitarian theology has, of necessity, drawn on a dazzling array of models, analogies, and metaphors to try to grasp the mystery of the three-in-one, recognising that these take us always (much) less than halfway to the ineffable truth. Some of these analogies are psychological (e.g., thinking of the three persons of the Trinity as analogous to human memory, understanding, will), some are social (e.g., thinking of the Trinity as a family or community). In this chapter, I employ the model of utterance: thinking of the three persons of the Trinity as analogous to the activity of uttering, specifically as utterer, word, and breath.[14] This has the advantage of biblical warrant: God utters; the second person is the Word; the third person is the Holy Breath.[15] Theology has given plenty of attention to the verbal side of this analogy, sometimes lapsing into a logocentrism that conceals the place of the Spirit; in this chapter, I will attempt to include a complementary stress on the respiratory side. Inevitably, the data here are less vivid and concrete when compared to the Word, at times both elusive and allusive.[16] Nevertheless, both are

---

13   Lateran IV, Canon 2: 'inter creatorem et creaturam non potest tanta similitudo notari, quin inter eos maior sit dissimilitudo notanda' [between creator and creature there can be noted no similarity so great that a greater dissimiliarity cannot be seen between them], in *Decrees of the Ecumenical Councils*, ed. by Norman P. Tanner, 2 vols (Washington, DC: Georgetown University Press, 1990), I, pp. 232–33.

14   I will use 'utter' (rather than 'say' and 'speak') because it encompasses a variety of options (including saying, speaking, and singing), while also retaining a more immediate sense of vocal activity. See also Gerard Manley Hopkins in his poem 'Margaret Clitheroe':
   'She caught the crying of those Three,
   The Immortals of the eternal ring,
   The Utterer, Utterèd, Uttering,
   And witness in her place would she'.

15   On the idea of 'Breath' as the proper name of the third person (as compared to 'Love' or 'Gift'), see Etienne Vetö, *The Breath of God. An Essay on the Holy Spirit in the Trinity* (Eugene, OR: Cascade, 2019), pp. 29–42.

16   On the 'fluidity' of (language about) the Spirit, see ibid., pp. 12–22.

needed: Christology is incomplete without pneumatology, and vice versa. Like a good singer, the theologian has to pay attention to both word and breath.

In Frederick Bauerschmidt's words, 'the God who is love is not a "thing" but an activity'.[17] In the eternal now of the Trinity, the unbegotten Father begets his Son, uttering his entire understanding of himself in his Word. For Rowan Williams, in this eternal now, 'God shares, God offers, himself in an eternal act that we can only think of as if it were a great primal utterance being poured out'.[18] This primal utterance is personal and consubstantial, the one who, according to the letter to the Hebrews, is the reflection of God's glory and the exact imprint of God's very being (Heb 1:3). For Robert Jenson, this means that 'the breaking of silence is eternally constitutive of God's triune life'; in other words, God is a 'talkative God'[19]—and therefore, despite what the hymn says, there is no 'silence of eternity'.

As every singer knows, you cannot utter a word without breath. Developing this observation, Yves Congar writes: 'There is no Word without a Breath: the Word would stay put in the speaker's throat and reach no one'. Congar then presses the analogy beyond its own immediate logic: 'There is no Breath without a Word: the Breath would be without content and would communicate nothing'.[20] For animals, it is quite possible to breathe without uttering words—we breathe in and out all the time, whether or not we are speaking or singing; it is not a problem for us that many of our breaths have no semantic content. But Congar is only talking about the Trinity and he wants to highlight the uniqueness of divine utterance: God exhales his entire self in uttering his Word; there is no more to be uttered, nothing else to be breathed, because all is contained in this one act of utterance.

This utterance is not received without reply. In the eternal now of the Trinity, the Son responds with the single and complete Word of his

---

17 Frederick Christian Bauerschmidt, *The Love That Is God: An Invitation to Christian Faith* (Grand Rapids, MI: Eerdmans, 2020), p. 14.
18 In the Foreword to Lucy Winkett, *Our Sound is Our Wound* (London: Continuum, 2010), p. ix.
19 Robert Jenson, 'Joining the Eternal Conversation: John's Prologue & the Language of Worship', *Touchstone Magazine*, November 2001, http://www.touchstonemag.com/archives/article.php?id=14-09-032-f
20 Cited in Vetö, *The Breath of God*, p. 50.

own self; all that he is, he returns to the Father. In the opening words of John's Prologue, the Word is said to be 'with God' (John 1:1). The Greek expression (*pros ton theon*) suggests not just being together with, but turned towards; it implies a face-to-face presence, a responsive movement. (One could say that the Son is 'antiphon' to the Father.) Here again, since a word cannot be uttered without breath, the returning self-utterance of the Word is borne to the Father on the divine Breath.[21]

This pattern in the eternal now—that the Word is uttered on the Breath by the Father and utters himself back to the Father, on the Breath—is the basis of all activity of the Trinity 'outside' of the Trinity, in time and history, in creation, redemption, and consummation. It provides the prototype of communication among creatures, including speech and song, as well as the *telos* of all authentic communication: eschatological participation in the communion of the Trinity. What follows is a selection of key moments from a trinitarian history of prayer and worship, highlighting the interaction of Word and Breath both in God's self-disclosure in creation and redemption (going out), and in the return path of prayer, worship, and thanksgiving (coming in).

III. In the Beginning

In the rhythmic incantation at the beginning of the book of Genesis, God is portrayed creating by his Word ('God said'). The New Testament picks up and develops this insight: all things were made through the Word ('All things came into being through him, and without him not one thing came into being'; John 1:3). But the Word acted in concert with the Spirit, who 'hovered over the chaos' (Gen 1:2). Early Christian writers saw this complementarity foreshadowed in the Psalms: 'By the word of the Lord the heavens were made, and all their host by the breath of his mouth' (Ps 33:6).[22] Made in the image and likeness of God (Gen

---

21 My approach here is indebted to Vetö, *The Breath of God*, and to Edward Kilmartin, *Christian Liturgy: Theology and Practice—I: Systematic Theology of Liturgy* (Kansas City, MO: Sheed and Ward, 1988).

22 For a survey of patristic, medieval, and early modern interpretations of this verse, see Geoffrey Wainwright, 'Psalm 33 Interpreted of the Triune God', *Ex Auditu* 16 (2000), 101–20. See also chapter 6, 'Psalm 33', in Geoffrey Wainwright, *Embracing Purpose: Essays on God, the World, and the Church* (Eugene, OR: Wipf and Stock, 2012), pp. 105–25.

1:27), human beings were likewise endowed with word and breath: God breathed life into Adam's nostrils, and gave him the responsibility of naming the creatures (Gen 2:7). The second-century Targum Onkelos paraphrases the biblical text to bring this out explicitly: 'And the Lord God created Adam from dust of the ground, and breathed upon his face the breath of lives, and it became in Adam a Discoursing Spirit'.[23]

Hildegard of Bingen is heir to this tradition of thought and she reads it all as inherently musical.[24] For Hildegard, the goal of creation is to render honour and glory to God. This is a spiritual and a musical task. It is led by the angels who are precisely called spirits because of their affinity with the Spirit of God. At the beginning, Adam sang with them; in his innocence, 'before his transgression, his voice blended fully with the voices of the angels in their praise of God'.[25] When Adam sinned, and fell from Spirit-filled musical harmony, a Spirit-filled musical remedy was provided: the prophets, inspired by the Spirit, were called to compose psalms and canticles and to make musical instruments, 'to enhance these songs of praise with melodic strains'. Note that for Hildegard, the music is integral, not accidental, to this divine therapy. The spiritual restoration would be accomplished by both 'the form and quality of the instruments, as well as through the meaning of the words which accompany them'. This was restorative music, prophetic music that was able to lead the faithful 'beyond the music of this exile and recall to mind that divine melody of praise which Adam, in company with the angels, enjoyed in God before his fall'.

Hildegard combines two kinds of music here: the singing of the voice and the plucking of stringed instruments (lyre and harp). The

---

23 *The Targums Onkelos and Jonathan Ben Uzziel*, trans. by J. W. Etheridge, 2 vols (London: Longman, Green, Longman, Roberts, 1862), I, p. 38.

24 See William T. Flynn '"The Soul is Symphonic": Meditation on Luke 15:25 and Hildegard of Bingen's Letter 23', in *Music and Theology: Essays in Honor of Robin A. Leaver*, ed. by Daniel Zager (Lanham, MD: Scarecrow, 2007), pp. 1–8; William T. Flynn, 'Singing with the Angels: Hildegard of Bingen's Representations of Celestial Music', in *Conversations with Angels: Essays Towards a History of Spiritual Communication, 1100–1700*, ed. by Joad Raymond (London: Palgrave Macmillan, 2011), pp. 203–29; Tova Leigh Choate, William T. Flynn, and Margot Fassler, 'Hearing the Heavenly Symphony: An Overview of Hildegard's Musical Oeuvre with Case Studies', in *A Companion to Hildegard of Bingen*, ed. by Beverly Kienzle, Debra L. Stoudt, and George Ferzoco (Leiden: Brill, 2014), pp. 163–92.

25 'Letter to the Prelates of Mainz', in *Personal Correspondence of Hildegard of Bingen*, ed. Baird, p. 159. Quotations in the next paragraph are all from this page.

link between singing and breath is straightforward, and Hildegard supplements it by the image of the trumpet:

> Those who long to complete God's works ... can only sing the mysteries of God like a trumpet, which only returns a sound but does not function unassisted, for it is Another who breathes into it that it might give forth a sound.[26]

The sounds are Christ's, the disciple is the instrument on which Christ plays, through which his breath blows. For Hildegard, any ministry of the Word is founded on an openness to be a tube breathed through by God's Breath.

Hildegard ingeniously makes the same pneumatological claim for stringed instruments, drawing on the well-established metaphor of the Holy Spirit as the finger of God: 'People of zeal and wisdom [...] accompanied their singing with instruments played with the flexing of the fingers, recalling, in this way, Adam, who was formed by God's finger, which is the Holy Spirit'.[27] A plucked string evokes the in-breathing of the Holy Spirit at creation, the giving of breath that makes possible all human speech, singing, praise, and prayer. Thus, not only in their songs but also in the music of lyre and harp, the Holy Spirit has indeed, as the Nicene Creed asserts, 'spoken through the prophets'. In all this, the creator Spirit does not exist and operate in a vacuum. Rather, the Spirit hovers over chaos and is breathed into clay. For liturgical theologian Louis-Marie Chauvet: 'What is most spiritual always takes place in the most corporeal'.[28] And by 'corporeal' Chauvet does not just mean our flesh and blood, but also our communities and societies, cultures and rituals, histories and traditions, and the institutions to which we belong—and that includes our musicking.

---

26 'A Fellow Visionary' [= Correspondence with Elizabeth of Schönau], in *Personal Correspondence of Hildegard of Bingen*, ed. Baird, pp. 104–05.
27 Ibid. In the Sequence for Pentecost, *Veni Creator Spiritus*, the Spirit is the finger of God's right hand ('digitus paternae dexterae'). This metaphor evidently lies behind Michelangelo's famous depiction of the creation of Adam, where the in-breathing of the Spirit is represented by the out-stretched finger of God's right hand. This metaphor seems to derive from a creative reception of two gospel texts: Luke 11:20, 'But if it is by the finger of God that I cast out the demons, then the kingdom of God has come to you', and Matthew 12:28, 'But if it is by the Spirit of God that I cast out demons, then the kingdom of God has come to you'.
28 Louis-Marie Chauvet, *The Sacraments: The Word of God at the Mercy of the Body* (Collegeville, MN: Liturgical Press, 2001), p. xii. The original subtitle is: *Parole de Dieu au risque du corps*.

IV. In the Fullness of Time

In the fullness of time, God's Word was born of a woman, uttered into the ebb and flow of creation. God had now 'spoken to us by a Son' (Heb 1:1–2). This Word is the unique and complete revelation of the Father, his first, only and last Word. In the powerful expression of John of the Cross:

> In giving us his Son, his only Word (for he possesses no other), he spoke everything to us at once in this sole Word—and he has no more to say ... because what he spoke before to the prophets in parts, he has now spoken all at once by giving us the All Who is His Son.[29]

Luke's account of the annunciation may be read in this light. The Holy Spirit brings about the advent of the Word into history, overshadowing the Virgin Mary at the dawn of the New Creation as it had hovered over the face of the waters at the first creation. In the angel Gabriel's words: 'The Holy Spirit will come upon you, and the power of the Most High will overshadow you; therefore the child to be born will be holy; he will be called Son of God' (Luke 1:35). Although it is the Spirit who comes upon Mary, she does not conceive and give birth to the Holy Spirit; the Breath in her brings forth the Word made flesh. As Chauvet puts it, 'the Spirit appears as the agent of God's embodiment: it gives a body to the Word'.[30]

Hildegard paraphrases and expands on the angel's greeting in a most striking meditation on the incarnation, making it explicitly musical. In the antiphon 'Ave generosa', Hildegard rejoices that heavenly music, which is the Son, is enclosed in Mary's womb, sounding forth from her flesh:

> Your womb truly held joy,
> when all the celestial symphony
> sounded from you,
> for you, Virgin, bore the Son of God,
> when your purity became luminous in God.
> Your flesh held joy,
> like grass upon which dew falls,

---

29 John of the Cross, *Ascent of Mount Carmel*, II, p. 22, cited in *Catechism of the Catholic Church*, 2nd ed. (Vatican City: Libreria Editrice Vaticana, 2019), §65.
30 Chauvet, *The Sacraments*, p. 166.

> pouring its life-green into it,
> even as it happened in you,
> O Mother of all joy.[31]

Through the workings of the Spirit, Christ becomes the 'song that puts heaven and earth into harmony'.[32] Mary's conception is likened to the dew falling on the grass and giving it life and vitality (Hildegard's famous 'viriditas' [greenness]). Again, Hildegard's allusion to the working of the Holy Spirit draws on a well-established biblically-inspired metaphor: among other texts, the dew on Gideon's fleece (Judg 6:36–40) was taken by Irenaeus, Origen, Chrysostom, and others to prefigure the descent of the Holy Spirit at the annunciation.[33]

Here we should pause and take stock of the way our analogy has been stretched. Because the Word has been made flesh, the 'utterance' of the Word takes the form of a pregnancy and a childbirth. The Word is not simply letters to be read off a page, a textual assertion about the love of God, but an incarnate, embodied revelation of the love of God. The Word became body language. Jesus revealed the Kingdom of God in his teaching and preaching, but also when he took children in his arms, when he touched and healed those who were sick, when he looked on the rich young man with love, when he looked on Peter his betrayer, when he allowed the woman to anoint his feet, when he laid down his life for his friends, and when he breathed on his disciples after his resurrection. The Word is not only 'what we have heard', but is also 'what we have seen with our eyes, what we have looked at and touched with our hands' (1 John 1:1). The Second Vatican Council, in its decree on divine revelation, underlines the presence of non-verbal communication, of body language, in the Word made flesh. This culminates in the paschal mystery of his death and resurrection:

---

31 'Venter enim tuus gaudium habuit, / cum omnis celestis symphonia / de te sonuit, / quia, Virgo, Filium Dei portasti, / ubi castitas tua in Deo claruit. / Viscera tua gaudium habuerunt, / sicut gramen, super quod ros cadit, / cum ei viriditatem infudit, / ut et in te factum est, / o Mater omnis gaudii'. Text and translation from Barbara Newman, *Symphonia: A Critical Edition of the Symphonia Armonie Celestium Revelationum*, 2nd ed. (Ithaca, NY: Cornell University Press, 1998), pp. 122–25.

32 Christina Labriola, 'Recalling the Original Harmony of Paradise', in *Music, Theology, and Justice*, ed. by Michael O'Connor, Hyun-Ah Kim, and Christina Labriola (Lanham, MD: Rowman and Littlefield, 2017), 163–79, at 168.

33 Paul Ladouceur, 'Old Testament Prefigurations of the Mother of God', *St Vladimir's Theological Quarterly* 50.1–2 (2006), 5–57, see 23–26 for the dew on Gideon's fleece.

> Jesus perfected revelation by fulfilling it through his whole work of making himself present and manifesting himself: through his words and deeds, his signs and wonders, but especially through his death and glorious resurrection from the dead and final sending of the Spirit of truth.[34]

Jesus is the icon of the invisible God (Col 1:15), not only making the invisible God visible, but also making the intangible God tangible, the inaudible God audible. This is the height and depth of the one Word that is uttered on the breath of the Spirit, accomplished through the agency of the Spirit, breathing the Word into time and space, history and culture, a baby born of Mary.

At the same time as he embodied God's word to the world, Jesus gathered to himself an ecclesial body, so that he might, as the first-born of many, return to the Father a chorus of prayer, praise, thanksgiving. He is the way, the mediator through, with, and in whom, creation comes before the Father. He had come from God and was returning to God (John 13:3, *pros ton theon* again), but he did not return empty; the Word accomplishes 'all that it was meant to do'.[35] A glimpse of this is shown in this prayer in Luke:

> Jesus rejoiced in the Holy Spirit and said, 'I thank you, Father, Lord of heaven and earth, because you have hidden these things from the wise and the intelligent and have revealed them to infants; yes, Father, for such was your gracious will'. (Lk 10:21)

As in all the instances where the gospels relate the words of Jesus in prayer (the words of the Word), he does not pray to the Spirit but always to the Father. He rejoices in the Spirit and addresses the Father. This is not an additional activity, tacked onto his person, but something that describes his ontology as Word antiphonal to the uttering Father: Jesus

---

[34] Second Vatican Council, 'Dei Verbum', 18 November 1965, 1, §4, https://www.vatican.va/archive/hist_councils/ii_vatican_council/documents/vat-ii_const_19651118_dei-verbum_en.html

[35] 'For as the rain and the snow come down from heaven, and do not return there until they have watered the earth, making it bring forth and sprout, giving seed to the sower and bread to the eater, so shall my word be that goes out from my mouth; it shall not return to me empty, but it shall accomplish that which I purpose, and succeed in the thing for which I sent it' (Is 55:10–11).

is prayer in person, he is 'sheer prayer'.[36] This is the dramatic playing out in history of his eternal relationship to the Father in the Spirit. And it holds true when joy gives way to sorrow. Compare these two texts:

> In the days of his flesh, Jesus offered up prayers and supplications, with loud cries and tears, to the one who was able to save him from death, and he was heard because of his reverent submission. (Heb 5:7)
> ... how much more will the blood of Christ, who through the eternal Spirit offered himself without blemish to God, purify our conscience from dead works to worship the living God! (Heb 9:14)

Even in the hour of his agony, when his prayer was not rejoicing but anguish, his antiphonal return to the Father, was offered 'through the eternal Spirit'. In death, he 'gave a loud cry and breathed his last' (Mark 15:37), he 'bowed his head and gave up his Spirit' (John 19:30).

V. In These Last Days

From the first monks in the Syrian Desert to the megachurch congregations of today, Christians believe that they encounter Christ when they come together to worship: 'Where two or three are gathered together in my name, there am I in the midst of them' (Mt 18:20). The Second Vatican Council employs this text when talking of different modes of the presence of Christ in the liturgy. It affirms that he is present in the Eucharist and other sacraments, in the person of the minister, in the proclaimed word, and in the gathered assembly—specifically when it 'prays and sings'.[37] Christ faces in two directions at once: he is the

---

36 Jesus 'is not first of all an individual person who then prays to the Father, his prayer to the Father is what constitutes him as who he is. He is not just one who prays, not even one who prays best, he is sheer prayer' (Herbert McCabe, *God Matters* (London: Chapman, 1987), p. 220).

37 'To accomplish so great a work Christ is always present in his church, especially in liturgical celebrations. He is present in the sacrifice of the Mass both in the person of his minister, "the same now offering, through the ministry of priests, who formerly offered himself on the cross" [Council of Trent], and most of all in the eucharistic species. By his power he is present in the sacraments so that when anybody baptises it is really Christ himself who baptises. He is present in his word since it is he himself who speaks when the holy scriptures are read in church. Lastly, he is present when the church prays and sings, for he has promised "where two or three are gathered together in my name there am I in the midst of them" (Mt 18:20)' (Second Vatican Council, 'Sacrosanctum Concilium', 4 December 1963,

Word coming from the Father (as proclamation and gift) and he is the Word returning to the Father (as prayer and song). The Council stressed that Christ's presence is not an abstract presence but is made manifest through sensible signs:

> In the liturgy the sanctification of women and men is given expression in symbols perceptible by the senses [*signa sensibilia*] and is carried out in ways appropriate to each of them. In it, complete and definitive public worship is performed by the mystical body of Jesus Christ, that is, by the Head and his members.

It is clear here that the sensible signs are not restricted to the canonical sacraments but comprise the whole environment of ritual worship. In this context, liturgical singing, carried out according to its own musical integrity, is drawn into the movement of worship and sanctification.

All of this is the sign of the presence of the Spirit of Pentecost in the Christian community. There is a pattern here. The Spirit dwells within the baptised (and confirmed) and they become not other Spirits, but other Christs and members of his body; the Spirit 'inspires' (breathes into) the apostolic writers and their words become the Word of God; the Spirit comes upon the bread and wine, and they become the body and blood of Christ.[38] The Holy Breath gives a body to the Word. Paul is explicit: 'No one can say "Jesus is Lord" except by the Holy Spirit' (1 Cor 12:3). As at the annunciation when Mary received the Spirit and bore the Word, so on the brink of Pentecost, Mary waited in prayer with the disciples for the Spirit that would make them into the Body of Christ. Willie Jennings notes the parallels, but highlights the difference: as the 'agent of embodiment', the Spirit forms not a single body for the Word but an ecclesial body, a fellowship, a community:

---

§7, https://www.vatican.va/archive/hist_councils/ii_vatican_council/documents/vat-ii_const_19631204_sacrosanctum-concilium_en.html). See also United States Conference of Catholic Bishops, *The Roman Missal* (Washington, DC: USCCB, 2011), 'General Introduction', §27.

38 The image of the dew appears here, falling on the bread and wine this time to transform them into the eucharistic presence of Christ: 'Make holy, therefore, these gifts, we pray, by sending down your Spirit upon them like the dewfall, so that they may become for us the Body and Blood of our Lord Jesus Christ' (Eucharistic Prayer II, in *Roman Missal*, 'Order of Mass', §101).

> This moment echoes Mary's intimate moment. The Holy Spirit again overshadows. However this similar holy action creates something different, something startling. The Spirit creates joining. The followers of Jesus are now being connected in a way that joins them to people in the most intimate space—of voice, memory, sound, body, land, and place.[39]

Jennings specifically highlights the sonorous capacity of that body, united in voice and sound. Hildegard spells out the musical parallels and the difference:

> Consider too that just as the body of Jesus Christ was born of the purity of the Virgin Mary through the operation of the Holy Spirit so too the canticle of praise, reflecting celestial harmony, is rooted in the Church through the Holy Spirit. ... Whence, in metaphor, the prophetic spirit commands us to praise God with clashing cymbals and cymbals of jubilation, as well as other musical instruments which men of wisdom and zeal have invented, because all arts pertaining to things useful and necessary for mankind have been created by the breath that God sent into man's body. For this reason it is proper that God be praised in all things.[40]

Conclusion

Through a trinitarian theology of liturgical singing, this chapter provides a thought experiment, a paradigm for the study of music and spirit, adaptable to a variety of other (non-liturgical, non-religious) contexts. There are three outcomes that are worth underlining: first, for many Christians, it is a conviction of faith that they experience the divine in worship. Since, in this approach, the Spirit 'epiphanizes in flesh and blood',[41] we should expect to find spiritual realities not beyond the material or physical, but through, with, and in them. If music is the 'most spiritual of the arts' this cannot mean that it is the 'least physical of the arts'. Second, while this approach does not rule out extraordinary or liminal experiences of music and spiritual realities, it expects that a singing, praying assembly is 'routinely' in spiritual communion with God. Every Sunday, people sing to the Lord, and expect to encounter

---

39   Willie Jennings, *Acts* (Louisville, KY: Westminster John Knox, 2017), p. 28.
40   *Personal Correspondence of Hildegard of Bingen*, ed. Baird, pp. 160–61.
41   Geoffrey Preston, Faces of the Church: Meditations on a Mystery and its Images (Edinburgh: T&T Clark, 1997), p. 281.

Christ, to hear the Word of God, to breathe in the Holy Breath of God. Through the practice of liturgical singing, a sensible sign that participates in the trinitarian work of worship and sanctification, the Spirit makes the body of Christ breathe. Taken together, these two points raise the question of how this spiritual presence is known. Alongside empirical studies on the potential spiritual effects of music, we might fruitfully consider the cluster of traditional methods of spiritual discernment developed in monastic and Ignatian circles. Third, this approach argues against drawing a strong line separating bodily respiration and corporate spirituality. On the negative side, this is implicated in our responses to COVID-19: the ongoing presence of an airborne pathogen makes worship services potential super-spreader events (likewise choral and wind-band concerts, karaoke nights, opera, etc.). The exchange of breath that facilitates sharing the Word is compromised by a new and evolving airborne pathogen that has proved fatal to millions, has reduced life expectancy around the world, and is increasingly seen to cause long-term disability—we will be seeing consequences for choristers and congregations who cannot sing as well as before, and church members, of all ages, increasingly asking to join worship online because they are not well enough to get to church. If worship is to be life-giving, then churches must be places where the air can be trusted. On the positive side, COVID-19 has reminded us in a new way of an old truth: that all things are connected and interdependent, that the material and the spiritual intermingle in ways that often lie outside of our attention. Worship spaces, where we share the Holy Breath, can be spaces where such respiratory interaction promotes *viriditas*.

4. An Adorative Posture towards Music and Spiritual Realities

Férdia J. Stone-Davis

In the preface to the *Proslogion*, Anselm (d. 1109) notes that he wrote the work 'from the point of view of one trying to raise his mind to the contemplation of God and seeking to understand what he believes'.[1] This idea of 'faith seeking understanding' is a complex one. However, if we take our cue from accounts that suggest that reason and faith do not have to be separated but are, at their foundation, inseparable, we may find a fruitful way into the connection between music and spiritual realities, and perceptions thereof. How so? In the first instance, the connection between faith and understanding indicates the positionality of any assertion that music might be theological, religious, or spiritual, thereby delimiting the kind of 'demonstration' that might be possible.[2] Indeed, 'faith *seeking* understanding' may intimate that attention to how we approach the question of the relationship between music and such realities may be more productive than 'demonstration' of that relationship per se. In the second instance, the connection between faith and understanding might suggest a particular relationship between music's materiality and our imaginative engagement with it, one that transforms sound into music and more broadly instantiates (or exemplifies) faith in 'something more'. Finally, and in the third instance,

---

1   Anselm, 'Proslogion', in *Anselm of Canterbury: The Major Works*, ed. by Brian Davies and Gillian Evans (Oxford: Oxford University Press, 2008), pp. 82–104, at 83.
2   Given the importance of positionality in this chapter, it is only fair to be transparent about my own, which is broadly speaking Catholic, and thus sacramental in approach.

this relationship may usefully be unpacked in terms of a movement that ultimately marks a shift towards the 'adorative' (one that proceeds in and through the material), that is, our elevation towards God.

I. Positionality

In relation to the first point—the recognition embedded within the claim 'faith seeking understanding' that any assertion of theological, religious, or spiritual meaning in music is always and already embedded in a prior set of commitments—it is helpful to recall the intimate relationship between music and transcendence. In some sense music has transcendence built into its very structure, since its meaning is irreducible, resisting paraphrase or concise explication. Whilst this is true of all artforms to an extent—with linguistic paraphrase only scratching the surface of how and in what way a particular artform means—the case seems to be more pronounced in the instance of music, with questions of 'ineffability' coming more readily to the fore.[3] The nature of the ineffability remains in question, however, since there is ambiguity as to whether the resistance characteristic of music relates to an epistemological transcendence (that is, the recognition that access to 'reality' broadly conceived is limited and incomplete) or an ontological transcendence (which entails the idea that there is an entity or realm that is inaccessible to human reason).[4]

Not only is music's structure bound up with the idea of transcendence, but music enables humans to 'transcend' in diverse ways that are differently conceived across time, in distinct contexts and according to individual and social perspectives.[5] In this sense there is

---

3   For an extended consideration of music's ineffability, see Michael Gallope, *Deep Refrains: Music, Philosophy and the Ineffable* (Chicago, IL: Chicago University Press, 2017). For an example of some of the ways in which music 'resists' particular meanings, see Morag J. Grant and Férdia J. Stone-Davis, *The Soundtrack of Conflict: The Role of Music in Radio Broadcasting in Wartime and in Conflict Situations* (Hildesheim: Olms Verlag, 2013).

4   For an articulation of these two types of transcendence in relation to the sublime, see Guy Sircello, 'How is a Theory of the Sublime Possible?', *The Journal of Aesthetics and Art Criticism* 51.4 (1993), 541–50.

5   Music sociologist, Tia DeNora, has written widely on the ways in which music allows us to go beyond, using music, in her terms, as a 'technology of the self'. See Tia DeNora, *Music in Everyday Life* (Cambridge, UK: Cambridge University Press,

no one understanding of music's transcendence that outdoes another. This is especially the case given our present concern. If the category of 'spiritual' is incorporated into the remit of the kinds of reality that music affords,[6] the notion of transcendence ought to remain purposively fluid as a category. This is because spirituality itself is multifaceted and broad in scope, and so too the conceptions of transcendence connected to it. For, understandings of transcendence differ according to what individuals take to be the ultimate value or end of their spirituality.[7]

The open scope of music's meanings is also bound up with the idea of transcendence itself. To transcend is to go beyond. Understood as such, the term has a wide application to a variety of phenomena and across a range of disciplines.[8] Within the domains of theology and philosophy (and discussions between the two) the idea of transcendence has acquired particular relevance, as it has also in discussions of music and sense-making. Within such discussions, two understandings tend to prevail: transcendence is either conceived in vertical terms, situated in

---

2000), pp. 46–74; and Eadem, *Music Asylums: Wellbeing through Music in Everyday Life* (Burlington: Ashgate, 2013). Philosopher Andrew Bowie frames music's capacity to enable transcendence in relation to freedom and the overcoming of obstacles: 'The transcendence at issue here is, then, anchored in a thoroughly realistic (though not in the current philosophical sense) sense of finitude and limitations of embodied human existence. It serves as a reminder that any current or dominant form of human existence can become a ground from which one may need to liberate oneself. In modernity, it seems that art may often provide more effective ways of achieving transcendence that many forms of philosophy' (Andrew Bowie, 'Music, Transcendence, and Philosophy', *Music and Transcendence*, ed. Stone-Davis, pp. 213–23 (at 223)).

6 For my use of 'affordance', see James J. Gibson, 'Theory of Affordances', in *The People, Place, and Space Reader*, ed. by Jen Jack Gieseking et al. (London: Routledge 2014), pp. 56–60 ('The affordances of the environment are what it offers the animal, what it provides or furnishes, either for good or ill'; p. 56). Eric F. Clarke applies the term 'affordances' to music in Eric F. Clarke, *Ways of Listening: An Ecological Approach to the Perception of Musical Meaning* (Oxford: Oxford University Press, 2005).

7 Here, one might take Sandra Schneider's definition as indicative, where spirituality is the 'experience of conscious involvement in the project of life-integration through self-transcendence toward the ultimate value one perceives' (Sandra M. Schneiders, 'The Study of Christian Spirituality: Contours and Dynamics of a Discipline', *Studies in Spirituality* 8 (1998), 38–57 (at 39)).

8 See also Jeremy Begbie, *Redeeming Transcendence in the Arts: Bearing Witness to the Triune God* (London: SCM Press, 2018); John D. Caputo and Michael J. Scanlon, eds, *Transcendence and Beyond: A Postmodern Enquiry* (Bloomington, IN: Indiana University Press, 2007); and Fergus Kerr, *Immortal Longings: Versions of Transcending Humanity* (London: SPCK, 1997).

relation to an 'absolute' that lies beyond the material, or is unpacked in horizontal terms, remaining situated within the 'immanent' and the material. Mark Johnson helpfully conceptualises the vertical and horizontal forms of transcendence thus: vertical transcendence is the 'alleged capacity to rise above and shed our finite form and to "plug into the infinite"'. Horizontal transcendence 'recognises the inescapability of human finitude and is compatible with the embodiment of meaning, and personal identity. From this human perspective, transcendence consists in our happy ability to sometimes "go beyond" our present situation in transformative acts that change both our world and ourselves'.[9] All this is to say that music can accrue significance by lifting us out of certain situations, charging and changing certain frames of meaning and transforming our perspective—although it does not necessarily do so, or do so uniformly or universally—and this process can be understood and elaborated in various ways, theological, religious, and spiritual (as well as ways that are not thus classed).

Given the backdrop of the dictum 'faith seeking understanding' and the fluid nature of musical meaning (which, as has been suggested, it may differ from person to person and evolves over time), and the inchoate character of transcendence, it seems unreasonable to delimit *a priori* how and in what way music enables transcendence. Furthermore, making authoritative claims about the kind of transcendence that is entailed by any one experience seems unwarranted. If by demonstration we mean something akin to a certain scientific method that aims towards causal knowledge and general truths via an inductive and empirically grounded procedure, the very fluidity of music's meaning suggests that 'demonstration' is not the most fruitful way of discussing music in relation to theological, religious, and spiritual realities.[10] This is because the slipperiness of music and our experience of it prevents the

---

9   Mark Johnson, *The Meaning of the Body: Aesthetics of Human Understanding* (Chicago, IL: Chicago University Press, 2007), p. 281.

10 See here Steven Shapin, *The Scientific Revolution* (Chicago, IL: University of Chicago Press, 1996), p. 92. Communication is central to this process of demonstration. Shapin notes (pp. 107–08) the importance of public witnessing of experimental performances (something which became a regular feature of meetings of the Royal Society), detailed instructions to enable physical replication, and then virtual witnessing (that is indirect witnessing through reading reports of experiments and finding 'adequate grounds to trust their accuracy and veracity'; p. 108). This last feature is discussed particularly in relation to Robert Boyle. This

possibility of 'proving' in any categorical sense that applies at a generic level to all music and/or all theological, religious, or spiritual realities (or any conflation of these) in all instances. The idea of demonstration may be more relevant if we take it to mean 'pointing out' and 'drawing attention to' features of a particular music experience that by virtue of certain characteristics can be tethered to theological, religious, or spiritual concepts and considerations (such that one can say, for example, 'this is how I felt at this point in the music and this is how I understand this feeling'). If we construe the role of demonstrating thus, we can discuss music's meanings, and identify potential points of convergence (even if differently elucidated).[11] It may be, however, that speaking in terms of how we 'approach' the question of how music relates to theological, religious, and spiritual realities has a certain advantage over demonstration, one also that does not entail the conflict of horizontal and vertical senses of transcendence but allows their coexistence, as we shall see.

II. Materiality

To the second point, 'faith seeking understanding' might suggest a particular relationship between music's materiality and our imaginative engagement with it, one that is involved in transforming sound into music and that involves orienting us in a way that 'looks through and beyond' the physical. The thought of Roger Scruton on music is helpful in this regard. The relationship between music and sound is of a piece with the cognitive dualism Scruton upholds, that is, the recognition that the world can be understood in two incommensurable ways, 'the way of science, and the way of inter-personal understanding'.[12] He suggests that, although music is constituted within and through the physical realm it is not explicable solely by means of it, something a 'resolutely physicalist

---

inductive approach was not accepted by all, see Shapin, *Scientific Revolution*, p. 110f.

11 Although in principle we must remain open to the possibility of multiple meanings—ones that extend to all faith traditions, and none—ensuring this in practice is another matter, necessitating an awareness of and reflection on implicit bias as well as issues of epistemic injustice.

12 Roger Scruton, *The Soul of the World* (Princeton, NJ: Princeton University Press, 2014), p. 34.

approach' would maintain.¹³ Rather, music emerges from sounds, becoming more than them. To explain: according to Scruton, sounds are not reducible to their causes and are therefore secondary objects. 'They are produced by physical disturbances, but are not identical with those disturbances, and can be understood without reference to their physical causes'.¹⁴ It is on this basis that Scruton posits sounds as 'pure events'.¹⁵ Sounds are 'things that happen, but which don't happen to anything'¹⁶ and it is this that enables humans to 'impose upon them an order that is quite independent of any physical order in the world'.¹⁷ Moreover, it is their detachability (in this sense) which grounds music:

> The ability of pure events to stand in perceived relations to each other independent of any perceived relations between their causes is a deep presupposition of music, in which note follows note according to the internal logic of the musical line, giving rise to a virtual causality that has nothing to do with the process whereby sounds are produced ... music is an extreme case of something that we witness throughout the sound world, which is the internal organisation of sounds as pure events.¹⁸

On the basis of the detachability of sound from its source, Scruton maintains that our experience of music is 'acousmatic'.¹⁹ In music, Scruton suggests, people focus on what can be heard in sounds: '[w]hat they then hear is not a succession of sounds, but a movement between

---

13   Roger Scruton, 'Sounds as Secondary Objects and Pure Events', in *Sounds & Perception: New Philosophical Essays*, ed. by Matthew Nudds and Casey O'Callaghan (Oxford: Oxford University Press), pp. 50–69 (at 50–51): 'Sounds, they [physicalists] argue, are identical with neither the waves that transmit them nor the auditory experiences through which we perceive them. They are identical with the events that generate the sound waves—physical disturbances in physical things, such as those that occur when the string of a violin vibrates in air'.
14   Roger Scruton, *Understanding Music: Philosophy and Interpretation* (London: Bloomsbury 2009), p. 5.
15   Ibid.
16   Ibid.: 'A car crash is something that happens to a car. You can identify a car crash only by identifying the car that crashed. Sounds, by contrast, can be identified without referring to any object which participates in them'.
17   Ibid.
18   Ibid., p. 28. See also p. 37: 'Musical understanding is not a form of theoretical understanding, and the kind of necessity that we hear in a musical phrase or sequence, when we hear that it must be so, is not the kind of necessity that we know from rule-following or mathematical proof'.
19   Ibid., p. 5.

tones, governed by a virtual causality that resides in the musical line'.[20] Thus, '[t]he first note of the melody brings the second into being, even though the first sound is produced by someone blowing on a horn at one end of the orchestra, the second by someone pulling a bow across a cello string at the other'.[21]

Now, whilst the extent to which Scruton articulates the distinction between sounds and music is problematic (on the one hand, it undermines his own cognitive dualism such that it verges on ontological dualism and, on the other hand, it prioritises the acousmatic to such a degree that the acoustic becomes peripheral to music-making, a claim that obscures as much about the musical experience as it elucidates),[22] what it valuably illuminates is the way in which we 'read into' or rather 'hear into' musical sounds, making sense of them.[23] That is, musical sounds are never simply given but are imaginatively engaged with, and this engagement can take many different forms, bring many different

---

20 Scruton maintains that within the musical experience a 'double intentionality' is at play such that '[y]ou hear a succession of sounds, ordered in time, and this is something you believe to be occurring—something you "literally hear". And you hear in those sounds a melody that moves through the imaginary space of music. This is not something you believe to be occurring, but something you imagine: just as you imagine the face in the picture, while seeing that it is not literally there' (ibid., p. 43). Given that I have been emphasising positionality, it is important to note that Scruton has a particular kind of music in mind: namely, music in the Western classical tradition. It is necessary to bear in mind that not all types of music are to be understood in terms of (or assimilated to) the 'logic' of Western classical music. Indeed, examining distinct traditions of music will be necessary to understand how 'hearing into' might be said to occur more broadly, if at all.

21 Ibid., p. 48.

22 See Férdia J. Stone-Davis, 'Making an Anthropological Case: Cognitive Dualism and the Acousmatic', *Philosophy: The Journal of the Royal Institute of Philosophy 90.352* (2015), 263–76.

23 See Martin Heidegger, *Being and Time*, trans. by Joan Stambaugh, rev. by Dennis J. Schmidt (Albany, NY: State University of New York Press, 1996), p. 153, cited in Jeff R. Warren, *Music and Ethical Responsibility* (Cambridge, UK: Cambridge University Press, 2014), p. 63: 'Hearkening is itself phenomenally more primordial than what the psychologist "initially" defines as hearing, the sensing of tones and the perception of sounds. Hearkening, too, has the mode of being of a hearing that understands. "Initially" we never hear noises and complexes of sound, but the creaking wagon, the motorcycle. We hear the column on the march, the north wind, the woodpecker tapping, the crackling fire. It requires a very artificial and complicated attitude in order to "hear" a "pure noise".' See also Warren, *Music and Ethical Responsibility*, p. 64: 'To hear a sound as "pure noise" requires a directedness to sound outside of everyday listening. Much of the work of John Cage, for example, is to encourage people to undo their "hearing-as" and "listen abstractly"'.

frames of reference (religious and otherwise) to bear, and enable different kinds of participation and attention.

If musical listening thus involves 'hearing into' sound, it is possible that in certain instances it can entail 'hearing beyond', in this sense moving past an understanding of music as an object to understanding music as a subject. To suggest that art might be viewed as person-like is not new. In his book *Seeing Things: Deepening Relations with Visual Artefacts* (2007), Stephen Pattison suggests that art and artefacts are usefully considered as full of intention and emotion and that it is advantageous to take seriously our person-like relationships with them, as well as their interaction in personal ways. This is on the basis that such artefacts have been created by human persons who have filled them with intention, emotion, agency, and communication (although the artefact transcends these human origins), as well as the observation that we do in fact treat some objects as having person-like qualities.[24] Pattison does not thereby suggest that every artefact is as important to the human moral community as every human being, nor hold that every artefact deserves the same respect and treatment as a sentient creature, but that they ought to be given due consideration.[25]

The person-like character of music has also been posited by Scruton, who suggests the fruitfulness of an analogy between musical understanding and interpersonal understanding. In each case, experience emerges in response to something that appears at the 'brink' of the empirical world. In the case of interpersonal understanding, I am addressed by another human person who, as such, is not only an object in the world but is also a subject. That is, like me, self-conscious. Within this interaction my awareness of the person extends beyond

---

24 Stephen Pattison, *Seeing Things: Deepening Relations with Visual Artefacts* (London: SCM Press, 2007), p. 204. Pattison also draws on the 'epistemological principle of mutual reciprocity between things and people' articulated by Lorraine Code, *What Can She Know? Feminist Theory and the Construction of Knowledge* (Ithaca, NY: Cornell University Press, 1991) pp. 164–65: '[A]fter Heisenberg's formulation of the "uncertainty principle", it is no longer possible to assert unequivocally that objects of study are inert in and untouched by the observational process even of physics. Once that point is acknowledged, it is no longer so easy to draw rigid lines separating responsive from unresponsive objects. Moving to a framework of "second person" knowledge ... calls ... for a recognition that rocks and cells, and scientists, are located in many relationships to one another, all of which are open to analysis and critique". See also Pattison, *Seeing Things*, p. 210.

25 Pattison, *Seeing Things*, p. 215.

what is immediately evident, that is, beyond the observable, and grasps towards an intentionality that can neither be captured by, nor reduced to, purely empirical investigation and causal explanation. As Scruton puts it: 'Each human object is also a subject, addressing us in looks, gestures and words, from the transcendental horizon of the "I". Our responses to others aim towards that horizon, passing on beyond the body to the being it incarnates'.[26]

Similarly, within its acousmatic space, music exhibits intentionality, operating by means of the freedom and necessity implied by its virtual causality. That is, in 'successful' works of music, 'there is a reason for each note, though not necessarily a reason that could be put into words. Each note is a response to the one preceding it and an invitation to its successor'.[27] On this basis, Scruton affirms the analogy between musical intentionality and human intentionality:

> It [music] moves as we move, with reasons for what it does and a sense of purpose (which might at any moment evaporate, like the purposes of people). It has the outward appearance of inner life, so to speak, and although it is heard and not seen, it is heard as the voice is heard, and understood like the face—as a revelation of free subjectivity.[28]

As we have seen, the idea of 'something more' is built into our engagement with the materiality of music in two ways. First, musical listening involves 'hearing into' sound, imaginatively creating a musical object that peels away from sound to create an intentional realm of musical movement. Second, musical listening facilitates 'hearing beyond' sound, attending to music as if it were a subject, a revelation of something beyond (but not detached from) what is presented to us. In both cases, one can understand how music might thus facilitate and cultivate an attention to, and trust of, that which resists and/or eludes definitive conceptualisation, and, in certain instances, how it might be associated with theological, religious, or spiritual realities.

---

26   Scruton, *Soul of the World*, p. 74.
27   Roger Scruton, 'Music and the Transcendental', in *Music and Transcendence*, ed. Stone-Davis, pp. 75–84 (at 82).
28   Scruton, *Soul of the World*, pp. 147–48.

III. Adorative Intellect

'Faith seeking understanding' is also a fruitful way to envisage the connection between music and theological, religious, and spiritual realities by positing a movement towards the 'adorative' (one that proceeds in and through the material), that is, our elevation towards God. In adopting this language, I am taking my cue from Jacob Sherman's account of Anselm,[29] building on the account of 'hearing in' and 'hearing beyond' outlined above, and working from two contextual markers surrounding Anselm's phrase. The first contextual marker concerns the relationship between faith and reason. In the pre-modern period, the two are not sharply divided. Grant Kaplan notes: 'The understanding arrived at through the rational, cogitative activity takes place on the same graced continuum as faith. Understanding—*intellectus*—does not mean the rational pursuit that humans undertake *on their own*'.[30] This ties in with the second contextual marker, which is the framing of Anselm's ontological argument within the context of prayer: 'You who give understanding to faith, grant me that I may understand, as much as You see fit, that You exist as we believe You to exist, and that You are what we believe You to be'.[31] Indeed, as has been observed by Marilyn McCord Adams:

> [T]he *Proslogion* alternates prayer exercises, designed to stir *the emotions and will* (in chapters 1, 14–18, and 24–26) so that the soul may seek by desiring and desire by seeking, with the hope of finding by loving and loving by finding, with sections of *intellectual* inquiry into the being of God (chapters 2–13 and 18–23) thereby focusing and refocusing the whole self as its investigation spirals upward toward increasingly inaccessible matters.[32]

What both of these contextual markers point towards is the fact that theological, religious and spiritual knowledge is not neutral and

---

29 Jacob Holsinger Sherman, *Partakers of the Divine: Contemplation and the Practice of Philosophy* (Minneapolis, MN: Fortress Press, 2014), pp. 75–130.
30 Grant Kaplan, *Faith and Reasons throughout Christian History: A Theological Essay* (Washington, DC: The Catholic University of America Press, 2022), p. 50.
31 Anselm, 'Proslogion', §2, p. 87.
32 Marilyn McCord Adams, 'Anselm on Faith and Reason', in *The Cambridge Companion to Anselm*, ed. by Brian Davies and Brian Leftow (Cambridge, UK: Cambridge University Press, 2004), pp. 32–60 (p. 36) (McCord Adams' italics).

detached—a matter of 'pure' intellectual speculation—but involves an orientation, both in terms of predisposition, but also in terms of transformation.

In this sense, John Cottingham's observation of the directional interrelation of praxis, faith, and truth is insightful: 'religious truth can only be accessed via faith, and faith can only be acquired via a living tradition of religious praxis'.[33] That is, knowledge arises from a way of being that is always and already anchored in a perspective on the world, an attitude towards it, and a practice within it. In his discussion of this, Cottingham reflects on Martha Nussbaum's essay 'Love's Knowledge'[34] and the idea she explores there of knowledge of love, which she does through the comparison of two contrasting stories, Marcel Proust's *A la recherche du temps perdu* and Ann Beattie's 'Learning to Fall'. As Cottingham glosses, Nussbaum suggests that 'there are certain kinds of truth such that to try and grasp them purely intellectually is to avoid them'.[35] Cottingham argues that religious knowledge is one such form of knowledge, drawing attention to a passage from Nussbaum's text to indicate how this is so:

> The attitude we have before a philosophical text can look, by contrast [to Ann Beattie's story], retentive and unloving—asking for reasons, questioning and scrutinizing each claim, wresting clarity from the obscure ... Before a literary work [of the kind described] we are *humble, open, active yet porous*. Before a philosophical work ... we are active, controlling, aiming to leave no flank undefended and no mystery undispelled.[36]

There is something about the posture involved in attending to literary texts, and in relation to religious knowledge, that is distinct from the kind of knowledge that aims to comprehend in a clear, absolute, and final way. Cottingham notes that it is because the truths of religion are 'beyond the direct comprehension of the human mind, that an attempt to grasp them head on via the tools of logical analysis is, in a certain

---

33 John Cottingham, *The Spiritual Dimension: Religion, Philosophy and Human Value* (Cambridge, UK: Cambridge University Press, 2005), p. 16.
34 Martha C. Nussbaum, *Love's Knowledge: Essays on Philosophy and Literature* (New York: Oxford University Press, 1990).
35 Cottingham, *The Spiritual Dimension*, p. 11.
36 Nussbaum, *Love's Knowledge*, p. 282 (cited in Cottingham, *The Spiritual Dimension*, p. 11).

sense, to evade them'.³⁷ Importantly, as is apparent from Nussbaum's account, the posture involved is not passive. It remains active, but is yielding, receptive, and open-ended. It involves a 'porousness' to what is encountered such that 'interior change' can take place. In the case of spiritual praxis, it is thus, for Cottingham, that the way is paved for 'the operation of grace'.³⁸

Influenced by Nussbaum, Cottingham's account resonates strongly with two interrelated moments of Sherman's account of Anselm on reason, which are of special importance. The first moment is the observation that for Anselm '[a]t its highest pitch, intellect is no longer domineering, but *adorative*. The intellect is itself suspended, but joyously so, by that which infinitely exceeds it and unceasingly gives it to itself'.³⁹ The second moment is the identification of the difference between Anselm and the Fool as a difference not of conceptual clarity but of 'orientation of heart'.⁴⁰ It is a matter of faith. In a similar way to Cottingham, Sherman explains that for Anselm, and the entire Patristic and early medieval tradition, affective and cognitive powers existed without division in the heart, such that '[t]he soul can only will what it (at least inchoately) thinks, but what it thinks *is governed by the propriety and energy of its loves and the history of its choices*'.⁴¹ That is:

> For Anselm, the adorative posture is the epistemological structure that prevents comprehension but enables knowledge. The adorative intellect avoids closure because it is not wholly determined by dialectical necessity but risks a sort of lyrical or artistic embellishment, a musement responsive to the lure of the Good.⁴²

---

37 Cottingham, *The Spiritual Dimension*, p. 12.
38 Ibid.
39 Sherman, *Partakers of the Divine*, p. 97.
40 Ibid., p. 98.
41 Ibid., my italics. See also McCord Adams, 'Anselm on Faith and Reason', pp. 35–36. This is echoed in more contemporary thought in the work of Iris Murdoch and the recognition that inner transformation is key, and that attention is formative to orientation in life, see Iris Murdoch, *Sovereignty of the Good* (London: Routledge, 1970). See also Mary Midgley, *Heart & Mind: The Varieties of Moral Experience* (London: Methuen, 1983).
42 Sherman, *Partakers of the Divine*, pp. 99–100. Kaplan points to the fact that both the *Monologion* and the *Proslogion* were meditations, which had a 'precise meaning in medieval learning and prayer'. Explaining this, he makes an analogy with Handel's 'Hallelujah' chorus from the *Messiah*: 'The chorus resembles a *meditation* in that it focuses on a specific word, sung every possible way, in order to extract every conceivable ounce of meaning from that word. Anselm wanted his monks

The affective and the cognitive are thus intertwined and propel one towards truth, as they draw on past experience but remain open to transformation. This conception suggests a certain modelling for our consideration of music experience and experience of theological, religious, and spiritual realities. In each case, the relationship is non-linear, since the adorative posture relies not only on the movement towards the object of our attention, but on its movement towards us. To illustrate this, Sherman reminds the reader of the parable of the prodigal son. He says: 'it is not, finally, we the prodigals who return to the father, but the father who sees us while still far off, loves us, and runs to embrace us'.[43] This is present in Anselm's statement 'Teach me to seek You, and reveal Yourself to me as I seek, because I can neither seek You if You do not teach me how, nor find You unless You reveal Yourself'.[44] Just as there is our own ascent, there is first of all the divine descent.

Conclusion

In this chapter, I have suggested that there is a certain parallel between the way of being, or posture, that is instilled in and through music, and the way of being that gives life to the pursuit of divine truth, one that might be called adorative. In this sense, it is possible that music's relationship to theological, religious, and spiritual realities operates at two levels. Music can cultivate an adorative attitude that involves seeing more, hearing more (and being more), and thereby offer a patterning that acts as a prolegomenon to the theological, religious, and spiritual enterprise. In opening out onto 'something more', music may also reveal the very same realities that it guides us towards and prepares us to receive. But this is not all. In practical terms, my account of the adorative posture may contribute to an understanding of the relationship between music and spiritual realities with three further considerations. First, it

---

to meditate on the being of God, to understand God more deeply as *one*, *true*, and *good*' (Kaplan, *Faith and Reasons*, p. 49). See also Geoff Dumbreck, 'Head and Heart in Christian Theology', in *Head and Heart: Perspectives from Religion and Psychology*, ed. by Fraser N. Watts and Geoff Dumbreck (West Conshohocken, PN: Templeton Press, 2013), pp. 19–48.

43 Sherman, *Partakers of the Divine*, p. 130
44 Anselm, 'Proslogion', §1, p. 86. See also McCord Adams, 'Anselm on Faith and Reason', p. 36.

resonates with the caution against attempts to delimit the relationship to any conceptually conclusive and general forms or rules which, as noted above, tend to eradicate the differences entailed by different positionalities and by different music experiences. Second, and in so doing, it moves us away from the understanding's tendency to control and dominate the object of its attention towards an attitude or mode of being that allows the object of attention to be, and embraces the inconclusive and the intractably open, thereby facilitating conversations about what is experienced in music, and how. Third, an emphasis upon the adorative allows a coexistence of immanent (horizontal) and absolute (vertical) forms of transcendence, since it encompasses within itself the materiality of music as well as its imaginative realms, and it does so open-endedly. As such, it indicates their situation along a vector that proceeds in and through the material and is driven by faith in 'something more' (and a way of being in the world), and suggests that discussions ought to include wider concerns with how music is embedded in practices and ways of life.

5. Religion, Science, and Music: An Augustinian Trinity

Bennett Zon

Although, as Sir John Templeton claims, 'god is revealing himself … through the astonishingly productive research of modern scientists',[1] it is fair to say that religion and science have not always seen eye to eye, particularly since the late nineteenth-century. Indeed, a culture of suspicion continues to haunt their relationship today despite valiant efforts, like Templeton's, to resolve their differences. Music can help. Music can bring religion and science together, and not simply because of its capacity to reveal spiritual realities, but because—as this chapter argues—music is intrinsically unifying. Music not only brings people together, it also brings ideas together, and it does so because it is itself unified by the very features of its own design. In this sense, music not only helps us discover spiritual realities; music is, as Augustine (354–430) suggests, those spiritual realities themselves; it is, as Templeton suggests, God revealing himself. This essay responds to those suggestions in two ways: firstly, by hypothesising a relationship between religion, science, and music today; and secondly, by testing that hypothesis against Augustine's theo-psychological understanding of music. The conclusion summarises my findings, and points to future plans, of which the present chapter may serve as a type of pilot.

---

1 Cited in John Templeton Foundation, 'Sir John Templeton 1912–2008', *John Templeton Foundation*, https://www.templeton.org/about/sir-john

I. Religion, Science, and Music

(a) Religion and Science

We begin with a presumption: 'Yes, there is a war between science and religion ... science and religion are not only in conflict ... but also represent incompatible ways of viewing the world'.[2] Reprising a nineteenth-century argument heavily disputed today in both theology and the history of science, Jerry Coyne claims that science and religion are not just incompatible, but have been at war since the beginning of science and religion themselves. Coyne's hostility to religion is nothing new. Richard Dawkins, for example, opens *The God Delusion* with an anti-prayer: 'If this book [*The God Delusion*] works as I intend, religious readers who open it will be atheists when they put it down'.[3] Dawkins does more than just evangelise science against religion, he also reinforces an historical stereotype that began with atheistic classics like *History of the Conflict between Religion and Science* (1875), *A History of the Warfare of Science with Theology in Christendom* (1896) and *Landmarks in the Struggle between Science and Religion* (1925).[4] These historical books not only christen what would become a long-standing stereotype, but by the middle of the twentieth century it had become scientific gospel—or so the likes of Coyne and Dawkins would have us believe. In fact, some thinkers make a strong and compelling counterclaim. They claim that 'it was possible to present a historical overview of the relationship between science and religion without relying on the conflict thesis'.[5] According

---

2   Jerry Coyne, 'Yes, There Is a War between Science and Religion', *The Conversation*, 21 December 2018, https://theconversation.com/yes-there-is-a-war-between-science-and-religion-108002.
3   Richard Dawkins, *The God Delusion* (Boston, MA, and New York: Houghton Mifflin, 2008), p. 11.
4   John William Draper, *A History of the Conflict between Religion and Science* (New York: D. Appleton and Company, 1875); Andrew Dickson White, *A History of the Warfare of Science with Theology in Christendom* (New York: D. Appleton and Company, 1896); James Young Simpson, *Landmarks in the Struggle between Science and Religion* (London: Hodder and Stoughton, 1925).
5   Bernard Lightman, 'Introduction', in *Rethinking History, Science and Religion: An Exploration of Conflict and the Complexity Principle*, ed. by Bernard Lightman (Pittsburgh, PA: University of Pittsburgh Press, 2019), pp. 3–16 (at p. 5); for other recent examples, see Peter Harrison and John H. Roberts, eds, *Science Without God?: Rethinking the History of Scientific Naturalism* (Oxford: Oxford University Press, 2019), and Alister McGrath, *The Territories of Human Reason: Science and Theology in an Age of Multiple Rationalities* (Oxford: Oxford University Press, 2019).

to John Hedley Brooke, for instance, there was no conflict; rather, the relationship of science and religion was 'complex'; as he says, 'Serious scholarship in the history of science has revealed so extraordinarily rich and complex a relationship between science and religion in the past that general theses are difficult to sustain. The real lesson turns out to be the complexity'.[6]

This chapter, and the project it recommends in conclusion, expands upon Brooke's complexity theory by using music 'to reveal something of the complexity of that relationship between science and religion as they interacted in the past'.[7] For Brooke, as for most historians of science today, there is 'no such thing as *the* relationship between science and religion'—only 'relationships'. But what are these relationships, and how should we understand them? Ian Barbour categorises them into four increasingly collaborative groups—conflict, independence, dialogue, and integration:[8]

1. *conflict* is relegated to historical prejudice 'perpetuated by the media'[9]

2. *independence* keeps science and religion apart by separating and differentiating their questions, domains, and methods[10]

3. *dialogue* 'portrays more constructive relationships between science and religion ... [by emphasising] similarities in presuppositions, methods, and concepts',[11] and, lastly,

4. *integration* calls 'for reformulations of traditional theological ideas', coming in three distinct versions—natural theology (science makes us more aware of design in nature), the theology of nature (science helps us reformulate theological ideas, such as creation and human nature), and a systematic synthesis (science and religion influence metaphysics).[12]

---

6   John Hedley Brooke, *Science and Religion: Some Historical Perspectives* (Cambridge, UK: Cambridge University Press, 2014), p. 6.
7   Ibid., p. 438.
8   See Ian Barbour, *Religion in an Age of Science* (San Francisco, CA: Harper and Row, 1990), and its expanded revision Ian Barbour, *Science and Religion: Historical and Contemporary Issues* (London: SCM Press, 1998).
9   Ian Barbour, *When Science Meets Religion: Enemies, Strangers, or Partners?* (San Francisco, CA: HarperCollins, 2000), p. 10.
10 Ibid., p. 17.
11 Ibid., p. 23.
12 Ibid., pp. 27–28.

The similarly-minded John Polkinghorne describes these same categories, but substitutes terminology in the last two from dialogue and integration to consonance and assimilation. In consonance, 'science and religions retain their due autonomies in their acknowledged domains, but the statements they make must be capable of appropriate reconciliation with each other in overlap regions';[13] in assimilation, 'there is an attempt to achieve the maximum possible conceptual merging of science and theology. Neither is absorbed totally by the other ... but they are brought closely together'.[14]

Regardless of terminology, if, as these categories suggest, complexity accounts for different types of relationships between religion and science, it is nevertheless curious that the term 'complexity' itself has received so little critical attention in the literature on their relationship. When Brooke describes their relationship as complex what exactly does he mean? What do we mean by the term 'complexity', and does it refer to more than just different levels of collaboration between science and religion? And when science and religion actually meet, how do we gauge their level of complexity accurately when the very circumstances of their relationship are so unique—when, as Brooke opines, 'there is no such thing as *the* relationship between science and religion'?[15] Bernard Lightman asks similar questions when he raises concerns over the very idea of the 'complexity thesis'. If it is 'actually a misnomer', he asks, 'then what kinds of stories can we tell about the relationship between science and religion?'[16]

(b) Religion, Science, and Music

How can music help us understand the complex relationship between religion and science?—and perhaps, more importantly, why should we even go to music for help? Why music, in other words? Firstly, because both science and religion believe that music 'is at the centre of what it

---

13 John Polkinghorne, *Science and Theology: An Introduction* (London and Minneapolis, MN: SPCK/Fortress Press, 1998), p. 22.
14 Ibid., p. 22.
15 John Hedley Brooke, 'Science, Religion, and Historical Complexity', *Historically Speaking* 8 (2007), 10–13 (at 11).
16 Lightman, *Rethinking History, Science and Religion*, p. 7.

means to be human':[17] indeed, for cognitive psychologist Daniel Levitin the 'embodied nature of music, [and] the indivisibility of movement and sound' makes it 'Evolution's #1 Hit';[18] and secondly, because music shows us how religion and science can cooperate in a way that no other art can. It gives us a template for cooperation, not warfare, and a model for collaboration. For science, music is 'a sacred cue',[19] and a window into the evolutionary neuroscience of perception and aesthetics;[20] for religion, it is 'social, biological and cultural, sensory and symbolic'.[21] Amalgamating these beliefs, ethnomusicologist Chris Small asserts that music has the unique capacity to express the relationship 'between person and person, between individual and society, between humanity and the natural world and even perhaps the supernatural world'.[22]

An obvious, if admittedly contentious, way to elaborate these considerations is to do what Brooke himself suggests: to look for the same thing across both disciplines—'to look for patterns behind the complexity,'[23] and this is exactly what this chapter aims to do, by using music effectively as an experimental 'constant'—as a common denominator against which patterns in the relationship of science and religion can be tested. This approach is unusual because historians of science and religion seldom venture outside the comfort-zone of their own home disciplines into the unknown territory of the arts—least of all into music. There are few exceptions: one is polymath, physicist, and natural philosopher Tom McLeish. In most of his work McLeish

---

17 Stephen Malloch and Colyen Trevarthen, 'The Human Nature of Music', *Frontiers of Psychology* 9 (2018), 1680.
18 Daniel Levitin, *This is Your Brain on Music: Understanding a Human Obsession* (London: Atlantic Books, 2007), p. 157.
19 Martin Lang, Panagiotis Mitkidis, Radek Kundt, Aaron Nichols, Len Krajčiková, and Dimitris Xygalatas, 'Music As a Sacred Cue?: Effects of Religious Music on Moral Behavior', *Frontiers in Psychology* 7 (2016), 814.
20 Mireille Besson and Daniele Schön, 'Comparison Between Language and Music', in *The Cognitive Neuroscience of Music*, ed. by Isabelle Peretz and Robert Zatorre (Oxford: Oxford University Press, 2003), pp. 269–93 (at 274).
21 Candace C. Alcorta, 'Music and the Miraculous: The Neurophysiology of Music's Emotive Meaning', in *Miracles: God, Science, and Psychology in the Paranormal*, ed. by J. Harold Ellens, 3 vols (Westport, CN, and London Praeger: 2008), III, pp. 230–52 (at 231).
22 Christopher Small, *Musicking: The Meanings of Performing and Listening* (Middletown, CN: Wesleyan University Press, 1998), p. 13.
23 Brooke, 'Science, Religion, and Historical Complexity', p. 11.

engages in what could be called 'scientific theology'.[24] But, following a recent trend in the development of Music Theology, in one of his last books *The Poetry and Music of Science* (2019) he connects directly with music (for example, Robert Schumann's *Konzertstück* for Four Horns and Orchestra (1849); or Johann Sebastian Bach's fugues).[25] Music Theology is the disciplinary descendent of Jon Michael Spencer's 'theomusicology'[26] (itself a descendent of Jaap Kunst's 'ethno-musicology'),[27] and it considers music—and by extension writings about music—to be intrinsically theological in nature.[28] Like most Music Theologians, McLeish never presses theological beliefs upon his readers, but tries to let the music speak for itself. Linking its structural characteristics (harmony, rhythm, tonality, and so on) to mathematical cosmology, he does with Schumann what this chapter, and its emergent project, intends to do more broadly—using music to illuminate patterns behind the 'complexity' characterising the relationship of science and religion.

Exploration of those same patterns has tended to elude scholarship because music has never been adequately triangulated. Ideological predisposition replicating the 'conflict theory', for example, often prevents musicology from accepting theological conclusions, for fear of lapses in scholarly objectivity. Published by the Society for Interdisciplinary Musicology, *The Journal of Interdisciplinary Music Studies* is emblematic, omitting only theology from its otherwise 'interdisciplinary' list of roughly forty contributing disciplines, despite claiming to include 'all subdisciplines or paradigms of musicology'.[29] The journal *The Psychology of Music* is not dissimilar, having only published three articles including the word 'theology' since it was

---

24   Thomas F. Torrance, *Reality and Scientific Theology* (Eugene, OR: Wipf and Stock Publishers, 2001).

25   Tom McLeish, *The Poetry and Music of Science* (Oxford: Oxford University Press, 2019).

26   Jon Michael Spencer, *Theological Music: Introduction to Theomusicology* (Westport, CT: Greenwood Press, 1991).

27   Jaap Kunst, *Musicologica: A Study of the Nature of Ethnomusicology, Its Problems, Methods, and Representative Personalities* (Amsterdam: Indisch Instituut, 1950).

28   See Bennett Zon, 'Music Theology as the Mouthpiece of Science: Proving It through Congregational Music Studies', in *Studying Congregational Music: Key Issues, Methods, and Theoretical Perspectives*, ed. by Andrew Mall, Jeffers Engelhardt, and Monique Ingalls (New York and London: Routledge, 2021), pp. 103–20.

29   Zon, 'Music Theology as the Mouthpiece of Science', p. 107.

founded in 1973. Recent work of mine illuminates the extent of this systemic cross-disciplinary distrust,[30] but also reveals an important underlying observation; namely, the fact that when various branches of musicology reach out to religion or science, they often do so in asymmetrically reciprocal disciplinary pairs. Perhaps inevitably, these tend to favour one disciplinary approach over the other—some, of the many, indicative examples of pairings include musicology and theology,[31] or theology and musicology;[32] ethnomusicology and theology,[33] or theology and ethnomusicology;[34] but owing to the nature of interdisciplinarity, and the way it seldom genuinely succeeds in achieving methodological parity, there are undoubtedly more pairings to be observed in other branches of religion, theology, and musical sciences.[35] There are, inevitably, more arguably symmetrical pairings as well—in Maeve Louise Heaney's *Music as Theology: What Music Says about the Word*,[36] or Chelle Stearns's *Handling Dissonance: A Musical Theological Aesthetic of Unity*,[37] to name just a few amongst a very wide range of, in many instances classic, examples. My own work is, similarly, aimed at resolving disciplinary disparities, by using musicology to converse with science,[38] with theology,[39] or with

---

30 Zon, 'Music Theology as the Mouthpiece of Science'.
31 See, for example, Julie Brown, *Schoenberg and Redemption* (Oxford: Oxford University Press, 2014).
32 See, for example, Richard Bell, *The Theology of Wagner's Ring Cycle I: The Genesis and Development of the Tetralogy and the Appropriation of Sources, Artists, Philosophers, and Theologians* (Eugene, OR: Cascade, 2020).
33 See, for example, Monique M. Ingalls, *Singing the Congregation: How Contemporary Worship Music Forms Evangelical Community* (Oxford: Oxford University Press, 2018).
34 See for example, Peter Ward, *Liquid Church* (Eugene, OR: Wipf and Stock, 2002).
35 See, for example, William Forde Thompson and Kirk N. Olsen, eds, *The Science and Psychology of Music: From Beethoven at the Office to Beyoncé at the Gym* (Santa Barbara, CA, and Denver, CO: Greenwood, 2021), especially pp. 140–204.
36 Maeve Louise Heaney, *Music as Theology: What Music Says about the Word* (Eugene, OR: Pickwick, 2012).
37 Chelle L. Stearns, *Handling Dissonance: A Musical Theological Aesthetic of Unity* (Eugene, OR: Pickwick, 2019).
38 See, for example, Bennett Zon, 'Evolution: Music in the Autobiologies of Darwin and Spencer', in *The Oxford Handbook of Music and Life Writing*, ed. by Paul Watt and Michael Allis (Oxford: Oxford University Press forthcoming); and Bennett Zon, *Evolution and Victorian Musical Culture* (Cambridge, UK: Cambridge University Press, 2017).
39 See, for example, Bennett Zon, 'Elgar *as* Theology', *The Oxford Handbook of Music and Christian Theology*, ed. by Steve Guthrie and Bennett Zon, 5 vols (Oxford:

both theology and science.[40] Regrettably, this same aspiration is not evident in chronologically broad interdisciplinary histories of music;[41] and neither do histories of religion and science ever seem to enter musicological territory.

(c) Methodologies

In the broadest possible sense, this chapter (and its larger project) responds to those challenges by using music to debunk the idea that religion and science were—and are to this very day—locked in some

---

Oxford University Press, forthcoming), III, 'Context'; and Bennett Zon, 'Music', in *Handbook of Religious Culture in Nineteenth-Century Europe*, ed. by Anthony J. Steinhoff and Jeffrey T. Zalar (Berlin: De Gruyter, forthcoming).

40 Zon, 'Music Theology as the Mouthpiece of Science'; Bennett Zon, 'Religion and Science', in *The Oxford Handbook of Music and Intellectual Culture*, ed. by Michael Allis, Sarah Collins, and Paul Watt (Oxford: Oxford University Press, 2020), pp. 387–408; Bennett Zon, 'Evolution', in *Edinburgh Critical History of Nineteenth-Century Theology*, ed. by Daniel Whistler (Edinburgh: Edinburgh University Press, 2018), pp. 124–42; and Bennett Zon, 'Music', in *The Oxford Handbook of Nineteenth-Century Christian Thought*, ed. by Joel D. S. Rasmussen, Judith Wolfe, and Johannes Zachhuber (Oxford: Oxford University Press, 2017), pp. 459–70.

41 See, for example, (1) long histories of music and cosmology: Michael J. Montague, *The Science of Music and the Music of Science: How Music Reveals Our Brain, Our Humanity and the Cosmos* (St Louis MO: Cosmic Music, 2019); Jamie James, *The Music of the Spheres: Music, Science, and the Natural Order of the Universe* (New York: Copernicus, 1993); Joscelyn Godwin, *The Harmony of the Spheres: A Sourcebook of the Pythagorean Tradition in Music* (Rochester NY: VM, Inner Traditions International, 1993); Joscelyn *Godwin, Harmonies of Heaven and Earth: Mysticism in Music from Antiquity to the Avant-Garde* (Rochester VM: Inner Traditions International, 1987); (2) sources on the historical and cultural relationship of music and science: Michael Spitzer, *The Musical Human: A History of Life on Earth* (London: Bloomsbury, 2022); Peter Townsend, *The Evolution of Music through Culture and Science* (Oxford: Oxford University Press, 2020); Alan Harvey, *Music, Evolution, and the Harmony of Souls* (Oxford: Oxford University Press, 2017); Adam Ockelford, *Comparing Notes: How We Make Sense of Music* (London: Profile, 2017); Gary Tomlinson, *A Million Years of Music: The Emergence of Human Modernity* (Princeton NJ: Princeton University Press, 2015); and (3) academic studies with a chronologically narrower focus: Jacomien Prins and Maude Vanhaelen, *Sing Aloud Harmonious Spheres: Renaissance Conceptions of Cosmic Harmony* (Routledge: Abingdon and New York, 2019); Andrew Hicks, *Composing the World: Harmony in the Medieval Platonic Cosmos* (Oxford: Oxford University Press, 2017); Philipp Jeserich, Michael J. Curley and Steven Rendall, *Musica Naturalis: Speculative Music Theory and Poetics from Saint Augustine to the Late Middle Ages in France* (Baltimore MD: Johns Hopkins University Press, 2013); and Alexander Rehding and Suzannah Clark, *Music Theory and Natural Order from the Renaissance to the Early Twentieth Century* (Cambridge: Cambridge University Press, 2001).

kind of mortal conflict, or what Steven Jay Gould famously calls 'non-overlapping magisteria'.[42] Instead, I aim to show how the unity of music can, to paraphrase Barbour, be shown to resolve their conflict; reconcile their independence; illustrate their dialogue; and exemplify their integration. It does that by building upon two intersecting methodologies.

The first methodology adapts a thesis argued in Michael Hanby's *No God, No Science?: Theology, Cosmology, Biology*.[43] Hanby makes a simple claim evident in the title of his book—that science cannot exist without God: that science fails to recognise the metaphysical underpinnings of its own methodology, and that nature cannot be studied objectively when the scientist is part of nature itself (a good example, frequently cited, is Dawkins, in his emblematic book *The God Delusion* (2006)). This essay extends Hanby's argument by treating Augustine as one of religion's first 'music psychologists', and claiming that music cannot be understood—it cannot even exist—outside the collaborative relationship of science and religion.

The second methodology comes from the work of David Christian and his concept of 'Big History'.[44] Although this essay focuses on Augustine, it also aims to create a methodology that uses music to explore the relationship of religion and science within the longest possible chronological framework. Admittedly contentious—and even criticised by historians of science for emplotting evolutionary history[45]— according to Christian, Big History enables us to ask big questions inaccessible through smaller timescales. One set of questions concerns the relationship between the personal and universal: 'who am I?', he asks, 'where do I belong? what is the totality of which I am a part?'[46]

---

42 See Stephen Jay Gould, 'Nonoverlapping Magisteria', *Natural History*, 106 (March 1997), 16–22.

43 Michael Hanby, *No God, No Science?: Theology, Cosmology, Biology* (Oxford: Wiley-Blackwell, 2013).

44 David Christian, *Maps of Time: An Introduction to Big History* (Berkeley, LA: University of California Press, 2005); David Christian, Cynthia Stokes Brown, and Craig Benjamin, *Big History: Between Nothing and Everything* (New York: McGraw-Hill Education, 2014); David Christian, *Origin Story: A Big History of Everything* (London: Penguin, 2019).

45 Ian Hesketh, 'The Story of Big History', *History of the Present* 4.2 (Fall 2014), 171–202.

46 Christian, *Maps of Time*, p. 1.

Big, comparable questions are also asked in science and religion—for example, 'How did the universe begin'; 'Is evolution compatible with creation'; 'Is science the only true path to truth'; or 'Has science made God obsolete'?[47]—and almost identical questions are asked in music: 'what is music?', 'what does it signal?', and 'what does it mean?'—'why is it important?', and 'what can music tell us about our ourselves, our human evolutionary origins and the origins of the world?'; 'what can it tell us about where we belong, and what part we play in the greater totality of life on earth?'; 'does it just point to God, or is it, as Augustine suggests, God himself?' Again, 'is music God revealing himself: is it a spiritual reality itself?' Let us ask Augustine.

II. Augustine

> Yet if I have the experience of being moved more by the singing than by the subject matter, I admit that I am sinning and deserve punishment and then would prefer not to listen to the singer. Just look at the state I am in! Weep with me and weep for me ... O Lord my God, listen! Look and see and have mercy and heal me; before your eyes I have become a puzzle to myself, and this itself is my weakness.[48]

So Augustine anguishes over the effect music has on his life. For Augustine that effect occurs through two forms of music: through the ordinary music we perform, compose, listen to, and dance to—the music that makes us weep; and through the extraordinary music that regulates the world—harmony, you might say: a sense of attunement with the world, or moving well—being 'groovy', if you will. The two forms of music are interrelated. Ordinary music is created by human beings, themselves created by God, and extraordinary music is directly created by God to reflect and embody the perfection of his unity. Augustine's musical project is to explain how they can be brought together—how the ordinary helps us to understand the extraordinary—the earthly, the spiritual—and how, in fact, we can ascend from one to the other, from the ordinary to the extraordinary. Current research on their relationship is

---

47 See the chapter headings in Keith Ward, *The Big Questions in Science and Religion* (West Conshohocken, PA: Templeton Foundation Press, 2008).
48 Augustine, *Confessions Books 9 to 13*, ed. and trans. by Carolyn J. B. Hammond (Harvard, MA: Loeb Classical Library, 2016), 10.33.50, p. 155.

wide-ranging, if arguably inconclusive. Giosuè Ghisalberti, for instance, focuses on Augustine's tears as an expression of mourning in Book 9 of his *Confessions*, but merely rehearses Platonic reservations over music's capacity to suppress reason's ability to control emotion.[49] James Jirtle and Brian Brennan, conversely, read Augustine through virtue ethics and the ability to positively harness musical emotion, rather than negatively subordinate it;[50] and Carol Harrison's recent work is in much this same vein, using 'affective cognition' to reassess the nature of Augustine's musical experience and its theoretical import.[51] But altogether this research omits a crucial element in our understanding of Augustine's notion of musical ascent: music brings us closer to the Trinity, and the Trinity brings us closer to God.

(a) The Trinity

Augustine traces this effect mainly in two correspondingly Trinitarian works, the *Confessions* and *De Musica*. The *Confessions* comprise thirteen books: the first nine are autobiographical; the remaining four, philosophical. According to Colin Starnes, books 1 to 9 represent the Father; book 10, the Son; and books 11 to 13, the Holy Spirit, 'while each of the bigger sections can be seen as consisting of three smaller sections, each in turn devoted to one of the three persons of the Trinity'.[52] Some theologians allocate Trinitarian structure differently; some perceive the structure as representing a form of Christian-Platonic spiritual ascent, from autobiography to metaphysical and theological issues, while others, still, see in its two-part division a structure based loosely around philosophical questions over God's omnipresence and transcendence.[53] In many ways *De Musica* is the intellectual yin to the *Confessions*' emotional yang. Trenchantly metaphysical (many would

---

49   Giosuè Ghisalberti, 'Listening to Hymns and Tears of Mourning in Augustine's *Confessions*, Book 9', *Early Music* 43.2 (2015), 247–53.
50   James V. Jirtle, 'Using Music Well: Reassessing Perception in Augustine's *De Musica*', *Augustiniana* 60.3–4 (2010), 263–81; Brian Brennan, 'Augustine's *De Musica*', *Vigiliae Christianae* 42.3 (1988), 267–81.
51   Carol Harrison, *On Music, Sense, Affect and Voice* (London: T&T Clark, 2019), p. 68.
52   Annemaré Kotzé, 'Structure and Genre of the Confessions', in *The Cambridge Companion to Augustine's 'Confessions'*, ed. by Tarmo Toom (Cambridge, UK: Cambridge University Press, 2020), pp. 28–45 (at 37)
53   Kotzé, 'Structure and Genre of the Confessions', pp. 28–45.

say, incomprehensible), *De Musica* mirrors, in part, the spiritual ascent of the *Confessions* but without much of its breezy human accessibility. Written not long after Augustine's conversion in 386 AD (sometime between 387 and 391 AD),[54] as part of a projected set of works on the liberal arts, *De Musica* comprises six books, of which the first five discuss the technicalities of rhythm, metre, and verse; the last, sixth book—the vaguely comprehensible one—addresses the ascent of the soul through music.

Amongst other things, the *Confessions* is renowned for Augustine's legendary ambivalence towards ordinary music: 'The pleasures of the ear', he cries, 'had a more tenacious hold on me, and had subjugated me; but you [God] set me free and liberated me ... my physical delight, which has to be checked from enervating the mind, often deceives me when the perception of the senses is unaccompanied by reason, and is not patiently content to be in a subordinate place ... I have sometimes gone so far as to wish to banish all the melodies and sweet chants commonly used for David's psalter from my ears and from the Church as well'.[55] That tension is never really resolved, and theories explaining his predicament abound. One of the more compelling theories concerns the evolutionary 'selfishness' of language. According to Marica Colish, Augustine felt that, as human beings, we are congenitally predisposed to use language to exert control over our environment.[56] Augustine certainly gives that impression throughout the *Confessions*—'By groans and various sounds and various movements of parts of my body I would endeavour to express the intentions of my heart to persuade people to bow to my will'[57]—but his mistrust of language goes further. Fuelled by a pervasive mistrust of the seemingly truthless emptiness of rhetorical logic (i.e., form over content), he rails against his former self for allowing

---

54 For research on the dating of *De Musica*, see Martin Jacobsson and Lukas J. Dorfbauer, 'Introduction', in *Augustinus, De Musica*, ed. by Martin Jacobsson, Corpus Scriptorum Ecclesiasticorum Latinorum 102 (Berlin and Boston, MA: de Gruyter, 2017), pp. 1–10.
55 *Saint Augustine Confessions*, trans. by Henry Chadwick (Oxford: Oxford University Press, 1991), book 10, xxxiii (49), p. 207; and ibid., book 10, xxxiv (50), p. 208.
56 Marcia Colish, *The Mirror of Language: A Study of the Medieval Theory of Knowledge* (Lincoln, NE: University of Nebraska Press, 1983), p. 19.
57 Augustine, *Confessions*, book 1, viii (13), p. 10.

his education to be 'aimed more at teaching eloquence than morality'.[58] The link to music is obvious because music and rhetoric are both linguistic. Both have the capacity for abuse, and both have the power to exert control over reason without authority; both, more concerningly, appear doubly entwined in vocal music. The problem for Augustine is moral, as much as it is psychological—when the music is loved more than the meaning its message conveys, and more especially when the message is itself considered to be morally unsupportable: 'woe to you', Augustine opines, 'if you have loved the creatures and abandoned the Creator!'[59] In many respects, Augustine's understandable fear is entirely unextraordinary, and it is easy to stop there at any explanation, but there is more to it than meets the eye, or ear, and it has to do with Augustine's notion of divine simplicity—and the way it unites his theology and psychological science.

(b) Simplicity

When Augustine worries over our sometimes-misguided love for creatures over their Creator, he invokes a relationship borne of divine simplicity; in other words, the hypostatic relationship of the Trinity, and the Trinity's relationship to God's creation. For Augustine, creation and the substance of God are one: 'God is simple, that is, in God all qualities are identical with God's essence'.[60] For Scott Dunham, that means that human participation in creation—being, in as many words—occurs only through our participation in God.[61] Dunham raises an interesting point with implications for Augustine's musical predicament. For Augustine there is a potentially threatening spiritual disconnect, when we allow ourselves to separate the music from the meaning of its messenger—the ordinary from the extraordinary; the

---

58 Calvin R. Stapert, *A New Song for an Old World: Musical Thought in the Early Church* (Grand Rapids, MI, and Cambridge, UK: Eerdmans, 2007), Kindle Location 2312.
59 Augustine, 'Tractate 2', in *Tractates on the First Epistle of John*, trans. by John W. Rettig, The Fathers of the Church 92 (Washington, DC: Catholic University of America Press, 1995), p. 153.
60 Lewis Ayres, 'The Fundamental Grammar of Augustine's Trinitarian Theology', in *Augustine and His Critics: Essays in Honour of Gerald Bonner*, ed. by Robert Dodaro and George Lawless (London and New York: Routledge, 2000), pp. 54, 60 and 62.
61 Scott A. Dunham, *The Trinity and Creation in Augustine: An Ecological Analysis* (Albany, NY: State University of New York Press, 2008), p. 83.

created from the Creator—because it breaks the bonds of God's divine simplicity. If the Trinity is itself meant to have created the world, it also subverts the principle of the Trinity: 'at the core of Augustine's analogical practice are two basic foci: the created order as a reflection of its threefold Creator; the threefold structure of the process by which the mind is reformed towards God ... [This is already] implicit in this earliest material, but only drawn out more fully in the *Confessiones*'.[62] What this suggests is that Augustine's anxiety over music is in fact representative of a much broader concern to epitomise creation as divine simplicity, and divine simplicity as the only tenable means of interpreting a Trinitarian Godhead. Music, in other words, is a metaphor, and one with uniquely transformative—even redemptive—spiritual powers: as we read elsewhere in the *Confessions*, 'the musical metaphor enables him [Augustine] to encapsulate how a will transformed over time is and remains a fundamentally unified life. It is one song, the "new song" of Christ'.[63]

(c) Simplification

'Why', then, as Harrison asks, 'did Augustine Sing?', if not to become one with the new song: the answer is that, according to Augustine, the soul is 'all too often distracted, fragmented and weighed down by its necessary involvement in sense perception ... the soul should direct its focus towards eternal and immutable rhythms whilst unconsciously attending to the temporal, mutable rhythms of sense perception; it should engage with sense perception—in this case, listening to the line of a hymn being sung—as it were, without noticing it and without allowing it to evoke any reaction from it'.[64] That prescription for simplification does make Augustine sound like a therapist, a psychologist, or even a 'scientist' in the broadest sense;[65] after all, he does define music as

---

62 Lewis Ayres, *Augustine and the Trinity* (Cambridge, UK: Cambridge University Press, 2010), p. 280.
63 Alex Fogleman, 'Becoming the Song of Christ: Musical Theology and Transforming Grace in Augustine's *Enarratio in Psalmum 32*', *Augustinian Studies* 50.2 (2019), 93–116 (at 144).
64 Carol Harrison, 'Getting Carried Away: Why Did Augustine Sing?', *Augustinian Studies* 46.1 (2015), 1–22 (at 7).
65 See *Augustine and Science*, ed. by John Doody, Adam Goldstein and Kim Paffenroth (Lanham MD: Lexington Books, 2012).

the science of modulating, or moving, well, and he does, as Harrison reveals, provide us with extraordinary insight into Patristic thinking on sense, emotion, memory, and mind, and many other things to do with 'affective cognition'. Those things, in themselves, do not necessarily make his opinion scientific, according to our modern understanding of the term, however. Controversially, philosopher Alvin Plantinga nevertheless calls for an 'Augustinian science' that accepts the non-neutrality of science; in other words, a science used 'in the service of a broadly religious vision of the world'[66] and from 'an explicitly theistic or Christian point of view'.[67] Others are more sceptical, and Josh Reeves even argues that Augustine would himself be suspicious of 'Augustinian science'.[68] While 'of its time', however, Augustine's own view on the utility and objectivity of empirical observation was largely favourable.[69] Augustine himself claims that 'Often a non-Christian knows something about the earth, the heavens, and the other parts of the world, about the motions and orbits of the stars and even their sizes and distances ... and this knowledge he holds with certainty from reason and experience. It is thus offensive and disgraceful for an unbeliever to hear a Christian talk nonsense about such things, claiming that what he is saying is based in Scripture'.[70]

Augustine's contempt for that kind of position is palpable because he sees no fundamental contradiction between the material and spiritual world, or indeed between what we would call today theology and science. For Augustine, the created and the Creator, the ordinary and the extraordinary, cannot be anything but simple, and simple in the clearest possible Trinitarian and incarnational terms. So when, in the course of spiritual ascent, Augustine gives the impression of

---

66 Alvin Plantinga, 'Science: Augustinian or Duhemian?', *Faith and Philosophy* 13.3 (1996), 368–94 (at 370).

67 Ibid., 369.

68 Josh A. Reeves, 'Science and Christianity: The Three Big Questions', *Journal of Biblical and Theological Studies* 2.2 (2017), 157–69 (at 164).

69 David C. Lindberg, 'The Medieval Church Encounters the Classical Tradition: Saint Augustine, Roger Bacon, and the Handmaiden Metaphor', in *When Christianity & Science Meet*, ed. by David C. Lindberg and Ronald L. Numbers (Chicago, IL: University of Chicago Press, 2003), pp. 7–32 (at 15).

70 Augustine, *On Genesis: A Refutation of the Manichees, Unfinished Literal Commentary on Genesis, The Literal Meaning of Genesis*, ed. by Boniface Ramsey and trans. by O.P. Hill (Hyde Park, NY: New City, 2004), p. 186.

'escaping reality' (i.e., the temptations of the physical world—like ordinary music) in pursuit of higher spiritual communion with God, in fact he does quite the opposite. His is, arguably, an incarnational approach in which the created and the Creator—the ordinary and the extraordinary—are fused as one—they are effectively 'creatored': 'Augustine sees the Incarnation as the primary model for signification, for this path from the physical to the spiritual, from *signum* to the *res*'.[71] Some of his language is perhaps unhelpful, portraying spiritual ascent as linear—as a path from A to B—when in fact the linearly vertical imagery of the ladder of ascent is more complex than that. Inherited from his Platonic days, Augustine's ladders of ascent ascended, or evolved, from the contemplative self-sufficiency of the philosopher to the loving grace of the Christian. According to Martha Nussbaum, at the same time 'it situates ascent within humanity and renounces the wish to depart from our human condition'.[72] In other words, ascent is actually marked not by progression but expansion: by loving God we love his creation; by loving God in humanity we see all humans as equal; and by seeing humans as equal we seek their equality.[73]

Nussbaum focuses on emotion in much the same way Harrison focuses on affect—as something Augustine sees as intrinsically good (because it is part of creation) but potentially bad if it becomes an end in itself. If something becomes an end in itself it tries to separate itself from God's creation and its Creator, and if something tries to separate itself from God it, ipso facto, creates complexity, or compositeness; i.e., the opposite of simplicity. Augustine hints at this when he fears 'the experience of being moved more by the singing than by the subject matter'.[74] Augustine considers it a sin: 'I admit that I am sinning', he opines, 'and deserve punishment and then would prefer not to listen to the singer'.[75] However defined,[76] it is universally agreed that sin

---

71 John Norris, 'Augustine and Sign in Tractatus in Iohannis Evangelium', in *Augustine: Biblical Exegete*, ed. by Frederick Van Fleteren and Joseph C. Schnaubelt (New York: Peter Lang, 2004), pp. 215–32 (at 215).
72 Martha C. Nussbaum, *Upheavals of Thought: The Intelligence of Emotions* (Cambridge, UK: Cambridge University Press, 2001), p. 547.
73 Ibid., p. 548.
74 Augustine, *Confessions Books 9 to 13*, p. 155.
75 Ibid.
76 See Jesse Couenhoven, *Stricken by Sin, Cured by Christ: Agency, Necessity, and Culpability in Augustinian Theology* (Oxford: Oxford University Press, 2013); Pier

creates separation from God; for Augustine it is 'any transgression in deed, or word, or desire, of the eternal law. And the eternal law is the divine order or will of God, which requires the preservation of natural order, and forbids the breach of it'.⁷⁷ Augustine's sin is a sin against divine simplicity, and that makes music dangerous. When music ceases to 'harmonise' with, and like, the Trinity, or to move well, it also breaks the relational bond of sense and meaning; for Augustine, 'whatever has pleasing sound, that it is which pleases and entices the hearing itself. What is really signified by that sound is what is borne to the mind through the messenger of our hearing … our praise of the meter is one thing, but our praise of the meaning is something else'.⁷⁸ When music does move well, however—when it moves well itself, and when it moves us well—it can heal the sinful disconnect between sense and meaning, between created and Creator. By healing us, music, for Augustine, also simplifies us so that we can, incarnationally like Christ, become music itself—the 'new song'. Music unifies us, not just within ourselves individually and with one another, but with our cosmic creator and the Trinity.

Augustine begins and ends book 6 of *De Musica* with a discussion of Ambrose's famous hymn *Deus Creator Omnium*—God Creates All. Why choose that hymn; why there, and in those places? Many have asked that question, often focusing on Augustine's emotional, psychological reason. His mother Monica had just died, and the hymn was a consolation.⁷⁹ But there are, of course, other reasons. In extended discussions of the hymn, Harrison and Guthrie make much the same

---

Franco Beatrice, *The Transmission of Sin: Augustine and the Pre-Augustinian Sources*, trans. by Adam Kamesar (Oxford: Oxford University Press, 2013); or Eric L. Jenkins, *Free to Say No?: Free Will in Augustine's Evolving Doctrines of Grace and Election* (Eugene, OR: Wipf & Stock, 2012).

77 Augustine, 'Contra Faustum Manichaeum', ed. by Philip Schaff and trans. by Richard Stothert, 22 (27), p. 388, http://www.documentacatholicaomnia. eu/03d/0354-0430,_Augustinus,_Contra_Faustum_Manichaeum_%5BSchaff%5D,_EN.pdf

78 Augustine, *On Order*, 2.11.34, cited in Carol Harrison, 'Augustine and the Art of Music', in *Resonant Witness: Conversations between Music and Theology*, ed. by Jeremy Begbie and Steven Guthrie (Grand Rapids, MI: W. B. Eerdmans, 2011), pp. 27–45 (at 44).

79 For example, Brennan, 'Augustine's *De Musica*', p. 269; Ghisalberti, 'Listening to Hymns and Tears of Mourning in Augustine's *Confessions*', p. 252; and Steven R. Guthrie, 'Carmen Universitatis: A Theological Study of Music and Measure' (unpublished doctoral thesis, University of St Andrews, 2000), p. 291.

claim. Both describe Augustine's variable (five-, sometimes six-stage) process of spiritual ascent as psychologies of perception,[80] engaging both the physical and spiritual (i.e., mental) resources of our soul. Guthrie helpfully summarises them in five concise questions: is music (1) in the sound—latent in the vibrations of the string itself; (2) in the hearer's sense—passively sensed; (3) in the act of the reciter—given the norms of performance; (4) in the memory because we have learnt it—a conditioned response to sound; or (5) in the judgment—actively constructed by the listener?[81] Augustine himself writes that 'When this verse . . . is sung [(1) in the sound] . . . We both hear [(2) in the hearer's sense] it with occurring rhythms [(2) in the hearer's sense/(3) in the act of the reciter], and recognize it [(3) in the act of the reciter/(4) in the memory because we have learnt it] with the memorized rhythms [(4) in the memory because we have learnt it], and enjoy it with these judicial rhythms [(5) in the judgment], and evaluate it with some others [(5) in the judgment]'.[82] Both Guthrie and Harrison also advocate a holistic interpretation of Augustine's spiritual ascent. For Guthrie, 'Augustine advances a polyphonic account of music: music perception is presented as a unified whole, composed of differentiated parts';[83] for Harrison, 'His [Augustine's] point is that this cosmic harmony—what he here [*De Musica*] calls "equality" (*aequalitas*)—owes its existence to God, the *Deus Creator Omnium*, the Creator of All ... it is through equality that we are able to apprehend Him, for He *is* perfect equality'.[84] Harrison and Guthrie both make an important point: *Deus Creator Omnium* is not just an illustration of music; it is music, and it represents it as well. It is the creation, and it represents it as well; it is God, and it represents him as well—because God the Creator is indivisible from his creation: it is 'a statement of the complete dependence of created reality upon the Creator of All, the *Deus Creator Omnium*'.[85]

---

80 Guthrie, 'Carmen Universitatis', p. 264; Harrison, *On Music, Sense, Affect and Voice*, p. 36.
81 Guthrie, 'Carmen Universitatis', p. 263.
82 Augustine, *De Musica*, 6.8.23, cited in Harrison, *On Music, Sense, Affect and Voice*, p. 38.
83 Guthrie, 'Carmen Universitatis', p. 264.
84 Harrison, *On Music, Sense, Affect and Voice*, p. 42.
85 Ibid.

(d) Simplification Today

Harrison ends where Augustine ends, with reference to *Deus Creator Omnium* and his concluding statement on the Trinity. But neither she nor other theologians invoke the term 'simplicity' to describe *De Musica*, or the *Confessions*, or other musical references for that matter. If musical ascent is indeed equivalent to a process of spiritual 'simplification', what does that mean exactly, and does it make Augustine any more 'scientific' in his approach?

That Augustine presents a psycho-scientific model of perception is fairly indisputable. Harrison describes it through modern emotion theory—'affective cognition'—but, as she herself admits, there are plenty of other ways to theorise it, and many other 'scientific' angles we could take on Augustine more generally (some of which have already been discussed). Admittedly, neither theology nor science has arrived at any consensus on Augustine's modern scientific credentials, least of all his seemingly 'scientific', if impenetrable, approach to music. So let me throw my hat in the ring. I think Augustine is concerned about simplicity—divine simplicity—and the relationship of God and his creation. Music is a part of creation, both in its ordinary and extraordinary forms. In all its forms music represents cosmic harmony—it moves well—but only while we, as created human beings, remain united to God our Creator. Being united to God our Creator means being united to more than the cosmos, however; it also means being united to God the Trinity and through the Trinity to the Incarnation of the Son. This makes Augustine's process of musical ascent an almost cyclical process of simplification, not just a spiritual elevation, in which we progress (or rather, *expand*) from our own human complexity to the simplicity of our own creation in God. The simpler we become, the more musical we become, and the more musical we become, the more unified (i.e. harmonised) with our God and His creation.

Simplification comes in many forms, scientifically, as James B. Glattfelder observes:

> Here on Earth, complexity is found everywhere. However, only recently has the human mind deciphered the simple rules behind complex phenomena. This insight came hand in hand with the emergence of information technology, allowing this new domain to be algorithmically

charted. The prototypical complex system is biological. However, the vast complex systems we humans have created, especially in finance and economics, require a detailed and in-depth discussion. Today, they affect every aspect of life on Earth.[86]

Glattfelder's comments apply equally well to theology. According to Wil Derske, simplicity has as much to do 'with the ordering of the complex', as it does with beauty and transcendence of some kind.[87] Scientists, for example, often refer to their discoveries or experiments in terms of beauty; for Thomas Dubay, it is where science and theology meet.[88] Science and theology also meet in Augustine's musical simplicity because music has the capacity to simplify our lives by focussing on less and less complexity. Decluttering, mindfulness, stress-reduction—these, whether religious or not, are all science-based, empirically-based movements designed to simplify our lives and return it to a more meaningful, essentialised, unified state of existence—to remove the noise and help us concentrate on the true meaning of life. Does Augustine help us declutter? Anita Higman and Hillary McMullan think so.[89] Is Augustine mindful? Jim Highland thinks so, as do others.[90] What about stress-reduction? Bob Stahl and Elisha Goldstein believe that too.[91] What all these people have in common is the basic belief that Augustine teaches simplification, be it theological, scientific, or just plain self-help. If Augustine's psychology of music perception—his 'science' of the science of moving well—is

---

86   James B. Glattfelder, 'The Simplicity of Complexity', in James B. Glattfelder, *Information—Consciousness—Reality: How a New Understanding of the Universe Can help Answer Ago-Old Questions of Existence*, The Frontiers Collection (Cham: Springer Open, 2019), pp. 181–214 (at 206).

87   Wil Derkse, 'Nice Work: Beauty and Transcendence as Factors in Scientific Practice', in *The Concept of Nature in Science and Theology, Part II*, ed. by Niels Henrik Gregersen, Michael W. S. Parsons, and Christoph Wassermann (Geneva: Labor et Fides, S.A., 1996), pp. 47–55 (at 49).

88   See Thomas Dubay, S.M., *The Evidential Power of Beauty: Science and Theology Meet* (San Francisco, CA: Ignatius Press, 1999).

89   Anita Higman and Hillary McMullan, *Daily Grace for Daily Life: Encouragement for Women* (Uhrichsville, OH: Barbour, 2013).

90   Jim Highland, 'Transformation to Eternity: Augustine's Conversion to Mindfulness', *Buddhist-Christian Studies* 25 (2005), 91–108; and L. Vandenberghe and F. Costa Prado, 'Law and Grace in Saint Augustine: A Fresh Perspective on Mindfulness and spirituality in Behaviour Therapy', *Mental Health, Religion & Culture* 12.6 (2009), 587–600.

91   Bob Stahl and Elisha Goldstein, *A Mindfulness-Based Stress Reduction Workbook* (Oakland, CA: New Harbinger, 2010), p. 16.

about anything, it is about helping to re-unite us with ourselves, even as a first step in the spiritual healing process, because we, too, are music when both it and we move well together.

Conclusion

Brooke suggests that we understand the relationship of science and religion only by looking 'for patterns behind the complexity'.[92] This essay extends that principle to music, using it as a common denominator against which patterns in science and religion can be tested. Theologian, therapist, psychologist—scientist in the broadest sense—Augustine provides a good example through an important, if controversial, theological concept of divine unity—the doctrine of divine simplicity. Encapsulated in the theology of the Trinity, the doctrine of divine simplicity describes the paradox of a God who is both three and one, Father, Son and Holy Spirit, yet one single and indivisible God.[93] St Augustine explains how three Persons can be one God (the Trinity); how the Second Person can be both God and Man (simple and complex); and how music both represents —and actually is —their perfect 'cosmic' relationship. In Templeton's words: 'god is revealing himself' through music.

For Augustine this involves understanding a psychological process of 'simplification' in which 'all finite reality is an image of ultimate reality'[94]—a process scientifically replicated today in Augustinian-influenced programmes of advice on decluttering, mindfulness, and stress-reduction. Are there other examples? There are, and it remains to explore them in a comprehensive 'Big History' using music to map the relationship of science and religion—from what physicist Marcus Chown calls the 'deep hum' of the Big Bang[95] to the latest 'world in a

---

92 Brooke, 'Science, Religion, and Historical Complexity', p. 11.
93 See for example, Steven J. Duby, *Divine Simplicity: A Dogmatic Account* (London: Bloomsbury, 2015).
94 Gerald P. Boersma, *Augustine's Early Theology of Image: A Study in the Development of Pro-Nicene Theology* (Oxford: Oxford University Press, 2016), p. 135.
95 Marcus Chown, 'Big Bang Sounded Like a Deep Hum', *New Scientist*, 30 Oct 2003, https://www.newscientist.com/article/dn4320-big-bang-sounded-like-a-deep-hum/

roar'[96] of modern composer Sir James MacMillan. What will that history tell us? It will tell us how music can help; how it can help bring religion and science together; how it can bring people together; and how it can bring each of us closer to God. It will tell us not only how, as Templeton claims, modern scientific research can illuminate spiritual realities, but how God reveals himself through music.

---

96 See Michael Capps, 'Warld in a Roar: The Music of James MacMillan, *Image* 54 (2007), 95–108, https://imagejournal.org/article/warld-in-a-roar-the-music-of-james-macmillan/

6. Dissonant Spirituality: A Hermeneutical Aesthetics of Outlaw Country

C.M. Howell

While, given the multiplication of uses of the term 'spiritual', no general definition can be determined, hermeneutical aesthetics offers a constructive framework to interrogate its meaning. Although this methodological framework emphasises a concrete set of particulars as the basis for its claims, it does so without being reduced to empirical data, allowing immaterial aspects to stand on an equal footing with any of their material (or even quantifiable) counterparts. Art is an event. It gathers a context, a meaningful world. It shifts being. As such, all relevant dimensions for the question at hand are drawn into view, including the psychological (i.e., the so-called 'subjective' dimension),[1] but also the tangible aspects of the aesthetic phenomena, as well as an underlying ontological dimension. The 'meaning' of spirituality happens in the relationships between these dimensions, as they appear all at once, and never alone. The first part of this chapter outlines a theoretical account of aesthetic cognition through some key thinkers of the tradition, and a corresponding account of contemporary spirituality through the work of Charles Taylor. The second part employs this method by tracing the meaning of spiritual in the tradition of American music known as outlaw

---

1   Although there is an obvious affinity with an aesthetics of 'event' and Lawrence Kramer's work on meaning in music, the decisive distinction is his focus on a subjectivity. Lawrence Kramer, *Musical Meaning: Towards a Critical History* (Berkeley, CA: University of California Press, 2002), pp. 3f., 146–72.

country. The genre was founded during the 1970s as well-established musicians in country music—Willie Nelson, Waylon Jennings, Kris Kristofferson to name a few—sought a freedom for the craft from the overly mechanised production of the Nashville sound. The term 'outlaw' was affixed to the style by the promoter Hazel Smith, who intended the meaning 'living on the outside of the written law'.[2] It is expressive of a disposition that is a step removed from outright transgression, but equally discontent with standing norms. The founding of outlaw country came at the tail end of the spiritual revolution in the late-1960s, which served as an impetus for the artists' newly claimed freedom. While allusions and explicit references to God and religion are longstanding features of country music, outlaw country presents these concerns through a hermeneutic of the advancements of spirituality. The meaning of spirituality presented is not quite a rejection of traditional religion, standing just at its boundary. Combined with its popularity—producing country music's first platinum record—this makes the genre a formative site for the meaning of spirituality in American culture.[3]

I. Music, Meaning, and Spirituality

It is often noted that 'spirituality' is inherently vague.[4] The term can indicate a transcendent realm that stands apart from, but is simultaneously

---

2   Michael Streissguth, *Outlaw: Waylon, Willie, Kris, and the Renegades of Nashville* (New York: itbooks, 2013), p. 153.

3   The steady stream of literature on pop music appears to indicate that the once controversial and neglected musical field has been accepted in the discourse of theology and the arts at least in terms of its cultural impact. For such examples, see Robin Sylvan, *Traces of the Spirit: The Religious Dimensions of Popular Music* (New York: New York University Press, 2002), pp. 2–13; Michael Bull, *Sound Moves: Ipod Culture and Urban Experience* (New York: Routledge, 2007); Eric Clark, Nicola Dibben, and Stephanie Pitts, *Music and Mind in Everyday Life* (Oxford: Oxford University Press, 2010); Tia DeNora, *Music Asylums: Wellbeing through Music in Everyday Life* (Aldershot: Ashgate, 2015), p. 170ff; David Brown and Gavin Hopps, *The Extravagance of Music* (Cham: Palgrave Macmillan, 2018).

4   Cheslyn Jones, Geoffrey Wainwright, and Edward Yarnold, 'Preface', in *The Study of Spirituality*, ed. by Cheslyn Jones, Geoffrey Wainwright, and Edward Yarnold (London: SPCK, 1986), pp. xxi–xxvi (at xxii–xxvi); Meredith B. McGuire, 'Mapping Contemporary American Spirituality: A Sociological Perspective', *Christian Spirituality Bulletin* 5 (1997), 175–82; Peter R. Holmes, 'Spirituality: Some Disciplinary Perspectives', in *A Sociology of Spirituality*, ed. by Kieran Flanagan and Peter C. Jupp (Surrey: Ashgate, 2007), pp. 23–42 (at 24f); Philip Sheldrake,

tethered to, the material world of sensual perception.[5] It can reference a kind of existential orientation that occurs through a process of seeking outside the bounds of traditional religion.[6] Even within the solid boundaries of Christian discourse, spirituality can speak to a personal, inner life distinguished from public forms of religious expression.[7] Or, it can refer to a form of mystical thought that lives beyond rationally determined limits.[8] These meanings are typically overlaid upon a network of innately dialectical categories—such as immanence/transcendence, sacred/secular, inner/outer, active/passive, etc.—which, while invoked to clarify matters, ultimately result in confounding an already complex semantic range. Despite this ambiguity, there is an ever-increasing use of the term spirituality. Indeed, the term's ambiguity, rather than being perceived as a deficiency, appears to be part of its strength and appeal. Its ambiguity allows the concept to be employed in a variety of ways. The indefinite openness of 'spirituality' is the stability of its hermeneutical horizon. This implies that the meaning of spirituality is

---

'A Spiritual City: Urban Vision and the Christian Tradition', in *Theology in Built Environments: Exploring Religion, Architecture, and Design*, ed. by Sigurd Bergmann (London: Routledge, 2009), pp. 151–72 (at 151–52).

5   Mircea Eliade, *The Sacred and the Profane: The Nature of Religion* (New York: Harcourt Brace Jovanovich, 1987), p. 11; Gerardus van der Leeuw, *Sacred and Profane Beauty: The Holy in Art* (New York: Oxford University Press, 2006), pp. 231–61; Sylvan, *Traces of the Spirit*, pp. 39–44.

6   Paul Heelas and Linda Woodhead, *The Spiritual Revolution: Why Religion Is Giving Way to Spirituality* (Malden, MA: Blackwell Publishing, 2005), p. 1f; Bryan S. Turner, 'Post-Secular Society: Consumerism and the Democratization of Religion', in *The Post-Secular Question: Religion in Contemporary Society*, ed. by Philip S. Gorski, et al. (New York: Social Science Research Council and New York University Press, 2012), pp. 135–58 (at 136); June Boyce-Tillman, *Experiencing Music—Restoring the Spiritual: Music and Well-Being* (Bern: Peter Lang, 2016), p. 25ff; Peter Jan Margry and Daniel Wojcik, 'A Saxophone Divine: Experiencing the Transformative Power of Saint John Coltrane's Jazz Music in San Francisco's Fillmore District', in *Spiritualizing the City: Agency and Resilience of the Urban and Urbanesque Habitat*, ed. by Victoria Hegner and Peter Jan Margry (London: Routledge, 2017), pp. 169–94 (at 169).

7   Philip Sheldrake, *Spirituality and Theology: Christian Living and the Doctrine of God* (London: Darton, Longman, and Todd, 1998), p. 6; Wade Clark Roof, *Spiritual Marketplace* (Princeton, NJ: Princeton University Press, 1999), p. 137; Sandra M. Schneiders, 'Approaches to the Study of Christian Spirituality', in *The Blackwell Companion to Christian Spirituality*, ed. by Arthur Holder (Malden, MA: Blackwell, 2005), pp. 15–34 (at 16–17).

8   Barbara Quinn, 'Leading to the Edge of Mystery: The Gift and the Challenge', *Spiritus: A Journal of Christian Spirituality* 22 (2022), 3–19 (at 4); Sheldrake, *Spirituality and Theology*, pp. xi; 14–32.

always involved in a process of interrogation. Its meaning happens in certain moments, as a dialectical reflexivity is negotiated. On the one hand, this claim coincides with uses of spirituality which speak to some ethical or dispositional formation.[9] On the other, this openness places the meaning of spirituality beyond the sure footing of scientific inquiry. In fact, it arguably pushes the inquiry into the domain of aesthetics.

The mode of thought that corresponds to the value of the aesthetic sphere is often termed 'symbolic', which indicates both a similarity and dissimilarity to rational cognition. Symbolic thought is not, however, irrational. It merely operates by analogy rather than propositional predication. It is akin to contemplation, which has been held at various points in the Western tradition as a higher form of thought than reason. Given the reflexive nature of spirituality, the element of difference in analogy—or, in musical terms, the dissonance within harmony—is a vital feature of its realisation. Dissonance, indeed, will be a controlling metaphor in what follows, even if the term occasions a 'certain odor of sinfulness'.[10] It is meant here in the somewhat traditional sense of a tension within the harmonious relationships of music, resonating with the ambiguity of the meaning of spirituality.[11] Unlike its modern usage, such as in Arnold Schoenberg's atonal 'emancipation of dissonance', classical dissonance works in complementing consonance in a certain way.[12] Dissonance, more pointedly, 'names the palpable presence of an enduring difference'.[13] Its effect is not chaos or ugliness, but rather

---

9   Charles Taylor, *A Secular Age* (Cambridge, MA: Harvard University Press, 2007), pp. 544–46.
10 Igor Stravinsky, *Poetics of Music* (Cambridge, MA: Harvard University Press, 1942), p. 34.
11 As with the term 'spirituality', the lack of concise definition of 'dissonance' is commonly highlighted. James Tenney, *A History of 'Consonance' and 'Dissonance'* (New York: Excelsior Music, 1988), p. 32, n. 6.
12 For accounts of spirituality in Schoenberg's modern sense of dissonance, see Carl Dahlhaus, 'Schoenberg's Aesthetic Theology', in *Schoenberg and the New Music*, ed. by Carl Dahlhaus (Cambridge, UK: Cambridge University Press, 1999), pp. 81–93; Pamela Cooper-White, *Schoenberg and the God-Idea: The Opera 'Moses and Aron'* (Ann Arbor, MI: UMI Research, 1985); Alexander L. Ringer, *Arnold Schoenberg: The Composer as Jew* (Oxford: Clarendon, 1990). For a critical analysis of Schoenberg's spirituality from the perspective of Trinitarian theology, see Chelle L. Stearns, *Handling Dissonance: A Musical Theological Aesthetic of Unity* (Eugene, OR: Pickwick Publications, 2019), p. 13f.
13 Sean Alexander Gurd, *Dissonance: Auditory Aesthetics in Ancient Greece* (New York: Fordham University Press, 2016), p. 11.

'extra audible information in the form of "beats" or "roughness", a richer, grainier, less-polished sound'.[14] In fact, by assuming its place alongside consonance, it leads to an 'enhancement of the audible', forcing attention to the aesthetic presence of music.[15] The disruption of consonance causes the listener to lean in, to focus, to concentrate. It produces an awareness of the tacit activities already in play in the listening experience. Dissonance reveals music.

(a) Post-Metaphysic Aesthetics and Cognition

Hermeneutical aesthetics develop from a tradition that held music in a negative light precisely because it apparently circumvents reason and stirs the emotions. Gottfried Wilhelm Leibniz, for example, stated that although 'music charms us' through the tacit tracking of 'harmonies of numbers and in the counting ... of the beats or vibrations of sounding bodies' it remains, essentially, a confused form of cognition.[16] In Immanuel Kant, music is a subordinate form among the arts, evoking a degraded sense of mental pleasure in place of the harmonious mental activity spurred by beauty.[17] Even in thinkers who give a much more positive cognitive function to music, such as Arthur Schopenhauer, poetry retains a high place in the arts due to its rational-linguistic structure.[18]

As ontology (the study of being) began to overtake epistemology (the study of knowledge) in the tradition, the relationship between reason and the arts also shifted.[19] Rather than being relegated to a domain beyond reason, aesthetics and hermeneutics became the basis for thought in general. In some sense, the broadening of the influence of music is congruent with the earlier rationalist accounts. The arts

---

14   Ibid. Cf. Patrick Colm Hogan, *Cognitive Science, Literature, and the Arts: A Guide for Humanists* (New York: Routledge, 2003), p. 8.
15   Gurd, *Dissonance*, p. 11.
16   Gottfried Wilhelm Leibniz, 'Principles of Nature and of Grace, Founded on Reason', in *Monadology and Other Philosophical Writings* (London: Oxford University Press, 1925), pp. 405–24 (at 422).
17   Immanuel Kant, *Critique of the Power of Judgment* (Cambridge, UK: Cambridge University Press, 2000), pp. 205–07 (5:328–30).
18   Arthur Schopenhauer, *The World as Will and Representation, Volume 1*, trans. by E. F. J. Payne (New York: Dover Publications, 1969), pp. 242–67 (§§51–52).
19   Cf. Taylor, *A Secular Age*, p. 557f.

penetrate the spirit of humanity, evoking emotions alongside reason. The difference is that for later thinkers this formative effect does not lead to deficient modes of cognition, but to a reconnection to the fullness of reality. Thought is now considered as an occurrence within the dynamic correspondence of a meaningful world. Aesthetic events establish this meaning by gathering various aspects of life-contexts—writer, performer, audience, instruments, speech, sound, other contextual features, etc.—into a single place.[20] They create a harmonious whole in their sheer existence.

One of the more distinguishing characteristics of hermeneutical aesthetics is that the creative essence of art is not reduced to artistic expression.[21] As Martin Heidegger points out, the 'work' of art gives an identity to the artist as much as the artist is the 'origin of the work'.[22] The artwork does not spontaneously appear, of course, but it is removed from the causal connection between human production and the force of its gathering. Art is always out ahead of the artist, often leading their creative insights and technical abilities to new possibilities. Art *happens* in the work of art as an ontological dimension is realised through the harmonious whole. Events create an intelligible context. To develop this standpoint, a broader meaning of λόγος is retrieved. Heidegger thus sees hermeneutics as a mediating realm between the coming to presence and apprehension of phenomena, the latter of which are particular instances in and through which being is revealed.[23] Paul Tillich revives λόγος in his concept of 'ontological reason', or 'the structure of the mind which enables it to grasp and shape reality'.[24]

---

20 This concept of 'event' is distinguished from 'musicking' in that it is not so much speaking to the real-life performance of a musical piece (although it certainly includes this), but more to a shift in meaning from the occasion. In other words, not all performances are aesthetic events. Cf. Christopher Small, *Musicking: The Meanings of Performance and Listening* (Middletown, CT: Wesleyan University Press, 1998), p. 9.

21 Cf. Nicholas Wolterstorff, *Art in Action: Towards a Christian Aesthetic* (Grand Rapids, MI: Eerdmans Publishing Company, 1980), pp. 50–58.

22 Martin Heidegger, 'The Origin of the Work of Art', in Martin Heidegger, *Poetry, Language, Thought* (New York: Harper & Row, 1971), pp. 15–86 (at 17).

23 Martin Heidegger, *Being and Time* (Albany, NY: State University of New York Press, 2010), pp. 30–37 (§7).

24 Paul Tillich, *Systematic Theology: Volume I: Reason and Revelation, Being and God* (Chicago, IL: University of Chicago Press, 1951), p. 83; cf. Jeremy Begbie, *Voicing Creation's Praise: Towards a Theology of the Arts* (London: T & T Clark, 1991), pp. 35–40.

Debates do continue, however, about the relationship between language and music, primarily concerning the degree of intelligibility within hermeneutics. What is typically agreed upon is that music exerts a positive influence on aesthetic intelligibility through its symbolic nature. Aesthetic presences (as well as phenomena in general) are not understood as beings with a definite and constant substance which thought penetrates through analysis and grasps through conceptual apprehension. In this post-metaphysical landscape, being (*Sein*) is relational, that is, all beings (*Seiendes*) are constituted through a referential network. In inquiring into the intelligibility of music, its symbolic nature is not a deviation from this basic framework. In fact, aesthetic presences are symbolic in that they make the relationality of being more obvious. They are, in a sense, truer to reality by their symbolic nature.[25]

Hans-Georg Gadamer explains the symbolic nature of aesthetic presences as an 'intricate interplay of showing and concealing'.[26] The essence of a symbol is an active negation. It ontologically participates in the reality toward which it points, revealing a hiddenness within its own presence. In doing so, symbols force a reflection on the relationality of being. A symbol is thereby not a poor 'substitute for the real existence of something', but a revealing of the reality of all things.[27] For the question

---

25 Cf. Eberhard Jüngel, '»Auch Das Schöne Muß Sterben«—Schönenheit Im Lichte Der Wahrheit. Theologische Bermerkungen Zum Ästhetischen Verhältnis', in Eberhard Jüngel, *Wertlose Wahrheit: zur Identität und Relevanz des Christlichen Glaubens,* Theologische Erörterungen 3 (Tübingen: J. C. B. Mohr (Paul Siebeck), 2003), pp. 378–96 (at 388): 'Being-true means: *to be present to one's self* and precisely because of this *to be lucid*. It applies in the highest way to music, insofar as its truth does not lie in the agreement of *intellectus* and *rei*, but only in the *event* of its tones. The musical artwork is to the highest degree an actuality present in itself: it shines most purely in the light of its own being'.

26 Hans-Georg Gadamer, 'The Relevance of the Beautiful', in *The Relevance of the Beautiful and Other Essays* (Cambridge, UK: Cambridge University Press, 1986), pp. 1–56 (at 33); cf. Paul Tillich, *Dynamics of Faith* (New York: HarperCollins, 1957), pp. 47–50.

27 Gadamer, 'The Relevance of the Beautiful', p. 35. Despite the similarities, this point in particular distinguishes Gadamer's theory of understanding (and those related) from that of aesthetic cognitivism. There, 'symbolic understanding' merely refers to the linguistic or pictorial representation of a claim, as (loosely) opposed to the actual claim in 'factual understanding'. See, Christoph Baumberger, 'Art and Understanding: In Defence of Aethetic Cognitivism', in *Bilder Sehen. Perspektiven Der Bildwissenschaft*, ed. by Mark Greenlee et al. (Regensburg: Schnell & Steiner, 2013), pp. 41–67 (at 43f.); Catherine Z. Elgin, *Considered Judgment* (Princeton, NJ:

of aesthetic cognition, Gadamer explains, 'there is more to the work of art than a meaning that is experienced only in an indeterminate way'.[28] That is, its meaningful contents are not 'traces of conceptual meaning'.[29] Symbols make meaning by their presence, doing so in manifesting a dynamic inner-relation.

Music accomplishes this in both its non-representative form, which is an even more radical feature of its being than with non-objective art, as well as in its re-presentation of relationality. As concerns the specific musical examples of outlaw country discussed below, the appearance of spirituality cannot be elucidated apart from the music itself. This is perhaps most explicit in Nelson's 1996 instrumental track title 'Spirit of E9', from the record *Spirit*. But even the examples below are events in which spirituality is taking form, becoming realised, rather than examples of an already established sense of the category. These songs add a dimension to the essence of spirituality that cannot be justified on rational terms.

On the one hand, their unique ability to present the self-negating activity of being 'calls on us to dwell upon [the artwork] and give our assent in an act of recognition'.[30] Symbols draw us in, offering the possibility of cognition by demanding the activity of interpretation. On the other hand, Gadamer is clear that the re-cognition here does not indicate a 'simple transference of mediation of meaning' which is elsewhere grounded in rational concepts.[31] The cognitive aspect of symbols is their freedom from reason. It, in fact, reminds reason of its limits. Symbols make meaning by inviting participation, all but

---

Princeton University Press, 1996), pp. 170–204. A similar distinction can be made to theories which would attribute some non-rational symbolic meaning to music, but a kind of meaning most closely associated with emotions. For an overview of these kinds of theories, see Maeve Louise Heaney, *Music as Theology: What Music Says About the Word* (Eugene, OR: Pickwick, 2012), p. 21f.

28 Gadamer, 'The Relevance of the Beautiful', p. 34.
29 Ibid. p. 38.
30 Ibid., p. 36. For a more developed account of music in Gadamer's aesthetics, see Beate Regina Suchla, 'Gadamer', in *Music in German Philosophy: An Introduction*, ed. by Stefan Lorenz Sorgner, Oliver Furbeth, and Susan H. Gillespie (Chicago, IL: University of Chicago Press, 2011), pp. 211–32 (at 219–22).
31 Gadamer, 'The Relevance of the Beautiful', p. 37.

compelling thought to search for a resolution from their inherent tension; concepts, in contrast, are meaningful in their precision and usefulness.[32]

The relationship of symbols to rational concepts reveals that meaning (and its cognition) stems from a more fundamental dimension of reality than what can be captured by reason. Tillich speaks of this as a 'Spiritual Presence' of the ontological structuring of love, which both produces and sustains ultimate meaning within being.[33] The meaning music gives to spirituality cannot be understood in this framework as music 'explaining' spirituality. Meaning, here, indicates something other than information. It is the gathering required for conceptual analysis.

(b) The Indeterminate Dimensions of a Secularised Spirituality

It is in this vein that Charles Taylor describes spirituality as an experience with 'fullness' that evokes a sense of enduring strength through bringing various features of existence into a harmonious order.[34] Taylor analyses the historical conditions of such an encounter with fullness in light of modern secularity,[35] devising the concept of an 'immanent frame' to explicate the conditions of belief unique to contemporary society.[36] For Taylor, this 'immanent frame' is generally shared by the inhabitants of Western culture, it forms a starting point for all spiritual experiences (akin to the role of experience and tradition mentioned above), and it is nonetheless constituted by a set of features that were historically understood as pitted against transcendence. Among these features is an axiomatic valuing of 'instrumental reasoning', or a mode

---

32 Hans-Georg Gadamer, *Truth and Method*, 2nd rev. ed. (London: Sheed & Ward, 1989), pp. 33–35. For a development of a similar point concerning Gadamer's distinction of 'understanding' (*verstehen*) and 'knowledge' (*erklärung*) and music, see Cynthia Lins Hamlin, 'An Exchange between Gadamer and Glenn Gould on Hermeneutics and Music', *Theory, Culture & Society* 33.3 (2015), 105–07.

33 Paul Tillich, *Systematic Theology: Volume III: Life and the Spirit, History and the Kingdom of God* (Chicago, IL: University of Chicago Press, 1963), pp. 160–61.

34 Taylor, *A Secular Age*, p. 6. In fact, he points to Friedrich Schiller's fundamental role of 'play' as an archetypal example, which Schiller describes as an 'ästhetische Stimmung des Gemüths' [aesthetic attunement of the mind/soul]. See Friedrich Schiller, 'Über Die Ästhetische Erziehung Des Menschen', in Friedrich Schiller, *Briefen. Werke* (Stuttgart & Tübingen: Gottaschen Buchhandlung, 1959), p. 90.

35 Taylor, *A Secular Age*, p. 20.

36 Ibid., p. 542.

of understanding which sees the meaning of things only in terms of causality or moral formation.[37] Taylor argues that this feature is naively presupposed in two broad kinds of reactions to the conditions of modern secularity, which he refers to as the 'spins' of 'open' and 'closed' postures. An 'open' posture posits an immediate access to some other realm of existence, invoking a view from nowhere often retrieved from a classical tradition, albeit employed in a new way against the immanent frame. A 'closed' posture inhabits the immanent frame fully, particularly its character of providing an 'order which can be understood in its own terms, without reference to the "supernatural" or "transcendent"'.[38] And yet it tenuously retains the language of spirituality (along with related terms), its meaning radically oriented to socio-cultural conditions; in the 'closed' posture, there can still be experiences of fullness, but their interpretation and explanation happen without reference to a transcendent realm.

Both the 'open' and 'closed' postures are 'spins' in the sense that they are influential narratives through which 'one's thinking is clouded or cramped by a powerful picture which prevents one seeing important aspects of reality'.[39] That is, they confuse the justifications for their own position without taking into account the experiences which led to the establishing and/or adopting of such a position. Neither spin is entirely persuasive. As Taylor notes, both require an element of 'anticipatory confidence', or a 'leap of faith', which catapults meaning into the search for rational justification.[40] This 'anticipatory confidence' speaks to the kind of aesthetic meaning explicated above. Neither the 'open' nor the 'closed' spins are typically in full effect, moreover. Most people live in the 'cross-pressure' developed between their pulls.[41] This is a frame of

---

37 Ibid., p. 110. Cf. 96–99. Taylor lists materialism, instrumental reasoning (i.e., the methodology of the natural sciences), chronotic (versus chairiotic) time, and a constructed (i.e., not metaphysically grounded) social space as the other features of the immanent order.
38 Ibid., p. 594. Taylor explains that the 'closed' spin can seem more natural or obvious within the immanent frame but he demonstrates that it is as influenced by precognitive 'images' as the open spin. Among its tendencies is the desire for scientific quantification, grounded in empirical research. This implies, in turn, that the social imaginary has a strong influence on the methodology for investigating into such things as the meaning of spirituality.
39 Ibid., p. 551.
40 Ibid., p. 550.
41 Ibid., p. 555.

experience circumscribed by tension, the competing claims of spirituality, and its various dialectical categories: materialism, traditional religion, extra-rational meaning, corporate sense of identity, secularity, etc. To return to Taylor's notion of spirituality, aesthetic events (including music) participate in the development of new forms of identity that stem from this tension, a process he terms the 'nova effect' of modern spirituality.[42]

Two points should be highlighted before moving to a concrete example of this situation. First, music developed in this context establishes new forms of spirituality. These new forms draw in various ways from the dialectical relationships inherent to the term spirituality, opening a range of new spiritual positions. Astrology and new religious movements (NRMs) are good examples of this sort of spirituality, as well as more recent developments in which hallucinogenic experiences play a formative role. Equally, however, spirituality can embrace more traditional forms of religion, which are themselves reinterpreted through materialism or any of the other dimensions mentioned here. The 'Nones' of post-confessional religion are a paradigm case.[43] Aesthetic moments do not impart their constitutive force by declaring one or the other 'spins' in an unambiguous manner. They allow the tension of spirituality to appear.

II. A Mythological Spirituality in Outlaw Country

Turning to specific forms of aesthetic symbols, the meaning of spirituality is established in particular musical events. Specific songs form the material basis for experiences with fullness as defined by Taylor. Here, attention is given to the articulation of the topic at various points within the single musical tradition of 'outlaw country': Willie Nelson (b. 1933), Sturgill Simpson (b. 1978), and Cody Jinks (b. 1980), approaching each through discussion of one exemplary song: 'Hands on the Wheel', 'Turtles All the Way Down', and 'Holy Water' respectively. Key here is

---

42 Ibid., p. 299.
43 Cf. ibid., p. 509f.

musical dissonance, which has a particular impact on the presence of their symbolic meaning.

(a) Symbolic Meaning and the Dissonance of the Third

The symbolic meaning of music reduces the tendency to frame musical hermeneutics in terms of an opposition between language and 'absolute' music.[44] Poetic modes of language are just as cognitively symbolic as musical forms, giving only the illusion of something more stable. For both, meaning is rooted primarily in the happenings of aesthetic events, and only develops into more stable cultural-traditional forms through hermeneutical reflection. The dissonant moments of music can be the very impetus for the event, directing attention towards the accompanying lyrics. On a general level, we take notice of lyrics, and analyse their meaning, because of their appearance in the song as a whole. They are 'lyrics' because they are accompanied by music. At a more detailed level, specific moments within a song heighten its hermeneutical effect. As a deviation from composition norms takes place, as our attention is caught, meaning has already happened. Here, dissonance receives a technical meaning. Even when understood as a 'single wave', consonance is not a single note. It rather refers (at least in modern music) to a specific relationship of a triad that is organised by a single tonal centre. In country music, this occurs in the simultaneous presence of the tonic, mediant, and dominant tones, or the I, III, and V notes of a typically major scale. Dissonance is a select deviation from this basis. The tonic remains the tonal centre, but variations occur in either the mediant or dominant tones.

The inclusion of variations on the mediant tones is an important point, for two reasons. First, Schoenberg rejects such a claim. For him, dissonance is only produced by dropping the dominant tone a full step (forming a diminished chord, e.g. C-E-F) or raising it either a full step or three half steps (forming an augmented chord, e.g. C-E-A or C-E-A#). He designates the dominant with this special power because it shares the highest degree of 'overtones' with the tonic.[45] As such, it competes with the tonic, being 'able to threaten the hegemony of the fundamental

---

44 See, Heaney, *Music as Theology*, pp. 24–26.
45 Arnold Schoenberg, *Theory of Harmony* (London: Faber and Faber, 1978), p. 23f.

and claim its governing role'.[46] As James Tenney shows, however, there is a historical component to dissonance, which means that its perceived tension is relative to the dominant structures of the time. Schoenberg was himself aware of this idea, at one point declaring his 'hope that in a few decades audiences will recognize the *tonality* of this music today called *atonal*'.[47] At various points in history, dissonance included either the presence of multiple tones (regardless of their harmonious relationship), or a tonic accompanied by one or more tonal intervals, ranging from the third to the seventh. The inclusion of the third as a dissonant tone originates in the eleventh century as the gaining popularity of triads began to challenge the largely accepted 'truth' of Pythagorean scales.[48] Effectively, the third was dissonant because it was innovative. As with Schoenberg's atonal aspirations, however, it was eventually subsumed under consonance by the end of the fourteenth century, where dissonance was relegated to notes beyond thirds, fourths, fifths, and sixths.[49]

This leads to the second importance of the inclusion of variations on the mediant tones. Country music lives by thirds. The 'country sound' is largely constituted by the mixing of major and minor thirds (and their sixth counterparts) in an idiosyncratic manner. The outcome, however, is that the third is largely unsure of its presence. The (broadly) dissonant elements in this music chiefly arise from playing with the mediant tones either by dropping them a half-step to the minor, or raising them a half-step to form a suspended chord. The overall effect of this musical dissonance is a heightened awareness of the aesthetic event at hand. The selected presence of deviation gathers interest. As it directs attention in terms of perception (i.e., the event of listening) it heightens the resolution of the synthetic phenomena of lyrics and music. On the one hand, this draws a higher quality of attention to the meaning of the lyrical content. On the other, it augments the linguistic meaning through its dissonant tones. Even in an attempt to secure this meaning in the closed realm of rational concepts, the derivative process by which

---

46   Stearns, *Handling Dissonance*, p. 23.
47   Arnold Schoenberg, *Style and Idea: Selected Writings of Arnold Schoenberg* (New York: St Martin's Press, 1975), p. 283.
48   Tenney, *A History of 'Consonance' and 'Dissonance'*, p. 21f.
49   Ibid., p. 39.

those concepts are produced is infected with this musical inflection. Music's influence here goes beyond a tacit value of the concept, to a constituent feature of its fundamental sense. Dissonance becomes part of the cognitive judgement, leading along the norms of reason, and transforming them in its wake. The key feature remains: the dynamics of dissonance and consonance in music encourages listening. It heightens awareness, and, through its presence, helps to form a context in which meaning is found.

(b) Willie Nelson, 'Hands on the Wheel'

Willie Nelson's breakthrough album *Red Headed Stranger* (1974) established the structural features of how the genre approaches questions of spirituality. In fact, he is the 'most significant musical and spiritual legacy of the outlaw movement'.[50] The first generation of writers and artists became 'absolutely disciples' of Nelson, as Kristofferson recounts—a description which echoes throughout the tradition.[51] As one recent retrospective review puts it, the tracks of *Red Headed Stranger* 'carry Biblical levels of anguish on their slender shoulders'.[52] This sentiment reverberates a 1978 review that suggested the album should be filed 'next to the King James or Revised Standard Version',[53] going on to recite the testimony of meeting people 'who have driven hundreds of miles to touch the hem of [Nelson's] garment. Literally'.[54] Dissonance is established in Nelson's wake along three dimensions: the lyrical content and poetic form; the musicological aspect; and the contours

---

50   Streissguth, *Outlaw: Waylon, Willie, Kris, and the Renegades of Nashville*, p. 5.
51   Robert Oermann, *Behind the Grand Ole Opry Curtain: Tales of Romance and Tragedy* (New York: Center Street, 2008), pp. 296–97.
52   Robert Ham, 'Classic Album Review: Willie Nelson Turns Outlaw on the Seminal Red Headed Stranger', *Consequence*, 17 September 2019, https://consequence.net/2019/09/classic-album-review-willie-nelson-red-headed-stranger/
53   Quoted in Chet Filippo, 'Willie Nelson: Holy Man of the Honky Tonks. The Saga of the King of Texas, from the Night Life to the Good Life', *Rolling Stone*, 13 July 1978, p. 66; Blase S. Scarnati, 'Religious Doctrine in the Mid-1970s to 1980s Country Music Concept Albums of Willie Nelson', in *Walking the Line: Country Music Lyricists and American Culture*, ed. by Thomas Alan Holmes and Roxanne Harde (Lanham, MD: Lexington Books, 2013), pp. 65–76.
54   Filippo, 'Willie Nelson'.

of production.⁵⁵ These features are re-presented, in differing ways, in two albums over thirty years later: Sturgill Simpson's *Metamodern Sounds of Country Music* (2014) and Cody Jinks' *Lifers* (2018). These records bring this discussion into a more contemporary context. More importantly, the opening tracks of both these later albums signal two opposite experiences of the possibilities within the spiritual landscape. One embraces its ambiguity, the other reluctantly acknowledges it through anxiety. The most unique augmentation to the basic framework laid by Nelson in these newer articulations is an emphasis on a sort of sacramental symbolism, indicating an interesting shift in this limited corner of the social imaginary within the last decade.

Willie Nelson's role in establishing the genre of outlaw country is replicated in the interrogation of spirituality incumbent to this musical tradition.⁵⁶ His 1974 breakthrough album *Red Headed Stranger* is often pointed to as the beginning of outlaw country—being the first album where the artist had full creative control—and the song 'Hands on the Wheel' acts as a sort of historical precedence for the analysis at hand.⁵⁷ The lyrics themselves are written from a first-hand perspective of a spiritual seeker, and dissonance is present along the three dimensions listed above.

Beginning with the lyrical dissonance, Nelson enters an overtly traditional progression with a Nietzschean line, bringing the coming spiritual tension to a palpable presence. Along with a type of world 'unhinged from the sun', the taxonomy of 'believers', 'deceivers', and 'inbetweeners' maps onto Taylor notion of the spins of spiritual positions in modern secularity. As does the disorientated experience of the shift, which leaves the imagined spiritual seeker with 'no place

---

55   The 'Nashville sound' from which outlaw country was breaking free 'prescribed the length, the meter, and the lyrical content of songs as well as how those songs were recorded in the studio'. Streissguth, *Outlaw: Waylon, Willie, Kris, and the Renegades of Nashville*, p. 2.

56   Nelson records that Levi H. Dowling's *The Aquarian Gospel of Jesus the Christ: The Philosophical and Practical Basis of the Religion of the Aquarian Age of the World and the Church Universal* (London: L.N. Fowler and Company) held a large influence over his religious thought in general and its interpretation set forth in Stranger specifically. Willie Nelson and Bud Shrake, *Willie: An Autobiography* (New York: Cooper Square Press, 1988), pp. 114–16.

57   The conceptual album *Yesterday's Wine* (1971) is much more explicit with its questions of spirituality, yet, as per the regulation of aesthetic symbols, its reception is neither as immediate nor apparent. See, Scarnati, 'Religious Doctrine', p. 67.

to go'. A realisation of the conditions of belief articulated by Taylor underlies this disorientation. Nelson himself recounts that, although he always had a 'powerful spiritual urge', he would not define it as 'religious'.[58] What seemed to appear initially as an exciting venture into new horizons of transcendence, however, has turned out to be 'the same old song' of a morality grounded by the 'same damn tune' of some supernatural deity.

> At a time, when the world, seems to be spinning
> Hopelessly out of control
> There's believers, and deceivers, and old inbetweeners
> Who seem to have no place to go
> It's the same old song
> It's right and it's wrong
> And livin' is just something I do
> With no place to hide
> I looked to your eyes
> And I found myself in you
> I looked to the stars
> Tried all of the bars
> And I've nearly gone up in smoke
> Now my hands on the wheel
> Of something that's real
> And I feel like I'm going home
> Beneath the shade, of an oak, down by the river
> Sat an old man and a boy
> Setting sail, and spinning tails, and fishing for whales
> With a lady that they both enjoy
> It's the same damn tune
> It's the man in the moon
> And it's the way I feel about you
> With no place to hide?
> I looked to your eyes
> And I found myself in you.[59]

In a key chorus, Nelson establishes a set of common facets to the appearance of spirituality in outlaw country while he simultaneously discovers a grounding orientation for the existential dissonance of a secular age. Beginning with these facets, 'looked to the stars' (astrology), 'tried all of the bars' (alcohol), 'nearly gone up in smoke' (drugs)

---

58 Nelson and Shrake, *Willie*, p. 114.
59 Willie Nelson, 'Hands on the Wheel', *Red Headed Stranger* (Columbia Records, 1974).

become spiritual tropes in this tradition. They confirm Taylor's insight that spirituality is an experience with fullness, here articulated by a reinterpretation of natural phenomena and an extra-rational experience of self-consciousness. Even though each of these facets is primarily defined by their material characteristics, their importance is in what lies beyond this definition.

It is also important that none of these facets ultimately bring consonance to Nelson's spiritual dissonance. The harmony he seeks only comes about through love. 'With no place to hide', the disoriented seeker finds 'something real' by looking into the eyes of the beloved. Love replaces religion, 'the man in the moon', in a glimpse of the influence of the immanent frame. The stability of the meaning found in such a gaze is the basis for the second verse, where it overflows into a child. What ultimately resolves the spiritual dissonance, then, is a proper relationship—an experiential harmony which sets things into order.

Fig. 6.1 Transcription by author (2024), CC BY-NC 4.0

Musically, the dissonance occurs most powerfully in bars 41–43 of the B-section, where the guitar and bass walk down from the VI to the V. Almost without exception, when a VI chord appears in this genre it is in the form of either a seventh chord (with the voicing here of

F#-E-A#-C#) or a minor chord. The important difference is the third of either chord. If the song opts for the seventh chord, then the major third is present; otherwise, it is harmonically present by the minor third. In 'Hands on the Wheel', Nelson plays a disquieting fifth chord (F#-C#-F#) as the tempo begins to slow. His vocals remain on an A, filling in the missing third with a minor. A harmonica enters in bar 38, adding a surprising degree of dynamics to the overall quiet composition. It initially harmonises the vocals by adding the relative fourth (E/A-E/D#-F#/D-E/C#-D/B-C#/A), but slightly wavers (following a *portamento*) between an A# and A in bar 40. Following from the predictable composition thus far, the lack of a third in the guitar voicing seems suspended mid-step. Rather than resolving this tension in the next measure, he compounds it by introducing the major seventh note (F) in the bass of the voicing, yet keeping the A in the vocals, producing the almost atonal chord of F-A-C#-F#. The tempo slows further, before resolving into a major V chord awaiting the bass to walk back up to the I via the third (E-F#-G#). This moment of dissonance happens as the key lines of 'livin' is just something I do' and 'almost went up in smoke' are sung. Its effect is to gather attention, but does so without an immediate resolution. In the beats that pass between the walk down (F#-F-E) and the bass initiating the resolving consonance of a major triad, the meaninglessness of spirituality is re-presented, forming the basis for its symbolic articulation. As the context is gathered in this moment, the stage is set for the significance of love. The line which follows—'now my hands on the wheel...'—is most directly augmented by the musical dissonance.

These features take place, moreover, within a kind of production which was outright startling for the time. Perhaps the best description of the record is thin, almost silent.[60] When Nelson presented it to the record label, 'the instrumentation was so sparse and Willie's guitar

---

60 The sonic dimensions as emphasised in analyses of music by the methods of cognitive science could be helpful in articulating this point in a different manner. For example, Annette Wilke, 'Sonality', in *The Bloomsbury Handbook of the Cultural and Cognitive Aesthetics of Religion*, ed. by Anne Koch and Katharina Wilkens (London: Bloomsbury Academic, 2020), pp. 107–16 (p. 107f.). For another example, see, Martin Pfleiderer, 'Sound Und Rhythmus in Populär Musik. Analysemethoden, Darstellungsmöglichkeiten, Interpretationsansätze', in *Die Bedeutung Populärer Musik in Audiovissuellen Formaten*, ed. by Christofer Jost et al. (Germany: Nomos Verlagsgesellschaft, 2009), pp. 175–95 (esp. 178–88).

playing so splintered that [the label's] officials assumed it was unfinished'.⁶¹ Paul Nelson of *Rolling Stone* wrote that the meaning of the album was akin to a Hemingway novel, 'accessible only between the lines', in that space between material content.⁶² Yet, as it was reluctantly released and surprisingly shot up the charts, it became apparent that the record was a shift in the entire country scene. As one reviewer wrote about the record, 'As likely as not, you won't like it the first time through, but stick with it. It'll stick with you for a long time. Masterpieces are like that'.⁶³ Its greatness is a judgment that requires a period of attunement.

(c) Sturgill Simpson, 'Turtles All the Way Down'

I've seen Jesus play with flames
In a lake of fire that I was standing in
Met the devil in Seattle
And spent nine months inside the lions' den
Met Buddha yet another time
And he showed me a glowing light within
But I swear that god is there
Every time I glare into the eyes of my best friend

...

There's a gateway in our minds
That leads somewhere out there, far beyond this plane
Where reptile aliens made of light
Cut you open and pull out all your pain
Tell me how you make illegal
Something that we all make in our brain
Some say you might go crazy
But then again, it might make you go sane

Every time I take a look
Inside that old and fabled book
I'm blinded and reminded of
The pain caused by some old man in the sky

---

61 Streissguth, *Outlaw: Waylon, Willie, Kris, and the Renegades of Nashville*, p. 180.
62 Paul Nelson, 'Hemingway, Who Perfected', *Rolling Stone*, 28 August 1975); quoted in Streissguth, *Outlaw: Waylon, Willie, Kris, and the Renegades of Nashville*, p. 184.
63 Streissguth, *Outlaw: Waylon, Willie, Kris, and the Renegades of Nashville*, p. 184.

> Marijuana, LSD
> Psilocybin, and DMT
>
> They all changed the way I see
> But love's the only thing that ever saved my life
>
> So don't waste your mind on nursery rhymes
> Or fairy tales of blood and wine
> It's turtles all the way down the line
> So to each their own 'til we go home
> To other realms our souls must roam
> To and through the myth that we all call space and time.[64]

The basic structure Nelson established reappears in Sturgill Simpson's masterfully composed 'Turtles All the Way Down'.[65] Here, though, the conditions of the immanent frame are even more apparent in the search for meaning. Not only was Jason Seiler commissioned for the album artwork—notable for his portrait of Pope Francis that adorned the cover of *Time* magazine in 2012—but appreciation is given to Carl Sagan and Stephen Hawking in the liner notes. The album is a synthetic product of Simpson's 'nighttime reading about theology, cosmology, and breakthroughs in modern physics' alongside personal experience.[66] The meaning of traditional forms of religion still lingers, but only in the midst of a radical reinterpretation. The first sung words of the song make this clear.

Simpson documents a spiritual search for meaning that winds through Christianity, Buddhism, and other vaguely defined conceptions of God, before ultimately finding meaning in everyday relationships.

---

64 Sturgill Simpson, 'Turtles All the Way Down', *Metamodern Sounds in Country Music* (High Top Mountain and Loose Music, 2014).

65 Even though the title of Sturgill's album, *Metamodern Sounds in Country Music*, references Ray Charles' 1962 breakthrough release, *Modern Sounds in Country and Western Music*, the influence of Nelson's *Red Headed Stranger* on Simpson's *Metamodern Sounds* is (at least) alluded to in the album's cover art. See, Figure 6.1.

66 Ann Powers, 'God, Drugs and Lizard Aliens: Yep, It's Country Music', *The Record*, 17 April 2014, https://www.npr.org/sections/therecord/2014/04/17/304075384/god-drugs-and-lizard-aliens-yep-its-country-music. Simpson elsewhere references Pierre Teilhard de Chardin's concept of the 'Omega Point' as an influence. See Chris Richards, 'Sturgill Simpson: A Country Voice of, and out of, This World', *The Washington Post*, 17 March 2014, https://www.washingtonpost.com/lifestyle/style/sturgill-simpson-a-country-voice-of-and-out-of-this-world/2014/03/31/46277cce-b8f9-11e3-899e-bb708e3539dd_story.html

He later describes this meaning as love, 'the only thing that ever saved my life'. This is, significantly, a love which stands in contrast to the 'pain caused by some old man in the sky', of whom he's reminded when he searches in the pages of the Bible. Moving to the chorus of the song, what has 'changed the way' Simpson sees the spiritual landscape is his experiences with psychedelic drugs: 'Marijuana, LSD, Psilocybin, and', most importantly, 'DMT'.

In an interview with National Public Radio (NPR) on the inspiration behind both this song and the entire album, Simpson explains that he was extremely inspired by Rick Strassman's *DMT: The Spirit Molecule*.[67] In this work, Strassman documents a government-funded research project in which he injected several dozen participants with DMT, and subsequently tracked their experiences with specific attention toward notions of spirituality. Strassman argues that there is a correlation between the levels of DMT present in people's minds and their accounts of religious experiences. The background behind this song uncovers a remarkable insight. As is characteristic of Taylor's taxonomy of spiritual positions, Simpson is finding meaning of a transcendent quality within the immanent structure of clinical psychology. This is precisely what Taylor refers to as a form of 'motivational materialism'.[68] Returning to Simpson's lyrics, acting as a 'gateway in our minds', the DMT-induced altered consciousness is what reveals that 'love's the only thing that ever saved my life'. Love, as experienced in everyday life, an experience with an 'other', is a powerful source of meaning within the immanent frame. For Simpson, love has been unhinged from the traditional religious use in Western culture. In a Tillichean sense, it is simply a foundational feature of the world available through a plurality of cultural articulations, an immanent realm that is merely the 'myth we call space and time'. Upon discovering this insight, we can all 'go sane', and proclaim love as the salvation of the world. The great hope of the world is found in this understanding of love: 'to each their own 'til we go home/To other realms our souls must roam'. Yet,

---

67 Powers, 'God, Drugs and Lizard Aliens'; cf. Rick Strassman, *DMT: The Spirit Molecule: A Doctor's Revolutionary Research into the Biology of New-Death and Mystical Experiences* (Rochester, VT: Parker Street Press, 2001).

68 Taylor, *A Secular Age*, p. 595.

unlike in Nelson, this meaning does not eradicate the need for drugs. Love saves, but drugs shift perspective.

Dissonance in both the composition and production of 'Turtles' takes on a form of suspension and augmentation, which are relatively rare in country music. The tonic and semidominant chords (here, the I and IV in E) involve suspending the third up a half-step (A over the E; D over an A). This suspension is compounded on the IV chord as the fifth is also raised to the major sixth (over A, E is raised to F#). These voicings happen as the bass moves between the octaves, which is also a strange choice in the genre. The bass line compounds the suspension in the chords, intensifying the euphoric atmosphere of the track.

Fig. 6.2 Transcription by author (2024), CC BY-NC 4.0

The general use of suspended dissonance reaches a new level in Bar 11. The guitar continues the movement between a suspended E, while the bass sustains its octave line. The vocal melody rises to a D natural, adding a seventh to the major triad. The vocals began a descending scale as the guitar suspends the third. The scale starts on a C#, adding a sixth to the already suspended E. The intensified moment of dissonance attracts the ear, in a sense preparing the reception of its lyrical content, here speaking of the meaning of spirituality as an inner spark of divinity. When all these features are combined, a *Stimmung* (see Chapter 10 in this volume for further discussion of this term) comes to definition which replicates the psychedelic experience being described. The heavy use of reverb in the production adds to this, further driving home the potency of a chemically-induced spiritual experience.

(d) Cody Jinks, 'Holy Water'

I walk around on pins and needles
Around people I can't even name
I keep on passing church steeples
Praying that my God is still the same
I been wandering like a fool too blind to see
Maybe it ain't the bottle that I need

> I need a shot of holy water
> I need it to chase down my demons
> And burn 'em just a little bit hotter
> I've been having drinks with the devil in this neon town
> I need a shot of holy water to wash it down
>
> Lost in a land of smoke and mirrors
> I do my best to just stay clear of my yesterdays
> I've been running so long, now I'm running from myself
> Tired of running away
> I'm still tryin' to get through to the man I wanna be
> Maybe I'm not so gone that I can't see.[69]

While Simpson exchanges traditional religion in the American landscape for new avenues of spirituality, wholly grounded in a secularised sense of immanence, Cody Jinks ponders if he can still maintain the type of Christianity he knew as a child. Jinks reinterprets Nelson's emphasis on drugs and alcohol to a similar degree that Nelson and Simpson reinterpret Christianity. He also, interestingly, emphasises a sacramental nature of his spiritual experience. While Simpson warns 'don't waste your mind ... on fairy tales of blood and wine', Jinks sees a sacramental encounter—'a shot of holy water'—as the resolution to the dissonant cross-pressures of the immanent frame.

Simpson's experience of liberation in the secularised spiritual landscape is countered by Jinks' anxiety. The immanent 'other' here is seen more as a judging onlooker, than the source of salvation. In terms of Taylor's secularisation narrative, Jinks's more traditional understandings of spirituality place him in a precarious position within the fragmentation of a novel spiritual context. Jinks understands there are significant and compelling challenges to those old church steeples, stemming from unfamiliar social sources. Yet, rather than turning to some structure of immanence, such as Simpson's 'motivational materialism', Jinks doubles-down on his traditional beliefs, and 'prays' to the God who has been proclaimed as 'unchanging' throughout the centuries.

Furthermore, the closed posture of Jinks towards newer forms of spirituality is not necessarily based completely on some dogmatic allegiance. There are also powerful critiques against the positions that

---

69 Cody Jinks, 'Holy Water', *Lifers* (Rounder Records, 2018).

openly welcome the spiritual substitutions of the cultural topography. One such critique is the seeming inability of immanent structures to provide the 'fullness of human life' sought by so many individuals. Jinks describes this quest for fullness as the attempt 'to get through to the man I wanna be'. He reasons that this goal cannot be found in the 'land of smoke and mirrors' that is the source of his spiritual anxiety. Even though he recognises the influence of a secular world on his own beliefs, he also acknowledges that he's 'not so gone that [he] can't see' that the source of meaning in life still emanates from more traditional forms of religion.

Fig. 6.3 Transcription by author (2024), CC BY-NC 4.0

While Simpson employs psychedelics to guide him through the ever-shifting spiritual landscape, Jinks proclaims that what he needs is 'a shot of holy water'. Drinking 'with the devil in this neon town' has only led to meaninglessness, away from which Jinks is 'tired of running'. The source of meaning—for this 'closed' spin—cannot be found within the immanent frame, but only in a rupture of it. A sacramental aesthetic is its augmentation. It is notable that the material form of this transcendental encounter is in a shot of alcohol. Whisky has replaced wine. Further, Jinks' spirituality is also more individualistic than Nelson or Simpson. He seeks a sort of self-transcendence of maturation. A process which cannot be participated in without a sacramental encounter. Yet, this comes at a cost. The communal dimension of love is ironically absent in Jinks' return to God, perhaps indicating that the materialism of the immanent frame is still in control.

In terms of production and overall composition, Jinks' conversion to country music from metal betrays itself. The deviation from the tradition happens from the outset of the song, introducing the spiritual dissonance of its lyrical content rather than augmenting it as with the other two examples. A distorted guitar plays variations on power chords (i.e., absent of a third; here, A#-F-A#), following the somewhat unusual progression of VI-V-IV (A#-G#-F#). An acoustic guitar imitates the progression, but plays the thirds while oscillating between the two notes of C# and C in a sort of syncopated rhythm. So, on the VI chord the acoustic goes back and forth between a A# minor and a A# suspended chord (A#-C#/C-F#); on the IV between a F# major and an augmented major seventh (F#-A-C#/C-C#). The two guitars play in unison on the suspension of the V (bar 2), forming another interesting similarity with Simpson. The production overall is more in the front of the mix, which exerts an anxious mood given the distorted guitars and rock progression.

Conclusion: A Theological Postscript

A spiritual seeker navigating through the novel conditions of belief, an outright embrace of the immanent frame, and an anxious desire to return to traditional religion all appear as meanings of spirituality in outlaw country. Yet, at their core, they are united in a foundation of dissonance. As such, it is perhaps pertinent to note that, in its broad use, spirituality cannot be directly identified with a theological discourse of a traditional religion such as Christianity. There is no clear pathway from the experience of fullness with these songs to a particular deity. Its ambiguity prevents this. What the hermeneutical dissonance of spirituality does imply, however, is that its ambiguity reveals the fullness of life. In analogous correspondence to symbolic reasoning, spirituality shows the limits of its dialectical counterparts—materiality, traditional religion, fixed forms of dispositional formation, determinative reason— by standing at their boundaries. In doing so, spirituality gives rhythmic value to these more stable aspects. This rhythm does not negate these more determinative dimensions. Instead, it complements them in a certain way. It reveals that life spills over the limits of determination, into a realm that is most appropriately described as aesthetic. This spilling over is dynamic. It is perpetually happening. And, it is precisely this dynamic happening which becomes present in music.

II. EMPIRICAL METHODS

7. From the Sacred to the Ordinary through the Lens of Psychological Science

Yeshaya David M. Greenberg

Music and spirituality have been intertwined within the socio-cultural and religious activities of our human ancestors for millennia. Many of the religions in existence today—for example, Buddhism, Christianity, Hinduism, and Judaism—have historical accounts of music being embedded within the spiritual, and today the modern practices of these religions all continue to use music as a vehicle for self-transcendence and to experience the divine. Thus, spirituality-infused musical experiences impact at least four billion people worldwide and 51% of the world's population. Yet, when it comes to the realm of science, the terms 'music' and 'spirituality' are rarely uttered in the same breath and almost never appear together in any title or abstract in a peer-reviewed empirical study. Perhaps this would make sense for the more natural sciences, like physics, but not for the field of psychology, whose fundamental purpose is to understand human behaviour. In fact, in searching the literature of psychological science and its surrounding sub-disciplines, including the subject specialisms of music cognition and music psychology, the topic of music and spirituality is entirely missing. And yet, of all the topics of inquiry about music—from preferences and perception to universality and therapy—it is the topic of music and spirituality which most interests me. Perhaps this is because it taps deeply into a very essential core of human sonic experience, or even because of my own mystical encounters with music.[1] Regardless of my personal preferences and beliefs, however, understanding the mysterious links between music and spirituality poses an immense scientific challenge. Even though this topic is both mystifying and challenging, it does not mean that it is not worth inquiry from a scientific point of view. On the contrary, it is often the topics posing the greatest challenge that can deliver the greatest reward. In this chapter, I will raise issues for researchers to consider, including how to define terms and develop theories in this area. I will also present preliminary results from my own research programme on this subject matter.

Although many chapters in this volume explore how music relates to Christian theology and worship, this chapter thereby takes the opportunity to present theory, research, and findings outside of Christian worship, investigating how music relates to Jewish, Muslim, Hindu, and Buddhist spirituality. The findings presented in this chapter, indeed, are based on data from participants from multiple religions and faiths. The first study presents results from a large group of Jewish singers (from many denominations, including renewal, reform, and conservative Judaism, and modern orthodoxy) who sang wordless melodies together called nigunim, which has no origins in relation to Christianity. In fact, Jewish nigunim were vitalized in Eastern Europe within the historical context of brutal antisemitic pogroms, religious persecution from the Cossacks and others, and in some cases, forced Jewish conversion to Christianity. The second, third, and fourth studies present data from many religions and faiths, including those who identify as Buddhist, Christian, Hindu, Jewish, Muslim, and those who identify as non-religious, including Agnostic, Atheist, and not religious. Finally, the fifth study presents findings from an Israeli-Palestinian youth chorus which includes predominantly Jewish and Muslim participants. Thus, this chapter not only provides an extension beyond Christian worship,

---

1   My personal journey of faith began with many years of searching for my faith, my spiritual home, for a deeper understanding of who I am. My path led me to explore many religions and faiths, from Hinduism and Buddhism to Christianity and Sufism. But I still did not find what I was looking for. I was lost. After years of searching, through a series of mystical and synchronous events, I landed in the religion and faith of my grandparents, great-great grandparents, great-great-great grandparents, and so on, a lineage that hasn't been broken. I am a Jew, and would be called an observant or a modern orthodox Jew.

but also provides important insight into music of religious traditions that predate Christianity and that may have influenced the music of Christian theology and worship.

I. Setting the Stage

(a) From the Sacred to the Ordinary

The inextricable links between music and spirituality can be observed throughout multiple facets of human life. It can be observed from the most sacred of rituals within religion and shamanistic practices, to the most ordinary of rituals within modern culture. The first area to look in terms of observations about music and spirituality is within rituals and customs of religious practices. Indeed, anthropological and sociological evidence demonstrates that comparable musical styles are rooted in cultural histories originating from opposite ends of the globe. Recent empirical research from computational musicology and music cognition demonstrates how the forms and functions of music have persisted in non-Westernised societies, emphasising the presence of lullabies and the healing aspects the healing aspects of human song.[2]

In the mainstream and contemporary practice of religion, we observe parallels between musical attributes and their form and function. For instance, repetition, synchrony, and communal harmonising are frequently combined with communal rhythm. In Hinduism and Buddhism, a circular chant with a melodic form is used to attain meditative states that bring one closer to a divine sense.[3] In Sufism, the mystical branch of Islam, there are also circular repetitive chants that are chanted in unison, and these are accompanied by circular dances, commonly referred to as whirling dervishes.[4] In Christianity, Gregorian chants are less circular and more linear in their melodic progressions,

---

[2] Samuel A. Mehr, Manvir Singh, Hunter York, Luke Glowacki, and Max M. Krasno, 'Form and Function in Human Song', *Current Biology* 28.3 (2018), 356–68.e5; Samuel A. Mehr, Manvir Singh, Dean Knox, Daniel M. Ketter, Daniel Pickens-Jones, et al., 'Universality and Diversity in Human Song', *Science* 366.6468 (2019), eaax0868.

[3] Paramhansa Yogananda, *Cosmic Chants* (Los Angeles, CA: Self-Realization Fellowship Publishers, 1974).

[4] Hazrat Inayat Khan, *Mysticism of Sound* (London: Pilgrims Publishing, 1923).

but share similar intervallic and vocalised properties with Buddhist, Hindu, and Sufi music. Judaism combines the forms of the religions of the East and West in a wordless song called nigunim, which features the repetition of multiple phrases, is frequently accompanied by dance, and has both circular and linear aspects to the melodic and intervallic expression.[5] Nigunim are historically most prevalent in Orthodox Judaism and are typically heard in groups of males. However, there are egalitarian groups that feature singing by both males and women, albeit it is even more difficult to access these groups as a researcher, or to get data on them, since they occur in more naturalistic environments and are very rare.

Organised religion is not the only source, however, where we find music immersed with spirituality. Everyday cultural events such as concerts, community events, cultural rituals (for example, graduations or weddings), or even ordinary daily activities like sitting in transit on the bus listening to music with earbuds, can evoke a profound spiritual experience, turning the ordinary into the extraordinary. Given the breadth of contexts in which the intertwining of music and spirituality can be both experienced and observed, my preliminary research programme investigates this area across a spectrum from the sacred to the ordinary. Furthermore, given the similarities and differences that can be observed in music-based spirituality activities across religious and spiritual practices described above, my programme also investigates the universals and variations of spirituality and music. Before describing my research programme, I first take a step back to consider important issues about definitions and theory.

(b) Defining Terms

There are many obstacles to conducting research in this area, beginning with defining terms. What is 'spirituality', and how is it dissimilar to religiosity? What is music? And what is the combination of the two (the spirituality of music or the music of spirituality)? Due to their scope, these questions would warrant their own chapter; nevertheless, there are a few observations and conclusions we can make to find our footing.

---

5   DovBer Pinson, *Inner Rhythms: The Kabbalah of Music* (Northvale, NJ: Jason Aronson, 2000).

The John Templeton Foundation defines spiritual realities to include: '…love, compassion, purpose, creativity, time, mind, infinity, complexity, and understanding, to name just a few, and these are for Sir John just as real as, and perhaps—as in the case of Ultimate reality—even more real than, tangible objects or physical forces like gravity'.[6] From this interpretation of spiritual realities, we may understand spirituality to encompass an interest, exploration, and experience of non-physical realities. There are numerous additional locations from which we can define spirituality. For example, in the realm of psychological science, Ralph Piedmont and others argue that spirituality can be understood as an individual difference in personal characteristics.[7] That is, people differ in their levels of spirituality: while some may be extremely spiritual, others may not be spiritual at all. Here, Piedmont demonstrated that spirituality is a distinct dimension of human personality from the Five-Factor Model of Personality (also known as the Big Five Model), which is currently the most widely used and accepted model of personality. This was a significant step in research towards recognising spirituality as a particular orthogonal human construct distinct from other human personality traits, addressing potential criticisms that spirituality is merely an aspect or facet of a fundamental personality trait such as the trait 'openness', with which it is often correlated. Additional research has echoed this notion empirically showing that spirituality and religiosity should be measured and analysed in multivariate terms that distinguishes the two from standard taxonomies and constructs like personality traits.[8]

There are numerous resources where readers can find answers to queries about the definition of music, so I will not address it here. However, it is germane to this chapter to discuss which spiritual

---

6 Templeton Religion Trust, 'Request for Proposals', *Art Seeking Understanding*, March 2021, §2 https://templetonreligiontrust.org/wp-content/uploads/2021/03/TRT_Art_Seeking_Understanding_RFP2_Mar2021-1.pdf

7 Ralph L. Piedmont, 'Does Spirituality Represent the Sixth Factor of Personality? Spiritual Transcendence and the Five-Factor Model', *Journal of Personality* 67.6 (1999), 985–1013; Robert R. McCrae and Oliver P. John, 'An Introduction to the Five-Factor Model and Its Applications', *Journal of Personality* 60.2 (1992), 175–215; C. Robert Cloninger, Thomas R Przybeck, Dragan M Svrakic, and Richard D Wetzel, 'The Temperament and Character Inventory (TCI): A Guide to Its Development and Use', *The Psychology of Religion* 73.3 (n.d.), 1176–78.

8 Cloninger et al., 'The Temperament and Character Inventory (TCI)', 1176–78.

activities are regarded as musical. For instance, are sounds that are solely percussive and rhythmic but not melodic, as in a shamanic drum circle, or chants like 'OM' and repeated mantras, considered to be music? My initial conclusion on this matter is that there is indeed a threshold in which auditory noise or vocalisations become music. This threshold lies, on the one hand, with the intention of the composer or performer, and the perception of the listener; on the other hand, the organisation and variability of the audio configurations that are in question play a role. For example, I would argue that shamanic drum circles that are only percussive, with variations in rhythmic features, should be considered music. However, I would argue that a metronomic chant like 'OM' with a metronomic rhythmic pulse but no variations in rhythm, pitch, melody, or harmony, should not be considered music. But when it comes to a mantra like 'Om Namo Bhagavate Vasudevaya' which has alterations in both rhythm and melody (via intervallic shifts), I would argue that this is indeed music. Precise answers to these questions are needed, however, for the topic of music and spirituality to develop.

Another issue arising is how to describe the particular relationship between music and spirituality. Can a phrase like 'spirituality of music' be used? Probably not—music is not inherently something that can be spiritual or non-spiritual. The extent to which music is perceived as spiritual is dependent upon the perception of the observer, as well as the intention of the composer and performer. Therefore, the spirituality of music does not seem to be an appropriate term either. The term 'music of spirituality' also does not work, as it refers only to music that is used in spiritual contexts, and the empirical study of music and spirituality extends far beyond this. Therefore, the phrase 'music and spirituality' remains an ideal route in terms of a descriptive mechanism of the subject area for the time being.

(c) Theory and Hypotheses

This research area faces not only a problem of definitions but also a theoretical challenge. Scientific investigation is predicated on the development and testing of hypotheses, followed by the pursuit of replication and replication extensions across multiple studies to establish a scientific consensus regarding the theory's viability. The same is true regarding music and spirituality. But establishing theory and applying the scientific method poses difficulties because many aspects of spirituality are difficult to quantify. Suppose, for instance, I develop the hypothesis that synchronised singing during prayer can bring a person closer to God. From a scientific standpoint, it is impossible to prove or disprove this hypothesis because it is impossible to prove or disprove God's existence using the scientific instruments currently available. Therefore, to address this hypothesis, we need to turn to a field like psychology, which is accustomed to investigating concepts that are not visible to the human eye (e.g., human consciousness), non-conscious cognitive processes, and solely subjective phenomena in the mind of the subject being observed. Since the definition of spirituality implies observations about non-physical realities that cannot be observed tangibly, many hypotheses will need to rely on subjective and phenomenological experience. In order to test the synchronised singing hypothesis, for example, we would need to adjust the hypothesis to demonstrate that synchronised singing during prayer can increase a person's feeling of being close to their sense of God. Many of the questions we confront regarding music and spirituality will face similar challenges. It is important to note that theory testing is not the sole method for advancing scientific investigation. Conducting research studies without building on prior theory is, in my view, highly valuable. Indeed, one of the greatest scientific discoveries of the twentieth century was of the double helix by Watson and Crick. The immense importance of this discovery was not because it confirmed a prior theory, but because of its precise observation based on its advanced instruments and the methods of the time.

Given that many theories and hypotheses will be founded on the subjectivity of the observer, it is natural to locate the empirical study of music and spirituality within psychological science. There are numerous entry points within the field of psychology for research into music and spirituality. The topics of mysticism, self-transcendence, meaning in life, and awe have been well-received within the discipline of psychological science, and there are journals in this realm that specialise in spirituality, including the peer-reviewed journal, *Psychology of Religion and Spirituality*, published by the American Psychological Association.[9] Yet, based on a

---

9   On mysticism, see Ralph W. Hood and Leslie J. Francis, ' Mystical Experience: Conceptualizations, Measurement, and Correlates', in *APA Handbook of Psychology,*

search of the journal since 2008, the year when it was established, there have been no published studies on music. In fact, music is mentioned in just two abstracts: once as an example of a feature of shamanic rituals and another time not to do with music at all per se, but because it used 'MUSIC' as an acronym for the Multisite University Study of Identity and Culture.[10]

Interactionist theories, that posit that people seek external environments that reflect and reinforce their internal psychological states and traits, are helpful theoretical frameworks.[11] From how people construct their bedrooms to where they choose to live geographically, people choose to surround themselves with objects, people, and locations that reflect their personalities.[12] Interactionist theories have also been extended to the music with which people surround themselves.[13] More than two decades of research has convergently shown that musical preferences are reflective of people's personality traits. Even

---

Religion, and Spirituality i: Context, Theory, and Research', ed. by Kenneth I. Pargament, Julie I. Exline, and James W. Jones (Washington, DC: American Psychological Assoc., 2013), pp. 391–405; on self-transcendence, see David Bryce Yaden, Jonathan Haidt, Ralph W Hood, David R Vago, and Andrew B. Newberg, 'The Varieties of Self-Transcendent Experience', *Review of General Psychology* 21.2 (2017), 143–60; on meaning in life, see Michael F. Steger, Patricia Frazier, Shigehiro Oishi, and Matthew Kaler, 'The Meaning in Life Questionnaire: Assessing the Presence of and Search for Meaning in Life', *Journal of Counseling Psychology* 53.1 (2006), 80–93; on awe, see Dacher Keltner and Jonathan Haidt, 'Approaching Awe, a Moral, Spiritual, and Aesthetic Emotion', *Cognition & Emotion* 17.2 (2003), 297–314.

10 Amber R. C. Nadal, Sam A. Hardy, and Carolyn McNamara Barry, 'Understanding the Roles of Religiosity and Spirituality in Emerging Adults in the United States', *Psychology of Religion and Spirituality* 10.1 (2018), 30–43; Michael Winkelman, 'Shamanism as a Biogenetic Structural Paradigm for Humans' Evolved Social Psychology', *Psychology of Religion and Spirituality* 7.4 (2015), 267–77.

11 David M. Buss, 'Selection, Evocation, and Manipulation', *Journal of Personality and Social Psychology* 53.6 (1987), 1214–21.

12 S. C. Matz, M. Kosinski, G. Nave, and D. J. Stillwell, 'Psychological Targeting as an Effective Approach to Digital Mass Persuasion', *Proceedings of the National Academy of Sciences* 114.48 (2017), 12714–19; Markus Jokela, Wiebke Bleidorn, Michael E. Lamb, Samuel D. Gosling, and Peter J. Rentfrow, 'Geographically Varying Associations between Personality and Life Satisfaction in the London Metropolitan Area', *Proceedings of the National Academy of Sciences* 112.3 (2015), 725–30; Samuel D. Gosling, Sei Jin Ko, Thomas Mannarelli, and Margaret E. Morris, 'A Room With a Cue: Personality Judgments Based on Offices and Bedrooms', *Journal of Personality and Social Psychology* 82.3 (2002), 379–98.

13 Peter J. Rentfrow and Samuel D. Gosling, 'The Do Re Mi's of Everyday Life: The Structure and Personality Correlates of Music Preferences', *Journal of Personality and Social Psychology* 84.6 (2003), 1236–56.

further, research has shown that there exists a self-congruity effect of music whereby people seek out the music of artists who share similar personalities as themselves.[14]

It is not a far leap to extend this theory to spirituality, and therefore to suggest that people seek musical environments that reflect and reinforce their spirituality, and further, that these environments might fulfil their spiritual needs. The twentieth-century saxophonist, John Coltrane (1926–67), arguably one of the most influential musicians of modern times, said:

> My music is the spiritual expression of what I am—my faith, my knowledge, my being... When you begin to see the possibilities of music, you desire to do something really good for people, to help humanity free itself from its hangups ... I want to speak to their souls.[15]

Without intending to do so, Coltrane provides anecdotal support for the interactionist theory applied to music; namely, that musical expression can be a self-expression of spirituality, and this sets the stage for my research programme on the correlations between trait spirituality and music across many populations.

II. A Preliminary Research Programme

(a) The Sacred

To begin my investigation into the sacred, I first examined the psychological effects of wordless sacred melodies called nigunim, mentioned earlier in this chapter. These melodies are a preserved musical form that exists in many Jewish communities today. Although there is some musicological and religious literature about them, there is no empirical literature. Nigunim is one of the oldest musical styles in Judaism. It was revived by Chassidism, an Eastern European Jewish sect

---

14 David M. Greenberg et al., 'Universals and Variations in Musical Preferences: A Study of Preferential Reactions to Western Music in 53 Countries', *Journal of Personality and Social Psychology* 122.2 (2022), 286–309; David M. Greenberg, Sandra C. Matz, H. Andrew Schwartz, and Kai R. Fricke, 'The Self-Congruity Effect of Music', *Journal of Personality and Social Psychology* 121.1 (2020), 137–50.

15 As quoted in Chris DeVito, *Coltrane on Coltrane: The John Coltrane Interviews* (Chicago, IL: Chicago Review Press, 2012).

that arose in the eighteenth century, and which is a form of Judaism that significantly incorporates Kabbalistic concepts. The nigun (the singular form of nigunim) is the focal point of Chassidic devotion. In the most traditional sense, a nigun is an endlessly repeated melody without words. The melody can be simple or complex, and while nigunim can be performed solo, they are typically sung in groups to enhance their effect. Nigunim are traditionally chanted without instruments; however, contemporary musicians have begun to incorporate harmonic, rhythmic, and melodic instruments into their performances. The iteration of a nigun can induce a communally experienced ecstatic state, frequently involving dance and movement, and one such Chassidic sect was so profoundly affected by the nigun that they would perform somersaults out of euphoria.[16]

In 2019, I conducted research with participants attending a three-day workshop with an egalitarian organisation in New York City, where they sang nigunim in large groups in concentric circles. At the workshop, 200 members of the Jewish faith gathered to sing nigunim from 9 a.m. to 5 p.m. This is an unusual amount of time to be immersed in music, particularly when it involves music of a single form or genre and a form that features much repetition. Over the course of three days, I administered psychometric questionnaires to the group and obtained saliva samples before and after singing sessions that lasted an hour and a half in duration. Even though the saliva samples to measure hormones were interrupted by the COVID-19 pandemic (we are still in the process of analysing the samples), the psychometric test results have been analysed. These tests included the Inclusion in Community Scale (ICS)[17] and the Center for Epidemiologic Studies Depression Scale Revised (CESD-R-10).[18]

Initial findings indicate, as discussed in my TEDx talk in 2021, that over the course of three days, a sense of community inclusion among

---

16 Pinson, *Inner Rhythms*.
17 Mashek, Debra, Lisa W. Cannaday, and June P. Tangney, 'Inclusion of Community in Self Scale: A Single-Item Pictorial Measure of Community Connectedness', *Journal of Community Psychology* 35.2 (2007), 257–75, http://dx.doi.org/10.1002/jcop.20146.
18 Thröstur Björgvinsson, Sarah J. Kertz, Joe S. Bigda-Peyton, Katrina L. McCoy, and Idan M. Aderka, 'Psychometric Properties of the CES-D-10 in a Psychiatric Sample', *Assessment* 20.4 (2013), 429–36.

participants increased by 37% and depression symptoms decreased by 33%.[19] Additional analysis indicated that people's self-descriptions of spirituality and ratings of spiritual emotions increased from day one to day three. Furthermore, participants indicated that, on average, spiritual emotions were evoked more than either positive emotions or negative emotions. These findings are consistent with prior biological evidence demonstrating that group singing can increase oxytocin, which contributes to a sense of social connectedness, and decreases cortisol, which is associated with stress.[20] This study, in addition to observing a preserved sacred activity, provided a unique opportunity to observe the collective impact that singing in a very large group can have. The research also raises important questions about the intrinsic musical elements that facilitate the positive effects of collective group singing, along with the role of individual differences in personal characteristics that may contribute to these effects. Further, it raises questions about the role of music and spirituality within frameworks of human evolution and human song, including the credible signalling hypothesis (which is an extension of the coalition signalling hypothesis), the social bonding hypothesis, and the theory of human herding.[21] It also raises questions about how these positive effects might manifest within peak spiritual experiences that are less confined to sacred spaces and that may be present in contemporary Westernised cultures.

---

19 David Greenberg, 'How Music Can Break Social Barriers | Dr. David Greenberg | TEDxRamatAviv', online video recording, *YouTube*, 3 December 2021, https://www.youtube.com/watch?v=evVRxrOo5iw

20 Arla Good and Frank A. Russo, 'Singing Promotes Cooperation in a Diverse Group of Children', *Social Psychology* 47.6 (2016), 340–44; Jason R. Keeler et al., 'The Neurochemistry and Social Flow of Singing: Bonding and Oxytocin', *Frontiers in Human Neuroscience* 9 (2015), 518; Gunter Kreutz, 'Does Singing Facilitate Social Bonding?', *Music and Medicine* 6.2 (2014), 51–60; D. Fancourt and R. Perkins, 'Effect of Singing Interventions on Symptoms of Postnatal Depression: Three-Arm Randomised Controlled Trial', *The British Journal of Psychiatry* 212.2 (2018), 119–21.

21 See for examples of these hypotheses and theories Edward H. Hagen and Gregory A. Bryant, 'Music and Dance as a Coalition Signaling System', *Human Nature* 14.1 (2003), 21–51; Samuel A. Mehr, Max M. Krasnow, Gregory A. Bryant, and Edward H. Hagen, 'Origins of Music in Credible Signaling', *Behavioral and Brain Sciences* 44 (2020), e60; Patrick E. Savage et al., 'Music as a Coevolved System for Social Bonding', *Behavioral and Brain Sciences* 44 (2020), e59 https://doi.org/10.1017/s0140525x20000333; David M. Greenberg, J. Decety, and I. Gordon, 'The Social Neuroscience of Music: Understanding the Social Brain through Human Song', *American Psychologist* 76.7 (2021), 1172–85.

(b) Peak Spiritual Experiences

Abraham Maslow, one of the first researchers of peak experiences, defined it as 'a sensory and perceptual experience, usually brief and profound, accompanied by enhanced perception, appreciation, and comprehension'.[22] Several years later, Alf Gabrielsson expanded the concept's terminology to include 'Strong Experiences of Music' (SEM) when he adopted it for the study of music.[23] Gabrielsson argued that the term 'peak' was normally only attached to positive experiences. In fact, Maslow himself characterised peak experiences as 'the moment of the greatest happiness and fulfillment'.[24] Gabrielsson acknowledged, however, that such phenomenological experiences are not always regarded as positive and can be accompanied or dominated by intense emotions that are not necessarily positive or euphoric. Therefore, Gabrielsson asked his research participants to characterise 'the strongest, most intense' musical experience they have ever had.[25] This research has been replicated and expanded upon in a number of studies.[26]

My prior research into individual differences of musical engagement involved inquiring into people's daily experiences of music when listening attentively to it. I asked participants from multiple cultures, including Pakistan, Japan, the United States, and the United Kingdom, the following: 'Describe in your own words the most powerful, intense musical experience you have ever had. Please write as much as you'd like...' I observed that many of the responses contained both explicit spiritual overtones and implicit spiritual undertones. Participants from

---

22 Abraham Maslow, *Religions Values and Peak-Experiences* (n.p.: Rare Treasure Editions, 1964).
23 Alf Gabrielsson, 'Emotions in Strong Experiences with Music' in *Handbook of Music and Emotion: Theory and Research*, ed. by Patrik N. Juslin and John A. Sloboda (Oxford: Oxford University Press, 2010), pp. 547–604.
24 Abraham Maslow, *The Farther Reaches of Human Nature* (New York: Viking Press, 1971).
25 Gabrielsson, 'Emotions in Strong Experiences', pp. 547–604. Alf Gabrielsson, *Strong Experiences with Music: Music Is Much More than Just Music* (Oxford, UK: Oxford University Press, 2011); Alf Gabrielsson and L. S. Wik, 'Strong Experiences Related to Music: A Descriptive System', *Musicae Scientiae*, 7 (2003), 157–217.
26 See, for example, Alexandra Lamont, 'University Students' Strong Experiences of Music: Pleasure, Engagement, and Meaning', *Musicae Scientiae* 15.2 (2011), 229–49; Alexandra Lamont, 'Emotion, Engagement and Meaning in Strong Experiences of Music Performance', *Psychology of Music* 40.5 (2012), 574–94.

each of the countries I observed exhibited this pattern. To replicate and extend these findings, I obtained new data from over 600 participants. The same SEM question was administered, but this time I also asked respondents to rate each experience on a scale from 1 (not at all spiritual) to 5 (very spiritual). This permitted spiritual and non-spiritual experiences to be categorised separately. Initial findings indicated that the levels of depth attributed to the music, as well as the rhythmic and cathartic aspects of engagement, were the most significant predictors of whether a strong musical experience was described as spiritual or not. Further, none of the Big Five personality traits, including the trait openness, contributed significantly to the statistical model. The results from this study suggested that musical aspects of strong experiences are more important than psychodemographic information in determining whether the experience was spiritual or not.

(c) Spirituality and Music in Everyday Life

When it comes to studying the uses and effects of music in daily life, musical preferences and musical engagement are frequently evaluated. As discussed above, strong musical experiences revealed that both musical attributes and musical engagement contribute to the spirituality of musical experiences. Next, I aimed to determine if there were any correlations between people's everyday musical preferences and engagement and aspects of their spiritual lives. To measure preferences, an audio-based musical preferences test was administered to over 2,800 people. This preference test, which has been used frequently in previous research, asks individuals to listen to fifteen-second excerpts from Western music and to rate their liking for each.[27] There were twenty-five administered excerpts, which represented sixteen genres and sub-genres. Based on prior theory and research, the arousal-valence-depth model can be applied to this test to derive three broad factors of musical

---

27 Kai R. Fricke, David M. Greenberg, Peter J. Rentfrow, and Philipp Y. Herzberg, 'Computer-Based Music Feature Analysis Mirrors Human Perception and Can Be Used to Measure Individual Music Preference', *Journal of Research in Personality*, 75 (2018), 98–102; David M. Greenberg et al., 'The Song Is You', *Social Psychological and Personality Science* 7.6 (2016), 597–605; Gideon Nave et al., 'Musical Preferences Predict Personality: Evidence From Active Listening and Facebook Likes', *Psychological Science* 29.7 (2018), 1145–58.

attribute preferences.[28] The Engagement with Musical Inventory (EMI) was also administered, which measures attentive listening engagement and identifies five listening dimensions: analysing, healing, dancing, narrative, and bonding.[29] Participants were asked to complete the Awe Scale (AWE-S),[30] the Self-Transcendence factor of the Temperament and Character Inventory (TCI),[31] and a short version of Hood's Mysticism Scale (M-scale).[32] In addition, participants completed a measure of the Big Five personality traits and demographic information. Over 2,800 individuals completed all measures. Initial findings indicate that musical engagement explains more variance in all three spiritual measures than either personality traits or demographics. The findings suggest that musical preferences and engagement may be better indicators of spirituality than other psychological factors such as personality.

III. Extensions and Future Directions

(a) Universals and Variations of Spiritual Experiences

In recent years, questions regarding the universality of music have emerged. The literature has advanced well beyond the question of whether or not music is a human universal, of which the consensus is both 'yes and no'. The current questions in this research area focus on which aspects of musical experience are universal and which are

---

28 Greenberg et al., 'The Song Is You', 597–605; Kai R. Fricke, David M. Greenberg, Peter J. Rentfrow, and Philipp Y. Herzberg, 'Measuring Musical Preferences from Listening Behavior: Data from One Million People and 200,000 Songs', *Psychology of Music* 49.3 (2019), 371–81.

29 David M. Greenberg and Peter J. Rentfrow, 'Rules of Engagement: The Structure of Musical Engagement and Its Personality Underpinnings', in *Proceedings of the Ninth Triennial Conferences of the European Society for the Cognitive Sciences of Music*, ed. by J. Ginsborg et al. (Manchester, 2015).

30 David B. Yaden et al., 'The Development of the Awe Experience Scale (AWE-S): A Multifactorial Measure for a Complex Emotion', *The Journal of Positive Psychology* 14.4 (2019), 474–88.

31 Cloninger et al., 'The Temperament and Character Inventory (TCI)', 1176–78.

32 Heinz Streib, Constantin Klein, Barbara Keller, and Ralph Hood, 'The Mysticism Scale as a Measure for Subjective Spirituality: New Results with Hood's M-Scale and the Development of a Short From', in *Assessing Spirituality in a Diverse World*, ed. by Amy L. Ai et al. (Cham: Springer, 2021), pp. 467–91.

variant. There are universals in the form and function of music;[33] pitch perception;[34] subjective affective responses to music;[35] and preferences for Westernised music[36] (but not the distinct in preference for consonant and dissonant sounds).[37]

Testing universality necessitates the use of enormous datasets that are geographically diverse and representative of numerous nations and societies. The Musical Universe project has been a public engagement platform since 2017 where people around the world have been able to take music and psychometric tests.[38] More than 350,000 people have taken tests about musical preferences, personality traits, musical engagement, and more. Participants completed a single-item global assessment of their spirituality that asked, 'How spiritual are you?' with answer options ranging from 1 (not at all spiritual) to 5 (very spiritual). Single-item measures to assess spirituality and religiosity are standard practice and single-item measures in general are found to be reliable and valid across multiple psychological domains.[39]

---

33   Samuel A. Mehr, Manvir Singh, Hunter York, Luke Glowacki, and Max M. Krasnow, 'Form and Function in Human Song', *Current Biology* 28.3 (2018), 356–68.e5; Samuel A. Mehr et al., 'Universality and Diversity in Human Song', *Science* 366.6468 (2019), eaax0868.
34   Nori Jacoby et al., 'Universal and Non-Universal Features of Musical Pitch Perception Revealed by Singing', *Current Biology* 29.19 (2019), 3229–43.e12; Alan S. Cowan, Xia Fang, Disa Sauter, and Dacher Keltner, 'What Music Makes Us Feel: At Least 13 Dimensions Organize Subjective Experiences Associated with Music across Different Cultures', *Proceedings of the National Academy of Sciences* 117.4 (2020), 1924–34.
35   Jacoby et al., 'Universal and Non-Universal Features of Musical Pitch Perception Revealed by Singing', 3229–43.e12; Cowen et al., 'What Music Makes Us Feel', 1924–34.
36   Greenberg et al., 'Universals and Variations'.
37   Josh H. McDermott, Alan F. Schultz, Eduardo A. Undurraga, and Ricardo A. Godoy, 'Indifference to Dissonance in Native Amazonians Reveals Cultural Variation in Music Perception', *Nature* 535.7613 (2016), 547–50.
38   *Musical Universe*, https://www.musicaluniverse.io
39   See, for example, Richard L. Gorsuch and Sam G McFarland, 'Single vs. Multiple-Item Scales for Measuring Religious Values', *Journal for the Scientific Study of Religion* 11.1 (1972), 53–64; Ellen L. Idler et al., 'Looking Inside the Black Box of "Attendance at Services": New Measures for Exploring an Old Dimension in Religion and Health Research', *The International Journal for the Psychology of Religion* 19.1 (2009), 1–20; Shalom H. Schwartz and Sipke Huismans, 'Value Priorities and Religiosity in Four Western Religions', *Social Psychology Quarterly* 58.2 (1995), 88–107; Susan Sprecher and Beverley Fehr, 'Compassionate Love for Close Others and Humanity', *Journal of Social and Personal Relationships* 22.5 (2005), 629–51; Karen B. DeSalvo et al., 'Assessing Measurement Properties of Two Single-Item

There was data for over 76,000 participants. The initial results showed that when compared to personality traits, demographics, and other musical factors, including musical importance, preferences for low arousal in music (with slower tempos, calming and relaxing attributes) were most strongly associated with trait spirituality. There were sixty-four nations represented with at least sixty-seven participants, which is the minimum required for a power analysis to assess correlation in G*Power.[40] The associations between trait spirituality and a preference for low arousal in music were largely consistent across nations. Regarding musical engagement, there were only fourteen nations in which there was sufficient data available. Here, the associations between trait spirituality, storytelling engagement (i.e. focusing on the narrative and symbolic elements of music), and healing engagement (affective responses to music including catharsis) were largely consistent with trait spirituality. Results indicate that associations between spirituality traits and music in daily life are essentially universal. These initial findings from the preliminary research programme are the first to show that there are universal features to aspects of music and spirituality.

(b) Social Conflict between Religions and Cultures

Understanding that music has universal characteristics has implications for social psychology and group processes, including the function of music in reducing social, cultural, and religious conflict. Intergroup cultural conflict is a serious threat to the social fabric worldwide, and it is often rooted in religious ideology and differences.[41] The

---

General Health Measures', *Quality of Life Research* 15.2 (2006), 191–201; Richard W. Robins, Holly M. Hendin, and Kali H. Trzesniewski, 'Measuring Global Self-Esteem: Construct Validation of a Single-Item Measure and the Rosenberg Self-Esteem Scale', *Personality and Social Psychology Bulletin* 27.2 (2001), 151–61; John P. Wanous and Arnon E. Reichers, 'Estimating the Reliability of a Single-Item Measure', *Psychological Reports* 78.2 (1996), 631–34; John P. Wanous, Arnon E Reichers, and Michael J Hudy, 'Overall Job Satisfaction: How Good Are Single-Item Measures?', *Journal of Applied Psychology* 82.2 (1997), 247–52; John P. Wanous and Michael J. Hudy, 'Single-Item Reliability: A Replication and Extension', *Organizational Research Methods* 4.4 (2001), 361–75.

40 Franz Faul, 'Statistical Power Analyses Using G*Power 3.1: Tests for Correlation and Regression Analyses', *Behavior Research Methods* 41 (2009), 1149–60.

41 World Economic Forum, *The Global Risks Report 2020 Insight Report* (Geneva: WEF, 2010), https://www3.weforum.org/docs/WEF_Global_Risk_Report_2020.pdf

Israeli–Palestinian conflict, in particular, has been among the most complex and persistent social, cultural, and political conflicts in the world.[42] This conflict has well-known negative effects on mental health, physiology, and behavior.[43]

Earlier in this chapter, I described similarities between Chassidic and Sufi musical elements — Chassidism being the mystical sect of Judaism and Sufism being the mystical sect of Islam. Bringing religions and cultures together through music can provide a platform for communicating and exchanging ideas in a safe environment that necessitates listening to each other, and the area of music and spirituality is ideally situated to be a medium in which to both study and apply this concept.

I began this line of inquiry with a pilot study of the Jerusalem Youth Chorus (JYC), which brings together Arab-Palestinians and Jewish-Israelis who are adolescents and young adults from East and West Jerusalem. The chorus members are both religious and secular. In the study, I administered psychometric measures to alumni members during a three-day workshop. The measures included both assessments of community inclusion and depression/anxiety. The initial results showed an increase in a sense of community inclusion by 18% and decreased their depressive symptoms by 17%. Intriguingly, these percentages are lower than those observed in the more homogeneous group of egalitarian Jewish participants in the first study I described in this chapter, but this is expected given the heterogeneity disparities between the groups.

In addition, participants were asked to evaluate their prior experience with the chorus using a variety of psychometric tests. Participants

---

42 Daniel Bar-Tal, 'Societal Beliefs in Times of Intractable Conflict: The Israeli Case', *International Journal of Conflict Management* 9.1 (1998), 22–50; Darcy R. Dupuis, Roni Porat, and Michael J. A. Wohl, 'Collective Angst in Intractable Conflicts: How Concern for the Ingroup's Future Vitality Shapes Adversarial Intergroup Relations', in *The Social Psychology of Intractable Conflicts, Celebrating the Legacy of Daniel Bar-Tal, Volume I*, ed. by Eran Halperin and Keren Sharvit, Peace Psychology Book Series 27 (Cham: Springer, 2015), pp. 131–42.

43 Jonathan Levy et al., 'Adolescents Growing up amidst Intractable Conflict Attenuate Brain Response to Pain of Outgroup', *Proceedings of the National Academy of Sciences* 113.48 (2016), 13696–701; Ruth Pat-Horenczyk et al., 'Posttraumatic Symptoms, Functional Impairment, and Coping among Adolescents on Both Sides of the Israeli–Palestinian Conflict: A Cross-Cultural Approach', *Applied Psychology* 58.4 (2009), 688–708.

indicated that during their time in the chorus, their social bonding and perception of chorus members from the 'other side' increased. In addition, participants reported improvements in social behaviours, such as empathic abilities and the capacity to navigate complexity during their time in the chorus. Further, participants rated the music elements of the chorus as being more important than the dialogue elements in terms of their changes in social bonding, while they rated the dialogue elements as being more important than the music elements in terms of their changes in social perception. The tentative conclusion is that side-by-side singing and face-to-face dialogue can enhance how Jewish-Israelis and Arab-Palestinians perceive and interact with one another. This study needs to be replicated on a larger scale and with more complex designs, including randomisation. In addition, this research should be expanded to include participants who are exclusively religious, including more right-wing segments of each religion who are more reluctant to engage with the 'other side'.

(c) God in the Brain

The programme's findings to date have established individual and group-level associations between music and spirituality. Music appears to serve at least two primary functions in spiritual contexts: (1) to facilitate a sense of communal bonding and (2) to be a vehicle for self-transcendent and divine experiences. A crucial next step for this research is to examine the relationship between music and spirituality at the level of the brain. Similar to psychological science, neuroscience lacks research on the links between music and spirituality. The closest volume of research is the neurobiology of chanting based on electroencephalogram (EEG) and functional magnetic resonance imaging (fMRI) studies, primarily conducted by Gao and colleagues.[44] The findings suggest that

---

44 Junling Gao et al., 'Repetitive Religious Chanting Invokes Positive Emotional Schema to Counterbalance Fear: A Multi-Modal Functional and Structural MRI Study', *Frontiers in Behavioral Neuroscience* 14 (2020), 548856; Junling Gao et al., 'Repetitive Religious Chanting Modulates the Late-Stage Brain Response to Fear- and Stress-Provoking Pictures', *Frontiers in Psychology* 7 (2017), 2055; Junling Gao, Hang Kin Leung, Bonnie Wai Yan Wu, Stavros Skouras, and Hin Hung Sik, 'The Neurophysiological Correlates of Religious Chanting', *Scientific Reports* 9.1 (2019), 4262.

the neurophysiological correlates of religious chanting differ from those of meditation and prayer; consequently, religious chanting may induce distinct psychotherapeutic effects.[45] If music serves the dual purpose of facilitating transcendent experience and social connection, it will be crucial to distinguish the context in which spiritual and secular music is performed. Is it utilised for worship or other purposes? Furthermore, is it employed singularly or in combination? Based on prior research from brain studies during meditation, we might hypothesise that the default brain network is involved, and based on prior research on social neuroscience, we may hypothesise that oxytocinergic and dopaminergic pathways, along with brain regions responsible for reward and motivation, may also be at play.[46]

Conclusion

Some of the most influential and renowned musicians of the past century (such as John Coltrane and The Beatles), including those who were not explicitly religious (such as Leonard Cohen), used music in their own search for life's meaning and spiritual growth. Coltrane, in particular, exemplifies this, integrating his artistry with spirituality to impact not just the realm of music, but also political and socio-cultural issues of his time. Coltrane said:

> The true powers of music are still unknown. To be able to control them must be, I believe, the goal of every musician. I'm passionate about understanding these forces. I would like to provoke reactions in the listeners to my music, to create a real atmosphere. It's in that direction that I want to commit myself and to go as far as possible.[47]

These were the directives that Coltrane gave to current and future generations of musicians. Through Coltrane's music and well-known rigorous work ethic, this sentiment has served as an anthem for subsequent generations of musicians. I contend that these words from

---

45 Gao et al., 'The Neurophysiological Correlates of Religious Chanting', 4262.
46 Britta K. Hölzel et al., 'How Does Mindfulness Meditation Work? Proposing Mechanisms of Action from a Conceptual and Neural Perspective', *Perspectives on Psychological Science* 6.6 (2011), 537–59; Greenberg et al., 'The Social Neuroscience of Music', 1172–85.
47 As quoted in DeVito, *Coltrane on Coltrane*.

Coltrane should also be the directors for current and future researchers in not just music and spirituality, but in the music sciences more generally. To discover the most profound abilities and effects that music has and can have, researchers must be willing to delve into the innermost recesses of the human mind. This begins with the study of music and spirituality, which I believe to be the key to unlocking new possibilities regarding the function of music in individuals and society.

8. An Inquiry into Musical Trance

Dilara Turan

> Well, there's one thing to try
> Everybody knows
> Music gets you high
> Everybody grows
> And so it goes...[1]

That music accompanies spiritual experiences is a cross-cultural phenomenon. Manifesting itself through a wide variety of cultural practices, it is the focal point of numerous religious, philosophical, and aesthetic doctrines. The present study attempts to uncover empirically the ways in which this prevailing connection between music and spiritual experiences might and can be demonstrated. This endeavour is challenging due to our current research paradigm, which gives rise to several complicating factors. First, there are diverse ways in which spiritual experiences are conceptualised, leading to further questions about how to establish ecologically valid empirical observations on the subject. As William James observes, mystical experiences are often considered ineffable and transient phenomena.[2] How, then, can we account for an experience that is temporary and already beyond language? It is essential, therefore, to clarify the underlying concepts before exploring the connection between music and spiritual experiences further. In the first part of this paper, I establish a framework for the investigation by adopting specific ontological positions on spirituality

---

1 Graham Nash, 'And So It Goes', *Wild Tiles* (Atlantic Records, 1974).
2 William James, *Varieties of Religious Experience A Study in Human Nature* (New York: Longmans, Green & Co., 1902; repr. London and New York: Routledge, 2002), p. 295.

and empiricism. In the second part, I provide a cross-cultural inquiry, examining documented examples of music accompanying spiritual experiences. Drawing on traditional trance rituals as a case of altered states of consciousness, I present a multi-layered understanding of the intricate relationship between music and spiritual experiences, accounting for cognitive, psychological, and socio-cultural contextual factors. By so doing, I suggest guidelines for identifying patterns in this relationship, providing a pool of examples and potential hypotheses on the question for future research.

I. Paradigms for the Study of Music and Spirituality

At least since the late seventeenth century, in the wake of John Locke's grand layout of material and mental substance and how they interact, empiricism has been a driving force behind the outstanding accomplishments of civilisation. As Werner Heisenberg documents in his survey, Locke, countering the claims of René Descartes, asserted that all knowledge ultimately originates from experience, which can be either sensation or the perception of our mental activities.[3] George Berkeley further developed this idea by arguing that if all knowledge stems from perception, the concept of real existence becomes meaningless, as it makes no difference to the presence or absence of things whether or not they are perceived. Thus, Berkeley equated being perceived with existence, i.e., subjective perceptions as reality. David Hume took this line of reasoning to an extreme form of scepticism and eventually rejected induction and causation. Hume's powerful critique was nonetheless accommodated as an exegesis within empiricist thought, a warning about the reductive use of the term 'existence'; the initial divisions of material–mental and subject–object remained a part, then, of empirical thought.

While Immanuel Kant played a significant role in reconciling the concept of existence, the early twentieth century was marked by the anti-metaphysical movement of logical positivism, initially led by Bertrand Russell and other figures of the Vienna Circle. For Hilary

---

3   Werner Heisenberg, *Physics and Philosophy, The Revolution in Modern Science* (New York: Harper, 1958), p. 83.

Lawson, this movement aimed 'to replace Victorian metaphysical philosophy with science and logic', setting an anti-metaphysical trend that also shaped the scientific method.[4] Prioritising the role of evidence and experience over abstract theories and dogma helped establish a more rigorous and rational approach to understanding the world around us, leading to significant advances in science, medicine, and the development of modern social and political systems. However, it also established an object-based ontology of a material reality which can only account for measurable and rational phenomena, leaving out a whole region of human experience. Only later in the twentieth century did empiricism become the central subject of debate among scientists and philosophers, as a shortcoming of logical positivism. In his later work, Ludwig Wittgenstein criticised the positivist idea that all meaningful statements must be empirically verifiable, arguing that this principle is a non-empirical statement that cannot be verified by empirical means. Likewise, Thomas Kuhn focused on the process of scientific revolutions and observed that the nature of the scientific process involves large leaps from one value system to another. Rather than a continuous process of uncovering reality that is objectively out there, Kuhn realised the socially constructed or warranted nature of scientific knowledge. This provided a much better lens to approach empirical demonstration with the tools at hand, opening up a new space for the recognition of formerly neglected areas of human experiences. As reported in Horgan's documentation,

> Kuhn argued that our paradigms keep changing as our culture changes. Different groups, and the same group at different times can have different experiences and therefore in some sense live in different worlds. Obviously, all humans share some responses to experience, simply because of their shared biological heritage, but whatever is universal in human experience, whatever transcends culture and history, is also 'ineffable', beyond the reach of language.[5]

One of the profound attempts to establish a fully developed new metaphysics came from outside academic circles through American writer and philosopher Robert M. Pirsig's study, known as Metaphysics

---

4   Hilary Lawson, '21st Century Metaphysics: Leaving Fantasy Behind', *Institute of Art and Ideas News*, 23 January 2023, https://iai.tv/articles/21st-century-metaphysics-leaving-fantasy-behind-auid-2367

5   John Horgan, 'What Thomas Kuhn Really Thought about Scientific "Truth"', *Scientific American*, 23 May 2012, https://blogs.scientificamerican.com/cross-check/what-thomas-kuhn-really-thought-about-scientific-truth

of Quality (MoQ). In his first book, Pirsig introduces his central term Quality as the undefined source of subjects and objects and suggests that everything that exists can be considered as value.[6]

Pirsig's approach diverges from the traditional way of understanding the world, where reality is typically based on either object (materialism) or mental substance (idealism). Instead, Pirsig sees values as the fundamental building blocks of reality itself and breaks reality into two categories: Dynamic Quality and static quality.[7] Dynamic Quality is a term that describes the ever-changing and immediate experience of reality, while static quality refers to any concept that is derived from this experience. The word 'Dynamic' highlights the fact that this experience is not fixed or static and cannot be fully defined; it is prior to conceptualisations. Therefore, an accurate understanding of Dynamic Quality can only be gained through direct experience:

> At the moment of pure Quality perception, or not even perception, at the moment of pure Quality, there is no subject and there is no object. There is only a sense of Quality that produces a later awareness of subjects and objects. At the moment of pure Quality, subject and object are identical. This is the *tat tvam asi* truth of the Upanishads.[8]

While recognising the undefined, immediate, and pre-intellectual Dynamic Quality, MoQ also accounts for static quality patterns, which Pirsig conceptualised in four layers in an evolutionary hierarchy: inorganic value patterns, biological value patterns, social value patterns, and intellectual value patterns. He argued that the static patterns cover the traditional Western duality of subjects and objects, with inorganic and biological values corresponding to what have traditionally been considered objective, and social and intellectual values to subjective. Contrary to Dynamic Quality, which is undefinable, the static quality layers are rational and understandable. MoQ alters the metaphysical ground by containing the subject–object division within static layers

---

6   Robert M. Pirsig, *Zen and the Art of Motorcycle Maintenance: An Inquiry into Values* (London: Vintage, 1974).
7   Dynamic Quality serves as the monistic, fundamental, and undefined reference in the Metaphysics of Quality (MOQ). Therefore, it is capitalized to denote its significance in the primary texts. On the other hand, static quality refers to definable patterns within MOQ, holding a secondary status compared to Dynamic Quality, and thus is not capitalized.
8   Ibid., p. 294.

without conflicting with the existing positivist observations; it also enables, however, an account of formerly neglected experiences of reality.

> The Metaphysics of Quality subscribes to what is called empiricism. It claims that all legitimate human knowledge arises from the senses or by thinking [based on] what the senses provide. Most empiricists deny the validity of any knowledge gained through imagination, authority, tradition, or purely theoretical reasoning. They regard fields such as art, morality, religion, and metaphysics as unverifiable. The Metaphysics of Quality varies from this by saying that the values of art and morality and even religious mysticism are verifiable and that in the past have been excluded for metaphysical reasons, not empirical reasons. They have been excluded because of the metaphysical assumption that all the universe is composed of subjects and objects and anything that can't be classified as a subject or an object isn't real. There is no empirical evidence for this assumption at all.[9]

MoQ not only encompasses spiritual experience but also places it at its centre. Pirsig further elaborates on the interchangeability of his central term Quality with value and spirituality. Recognising both the Dynamic, ineffable experience and the static (patterned) experiences of spirituality, he provides a comprehensive account of spiritual experiences in MoQ:

> Quality and spirituality are synonymous, so that a metaphysics of quality is in fact a metaphysics of spirituality. There is Dynamic spirituality, which is undefinable; and static spirituality, which consists of intellectual spirituality (theology), social spirituality (church), and biological spirituality (ritual).[10]

An empirical demonstration of spiritual reality would have no place in object-based metaphysics, as such a demonstration cannot extend its investigation beyond the realm of subjective experiences and, therefore, cannot be a subject of scientific research However, through the lenses of MoQ, we can reconcile reality and Quality, or spirit. The question at hand, in turn, can be rephrased: how can we explore the connection between the Dynamic spirituality and static spirituality that involves musicking?

---

9   Robert M. Pirsig, *Lila; An Inquiry into Morals* (New York: Bantam Books, 1991), p. 121.
10 Robert M. Pirsig, *On Quality: An Inquiry into Excellence: Unpublished and Selected Writings*, ed. by Wendy K. Pirsig (New York: HarperCollins, 2022), p. 104.

II. An Inquiry into Musical Trance

MoQ allows us to observe music's involvement in each static pattern and their relation to each other. This study adopts a modular and systematic approach, utilising a multidisciplinary perspective to observe musical trance phenomena from three different angles. The first sub-section focuses on cognitive and psychological theories of spiritual experiences and examines music's role in the patterns of biological spirituality. Borrowing the term altered states of consciousness (ASC) from cognition and psychology literature, this section seeks to understand the brain mechanisms and cognitive functions during spiritual experiences. Considering musical trance as a sub-category of altered states of consciousness, it delves into cognitive theories of musical trance, exploring auditory processing mechanisms and emotional arousal. The second sub-section observes intellectual and social patterns in cross-cultural examples of musical trance. By presenting a collection of examples from various parts of the world, it delves into the belief systems and social contexts of rituals and how they shape the overall spiritual experience. The third sub-section takes a music analytical approach, providing a detailed examination of the musical activity and its psychoacoustic and perceptual capacities. Utilising perceptual music analysis of recordings, I will discuss prominent sonic events and common means of musical signification in spiritual experiences. By examining musical trance as a case of music and spirituality, where music accompanies non-ordinary experiences, the study embraces a framework that accommodates both the ineffable and observable, allowing for a deeper understanding of the intricate relationship between music and spiritual experiences.

(a) Music and Altered States of Consciousness

ASC refer to significant deviations in subjective experience from the normal functioning of waking consciousness, induced by physiological, pharmacological, or psychological factors.[11] These alterations are linked to changes in the default mode network (DMN), a large-scale brain network responsible for higher-level cognitive processes like

---

11 Arnold M. Ludwig, 'Altered States of Consciousness', *Arch Gen Psychiatry* 15.3 (1966), 225–34.

self-referencing, social cognition, and theory of mind. The DMN's regular functions, involving the preservation of our sense of self and autobiographical memory, remain largely unchanged during waking states due to its high metabolic rate and energy consumption.[12] During ASC, the coupling between the posterior cingulate cortex (PCC) and the prefrontal cortex (PFC) can decouple, as it was observed in a psilocybin research study.[13] PCC deactivates, leading to decreased meta-cognitive functions such as self-referencing and mind wandering, while PFC activity enhances, resulting in increased integration of input data and attention level in goal-oriented tasks. The study also suggests that during ASC, various brain oscillatory rhythms, such as alpha, theta, and gamma, can promote the structured activity of the DMN and influence the sense of self. They observed that during psilocybin-induced ASC, alpha activity in PCC decreased, and theta activity increased, correlating with a weakened sense of self and an experience of the supernatural. Another observation during ASC is the decoupling of the DMN and the medial temporal lobe (MTL), which includes hippocampal structures responsible for declarative memory. This decoupling reduces the synchronisation and organisation of DMN activity, impacting the integrated sense of self and clock time perception.[14]

We can observe two main approaches to the question of the functions of music in altered consciousness states: particularist and mechanistic. The particularist approach of ethnomusicology highlights emotional arousal as the link between music and trance. Ethnographers often report from the field that the emergence of ASC in ritual settings primarily depends on communally shared cosmology. Individual participants of the ceremony share the same predictable expectations, intentions, and behaviours, which create a social/communal space. This predictability and intentionality enable the trancers, especially those in charge of leading the ritual and music, to interact with the music in response to their emotional states for the emergence of trance possession. In other words, trancers often know how to alter

---

12 Marcus E. Raichle and Abraham Z. Snyder, 'A Default Mode of Brain Function: A Brief History of an Evolving Idea', *NeuroImage* 37 (2007), 1083–90.
13 Carhart-Harris et al., 'The Entropic Brain: A Theory of Conscious States Informed by Neuroimaging', *Frontiers in Human Neuroscience* 8 (2014), 20.
14 Ibid., p. 20.

their consciousness via interactions within that extremely static ritual setting. Concerning the importance attributed to pre-set cognitive familiarity, music functions as a catalyst for trance experiences and not as a direct element of induction. Thus, ethnographers do not propose a causal relation between the trance state and the specific properties of music specifically. Instead, music, combined with all the other psychological factors of a ritual setting, creates strong emotions, which cause chemical alterations in serotonin, dopamine, and oxytocin levels in brain structure. Thus, this theory suggests that the whole process might give way to alterations in consciousness and the frequently mentioned effects, such as loss of sense of self and other changes in attention, alertness, or time perception.[15]

The emotional arousal theory of trance explains many common features of trance rituals, such as communal settings, shared cosmology, or religious context, and the importance of cultural and social familiarity between the trancers and strictly followed ritual conventions. It also elucidates why some ritual settings promote the emergence of ASC experiences for some people, while the same music and setting might be meaningless, boring, or disturbing for others. Gilbert Rouget and Judith Becker highlight the great diversity and specification in the musics and ritual settings of various cultures concerning the particularistic point of view. Due to such effective involvement of cultural variables, they also stress the problems of making direct causal relations between musical qualities and trance induction. Both Rouget and Becker attribute a psychological function to music, which enables the person to break his or her self-perception and identify with the spiritual experience. In this way, music has a culturally shaped mediator function as a catalyser to overall experience rather than a sonic inducer with formal musical characteristics. While avoiding music-specific induction theories of trance applicable to different cultures, they also agree that cross-cultural examples depict a distinction between high and low arousal-emotional states. High arousal emotional states are expressed by extremely active body movements and caused by over-sensory stimulation in communal religious/ritual settings. Ecstasy, on the other hand, is characterised by top-down processes like meditation or contemplation, with low-arousal

---

15 Judith Becker, *Deep Listeners Music, Emotion and Trancing* (Bloomington and Indianapolis, IN: Indiana University Press, 2004), p. 56.

emotional states that result in immobility, silence, solitude, sensory deprivation, and relaxation.[16]

However, a more mechanistic point of view was introduced in the 1960s. Rodney Needham pointed out the predominant use of percussion instruments and rhythmic devices in ritual settings across different cultures, suggesting that drumming specifically affects the brain and body, inducing altered states.[17] Similarly, Neher conducted experiments on the relationship between brainwaves, particularly theta and alpha ranges, and sound waves similar to drumming sounds of traditional rituals in terms of drumming frequencies.[18] He proposed that loud sound waves at very low frequencies travel bottom-up the afferent auditory pathways and entrain with the brainwaves. By imitating the electroencephalogram (EEG) correspondence of theta and alpha patterns, which are 3–8 Hz drumming beats per second (theta) and 8–13 Hz (alpha), he observed observable brainwave responses to drumming via scalp electrodes. In a relatively recent study, Melinda Maxfield also observed that drumming has specific neurophysiological effects on listeners, including a loss of the time continuum, alterations in body temperature, emotional arousal, extraordinary imagination, and possible entry into ASC.[19] Later, Jörg Fachner suggested that music is capable of shaping our subjective time perception concerning the amount of sensory information per minute.[20] Currently, the mechanistic view is often referred as brainwave entrainment (BWE) which suggests that a rhythmic sonic stimulus can synchronise with and influence brainwaves. BWE involves using pulsing patterns in stimuli to elicit a frequency-following response in brainwaves, aiming to match the frequency of the stimulus. Entrainment can be achieved through

---

16   Ibid., pp. 51–54; Gilbert Rouget, *Music and Trance: A Theory of the Relations between Music and Possession*, trans. by B. Biebuyck (Chicago, IL: University of Chicago Press, 1985), pp. 10–11.
17   Rodney Needham, 'Percussion and Transition', *Man* 2.4 (1967), 606–14.
18   Andrew Neher, 'Auditory Driving Observed with Scalp Electrodes in Normal Subjects', *Electroencephalography and Clinical Neurophysiology* 13.3 (1961), 449–51.
19   Melinda C. Maxfield, 'Effects of Rhythmic Drumming on EEG and Subjective Experience' (unpublished doctoral dissertation, Institute of Transpersonal Psychology, 1990), https://www.proquest.com/dissertations-theses/effects-rhythmic-drumming-on-eeg-subjective/docview/303885457/se-2
20   Jörg Fachner, 'Time Is the Key: Music and Altered States of Consciousness', in *Altering Consciousness: A Multidisciplinary Perspective*, ed. by Etzel Cardeña and Michael Winkelman, 2 vols (Santa Barbara, CA: Praeger, 2011), I, 355–76 (at 367).

auditory, photic, or combined stimuli.²¹ The mechanistic view of music and trance is often criticised for its reductive approach to the involvement of cultural and psychological factors while assigning a strong emphasis to the sonic qualities. In fact, the early studies on drumming effect later raised the famous critique of experienced ethnomusicologist Rouget, who suggested that if it is true, then 'half of Africa would be in a trance from the beginning of the year to the end'.²²

Returning to the inquiry into whether sound can induce or facilitate ASC, the auditory entrainment theory offers a basis for hypothesising a musically induced form of altered states. While laboratory studies explore sound as a potential cue in entraining brainwaves during ASC, the particularist perspective tends to reject the idea of inherent sound effects. Nonetheless, both viewpoints cannot be entirely disregarded, as establishing a causal relationship at the initial point remains challenging. It is worth noting that the association of music with religious and ritual contexts is a pervasive feature in the context of musical performances²³, suggesting that auditory entrainment as a phenomenon may be attributed to cultural memories of musical trance acquired over centuries, rather than being an innate aspect. Nevertheless, this does not necessarily discount the possibility of a biological experience of sound and its impact on the body at more fundamental levels, such as bodily responses to low-frequency loud sounds or repetitive exposure. The particularist approach emphasises the cultural and social context of music in trance rituals, while the mechanistic perspective explores the direct effects of sound on the brain and body. However, I argue that these two perspectives are not mutually exclusive. Rather, music simultaneously engages in both layers, with the particularist view highlighting its involvement in social and intellectual static patterns, and the mechanistic view explaining its role in biological static patterns.

---

21 Tina L. Huang, and Christine Charyton, 'A Comprehensive Review of the Psychological Effects of Brainwave Entrainment', *Alternative Therapies* 14.5 (2008), 38–50.

22 Gilbert Rouget, *Music and Trance: A Theory of the Relations between Music and Possession*, trans. by Brunhilde Biebuyck (Chicago, IL: University of Chicago Press, 1985), p. 175.

23 Steven Brown and Joseph Jordania, 'Universals in the World's Musics', *Psychology of Music* 41.2 (2011), 240–41.

(b) A Cross-Cultural Overview

Building on the concepts discussed above, the following sections explore trance examples traditionally associated with altered states of consciousness. The objective is to observe the co-occurrence of various sounds and trance behaviours in light of the theories of musical trance presented above. To collect relevant examples, a two-step process, along with an additional strategy, is employed (see Figure 8.1). In the first step, controlled words that could potentially lead to the identification of musics and musical traditions associated with ASC are scanned in the indexes of the *Garland Encyclopedia of World Music* volumes, except for Volume 8: Europe.[24] Subsequently, the same list of controlled words is used to search the Alexander Street Press Online Music Library, with each region's name, and the results are filtered based on the information provided in the liner notes before including them in the sample set. Given that trance rituals are frequently encountered without explicit tags from the initial list of control words, but instead are described using original culture-specific terminology, such as 'dhikr' (a devotional practice aiming to induce a type of ASC called 'hal'), the process led to the development of region-specific secondary lists of control words.

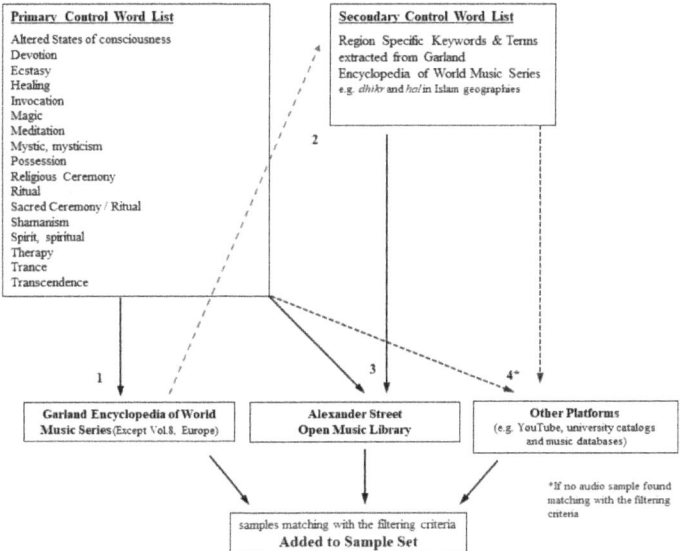

Fig. 8.1 Sampling methodology. Created by author (2017), CC BY-NC 4.0

---

24 *Garland Encyclopedia of World Music*, ed. by Bruno Nettl, Ruth M. Stone, James Porter, and Timothy Rice, 10 vols (New York: Routledge, 1998–2002).

In order to examine comprehensively the involvement of socio-cultural contexts, I conducted an analysis of various factors that shape the surface setting and ritual behaviours, including the belief systems providing the theological background for these customs and the modes of interactions through which individuals engage with these cultural ties. To observe these aspects systematically, a set of questions was formulated for each sample and available information was organised into clusters using open coding. These questions were as follows:

- What belief system, religion, and theology form the conceptual foundation of the experience?
- What type of ceremony is it, and what are the defining characteristics of the cultural context of the ritual at the level of action and surface setting? How is the ceremony named?
- How is the experience conceptualised, and what are the motivations and intentions behind the ritualistic practices leading to an ASC?
- Is the experience predominantly a collectively shared group experience or more individual in nature?
- Based on the general categorisation of musical trance types according to emotional states (high arousal/active and low arousal/still), which type of musical trance best describes the given example?

As can be seen from Figure 8.2, for each example, a religion or belief system is indicated as the central underlying theme shaping the ritual context. Among the observed religious practices, it is salient that the traditional belief systems of regional cultures constitute the largest category compared to the Abrahamic religions. Secondly, the two largest categories of ritual context are spirit possession and devotional ceremonies, as shown in Figure 8.3. The culture-specific definitions of these ritual categories suggest a certain level of mental readiness and attentiveness required from the participants.

8. An Inquiry into Musical Trance   171

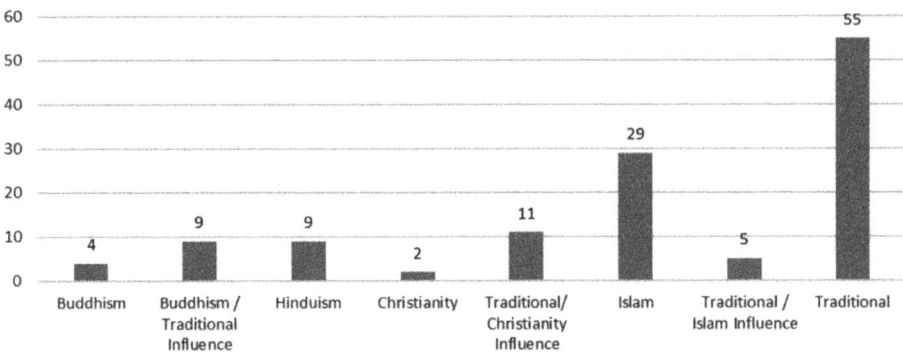

Fig. 8.2 Number of examples by religion/belief system. Created by author (2017).

Furthermore, in addition to the theological aspects, the phenomenon of musical trance also exhibits associations with social patterns and ordinary life events. As evident in Figure 8.3 and Figure 8.4, the examples indicate that participants have specific objectives and structured practices in advance while engaging in trance activities. Notably, the largest category of these objectives revolves around physical or psychological healing (see Figure 8.4), followed by invocations of deities to address practical issues like drought, security concerns, or individual matters. This suggests a well-defined cultural aspect of trance practices as a social pattern where participants organise the experience, and anticipate positive outcomes, leading to enriched meanings and emotional states associated with the ritual.

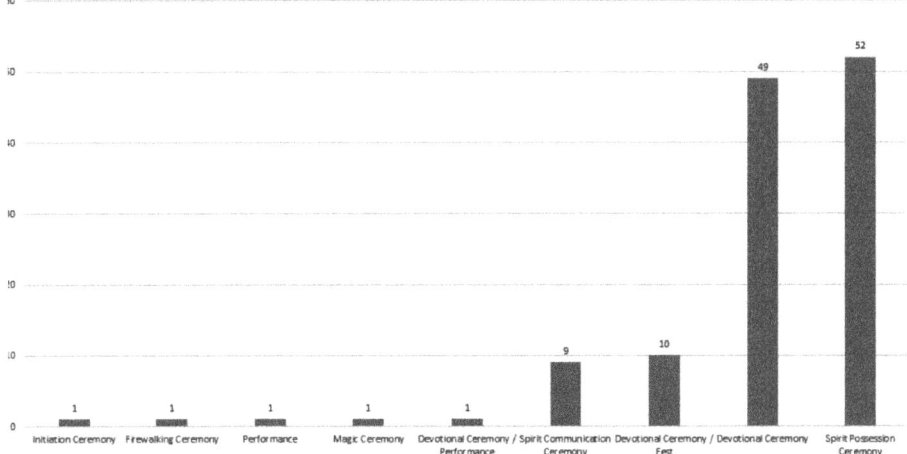

Fig. 8.3 Number of examples by ritual context. Created by author (2017).

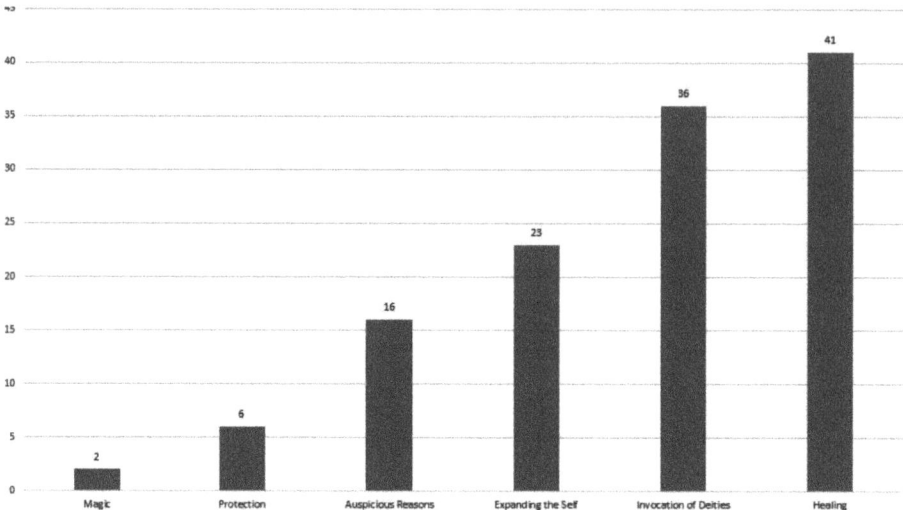

Fig. 8.4 Number of examples by ritual function. Created by author (2017).

Another noteworthy aspect is the prevalence of communal social settings in many examples, emphasising the significance of shared ritualistic behaviour and psychological dynamics. As Fig. 8.5 shows, it is more often the case that trance rituals are held in communal settings.

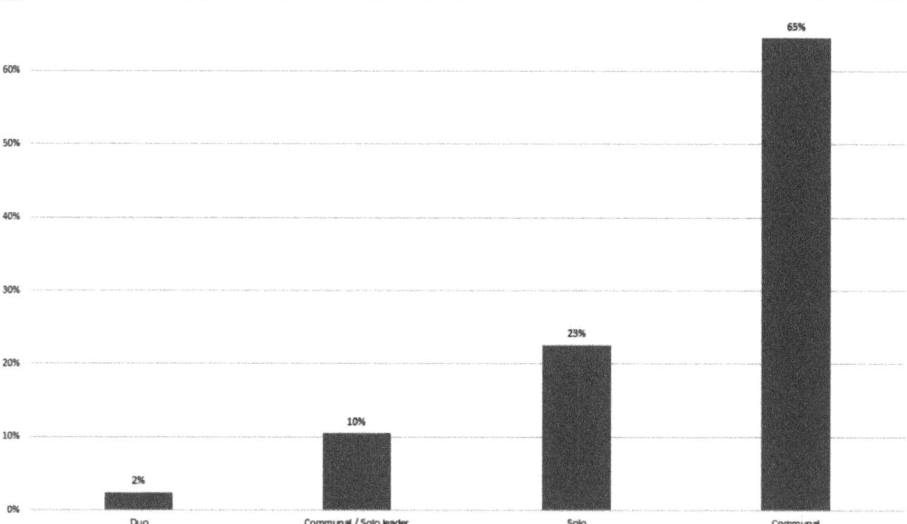

Fig. 8.5 Examples by social setting of ritual. Created by author (2017)..

The existence of such static patterns, including ritualistic behaviour and the underlying theological context, empowers trancers with the knowledge and means to alter their consciousness, as postulated by Becker.

(c) Sonic Signification in Musical Trance

The culturally-oriented perspective, however, overlooks the direct influence of organised sounds on the bodily experience of trance. This neglect of the biological experience of sound events and their psychoacoustic impact on consciousness calls for a closer examination of sonic parameters to bridge the gap between cultural and musical explanations. Such analysis addresses the signification of sounds in the auditory experience, following Bob Snyder's three-part model of auditory processing.[25] Given the importance of auditory entrainment theory for understanding the relationship between music and ASC, specific focus is placed on sonic properties related to temporal aspects, such as pulsation, tempo, rhythmic groupings, and the arrangement of musical layers. Timbral and textural features are also considered. The analysis process consists of two main steps. First, a subjective ear-based analysis is conducted, accompanied by a comprehensive review of ethnographic notes to gather basic information, such as instrumentation or duration. Subsequently, the samples undergo sound analysis using the Sound Visualiser, where the Constant-Q Spectrogram is employed to analyse texture, layering, and repetition, while the Tempo and Beat Tracker Onset Detection Function is utilised for tempo and beat detection.

The prevalent sonic qualities observed in musical trance are closely tied to temporality and can be understood as manifestations of statistical regularity, representing various static sound units. In music, regularity is commonly discussed in the context of repetition, which often involves repetitive pitch content like ostinato lines or refrains. However, in the context of musical trance, regularity units manifest in a variety of forms, including but not limited to steady pulsations, repetitive short figures, drone tones, interlocked textures, siren or signal-like motions, drumming spectra, as well as simple melodies or short percussive loops.

Statistical regularity plays a significant role in auditory functions, encompassing tasks like streaming musical layers, maintaining auditory continuity, detecting temporal values, and facilitating musical memory.[26]

---

25 Bob Snyder, *Music and Memory: An Introduction* (Cambridge, MA: The MIT Press, 2001), pp. 12–15.
26 Diana Deutsch, 'Grouping Mechanisms in Music', in *The Psychology of Music*, ed. by Diana Deutsch (San Diego, CA: Elsevier, 2013), pp. 183–248.

Accordingly, it suggests that sonic events with recurrent patterns are more accessible to auditory processing, and this cognitive ease facilitates embodiment, anticipation, memorisation, and participation during musical trance experiences. By providing ease in auditory processing, the prevalence of regular sonic elements imparts a sense of 'freedom, luxury, and expansiveness' as aptly expressed by John Ortiz.[27]

One of the static sound units observed in musical trance is the melody. In the majority of collected examples, a single specific melody is prominently present, with approximately 78.4% of instances being sung. Repeating melodies are often formed as a single motivic figure that is no longer than the period of short-term memory processing, and they are simple by having a small number of pitches moving by smaller intervals, repeated through the flow without a significant change (see Figure 8.6). These melodies incorporate a verbal context that relates to the cultural content of the trance experience, encompassing curing songs, spirit songs, and modes and melodies associated with deities. Because melodies, in general, tend to be listened to and perceived through 'mental schemas, developed from early childhood in the course of hearing many of the culture's melodies' with this joining of the musical and semantic content, melodic units serve as effective sonic signifiers.[28]

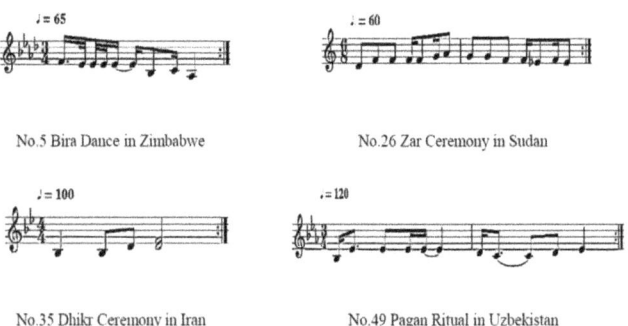

Fig. 8.6 Melody transcriptions of examples No. 5, 26, 35, and 49.[29] Created by author (2024), CC BY-NC 4.0.

---

27 John M. Ortiz, *The Tao of Music: Sound Psychology Using Music to Change Your Life* (Boston, MA: Weiser Books, 1987), p. 275.

28 W. Jay Dowling and Dane L. Harwood, *Music Cognition* (Orlando, FL: Academic Press, 1986), p. 152. For further information on the relationship between the melodic structures and the trance specific ritual context, see Dale A. Olsen, 'Shamanism, Music and Healing in Two Contrasting South American Cultural Areas', in *The Oxford Handbook of Medical Ethnomusicology*, ed. by Benjamin D. Koen (Oxford: Oxford University Press, 2008), pp. 343–46.

One other common observation is the employment of drumming effects. 98 out of 125 examples in the sample set employ at least one percussion instrument, and 86 out of those 98 examples utilise an idiophone (30) or a membranophone (26), or both (30). Those percussive instruments are primarily associated with sacred meanings relating to the contextual specification of trance rituals. The association of drumming and healing rituals is especially widespread across large geographies. The most frequently observed drumming instruments are frame drums, sticks, and maracas. Aerophones are the second most employed instruments. In most examples, drumming is utilised constantly as the most active and continuous layer in the overall flow. This parallels previous studies[30] on the associations of drumming as a sonic cue for spiritual experiences.

Pulsation (steady drumming) and rhythmic units (patterned drumming) are observed as the two most common units of temporal regularity. While pulsation and rhythmic units are mostly played on percussive instruments, they can also be voiced variedly on other instruments and the human voice, as in the case of Kecak of Bali (example numbers 77–78). Pulsation is the time level often conceptualised as points in musical time that we can easily detect and tap into, which is also considered as a stimulus for auditory entrainment. On the other hand, rhythmic units differ from pulsation having a more figurative character (patterned) in contrast to the steadiness of the pulse. Pulsation mostly uses isochronal and non-accentuated ways, resulting in pure steadiness. They are distinctive in the entire sound because of their higher volume at lower frequencies, especially when played in frame drums, and they rarely go silent during the musical flow. No. 10 and No. 110 are examples of this periodic membranophone pulsation. When the steady pulse is signified in sticks like light idiophone percussions, its sound is distinguishable, resembling a metronome beating, as No. 2, No. 51, or

---

29 Author-transcribed melodies without tuning system specifications. The transcriptions provide reductive representations of the original melodies, excluding spectral and temporal details, with the sole purpose of demonstrating contours. For more detailed renditions, please refer to the recordings cited in the discography at the end of this chapter.

30 Alongside Neher and Needham's previously cited experimental studies on drumming and altered states of consciousness, also see Peter Michael Hamel, *Through Music to the Self*, trans. by P. Lemesuer (Shaftesbury: Element Books, 1978), pp. 76–79.

No. 87. Pulsation can also be signified via hand clapping and other body percussions, as in the case of No. 40.

Rhythmic units observed through the sample set significantly differ in temporal structure. Except for drone-based examples, almost all the examples employ at least one layer of a rhythmic unit in a percussive manner, and most have at least two simultaneous layers of patterned rhythms (beside pulsation). The internal structure of rhythmic units in musical trance is mostly short in duration, simple in temporal divisions, and grouped with the pulse level, allowing ease in entrainment. Rhythmic units also function as accompaniment layers filling the texture. Example numbers 5, 13, 24, 29, 58, 63, and 79 explicitly show the accompaniment function of rhythmic units in the drumming layer.

Although the static units in musical trance are often short in length and simple in internal structure, the way they relate to each other, the texture, offers a unique listening experience. In most examples, units are temporally interlocked to each other, creating a synchronised overall beating pattern formed by all the sounding parts of the texture, often called composite rhythm. The composite rhythm can be audible or implied via the functions such as auditory continuity and temporal streaming.[31] The synchronisation of units is dense as units are linked in more than one way to each other. The interlocked texture in musical trance offers enough comfort in streaming yet also creates a unique experience of musical time, allowing multiple dimensions simultaneously. Such a perception of musical time is termed as the 'pure' ostinato 'cyclic' time category in Michael Tenzer's cross-cultural topology of musical time. Ostinato cyclic time refers to the extremely 'statis' type of musical time in which the pulsation 'structurally' matches with other units in the higher temporal hierarchies, and 'the unchanging identity' of rhythmic and melodic units creates the 'static aspects'.[32]

The combination of these tendencies, at extreme degrees, promises a higher potential of musically induced trance states due to their

---

31 Daniel J. Cameron, Jocelyn Bentley, and Jessica A. Grahn, 'Cross-Cultural Influences on Rhythm Processing: Reproduction, Discrimination, and Beat Tapping', *Frontiers in Psychology* 6 (2015), 366.

32 Michael Tenzer, 'A Cross-Cultural Topology of Musical Time: Afterword to the Present Book and to *Analytical Studies in World Music* (2006)', in *Analytical and Cross-Cultural Studies in World Music*, ed. by Michael Tenzer and John Roeder (Oxford: Oxford University Press, 2011).

compatibility with the general principles of sound processing and auditory entrainment. Based on this observation, we can hypothesise that the possibility of a sound-induced trance experience increases according to the varying employment of the means of sonic signification listed. Numbers 1, 8, 10, 26, 28, 44, 58, and 110 are examples of such strong combinations of sonic qualities.

Another unit under examination is tempo, which plays a significant role in musical trance. Faster tempo examples, ranging between 80 and 150 beats per minute (bpm), correspond to high arousal bodily active states, and the majority of the examples are in this category. However, there exists a smaller group of examples characterised by extremely slow tempi, ranging from 20 to 50 bpm, indicative of low arousal meditative states. These diverging tempi in extreme ranges, either slow or fast, align with the conventional types of trance and serve as indicators of low- or high-arousal emotional states. While the examples with slow tempi lack pulsation or any indication of periodic beats, making them seemingly incompatible with auditory entrainment theory, they still conform to the essential idea of statistical regularity. With an impression that the music might stop, they contribute to the overall sonic regularity observed. Drones, for instance, are simply the exact perpetual sounding of a single tone. It is also true that the continuum-like melodies have a static character since the frequencies are changing too slowly to form a perceivable patterned order. Conceptually, the vertical temporality percept caused by the fast tempo-pulsation stream is replaced with a single sonic event that is the very slow continuum. The smoothly and slowly changing frequency content is the only motion of shift. Although it favours a comparatively more linear time perception because of its form of a continuum, it also allows for a unique experience of musical verticality by slowing down the time percept as though it will stop.

Many of those slower tempo examples are performed in a communal setting where the participants mostly chant in a monophonic texture. We can point out two important psychological and perceptual effects of communal chanting as a means of sonic signification in trance experiences. First, it is a very effective way of creating a shared musical atmosphere, providing a single-line sonic experience sung and heard by all. Additionally, because of its semantic content, chanting can also be a cue to the shared theology and social side of ritual activity. The following lines describe the communal chanting experience in Kirtan singing:

> The auditory space resonates synchronously with the beat of the heart. The tactile sensibilities are equally in operation as people sit close together singing. Boundaries dissolve as the skin of individuals touches, and their discreate voices merge in unison. The intense emotion and devotion that results creates an altered perception and an indomitable community spirit. In such settings, the embodiedness of each listener 'carries an anticipation of others' bodies'.[33]

Group chanting psychology is often associated with the common themes of religious altered state experiences, such as the unity in the Oneness or the dissolution of the sense of self. With regard to Buddhist music, Williams comments:

> Chanting certainly is capable of assisting in the creation of a heightened state of consciousness in the performer. When a person performs Buddhist music as a part of crowd of chanters, the individual self disappears into the Sanga, or community ... Group chanting, mostly in unison, causes the self to become absorbed into the community.[34]

Besides the socio-psychological effect that it provides for ritual setting, it is also true that certain sonic qualities in communal chanting might relate to the issue of musical trance. It is often the case that even though the chanting is primarily signified in monophonic texture with a linear continuum, the spectra of the entire sound are not information-poor perceptually, since the communal singing, especially in unison, creates its own density in a type of heterophonic texture. Often the listening experience of communal chanting is highly tense because of the high-volume level, enriching the spectra. It is also true that frequencies used in monophonic chanting tend to be at lower ranges of spectra, creating a more elaborate experience of overtones and other spectral details

---

33 Sukanya Sarbadhikary, 'Hearing the Transcendental Place: Sound, Spirituality and Sensuality in the Musical Practices of an Indian Devotional Order', in *Music and Transcendence*, ed. by Ferdia J. Stone-Davis (Farnham: Ashgate, 2015), pp. 23–34 (at 26).

34 Sean Williams, 'Buddhism and Music', in *Experiencing Music in World Religions*, ed. by Guy. L. Beck (Ontario: Wilfrid Laurier University Press, 2006), pp. 169–89 (at 186).

of the sonic event. These lower-frequency sounds are also favourable in a musical trance since they are more effective regarding the bodily experience of sound.

Conclusions

Neither the listed sound components nor their statistical dominance in the sample set can prove a causal relationship between sound-specific aspects and trance experiences in terms of inducement. However, the presence of the listed tendencies in musical trance examples indicates a high potential for facilitating trance states. The decreased activity of the PCC in DMN, which is generally associated with the meta-cognitive functioning in higher brain regions and long-term memory, has parallels with the preference for using short and basic sonic materials that are processed easily in the early chains of auditory processing. Pulsation and drone continuums are extremes of this type of directly detected sonic units without referencing the long-term musical memory storages. Additionally, the simple and reoccurring character of melodies in musical trance might reduce the need for a re-entrance process in higher brain regions. In comparison with musics such as Eurogenetic art compositions or popular songs, it can be said that in trance music, there is a tendency to use sonic materials that are processed concerning veridical perception, which is the direct perception of stimuli as it exists in the given moment, unlike the schematic expectations that are the result of long-term memory formed by earlier exposure to music.[35] The excessive use of statistical regularity or repetition in trance music and its vertical time perception might be related to the increased activity of the PFC functions in integrating input data and attention during the trance states. It is true that non-progressive music has more potential in directing attention to the very moment of the musical flow rather than the linear movement. The predominant use of short static sonic events over the linearly patterned ones might contribute to a more focused, moment-to-moment musical experience of the composite sound.

---

35   Deutsch, *The Psychology of Music*, p. 213.

Another deviation in the brain regions observed during altered states of consciousness is the decoupling of the MTL with the DMN system, and it is proposed that it might distort the perception of clock time, which also contributes to the sense of self. Similarly, it is observed that most of the sound-specific aspects are related to the temporal qualities in musics. As is indicated, there is a tendency to use non-harmonic sounds caused by the predominant use of percussive sounds rather than harmonic pitch patterns. This directly leads the attentional focus to time-related aspects, such as the pulse, rhythms, tempi, and flow, which can be considerably more effective in altering the time perception. These sound-specific tendencies observed in the sample set are proposed as the psychoacoustic correspondences of the musical trance experiences. The predominance of temporal parameters in the featured tendencies provides a compatible ground between sound and the brain/body mechanisms of ASC phenomenon with music in terms of perceptual qualities. While they are not suggested as the inducers of the trance states, they can be hypothesised as the sonic cues with a high potential to alter the conscious state because of their relation to auditory processing mechanisms. Nevertheless, it is also true that specific socio-cultural codes and specificities of contextual meanings related to the trance rituals are also observed not only in a variety of ritual settings but also in music-specific aspects, such as the verbal and motivic associations of melodies with the intentions behind the ritual, or the use of specific timbres to indicate the specific ritual.

The simultaneity of the psychoacoustic and socio-cultural aspects in association with musical trance suggests a *via media* between scholars who would stress one side to the exclusion of the other. The present study brings out the core ideas of each perspective and, I hope, makes a distinctive contribution by demonstrating these diverse yet complementary factors in musical trance phenomena. This intermediate standpoint is also reflected in the choice of the term 'sonic signification'. One might question the precision of the term signification since it is often considered as including meaning and interpretation rather than the direct, quick cognitive responses with psychoacoustic foundations. While such a distinction in the levels of perception is beneficial in understanding the differential factors of any given phenomenon, it is also true that they are not independent of each other in the moment of experience. This problem of separating the biological foundations from the meaning-making processes and limiting the meaning to the socio-cultural verbal contexts is criticised in Paul Thibault's unified theory of eco-social semiotics. According to Thibault, meaning-making also includes cognitive states, bodily experiences, and all types of percepts (that is, objects of perception), along with social phenomena, such as linguistic models or cultural notions. Therefore, meaning-making is an integrated activity in an eco-social system formed by three factors; the individual mental processing, the material environment, and the linguistic models of the socio-cultural domain in which the individual is situated. Thibault suggests that even though the language base meanings on the cultural level are essential parts of the entire system, 'they have a secondary and derived status with respect to the activities in which they are made and in which they participate'.[36] Nevertheless, the meaning emerges as a composite in the individual experience at the focal point of this eco-social model.

In this chapter, I have discussed the qualities of the music accompanying trance rituals as integrated parts of sonic significations with both psychoacoustic and socio-cultural traces. Both function in the experience and the meaning-making process of sounds played and heard during trance rituals. They are signified by the people (human cognition) who are the focus of this eco-social model. While psychoacoustic tendencies and socio-cultural codes are different in terms of the way that they involve the emergence of the overall signification (the former is bottom-up, the latter is top-down), the sonic signification is an amalgam derived from the interactions of the human mind with both means. In this more holistic context, the present study should be considered as an effort to bring out the observable patterns in this entire signification process concerning many sides. From this standpoint, what makes music such a unique companion to spiritual experiences is its temporality, its capacity to hold a variety of layers within unity and to carry them simultaneously into the very moment of experience.

---

36 Paul Thibault, *Brain, Mind, and the Signifying Body* (New York: Continuum, 2004), p. 3

Discography

1	D. Bernez [Performer], 'Na Go De' [Liner notes and recordings by Scott Kiehl]. On *Akom: Art of Possession*, Track Number 19 [CD] (Village Pulse VPU-1009, 2000).
2	'An Evening with the Flute Ensemble' [Liner notes and recordings by Artur Simon]. On *Berta—Waza, Bal Naggaro, Abangaran—Die Musik Der Berta Am Blauen Nil—Music of the Berta from the Blue Nile*, Track Number 15 [CD], Museum Collection Berlin (WERGO—SM 17082, 2003).
3	'Bartha, the Winner' [Liner notes and recordings by Artur Simon]. On *Berta—Waza, Bal Naggaro, Abangaran—Die Musik Der Berta Am Blauen Nil—Music of the Berta from the Blue Nile*, Track Number 14 [CD], Museum Collection Berlin (WERGO —SM 17082, 2003).
4	'The Bata Repertoire for Shango in Sakété: Oba Koso' [Liner notes and recordings by Carol Hardy, compilation by Marcos Branda-Lacerda]. On *The World's Musical Traditions, Vol. 8: Yoruba Drums from Benin, West Africa*, Track Number 7 [CD] (Smithsonian Folkways Recordings 40440, 1996).
5	Matsuhira Yuji [Screen name], 'Bira Dance at Great Zimbabwe', *YouTube*, 20 January 2013 [online video recording], https://www.youtube.com/watch?v=Pbs80p4-nGM
6	'La Cérémonie Du Bobé' [Produced by Caroline Bourgine]. On *Congo: Cérémonie du Bobé*, Track Number 2 [CD] (Ocora W 560010, 1991).
7	'Le Bobé S'est Rapproché' [Produced by Caroline Bourgine]. On *Congo: Cérémonie du Bobé*, Track Number 3 [CD] (Ocora W 560010, 1991).
8	'Musique de Divination Diye' [Liner notes and recordings by Simha Arom]. On *Anthologie de la musique des Pygmées Aka = Musical anthology of the Aka Pygmies*, Disc 2, Track Number 9 [CD] (Ocora C 560171/72, 2002).
9	Foundation for Hausa Performing Arts, 'Dodorido Koroso Dance Drama Segment 2 Bori Adept', 8 January 2012 [online video recording], https://www.youtube.com/watch?v=hpjrw_VRW1Y
10	'Music for the Buma Dance' [Liner notes and recordings by Simha Arom & Patrick Renaud]. On *Cameroon: Baka Pygmy Music*, Disc 1, Track Number 1, 10 [CD] (Smithsonian Folkways Recordings/UNESCO, 1977).

11	'Le Jeune Eland (Nang Tzema Tzi)' [Liner notes by Emmanuelle Olivier]. On *Namibia: Songs of the Ju'hoansi Bushmen*, Track Number 18 [CD] (Ocora C 560117, 1997).
12	'Oryx (Go'e Tzi)' (1997) [Liner notes by Emmanuelle Olivier]. On *Namibia: Songs of the Ju'hoansi Bushmen*, Track Number 19 [CD] (Ocora 560117, 1997).
13	Mtendeni Maulid Ensemble, 'Dahala 3: Marihaba / Hua Maulana / Salat / Jalla Jalaluh / Khamsa Arkan / Man A'ala / Leo Mambo' [Liner notes by Aïsha Schmitt]. On *Zanzibara, Vol. 6—A Sufi Performance from Zanzibar*, Track Number 3 [CD] (Buda Musique 860219, 2012).
14	'Hadra Song: "Al hamdou lillahAlgeria"' [Liner notes and recordings by Pierre Augier]. On *Algeria: Sahara - Music of Gourara* Disc 1, Track Number 3 [CD] (Smithsonian Folkways Recordings/UNESCO, 1975).
15	'Jinele: chant de divination' [Liner notes by Jean L. Jenkins, Ralph Harrisson and Ragnar Johnson]. On *Ethiopie: musiques vocales et instrumentales*, Disc 2, Track Number 10 [CD] (Ocora C 580055/56, 1994).
16	'Būderbāla / Būḥāla'. On *The Music Of Islām—Volume Six: Al-Maghrib, Gnāwa Music, Marrakesh, Morocco*, Track Number 4 [CD] (Celestial Harmonies 13146-2, 1997).
17	Matsuhira Yuji [Screen name], 'The Mbira Ceremony', *YouTube*, 18 May 2012 [online video recording], https://www.youtube.com/watch?v=OXBQbn6wZeQ
18	'Molimo Song of Devotion to the Forest' [Liner notes and recordings by Colin Turnbull and Francis S. Chapman]. On *Mbuti Pygmies of the Ituri Rainforest*, Track Number 26 [CD] (Smithsonian Folkways Recordings 40401, 1997).
19	'Molimo Song: Darkness Is Good' [Liner notes and recordings by Colin Turnbull and Francis S. Chapman]. On *Mbuti Pygmies of the Ituri Rainforest*, Track Number 25 [CD] (Smithsonian Folkways Recordings 40401, 1997).
20	Gnawalux Brussels [Screen name], 'Stambali 1—Gnawa Tunisie', *YouTube*, 27 August 2008 [online video recording], https://www.youtube.com/watch?v=wK-UasuUtdo
21	'Tazenkharet' [Liner notes and recordings by Finola Holiday & Geoffrey Holiday]. On *Tuareg Music of the Southern Sahar*, Disc 1, Track Number 13 [CD] (Ethnic Folkways Library FE 4470, 1960).
22	'Timgui' [Liner notes and recordings by Charles Duvelle]. On *Bariba—Bénin*, Track Number 5 [CD] (Philips Music Group France 538721-2, 1999).

23	Mwizenge Tembo [Screen name], 'Vimbuza Dance Ritual Ceremony', *YouTube*, 20 July 2008 [online video recording], https://www.youtube.com/watch?v=6wpsNQp1ci4
24	'Alto Bung'o Horn (Kenya)' [Compiled by Stephen Innocenzi]. On *Africa, Music from the Nonesuch Explorer Series*, Track Number 1 [CD] (Nonesuch Records 7559-79793-2, 2002).
25	Ivo Biegman. [Screen name], 'Zar ritual in Egypt', *YouTube*, 19 May 2011 [online video recording], https://www.youtube.com/watch?v=YNiUc4W5Kzo&list=RDYNiUc4W5Kzo#t=517
26	'Zar Omdurman' [Liner notes and compilation by Peter Verney]. On *Rough Guide to Sudan*, Track Number 7 [CD]. (World Music Network—RGNET 1152, 2005).
27	'Danse, Bozok Semahi' [Liner notes by Jean During and Jerome Cler]. On *Turquie: Ceremonie du Djem Alevi* (*Turkey: Djem Alevi Ceremony*), Track Number 12 [CD] (Ocora C 560125, 1998).
28	kabultransit [Screen name]. 'Kabul Transit—Zikr', *YouTube*, 7 November 2007 [online video recording], https://www.youtube.com/watch?v=_BvSLgJSBBY
29	'Zikr' [Liner notes by Jean During]. On *Kurdistan: Zikr et chants soufis*, Disc 2, Track Number 2 [CD] (Ocora C 560071/72, 1994).
30	Iraqi Maqam [Screen name], 'Dhikr Ceremony in Iraq', *YouTube*, 1 January 2009 [online video recording], https://www.youtube.com/watch?v=yyrK-oAo3DM&list=PL5B186F663D6F3052&index=2
31	Iraqi Maqam [Screen name], 'Qadiri Dhikr—God is Eternal', *YouTube*, 8 December 2008 [online video recording], https://www.youtube.com/watch?v=lV52djNFcKk&index=1&list=PL5B186F663D6F3052
32	'Zikr/ Du'a / Tekbir' [Liner notes and recordings by Bernard Mauguin]. On *Islamic Ritual from Kosovo*, Track Number 2 [CD] (Smithsonian Folkways Recordings/ UNESCO-UNES08055, 1974).
33	'Islamic Ritual Zikr' [Liner notes by Christian Poché, recordings by Jochen Wenzel]. On *Syria: Islamic Ritual Zikr in Aleppo*, Track Number 2 [CD] (Smithsonian Folkways Recordings/ UNESCO-UNES08013, 1975).
34	'Zikr' [Liner notes by David Stevens]. On *Turquie: Musique Soufi*, Track Number 1 [CD] (Ocora C559017, 1987).
35	'Zikr-e Allah et percussions' [Liner notes by Jean During]. On *Kurdistan: Zikr et chants soufis*, Disc 2, Track Number 1 [CD] (Ocora C 560071/72, 1994).

36	H. Shakkûr & Ensemble Al-Kindî [Performer], 'Meditation' [Liner notes by Peter Pannke]. On *Sufi Soul* (*Echos Du Paradis*), Disc 1, Track Number 2 [CD]. (Network Medien—26.982, 1997).
37	Muhammad Al Ashiq [Performer], 'Qasida: Saluha Limadha' [Liner notes by Andre Jouve and Christian Poche]. On *Archives De La Musique Arabe Vol. 1*, Track Number 2 [CD] (Ocora C 558678, 1987).
38	Mobarak & Molabakhsh Nuri [Performer], 'Qalandari Tune'. On *Troubadours of Allah: Sufi Music from the Indus Valley*, Disc 1, Track Number 2 [CD] (Wergo SM 16172, 1999).
39	Yâr Mohammad [Performer], 'Qalandari Tune (Khorasani)' [Liner notes by Peter Pannke]. On *Sufi Soul* (*Echos Du Paradis*), Disc 2, Track Number 10 [CD] (Network Medien—26.982, 1997).
40	'Tamburah (Voice of the Lyre)' [Liner notes and recordings by Dieter Christensen]. On *Oman: Traditional Arts of the Sultanate of Oman*, Track Number 7 [CD] (Smithsonian Folkways Recordings/UNESCO-UNES08211, 1993).
41	O. Y. Traibi [Performer], 'Zar' [Liner notes by Christian Poché, recordings by Jochen Wenzel]. On *Yemen: Traditional Music of the North*, Track Number 3 [CD] (Smithsonian Folkways Recordings/UNESCO-UNES08004, 1978).
42	Ozman Khaled [Screen name], 'ZAAR Ceremony at Qeshm', *YouTube*, 18 April 2016 [online video recording], https://www.youtube.com/watch?v=gifUSI1RFCQ
43	'Zikr' [Liner notes and production by Jean During and Ted Levin]. On *The Silk Road: A Musical Caravan*, Disc 2, Track Number 19 [CD]. (Smithsonian Folkways Recordings SFW40438, 2002).
44	Aznash Ensemble [Performer]. Konya Mystic Music Festival [Screen name], 'Aznash Ensemble', *YouTube*, 5 August 2013 [online video recording], https://www.youtube.com/watch?v=TiPqB4GNzT0&list=RDtx6dwa4u8Lg&index=11
45	Swiatoslaw Wojtkowiak [Screen name], 'Chechen Female Zikr: Opening', *YouTube*, 16 December 2010 [online video recording], https://www.youtube.com/watch?v=tx6dwa4u8Lg
46	S. Aqmoldaev [Performer], 'Kertolghau' [Liner notes and production by Jean During and Ted Levin]. On *The Silk Road: A Musical Caravan*, Disc 2, Track Number 16 [CD] (Smithsonian Folkways Recordings SFW40438, 2002).
47	T. S. Qalebov and S. Tawarov [Performer], 'Madh' [Liner notes and production by Jean During and Ted Levin]. On *The Silk Road: A Musical Caravan*, Disc 2, Track Number 18 [CD] (Smithsonian Folkways Recordings SFW40438, 2002).

48	Supergnak [Screen name], 'Le tour du monde en musique: Kazakhstan—Le kobyz du chaman', *YouTube*, 14 January 2010 [online video recording], https://www.youtube.com/watch?v=5M6DA5w6aCc
49	'Shod-i Uforash and Ufor-i Tezash: Dilbaram Shumo' [Liner notes and recordings by Ted Levin]. On *Bukhara: Musical Crossroads of Asia*, Track Number 1 [CD] (Smithsonian Folkways Recordings SFW40050, 1991).
50	'Cérémonie De Propitiation De Nag-Zhig' [Liner notes and recording by Ricardo Canzio]. On *Tibet: Traditions Rituelles Des Bonpos*, Track Number 2 [CD] (Ocora C 580016, 1993).
51	'Shamanic Bear Session' [Liner notes and recording by Henry Lecomte]. On *Siberia, Vol. 1—Shamanic & Narrative Songs of Siberian Arctic*, Track Number 12 [CD] (Buda Musique—925642, 1995).
52	O. A. Njavan [Performer], 'Song, Kkas Drum and Jampa Jingle Belt, Imitation of Kamlanie' [Liner notes and recording by Henry Lecomte]. On *Siberia, Vol. 6: Sakhalin—Vocal & Instrumental Music, Nivkh Ujl'ta*, Track Number 8 [CD] (Buda Musique—927212, 1998).
53	'Chant Chamanique' [Liner notes and recording by Henry Lecomte]. On *Siberia, Vol. 5—Shamanic & Daily Songs from the Amur Basin*, Track Number 8 [CD] (Buda Musique—926712, 1997).
54	'Chant Chamanique' [Liner notes and recording by Henry Lecomte]. On *Siberia, Vol. 5—Shamanic & Daily Songs from the Amur Basin*, Track Number 27 [CD] (Buda Musique—926712, 1997).
55	'Pei-tou Liturgy (Great Bear Liturgy)' [Produced by John Levy]. On *Chinese Buddhist Music*, Track Number 6 [CD] (Lyrichord—LLST 7222, 2004).
56	'Dai Hannya Tendoku E' [Liner notes by Toshiro Kido and Pierre Landy]. On *Japan: Shomyo Buddhist Ritual—Dai Hannya Ceremony*, Track Number 1, 17:00–31:42 [CD] (Smithsonian Folkways Recordings/UNESCO-UNES08036, 1975).
57	'Sinawi' [Liner notes and recording by Kwon Oh Sung]. On *Korea: Folkloric Instrumental Traditions, Vol. 1: Sinawi and Sanjo*, Track Number 1 [CD] (JVC Ethnic Sound Series #25, JVC VID- 25020, 1988).
58	O-Suwa-Daiko [Performer]. 'Ama-No-Naru Tatsu-O Dai-Kagura' [Liner notes by Iyori Takei]. On *Japan: O-Suwa-Daiko Drums*, Track Number 3 [CD] (Smithsonian Folkways Recordings/UNESCO-UNES08030, 1978).

59	'Rimse' [Liner notes and recording by Jean-Jacques Nattiez and Kazuyuki Tanimoto]. On *Japan: Ainu Songs*, Track Number 4 [CD] (Smithsonian Folkways Recordings/UNESCO-UNES08047, 1980).
60	M. K. Seo [Author and Recorder], 'Tangak'. In the CD of the book *Hanyang Kut: Korean Shaman Ritual Music from Seoul* (*Current Research in Ethnomusicology: Outstanding Dissertations*), Track, Number 20, pp. 165, 171, and 194 (New York & London: Routledge, 2002).
61	B. Salchak [Performer], 'Kham [Shaman Ritual]' [Liner notes and recording by Dina Oiun]. On *Voices from the Distant Steppe*, Track Number 16 [CD] (Real World Records—CDRW41, 1994).
62	K. Yokoyama [Performer], 'Ko-ku (Vacuity)' [Liner notes by Akira Tamba]. On *Japon, Kinshi Turata—Katsuya Yokoyama*, Track Number 2 [CD] (Ocora C 558518 1994).
63	V. G. Anastasija [Performer], 'Vocals and Jajar Frame Drum: A Song for the Khololo Celebration' [Liner notes and recording by Henry Lecomte]. On *Siberia, Vol. 4 Kamtchatka: Dance Drums from Siberian Far East*, Track Number 15 [CD] (Buda Musique—925982, 1994).
64	'Tus' [Liner notes and recording by Jean-Jacques Nattiez and Kazuyuki Tanimoto]. On *Japan: Ainu Songs*, Track Number 10 [CD] (Smithsonian Folkways Recordings/UNESCO-UNES08047, 1980).
65	'Upopo' [Liner notes and recording by Jean-Jacques Nattiez and Kazuyuki Tanimoto]. On *Japan: Ainu Songs*, Track Number 2 [CD] (Smithsonian Folkways Recordings/UNESCO-UNES08047, 1980).
66	'Smaon' [Liner notes by John Schaefer and recording by David Parsons]. On *The Music of Cambodia* (*Royal Court Music*), Track Number 19 [CD] (Celestial Harmonies 13075-2, 1993).
67	'Beliatn Sentiyu Suite' (excerpt) [Liner notes and recording by Philip Yampolsky]. On *Music of Indonesia, Vol. 17: Kalimantan: Dayak Ritual and Festival Music*, Track Number 14 [CD] (Smithsonian Folkways Recordings SFW40444, 1998).
68	P. Pargi Mina [Performer] (1984), 'Devi Ambav ro dhak' [Recording by David Roche]. On *The Garland Encyclopedia of World Music, Vol. 5: South Asia: The Indian Subcontinent Audio*, Track Number 13 [CD] (Garland Publishing, 2000).
69	'Buddhist Ritual Music and Chant in Honor of A-phyi' (1976). [Recording by Mireille Helffer]. On *The Garland Encyclopedia of World Music, Vol. 5: South Asia: The Indian Subcontinent Audio*, Track Number 24 [CD] (Garland Publishing, 2000).

70	'Ritual Chanting (Ngāyung) of Mediums (to Rid the Settlement of Malign Forest Spirits) [Produced by Harold C. Conklin]. On *Hanunóo Music from the Philippines*, Side 1, Band 11 [LP] (Ethnic Folkways Library FE 4466, 1956).
71	'Châu Văn' [Liner notes by Trần Văn Khê]. On *Viêtnam Musique de Huê: Chants de Huê et Musique de Cour*, Track Number 18 [CD] (Inedit—W 260073, 2005).
72	'Dabuih' [Produced by Margaret J. Kartomi]. On *The Music of Islam, Vol. 15: Muslim Music Of Indonesia, Aceh And West Sumatra*, Disc 1, Track Number 16 [CD] (Celestial Harmonies 14232, 1998).
73	'Dzikir Samman: Allahu Allah' [Produced by Philip Yampolsky]. On *Music of Indonesia, Vol. 19: Music of Maluku: Halmahera, Buru, Kei*, Track Number 17 [CD] (Smithsonian Folkways Recordings SFW40446, 1999).
74	'Gamelan Salunding, Tenganan—Gending Sekar Gadung' [Liner notes and recording by David Lewiston]. On *Bali: Gamelan & Kecak*, Track Number 5 [CD] (Elektra Nonesuch—9 79204-2, 1989).
75	'Musique des anciennes cérémonies religieuses avec une guru sibaso: Begu deleng/ Odak-odak/ Pertang-tang sabe/ Peseluken' [Liner notes by Artur Simon]. On *Sumatra: Musiques Des Batak Karo, Toba, Simalungun*, Track Number 2 [CD] (Inedit—W 260061, 1995).
76	'Gondang "Pangelek-elek Ni Jujungan Ro"' [Liner notes by Artur Simon]. On *Sumatra: Musiques Des Batak Karo, Toba, Simalungun*, Track Number 5 [CD] (Inedit—W 260061, 1995).
77	'Kecak From Blakiuh Near Mengwi' [Liner notes by Wolfgang Hamm and Rika Reissler]. On *Bali: A Suite of Tropical Music and Sound*, Track Number 9 [CD] (World Network 35, 1995).
78	'Sekaha Ganda Sari, Bona—Kecak' [Liner notes and recording by David Lewiston]. On *Bali: Gamelan & Kecak*, Track Number 8 [CD] (Elektra Nonesuch—9 79204-2, 1989).
79	'Kuda Kepang'. On *The Ethnic Sampler 4*, Track Number 25 [CD] (APM Music, Sonoton—SAS 107, 1995).
80	'Phléng khlom' [Liner notes and recording by Jacques Brunet]. On *Cambodia: Folk and Ceremonial Music*, Track Number 12 [CD] (Smithsonian Folkways Recordings/ UNESCO-UNES08068, 1996).
81	'Pheng Phi Fa' [Liner notes and recording by Jacques Brunet]. On *Laos—Traditional Music Of The South*, Track Number 1 [CD] (UNESCO—D 8042, 1992).

82	'Nanduni Pattu—Song to Bhadrakali' [Liner notes and recordings by Rolf Killius]. On *Ritual Music of Kerala*, Track Number 5 [CD] (Archives and Research Centre for Ethnomusicology—ARCE00028, 2008).
83	'Burmese "Pwe"' [Liner notes and recording by the collection of La Meri]. On *Exotic Dances*, Track Number 4 [LP] (Folkways Records FP 52, 1950).
84	'A Healing Ceremony at Kg' [Liner notes and compilation by Marina Roseman]. On *Dream Songs and Healing Sounds in the Rainforests of Malaysia*, Track Number 10 [CD] (Smithsonian Folkways Recordings SFW40417, 1995).
85	'Piphat Mon: Spirit Dance' [Liner notes by Andrew Shahriari]. On *Silk, Spirits and Song—Music from North Thailand*, Track Number 12 [CD] (Lyrichord—LYRCD 7451, 2006).
86	'Perdjuritan (Soldiers Dance)' [Edited by Henry Cowell]. On *Music of Indonesia*, Track Number 7 [CD] (Folkways Records FE 4537, 1961).
87	'Invocation to the Goddess Yeshiki Mamo (Tantric Puja) Part II' [Recording by Manfred Junius and P. C. Misra]. On *The Lamas of The Nyingmapa Monastery of Dehra Dun—Tibetan Ritual*, Track Number 2 [CD]. (UNESCO Collection of Traditional Music of the World Series, Auvidis – D 8034, 1991).
88	'Salai Jin, Pt. 2' [Produced by Margaret J. Kartomi]. On *Music of Indonesia: Maluku & North Maluku*, Disc 1, Track Number 5 [CD] (Celestial Harmonies 14232, 2003).
89	'Bandina Devi ninna charana' [Liner notes and recordings by Luisse Gunnel]. On *Inde: Rythmes et Chants du Nord—Karnataka, Rythmes—Comptines, Chants dévotionnels*, Track Number 43 [CD] (Buda Musique—1978542, 2001).
90	'Tovil (Drum Dance)'. On *Sri Lanka, Nepal & Bhutan: Ritual, Festival, Masked Dance and Drum Traditions*, Track Number 1 [CD] (Music of the Earth, 2015).
91	'Kohomba Kankariya (Dance Ritual)'. On *Sri Lanka, Nepal & Bhutan: Ritual, Festival, Masked Dance and Drum Traditions*, Track Number 2 [CD] (Music of the Earth, 2015).
92	'Baha Festival Dance' [Liner notes and recordings by Deben Bhattacharya (1973)]. On *Music of the Santal Tribe*, Track Number 11 [CD] (ARC Music Productions EUCD2510, 2014).
93	'Uunu' [Liner notes and recording by Hugo Zemp]. On *Solomon Islands: Fataleka and Baegu Music from Malaita*, Track Number 1 [CD] (Smithsonian Folkways Recordings/UNESCO-UNES08027, 1973).

94	'Kabu Kei Conua Group [Performer], 'Yavulo, Yavulo, Vuni Maqo E Buto' [Liner notes by Ad Linkels]. On *Viti Levu: The Multicultural Heart of Fiji*, Track Number 14 [CD] (Pan 2096, 2000).
95	'Seance Gisalo Song by Aiba with Weeping' [Liner notes and recording by Steven Feld]. On *Bosavi: Rainforest Music from Papua New Guinea*, Disc Number 3, Track Number 4 [CD] (Smithsonian Folkways Recordings SFW40487, 2001).
96	'Songs of the Spirits (Newet)—Lo, Torres' [Liner notes by Alexandre François and Monika Stern]. On *Music of Vanuatu: Celebrations and Mysteries*, Track Number 39 [CD] (Inedit—W 260147, 2013).
97	'Alujà de Xangô Aira' (2005). On *Brésil: Les Eaux D'Oxala—Afro-Brazilian Ritual: Candomblé*, Track Number 8 [CD] (Buda Musique 92576-2, 1973).
98	'Shipibo Song' [Produced by Alan Jabbour and Mickey Hart]. On *The Spirit Cries: Music of the Rain Forests of South America & The Caribbean*, Track Number 12 [CD] (Rykodisc—RCD 10250, 1993).
99	'Selk'ham-Tierra del Fuego-Arrow Ordeal Chant' [Produced by Alan Lazar]. On *Anthology of Central and South American Indian Music*, Disc 2, Track Number 14 [CD] (Smithsonian Folkways Recordings/Folkways Records FW04542/FE 4542, 1975).
100	'Kumanti' [Produced by Alan Jabbour and Mickey Hart]. On *The Spirit Cries: Music of the Rain Forests of South America & The Caribbean*, Track Number 20 [CD] (Rykodisc—RCD 10250, 1993).
101	'Warao Male Hoarotu Shaman's Curing Song' [Recorded by Dale A. Olsen]. On *The Garland Encyclopedia of World Music, Vol. 2: South America, Mexico, Central America, and the Caribbean Audio CD*, Track Number 3 [CD] (Garland Publishing, 1998).
102	'Curing Ritual' [Produced by Alan Lazar]. On *Anthology of Central and South American Indian Music*, Disc 1, Track Number 19 [CD] (Smithsonian Folkways Recordings/Folkways Records FW04542/FE 4542, 1975).
103	'Warao Male Wisiratu Shaman's Curing Song' [Recorded by Dale A. Olsen]. On *The Garland Encyclopedia of World Music, Vol. 2: South America, Mexico, Central America, and the Caribbean Audio CD*, Track Number 3 [CD] (Garland Publishing, 1998).
104	'Yanomamö Male Shaman's Curing Song' [Recorded by Pitts Collection]. On *The Garland Encyclopedia of World Music, Vol. 2: South America, Mexico, Central America, and the Caribbean Audio CD*, Track Number 1 [CD] (Garland Publishing, 1998).

105	'Yekuana Male Shaman's Curing Song' [Recorded by Walter Coppens]. On *The Garland Encyclopedia of World Music, Vol. 2: South America, Mexico, Central America, and the Caribbean Audio CD*, Track Number 2 [CD] (Garland Publishing, 1998).
106	'Healing Song' [Produced by Alan Jabbour and Mickey Hart]. On *The Spirit Cries: Music of the Rain Forests of South America & the Caribbean*, Track Number 11 [CD] (Rykodisc—RCD 10250, 1993).
107	'Shango Cult: Annual Ceremony in a Rural Area' [Liner notes and recordings by George Eaton Simpson]. On *Cult Music of Trinidad*, Track Number 7 [CD] (Smithsonian Folkways Recordings/Folkways Records FW04478/FE 4478, 1961).
108	'Shamanistic Ritual: The Dance' [Liner notes and recordings by Peter Kloos]. On *The Maroni River Caribs of Surinam*, Track Number 11 [CD] (Pan PANKCD4005, 1997).
109	'Winti Medley' [Liner notes and recordings by Clifford Entes]. On *Creole Music of Surinam*, Track Number 8, 33:25' [CD] (Smithsonian Folkways Recordings/Folkways Records FW04233/FE 4233, 1978).
110	'Abelagudahani' [Produced by Alan Jabbour and Mickey Hart]. On *The Spirit Cries: Music of the Rain Forests of South America & the Caribbean*, Track Number 1 [CD] (Rykodisc—RCD 10250, 1993).
111	Gropo Laka [Performer], 'Danca de tambor pulaya / Pulaya Drum Dance' [Liner notes and production by Sten Sandahl]. On *Music from Honduras*, Disc 1, Track Number 3 [CD] (Caprice Records CAP 21632, 2000).
112	'Salve' [Recorded and produced by Isidro Bobadilla and Morton Marks]. On *Afro-Dominican Music from San Cristobal, Dominican Republic*, Track Number 3 [CD] (Smithsonian Folkways Recording/Folkways Records FW04285/FE 4285, 1983).
113	'Kumina "Bailo"' [Recorded and produced by Edward P.G. Seaga]. On *Folk Music of Jamaica*, Track Number 4 [CD] (Folkways Records FW04453/FE 4453, 1956).
114	Jo Leh [Recorded and produced by Kenneth M. Bilby]. On *Drums of Defiance: Maroon Music from the Earliest Free Black Communities of Jamaica*, Track Number 14 [CD] (Smithsonian Folkways Recordings SFW40412, 1992).
115	'Vodoun Dance (Three Vodoun Drums)' [Liner notes and recordings by Harold Courlander]. On *Music of Haiti: Vol. 2, Drums of Haiti*, Track Number 1 [CD] (Smithsonian Folkways Recordings/Folkways Records FW04403/FE 4403, 1950).

116	'Petro Dance (Two Drums)'. On *Music of Haiti: Vol. 2, Drums of Haiti*, Track Number 5 [CD] (Smithsonian Folkways Recordings/ Folkways Records FW04403/FE 4403, 1950).
117	'Bear Dance' [Produced by Gertrude Prokosch Kurath]. On *Songs and Dances of the Great Lakes Indians*, Disc 1, Track Number 7 [CD] (Smithsonian Folkways Recordings/Folkways Records FW04003/FE 4003, 1956).
118	'Peyote Song: First Song Cycle' [Produced by Michael Asch]. On *Anthology of North American Indian and Eskimo Music*, Disc 1, Track Number 13 [CD] (Smithsonian Folkways Recordings/ Folkways Records FW04541/FE 4541, 1973).
119	'Peyote Song' [Produced by John Bierhorst]. On *Cry from the Earth: Music of the North American Indians*, Disc 1, Track Number 31 [CD] (Smithsonian Folkways Recordings/Folkways Records FW37777/FA 37777, 1979).
120	'Crown Dance' [Produced by Charlotte Heth and Terence Winch]. On *Creation's Journey: Native American Music*, Track Number 4 [CD] (Smithsonian Folkways Recordings SFW40410, 1994).
121	'Drum Dance' [Produced by John Bierhorst]. On *Cry from the Earth: Music of the North American Indians*, Disc 1, Track Number 12 [CD] (Smithsonian Folkways Recordings/Folkways Records FW37777/FA 37777, 1979).
122	Peter Webster [Performer], 'Medicine Man Song' [Liner notes and production by Ida Halpern]. On *Nootka Indian Music of the Pacific North West Coast, Disc 1*, Track Number 4 [CD] (Smithsonian Folkways Recordings/Folkways Records FW04524/FE 4524, 1974).
123	'Huichol—Peyote Dance' [Produced by Henrietta Yurchenco]. On *Indian Music of Mexico*, Track Number 9 [CD] (Smithsonian Folkways Recordings/Folkways Records FW04413/FE 4413, 1952).
124	'Yaqui—Deer Dance' [Produced by Henrietta Yurchenco]. On *Indian Music of Mexico*, Track Number 8 [CD] (Smithsonian Folkways Recordings/Folkways Records FW04413/FE 4413, 1952).
125	'Wolf Dance' [Liner notes and production by Ida Halpern]. On *Nootka Indian Music of the Pacific North West Coast, Disc 2*, Track Number 2 [CD] (Smithsonian Folkways Recordings/Folkways Records FW04524/FE 4524, 1974).

9. An Ethnomusicology of Spiritual Realities

Jeffers Engelhardt

In reflecting on the connection between music and spiritual realities, I begin this chapter by revisiting a performance of The Campbell Brothers at Amherst College in the mid-2000s. This brings me into a consideration of ethnomusicology's attitude toward religion and other-than-human agency in its disciplinary history and practices. As the field has moved from its positivist, comparative origins through its cultural turns and into non-secular methodologies, its story has been one that moves from disentangling music and religion as exchangeable secular categories toward recognising the entanglements of sound, spiritual realities, and ethnomusicologists. To make this movement tangible, I bring into conversation two ethnomusicologists of music and religion—Jeff Todd Titon and Melvin L. Butler—whose scholarly works exemplify 'disentangled' and 'entangled' ethnomusicology respectively. In conclusion, I connect their methodological positions back to the world of The Campbell Brothers.

I. The Campbell Brothers: 'Can You Feel It?'

The Campbell Brothers are widely celebrated bearers of the sacred steel gospel music tradition nurtured since the 1930s in the House of God (Keith Dominion) and Church of the Living God (Jewell Dominion) churches—African American Holiness-Pentecostal denominations found across the United States. Sacred steel gospel gets its sound and name from the foundational presence of pedal and lap steel guitar in the style, introduced into the Keith Dominion by brothers Troman, Willie, and Henry Eason in the late 1930s/early 1940s and the Jewell Dominion by Lorenzo Harrison in the early 1940s. Steel guitars' presence in Keith and Jewell Dominions was part of the 'Hawaiian guitar' (kikā kila) vogue emerging from Joseph Kekuku's kī hōalu or slack-key style that transformed popular music in the United States in the early decades of the twentieth century.[1] In the following decades, Henry Nelson, Robert Randolph, Glenn Lee, Sonny Treadway, Aubrey Ghent, and The Campbell Brothers brought sacred steel closer to the gospel mainstream and, to varying degrees, into spaces beyond House of God and Church of the Living God worship.

At their Amherst performance, The Campbell Brothers—Chuck, Phillip, Carlton, and Darick Campbell—played material from their 2005 Ropeadope release *Can You Feel It?*[2] and gospel classics but not the 'praise', 'shout', and 'jamming' music of Holiness-Pentecostal worship that creates atmospheres in which listeners can 'fall out' in Holy Spirit-infused dance and glossolalia. The powers of sacred steel are many: the kinetic effects of up-tempo backbeat 'framming', the at-ease shuffle of a mid-tempo gospel hymn, or unexpected harmonic moves around a beloved melody. But it is the steel guitar's capacity to speak, sing, growl, sweeten, quake, and run melodically;[3] to weave around a rhythmic groove, flash across the fretboard, and tarry around pitches; and to dominate in volume, tone, and sound a church or performance venue in the hands of a master artist like the late Darick Campbell that defines the world of sacred steel. With exacting knob and pedal control over the onset and tonal qualities of their sound and the liquid slide of pitches under the steel bar, sacred steel guitars can sing as song surrogates in familiar hymns and gospel treatments—Darick Campbell's rendering of Sam Cooke's 'A Change Is Gonna Come'[4] spoke in this non-metaphorical sense to the Amherst audience. Sacred steel's proximity to the human

---

[1] Robert Stone, *Sacred Steel: Inside an African American Steel Guitar Tradition* (Urbana, IL: University of Illinois Press, 2010).

[2] The Campbell Brothers, *Can You Feel It?* (Ropeadope, 2005).

[3] See Arhoolie Foundation, 'SACRED STEEL' [41:43], online video recording, *YouTube*, 6 April 2020, https://www.youtube.com/watch?v=yRZS86tmvDA&t=2501s&ab_channel=ArhoolieFoundation

[4] See Del Grace, 'Gospel of Sacred Steel—the Campbell Brothers 2020' [16:24], online video recording, *YouTube*, 25 February 2020, https://www.youtube.com/watch?v=SGqaWjw1wyI&t=984s&ab_channel=DelGrace

voice centres it in House of God and Church of the Living God prayer and meditation by channelling a player's testimony, understanding of, and material contact with the word like a gospel singer. Famously, singers would stop singing to hear Henry Nelson speak through a sacred steel gospel hymn. Their tonal turns, articulations, and breathing rhythms intertwine the instrument, body, and familiar lyrics into an amplified, extended voice.[5] At other moments, sacred steel guitarists translate ecstatic gestures of praise and shout to their instrument through electrifying vibrato, growling sonorities, feverish accelerations of tempo and intensifying harmonic textures, and acrobatic leaps that both sonify and guide the holy dancing at the front of a church or, like at Amherst, the movement of bodies in a club space during the breakdown of a gospel blues number.

The sonic–spiritual power of sacred steel gospel moves from word to body and from Holiness-Pentecostal worship to non-church performance venues and back again, tracing 'interworldly'[6] paths between the spiritual and the material and transitions between forms of 'deep listening'[7] that may or may not involve relationships with other-than-human beings. Moving alongside one another, entrained by sacred steel's driving grooves, mentally taking up the words the guitar speaks, the bodies present at a Campbell Brothers performance foreground the 'problem' of musical experience and spiritual realities not only for scholars, but for believing musicians, non-religious audiences, and those positioned otherwise. This 'problem' is, of course, an artifact of a secularity that draws strong distinctions between spaces of religion and non-religion—a historically limited form of social imagination that nevertheless shapes music studies profoundly.

The Campbell Brothers spoke to this in conversation at Amherst, rearticulating histories of play between Saturday night and Sunday morning in Black music and the Black church, the misgivings of others

---

5 See Ashon T. Crawley, *Blackpentecostal Breath: The Aesthetics of Possibility* (New York: Fordham University Press, 2016); Elisabeth Le Guin, *Boccherini's Body: An Essay in Carnal Musicology* (Berkeley, CA: University of California Press, 2005); and Maurice O. Wallace, *King's Vibrato: Modernism, Blackness, and the Sonic Life of Martin Luther King Jr.* (Durham, NC: Duke University Press, 2022).

6 Braxton D. Shelley, *Healing for the Soul: Richard Smallwood, the Vamp, and the Gospel Imagination* (New York: Oxford University Press, 2021), p. 35.

7 Judith Becker, *Deep Listeners: Music, Emotion, and Trancing* (Bloomington, IN: Indiana University Press, 2004).

about gospel musicians performing in non-church venues for the unsaved or extractive white listeners, and the personal and spiritual challenges they face because of their careers. Chuck Campbell, pedal steel player in The Campbell Brothers and, along with his brothers, raised in the family of Bishop Charles Campbell, described the dynamic of non-church performances: embodied responses to their music are outwardly similar in church and non-church atmospheres—hypothetically, a Holiness-Pentecostal believer and an unsaved fan could be dancing and moving the same way, side by side, expressing sonic experiences that index spiritual movement and/or performers' mastery. The ambiguity of these scripted, predictable movements in the affective atmospheres of church (is the shout 'authentic'?) and non-church (is that a fan or a believer?) performance was an everyday part of Chuck Campbell's musicking and religious life, and reconciling other-than-human agency and musical charisma in non-church sacred steel performance was something Campbell was happy to leave undone. For this reason, others in the House of God and Church of the Living God communities forestall the threat of ambiguity by swearing off non-church sacred steel performance, keeping the words it gives and the bodies it moves in the interworld of Holiness-Pentecostal worship.

II. Humans and Other-Than-Humans

My experience with The Campbell Brothers as a fan and in conversation helps clarify what is at stake in the ethnomusicology of spiritual realities. In my current work, I am grappling with ethnomusicology's attitude toward religion as a whole through the frame of other-than-human agency. A formidable question at the centre of this project cuts across music studies, anthropology, and theology: can other-than-human beings enter directly into ethnomusicology's record, or are they only ever present second-hand through the relational ontologies of humans and other-than-humans? It is possible to sit with Chuck Campbell's both/and position, a position echoed in ethnomusicology's current moment, emerging from its foundations in comparative positivist and exclusively human culturalist approaches. Ethnomusicology's both/and position might be: divine, other-than-human beings and sacred objects are agents in the world with social and sonic relationships to humans.

Divine, other-than-human beings and sacred objects become agents in the world through the sounds of ritual practice. Sacred sound, whether composed by humans or revealed to them, mediates—is in the midst of, as infrastructure—the binds between humans, the divine, and other-than-human beings. Performing sacred traditions can be an expedient means of accessing or strengthening social networks. Similarly, sacred sound realises transitions into life and into death, giving voice to the cosmologies, memories, and spaces of which it is part.

The invitation to address connections between music and spiritual realities is a timely one for me, writing here as an ethnomusicologist whose research and teaching never stray very far from music, religion, and questions of secular methods and critique. Ethnomusicologies at the intersections of music studies, sound studies, religious studies, and theology have, over the past decade or so, begun a turn toward non-secular methodologies and modes of representation. This is a continuing departure from much of ethnomusicology's disciplinary histories and extensive prehistories. Alongside its kindred, methodologically atheist or methodologically agnostic disciplines in the social sciences, mainstream ethnomusicology proceeded through the twentieth century on the basis of music being a 'humanly organised' category of sound.[8] The musicalisation of sound in this frame is an inherently secular move: music mediates human relationships, expression, and experience, and other-than-human agents are written out of ethnomusicology, scare-quoted as the 'voices of deities' or 'songs of spiritual beings' or 'revealed sounds'. In the field of ethnomusicology, which has carved out space for itself in the academy as a 'sciencing about music',[9] the sonic agency of other-than-human beings as listeners, gift-receivers, composers, sharers of knowledge, and communicators through sacred voice and materials had almost no place. For ethnomusicologists operating in worlds of secular critique and reproducible, rigorous analysis, other-than-human agency and one's position as a religious insider or as vulnerable to spiritual powers were framed out of the discipline. Ethnomusicologists could report on research participants' descriptions

---

8   John Blacking, *How Music Is Man?* (Seattle, WA: University of Washington Press, 1973).

9   Alan P. Merriam, *The Anthropology of Music* (Evanston, IL: Northwestern University Press, 1964), p. 25.

of the spiritual power and divine origins of music,[10] but they could not leverage sonic theologies or the knowledge of divine encounter. Theirs was a knowledge about practice rather than of practice; functionalist interpretations of divine audiences and ritual propriety rather than knowledge of the sonic–spiritual entanglements of human and other-than-human beings. For much of ethnomusicology's histories, then, addressing connections between music and spiritual realities meant wielding the blunt instrument of 'music' on the secular oxymoron of 'spiritual realities'.

III. Ethnomusicology, Religion, and Spiritual Realities

Ethnomusicology's histories are rooted in positivist anthropological, ethnological, and national/regional folklore collection projects and fraught comparative musicological projects in the nineteenth and twentieth centuries. Since its beginnings, ethnomusicology has had an abiding connection to religion as a culturalised, secular category of practice and experience; a category of difference in which music is (nearly) exclusively human, with gods, spirits, and other-than-humans disentangled from musical sound, behaviour, and experience. Unlike the concept of music, which has long been critiqued and rethought in light of different lexicons and ontologies and, more recently, as a discrete sonic object and kind of species-specific social practice within a broader field of sound, the concept of religion is, by and large, still taken as second nature within much ethnomusicology, despite a rich body of social scientific and humanistic work examining its particular Enlightenment, colonial, and secular genealogies.[11] There is not yet a strong sense of the extractive, colonising tendencies of designations like

---

10 See, for instance, David P. McAllester, *Enemy Way Music: A Study of Social and Esthetic Values as Seen in Navaho Music* (Cambridge, MA: Peabody Museum of American Archeology and Ethnology, 1954); Kristina Nelson, *The Art of Reciting the Qur'an* (Cairo: American University in Cairo Press, 1985); Regula Burckhardt Qureshi, *Sufi Music of India and Pakistan: Sound, Context and Meaning in Qawwali* (Cambridge, UK: Cambridge University Press, 1986).

11 Jim Sykes, *The Musical Gift: Sonic Generosity in Post-War Sri Lanka* (New York: Oxford University Press, 2018).

Jewish music, music and Islam, Christian musical repertoires, or Vedic music theory, for instance. And, crucially, there is not yet a strong sense of how ethnomusicologists have written with and against the concept of religion as they attune themselves to sacred voices and places, endeavour to be 'with the gods in a musical way',[12] and preserve in-between spaces in which they are neither 'unwelcome inquisitors' in others' worlds nor renderers of those worlds in spaces ethnomusicologists 'dominate utterly'.[13]

At the same time, the sacredness of sound (its material and perceptual links to divine powers and right intentions)—established, in part, through the globalised origins and reach of Abrahamic and Dharmic tradition—has ingrained in ethnomusicologists a tendency to think in terms of religions (sometimes without enough distance from the transcendental aesthetics of European Romanticism that shape their habits of thought). Ethnomusicology operates through the making and recognition of religious genres, histories, repertoires, instruments, performers, and listeners or the common interpretive move of describing religious/secular/spiritual boundary maintenance and crossing. Although music and spiritual realities are entangled, secular ethnomusicologies disentangle them through the frame of religion. Beyond the mainstream of twentieth-century European and North American ethnomusicology, however, the situation can be different, with the connection between music and spiritual realities being commonplace. Some of the first 'musicologies' were 'sonic theologies'[14] described in the scriptural, poetic, and literary language of the Rig Veda,

---

12   Steven M. Friedson, *Remains of Ritual: Northern Gods in a Southern Land* (Chicago, IL: University of Chicago Press, 2009), p. 8.
13   Richard C. Jankowsky, 'Music, Spirit Possession and the In-Between: Ethnomusicological Inquiry and the Challenge of Trance', *Ethnomusicology Forum* 16.2 (2007), 185–208 (at 191).
14   See Andrew Alter, 'Expressing Sonic Theology: Understanding Ritual Action in a Himalayan Festival', *Ethnomusicology Forum* 28.3 (2019), 321–37; Guy L. Beck, *Sonic Theology: Hinduism and Sacred Sound* (Charleston, SC: University of South Carolina Press, 1993); Katherine J. Hagedorn, 'Toward a Theology of Sound', *Harvard Divinity Bulletin* 34.2 (2006), https://bulletin.hds.harvard.edu/toward-a-theology-of-sound/; Eadem, '"Where the Transcendent Breaks into Time": Toward a Theology of Sound in Afro-Cuban Regla de Ochá', in *Theorizing Sound Writing*, ed. by Deborah Kapchan (Middletown, CT: Wesleyan University Press, 2017), pp. 216–32; and Jacob Neusner, *Judaism's Theological Voice: The Melody of the Talmud* (Chicago, IL: University of Chicago Press, 1995).

Gītassara Sutta, Psalms of David, Epistles of Paul, and Sura 96 al-'Alaq. Texts like these, in turn, shaped the thinking of figures like Purandara Dasa, Yunqi Zhuhong, Maimonides, Augustine, and al-Ghazālī, who are central to sacred musicological traditions in their own right.

One can observe ethnomusicology shifting—however incompletely and in fits and starts—from a secular approach disentangling religion and music along cultural lines to a non-secular approach embracing the entanglements of humans and other-than-humans in ethnomusicological knowledge. Disentangling music and religion is a culturalist project ethnomusicology has been invested in for most of its history; entangling sound, humans, and other-than-humans is an ethnomusicology that transforms the secular relationship of music and religion. Simply put, the connection between music and spiritual realities is located in those entanglements.

To locate the transitions between disentangled and entangled ethnomusicologies, I will spend a moment here contrasting work that represents those approaches. Jeff Todd Titon and Melvin L. Butler are ethnomusicologists who theorise positionality, stance, belief, and secular/non-secular methodologies with great care in their scholarship. The two decades of overlap in Titon's and Butler's work (2000s–20s) offer us compelling models of disentangled and entangled ethnomusicologies inhabiting a common disciplinary moment within radically diverse soundscapes of Baptist and Pentecostal Christianities in the United States and the Caribbean and different scholarly projects. Titon, whose work I would characterise as secure in its agnostic methodology, is committed to bracketing off religious experience and other-than-human agency in understanding 'people making music';[15] Butler, whose work I would characterise as verging with a light touch into methodological theism, is committed to integrating his life as 'an academic and spiritual being'[16] through an epistemology grounded in musicking and the Holy Spirit. For a fuller accounting of how Titon's and Butler's held identities and positions shape their work, one must, of course, engage with the richness of their scholarship as a whole.

---

15 *Worlds of Music: An Introduction to the Music of the World's Peoples*, ed. by Jeff Todd Titon (New York: Schirmer Books, 1992), p. xxi.

16 Melvin L. Butler, 'Musical Style and Experience in a Brooklyn Pentecostal Church: An "Insider's" Perspective', *Current Musicology*, 70 (2000), 33–60 (at 38).

IV. Disentangled and Entangled Ethnomusicologies: Jeff Todd Titon and Melvin L. Butler

In *Powerhouse for God: Speech, Chant, and Song in an Appalachian Baptist Church*, and multiple theoretical reflections on ethnomusicological fieldwork in religious communities, Titon makes the case for a disentangled ethnomusicology that is deeply sympathetic to accounts of other-than-human agency in musical creation and relationship in religious experience.[17] At the same time, Titon, informed by decades of fieldwork with Baptist and Pentecostal Christians in the United States, approaches 'religious belief and practice as a cultural system'— religion as a secular form of difference in the culturalist vein familiar to ethnomusicology.[18] In other words, religion is not a different kind of difference. Titon's conviction is that a Husserlian bracketing of other-than-human agency and experiences of the sacred within the frame of culture is essential to ethnomusicology as a social science (as opposed to theology): 'I mean to be phenomenologically agnostic, "bracketing" or setting aside the question of whether their worldview is true or false outside of their cultural setting while representing them as if it is true within it'.[19] This means that Titon encounters the testimony of someone like Brother Belvin Hurt receiving a gospel song from the Holy Spirit as an element of religious belief to be examined for its relationship with musical behaviour.[20] Ethnographic accounts of other-than-human agency are bracketed and disentangled, with Titon moving on to an ethnomusicological analysis of the structure and lyrical content of Brother Hurt's song apart from his 'passive role'[21] in the composition

---

17 Jeff Todd Titon, *Powerhouse for God: Speech, Chant, and Song in an Appalachian Baptist Church*, 2nd ed. (Knoxville, TN: University of Tennessee Press, 2018).

18 Jeff Todd Titon, 'Reflexivity and the Study of Religious Folklife', revised response delivered at the Annual Meeting of the American Folklore Society, 1989 (Unpublished manuscript, 1991), p. 5.

19 Ibid., 9. See also Titon, *Powerhouse for God*, pp. 477–78; and Jeff Todd Titon, 'Ethnography in the Study of Congregational Music', in *Studying Congregational Music: Key Issues, Methods, and Theoretical Perspectives*, ed. by Andrew Mall, Jeffers Engelhardt, and Monique Ingalls (New York: Routledge, 2021), pp. 64–80 (at 65).

20 Jeff Todd Titon, 'A Song from the Holy Spirit', *Ethnomusicology* 24.2 (1980), 223–31.

21 Ibid., 228.

process under the 'anointment of the Spirit'. Might the 'unusual'[22] structure of Brother Hurt's gospel song be attributed to the Holy Spirit, one wonders?

In an ethnomusicology where other-than-human agency is bracketed off, the humanness of musicking is definitive, and testimonies like Brother Hurt's become part of worldviews and culture. The bracketing moves of an agnostic methodology reserve the social scientific takeaways for human-centred, exclusively human explanations. 'No ethnomusicologist could maintain a scholarly reputation', Titon suggests, 'if he attributed the cause of the religious music and behavior he observed in the field to God. Instead, scholarly reputations have been built on insisting the opposite'.[23] But Titon is also unsatisfied with the exclusive secularity of a scientific paradigm that 'must absolutely reject all absolutist claims to truth'.[24] In later work, Titon seeks to understand the breath-based integration of Old Regular Baptist congregational singing in eastern Kentucky[25] being 'tuned up with the grace of God'— 'in step and deliberately just a bit out of phase'.[26] Early on, Titon did not apprehend how Old Regular Baptists' language of religious experience 'might serve as an explanation of what I considered a technical problem: the integration in their music'.[27] After some time, however, Titon arrives at a different place: 'Was it really metaphor when they spoke of being tuned up with the grace of God? When they spoke of how the Holy Spirit made a melody? Or was it not metaphor at all but their habitual way of thinking, their quite literal belief?'.[28]

This might be as far as an agnostic, disentangled ethnomusicology can take us without admitting the agency of other-than-humans. By listening for and identifying Old Regular Baptists' 'unerring sense for a long period', Titon brings us to the musicalisation of their belief in

---

22   Ibid., 226.
23   Jeff Todd Titon, 'Stance, Role, and Identity in Fieldwork among Folk Baptists and Pentecostals', *American Music* 3.1 (1985), 16–24 (at 22).
24   Ibid., 23.
25   See Various, *Songs of the Old Regular Baptists, Vol. 2* (Smithsonian Folkways, 2003).
26   Jeff Todd Titon, '"Tuned Up with the Grace of God"': Music and Experience among Old Regular Baptists', in *Music in American Religious Experience*, ed. by Philip V. Bohlman, Edith L. Blumhofer, and Maria M. Chow (New York: Oxford University Press, 2006), pp. 311–34 (at 320).
27   Ibid., p. 326.
28   Ibid., p. 328.

a divine presence in their singing.²⁹ Their belief is still bracketed in relativist, cultural terms, however. Religion is, in Titon's final analysis, disentangled in the disciplinary norms of a secular ethnomusicology, mapping onto an emic/etic distinction at the boundary of religious belief.³⁰ Religion-as-belief, then, is a frame that fundamentally shapes Titon's ethnomusicology, and belief, it seems, extends to admitting the agency of other-than-humans into an ethnomusicological paradigm. While Titon is quick to point out that the difference across which the bracketing of belief operates is productive,³¹ he leaves us at a firmly drawn disciplinary boundary: 'By resolutely projecting my role and maintaining my identity as a professional ethnomusicologist', Titon writes, 'I take my place among the unsaved'.³²

But what about the professional ethnomusicologist who has a place among the saved in a community of religious belonging and practice,³³ whose 'epistemological home'³⁴ is at once inside the discipline of ethnomusicology and the world of Pentecostal saints, as in Butler's case? In *Island Gospel: Pentecostal Music and Identity in Jamaica and the United States* (2019) and multiple theoretical meditations on 'observant participation'³⁵ as a believing scholar, Butler models what a theistic methodology can mean for ethnomusicology. 'Because I share the religious beliefs of those whom I am studying', Butler writes, 'I must necessarily hold, for example, that the Holy Spirit is indeed real and is manifested through music. Furthermore, this manifestation is not subject to an individual's "belief" in it, nor is it limited to the "worldview" of a particular group of people'.³⁶ For Butler, there is no bracketing off of other-than-human agency, his religious experience, and the religious experiences of those

---

29 Ibid., p. 330.
30 Marcia Herndon, 'Insiders, Outsiders: Knowing Our Limits, Limiting Our Knowing', *The World of Music* 35.1 (1993), 63–80.
31 See Titon, 'Stance, Role, and Identity', 19. On the nuance this brings to essentialisms of religious insiders/outsiders, see Titon, 'Reflexivity and the Study of Religious Folklife', 8.
32 Titon, 'Stance, Role, and Identity', 18.
33 Melvin L. Butler, *Island Gospel: Pentecostal Music and Identity in Jamaica and the United States* (Urbana, IL: University of Illinois Press, 2019), p. 2.
34 Ibid., p. 13.
35 Barbara Tedlock, 'From Participant Observation to the Observation of Participation: The Emergence of Narrative Ethnography', *Journal of Anthropological Research* 47.1 (1991), 69–94.
36 Butler, 'Musical Style and Experience in a Brooklyn Pentecostal Church', 38.

he works with in an entangled ethnomusicology. His is a flat ontology in which other-than-humans are agents and in relationship with humans not as artifacts of belief (a culturalist approach in which religious beliefs and worldviews are attributes of secular difference, which Butler views as 'ontological colonialism'[37]), but as part of the real. What is bracketed in an entangled, non-secular ethnomusicology, in other words, is the question of cultural difference.

This effects a shift in perspective regarding questions that vex an exclusively secular ethnomusicology—questions of epistemology and ethnographic limits that are erased or bracketed through atheistic, agnostic, and ludic methodologies. Butler describes a moment of 'observation-as-worshipping' at the Glorious Rock Worship Center in Port-au-Prince, Haiti when

> ...a woman at the front right side of the sanctuary began to flail her arms and let out a series of shrieks. Falling to the ground and out of the view of all but those next to her, the woman was experiencing either the joyous touch of the Holy Spirit or an attack of an evil spirit—at least those are the two options into which most churchgoers would relegate her experience. But other Haitian Christians see the woman's apparently involuntary behavior in more nuanced terms. Perhaps it evidenced a spiritual experience more properly situated in the cracks of a rigid holy-evil dichotomy. Or perhaps this was, heaven forbid, a learned behavior—a performance of Pentecostal faith motivated by a desire to express a natural emotion.[38]

A secular approach to this moment moves quickly to questions of the veracity and pragmatism of the woman's experience of or response to 'heated' worship. In this paradigm, her actions were either an authentic expression of 'spiritual transcendence' (a term Butler prefers to 'trance' or 'possession' given his 'belief in the validity of Pentecostal experiences in general'[39]) and, therefore, bracketed beyond what is knowable, or a functional 'distractive outburst'[40] through which she could navigate

---

37 Ibid.
38 Melvin L. Butler, 'Performing Pannkotis Identity in Haiti', in *The Oxford Handbook of Music and World Christianities*, ed. by Suzel Ana Reily and Jonathan M. Dueck (New York: Oxford University Press, 2016), pp. 606–28 (at 616).
39 Melvin L. Butler, '"Nou Kwe nan Sentespri" (We Believe in the Holy Spirit): Music, Ecstasy, and Identity in Haitian Pentecostal Worship', *Black Music Research Journal* 22.1 (2002), 85–125 (at 93, n. 9).
40 Butler, 'Performing Pannkotis Identity in Haiti', p. 617.

the social and spiritual textures of the moment. For Butler, being both the 'Pentecostal researcher' and 'researching Pentecostal',[41] however, this moment landed differently. Given the reality of other-than-human agents, Butler does not need to jump to questions of veracity and pragmatism; the presence of the Holy Spirit in that moment is not contingent on human belief or the authentic manifestation of spiritual transcendence. Instead, Butler's entangled ethnomusicology leads him to a critically nuanced understanding of the woman's 'distractive outburst as an element contributing to the worship service's success. It may have served to outline the limits of exuberance and/or as constructive evidence of the tangibility of spiritual forces'.[42] What gets him there? 'My past experiences in a wide variety of heated worship services', Butler writes,

> ...had prepared me not to know, to accept the uncertainty of it; I had gained a level of intellectual comfort that, despite (or perhaps because of) my allegiance to the faith, the 'legitimacy' of these kinds of practices—the question of whether they really 'are' spiritual manifestations—must lie outside my analytical frame.[43]

I read this 'outside' not as an agnostic bracketing off religion but as an outcome of Butler's epistemology of faith. Could one understand the effects of the woman's actions with such critical nuance within a secular ethnomusicology? Certainly so, and that is precisely my point here: an entangled ethnomusicology can arrive at a critical understanding of religious musicking whose place within the discipline is untroubled and untroubling. Without trying to represent another's subjective experience and lifeworld (or dispel the reality of other-than-human agency by reducing the woman's actions to performance), Butler unites epistemological humility and the reality of other-than-human agency known through not-unscientific methods of experience.[44] His alternation between first- and third-person ethnography is one of the

---

41 Butler, *Island Gospel*, p. 13.
42 Butler, 'Performing Pannkotis Identity in Haiti', p. 617.
43 Ibid., p. 616.
44 Melvin L. Butler, 'Researching Black Congregational Music from a Migratory Point of View: Methods, Challenges, and Strategies', in *Studying Congregational Music: Key Issues, Methods, and Theoretical Perspectives*, ed. by Andrew Mall et al. (London and New York: Routledge, 2021) pp. 174–92 (p. 184).

ways Butler negotiates a theistic methodology, weaving together the 'I' of experiential and faith-born knowledge with the 'they' of theological and positional difference.[45] For Butler, music is the sounding of human/other-than-human relationships irreducible to culture, and his non-secular approach is part of a broader turn in ethnomusicology (including Titon's recent work in eco-ethnomusicology) that opens the discipline to networks of actors, ways of musical knowing, and positioned research less exclusive of other-than-human beings.

Conclusion

Past approaches to the question of what makes religious music religious[46] focused, by and large, on the humanness of music and the powers of sound to forge and bind religious communities or transmit religious ideologies. Style and tradition matter most here: an ethics of style in which what *sounds* good and right *is* good and right[47] and the reproduction of musical traditions that connect to religious orthodoxies and authentic routes of transmission.[48] Recent decolonising turns toward flat ontological approaches have begun to displace the centrality of the human in ethnomusicology. 'Taking, however, our research associates seriously', writes Bernd Brabec de Mori,

> ...we have to apply an ontological pluralism: Although we 'know' that spirits do not exist outside of the human mind, people in the community in question may likewise 'know' that they do exist, and that it is possible, and in certain circumstances perfectly reasonable, to socialize with a tree.[49]

---

45 Butler, '"Nou Kwe nan Sentespri" (We Believe in the Holy Spirit)', 94–95, n. 12.
46 Lois Ibsen al Faruqi, 'What Makes "Religious Music" Religious?', in *Sacred Sound: Music in Religious Thought and Practice*, ed. by Joyce L. Irwin (Chico, CA: Scholars Press, 1983), pp. 21–34; Philip V. Bohlman, 'Is All Music Religious?', *Black Sacred Music* 8.1 (1994), 3–12.
47 Timothy Rommen, *Mek Some Noise: Gospel Music and the Ethics of Style in Trinidad* (Berkeley, CA: University of California Press, 2007).
48 Jeffers Engelhardt, *Singing the Right Way: Orthodox Christians and Secular Enchantment in Estonia* (New York: Oxford University Press, 2015); Jaime Jones, 'Music, History, and the Sacred in South Asia', in *The Cambridge History of World Music*, ed. by Philip V. Bohlman (Cambridge, UK: Cambridge University Press, 2013); Anna Schultz, *Singing a Hindu Nation: Marathi Devotional Performance and Nationalism* (New York: Oxford University Press, 2013).
49 Bernd Brabec de Mori, 'Musical Spirits and Powerful Voices: On the Origins of Song', *Yearbook for Traditional Music* 49 (2017), 114–28 (at 189).

I encounter this turn toward flat ontologies in the careful wording of scholars like Katherine Hagedorn who, in theorising a theology of sound in oricha worship, centres other-than-human agents unproblematically and without qualification:

> The batá drums are crucial in this performance process, because they not only respond to the praise songs offered by the lead singer and guide the movements of the congregants, but also speak to the orichas 'in their own language'. Consecrated batá drums are inhabited by an oricha known as Añá, who has the power to make the rhythms of the drums intelligible to the other orichas, so that the earthly pleas for manifestation of the deities through possession performance may be heard and understood by these divine entities.[50]

Positioned as an ethnomusicologist and Santería initiate, Hagedorn models in her non-secular methodology not only a connection between music and spiritual reality, but the selfsameness of sound, spirits, consecrated material, 'divine utterances',[51] and the real.

Returning to The Campbell Brothers, Chuck Campbell's clarification of his E-ninth tuning system being revealed or gifted by God is an invitation to listen and be moved through the sonic-material expression of other-than-human agency. In an interview with sacred steel scholar Robert Stone, Campbell speaks of his tuning system:

> Right, and it had a sound, the country western players didn't like. But it was the most beautiful sounding guitar I've ever had for church. And at that point, what I did then was had an E ninth up top, and I had it and the way I got my tuning, which is from God. You got to be.[52]

To turn from an ethnomusicology that humanises sound as music toward a flat ontology in which Campbell's tuning system 'from God' is as real as the dancing bodies of agnostic clubgoers gets us to a kind of ethnomusicology more capable of addressing the spiritual reality of music (not least as it pivots from humanist identity paradigms).[53] As

---

50   Hagedorn, 'Toward a Theology of Sound'.
51   Katherine J. Hagedorn, *Divine Utterances: The Performance of Afro-Cuban Santería* (Washington, DC: Smithsonian Institution Press, 2001).
52   Robert L. Stone, 'Interview with Chuck Campbell', *Arhoolie Foundation*, 13 June 1996, https://arhoolie.org/sacred-steel-archive-chuck-campbell-interview/
53   See Lanlan Kuang, '(Un)consciousness? Music in the Daoist Context of Nonbeing', in *Music and Consciousness 2: Worlds, Practices, Modalities*, ed. by Ruth Herbert, David Clarke, and Eric Clarke (New York: Oxford University Press, 2019), pp.

someone who may never be able to incorporate firsthand knowledge of other-than-human agency in their scholarship as meaningfully as Butler and Hagedorn have (I am not a sonic theologian), I am, nevertheless, committed to the decolonising non-secularity of their kind of ethnomusicology—an ethnomusicology that is not troubled by the reality of secular and non-secular positions at a Campbell Brothers performance and, crucially, is not burdened to prove the reality of the secular (the theoretical and organological genealogies of Chuck Campbell's tuning system) at the expense of the non-secular (the power of his tuning system to bring people into the Spirit). Human beings, of course, make music in performance and scholarship; but music, as a sonic channel of other-than-human agency, knowledge, and sense making, also makes us. That, for me, is the connection between music and spiritual realities music studies is beginning to address, transforming itself along the way.

306–34; Heather MacLachlan, 'Burmese Buddhist Monks, the Seventh Precept, and Cognitive Dissonance', *Asian Music* 53.1 (2022), 34–55.

10. The Concept of 'Atmosphere' as a Bridge between Music and Spirituality

Bernard Łukasz Sawicki OSB

Although we naturally intuit a close relationship between music and spirituality, it is difficult to specify exactly in what it consists. The concept of 'atmosphere', as developed by authors such as Hermann Schmitz, Gernot Böhme, and Tonino Griffero can help here. It is about a feedback relationship with the environment, about feeling and reacting to the mood and its reciprocal effects. It is thus a matter of integrative interaction between the subject and the environment: in the case of music, it will be the experience of being composer, performer, or listener; in the case of spirituality, it will be a spiritual experience, involving and connecting the subject with spiritual reality (in a religious key or not). In both cases, there is a synaesthetic synthesis of cognition and feeling, perception and activity. This brings us to the common structure of spiritual and musical experiences, which turns out to be a unique and transformative participation in something that transcends matter. The notion of atmosphere adds a new dimension to metaphors and symbols attempting to describe both musical and spiritual experience. It evokes new areas of meaning, already present in the scholarly literature on both domains, but now integrable. These areas include concepts such as mood, presence, inhabitation, and landscape. Their meaning takes on a new quality, moving symbolism into the realm of concrete experiences. Speaking finally of atmosphere, the discourse on music and spirituality itself moves from the purely descriptive sphere into the realm of experience, shedding new light on its specificity and effects. Consequently, one can speak of a reinterpretation for spirituality and theology of such key concepts as the body, incarnation, and transformation (conversion). Music can help us to understand and express such concepts more effectively.

I. The Definitions of 'Atmosphere'

Let us first clarify what is meant by the term 'atmosphere' in these deliberations, especially when we want to apply it to aesthetic issues. Böhme, the pioneer of atmosphere research, observes:

> The introduction of "atmosphere" as a concept into aesthetics should link up with the everyday distinctions between atmospheres of different character. Atmosphere can only become a concept, however, if we succeed in accounting for the peculiar intermediary status of atmospheres between subject and object.[1]

Its natural linguistic connotation plays an important role in understanding the concept. Gumbrecht and Butler note:

> English offers 'mood' and 'climate'. 'Mood' stands for an inner feeling so private it cannot be precisely circumscribed. 'Climate', on the other hand, refers to something objective that surrounds people and exercises a physical influence. Only in German does the word connect with *Stimme* and *stimmen*. The first means 'voice', and the second 'to tune an instrument'; by extension, *stimmen* also means 'to be correct'. As the tuning of an instrument suggests, specific moods and atmospheres are experienced on a continuum, like musical scales. They present themselves to us as nuances that challenge our powers of discernment and description, as well as the potential of language to capture them.[2]

As can be seen, in addition to the original etymological meaning of the term 'atmosphere', it also carries a strong musical component, which is present in the German term *Stimmung*. This term technically denotes a tuning but, in a wider sense, suggests a mood, an ambience;

---

1   Gernot Böhme, *The Aesthetics of Atmospheres* (London and New York: Routledge, 2017), p. 12.
2   Hans Ulrich Gumbrecht, *Atmosphere, Mood, Stimmung: On a Hidden Potential of Literature*, trans. by Erik Butler (Redwood City, CA: Stanford University Press, 2012), p. 3.

for instance, it gestures towards a kind of congruence, a harmony that can arise between two subjects, between two objects, or between an object and a subject. Here the first meaning of 'atmosphere', a meaning simultaneously spiritual and ethical, is revealed: the experience of closeness, or at least the search for it; the possibility—or perhaps rather the longing—for intimacy. As Gumbrecht notes,

> The yearning for *Stimmung* has grown, because many of us—perhaps older people, above all—suffer from existence in an everyday world that often fails to surround and envelop us physically. Yearning for atmosphere and mood is a yearning for presence—perhaps a variant that presupposes a pleasure in dealing with the cultural past. To quell this yearning, we know, it is no longer necessary to associate *Stimmung* and harmony.[3]

This musical dimension of 'atmosphere' is clearly present in Böhme's definition which, alongside tuning, refers to 'resonance':

> The atmosphere is henceforth a space with its own emotional tone, i.e. what suggests a certain impression here is a mood. That is, first of all, not as my mood, but rather as the arrival of a mood as something I perceive precisely by entering into a mood. We have thus identified a further peculiar element of atmospheres: they are dispositions of mind indefinitely extended in objective space. But there is also another experience of atmospheres, one that is based on discrepancy. What is meant here is that because of an atmosphere I experience an urge to turn to a different disposition of mind from the one I am in. ... This is an experience that has something paradoxical about it if one wants to understand the perception of atmospheres as a kind of resonance phenomenon.[4]

Thus, the 'atmosphere' necessarily has both an ethical and a spiritual dimension, located in the 'in-between' space explored ever more boldly and fruitfully by philosophers and theologians.[5] It is the space where

---

3   Ibid., p. 20.
4   Gernot Böhme, *Atmosfere, estasi, messe in scena. L'estetica come teoria generale della percezione* (Milano: Marinotti, 2010), p. 84.
5   See, for example, William Desmond, *Being and the Between* (Albany, NY: State University of New York Press, 1995); William Desmond, *God and the Between* (Hoboken, NJ: Willey-Blackwell, 2008); William Desmond, *Ethics and the Between* (New York: State University of New York Press, 2001); Carl F. Starkloff, *A Theology of the In-Between: The Value of Syncretic Process* (Milwaukee, WI: Marquette University Press 2002).

our relationships and interactions are born, and consequently it locates our emotions and our 'being-in-the-world'. Not coincidentally, Böhme refers to Martin Heidegger:

> Specifically, I am referring to Heidegger's view of temporality as a constitutive feature of atmospheres and moods. To explain what he means by *Stimmung*, Heidegger writes of 'fear' and 'anger', 'hope', 'joy', 'enthusiasm', 'cheer', and 'boredom'. Then he declares, somewhat surprisingly, that analysis of these different moods will lead to a particularly profound understanding of the 'throwness' of human existence—that is, to a position between 'ecstatic' dimensions of time: a future that has nothing to offer but 'nothing', and the past, which, as 'tradition', has always already limited and determined what we may do in the present. Answering the question—'What do the various *Stimmungen* have to do with "time"?'—Heidegger seeks to show how, in different ways, they are all formed by something belonging to the existential dimension of the past.[6]

In this sense, atmospheres are unavoidable ways of our being in the world and contacting it, as well as the world's effect on us.

Böhme then distinguishes five 'generators' of atmospheres:

> a) the states of mind produced by so-called 'mise-en-scène'; b) synesthesia, the effectiveness of which is explained on the example of Goethe's conception of the sensible and moral effects of colours (probably one of the main inspirational motifs of the entire Bohemian philosophy) and of the evocative as well as almost forgotten 18th-century reflections on the art of gardens; c) the motor impressions in the assumption of a precise pathic counterpart to the presence of forms and volumes; d) the social characters, arouse—be they power, wealth, elegance, etc.—especially by insignia and symbols—finally e) communicative characters, which include gestures, mimicry, timbre of voice, physiognomic traits in the broadest sense.[7]

Our emotions, impressions and interactions with the world are constituted on the basis of these five categories. They encompass a wide range of feelings and our entire psycho-physical structure. At the same time, there is a constant interplay between the appearance and the

---

6 Gumbrecht, *Atmosphere, Mood, Stimmung*, p. 92.
7 Böhme, *Atmosfere, estasi, messe in scena*, p. 22.

concreteness of our experiences, often with profound consequences.[8] In the paradoxical nature of its identity, atmosphere is akin to music, which also 'appears' (resounds) in a way that is difficult to define, but which leaves such a lasting mark on the heart and on life.[9]

Atmospheres allow us to feel the concreteness of the objects that surround us and the situations in which we find ourselves. They are in a sense, therefore, the natural tissue of human bonds. In this way, atmospheres become the core of all aesthetic experience, situating it simultaneously at the heart of all our relationships. Again, according to Böhme:

> The primary subject of sensuality is not the things you perceive, but what you feel—the atmospheres. When I step into a room, I am in some way tuned by that room. Its atmosphere is decisive for how I feel. Only when I am in the atmosphere, so to speak, will I also identify and perceive this or that object. Atmospheres, as they are felt in environments, but also in things or in people, are—this is my second thesis—the central theme of aesthetics.[10]

> Atmosphere as that which emanates from things and people, which fills spaces with affective tint, is at the same time that which the subject, by being in such and such a place, becomes aware of its own presence. With the basic theme of atmospheres, aesthetics becomes itself more than ever: The doctrine of aesthesis.[11]

Moreover, an atmosphere is born between the objective and the subjective—yet another dimension of the 'in-between'!—both levelling and transforming them into a new quality. This is another of the spiritual dimensions of atmosphere: the experience of presence, which, while being something very personal, is at the same time always something very concrete. As Böhme argues:

---

8   All that touches us affectively, that we feel threatening, depressing, moving, exciting, that involves us, all that is the world of appearances. But all of this in itself is also the world of mere appearance, the world of play, which only becomes something serious when it calls into question physical reality, which is also perceived as such. See Böhme, *Atmosfere, estasi, messe in scena*, p. 240.
9   This touches on the fractious subject of the identity of a musical work, cf. Roman Ingarden, *The Work of Music and the Problem of Its Identity* (Berkeley, CA: University of California Press, 1986).
10 Gernot Böhme, *Atmosphäre, Essays zur neuen Ästhetik* (Berlin: Suhrkamp, 2013), pp. 15–16.
11 Böhme, *Atmosphäre*, p. 147.

> The atmospheres are thus conceived neither as something objective, namely properties that things have, and yet they are something thing-like, belonging to the thing, insofar as things are conceived through their properties as ecstasies—articulating the spheres of their presence. Atmospheres are still something subjective, such as determinations of a state of soul. And yet they are subjective, belong to subjects, insofar as they are felt in bodily presence by people and the feeling is at the same time a bodily feeling of the subjects' space.[12]

This presence seems to be nothing more than experiencing specific situations, occurring in different spaces and contexts.[13] The correlation of atmosphere to music is clear, as music is also a carrier of past emotions and memories, feeding on memory itself. And yet, music has been accompanying various situations since time immemorial, giving them colour, hues, flavour, and being, as it were, an organic component of their atmosphere. Böhme recognises this aspect as well:

> The term atmosphere originates from the logical realm and refers to the upper air envelope that is susceptible to weather. Only since the 18th century has it been used metaphorically, for moods that are 'in the air', for the emotional tone of a room. Today, this expression is common in all European languages, no longer seems artificial and is still regarded as a metaphor. One speaks of the atmosphere of a conversation, the atmosphere of a landscape, of a house or the atmosphere of a celebration, of an evening, of a season. Yet the way we talk about atmospheres is highly differentiated—even in everyday language. An atmosphere is tense, cheerful or serious, oppressive or uplifting, cold or warm. We also speak of the atmosphere of the petty bourgeoisie, the atmosphere of the 1920s, the atmosphere of poverty.[14]

Another dimension of the encounter between music and atmosphere is the way it interacts with space: filling it, managing it, and thus making sense of it. Our lives run in specific places. Various situations and encounters also have specific spatial contexts, both coloured by and through them. Our every presence has a spatial character. For Schmitz,

---

12 Ibid., pp. 33–34.
13 Ibid., p. 167: 'Voice is the atmospheric presence of something or someone, it is one of the dimensions in which something or someone emerges from itself and the atmosphere in the environment is essentially emotionally tinged. In contrast to verbal forms of expression, it is highly individual, so that the atmosphere it determines can be described and recognised as one's own'.
14 Ibid., pp. 101–02.

atmosphere *occupies* space in a way that gives articulation to both positive and negative experiences:

> Feelings are spatially poured atmospheres and bodily gripping powers. What is meant here by 'atmosphere', 'spatial' and 'bodily' must first be specified. I refer to the occupation of a space or area without surface in the realm of experienced presence as atmosphere. I speak of occupation instead of fulfilment so that there is also room for an atmosphere of emptiness.[15]

Another way to speak of this kind of space is in the latent yet constant search for safe places to live, to 'be at home', even when continually wandering from one place of residence to another; a constant longing to be rooted. Space is necessary, moreover, for a musical phenomenon to exist. Without it, there is no resonance. Our well-being, the first direct and often intuitive effect of the atmosphere, is precisely linked to the experience of space, either positively or negatively. Every concrete space in which man finds himself, be it outer space or inner space, has as such a certain character of emotional tonality (*Stimmung*); it has, so to speak, its own human qualities which, in turn, condition, among other things, the form of the most elementary determinations, the experiences of narrowness and vastness of a certain space.[16]

There is no experience of space without a concrete experience of the body. The body is the axis of every experience of atmosphere. It is the body that allows all the aforementioned generators of atmosphere to function. Atmosphere allows us to feel our own body concretely, in all its rich context. For Griffero, this means that 'to perceive the atmospheric always means to co-perceive (pre-categorically, synesthetically, kinesthetically) one's own affective own-body situation and to ascertain how one feels in a certain place by means of a bilateral perception that has nothing metaphorical about it'.[17]

Another musical dimension of atmosphere is also worth mentioning: the so-called 'soundscape'. The sounds around us, to which we have become so accustomed that we no longer notice them, are an important component of the atmosphere of the places in which we live, be they

---

15 Hermann Schmitz, *Atmosphaere* (Freiburg/München: Karl Alber, 2014), p. 30.
16 Tonino Griffero, *Atmosferologia. Estetica degli spazi emozionali* (Sesto San Giovanni, MI: Mimesis Edizioni, 2017), p. 849.
17 Ibid., p. 3009.

voices from the street, birds singing in the forest, bells from a distant church, or, even, the footsteps or other sounds of life of the neighbours living one floor above us. Böhme describes it thus:

> What is generally true for atmospheres is an everyday reality for acoustic atmospheres: The characters of a space are responsible for how one feels in a space. In the meantime, it has been discovered that the feeling of home is essentially conveyed by the sound of a region and that the characteristic feeling of a lifestyle, of an urban or rural atmosphere is essentially determined by the respective acoustic space.[18]

Canadian composer R. Murray Schafer popularised the term 'soundscape', and regularly used immersive environments in his compositions. As Schafer explains:

> The keynote sounds of a given place are important because they help to outline the character of men living among them. The keynote sounds of a landscape are those created by its geography and climate: water, wind, forests, plains, birds, insects and animals. Many of these sounds may possess archetypal significance; that is, they may have imprinted themselves so deeply on the people hearing them that life without them would be sensed as a distinct impoverishment. They may even affect the behaviour or life style of a society.[19]

Therefore, in many musical works, the soundscape resonates in a variety of ways. Many composers besides Schafer have admitted to being inspired by it. After all, it can be the hallmark of their national and cultural identity. Filtered through their personality, it becomes the basis of a unique personal style, well distinguishable, at once local and universal.

II. The 'Atmospheric' Dimension of Music

As we have seen, atmospheres are closely related to music. However, music itself can also be a source of atmosphere. Atmosphere is a part of the nature of music, both in music's connection to and in its participation in life. This bond between music and life is written into the structure of

---

18 Böhme, *Atmosphäre*, p. 267.
19 R. Murray Schafer, *Soundscape. Our Sonic Environment and the Tuning of the World* (Rochester, VT: Destiny Books, 1977), p. 245.

atmosphere; it is, as it were, its genetic code. Increasingly, one could say that music is being consciously used to generate atmosphere in order to 'help life' and to make the various situations in which we find ourselves more easy or more pleasant. This is a phenomenon well known to music psychologists. They recognise that 'people can play mental songlists to alter mood, including in difficult conditions such as isolation or during extreme stress'.[20] The imagination is involved, which in turn 'draws' other areas of our personality and psyche into the musical experience. In this sense, everything that happens during the resounding of music has its repercussions in the imagination and, consequently, in our perception of the atmosphere. As Rolf Godøy suggests, 'we may assume that there are variable degrees of acuity in such mental images, for example, that they may be vague recollections of overall "sound" or "mood" of large-scale works, or they may be salient images of particular details'.[21]

Atmosphere in music, then, is mainly the fruit of imagination, which naturally links our musical perception with extra-musical reality. This is how emotions similar to those brought about by the various 'non-musical' situations of our lives are born. Music visualises this emotional dimension of the atmosphere:

> The contrast between the emotion or mood that music induces in listeners, and the emotion a listener understands some musical performance to express, is complicated by the fact that the listener also often gets a certain satisfaction from the music whatever emotion it is conveying. Furthermore, such satisfaction occurs even when nothing that could be called an emotional state is felt or understood by the listener.[22]

Let us try to identify, therefore, a provisional taxonomy of the atmospheric dimensions of music. These atmospheric dimensions would include: a) tonality (modality); b) the event of performance (and particularly the relationship between performer and listener); and c) the role of the title and of the biography of the composer or performer in musical perception.

---

20 Andrea R. Halpern, 'Foreword', in *Music and Mental Imagery*, ed. by Matts B. Küssner, Liila Taruffi, and Georgia A. Floridou (London & New York: Routledge, 2023), pp. xviii-xx (at xix).

21 Rolf Inge Godøy, 'Intermittent Motor Control in Volitional Musical Imagery', in *Music and Mental Imagery*, ed. Küssner, pp. 42–53 (at 46).

22 Siu-Lan Tan, Peter Pfordresher, and Rom Harré, *Psychology of Music: From Sound to Significance* (London and New York: Routledge, 2018), p. 264.

(a) Tonality (Modality)

Since the beginning of musical history, the sound material from which a piece of music was created—scales, modes, or tonalities—has always played a fundamental role in musical expression, especially in Europe. Two salient examples are the scales of ancient Greece[23] as well as the modes of Gregorian chant.[24] Aware of the expressive potential and ethos of scales from other musical traditions as well, and of the fact that this is an area for further exploration, we will limit our considerations to Gregorian modality, illustrating thereby how much the strictly musical structure intermingles with various aspects of our lives in the phenomenon of the mode.

At this point, the peculiar 'problematic nature' of Gregorian chant must be mentioned. We know it today mainly from reconstructions created initially in monastic circles (as at Solesmes Abbey) and now in the studios of lay singer-musicologists. Gregorian chant, steeped in various myths, is, therefore, an area of constant research.[25] Nevertheless, its modal dimension, which we would like to address, seems to be the element of expression that has survived rather unchanged through the various turbulences of history, and especially in the face of the turmoil over its identity that has taken place in recent decades.[26]

---

23 Curt Sachs, *The Rise of Music in the Ancient World. East and West* (New York: Dent, 1943), pp. 216–72; Thomas J. Mathiesen, 'Harmonia and Ethos in Ancient Greek Music', *The Journal of Musicology* 3.3 (1984), 264–79.

24 Jean Claire, 'Évolution modale des antiennes provenant de la corde-mère DO', *Revue grégorienne* 41 (1963), 49–62; Jean Claire, 'Évolution modale des antiennes provenant de la corde-mère MI', *Revue grégorienne* 41 (1963), 77–102; Jean Claire, 'L'évolution modale dans les répertoires liturgiques occidentaux', *Revue grégorienne* 40 (1962), 196–211, 229–45; Alberto Turco, *Il canto gregoriano. Toni e modi* (Rome: Edizioni Torre d'Orfeo, 1996); Daniel Saulnier, *Les modes grégoriens* (Solesmes: Éditions de Solesmes, 1997).

25 See Enrico Correggia, 'Inaudite banalità sul Canto Gregoriano: ovvero della necessità di osservare sempre le piccole ovvietà', in *VII Ciclo di Studi Medievali. Atti del Convegno 7–10 giugno 2021* (Florence: NUME, 2021), pp. 623–27. About the reconstruction of Gregorian chant, see Marcel Pérès and Jacques Cheyronnaud, *Les voix du plain-chant* (Paris: Desclé de Brouwer, 2001); Fulvio Rampi and Alessandro De Lillo, *Nella mente del notatore. Semiologia gregoriana a ritrorso* (Rome: Città del Vaticano, Libreria Editrice Vaticana, 2019).

26 Bernard Sawicki, 'Chorał gregoriański—dziedzictwo coraz bardziej … problematyczne?', *Teofil* 1.41 (2024), 81–105 (at 105): 'Looking at the complicated status of chant and the ambiguous perception of its identity today, it is impossible not to feel a sense of concern. Despite the many activities in the various fields

A scale (modus) is a group of sounds characterised by the distinction of at least one of them as central, and by a specific configuration of intervals. It is the arrangement of these intervals that determines the expressive and, therefore, the emotional profile of works based on any given scale. These intervallic arrangements have their own characteristics, style—or, using today's terminology, tonality. In fact, today's Western tonalities are derived from the modal system; although, due to their even temperament, they do not differ in the arrangement of intervals, they have their own character, not to say 'colour', which is felt by many musicians.[27] The modal ethos is thus an expression of synaesthesia, one aspect, as we noted above, of the atmosphere.

Let us investigate what constitutes the atmospheric dimension of the modus by analysing a description of the first of the Gregorian modes:

> It is described as *gravis*, which means heavy, serious. After all, there is more maturity and responsibility in it than overwhelming heaviness. It has something of dignity and nobility about it. It is reflective, but also full of energy. It expresses piety without sentimentality. It befits great things, though it is far from pompous. There is much grandeur in it, but also richness, as well as inner depth. There is something solid and reliable about it — dependability and certainty, groundedness in what is important, adult and credible, momentum and solemnity. It is not lacking in brilliance, but also in persuasiveness, often leading to enthusiasm.
>
> The compositions resounding in this tone are an expression of clearly stated principles, as well as an accompanying awareness of the ever-present tensions in life. The basic polarity marking the character of this tone is always a sharply delineated fifth *re - la*. According to Ansermet's

---

of chant, it is difficult to see its future clearly. Perhaps we should rejoice in the fact that it has not disappeared after all, that it invariably inspires and seeks new ways and forms of existence? It remains a legacy, but... whose legacy? There is a problem here too. "Certainly it remains the Roman liturgy's own chant" (SSC 116), but in practice banished from it, it is constantly being rediscovered as a heritage of European culture and spirituality, and even world culture and spirituality'.

27 See, for example: Chris Caton-Greasley, 'A Mapping Between Musical Notes and Colours', *Stalybridge Music Academy*, 20 June 2020, https://www.stalybridgemusicacademy.com/post/colours-and-keys; Katie Gutierrez, 'The Colors of Music', *Bright Star Musical*, 24 October 2022, https://web.archive.org/web/20221024225859/https://brightstarmusical.com/the-colors-of-music-do-musical-notes-have-color/. It works in both directions: Science of Colour, 'Tonality of Colors in Painting', *Science of Colour*, https://sites.google.com/site/scienceofcolour/tonality-of-colors-in-painting

typology,[28] the positional tension of the ascending fifth has an active extravertedness in its character, as it is carried by an active determination of the self to occur in the future. The descending fifth, on the other hand, appears as its immediate past, characterised by a positional tension that is passive and introverted in its reflexive return to itself and in its reference to the past only on the basis of its 'recognition'. The value of this tension is 1. The presence of the fifth is an expression of boldness and determination, of courageously looking the truth in the eye — including the truth about life, about the uneasy tension between its practice and theory, the starting point and the arrival point. Here we have a definite distinction between what is necessary and asked for and what is possible or what one would like. In comparison to the movement of the seconds, prevailing in chorale melodies, the intonation of the fifth requires effort and a greater concentration of imagination. This results in a kind of independence and greater internal coherence for it, compared to the relationship linking the notes that make it up to the other notes of the scale. It is also not surprising that the intonation of the ascending fifth, typical of the first tone, is usually marked by a single emphatic mark (*pes*).

The stability and predictability of this tone is due to the embedding of the *finalis* sound between notes a whole tone away from it (*do* and *mi*). The dominant, on the other hand, is ambivalent in character. Depending on whether there is a *si* (B) sound over it (and thus distant by a whole tone), or *sa* (B flat distant by a semitone), it can lean upwards (usually even towards the *do* sound) or gravitate towards the *finalis*.

In such an arrangement, the role of the *finalis* as both base and target point is reinforced. The possibility of deviating from stability or shaking it up always brings a semitone. In the first tone, it appears exactly midway between the *finalis* and the dominant. Thus, it cannot directly affect either of the two, but remains an expressive quality in its own right. However, it never manages to be able to surpass the expressive power of the *la-sa* semitone, if it appears in the melody, as well as — although to a much lesser extent — the *si-do* semitone. Everything in the first tone — is therefore forced to revolve around this crucial and unshakeable fifth of the *re-la*. Certainty and decisiveness are firmly at their basis here. Combined with the expressive liveliness of the aforementioned semitones adding to this fifth, they give an image of positive seriousness and boldness without audacity. This is music of conscious planning, of good discernment of one's own possibilities, of a vision concretely supported. Everything

---

28   Cf. Ernest Ansermet, *Les fondments de la musique dans la conscience humanie et autres écrits* (Paris: Robert Lafont, 1989), pp. 491–502.

is under control, however, allowing some elements of freedom (the movement and striving of the semitones). Hence a sense of security, peace and even trusting and responsible love. There is a mobilizing and dynamiting festivity in this tone, a kind of opening towards great things.[29]

In this description, many images and metaphors carry unambiguous emotional associations: heaviness, seriousness, tension, bold determination, and so on. They outline a particular attitude, which has a clear ethical dimension. In this way, the configurations of the intervals and their relationships become a network of metaphors: 'swollen', or rather saturated, with life. In a medieval treatise by William of Auxerre, the meaning and atmosphere of the first modus grows out of the symbolism of the number of that modus (the number 1). This extends beyond a purely musical sense, and undoubtedly alludes to the Pythagorean tradition according to which numerals express the harmony and sense of music:

> The first tone can allude to the semantic area of the beginning, of the origin and, in fact, we can highlight four allegorical references which express just that. Two of them use the neuter noun *principium* which sees *primus* in its etymology, one sees the use of alpha and a further the same *primus*. Of these, three are clearly Christological and see the principle associated with the antithetical counterpart, i.e. with the end: *principium et finis, primus et nouissimus* and *alpha et omega*. The remainder, of a moral nature, sees conversion as the *principium*, the starting *locus* of the good life The first tone can also symbolize the day of the Resurrection. In fact, we find in three points a precise connection to the first day after Saturday: *mane prima sabbati, prima die* and *valde mane*. Finally, we meet two further temporal references symbolized by the *protus authenticus*. William, in fact, associates it both with the first Resurrection, that which, as Augustine also explains, belongs to souls, both at an early age, that is, still according to Augustinian presentation, infancy.[30]

Symbols, especially numerical symbols, are the natural language of theology. Through abstraction, they are able to transcend the natural limitation of matter—be it linguistic, conceptual or, as in our case, musical. Thus, the very structure of the musical matter (scale, modus),

---

29 Bernard Sawicki, *W chorale jest wszystko* (Kraków: Tyniec Wydawnictwo Benedyktynów, 2014), pp. 102–03. English translations are my own, unless otherwise stated.
30 Claudio Campesato, *Allegoria modale* (Vienna: LIT Verlag, 2021), pp. 86–88.

if put in order, gives place to numbers that give it a higher meaning and introduce a corresponding atmosphere.

We have deliberately quoted these lengthy descriptions of the first Gregorian modus to demonstrate the multi-layered nature of its atmosphere. Most importantly, everything grows out of a pure configuration of sounds and the interval relationships between them. The rest, through associations with life, is completed by the imagination.

(b) The Event of Performance

As for the impact of the work itself, that is, the interaction with the listener that takes place over the perceptual space, this is not as easily grasped as the structure and sonic configurations of the scale. It has the character of personal, subjective sensations and feelings, often difficult to express. We can be helped in documenting such impressions by literature and texts that are devoted exclusively to music. They are not few in number, and usually describe the author's impressions of listening to or perceiving a particular work.

Here follow three such examples of the transfer, or rather the rendering, of musical atmosphere in literary prose. The first dates from over half a century ago and is a description of one of Frédéric Chopin's special works, the Barcarolle in F-sharp major, Op. 60. We are dealing here more with the atmosphere of the work itself rather than of a specific performance:

CHOPIN'S BARCAROLLE

> Some works of art give the impression of greatness because they enclose something unknown and undefinable, which acts on man in a liberating way, communicating to him with another world, the existence of which we would not know if the works of certain artists did not become such a revelation. The elements that cause such a revelation can also sometimes be other aesthetic or artistic things: nature or a work of craftsmanship. It is extremely difficult for an artist, and even more so for a critic, to notice and capture and finally recreate this element that opens up the spaces of artistic revelations; Proust's description of church towers (*les clochers de Martain-ville*) is unforgettable in this respect, which — suddenly appearing during a horse walk against the sky purple from the west — become for the artist a discovery of his world and his ability to feel, leading to creativity. What is this element that the author puts

into the work so that it penetrates us with fear and longing? Is it only fear and longing, as Spengler means it? Anxiety created in the pre-existence of genus, when the murmur of an unfamiliar stream or the sight of an unfamiliar tree on the horizon evoked deep traumas in the primitive soul, traumas implanted in our genus and awakened to this day in the artist, terrified by an unfamiliar sight? It is a longing... but for what? To the paradise from which we were expelled, or to impossible realizations, or to a sense of community and oneness with people or with God? Where to look for explanations, we do not know, and we search in vain. Neither Nietzsche nor Spengler nor Proust explain this to us. At most, they can point us to certain phenomena taking place in artists and through their works that affect us, the listeners; inexplicably frightening us, *pavor nocturnus*. It is a fear that fills us with sweetness, like the thought of walking on dark water on a summer night. Imagine a black sheet of water and stars above the water and clouds, all immersed in the night as in a great day, distant and taking away our sense of reality. Echoes of childhood expeditions will now resound in us, be it delayed walks in the woods or unnecessary stops by dark water; or simply sitting on the front porch as the nightingale sings in the shadows, the frogs croak, the fragrant 'night ornaments' open as witnesses to the unknown nocturnal activities taking place beyond us. Those old memories, and then the fears of youth, when we first become aware of the power and omnipresence of the eternal night, we notice in this night passing in the mirror of water, in everything that surrounds us. It detaches our body from us, and we remain disembodied as our boat floats noiselessly over the ink. The murmur of trees set like shadows on the edges reaches us as a fragrance, rather a scent of leaves, soft and noisy, a greeting to that which is green by day and rustling by night. The nearby reeds do not tie us to the ground with their frail threads and we walk on water into nothingness. Everything is already in such a range that death ceases to bother us. Chopin's "Barcarolle" is more or less such a walk.[31]

This is a description of a certain existential state, which consists of a deep and multifaceted interaction with the environment caused by a particular interaction of imagination, memory, and reflection. This interaction has a great impact on the person experiencing it—both the listener and the performer: it opens new horizons, it engages, it transforms. It is thus the evident germ of an experience that goes beyond acoustic and artistic matter, thus acquiring a spiritual character.

---

31   Jarosław Iwaszkiewicz, 'Barkarola Chopina', in Jarosław Iwaszkiewicz, *Pisma muzyczne* (Warsaw: Czytelnik, 1958), pp. 522–27.

Atmosphere becomes an introduction to a deeper experience, permeating the whole person and even capable of permeating all of life. It helps to make the experience of the environment, the space around the listener, more profound and concrete. By inspiring the imagination, atmosphere gives this space a broader character that goes beyond the moment of listening to the piece. It is a space tinged with the emotions of relationships and related reflections. These are what give it meaning, colour, and flavour. Synaesthetic sensory experiences lead to interaction, leaving a lasting, transformative mark on the heart. The structure of the musical experience configures the imagination and the images and sensations that arise, collecting various memories from the past and catalysing them into an acoustic experience.

In the following examples, we are presented with descriptions of an imaginary piece, which, however, aptly capture the process of the interweaving of musical and imaginary experience leading to the creation of an atmosphere; namely, the experience of a specific extra-musical situation:

> How beautiful the dialogue which Swann now heard between piano and violin, at the beginning of the last passage! The suppression of human speech, so far from letting fancy reign there uncontrolled (as one might have thought), had eliminated it altogether; never was spoken language so inexorably determined, never had it known questions so pertinent, such irrefutable replies. At first the piano complained alone, like a bird deserted by its mate; the violin heard and answered it, as from a neighbouring tree. It was as at the beginning of the world, as if there were as yet only the two of them on the earth, or rather in this world closed to all the rest, so fashioned by the logic of its creator that in it there should never be any but themselves: the world of this sonata. Was it a bird, was it the soul, as yet not fully formed, of the little phrase, was it a fairy—that being invisibly lamenting, whose plaint the piano heard and tenderly repeated? Its cries were so sudden that the violinist must snatch up his bow and race to catch them as they came. Marvellous bird![32]

The arietta theme, destined for adventures and vicissitudes for which, in its idyllic innocence, it seems never to have been born, is immediately called up and for sixteen bars says its piece, reducible to a motif that emerges toward the end of its first half, like a short, soulful cry-just

---

32 Marcel Proust, *In Search of Lost Time*, trans. by C. K. Scott Moncrieff (New York: Modern Library Edition, 1992), p. 481.

three notes, an eighth, a sixteenth, and a dotted quarter, that can only be scanned as something like: 'sky of blue' or 'lover's pain' or 'fare-thee-well' or 'come a day' or 'meadow-land' — and that is all. But what now becomes of this gentle statement, this pensively tranquil figure, in terms of rhythm, harmony, counterpoint, what blessings its master bestows upon it, what curses he heaps upon it, into what darknesses and superilluminations, where cold and heat, serenity and ecstasy are one and the same, he hurls and elevates it-one may well call it elaborate, miraculous, strange, and excessively grand without thereby giving it a name, because in actuality it is nameless.[33]

Literature provides many such descriptions, aptly demonstrating the fecundity of music for our imagination and affectivity, the main components of atmosphere in exploration of the 'in-between' space, the sense of presence, the longing for rootedness, and the particular experience of one's own body. In this approach to music, we can simultaneously find the five 'generators' of atmosphere. The imagination develops and expands the landscape in which the atmosphere appears, thereby intensifying it. A synaesthetic sensory interaction with the environment interacts with this, organically linking to the motor response of the body. In this way, the experience of presence is concretised and communicated.

One does not necessarily need literary texts to portray the atmosphere associated with musical experience, although these too still play a great role; for instance, in Riku Ondas' *Honeybees and Distant Thunder*.[34] Communicating the atmospheric experience of music is most often done at the level of reviews or even short quotations from them. Here are some examples from two short review describing the pianism of a recent winner of the Van Cliburn International Piano Competition (2022), Yunchan Lim:

> The sighing phrases of the Dowland were transmuted into subtly coloured, immaculately voiced arcs, while the Bach miniatures were imaginatively dispatched with a different mood or temperament for each — jaunty, good-humoured, pensive and so forth — ending with a poignant reading of the F minor, with its anguished chromaticisms. (Barry Millington, *Evening Standard*)

---

33   Thomas Mann, *Doctor Faustus*, trans. by John E. Wood (New York: Vintage Books, 1999), p. 58.
34   Riku Ondas, *Honeybees and Distant Thunder* (New York: Doubleday, 2023).

> There was, in his performance of Rachmaninoff's Piano Concerto No. 3, the juxtaposition of precise clarity and expansive reverie; the vivid scenes and bursts of wit; the sense of contrasting yet organically developing moods; the endless and persuasive bendings of time—the qualities that tend to characterize night-time wanderings of the mind. (Zachary Woolfe, *New York Times*)[35]

The word 'mood' appears in both these descriptions, as well as associations with nature and space, and various metaphorical depictions of movement.

(c) The Role of Title and Biography

Musical works function in a broader historical, social. or cultural context. They are usually inextricably linked to their creator, so that when performing a piece — or even thinking about it — we naturally enter the space of the composer's life, conveyed through various stories that create a special and unique atmosphere around this figure and, in effect, their works. In a sense, the composer functions as a 'brand', signifying with its own character all its products, offering what in advertising is called a mood-board.

In the history of music, we have many examples of composers' biographies or even titles of works functioning in this way. They carry with them particular stories, associations, situations, emotions. For instance, the lives of Wolfgang Amadeus Mozart, Ludwig van Beethoven, Franz Schubert, or Frédéric Chopin demonstrate how genius is combined with the extraordinary fragility of the human condition, the difficulty of material situation, or the hostility of the environment. This creates an atmosphere of sensation and emotion at the same time, awe and horror, compassion and reflection. The atmosphere generated by a brilliant personality and his interaction with the world when creating masterpieces is interwoven through the history of mankind and art — from saints to artists to contemporary celebrities. The atmosphere evoked by one person can include a multiplicity of situations, their associated emotions engaging, attracting, and transforming at the same time. Perhaps this is why there is such a commitment to finding details

---

35 IMG Artists, 'Yuanchan Lim', *IMG Artists*, https://imgartists.com/roster/yunchan-lim/

from the lives of musicians, so that their creations take on a new and deeper human dimension.

This, then, is the all-important interaction of atmosphere with music. Growing out of life, it expresses itself in the sound configuration but then it is also needed so that the full meaning of this configuration can be understood. This is well illustrated by an episode from Glenn Gould's private, affective life accompanying his recording of Brahms' Intermezzi. If a listener is familiar with this episode, he or she can get a better feel for the atmosphere of these interpretations—and thus understand and absorb it better:

> Back in Toronto in 1959–60, Gould introduced Sandercock to what she would call her and Gould's music—Brahms' Intermezzi. It was an intimate, personal album he was preparing to record in New York, and he had only played samples of it in live concerts. 'We were at his St. Clair apartment one night when he played it all for me', Post said. 'He was going to New York the next day to record it and he was excited. When he finished playing, he said to me, "God, wasn't that sexy!" I thought to myself, "This music is mine!"' What she didn't realize was that the Chickering piano Gould used for the seductive music had once belonged to his former girlfriend Frances Batchen.
>
> Later he told an interviewer that he played the Intermezzi, 'as though I were really playing for myself, but left the door open ... I have captured, I think, an atmosphere of improvisation which I don't believe has ever been represented in a Brahms recording before'. Gould never said that Verna influenced his music, but he was usually slow to credit people and the influence they had on him. Critics noted that Gould's version of the Brahms Intermezzi created an atmosphere of nostalgia, intimacy and melancholy, although John Beckwith in the Toronto Daily Star dismissed it as 'supper music'.[36]

In listening to this recording and learning about Gould's story, we enter a space of something more than a purely musical experience—we are touched by the discreetly delineated intimacy of the artist and its unique expression. It thus becomes more concretely present to us, more moving.

At the same time, many 'in-between' spaces are activated—from the intimate, interpersonal one, to the one connecting the performer to the score, to the listener's reception. They all intertwine and interpenetrate

---

36 Michael Clarkson, *A Secret Life of Glenn Gould* (Toronto: ECW Press, 2010), pp. 83–84.

each other, creating a rippling web that delights, entwines and moves: here we feel that we are in front of something extraordinary, one of a kind, and we do not want to part with it. The music has to reverberate, of course, but its lasting imprint in the heart remains and we cannot help but return to it, and the atmosphere of this performance becomes part of us.

In such a perception of music, its extra-musical context—knowledge of the culture, life, history of the creator or works—plays an important role. At this point we become involved in the classical dispute between absolute and programmatic music, most intensified in the second half of the nineteenth century.[37] All human experience of music, however, needs to be hooked into a non-musical reality: the atmosphere. Therein lies the greatness and at the same time the irrevocably human character of music.

The historical, cultural, and biographical contextualisation of a musical work expands the palette of its perception, enriching it with a symbolic dimension. In this way, the atmosphere transcends a specific time and place, rooting the piece or musical experience in a wider area of social or national consciousness. From symbolism it is a short step to spirituality, which it provides a natural key. This establishes another link between atmosphere and spirituality, an example of which we have in Cyprian Norwid's poem describing Chopin's music:

> And then, when you played—what? said the tones—
> what? will they say,
> Though stand the echoes might in different array
> Than when your own hand's benediction made
> Quiver each chord your fingers played—
> And when you played, there was such simplicity—
> Periclean—perfection—sublime
> As if some Virtue from Antiquity
> Stepped into a country cottage's confine
> And on the simple threshold swore:
> 'This day in Heaven I was reborn:
> The cottage door—a harp to me;
> My ribbons—the winding lane;

---

37 See Eduard Hanslick, *Vom Musikalisch-Schönen. Ein Beitrag zur Revision der Aesthetik der Kunst* (Leipzig: Rudolph Weigel, 1865); Carl Dalhaus, *The Idea of Absolute Music* (Chicago, IL: University of Chicago Press, 1991).

> The Holy Host—in the corn I venerate
> And Emmanuel will reign
> On Tabor incarnate!'[38]

Here we are presented with an eloquent depiction of a specific space—a country house, shrouded in the serene glow of the sky, which also becomes the setting for an Arcadian idyll. This is superimposed on a similar tonal image (sky glow, grain) of the Transfiguration of Jesus which, according to tradition, took place on Mount Tabor. In this case, the music, through the personal context of the composer (Polish countryside), opens up an atmosphere of not only spiritual, but also religious, mystical character. At the same time, all the spiritual atmospheric references of the previously presented musical atmospheres are present here. Being aware of their transience and complexity at the same time, we can now—carefully and gently—try to outline their spiritual orientation.

III. The Spiritual Overtones of Atmosphere

In the above descriptions one can perceive a transcending of the materiality of events and situations. The descriptions are evocative, emotionally saturated, and yet lead on somewhere beyond, directing the attention to a transcendent dimension. It is good to recognise and support this dimension today, otherwise music and the experience of it can be reduced to a background or a mere superficial stimulation of affectedness.[39] It is therefore useful to link atmospheres with the concept of spirituality. To do so, let us juxtapose different insights, more intuitive than scientific, with what we understand by 'spirituality'. We will refer here to Kees Waaijman's definition:

> 'Spirituality' is the basic word which has forced all other names for the field of spirituality into the background. The basic word 'spirituality'

---

38 Cyprian K. Norwid, 'Chopin's Grand Piano', trans. by Teresa Bałuk, *Visegrad Literature*, https://www.visegradliterature.net/works/pl/Norwid%2C_Cyprian_Kamil-1821/Fortepian_Szopena/en/1593-Chopin_s_Grand_Piano

39 On this, see, for example, Douglas Bachorik Jr, *Emotion in Congregational Singing: Music-Evoked Affect in Filipino Churches* (Durham, NC: Durham University Press 2019): 'the use of music for the creation of atmosphere, the attraction of a specific demographic of people, and a powerful sense of worship or an experience with God' (p. 89); 'the overall affective atmosphere of the church service' (p. 214).

has a comprehensive semantic range: it embraces the divine and human spirit; overarches asceticism and mysticism; integrates biblical traditions (*ruach*) with Hellenistic intuitions (*nous*); exceeds the boundaries of religions and philosophies of life. The core process evoked by the term 'spirituality' is the dynamic relation between the divine Spirit and the human spirit.[40]

Thus, Waaijman identifies 'spirituality' with 'the rational process between God and man', adding that 'this relational process is understood as an intensive, purifying and unifying process of interiorisation (*kabbala*, inner life, mysticism)'. Waaijman also delineates three further features of the spiritual: first, 'the spiritual stands for a sphere of its own with language and logic of its own, one that exists in tension with the rational theology of universities and the instrumental rationality of Western culture'; second, 'the spiritual "way" includes the purification of one's faculties (intellect, will, memory) and the formation of one's conduct'; and, third, 'spirituality is situated in the intimacy of the relational process (*kabbala*, mysticism) and in the inwardness of the human spirit (inner life, spirituality); it withdraws itself from the external world: from public order and from objectivity'.[41] In these definitions, spirituality is firmly located in the various 'in-between' spaces, having as its task the dynamic integration of different polarities, permeating all the powers of the human personality, involving the whole person and influencing his or her behaviour.

One cannot deny that the concept of atmosphere functions best in the spirituality of religions based on personal contact with God. Not only does spirituality spring from such contact, but, in its own way, spirituality is an opportunity for the development of intimacy with God. In the case of music, its personal character is clear. At the same time, the concept of 'atmosphere' is not merely descriptive. It can have a practical dimension, stimulating both the musical or spiritual experience and at the same time facilitating its interpretation by opening it up, through synaesthesia, to the sensations and language of other arts.

The intimate relationship of presence in relation to a transcendent being—God—is the ultimate bearing of this spiritual experience. We

---

40 Kees Waaijman, *Spirituality. Forms, Foundations, Methods*, trans. by John Vriend (Leuven: Peeters Publishers, 2002), pp. 360–61.
41 Ibid., p. 364.

can therefore read the reality of the 'atmosphere' as a spiritual key, facilitating an opportunity to open up in a special way, and augmenting our sensitivity and hospitality with regard to meeting the Other and experiencing his presence to the fullest. In the broadest possible sense, this would not only be an encounter with another person, but also a deepened experience of the world and, ultimately, an encounter with God. Here, the common resonance of atmosphere and music, along with their mutual, inseparable relationship, can lead naturally toward the realm of mysticism, where it is not so much the atmosphere itself that matters, but the sheer, pure experience of presence in its deepest form: loving union. Then the full meaning and integrity of the 'musical matter', its historical, social, and cultural context and the workings of the imagination, are revealed. Then, perhaps, all questions about their interrelationship will find a final answer.

11. Spiritual Subjects: Musicking, Biography, *and* the Connections We Make

Maeve Louise Heaney VDMF

Introduction

In one of the best talks I have heard addressing the connection between the arts and spirituality, the Irish poet and writer Aidan Matthews pays special attention to the inobtrusive connecting word between the two, that small three-letter word 'and', describing it as 'a humble, understated' word, which hides as much as it says, since it is the nature of the connection between what we seek to understand that is important.[1] As I approach this chapter on music and spirituality, it occurs to me that the same is true here: just how we connect the musical and the spiritual is important, and the reality is that this connection is a personal one. Music—better described as 'musicking' (the useful term coined by Christopher Small to refer to every aspect of the reality of how music happens)—and spirituality are either human phenomena or they are perceived and performed by human beings. I am not suggesting that the world is an unspiritual place or that creation lacks musicality, but in seeking to explore the relationship between music and the spiritual, attention to *who* is doing the connecting, as well as to *how* and *why* they

---

1   Aidan Matthews speaking at 'The Arts and Spirituality', speech given at the Manresa Jesuit Retreat Centre, Dublin, August 2007.

are interested in doing so, is paramount. In this way, exploration in the field of music and spirituality is analogous to work on faith and science. Australian theologian Denis Edwards, who dedicated much of his life to this area, explained that there are three types of people active in that interdisciplinary space: scientists with an interest in religion and theology; theologians with an interest in science; and those who have interest and expertise in both.[2] Similarly, the commonly-perceived links between music and spirituality are primarily seen by three groups: those aware of spirituality (whether they name it in this way or not) with an interest in music; musicians with an interest in spirituality; and people with an authoritative foot in both camps. A core invitation of this chapter is to interrogate critically *how* we pay attention to the subjective source of our thought.

In inviting us to adopt this lens, however, it is also important to realise that my use of the word 'subjective' or 'subject' in this context is not to be understood as the opposite of 'objective'. Rather, it recognises the fact that every human perception or thought has a subject as its source. It also challenges the conventional notion of 'objectivity' in the history of Western thought—emphasising, as it does, reason over emotion, and the natural sciences over the humanities—and suggests that 'objectivity' is, at best, unattainable (since only 'someone' outside the socio-historical reality of human life—the divine, in theological terms—could ever have twenty-twenty vision over what is being understood), and, at worst, false. From a human perspective, the perception of truth is only possible through the lens of shared, critical reflection; in the words of Bernard Lonergan, a philosopher and theologian who has explored extensively the reality of how we come to know, 'genuine objectivity is the fruit of authentic [shared] subjectivity'.[3] My own lens, then, is that of a female Irish Roman Catholic theologian who is also a musician and composer.

In this chapter, I offer some initial definition of our core terms as I understand them, and I provide an overview of some relevant insights from my past and current research, in five steps or sections. First, I

---

2   Denis Edwards, 'Story of a Theologian of the Natural World', in *God and the Natural World: Theological Explorations in Appreciation of Denis Edwards*, ed. by Ted Peters and Marie Turner (Adelaide: ATF Press, 2020), pp. 21–30.
3   Bernard J. F. Lonergan, *Method in Theology* (New York: The Seabury Press, 1972), p. 292.

define the terms of music and spirituality with which I am working. Second, I explore some key theological truths that are important, if not essential, foundations for an understanding of how music and spirituality connect. Third, I name some interdisciplinary lenses at play in work in this field. Fourth, I introduce the importance of narrative and autobiographical awareness in all scholarship, and explore the insightful work of Lonergan in this regard, through a multifaceted understanding of what he calls 'conversion'. Finally, I exemplify how this might be helpful in a short case study involving scholars currently collaborating on a *Handbook of Music and Christian Theology*.[4] Based on that research experience, I conclude with some initial explorations into this subject which will be an essential element of future work in this field: the connection between scholarly work and biography, that is, the connection between our persons as scholars (life, culture, concerns, religious affiliation, etc.), and the research areas and methods to which we are drawn.

I. Defining our Terms: 'Musicking' and 'Spirituality'

Such a broad and open research question as the one addressed here needs to adopt an equally wide-ranging and inclusive definition of what music is, in its creation, performance, and enjoyment. Christopher Small's definition of 'musicking'—emphasising music as a human activity to which people contribute in many and various ways—is helpful: 'To music is to take part, in any capacity, in a musical performance, whether by performing, by listening, by rehearsing or practising, by providing material for performance (what is called composing), or by dancing', a definition he extends to those involved in the essentially non-musical tasks of taking our tickets or setting up the stage.[5] This open definition allows space to explore more specifically, and with hermeneutic awareness, *when*, *how* and *why* musicking occurs.

---

4   I am grateful to its general editors, Bennett Zon and Steve Guthrie for their willingness to support and collaborate in this with me.
5   Christopher Small, *Musicking: The Meanings of Performing and Listening* (Hanover, NH: University Press of New England, 1998), p. 9.

A similarly broad approach is needed for our understanding of the spiritual, described twice in this project's introduction as a dimension or perceived area of human experience 'beyond the material'.[6] The expression is an interesting one that creatively collides with my own lived experience and what Roman Catholic theology calls sacramentality—a worldview in which the material world mediates the divine such that revelation and access to what Christianity calls 'God' *happens through* matter. The nature of musicking resonates well with this tensive understanding of the spiritual and material worlds. In terms of definitions, my starting point is that of scripture and spirituality scholar, Sandra Schneiders, who describes human spirituality as 'the actualization of the basic human capacity for transcendence ... the experience of conscious involvement in the project of life integration through self-transcendence toward the horizon of ultimate value one perceives'.[7] While the definition is broad and inclusive in recognising the basic human quest for more, its focus on intentionality, ultimate value, and 'conscious involvement' underlines the centrality of conscious meaning-making in human living for an understanding of what spirituality might mean. Schneiders' definition carries an implicit challenge to anyone considering a kind of human drifting in positive, spiritual terms; an important insight. Schneiders suggests that spirituality can be defined more specifically as Christian spirituality when the triune God revealed in Christ is the ultimate concern of one's life; self-transcendence refers to modelling one's life after the life of Jesus; and the 'spirit in spirituality is identified with the "Holy Spirit", all lived out in the community of the Church'.[8]

The way Schneiders connects *and* differentiates spirituality to and from its Christian expression is another example of the importance of how our key term 'and' is negotiated. I would similarly recognise and uphold both the reality that spirituality can be found wherever the human spirit is invested in life and open to the quest for truth and human dignity, and the fact that *Christian* spirituality implies a particular experience

---

6   George Corbett and Sarah Moerman, 'A Toolkit to Measure the Spiritual', A Toolkit to Measure the Spiritual', *University of St Andrews*, https://music-spirituality.wp.st-andrews.ac.uk/a-toolkit-to-measure-the-spiritual/

7   Sandra M. Schneiders, 'Approaches to the Study of Christian Spirituality', in *The Blackwell Companion to Christian Spirituality*, ed. by Arthur Holder (Oxford: Blackwell Publishing Ltd, 2005), pp. 15–33 (at 16).

8   Ibid., p. 17.

and understanding of the God revealed in Christ. While this may seem distant from the theme at hand of music and spirituality, I suggest it is actually at its essence. To explore how music and the spiritual intersect from a Christian perspective implies reflecting on, and defining, how an author positions themselves at this intersection; in Christian terms, the core question could be formulated as follows: can the God revealed in Jesus Christ leave traces in, or be experienced through, the world of music *outside* the context of explicit Christian practice and belief? If so, how do we explain this without overreaching or imposing our Christian interpretative perspectives on the musickings of someone who does not self-identify with the Christian faith? Analogous questions could be posed from within other religious worldviews.

II. Theological Soundbites: Grace, Trinity, and the Ascended Body of Christ

At this intersection of Christianity and culture, I would name three theological 'truths' or doctrines that I think are fruitful in the exploration of music and spirituality, both in their own right and when we bring them together: first, a theology of grace that seeks to recognise the work of God in the world within and beyond the realms of the baptised community of Christian faith; second, our understanding of the ongoing incarnation of Jesus' ascended body in the world and beyond it, which different denominations call ascension theology or the mystical body of Christ; and, third, a trinitarian theology that seeks to take seriously and reimagine the nature and order of how God interacts with the world.

A theology of grace makes it possible to hold together Christian belief in salvation through Jesus with the presence of grace encountered beyond the world of the baptised, because of the universal salvific will of God, whose gift of self to the world prepares and enables human openness to God. This presence of divine grace without (or before) needing to be named can ground our understanding of the arts as a *locus theologicus* of the Word; and, likewise, the obligation to listen to the 'signs of the times' therein lest we miss the work of God in the world. While this position is explored by various theologians, the key forerunner in Catholic theology is Karl Rahner and his understanding of grace as the 'universal existential' offered to all people and present in every personal act of knowing and loving, which has been developed in myriad ways since his work. The quest for grace in the non-Christian is a major focus in theological studies on different realms of contemporary music, although these are often focussed more on the lyrics, with the noteworthy exception of jazz, which has drawn interesting theological reflections on improvisation.[9]

Incarnational theologies that view music as an intersecting point of the material and the divine, of body and spirit, are central to many theologies of the arts. However, Augustine's (354–430) insight into the ascended body of Christ as the heart (or head) of sacramental theology, and the reality of Jesus' ongoing risen body 'in whom we live, move and have our being' (Acts 17:28) present in the world and mediating humanity and God (the reality is the Body of Christ, cf. Col 2:17) is, I suggest, the single most underestimated Christian truth of faith for both spirituality and music studies alike. That God entered the world is scandalous; that God has not left it, is world-changing and transformative.[10]

There are myriad ways in which trinitarian theology and spirituality connect, but one approach, I suggest, has potential to answer some of the questions about connection being raised here: a trinitarian theology which enables us to reimagine how God reveals Godself in the world. We normally name and 'image' God in the order of their theological-if-eternal 'originating' and Scriptural revelation to us: 'Father (Mother/Creator)—Jesus/Son—Spirit'. While this honours the 'order' of salvation in which Christians normally name God's interaction with our world, it

---

9 See the two foundational works: Karl Rahner, *Spirit in the World*, ed. and trans. by. W. Dych (London: Sheed and Ward, 1968); and Karl Rahner, *Hearers of the Word*, trans. by Rolands Walls (London: Sheed and Ward, 1969). However, the best access to this aspect of his thought can be found in chapters of his voluminous *Theological Investigations*. For example: Karl Rahner, 'Reflections on the Experience of Grace', in *Theological Investigations III*, ed. and trans. by Karl H. Kruger and Boniface Kruger (London: Darton, Longman & Todd, 1967), pp. 86–90; Karl Rahner, 'Anonymous and Explicit Faith', in *Theological Investigations XVI*, ed. and trans. by David Morland (London: Darton, Longman and Todd, 1979), pp. 52–59; Karl Rahner, 'Prayer for Creative Thinkers', in *Theological Investigations VIII*, ed. and trans. by D. Bourke (London: Darton, Longman and Todd, 1971), pp. 130–31.

10 See chapters four, five, and six of Maeve Louise Heaney, *Music as Theology: What Music Has to Say About the Word* (Eugene, OR: Pickwick Publications Wipf and Stock, 2012), pp. 135–305.

is often not the order in which we actually sense, experience, and come to know the divine in our lives. Rather, some would suggest, we move in the opposite direction: from the Spirit, through Jesus, to the Source and Origin of all life, whom we never fully grasp. The underlying theological category at stake in this theology of trinitarian grace is revelation: how God interrupts history and becomes present in the world. In the words of Lonergan (drawing on St Augustine):

> God becomes known to us in two ways: as the ground and end of the material universe; and as the one who speaks to us through Scripture and Tradition. The first manner might found a natural Religion. The second adds revealed Religion. For the first, one might say the heavens show forth the glory of God; what can mere words add? But for the second, one must answer that, however trifling the uses to which words may be put, still they are the vehicles of meaning, and meaning is the stuff of man making man [sic].[11]

In other words, there is an explicit categorical knowledge of God that is the fruit of 'Scripture and Tradition', but God goes beyond that, or better said, before that. Human existence is flooded with God's presence, a presence that precedes 'knowledge', and provokes faith. From the perspective of Christian theology, the backdrop of this understanding is Augustine's notion of the double mission of the Son and the Spirit, referring to them as the 'outer' Word and the 'inner' Word: the inner and invisible word of the Holy Spirit, poured out universally into our hearts by the Holy Spirit (*fides ex infusione*); the outer and visible Word of Christ in his historical mission (*fides ex auditu*).[12] And importantly, it is the inner Word that comes first.

These are three rich theological categories with which to imagine the felt spirituality at work in and through music. They allow us to reimagine and articulate our questions in creative ways: where does the

---

11 Bernard J. F. Lonergan, 'Theology in Its New Context', in *A Second Collection. Papers by Bernard J.F. Lonergan S.J.*, ed. by F. J. Ryan and B. J. Tyrell (London: Darton, Longman and Todd, 1974), pp. 55–68 (at 61–62).

12 See Frederick G. Lawrence, 'Grace and Friendship. Postmodern Political Theology and God as Conversational', *Gregorianum* 85. 4 (2004), 795–820 (at 818); Bernard J. F. Lonergan, 'Mission and the Spirit', in *Collected Works of Bernard Lonergan. A Third Collection.*, ed. by Robert M. Doran and John D. Dadosky (Toronto: University of Toronto Press, 1985), pp. 21–33; Frederick E. Crowe, 'Rethinking God-with-Us: Categories from Lonergan', *Science et Esprit* 16. 2 (1989), 167–88.

inner Word of the Spirit 'show up' in musicking? And how, if at all, can we name this? Does it only become 'Christian' mediation when words qualify and articulate the presence of the 'outer Word'? Is that not an excessively monotheistic way of how we might imagine divine action? In my own experience as musician and composer, I have at times related these dual inspirational sources of the Spirit and Jesus with the process of song writing when it moves from music or melody emerging from any given experience to lyrics that seem to express what the music was trying to 'say'—one tending to the other, incomplete without the other. This understanding of the Spirit present before words define things could also help us to name respectfully what takes place in music performed or shared by people of diverse religious experiences or none: music as a school and expression of love of the Spirit poured out into humanity (Rom 5:5) and implicitly known universally in human experiences of unconditional love. John Blacking began to name this years ago in connection with the corporal nature of human life and empathy, but there is more to be explored.[13]

III. Interdisciplinary Perspectives: Musical Semiotics, Hermeneutics, and History

These theological perspectives need, of course, to be complemented by interdisciplinary expertise into the nature of musicking. Three aspects have, to date, been important in my own research: musical semiotics, hermeneutics, and history.

Revelation and the Incarnation of God oblige us to take seriously the nature of the human. With regard to musicking, this implies qualitative attention to the fields of music studies, music theory, history, musicology, and ethnomusicology (in the measure that these can and should be distinguished). My own emphasis on the embodied nature of Christian faith and music has led me to draw extensively on the work of colleagues in musical semiotics, and, especially, on the work of Willem Marie Speelman, who applies the complex field of semiotics to

---

13 John Blacking, *How Musical Is Man?* (London: Faber, 1976).

the musical space.¹⁴ I think attention to and analysis of what is actually happening in the music (melody, tonality, harmony, lyrics, rhythm, etc.) for those who are involved is an ongoing essential element of its understanding; otherwise, we risk theorising away the actual meaning of musicking in each context in which we find ourselves.

Context, history, and a hermeneutical approach to all analysis are now central to any quest for understanding. In relation to our theme, the work of Jean-Jacques Nattiez helps name perspectives in musicking that challenges the discursive nature of philosophical hermeneutics and can therefore fruitfully be used in an ongoing way.¹⁵ If nothing else, these perspectives hold the analyst or interpreter accountable to the context and intentionality with which they approach their analysis, and it is surprising how often such awareness is absent. The intersection of human contexts, history, and interpretation is a necessary element of every study of music and spirituality. However, there is a more immediate, and, perhaps, underestimated perspective that needs to remain front and centre in our considerations: that is, the actual history of interaction between music and the theological, philosophical, and literary understandings of music over the history of human life. The fact is that musicking has been an essential element of human life in every human culture since we have awareness of human life, and of every religious tradition. Conversely, religious and philosophical strands of thought—in my context, the Judaeo-Christian Story—have deeply influenced our understanding, creation, and evaluation of musicking for centuries.¹⁶ Many of the polarising positions in Christian theology between right and left, 'conservative' and 'progressive', classical and contextual, also affect research into music and spirituality and music; these positions can often betray a type of amnesia of the bigger picture of the history of music and thought. Every individual study needs to be cognisant of the bigger shifts of which it is a part, especially the central

---

14 See Willem Marie Speelman, *The Generation of Meaning in Liturgical Songs* (Kampen: Kok Pharos Publishing House, 1995); Willem Marie Speelman, 'Music and the Word: Two Pillars of the Liturgy', *GIA Quarterly* 19.4 (2008), 14–45 (see 14–15, 44–45).

15 See, for example, Jean-Jacques Nattiez, *Music and Discourse. Toward a Semiology of Music* (Princeton, NJ: Princeton University Press, 1990).

16 This is true of both the development of what we might broadly call 'Western or European classical' music and the many strands of music emerging from Afro-American music, in all its variety.

historical questions affecting the history of interpretation: what was/ is important in this moment, and why? What got carried forward and what did not, and why?[17]

IV. The Biographical Nature of Work in Music, Theology, and Spirituality

Evaluating critically the biographical nature of work in the field of music and spirituality is essential, therefore, for clarity moving forward, and is a central concern of my current research. In one sense, it is a consequence of taking history and hermeneutics seriously in a felt quest for understanding or truth: every interpretative act is contextually situated and cannot be fully understood, therefore, without reference to its source. Even when named, however, it seems that awareness stays at the more impersonal level of socio-cultural influences or, as perhaps more recently, of gender and intersectionality, but what about the whole range of an individual's biography? Researchers and scholars tend to write themselves out of their reflections and conclusions so as not to corrupt the 'objective' nature of their work, but is that helpful or even possible? The spiritual 'subjects' of my title refer not only to the themes we address but the embodied and evolving persons that we are, from and through whom our musicking takes shape and our experience and thought reaches paper and publication.

Although underdeveloped, this theme is not new. Over fifty years ago, Johann Baptist Metz wrote a short piece on the biographical nature of theology entitled 'Excursus: Theology as Biography'. Adapted from a piece written on and for Rahner on the occasion of his seventieth birthday, it argues that Rahner's theology is intrinsically linked to his life and spirituality (which some have referred to as an 'everyday mysticism'); as such, it is 'a narrative, biographical dogmatic theology which is at the same time more objectively instructive than any other theology' of that time.[18] The influence of Rahner on the Catholic theological world,

---

17 The questions are drawn from Bernard Lonergan's understanding of the history of interpretation.
18 Johann Baptist Metz, 'Excursus: Theology as Biography', in *Faith in History and Society: Toward a Practical Fundamental Theology*, trans. by David Smith (London:

in shaping the *sensus fidelium* of the Church and the teachings of the Second Vatican Council, would back this claim. Metz's title 'excursus' is nonetheless deceptive, as it seems to suggest an afterthought, somewhat secondary in nature and limited to the thought of one person. For Metz, however, it is clearly more foundational than that. In the book of which it is a part—entitled *Faith in History and Society: Toward a Practical Fundamental Theology*—the 'Excursus' is situated at the end of the central chapter of three chapters addressing the three basic categories of his practical theology (memory, narrative, and solidarity). Metz's category of 'narrative' seeks to challenge the disconnection between story and theory as detrimental to any pretension to a scientific understanding of truth. Marginalising narrative as not critical or pre-critical leaves theology alienated from experience and therefore empty of its originating sources, since story is the very language of God's interruption in history (a definition of revelation initiated by Metz and taken on by others).[19] In order to overcome the unhelpful gap between religious experience and theology as a system, narrative, story, and biography are essential:

> Biographical theology introduces the subject into the dogmatic consciousness of theology. It does not in any sense propagate a new form of theological subjectivism. 'Subject' is not a term that can be exchanged at will in this context for any other. It is man [sic] involved in his experiences and history and capable of identifying himself [sic] again and again in the light of those experiences. Introducing the subject into dogmatic theology therefore means raising man [sic] in his religious experience and biography to the level at which he becomes the objective theme of dogmatic theology. In other words, it means that dogmatic theology and biography can be reconciled with each other and that theological doxography and mystical biography can be brought together.[20]

Written in 1977, Metz's assessment still holds true today, although how we might name the issues has, of course, changed. The very concepts of 'objective' and 'subjective' need more careful attention, as noted above. It is simply false to think that our personhood does not influence our

---

Burns and Oates, 1980), pp. 219–28 (at 224); Lieven Boeve, *God Interrupts History: Theology in a Time of Upheaval* (New York: Continuum, 2007). The statement challenges and complements historical emphases on the difference and disagreement between Metz and Rahner.
19 Metz, *Faith*, pp. 206–16.
20 Ibid., p. 220.

questions, processes, and conclusions, no matter what theme we are dealing with. It is also worth mentioning that the issue of the place of the scholar in research is not exclusive to theology: the social sciences, spirituality, and philosophy all grapple in some way with how this might be named and explored.[21]

For a research project that seeks to explore the connections we can and do make between music *and* spirituality, it is essential that we delve deeper into these underlying, implicit, and often unconscious or subconscious mechanisms that condition how we perceive, experience, and reason. Otherwise, there are undisclosed interests or influencing factors we are in danger of missing, which nonetheless affect and condition our perspectives and conclusions. We have all witnessed instances in academic discourse where the difficulty in reaching a consensus is more due to unacknowledged premises, unnamed biases or horizons of comprehensions, and undeclared interests than to any postmodern inaccessibility of truth. In musicking and spirituality, both domains in which taste, aesthetics, and non-verbal creativity are central, it becomes essential that we consciously seek and name unmentioned aspects of human sensibility.[22]

One way of addressing this in a systematic way in the world of theological investigation is that of Lonergan's exploration of human epistemology, its application to a systematic approach to theological method, and the work of those who continue to develop his thought.[23]

---

21 For example, the emergence of autoethnography in the social sciences, or the implication of the scholar in the academic discipline of Spirituality. See, for instance, Carolyn Ellis and Brydie-Leigh Bartleet, *Music Autoethnographies: Making Autoethnography Sing/Making Music Personal* (Bowen Hills: Australian Academic Press, 2010); Belden C. Lane, 'Writing in Spirituality as a Self-Implicating Act. Reflections on Authorial Discolsure and the Hiddenness of the Self', in *Exploring Christian Spirituality: Essays in Honor of Sandra M. Schneiders*, ed. by Bruce H. Lescher and Elizabeth Liebert (New York: Paulist Press, 2006), pp. 53–69.

22 Feminist (speaking broadly), queer, theopoetic, and post-colonial theologies excel in addressing this. Do the reading lists for the classes we teach incorporate such perspectives?

23 For his major study on how human beings come to know, see Bernard J. F. Lonergan, *Insight: A Study of Human Understanding* (Toronto: University of Toronto Press, 1957). There are a variety of what can be identified as 'Lonerganian' centres of thought, for example, at Boston College, Massachusetts (https://bclonergan.org/); Regis College, Toronto (http://www.lonerganresearch.org); Loyola Marymount University, Los Angeles (https://bellarmine.lmu.edu/lonergan/); Dublin (https://lonerganmorin.wordpress.com/2007/03/04/

It is a complex and compelling exploration of human epistemology and the quest for truth in our contemporary and plural world, which defies contemporary resistance to truth claims and systems in academic research while acknowledging the difficult and complex nature of the quest. It is also a closely knit system in terms of how its parts interact with and imply one another, which is impossible to fully present here. Despite this, I would name one aspect as particularly important for the music–spirituality–theology conversations: Lonergan's understanding of the person of the scholar (or the community of scholars) as foundational to all academic work (from the natural sciences to theology and religious studies).[24] He calls for considerable self-awareness and self-appropriation of the researcher in their work, which, in the sphere of studies into religious studies and theology, leads him to introduce the notion of 'conversion' as an essential guarantor of the quest for theological truth.

Lonergan's use of the term 'conversion' needs to be clarified, however, because he is not talking about 'conversion' in the biblical understanding of *metanoia* (turning back to God and spiritual transformation) but of the need to identify the horizons or worldviews of human experience and knowledge within which we position ourselves, the questions we raise, and the influences we welcome (socio-political, philosophical, religious,

---

dublin-lonergan-centre/); and at the Pontifical Gregorian University, Rome (https://www.unigre.it/it/ua/facolta/teologia/progetto-lonergan/).

24   Interestingly, James Wm. McClendon Jr presents a similar insight, albeit addressing it in a different way. See James Wm. McClendon, Jr, *Biography as Theology: How Life Stories Can Remake Today's Theology* (Nashville, TN: Abingdon Press, 1974). McClendon takes ethics as its entry point to respond to the changing reality of faith practice and knowledge, specifically an 'ethics of character' or 'theology of character': 'I claim here that the truth of faith is made good *in the living of it* or not at all; that living is a necessary condition of the justification of Christian belief. There is no foundational truth available apart from actual life, no set of timeless premises acceptable to believers and unbelievers alike, upon which Christian theology can once and for all found its doctrines ... By recognizing that Christian beliefs are not so many "propositions" to be catalogued or juggled like truth-functions in a computer, but are living convictions which give shape to actual lives and actual communities, we open ourselves to the possibility that the only relevant critical examination of Christian beliefs may be one that begins by attending to lived lives. Theology must be at least biography. If by attending to those lives, we find ways of reforming our own theologies, making them more true more faithful to our ancient vision, more adequate to the age now being born, then we will be justified in that arduous inquiry. *Biography at its best will be theology*' (*Biography as Theology*, pp. viii, 22).

and theological), as well the willingness to broaden them. Lonergan scholars name four such essential areas in need of attention. Although this is only one way among others to differentiate and sub-divide, these categories are insightful, and therefore a perhaps useful framework within which to situate our findings: religious, moral, intellectual, and psychic.[25]

Religious conversion refers not only to the explicit spiritual, religious, or denominational allegiance of the scholar (or lack thereof), although necessary. Rather, it suggests the reality of unconditional love that floods human life, whether the scholar is a believer, or a Christian, or not. The term 'religious conversion' is therefore perhaps misleading but interesting, as it seeks to recognise the 'ultimate concern' that can grasp human living and focus our intentionality, perception, and life. If and how a researcher positions themselves in relation to God or the Spirit or the world as a whole, or religious thought, and if and how they are open to the same, is an important conditioning element of their work. The connection between a person's spirituality, 'religious' experience and their interaction with music is, therefore, highly significant.

Moral conversion refers to how someone understands and embraces the fundamental reality of human freedom: are we living for self (and drifting), on the one hand, or seeking and choosing values and the common good over self and, in doing so, shaping our own lives and those around us, on the other? So, while 'moral conversion' embraces notions of personal accountability and social justice, it goes beyond moralism to the awareness of life as gift and task, and the contexts within which this plays out for each person. This is perhaps the aspect that most coincides with the insistence on the historical and socio-political contexts and background of our thought, with connections to theological and philosophical anthropologies, in feminist, liberation, and post-colonial theologies.

Lonergan's notion of 'intellectual conversion' is perhaps the hardest to access and therefore often the most controversial; its absence leads to difficulties in intellectual dialogue and in the discernment of the differences between persons or between schools of thought. It recognises the complicated epistemological history of the mainly

---

25   I have explored these more fully in chapter four of Maeve Louise Heaney, *Suspended God: Music and a Theology of Doubt* (London: Bloomsbury T&T Clark, 2022), pp. 104–08.

western intellectual tradition; Lonergan asks scholars to identity the epistemological worldview out of which they work, and to 'convert' or move to the insight that we are beings in a world in and of which we mediate meaning. In other words, 'intellectual conversion' positions itself against both idealism (reality is only in our minds) and empiricism (reality is only 'what is actually out there', in front of us), proposing, instead, a critical realism in which we understand the role of the meaning-making subject in the world we live in. While this may seem unduly abstract, the epistemological conundrums facing philosophy, theology, and current musicological debates are exacerbated by our unawareness of how our minds work, of how we think they work, and of the force of the intellectual traditions we buy into when we fail to acknowledge them. Since academics in religious and Christian traditions, as well as music theorists, often work out of these worldviews, naming them is essential for scholarly dialogue to move beyond the dual pitfalls of ideological animosity and a kind of beige tolerance and naïve optimism that all opinions are equal and can somehow co-exist.[26]

Psychic conversion refers to the symbolic and aesthetic awareness of our embodied selves, and how past experiences and wounds, their recognition, and their healing affect our thought much more than we realise. Given the centrality of musicking to human existence and development, I would suggest that attention to the connection between musicking and spirituality will uncover significant aspects of this symbolic dimension of human experience. Naming and critically reflecting on them can only help clarify our tastes, research foci, and collaborations.

V. A Small Preliminary Test Case

During the process of reflecting upon and writing this chapter, I asked a group of people with whom I am currently working in the field of

---

26 Kevin Ernst Korsyn describes this as the tension between the biblical image of the Tower of Babel and the Orwellian Ministry of Truth (from Orwell's novel *1984*), in chapter one of Kevin Ernst Korsyn, *Decentering Music a Critique of Contemporary Musical Research* (Oxford, UK: Oxford University Press, 2003), pp. 5–31; Kevin Ernst Korsyn, 'The Aging of the New Musicology', in *Approaches to Music Research: Between Practice and Epistemology*, ed. by Leon Stefanija and Nico Schüler (Frankfurt am Main: Peter Lang, 2011), pp. 9–23.

music and theology to write about their own motivations and influences in this research field. Colleagues were asked to identify the connections between themselves as scholars (life/biography; culture; concerns; spirituality/religious affiliation/theological education; and personal encounters or friendships), the research areas and methods they are drawn to, and their perception of the societal need, or the 'signs of the times', that required attention. The aim was to kickstart and test some initial reflections on the connections between biography and scholarship to see if more systematic research and analysis would be helpful. I received responses from 70% of those asked, and a further 20% expressed an interest in the project's future. The findings were deep and rich. In an initial (although attentive) reading, I have categorised their reflections into seven subjects which I describe here in the order that best reflects the connections I noticed being made. I have also named the conversions I sense implicit in these responses, although this is complex and not in any way comprehensive.

(a) Musicians *(Psychic)*

All the contributors were active musicians and/or composers interested in a wide variety of music-types, and often with a family background in music, which at times overlapped with their experience of faith and/or church. Most had chosen theology as their professional pathway, which is unsurprising given that my own world and network is more theological than musical, and the selection was drawn from people I intuited would be open to this initial exploration. A broader pool of scholars would allow us to better explore how this affects our work. Ideally, it would include a variety of scholars, at the intersection of music and spirituality/theology, analogous to the threefold typology noted above in Denis Edward's study of scholarship in faith and science.

(b) Music's Influence in Religious Faith/Practice *(Psychic/Religious)*

Most contributors identified an initial or even foundational experience of the connection between musicking and spirituality and/or religious affiliation, either personal or in their family origins. For example:

> We were Protestant, and went to church weekly. My father sang in a choir, and that sound touched me deeply...
>
> Music played a huge part in keeping me attached to church life while many of my peers dropped away...
>
> My music and experience of God always seemed intertwined. As a child, I would occasionally hear a tone inside my ear that I thought was God getting my attention. Today I accept that there may be other explanations, but I continue to experience these tones as gifts because they remind me of the mystery and closeness of God and the embodied yet ethereal mystery of sound and music.
>
> Amongst the things [my aunt] would often sing was a very particular version of the Aaronic blessing by Lowell Mason ... My grandfather was the leader of the choir in their Methodist church ... So, at the heart of things is my memory of so many hymns ... that I never remember learning that pour from my heart.
>
> The worship services in our church were filled with hymn singing and personal testimonies. Men and women would stand and testify through tears to their powerful experience of God's tenderness and closeness. We sang: 'He walks with me and talks with me/along life's narrow way....'

The personal and symbolic resonance of these passages is clear, making the connection between music and the religious and psychic dimensions of conversion stand out.

(c) Denomination (*Religious*)

All the contributors identified some form of religious affiliation and/or spirituality that influenced their thought. Some had struggled with the institutional church's resistance to insight or change—particularly in relation to women and power-struggles, and sought other pathways in spirituality (such as meditation, contemplative practices, etc.). Others recognised how they drew on that worldview in their work.

(d) Autobiography/Identity/Spirituality (*Religious/Psychic/Moral/Intellectual*)

Personal identity and history emerged as another fertile ground of awareness and insight, which highlighted a clear sense of how good and bad past experiences were constitutional in framing identities and research interests. For example:

> Music and the arts were where I found my voice in my early and school days. As a queer kid, it was a way into participation and belonging outside of sport and stereotypically gendered activities.

Named experiences included gender, sensibility to nature, solitude and friendships, family trauma and their consequences (such as eating disorders, depression, etc.), how the classroom may inform positively our curiosity and knowledgebase, and how abusive atmospheres in academic workplaces shape both research interests and our relationship to musicking.

(e) Theological or Other Background/Education (*Religious/Intellectual*) and Personal Encounters (*Religious/Moral/Psychic*)

A person's background and their encounters with others seem to overlap, as in many cases the influence of a person's intellectual passion and the expertise of their mentors was clear and moving. At times, the admired expertise was in *how* they connected music, spirituality, and theology, but the more common denominator in bringing people to research into music and theology was their own personal investment in music alongside a felt interest in *understanding* musicking.

(f) Cultural, Ecclesial, or Social Context (*Moral/Psychic*)

The positive and negative sides of cultural, ecclesial, or social contexts continually shaped how participants unpacked their research. An example of the former was the principle of sacramentality in Catholicism, which envisages the arts as mediators of revelation. But the more challenging aspects of these contexts seem even more influential in shaping the foci of people's research fields, as the unfinished or negative understanding of experience and thought leads to further exploration and/or pushback. For example, the unfinished and to a large extent, 'experimental liturgical reforms of Vatican II'; the historical (and still present) marginalisation of women in a Christian understanding; fundamentalist rigidity in welcoming socio-political issues; the inner manoeuvrings of the institutional church in liturgical matters, and its resistance to change. In the words of one researcher: 'I think this has made me more polemical/apologetic in my approach to my scholarship, and more committed to the axiom that the spiritual is political'.

(g) Music and Words: Tension and Dichotomy, and Mutual Enrichment (*Intellectual/Religious/Moral/Psychic*)

The dichotomy between experience and theory, mysticism and theology, musicking and music studies, emerges clearly in many of the contributions:

> There were dear people in my childhood church who warned me against going to seminary, because it would water down the mystery of my faith and steer the warmth of my devotion into too-neat categories. Likewise, some of the musicians in the bands I played in in high school warned me against going to music school, saying that it would make my playing stiff or too conventional.

A common trait was an awareness of the limits of words to fully express the divine, however that was named (faith, mysticism, mystery, etc.), combined with the desire to understand more analytically, which led people to the more academic work of music theory and theology.

> My religious upbringing meant that I never doubted that reality exceeded the realm of the linguistic, the empirical, or that which could be expressed in logical syllogisms.

> My whole life has been driven by a desire to communicate something of who God is, in music, in words, in both together.

> My own approach was somewhat bi-polar, inhabiting both sides of this dichotomy at different times …When musicking … I feel like a musician expressing and discovering my faith in music; when teaching or writing, I am a theologian expressing and discovering faith discursively and conceptually—even when the subject is music. The balance/proportion is not clear—I think it probably fluctuates—but since I have university credentials in theology, and not in music, I tend to find myself nudged in the direction of 'theologian' (by others but also by myself).

Also common was the felt tension in deciding which pathway to take as a life option, 'torn between music and pastoral ministry', or between music and theology. The option for the academy as a pathway was described relatively frequently as 'safer', although theory and musicking (in whatever form it takes) were usually described as mutually enriching:

> I see my musicking and my theology as mutually informing.

The insights into how scholars negotiate this dichotomy was profound. For example, in one songwriter-theologian's reflection on past music-making and her shift to theological language:

> What struck me when I listened to [songs written when younger] again is that to me they seem to express the voice of a child. I don't know what my adult voice sounds like, except in the words of books that are no longer musical. Sometimes I wish I could return to song-writing, yet there is a naiveté that has gone from me now.

Most show considerable awareness of how navigating the two affects and enriches their work:

> [I] find music a salient entry point to work in liturgical reform and renewal— ... for much of my career.

> That said, I am instinctively and incessantly analytical—music theory appeals, e.g., and so does theological method and things like theoretical physics. I like to plumb the depths, while also tearing down barriers to the experience of mystery

> I wonder how much of my theological work is an attempt to articulate my musical experience, even to set it on a firm footing.

And this in an ongoing way, not just as a past or even foundational dynamic. The factors reflected upon do not only merge as shaping the past, but also that of an ongoing process of interaction and influence.

> I am constantly re-inventing my music and my theology; I am constantly being interrupted.

This mutuality is not just personal but structural, since music performs 'sets of codes and conventions that have culturally semiotic meaning ... the profound interdependence of musicality and sexuality—music as a semiotics of desire—with all the political, socio-historical implications and interanimations this nexus entails'.

Provisional Conclusions and Further Questions

The above testimonies, categorised into seven subjects and implicit conversions, set the stage for a series of questions which emerge from this work, as starting points for further research. Indeed, the participants' own varied and fascinating questions are pertinent to this line of enquiry:

> Today many reject the religion of their parents in favour of a broader 'spirituality' or 'mindfulness'. There is a need to present religion (and for many it is Christianity) in ways that support spiritual exploration and integration, regardless of where the spiritual quest leads. Musicians have their creativity to draw upon for this sacred work, and musical theologians/spiritual directors are best suited to innovate ways to companion them on this journey.

> Much of my waking life is spent trying to work out, then, how 'God' can make sense in a world that has no memory of the kind of life that was lived when I was a child, no memory of music and God fused together.

> If music and musical interpretation are semiotics of desire, what deep dark desires drive exclusionary, conservative theologies thereof? ... Musico-erotic experiences (especially from the margins) save music from being a proof-text for Greek metaphysics or Calvinist doctrine.

> Why does anything sound good? Why is it that a vibrating string or a struck piece of leather should move me so profoundly? Why should song form such an essential element of our worship? ... My questions about music were more theological than musicological.

> The eclipse of community and of a sacramental worldview potentially make Christianity (and at least ritual worship) untenable... Can we still celebrate the Eucharist? Lament and the dark side of sacramentality need exploration. Processes of liturgical reform must be opened up and revitalised; local agency is essential; theologians need a place within the conversation that can inform 'official' change. Post-conciliar formation (liturgical and otherwise) of Catholics has failed; a Catholic fundamentalism endures. Expertise in engaging with primary sources in liturgical studies is diminishing; this makes informed engagement with tradition difficult.

> The gap between how Christianity expressed its worldview and how the world does so. This includes the epi-logos (post-word) nature of human meaning making and its challenge to Christianity's tenet of Truth/truths as accessible and eternal.

Although this is but an initial exploration into some scholars' own thoughts about what they are doing and why, I think it heralds an insightful and necessary focus for future work in the field. As noted above, it is incomplete in its representation, making the inclusion of other perspectives all the more attractive and necessary. This chapter's invitation to take the person and biography of the scholar more seriously seeks to lay a foundation for a more honest, nuanced, and fruitful understanding of the connection between musicking and spirituality.

The implicit but unnamed worlds of meaning and horizons of comprehension are often the 'elephant in the room', impeding us from moving towards understanding and, if not consensus, at least a harmony of sorts. However, welcoming biography into the space of scholarship has consequences, not least of which is that attention to narrative may change and disrupt the perceived 'eternal' nature of our conclusions, or the specific expertise we claim. Life moves and changes: people, events, encounters, and the process of human growth, which is never linear, can lead us to change direction. But then, here below 'to live is to change', as John Henry Newman put it, and musicking is part of the invasive, interruptive, and transformative symbolic revelation of God.

12. The Impetus to Compose: Where is Fantasy Bred?

Richard E. McGregor

I have spent the last thirty years or more trying to understand the decisions composers make during the process of composition. One might understand this as an analytical concern for what 'happens' during the composition of a musical work, and particularly how the first ideas take shape, where they come from and how they evolve, and also the largely unconscious decision-making processes that occur through the whole course of a work's composition. Sometimes this element is referred to as inspiration, a word which shares a common root with spirituality.[1] From quite early on I realised that there is, in most composers, a conflict between what is intuitive, and what is a product of processes which probably have their origin in early experiences, in study, and in personal understandings of musical shapes and forms. In this chapter, I first describe three personal experiences of composing—over a twenty-five year timespan—which have profoundly influenced my own view of musical composition. Second, I turn to Peter Maxwell Davies' eclectic approach to composition, an approach that has fascinated me, as a musicologist, for many years. Third, I widen my discussion to consider the compositional processes of a series of canonical and more contemporary composers, including James MacMillan and Wolfgang Rihm. Finally, I return to my own experiences again in light

---

1   Richard E. McGregor, '"Songs That Seem to Come from Nowhere": Composition: Inspiration and Spirituality May Share a Common Root, but Can We Talk about Them in the Same Breath?' (unpublished keynote lecture, Music and Spirituality conference, Middlesex University, 20 May 2022).

of my analysis of the differences, and points of similarity, between the compositional approaches of Davies, MacMillan, and Rihm.

I. Personal Context

I began composing in the early 1970s by trying to express the musical ideas which I had in my head in a coherent and communicative manner. For me, this was not the best time to start composing, however, as I felt caught between two polarities. Younger composers who had come to the fore in the 1960s had moved away from the strict serial music of the 1950s, and towards a more expressive form of writing (towards, indeed, a new post-expressionism, which was nonetheless typically technique-based, flowing from their previous engagement with serial orthodoxy). But then there were other composers who seemed to allow chance to determine the flow of musical ideas. The essence of my problem was that, on the one hand, I felt that music should have a structure and a logic behind it, while at the same time being capable of direct and free expression. For me, this came to a head in 1982 as the only non-Italian left in the Franco Donatoni composition summer school at Siena. I spent five weeks writing a piece for solo flute in which I could explain all the compositional decisions, choice of pitches, dynamics, form, and structure—sweating over every single pitch's relation to the whole. Having completed it, I then wrote, in an hour, completely freely, and with no planning ahead, a piece for solo oboe, which lasted almost the same length of time as the flute piece. This piece came straight out of my head. I called the former '...too much I' the sun' and the latter *Pietà*. This experience provoked questions for me that were profound and far-reaching. If I used my whole intellect, I could order and control every aspect of composition, but was that enough? And yet, I could also write down an oboe piece, as if automatically, with no conscious planning or forethought. How does one resolve the apparent tension between controlled order and spontaneous inspiration?

About twelve years later, I tried the same process using an early Atari computer with essentially the same result. This new piece, now transcribed as *Sarajevo 583* for strings, had an audible unity imposed by my brain, but I couldn't explain it. Finally, another decade or so on, I composed a fanfare for the newly created University of Cumbria.

I wrote several possible beginnings, and nothing was quite right, so I took it to one of my classes and explained my problem. A member of the class responded with the suggestion that I should not try and think of models but just let my brain be free to respond—in other words, use mindfulness. I sat down there and then, and composed an opening idea out of my head and, of course, that was the right one. There was twenty-five-year gap between the first and last of these incidents and something changed in the meantime. Quite simply, by that time it had become obvious to me that some underlying 'inspiration' and/or 'spirituality' was key to any understanding of musical processes, whether these were controlled by the conscious mind or not.

II. The Application of Musicology

In an attempt to answer some of these questions, I turned to the music of one composer whose eclectic approach had always intrigued me. My interest in the music of Peter Maxwell Davies had been sparked by the first performance of Davies' highly evocative work for soprano and orchestra *Stone Litany* at Musica Nova Festival in Glasgow in 1973, and through subsequently studying Davies' *Second Fantasia on John Taverner's 'In Nomine'* at Glasgow University, as a student of Stephen Arnold. Arnold had, in turn, been a pupil of Davies at Cirencester Grammar School when he taught there between 1959 and 1962, and Davies' influence on Arnold had been quite profound. Davies gave him copies of the sketches with the generating charts for the *Fantasia* (sketches which had been rescued from the fire that took place in his cottage in Dorset in 1969). The significance of these sketches and charts only became obvious to me somewhat later. On the face of it the musical content was quite simply what is known as transformation sets, where one musical idea or thematic entity is mutated into another, which could be, for example, the idea's own inversion. These charts do not give any indication, however, of how to deploy the generated material in a developing musical context, much less how the form and structure of the work is affected by them. On reflection, the process of thematic metamorphosis which is embedded within this compositional activity could be thought of as a process of transfiguration—thematic material undergoing a process of change, development, and progression.

However, that spiritual aspect of the work is effectively hidden from the listener as it operates as a structural framework underpinning the work rather than occurring overtly on the surface.

Looking back on Davies' career, one could suggest that these transformation processes were almost a musical metaphor of the changes that were happening within his own personality. The *Fantasia* was written during what he himself described in his later journals as 'the terrible years' when he had to confront the 'Antichrist' within himself.[2] There are no journals for the decade from 1962 but his statements suggest that at least part of it was to do with an acceptance of his sexuality. Certainly, the music of this period displays many psychological peculiarities, being both introvert and extrovert, showing extreme order on the one hand in some places, such as *Worldes Blis* for orchestra, and being freely extrovert and neo-expressionistic, as in *Eight Songs for a Mad King* on the other. This duality was only obvious to me much later.

Davies never felt comfortable, to put it mildly, with some of the aspects of formal religious practices within 'the church', but certainly his early conception of God was firmly tied to an understanding of his creativity. In a journal entry written in 1955 at the age of twenty-two, he declared, probably to himself at this time, 'I [write], because I am created anew in each work, & such renewal is satisfactory when one has hopes of ambition to eventually being created *perfect'. The '*perfect' is elaborated by a note in brackets presumably added a little later '*(in God's likeness?)'.[3] In 1974, and almost by way of explaining to himself, he wrote:

> I realise that my being alone, first in Princeton, then in Tollard Royal in Wiltshire, between '62 & '64 enabled me to come to living terms with the shattering upheaval which broke through the veneer of my attempts to interpret sound-images in terms of Christ, the Virgin Mary &c, & forced me to take into account the Antichrist in myself resulting [in] years of darkness, from which Hymnos [1967], Rev &Fall [1965–66], L'homme armé [1968] and probably (though late) Worldes Blis [1966–69] were the eventual surface manifestations, as well as the opera... Here, in Rackwick,

---

2   Peter Maxwell Davies, *Journal 2010–11*. Davies' private journals, which are housed at the British Library, are currently under embargo. I thank the Trustees of the Peter Maxwell Davies Trust for granting me permission to quote from them.

3   Peter Maxwell Davies, *Journal 21* [in fact, it is 23, apparently renumbered by composer] (1955–56).

> I feel I can better attempt to cope with what I can only describe in visual/sensual terms as a burning of whitening light, though this is inadequate; again, it has to do with a typus of sound-images.[4]

Of course, one must recognise that composers can, and do, create their own personal (and sometimes private) mythologies. At this stage in his life, Davies was not at all confident in his abilities and significance as a composer, and that, in truth, lasted most of his life. When writing in his later journals, he was perhaps conscious that they would be read at some time by others. At the age of forty, however, he was probably still writing for himself as a record, and the journal that he kept from 1976–78 was entirely in the personal 'invented script' which he developed at about the age of fourteen (and which I am now able to transliterate). He did later show this (but did not translate it) to Gerard McBurney in 1991, by which time he must have realised that it would eventually be read.[5] Rodney Lister, who was also shown this journal, reported that Davies said that 'some of his diaries [are] in his personal writing language, which, at least as I recall, he said he'd developed because he'd realized he was gay, and he didn't want anybody to be able to read his diaries and see that...'.[6]

Davies' reference to 'whitening light', a phrase which recurs as the title of his work *A Mirror of Whitening Light* (1977), gives a clue to two of his obsessions: an interest in alchemical associations, and superstition—aspects of his 'personality' which surface in some of his works—not primarily for the listeners' benefit but as compositional imperatives. Sometime in Autumn 1974 he wrote in his journal:

> ... every journey ... is part of this quest, which is a search for the CRUX whereby all these experiences will be able to be not only related—but transformed—each and every one—*caudâ pavonis**—ignious [sic] to gold. If it is to do with the recurrence of archetypal principles—generating principles—and recurrent forms—forms in movement, faces, cycles, number—images or constellations (probably based on natural forms, groped for slowly & painfully & dubiously with unsatisfactory results in the music)—unified in a relationship—sealing principle (called

---

4   Peter Maxwell Davies, *Journal 35* [the journal is incorrectly labelled 1966–71] (1974)
5   Peter Maxwell Davies, 'Letters to Gerard McBurney', Ms Mus 1779, October 1991, p. 6f (British Library, London), and personal communication with the author from McBurney, 17 March 1995.
6   Rodney Lister, email to the author, 23 November 2021. Permission granted.

Mercurius?) but which exists, not in time or space, which would mean that at one moment one could say it's achieved and at the next build up on the achievement, whereas in fact this MEANS is not perceived at any given moment or at any given place—but the principle exists behind both of these, &- enormous mechanical & spiritual effort is reqd to make it manifest behind any moment or spot of place, whereby moments in places can be illuminated by its presence, which is outside them.[7]

'Mercurius' hints at the magic square processes which would come to dominate his larger scale works from 1976 onwards. It has never been absolutely clear when Davies actually saw the work written by Gillian Whitehead, then his student, in which she used magic squares as pitch generators. That circumstance caused him to tell her that 'you've even made me think' because, apart from the patterns which can be created when substituting pitches for the number, there are both alchemical and, for Davies, personal associations attached.[8] As an example of such associations, when writing to Gerard McBurney in 1991, the composer refers to the four elements as symbolic: 'there are "cyphers" for the 4 elements (obviously!) & for polarities of states of mind, all entirely personal, but I hope their "meaning" comes over in the abstractions of the music'.[9] As to the exact mathematical abstractions into sound, however, there was usually a degree of circumspection:

> The forces generated during the composition of *The Lighthouse* [1979] and *Resurrection* [1986–87] on the other hand were such that I felt they had to be 'spiked'—I therefore introduce specific 'wrong' notes into various sequences including magic squares, to neutralize any Nekuomanteia (evocation of shades) ....

Even twenty years earlier, Davies had introduced 'superstitious deviations, something done first in *Prolation*, [1957/1958] where I broke absolutely perfect arithmetical symmetry out of a conviction that it was presumptuous—possibly even dangerous! —to attempt any exact imitation of higher natural perfection'.[10]

---

7   Davies, *Journal 35*, possibly 18 September 1974.
8   Gillian Whitehead (New Zealand composer), email to the author, 31 May 2016.
9   'Letters to Gerard McBurney', Ms Mus 1779, Davies to McBurney, 5.
10 Peter Maxwell Davies, 'A Composer's Point of View (I): On Music, Mathematics and Magic Squares', in *Peter Maxwell Davies, Selected Writings*, ed by Nicholas Jones (Cambridge, UK: Cambridge University Press, 2017), pp. 215 and 217.

What becomes apparent when one tries to interpret any spiritual impetus behind, or underpinning, Davies' work is that it is both complex and loaded with symbolism that provides a generating source for the musical expression. One such example of symbolism driving the genesis of a work is found in *Ave Maris Stella* [1975], seemingly the first composition in which Davies used a magic square to generate thematic and harmonic material for the work. This was not just any magic square but the square of the Moon (the 9 x 9 square) into which an adapted plainchant is woven. *Ave Maris Stella* is one of the plainchants (LU1259) from the *Liber Usualis* that Davies mined for sources, but it is also a direct link with the Virgin Mary through the *Catena Legionis* antiphon 'Who is she that comes forth as the morning rising, fair as the moon, bright as the sun', and Mary's liturgical birthday falls on September 8, Davies' birthday.

It is possible that the spiritual influence of these connections was a crucial personal point of origin for Davies' creativity and might have translated at times into more abstract conceptions—such as into 'Whitening Light' and the symbol-infused poetry of George Mackay Brown, a Roman Catholic convert. Davies wrote to Roderic Dunnett in 1974, presumably while actually composing *Ave Maris Stella* and his First Symphony, requesting a 'motto to go on an *ex-libris* sticker for the books here… make something poetic & concise to do with book but meaning (spiritual) water of life…'[11]

Intermedio

The above background illustrates how the process of coming to begin composing can be seen and understood, not analytically, but symbolically as a journey, which invokes spiritual elements of different types to allow work to proceed. Analysis of compositions by Maxwell Davies reveals that the formal structures he uses are not particularly unusual. To a degree his music works with recognisable sections, and in his scores, he even writes, albeit in his personal script, the words 'middle eight', 'reprise', 'durchführung' [development] for sections into which the pitch and

---

11 Peter Maxwell Davies, 'Correspondence with Roderic Dunnett', currently uncatalogued, acquired 2021 (British Library, London); Peter Maxwell Davies, 'Davies to Dunnett', 16 August 1974 (British Library, London).

rhythm processes from the magic square are placed. Such strict processes were only applied to the more formal works such as symphonies and concertos since, once he was sure of his technique, he allowed himself to express other ideas in a freer and less rigidly defined way.

III. Development

Working so intently and intensely on the music of Maxwell Davies suggested to me that whether consciously or unconsciously, the generating ideas for a composition need to be in place to allow the actual composition to proceed. I did not, at that stage, link such processes directly to some aspect or understanding of spirituality. However, at a certain point some twenty years ago, I took the decision to broaden my exploration of composers' works beyond that of Davies. The reasons for this decision are quite obvious: one cannot make any form of case for musical development based simply on one composer's work, but equally, and importantly, I had become interested in not just the creative process, not just inspiration, but what spiritual understandings contributed to the work of different composers. I began by considering composers' expressions of their spirituality, starting with the most obvious ones, such as Johann Sebastian Bach and Joseph Haydn, but also considering more contemporary composers such as Arvo Pärt, Francis Poulenc, and James MacMillan.[12]

At that time, the music of Pärt, along with that of others such as Henryk Górecki and John Taverner, was receiving some publicity and analytical discussion, although not always of a favourable kind, as when they were designated 'holy minimalists'. They followed, in a way, the example set by Olivier Messiaen whose music I knew well and, importantly, had also performed. However, at the time, no one had written anything of substance about the music that James MacMillan was composing. One understood that MacMillan was motivated by a strong Catholic faith which could not but be reflected in his music, and, one might expect to observe—as indeed is the case—that his personal spirituality would be quite obvious. In addition, I judged that to focus on just one composer again was not going to answer some of

---

12   Richard McGregor, '"Laus Deo?" On Composers' Expression of their Spirituality', *Spirituality and Health International* 6.4 (2005), 238–45.

the questions that had been raised by my studies of Maxwell Davies. I had the opportunity to go to the Paul Sacher Stiftung in Basel for an extended period, so I began looking at the sketches made by several composers from the collections held there.

I initially considered three composers: Harrison Birtwistle, Sofia Gubaidulina, and Wolfgang Rihm. Birtwistle's music was attracting a lot of analytical attention, particularly in the United Kingdom, but his work came out of the same artistic milieu as Davies'. Despite the very different personalities involved there was therefore a substantial degree of crossover, particularly in their first two creative decades, and, I felt, it might be difficult to find sufficient areas of difference to build upon. In addition, there were always elements of Davies' personality and writing which suggested at least some kind of spiritual understanding: an aspect of his personality which has been confirmed, though complexified, by study of his journals. I was less sure that I would find something comparable for Birtwistle.

Gubaidulina, on the other hand, undoubtedly exhibited clearly defined spiritual elements in her work and her compositional processes, and would have provided an interesting point of comparison with MacMillan's work, since the works of both composers seem more concerned with forms of expression which draw on a deeper spiritual core than appears to be the case with the 'holy minimalists' (but that is actually only a surface understanding of those composers' works). However, to really understand Gubaidulina one must understand not only Russian but her Russian temperament and motivation, and this latter can easily be misunderstood, as witness some critical reaction to Dmitri Shostakovich's work.

Rihm was a very different proposition coming out of what was, slightly disparagingly, called the *Neu-Einfachkeit* [New Simplicity] movement. This was a term coined by the German composer Aribert Reimann to categorise certain composers, whereas Rihm himself, writing in 1977, expressed a preference for the descriptors *Neue Vielfalt* [New Multiplicity] and *Neue Eindeutigkeit* [New Clarity/Uniqueness/ Explicitness].[13] Rihm's compositional process is often described as

---

13 Wolfgang Rihm, '"Neue Einfachheit"—Aus-und Einfälle', *Hifi-Stereophonie* 16.4 (1977), 420, reprinted in *Ausgesprochen Schriften und Gespräche*, ed. by Ulrich Mosch, 2 vols (Winterthur: Schott 1997), I, 354.

'intuitive'—meaning that he writes very few sketches and composes straight onto the page. In most cases, there is little evidence of change of mind, although on occasion a whole page of writing is rejected (this happened in the Fourth Quartet for example). Rihm was brought up a Catholic, although his later relationship to his faith is not clear. This made him an interesting parallel with MacMillan even though the cultural environment of each composer was so different. Particularly in his earlier works, moreover, Rihm did not seem to be concerned with expressing anything overtly spiritual but relied on his own inspiration. Do not these share, though, as we have seen, the same root?

In the context of a comparison between the creative impulses of MacMillan and Rihm there is an interesting statement made by Rihm in an interview with Kirk Noreen and Joshua Cody regarding his early years:

> I was very religious at the time and wanted to become a priest. Whenever I could, I made my way to the church. One reason was, of course, that I was deeply attracted by the rites (I was Catholic), the incense, the singing, the music as such—above all the organ. I wanted to compose a Mass and asked my mother for large-size manuscript paper. I must have been eight or nine years old.

He then goes on to describe how he was unable to write the music, but that he would improvise on the piano (something he apparently still does) so that 'the Mass was "in my fingers", but I could not yet put it down on paper. Indeed, improvisation was for quite some time to be my "salvation"'. It was, however, a short note that Karlheinz Stockhausen sent to him in 1970 that motivated his subsequent development:

Dear Wolfgang Rihm,

Please only heed your inner voice.

With kindest regards.

Yours,

Karlheinz Stockhausen[14]

---

14 'Wolfgang Rihm in Conversation with Kirk Noreen and Joshua Cody', *Sospeso*, 2006, http://web.archive.org/web/20060525100029/http://www.sospeso.com:80/contents/articles/rihm_p1.html

Although it was not obvious at first, it is now clear to me that I was drawn to understanding the creative impetus in composers who, somewhere in their background or foreground (as in MacMillan's case), had encountered religion in a positive way.

It is hard to make specific statements concerning a composer's methodology and what feeds their initial creative process if one looks at slighter works or smaller scale works, often written to commission. Rather, it is necessary to look at those works in which the composer feels that they have something to express of a more lasting, and usually more extensive and expansive nature. Religious works do not, of themselves, provide many answers. As Davies wrote when speaking about his religious works: 'As the authorities at Westminster Cathedral said to me ... they had commissioned Britten and he was not a Catholic, and they commissioned Vaughan Williams, who was an outspoken atheist' so why would they not choose him.[15] Davies is frequently characterised as an atheist but, as I have hinted, this is not really an accurate description of his spirituality.

The creative impetus can be most easily examined through the larger scale works, particularly the symphonies in the case of both Davies and MacMillan, Davies' and Rihm's string quartets, and Rihm's many large-scale orchestral works. Despite their quite different approaches and forms of musical expression, both MacMillan and Davies seem to need to locate their symphonic thought within some aspect of personal feelings or experience. In MacMillan's case, the symphonies often have an explicit religious/spiritual underpinning. As Phillip Cooke puts it in relation to his first symphony *Triduum III: Symphony (Vigil)* (1997): 'It is the work that relates to the Easter Vigil ... and by its very nature deals with the journey from darkness to light which the service traditionally represents', while the Fourth Symphony had a 'secret' programme which was decoded by Seán Docherty as a 'setting' of the Pauline Mass, no hint of which appeared in the composer's programme note.[16] However, in a deliberately direct message to his listeners, MacMillan's

---

15 Jones, ed., *Selected Writings*, p. 267.
16 Phillip A. Cooke, *The Music of James MacMillan* (Woodbridge: Boydell and Brewer, 2019), p. 110; Seán Doherty, 'The Mass "Transubstantiated" into Music: Quotation and Allusion in James MacMillan's Fourth Symphony', *Music and Letters* 99.4 (2018), 635–71.

programme note for his Fifth Symphony, subtitled *Le grand inconnu*, refers specifically to the third person of the Trinity which 'still feels like relatively unexplored territory, so perhaps now is the time to explore this mysterious avenue, where concepts of creativity and spirituality overlap...', the work being 'an attempt to explore the mystery discussed above in music for two choirs and orchestra'.[17]

Maxwell Davies, on the other hand, was drawn to more specifically personal resonances but some with an element of mystery or deeper spiritual significance behind them. The Fourth Movement of his Third Symphony was written at a time when his parents were ill and coming to the end of their lives. Knowing this to be the case generated a recurring dream of the:

> ...blackened Victorian gothic church [of Agecroft Cemetery], now abandoned, with shrubs growing from the broken roof, and crows cawing from the tower; in my dream these become the angels of death, calling with voices of inhumanly high trumpets across the gravestones from their fastness of fathomless nightmare.[18]

However, as Nicholas Jones points out, this same exact symbolism reappears throughout Davies' compositional career, from the *St Michael Sonata* (1957) via the Sixth Symphony (1996) to *Roma Amor* (2010). In addition, the Third Symphony shares with the Sixth Symphony a reference back to *Parade*, a piano work written when the composer was fifteen. *Parade* seems to symbolise for Davies some kind of understanding of his creative impulse as well as providing him with a starting point on which to build. Other symbolic elements which are embedded in the Third Symphony include his relationship with the actor Metin Yenal who is embodied within the thematic material subjected to the magic square of the sun (whose symbolism needs no explanation).

I found these personal connections in Davies' and MacMillan's works to be highly significant in my search to understand the creative process. However, on the face of it, the music of Rihm cannot be explained in the

---

17 James MacMillan, *Symphony No.5: 'Le grand Inconnu'* (*The Great Unknown*) (London: Boosey & Hawkes, 2018), https://www.boosey.com/cr/music/James-MacMillan-Symphony-No-5-Le-grand-Inconnu/102048

18 Peter Maxwell Davies as quoted in Nicholas Jones, 'Analytical Perspectives on the Third Symphony of Peter Maxwell Davies' (unpublished doctoral thesis, Cardiff University, 1999), p. 156.

same way. There are, nonetheless, important, if perhaps unconscious, spiritual concepts which underlie his approach. As a composer Rihm has a specific notion of transformation. Indeed, one might say that Rihm transfigures an idea/ideas/material—that is, literally 'carries [them] across'—from one work to another, particularly when the works could be conceived as forming some kind of cycle (an idea to which I will return shortly). As I have written before: 'though starting "at the beginning", both literally and metaphorically, has a certain logic [for Rihm], even this is an open concept for much of his work, since his predilection for cycles and continuations of material already explored make his music more like a continuum [my word] and less like discrete singularities having a beginning and an end'.[19] When I interviewed him in 2000 at the Huddersfield Contemporary Music Festival, Rihm said:

> Each piece has a different way. Sometimes a piece started, and I don't know where it belongs, this is what I do, and it becomes the middle of the piece and the following week it's the end, and the next day maybe it's the beginning. Sometimes the piece is written from the beginning to the end. Sometimes I need two years and sometimes I need two hours. Pieces are individuals.[20]

The idea of a continuum where there is no beginning and no end: a piece just starts and, at a certain point, it ends, has at least a feeling of the creative impetus underpinning the process. But with Rihm the process has to do with speed. What sketches he makes (and by sketches, I mean the notation of random musical ideas rather than a fully worked out draft) are clearly not placed according to any pattern—just located in whatever space happens to exist on the sheet of manuscript. This is particularly true of his earlier works, but even when he writes a work straight in, it is about speed. The 2008 programme booklet for *Deus Passus* quotes from the answer to a question put to him by Achim Heidenreich:

> Mein Kopf, meine Imagination, meine Ideen—das sind meine Hilfsmittel. Ich schreibe meine Partituren mit der Hand, mit dem Füller. Das geht viel schneller als über Taste und Computer. Das fliegende Vorankriechen

---

19 The article was entitled 'On Second Thoughts ... In the Beginning' (2006) and only now do I see that I was making spiritual connections.
20 Richard McGregor, 'Hunting and Forms: An Interview with Wolfgang Rihm', in *Contemporary Music: Theoretical and Philosophical Perspectives*, ed. by Max Paddison and Irène Deliège (Farnham: Ashgate Publishing Limited, 2010), pp. 349–60 (at 352).

darf ich mir nicht verlangsamen lassen. Das ist meine Vorgehensweise: kriechender Flug.[21]

[My head, my imagination, my ideas—these are my tools. I write my scores by hand, with a pen. It's much faster than using a keyboard or computer. I can't let the flying (?fleeting) creep forward (?progress) slow me down. That's my approach: creeping flight.]

It is therefore interesting that the sketches for his works to religious texts from the last decade and a half are much more extensive, and especially those for his *Missa brevis*—surprising for an unaccompanied work lasting just 20 minutes. The same is true for a work, *De profundis* for choir and orchestra, written shortly after and lasting five minutes less than the *Missa brevis*. The *Universal Edition* website for the online score of *De profundis* makes an interesting comment: 'as in *Deus Passus*, Rihm talks again about finalities with a deceptively simplified musical language; waiving technical difficulties does not at all preclude profound utterance—as often, the apparent simplicity is actually the difficulty'.[22]

IV. Ensemble and Finale

In reflecting on these three composers in tandem for this chapter, the aspect of Rihm's work which does seem to create a resonance with the other two, albeit expressed by them in different ways, is the concept of cycles—where one created work becomes the 'jumping off point' for the next and the third builds on the second, and so on. This means that the continuity of the first becomes the building block for the others: a process of continuing creation and recreation. We see the same sort of idea in Maxwell Davies' works expressed in the way that a work throws off satellite works which perhaps share origination material with the main 'planet'. The process might even go the other way and an

---

21 Achim Heidenreich and Wolfgang Rihm, '"Größtmögliche unschörfe": Wolfgang Rihm über das komponieren, das politische in der musik und sein neues Bühnenstück Das Gehege: ein Gesprach mit Achim Heidenreich', *Neue Zeitschrift für Musik* 168.1 (2007), 10–13. The translation below is my own.
22 Wolfgang Rihm, 'De Profundis', *Universal Edition*, 2015, https://www.universaledition.com/wolfgang-rihm-599/works/de-profundis-16963. The sketches for both works are held at the Paul Sacher Stiftung in Basel, Switzerland.

earlier work embeds itself within a larger work.[23] A similar idea occurs in MacMillan's music, and particularly in his earlier works, where a previous composition, not necessarily written by him, is like a spiritual presence within the work as a whole. Two examples of this are Robert Carver's setting of *O bone Jesu* which underpins MacMillan's work of the same name (2002), and the hymn *Veni, Veni, Emmanuel* which is at the heart of his work with that title (1992).[24]

The aspects of all three composers' approaches to composition which I have articulated here have some affinity with my own rather limited experience that I outlined above. There is an apparent tension between the free-flowing creative impetus, which one could perhaps readily equate with the essence of spirituality, and the actuality of both the writing down of the music (not just the time it takes), and its 'perceived' constraints—what one feels one must undertake for a specific work. When the ideas, the creative urge, the spirituality, flows freely, then the unconscious is allowed to become conscious.

It is quite striking how this compositional phenomenon parallels some of the characteristics of 'peak experience'. In his chapter 'Emotions in Strong Experiences with Music', Alf Gabrielsson draws on the initial articulation of this phenomenon by Abraham Maslow, who:

> ...found several characteristics of generalised peak experience, such as total attention on the object in question, complete absorption, disorientation in time and space, transcendence of ego, and identification or even fusion of the perceiver and the perceived. Peak experience is good and desirable; there is a complete loss of fear, anxiety, inhibition, defence, and control ...The experience may occasionally be described as sacred.[25]

---

23 The idea of satellites around a focus work was first expressed by Peter Owens in 'Revelation and Fallacy: Observations on Compositional Technique in the Music of Peter Maxwell Davies', *Music Analysis* 13 (1994), 161–202. The opposite way around—satellite 'before' planet—would be, for example, the overture *Time and the Raven* embedded within Symphony No. 6. and *Chat Moss* in Symphony No. 5—both carry elements of autobiography.

24 I have published analyses of both these works: Richard McGregor, 'James MacMillan's *O Bone Jesu*', *Scottish Music Review* 2.1 (2011), 88–114; Richard McGregor, 'Transubstantiated into the Musical: A Critical Exegesis on James MacMillan's *Veni Veni Emmanuel*', in *A Companion to Recent Scottish Music: 1950 to the Present*, ed. by Graham Hair (Glasgow: The Musica Scotica Trust, 2007), pp. 21–42.

25 Alf Gabrielsson, 'Emotions in Strong Experiences with Music', in *Music and Emotion: Theory and Research*, ed. by Patrik N. Juslin and John A. Sloboda (Oxford: Oxford University Press, 2001), pp. 547–604 (at 431).

I realise that any insights that I have gained into the processes of composition are insights personal to me because they illuminate long-standing questions that I harbour about the process of composition. It is one of the many paradoxes of musical composition that one can analyse, interpret, and understand, almost all the actual musical results, but the impetus for creation, the sustaining vision of the work, and intrinsic value or quality of a work are much harder, if not impossible, to define or articulate precisely in words. When, to this, one adds further elements (within the process of creation), which themselves defy verbal description—in our case, the notion of spirituality contained, implicit, or unconsciously expressed through a musical work—it becomes even more difficult.

Each of the three composers I have discussed, in their own ways, signposted for me elements of the creative impetus as an ongoing generative process. This helped me to understand the essential compositional block created for me through the opposition between order, logic, and control and creative freedom. The quality of a composer's 'inspiration' is clearly a result of intense study of other composers and the synthesising of compositional techniques—acquired through study, listening, and practice—these things then become embedded in the subconscious, and form one of the driving forces of musical composition. Perhaps the most successful composers are driven and compelled to write because of their brain's capacity to recreate ideas in new and individualistic forms while preserving resonances from the past. Re-synthesising ideas in a new and original form has been going on for centuries, even with Mozart, who wrote to his sister:

> Above us is a violinist, another one is below, next to us is a singing teacher giving lessons, in the last room across the hall is an oboist; it's all such fun for Composing! gives you lots of ideas.[26]

---

26 Cited in *Mozart's Letters: Mozart's Life*, ed. by Robert Spaethling (London: Faber & Faber 2000), p. 30.

III. CHRISTIAN WORSHIP

13. Music in Christian Services as a Means to Induce Religious Feelings

Melanie Wald-Fuhrmann

For centuries, the relationship between music and spirituality has been considered, and even systematised, in religious community rituals. Music is used in the worshipping practices of most religions. Its functions are manifold, but always include establishing a connection to the divine. It has long been assumed that listening to or making music facilitates access to spiritual realities and the divine—to discover, explore or experience them, to learn about them and to communicate with them. In this chapter, I will approach this relationship from the combined perspectives of the history of liturgical and sacred music in the Christian Churches of Western Europe, theoretical and empirical studies of post-conciliar practices of liturgical music in the Roman Catholic Church, and a conceptual framework called 'aesthetics of the liturgy',[1] drawing also from research of audiences' live music experiences in real-world contexts. My personal background as a practising Roman Catholic may also come into play. First, a three-fold taxonomy of the psychological effects of music in Christian worship ('social', 'spiritual', and 'dispositional') will be introduced, followed by a review of the existing empirical studies of such effects. Second, some of the key findings of a quantitative study on

---

1   See Klaus Peter Dannecker and Melanie Wald-Fuhrmann, 'Wirkungsästhetik: Ein neuer Ansatz für eine transdisziplinäre empirische Liturgieforschung', *Liturgisches Jahrbuch. Vierteljahreshefte für Fragen des Gottesdienstes* 68.2 (2018), 83–108.

the spiritual and social effects of singing in Catholic worship in German-speaking countries will be summarised. Third, I propose a new research programme to understand empirically the spiritual and dispositional effects of different kinds of 'musicking' in Christian worship.

I. Measuring the Psychological Effects of Music in Christian Services

In the Christian context, inducing or increasing religious feelings—such as devotion, love of God, feeling close to God, gratefulness, contrition, or repentance—is one type of function or effect music is expected to have across most denominations.[2] A reading of the present authoritative Roman Catholic documents on music in the liturgy allows us to extract a broad range of functions ascribed to music, and in particular singing. These documents include the conciliar constitution *Sacrosanctum Concilium* (SC, 1963),[3] the related instruction *Musicam Sacram* (MS, 1967),[4] as well as the preface to the reformed Roman missal, *Institutio Generalis Missalis Romani* (IGMR, 1975, 2002).[5] Alongside the pragmatic, semiotic, and decorative functions of singing and music, three types of psychological effects can be identified, which I have previously labelled 'spiritual effects', 'social effects', and 'dispositional effects'.[6]

---

2   See, for example, William T. Flynn, 'Liturgical Music', in *The Oxford History of Christian Worship*, ed. by Geoffrey Wainwright and Karen B. Westerfield Tucker (Oxford: Oxford University Press, 2006), pp. 769–92.
3   'Sacrosanctum Concilium', *Vatican.va*, 4 December 1963, https://www.vatican.va/archive/hist_councils/ii_vatican_council/documents/vat-ii_const_19631204_sacrosanctum-concilium_en.html (henceforth SC).
4   'Musicam Sacram: Instruction on Music in the Liturgy', *Vatican.va*, 5 March 1967, https://www.vatican.va/archive/hist_councils/ii_vatican_council/documents/vat-ii_instr_19670305_musicam-sacram_en.html (henceforth MS).
5   'Institutio Generalis Missalis Romani', *Vatican.va*, 13 November 2002, https://www.vatican.va/roman_curia/congregations/ccdds/documents/rc_con_ccdds_doc_20030317_ordinamento-messale_en.html (henceforth IGMR). For a detailed analysis of the IGMR, see Melanie Wald-Fuhrmann, 'Liturgische Aufführungsbestimmungen zwischen Semiotik und Ästhetik: Ein Durchgang durch die "Allgemeine Einführung in das Römische Meßbuch"', in *Wirkungsästhetik der Liturgie: Transdisziplinäre Perspektiven*, ed. by Melanie Wald-Fuhrmann et al. (Regensburg: Pustet, 2020), pp. 143–64.
6   Melanie Wald-Fuhrmann, 'Positive Aspekte des gemeinschaftlichen Singens: Ein Forschungsüberblick', in *Wirkungsästhetik der Liturgie*, ed. Wald-Fuhrmann et al., pp. 191–214. For an abridged English version, on which I also draw in this chapter,

Spiritual effects of singing include phrases like 'the sanctification of the faithful',[7] 'the raising of the minds of the congregation to heavenly things or to God',[8] and 'the embellishment of prayer'.[9] Social effects are addressed when it comes to 'promoting unanimity' and the connectedness of the congregants through singing.[10] Dispositional effects consist mainly of persuasion and emotional contagion through music and are connected to the church's belief that song or music has an enhancing effect on the words it accompanies, which also seems to be the primary justification for the 'pre-eminence' that is given to music over any other art in Catholic worship.[11] Concretely, the musical embedding of liturgical texts is supposed to direct the attention of the congregation to the words they sing and, in this way, to help the words penetrate the congregants' minds and souls. Thus, for example, attendants of Mass may make the meaning of the texts and their emotional tone their own in order to become the 'I' or 'We' that speaks in the chant.[12] While social and spiritual effects of singing and listening to music in Christian services have been extensively discussed in theological, liturgical, and music historical scholarship,[13] this dispositional function has often been overlooked. Furthermore, empirical studies that seek to explore the

---

see Melanie Wald-Fuhrmann, Sven Boenneke, Thijs Vroegh, and Klaus Peter Dannecker, '"He Who Sings, Prays Twice"? Singing in Roman Catholic Mass Leads to Spiritual and Social Experiences that are Predicted by Religious and Musical Attitudes', *Frontiers in Psychology* 11, 570189 (2020), 1–3.

7   MS, art. 5.
8   MS, art. 5 and 15.
9   SC, art. 112; MS, art. 5.
10 SC, art. 112; MS, art. 5.
11 SC, art. 112.
12 IGMR, art. 52 and 62. The arousal of spiritual and dispositional effects also serves as a key argument in theological discussions of sacred music more broadly, and additionally outside the liturgy, e.g., in the context of oratorios as a musical means for conversion. See Esma Cerkovnik, '...*Et nos immutabimur*'—*Music and Conversion in Rome in the First Half of the 17th Century* (Kassel: Merseburger, 2020).
13 See, for example, Jan Michael Joncas, *From Sacred Song to Ritual Music: Twentieth-Century Understandings of Roman Catholic Worship Music* (Collegeville, MN: The Liturgical Press, 1997); Christopher Page, *The Christian West and Its Singers: The First Thousand Years* (New Haven, CT: Yale University Press, 2010); Philipp Harnoncourt, 'Gesang und Musik im Gottesdienst', in *Die Messe: Ein Kirchenmusikalisches Handbuch*, ed. by Harold Schützeichel (Düsseldorf: Patmos, 1991), pp. 9–25; Mary E. McGann, 'Interpreting the Ritual Role of Music in Christian Liturgical Practice' (unpublished doctoral thesis, Graduate Theological Union, Berkeley, CA, 1996); Luigi Girardi, ed., *Liturgia e emozione* (Rome: Studi di Liturgia, 2015).

occurrence, extent, and conditions under which these effects occur in the present day are extremely rare.

Existing empirical studies on experiences and psychological effects of (group) singing and music listening that are relevant to the present topic can be sorted into three main groups: (1) religious (Christian) singing experience; (2) non-religious group singing; and (3) music listening.

Thus far, for Christian singing experiences, only qualitative studies exist. These studies provide rich and detailed descriptions of subjective singing experiences in various religious and musical contexts, and they seem to support the assumptions of Roman Catholic liturgical doctrine alluded to above.[14] There appears to be only one study that quantitatively examined spiritual singing experiences in the context of a specific Christian denomination.[15] The second group is formed by more psychologically and quantitatively oriented studies that mainly investigate group singing in amateur choir singers (outside religious services).[16] These studies have generated initial evidence for a broad

---

14 For studies in Protestant denominations, see Rebecca J. Slough, '"Let Every Tongue, by Art Refined, Mingle Its Softest Notes with Mine": An Exploration of Hymn-Singing Events and Dimensions of Knowing', in *Religious and Social Ritual. Interdisciplinary Explorations*, ed. by Michael B. Aune and Valerie DeMarinis (Albany, NY: State University of New York Press, 1996), pp. 175–206; Ellen S. Davis, 'The Multi-Faceted Phenomenon of Congregational Song: An Interdisciplinary Exploration of Interpretive Influences' (unpublished doctoral dissertation, Claremont Graduate University, Claremont, CA 1997); Marlene Kropf and Kenneth James Nafziger, *Singing: A Mennonite Voice* (Scottdale, PA: Herald Press, 2011); Gordan Alban Adnams, 'The Experience of Congregational Singing: An Ethno-Phenomenological Approach' (unpublished doctoral dissertation, Concordia University of Edmonton, Alberta, 2008); Hanns Kerner, *Die Kirchenmusik: Wahrnehmungen aus zwei neuen empirischen Untersuchungen unter evangelisch Getauften in Bayern* (Nürnberg: Gottesdienst-Institut der Evangelisch-Lutherischen Kirche in Bayern, 2008); Jochen Kaiser, *Singen in Gemeinschaft als ästhetische Kommunikation: Eine ethnographische Studie* (Berlin: Springer, 2017); McGann, 'Interpreting the Ritual Role of Music'; Kit Smith, 'The Singing Assembly: How Does Music Affect the Faith Life of a Worshipping Community?', *The Australasian Catholic Record* 87.3 (2010), 284–95.
15 Mandi M. Miller and Kenneth T. Strongman, 'The Emotional Effects of Music on Religious Experience: A Study of the Pentecostal-Charismatic Style of Music and Worship', *Psychology of Music* 30.1 (2002), 8–27.
16 The existing body of studies has been summarised and evaluated in several review articles. See, for example, Stephen Clift et al., 'Group Singing, Wellbeing and Health: A Systematic Mapping of Research Evidence', *Unesco Observatory* 2.1 (2010), 1–25; Imogen N. Clarke and Katherine Harding, 'Psychosocial Outcomes of Active Singing Interventions for Therapeutic Purposes: A Systematic Review

range of benefits for physical, mental, and social well-being for various communities. Social effects such as facilitating social bonding, and creating feelings of social connectedness or social participation, seem to be a particularly frequent and strong outcome of group singing.[17] Although there is a large body of quantitative psychological research on experiences during music listening, spiritual dimensions are only very rarely covered in this context.

However, no quantitative studies seem to exist so far that address dispositional effects of religious singing. And there is only a very small number of studies that touch upon related questions such as how the musical and textual elements of songs interact with each other regarding emotional and motivational effects. There is, however, a large and supposedly relevant research tradition dealing with the emotional effects of music listening.[18]

II. An Empirical Study of the Spiritual and Social Effects of Group Singing in Catholic Worship

To follow up on our theoretical analysis of liturgical documents and our review of existing research on the topic of psychological effects of group singing (in Christian services), Klaus Peter Dannecker, Sven Boenneke, and I conducted a survey on singing experiences in Mass as a first quantitative approach to the issue in question.[19] For this purpose,

---

of the Literature', *Nordic Journal of Music Therapy* 21.1 (2012), 80–98; Jing Kang et al., 'Review of the Physiological Effects and Mechanisms of Singing', *Journal of Voice* 32.4 (2017), 390–95; and Antje Bullack et al., 'Psychobiological Effects of Choral Singing on Affective State, Social Connectedness, and Stress: Influences of Singing Activity and Time Course', *Frontiers in Behavioral Neuroscience* 12 (2018), 223.

17 Gunter Kreutz, 'Does Singing Facilitate Social Bonding?', *Music and Medicine* 6.2 (2014), 51–60; Elluned Pearce et al., 'The Ice-Breaker Effect: Singing Mediates Fast Social Bonding', *Royal Society Open Science* 2.10 (2015), 150221; Bullack et al., 'Psychobiological Effects'; Genevieve A. Dingle et al., 'An Agenda for Best Practice Research on Group Singing, Health, and Well-Being', *Music and Science* 2 (2019), 1–15.

18 A widely-cited model on the different mechanisms underlying emotion induction through music listening can be found in Patrick N. Juslin, 'From Everyday Emotions to Aesthetic Emotions: Towards a Unified Theory of Musical Emotions', *Physics of Life Review* 10.3 (2013), 235–66.

19 Wald-Fuhrmann et al., '"He Who Sings, Prays Twice?"'.

we transformed the identified functions attributed to songs and singing in Catholic worship into three hypotheses, namely: (1) liturgical singing facilitates feeling connected to God; (2) it induces the feeling of social connectedness among congregants; and (3) singing religious texts is experienced as a form of personal prayer. We collected data from more than 1600 Catholics from German-speaking countries who completed an exhaustive questionnaire. The questionnaire's central part consisted of questions on whether and how often churchgoers actually experience the three types of effects when singing in Mass. For this purpose, we transformed each of the aforementioned hypotheses into several statements and asked the participants how often they have such experiences in church. In addition, participants answered a number of socio-demographic questions, but also questions regarding their religious and musical background, practices, and attitudes.

Overall, our participants reported having these experiences relatively frequently (mean values for all relevant items ranged from 3.5 to 4.4 on a 5-point scale with 1 = never and 5 = very often). Social feelings seemed to be experienced even more frequently than spiritual feelings and feelings of singing as praying. In a next step, we explored potential statistical relationships between the frequency of such singing experiences and a person's socio-demographic, religious, and musical background with the help of linear regression models. Significantly, while socio-demographic variables such as age, gender, or level of education were not related to singing experiences, religious, and musical practices were so related, and attitudes even more strongly so. Concretely, the frequency of spiritual experiences during singing in Mass was statistically related to a traditional understanding of the Mass, a positive attitude towards singing in Mass, and a personal practice of singing at home; together, these three factors explained 33% of the variance of our data. The feeling of singing as praying (i.e., a dispositional effect) was also related to a traditional understanding of Mass and a positive attitude towards singing in Mass, as well as–albeit to a weaker degree–having a musical office in Mass and a positive attitude towards one's own singing; here, 34% of the variance was explained by these factors. Social experience, on the other hand, could be less well explained (the final statistical model captured only 22% of the variance in the data), but was found to be related to a more secular understanding of Mass and a social motivation to attend Mass.

This survey appears to demonstrate that three core functions attributed to singing in Catholic worship–liturgical singing facilitates feeling connected to God, it induces the feeling of social connectedness, and it is experienced as a form of personal prayer–do generally hold true in practice, at least with respect to the population we studied. However, there are limitations to this survey and analysis which require further investigation. It may be misleading to take the high frequencies of such experiences at face value. As participation in the survey was voluntary, it may have been driven, at least in part, by prior interest in the topic of singing at Mass, and a generally positive attitude towards it. Further, the results show that the frequency of the experiences of interest depends to a significant degree on religious and musical attitudes. This highlights at least two things. First, the presence of music and singing does not automatically and uniformly lead to the expected effects (as the Church documents seem to assume, as they adopt a more 'pharmaceutical' understanding of musical effects on worship). Second, in addition to attitudes, the occurrence of such singing experience may also depend on the concrete forms of musical integration into a religious service, i.e., their actual aesthetic realisation. Yet, the influence of these factors could not be established by this survey, since questions had to be answered retrospectively, averaging across many services, and not related to a particular one. Acknowledging the limitations of this, and other existing studies, enables us to develop a revised understanding of the underlying research questions, and a revised formulation of an empirical approach to them, as will be discussed in the following section.

III. 'Musicking', and the Type, Intensity, and Likelihood of Spiritual Experiences in Christian Worship

So far, this chapter has mainly dealt with the theory and experience of active singing in Mass. However, there are many forms of music and musicking present at Christian services both within and across denominations, including, for example, (1) singing by individuals that perform a liturgical office; (2) singing by the whole congregation; and (3) instrumental music that the congregation listens to. There are also many other relevant distinctions, as between (1) forms of liturgical music that constitute liturgical acts of their own (like sung prayers or the chants of the ordinary) and (2) forms that accompany a liturgical act; and as between (3) communal chants and hymns that occur regularly in worship services, and (4) complex musical compositions performed by specialised ensembles.

Taken together, the question arises whether all these different forms of liturgical music have the same relation to the religious feelings they aim to arouse, or whether the type, intensity, and likelihood of such feelings vary depending on the type of music present in a service. For example, it might well be the case that listening to others singing a chant or song affords a weaker spiritual experience than when singing it oneself. And listening to or singing a well-known chant or song might provoke religious feelings more easily than an unfamiliar tune. Also, the basic assumption that a sung prayer is more emotionally effective than a spoken one has never been studied systematically. Therefore, one may think of a research design that combines theoretical, historical, and comparative approaches with an experimental research paradigm to study how concrete forms of music and musicking interact with religious feelings in Christian services (of one or more denominations).

The primary focus would be on spiritual and dispositional effects of music, but other types of religious feelings might also be found that are associated with sacred music. Among others, the influence of the following factors could be examined experimentally: (1) recitation versus singing; (2) singing versus listening; (3) familiar versus unfamiliar repertoires; and (4) spiritual intention versus internal intention. Possible digressions may touch upon the musical styles that are felt by people to be most associated with spirituality (e.g., gospel singing versus more traditional church songs), or the question of whether historical genres of liturgical music (such as motets, cantatas, or mass compositions) can still work in the context of religious services today or whether, instead, they create a sphere of spirituality in a context outside of religious services, such as in a concert performance.

In relation to these factors of influence, we may put forward the following provisional hypotheses. First, a sung prayer is more spiritually effective than a spoken one. This experimental hypothesis, founded on a common assumption ('he who sings prays twice'), has never been studied systematically in an empirical experiment. Second, singing a chant or hymn affords a stronger spiritual experience than when listening to others doing the same. It is of critical importance to test this widely held hypothesis empirically, not least due to the culture wars in Christian worship with regard to 'active participation' (i.e., to what extent active participation includes listening to music as well as singing or performing music). Third, listening to or singing a familiar chant or song provokes a more intense spiritual experience than listening to or singing an unfamiliar tune. The question of which repertoires to use during a service is also highly debated among church musicians and churchgoers. Based on large empirical evidence for the importance of familiarity in aesthetic contexts, we assume that familiarity will play a particularly important role with regard to the dispositional effect. Fourth, the presence of a repertoire that is commonly associated with the spiritual and religious sphere (e.g., Gregorian chant, Renaissance polyphony, gospel songs) will evoke spiritual experiences more strongly than other musical repertoires and styles. For the longest part in their history, church authorities in all Christian denominations have sought to control which musical styles and repertoires were allowed a role in public worship. Often, the reasons for this implied a belief in the spiritual qualities of certain stylistic properties. While this may not hold true, it can be assumed that the association of certain styles with the spiritual will act as a psychological top-down mechanism and thus afford a spiritual experience. Fifth, if a singer's intention is directed externally to the spiritual content of the music sung, the music will provoke a more intense spiritual experience in the listener than if the singer's intention is directed internally (focused exclusively on the voice, pitch, etc.). Other hypotheses could also be developed in relation to the factors of influence mentioned above and to further factors of influence explored.

While some of the relevant issues could be studied in a controlled laboratory environment, most of them would be addressed most effectively in ecologically valid contexts, i.e., during real religious services. Individual factors (such as an individual's musicality, musical attitudes, and religious background) will need to be controlled, as they are likely to moderate music effects. In such experiments, the factors of interest will be used to manipulate the experimental stimuli, which will be specific Christian services. For example, to study the effects of recitation versus singing, the same Christian service could be performed in two different ways: one, where all texts and prayers are recited, and the other, where those texts and prayers that can be sung are sung. To study the effects of familiarity and religious association, sung services could either feature only Gregorian chants or only modern pop-style songs.

To chart differences in the type or degree of spiritual experiences, one could adopt experimental approaches from studies of concert audiences. Here, three types of data have been collected that yielded meaningful results:[20] first, continuous psycho-physiological measures such as heart and breathing activity, as well as electrodermal activity. All of these are known to be related to the autonomous nervous system and to emotional experiences. It will be of interest to investigate event-related, i.e., momentary responses of individual study participants over the course of a service, but also to look for the degree of physiological synchronisation across participants. The second type of data is yielded from peak experience monitoring. One way to achieve this is to request participants to press a button sensor at moments of particular spiritual or affective experience during a worship service. After the service, the research team may refer the participant to these recorded moments in the service and ask them to describe the nature of the experience. The third type of data is qualitative and quantitative self-reported data, with participants filling in questionnaires about their experience immediately after the worship service. Study participants would ideally consist of congregations (ordinary participants of a service without a liturgical office) and liturgical singers (people who sing as part of their liturgical or religious office).

---

20 Melanie Wald-Fuhrmann et al., 'Music Listening in Classical Concerts: Theory, Literature Review, and Research Program', *Frontiers in Psychology* 12, 638783 (2021); Julia Merrill et al., The Aesthetic Experience of Live Concerts: Self-Reports and Psychophysiology', *Psychology of Aesthetics, Creativity, and the Arts* 17.2 (2021), 134–51; Anna Czepiel et al., 'Synchrony in the Periphery: Inter-Subject Correlation of Physiological Responses during Live Music Concerts', *Scientific Reports* 11.1 (2021), 1–16; Wolfgang Tschacher et al., 'Audience Synchronies in Live Concerts Illustrate the Embodiment of Music Experience', *Scientific Reports* 13 (2023), 14843.

Whatever the results of an experiment such as this, it will be important to consider, also, if they are specific to Christian contexts or if they may extend to other religions and their musico-religious practices. As empirical research of the purported psychological effects (and especially the spiritual and dispositional effects) of music in worship is very much in its infancy (with, as we have seen, few studies currently available), there is much scope for further empirical projects of the kind described and proposed in this chapter. Only when there is a greater breadth and depth of empirical studies can more reliable inferences be drawn both within particular religious communities, and across them.

14. Spiritual Cultures: Innovations in Choral and Classical Music

Jonathan Arnold

Recent research has revealed not only the continued growth of interest in traditional Western sacred music but also the development of new initiatives that respond to people's desire to experience spirituality through music. For example, the work of Kathryn King and Hanna Rijken has demonstrated, through empirical research, why choral Evensong in the Anglican tradition appeals to so many, and exactly who is attending and listening to these services, both in England and, perhaps surprisingly, in the Netherlands, where choral Evensong is a popular 'new' or 'fresh' expression of worship with a burgeoning English-style choral tradition. Written from my own perspective as an Anglican priest and musician in the classical tradition, in this chapter I will explore how these trends in choral Evensong have been mapped and what conclusions have been drawn using both quantitative and qualitative data. In addition, my own research through the 'Experience of Music' project, as well as analysis of non-liturgical or quasi-liturgical settings of both choral and instrumental classical music, have shown that there are social, ethical, and spiritual benefits to music experience. Such spiritual experience through music can point towards, and even reveal, a reality beyond our everyday human materiality.

I. Choral Evensong in England Today: An Immersive Study

Kathryn King's empirical study of choral Evensong has made an important contribution to the scholarly understanding of music listening as well as of the experiences of congregants at choral Evensong.[1] Using a multi-methodological approach, King makes essential findings about tranquillity, transcendence, and retreat, about the agency afforded by an attendee, and about the use of Evensong as an escape from everyday life and towards an ideal 'Evensong persona', in ways that allow attendees to regulate emotions and seek fulfilment. Locating Evensong within the framework of everyday life, King argues that it is a '... powerful and trusted technology of the self'.[2] King shows that the experience can evoke both emotional and cognitive transformation, which lead the attendee towards experiences of tranquillity, transcendence, and retreat.

King's research methodology incorporated forty-three ' ... in-depth interviews; an immersive, real-time experimental study involving twenty-six participants; two national surveys which elicited more than 2,100 responses; and two years of participant observation'.[3] The real-time experimental element, called the Immersive Evensong Study (IES) was an original methodology designed to ascertain how attendee participants thought and felt during an Evensong service.[4] Aware that '... situational factors are fundamental to listeners' experiences of music (Gabrielsson, 2011; Juslin et al., 2008), and that both music and emotion unfold over time, with thoughts and feelings changing continually and sometimes dramatically during the course of a listening experience (Schubert, 2010)', King sought out a 'real-time research method ... that could capture participants' evolving thoughts, emotions, and experiences—including the non-cognitive and unconscious embodied responses that are a common feature of musical experience—in a

---

1 Kathryn King, 'Tranquillity, Transcendence, and Retreat: The Transformative Practice of Listening at Evensong' (unpublished doctoral thesis, University of Oxford, 2021), https://ora.ox.ac.uk/objects/uuid:0772a6ce-d68e-4356-af39-dfab545ee108
2 Ibid., p. 11.
3 Ibid.
4 Ibid., p. 57.

controlled environment, so that the responses of multiple participants could be investigated consistently, and with a reasonable degree of ecological validity'.[5] The practical and ethical difficulties of obtaining representative and replicable data about attendee experience were overcome by using virtual reality or 'VR'.

The use of a virtual experience of choral Evensong allowed '... multiple participants, separated in time, to engage with exactly the same replica environment (Blascovich et al. 2002)'.[6] Participants in the IES study, which included myself, sat in a pew or stall in Magdalen College Chapel, Oxford. Through a VR headset and headphones I experienced a very high quality three-dimensional recording of a service, from May 2018, sung by the boy choristers and academical clerks (choral scholars). I stood and sat in all the correct liturgical places and faced east to speak the words of the creed. Through the headset I could see other members of the congregation who had been present when the 3D recording was made. Through sensors my heart rate, skin conductivity, and eye, or 'gaze', movement were also monitored. During the playback I was encouraged to think out loud about what I was thinking or feeling. After the recorded service was over the researcher asked me questions about the experience, including emotions or anything that had come to mind during my experience. It was a remarkable reproduction or representation of the 'real thing' that allowed for the research participant to express how they were experiencing the event that obviously would have been impossible during a live service, without disturbing other members of the congregation.

The potential of using VR is evident from studies on clinical, affective, and social neurosciences:

> A virtual environment provides the researcher with an ecologically valid platform for presenting dynamic stimuli in a manner that allows for

---

5   Ibid. Alf Gabrielsson, *Strong Experiences with Music: Music Is Much More than Just Music* (Oxford: Oxford University Press, 2011); Patrik N. Juslin, 'Emotional Responses to Music', in *The Oxford Handbook of Music Psychology*, ed. by Ian Cross et al. (Oxford: Oxford University Press, 2008), pp. 131–40; Emery Schubert, 'Affective, Evaluative and Collative Responses to Hated and Loved Music', *Psychology of Aesthetics, Creativity, and the Arts* 4.1 (2010), 36–46.

6   King, 'Tranquillity, Transcendence, and Retreat', p. 58; Jim Blascovich et al., 'Immersive Virtual Environment Technology as a Methodological Tool for Social Psychology', *Psychological Inquiry* 13.2 (2002), 103–24.

both the veridical control of laboratory measures and the verisimilitude of naturalistic observation of real-life situations ... Virtual environment-based assessments can provide a balance between naturalistic observation and the need for exacting control over key variables.[7]

The Evensong chosen for recording was selected because it was representative of a typical weekday Evensong, and because its music was without copyright limitations.[8] The IES research methods were chosen to encompass the three widely-recognised systems of monitoring human experience, which are '... physiological indicators; observable acts or behaviours; and language and other oral communication (M. M. Bradley and Lang 2002; P. J. Lang 1993)'.[9] King thus employed five research methods for the IES: thinking/speaking aloud, observation, gaze tracking, physiological monitoring, and post-IES follow-up interviews.

In addition to the data collected by the IES experience, King collected thousands of responses in two questionnaire surveys: 'Experiences of Evensong', conducted in 2019, and 'Absence of Evensong', conducted during the 2020 lockdown:

> The [Experiences of Evensong] survey asked 30 questions in five areas: (i) Evensong and other church attendance practices and motivations; (ii) the experience of being at Evensong; (iii) wider musical tastes, music listening habits, and musical training and performance practices; (iv) religious affiliation and faith; and (v) demographic factors. Questions were a combination of multiple choice, closed and open, and wording was constructed in line with established principles of social research surveys (e.g., De Vaus et al. 2013, 94–120). Multiple choice options were

---

[7] King, 'Tranquillity, Transcendence, and Retreat', p. 59; Thomas D. Parsons, 'Virtual Reality for Enhanced Ecological Validity and Experimental Control in the Clinical, Affective and Social Neurosciences', *Frontiers in Human Neuroscience*, 9 (2015), 600; Alice Chirico et al., 'Effectiveness of Immersive Videos in Inducing Awe: An Experimental Study', *Scientific Reports* 7.1 (2017), 1218; Giuseppe Riva et al., 'Affective Interactions Using Virtual Reality: The Link between Presence and Emotions', *CyberPsychology & Behavior* 10.1 (2007), 45–56.

[8] The recording can be viewed here: The Choir of Magdalen College, Oxford, 'The Choir of Magdalen College Oxford Sing Choral Evensong on Thursday...', online video recording, Facebook, 29 April 2019, https://www.facebook.com/watch/?v=370168640373718

[9] King, 'Tranquillity, Transcendence, and Retreat', p. 63; Margaret M. Bradley and Peter J. Lang, 'Measuring Emotion: Behavior, Feeling, and Physiology', in *The Cognitive Neuroscience of Emotion*, ed. by R. D. Lane et al. (Cary, NC: Oxford University Press, 2002), pp. 242–76.

determined by reference to pre-existing findings, and where possible the same wording used by the relevant comparator survey was adopted. Five open questions were included to ensure that views or themes of importance to respondents that might not have been addressed in the closed or multiple-choice options could be captured.[10]

The Absence of Evensong survey was on a smaller scale, asking seven questions concerning the effects of being unable to attend live Evensong and on experiences of online or other Evensong broadcasts.

Analysis of the Experiences of Evensong survey revealed '... two important overall themes in participants' reasons for attending Evensong ... (a) the music, and (b) the attainment of a sense of tranquillity. Furthermore, it was clear that for a large majority of survey respondents, these two factors are inextricably linked'.[11] Likewise, the Absence of Evensong survey suggested the same '... inter-relationship between music and self-regulation for relaxation'.[12] This is evident in the response of one survey participant, as well as a link between this kind of self-regulated relaxation and divine presence:

> Attending choral services used to be one of my primary outlets to aid my emotional well-being... not having this outlet available ... meant that it felt like there was no safety valve to help calm my emotions. ... times of feeling anxious, powerless, isolated, and cut off would have been assuaged by being able to share in Choral Evensong. There is a real sense of divine presence and calm in the service which works against the feelings I describe above. Evensong is utter mindfulness. The lack of it has removed a slice of peace.... A recording is not a substitute for the balm to the soul that is evensong.[13]

The connection between musical quality and an experience of tranquillity was also indicted by the fact that, overall, 85% of attendees reported having had musical instrument or voice training, and 82% responded that they attended Evensong in order to reflect, meditate, contemplate, or find peace and quiet.[14]

---

10   King, 'Tranquillity, Transcendence, and Retreat', pp. 76–77; David De Vaus et al., *Surveys in Social Research* (London: Taylor & Francis Group, 2013).
11   King, 'Tranquillity, Transcendence, and Retreat', p. 85.
12   Ibid., p. 90.
13   Ibid.
14   Ibid., p. 91.

King questions the extent to which this self-regulation might be called a 'technology of the self', a term coined by Michel Foucault to describe those who use resources in order to perform '... operations on their own bodies and souls, thoughts, conduct, and way of being, so as to transform themselves in order to attain a certain state of happiness, purity, wisdom, perfection, or immortality'.[15] Tia DeNora and Peter Rentfrow have identified music as such a resource used in 'creating, enhancing, sustaining and changing subjective, cognitive, bodily and self-conceptual states' (DeNora 1999, 34–35), and 'in a vast variety of situations, and for a range of social and psychological objectives (Rentfrow 2012)'.[16] Choral Evensong is not, however, an obvious technology of the self, as it is a live experience with its own rules of behaviour that cannot be manipulated or experienced on demand like a recording, it restricts the extent to which an attendee can participate or express themselves, and it is an act of worship. Nonetheless, King's findings indicate that there is an interwovenness between the use of the music and attendees' other motivations or objectives in attending, '... whether those objectives are religious and spiritual, self-directed as a means to attaining religious or spiritual ends, or focused on self-care without a religious or spiritual dimension'.[17] Those who do attend for 'spiritual' reasons, do so because they believe that the music will assist in their aim:

> Participants who attend to get in touch with a spiritual part of themselves, or with the spiritual in the abstract, widely believed that the music promotes spirituality; and participants who have no religious or spiritual goals, but are seeking tranquillity, often regarded the music an important resource in effecting the affective transformation they desire.[18]

Thus, King identifies that, in choral Evensong, music is a common factor in attendees who are there primarily for worship, or to achieve

---

15 Ibid., p. 101; *Technologies of the Self: A Seminar with Michel Foucault*, ed. by Luther H. Martin et al. (London: Tavistock, 1988), p. 16.
16 King, 'Tranquillity, Transcendence, and Retreat', p. 101; Tia DeNora, 'Music as a Technology of the Self', *Poetics*, 27.1 (1999), 31–56.
17 King, 'Tranquillity, Transcendence, and Retreat', p. 105. Peter J. Rentfrow, 'The Role of Music in Everyday Life: Current Directions in the Social Psychology of Music', *Social and Personality Psychology Compass*, 6 (2012), 402–16.
18 King, 'Tranquillity, Transcendence, and Retreat', p. 106.

tranquillity, or for a spiritual experience.[19] As such, Evensong-goers use music '... knowingly and deliberately to balance their active and passive engagement for the achievement of a plurality of varying emotional, spiritual, intellectual and embodied goals'.[20]

In addition to this use, King also discovered, through the ISE study, survey, and in-depth interviews, that transcendence was a common experience in Evensong.

> Experiences of transcendence at Evensong are not only surprisingly common, but for a very significant proportion of participants, they are intrinsic to their participation in the service. These experiences are not unique to people professing a religious belief: they are reported widely, and by people across the spectrum of religiosity and of faith, doubt, and certainty about the existence or absence of any sort of spirit or God.[21]

King's findings show that these widely felt experiences of transcendence are what motivates people to return to choral Evensong multiple times. Indeed, it is the benchmark for judging a 'successful' Evensong: 'Evensong has "worked" if transcendence has been achieved'.[22] Experiences of transcendence are manifested in a variety of ways. They can be short or long in duration, with different levels of intensity: 'Some are manifest as fleeting flashes of insight; others are prolonged plateaus of divine encounter with life-changing consequence'.[23] But in all cases, the 'self' and the 'world' are experienced in a way that is different from everyday living. King identifies seven, overlapping, types of transcendence experienced at Evensong, all of which are responses to the 'musical soundscape of the service, regardless of the musical background or training of the individual involved'.[24] These are: enlightenment, elevation, encountering God or the Other, being transported, losing and finding the self, flow, and disassociation. These porous categories are situated diagrammatically, in King's thesis, within the boundaries of transformation, transience, and ineffability.

---

19 Ibid.
20 Ibid., p. 120.
21 Ibid., p. 197.
22 Ibid.
23 Ibid.
24 Ibid., p. 198.

Although Anglican psalm chanting particularly appealed to survey respondents, all aspects of the service encouraged intellectual and emotional engagement from the attendees:

> Listening to the choral psalms, canticles, and prayers at Evensong involves an in-depth intellectual engagement with the sung text, through well-honed practices of concentration, interpretation, reflection, and meditation. The involving nature of these processes was frequently associated with transcendent experiences related to being transported, the loss of self, enlightenment, and encountering God.[25]

For instance, one respondent wrote of his experiences as 'like floating in the sea' with the choir, 'communicating a sense of one's own smallness and God's infinite goodness',[26] corresponding to Emilie Gomart and Antoine Hennion's sociology of attachment in which 'the user strives tentatively to fulfil those conditions which will let him be seized and taken over by a potentialized exogenous force'.[27] In addition to the music, the words of the Book of Common Prayer contribute to the sense of 'otherness' and mystery in the experience, which Rijken has also noted in her study of choral Evensong in the Netherlands.[28]

The intentions of the attendee were also noted as significance factors in prioritising meaning, 'with participants activating or mobilizing selected features of what they perceived in order to produce meanings and interpretations in accordance with what they felt they needed at particular moments'.[29] Moreover, some attendees intentionally wish to feel connected to a community of Evensong-goers across the centuries, corresponding to Georgina Born's 'musically imagined community'.[30] Another important finding was that there is no adequate substitute for

---

25   Ibid., p. 202.
26   Ibid., p. 203.
27   Emilie Gomart and Antoine Hennion, 'A Sociology of Attachment: Music Amateurs, Drug Users', *The Sociological Review* 47.1 (1999), 220–47, cited in King, 'Tranquillity, Transcendence, and Retreat', p. 203.
28   Hanna Rijken, *My Soul Doth Magnify: The Appropriation of Anglican Choral Evensong in the Netherlands* (Amsterdam: Vu Press, 2020), pp. 81–83; King, 'Tranquillity, Transcendence, and Retreat', p. 206.
29   King, 'Tranquillity, Transcendence, and Retreat', p. 202; cf. Tia DeNora, *Music in Everyday Life* (Cambridge, UK: Cambridge University Press, 2000), p. 38.
30   King, 'Tranquillity, Transcendence, and Retreat', p. 209; Georgina Born, 'On Musical Mediation: Ontology, Technology and Creativity', *Twentieth Century Music* 2.1, 7–36.

attending Evensong in person and having a live experience. King's much smaller survey regarding online services during lockdown found that respondents' opinions ranged from '...the best substitute, but nothing compared to being there' to '...remote and pointless... There is no substitute for being at a live musical service'. Indeed, many respondents actively sought in the broadcasts the same transformational effects they expected from attending Evensong, but instead reported finding them 'ridiculous' or voyeuristic.[31]

With regard to Evensong and well-being, King posits that there are several beneficial effects of attending Evensong, including a sense of escape, retreat, belonging, and a sense of home, sanctuary in certainty and stability, and security in Evensong's ongoing existence.[32] Contrary to Theofor Adorno and Jacques Attali's argument that listening to music for a sense of escape is a consumerist regressive trap created to childishly distract us from realities of life,[33] King finds that Evensong attendees find fortification from the service in order to face the realities of life thereafter, as evident in the words of one respondent, who found Evensong 'a time of contemplation and worship where my soul is filled and refreshed by the offering of prayers and music. It sets me up for the week ahead...'[34] Indeed, the 'sanctuary' of Evensong can enable human flourishing beyond the service itself:

> Evensong's role as a sanctuary extends beyond creating a retreat from the outside world. It also re-presents that world in a new way, that allows the exploration, expression, and development of dimensions of self and identity that can, in everyday life, be difficult to perform. Music is an important catalyst for these generative activities. Through musical sound, Evensong affords a space in which introversion and introspection can become platforms for flourishing.[35]

---

31 King, 'Tranquillity, Transcendence, and Retreat', p. 248.
32 Ibid., pp. 261–71.
33 Theodor W. Adorno, 'On the Fetish-Character in Music and the Regression of Listening', in *The Culture Industry: Selected Essays on Mass Culture*, ed. by J.M. Bernstein (London and New York: Routledge, 1991), pp. 29–60; Theodor W. Adorno, 'On the Social Situation of Music', in *Essays on Music*, ed. by Richard Leppert (Berkeley and Los Angeles, CA: University of California Press, 2002), pp. 391–436; Jacques Attali, *Noise: The Political Economy of Music* (Minneapolis, MN: University of Minnesota Press, 1985).
34 King, 'Tranquillity, Transcendence, and Retreat', p. 273.
35 Ibid., p. 299.

Overall, King finds that the majority of people are motivated to attend Evensong primarily for musical, religious/spiritual, or affective/cognitive reasons in varying degrees depending on the person. These motivations are all interrelated.[36] Moreover, attending Evensong was rarely perceived as a matter of indifference: 'It is not akin to attending a concert for entertainment, a historical building for awe or education, or a meditation class for relaxation', but rather a serious pursuit that seeks 'profound meaning, feeling, and transformation'.[37]

Three types of experience were found to be common: tranquillity, transcendence, and sanctuary.[38] Regarding musical experience, King found that attendees engage in 'multiple acts of agency in releasing and exploiting its [music's] potential. Specifically, they were shown to actively potentialize music to create the conditions for the experiences that they sought, before passing from activity to passivity in order to realise that experience through the relinquishment of agency'.[39]Thus, the listener moves from an active intentionality to a passive release of agency during the experience, where sounds of music and the words of the book of common prayer are 'heard as a de-personalised sound of Otherness', where a 'reassuring sense of calm' provides a path to transcendence.[40] Perhaps most surprisingly, the motivations for, and outcomes of, attendance at choral Evensong vary little due to 'religious affiliation, faith, or musical training and background'.[41] Rather, choral Evensong appealed to a wide variety of people with or without these attributes.

While DeNora has explored the routine use of music, especially recorded music, for 'affective and cognitive objectives in a range of settings',[42] King's research demonstrates that the 'live' experience of choral Evensong was used by many for self-regulation and 'affective scaffolding as part of everyday life', whether for listeners who wished to achieve a transformed state as a goal in itself, or those who aimed for

---

36 Ibid., pp. 301–02.
37 Ibid., p. 303.
38 Ibid.
39 Ibid., p. 304.
40 Ibid.
41 Ibid., p. 305.
42 DeNora, *Music in Everyday Life*, passim; King, 'Tranquillity, Transcendence, and Retreat', p. 298.

another goal, such as worship.[43] Because Evensong is not on demand like recorded music it is a different, and more effective, mechanism for self-management. The recorded Evensong services during lockdown, then, were an extremely poor substitute for the live experience.

> Specifically, participants took comfort from the knowledge that Evensong was not available on demand, because that afforded a sense that it was not 'all about me'. This was experienced as liberating and a relief, or as recalling or even prefiguring a simpler time, outside of consumerist rules of exchange. For some, the experience of having to await gratification on the timescale of the service schedule rather than on demand created a reassuring and calming awareness of a different sense of time and priorities, that in turn promoted patience and a different, broader cognitive perspective.[44]

Because Evensong is often a daily event in cathedrals and chapels, the service is 'not as a standalone event, but rather—in many cases—as the culmination of a potentially prolonged period of preparation, in an ever-repeating cycle'.[45]

People go to Evensong with 'self-regulation and affective objectives' in mind, like meditation or worship and enhanced well-being.[46] Attendees also 'engage in practices and behaviours in support of a transformation of their affective state at Evensong prior to, and during, the commencement of the event'. King also finds that Evensong is 'vital, central, and indispensable' in the affect it can afford people.[47] In concluding her study, King suggests that

> ...a comparative study of experiences of Evensong in the UK and in the Netherlands, where Evensong has a different history, cultural position, and relationship with religion, could be mutually informative about the motivations and experiences of Evensong participants in both cultures. The foundations for an international research project with this focus have already been laid, and it is hoped its findings will elaborate further on contemporary participation in Evensong, and the many varieties of experience that it affords.[48]

---

43 King, 'Tranquillity, Transcendence, and Retreat', pp. 305–06.
44 Ibid., p. 306.
45 Ibid., p. 307.
46 Ibid.
47 Ibid., p. 308.
48 Ibid., p. 324.

And so it is to the work of Hanna Rijken in the Netherlands that I turn now.

II. Choral Evensong in the Netherlands: A Ritual-Ethnographical Approach

When I was invited, by Dr Rijken of the Protestantse Theologische Universiteit in Amsterdam, to attend, and to speak at, the *Choral Evensong Symposium* in the Lutheran Church in Utrecht in February 2020, I was delighted to hear of the rise in popularity of Choral Evensong in the Netherlands with over one hundred choirs singing regular choral Evensongs up and down the land. I was privileged to attend the service of Choral Evensong, sung by the Kampen Boys' Choir in the packed cathedral, and immensely impressed by the high standard of liturgy and music-making at a professional level from the men and boys, even though I later learned that the singers are not paid for their services; on the contrary, they subscribe to the choir in order to resource it and its purposes. This only goes to demonstrate the enormous enthusiasm there is for the music and the liturgy, from clergy, musicians, and congregation alike. Of course, choral Evensong is not native to the Low Countries and there is no English cathedral choral tradition. Thus, the traditional choral service is seen as a 'fresh expression', a delightful phenomenon in Reformed and Lutheran Churches. It has also been described as the 'Anglican Virus.'[49]

How can something so ancient be 'fresh'? King's research would suggest that Evensong appeals 'afresh' to each new generation who seek the divine through liturgy, and Rijken herself has undertaken significant research into why choral Evensong is such a popular phenomenon in the Netherlands. Rijken asks:

> What is happening in the so-called secularized Netherlands? We notice something remarkable; overcrowded churches, chamber choirs which are transforming into evensong choirs and the establishment of 'Anglican' choir schools for boy and girl choristers.[50]

---

49 Hanna Rijken et al., 'The "Anglican Virus". The Emergence of Anglican Music in the Netherlands', *Jahrbuch für Liturgik und Hymnologie* 54 (2015), 131–52.
50 Ibid., p. 13.

In order to answer this question, Rijken takes a ritual-musical ethnographical approach which deploys an empirical process of mapping the field. Like King, Rijken chooses particular loci for investigation, conducts interviews, and draws on participant observation. This process includes an historical investigation of music within the church of the Netherlands, and of the 'cultural brokers' who introduced Anglican music in the Netherlands.[51] The research also involves a study of the use of language in choral Evensong, both English and Dutch, noticing that Evensong language is notably different to Sunday morning services in the Netherlands; the non-native archaic language of the prayer book, sung or spoken, can aid a transcendental experience, both through its sacrality and its rituality; an experience of 'otherness' lies in the use of a non-native ritual language, which evokes an unarticulated 'sens du sacré'; and, finally, the use of language in Evensong, from the prayer book and Bible, creates a noticeably different and ritualistic sacrality than a common choral concert.[52]

Rijken's empirical research programme also investigates the changing uses of ecclesiastical space, and where the choir is positioned in the building. Rijken calls this 'cathedralization', where buildings made for preaching have been changed with the introduction of choir stalls: the choir has moved from a concert layout (with the choir at the front and congregation in audience positions), to a more antiphonal mode (with Decani and Cantoris sides facing each other, and turning east to say the creed).[53] Choral Evensong choirs in the Netherlands have also appropriated Anglican liturgical dress, with cassocks and surplices, indicating a 'transformation in the way religion is expressed' in Protestant churches. 'A new form of religiosity', corresponding to Anton van Harskamp's observance of a 'new religious longing' in the Netherlands, is characterised by what W. B. H. J. van de Donk has called 'non-compulsory choice options'.[54]

---

51 Ibid., p. 60.
52 Ibid., pp. 82–83.
53 Ibid., pp. 87–105.
54 Ibid., p. 124; Anton Van Harskamp, *Het nieuw-religieuze verlangen* (Kampen: Kok, 2000), p. 48; W. B. H. J. van de Donk et al., *Geloven in het publieke domein: verkenningen van een dubbele transformatie* (Amsterdam: Amsterdam University Press, 2006), pp. 13–14.

In analysing interview material, Rijken identifies six different categories of metaphors which participants and attendees of choral Evensong use to describe their experiences: eschatological (such as 'heavenly', 'paradise'); aesthetical (such as 'beautiful', 'gorgeous'); sensorial (such as 'bright', 'light', 'transparent'); transcendental metaphors (such as 'lifted up', 'higher plain', or 'revelatory'); emotional (which can be evident in an attendee crying, or feeling emotional, or in physiological change related to emotion, such as 'your heart rate goes down'—a phenomenon that can occur during choral Evensong, as King has shown); and, finally, connective (where participants describe their experience as a connection, either between the singers and choir, or choir and congregation, or between other groups, or between heaven and earth).[55] Like King, Rijken finds that 'there are no strict boundaries between religious and musical experiences'. Thus, any antithesis between an experience as either 'beautiful' or 'sacred' becomes artificial. The metaphors used by participants demonstrate that the experience is many things at once, from religious to aesthetic.[56]

In the ritual appropriation of choral Evensong in the Netherlands, those who attend have typically been attracted by beauty, sacrality, rituality, a desire for transcendent experience and, closely related to this, a service that contrasts with the usual Sunday morning services. In her understanding of this phenomenon, Rijken draws on Paul Post's notion of ritual-sacral practice, where 'ritual and sacrality go hand in hand',[57] whether in religion, marking and remembering, culture or leisure. Choral Evensong is popular 'because of the possibility of appropriating this ritual-musical form in diverse ways (religion, arts, leisure)'.[58] But this does not fully explain the phenomenon for Rijken, and she draws also, therefore, on the concept of 're-enchantment', as mentioned in Erika Fischer-Lichte's observations regarding aesthetic experiences that can lead to a re-enchantment of the world, and Andrew Burnham's call

---

55 Rijken, 'The "Anglican Virus"', p. 134.
56 Ibid., pp. 142–43.
57 P. G. J. Post, 'From Identity to Accent: The Ritual Studies Perspective of Fields of the Sacred', *Pastoraltheologische Informationen* 33.1 (2013), 149–58 (at 149); Rijken, 'The "Anglican Virus"', p. 155.
58 Rijken, 'The "Anglican Virus"', p. 157.

for a re-enchantment of the liturgy.[59] In addition, Rijken finds resonance with Charles Taylor's call for a 'transcendent humanism', which is a 'liberating alternative to the exclusive, secularist humanism on the one hand and religious dogmatism on the other. For Taylor this is a new Christian humanism which is open to transcendence, an attempt to 'believe again'.[60] Richard Kearney calls this 'anatheism', which is 'the space where an open theism and an open atheism can come into dialogue'.[61] Rijken also finds common ground with Pieter Villiers who has applied the notion of re-enchantment to theology, and who pleads for a 're-enchantment of theology by beauty and mysticism', through aesthetics.[62]

Thus, the churches of the Low Countries, ringing out with the sounds of voices lifted up in choral praise, can act as spiritual centres in their communities, opening their doors to people of all faiths and none, offering musical and liturgical excellence. If you pop in to one you may well find an inclusive spirit of welcome, prayerful worship, and aesthetic beauty. Choral music within the liturgy has long been one of Britain's greatest cultural and religious heritages. Thus, I now turn to consider the results of a UK national live music survey and those of my own research survey on the experience of music.

III. 'Experience of Music' Surveys in England

The twenty-first century has seen a rise in attendance at English cathedral services. Sunday service attendance has risen by a few thousand, but midweek service attendance has increased dramatically, from 7,000 in 2000 (when first reported) to a peak of 19,900 in 2015, since when it has remained basically stable until 2020. The number of

---

59   Erika Fischer-Lichte, *The Transformative Power of Performance: A New Aesthetics*, trans. by Saskya I. Jain (London, New York: Routledge, 2008); Andrew Burnham, *Heaven and Earth in Little Space: The Re-Enchantment of the Liturgy* (Norwich: Canterbury Press 2010), p. 129.
60   Richard Kearney and Jens Zimmerman, eds, *Reimagining the Sacred: Richard Kearney Debates God* (New York: Columbia University Press, 2013). Kearney in conversation with Charles Taylor, author of *A Secular Age* (Cambridge, MA: Harvard University Press, 2007), p. 77 (cited in Rijken, 'The "Anglican Virus"', p. 160).
61   Ibid., p. 80 (cited in Rijken, 'The "Anglican Virus"', p. 160)
62   Pieter G.R. de Villiers, 'Re-Enchanted by Beauty: On Aesthetics and Mysticism', *HTS Teologiese Studies/Theological Studies* 72.4 (2016), 1–7.

people hearing sacred music in these ancient buildings by attending both Sunday and weekday services has almost returned to 2019 levels, following the pandemic.[63] In two surveys I conducted, also in 2018, I collected qualitative data from people who had attended performances of sacred music. One survey focussed on those listening to sacred music in a liturgical context and the other survey collected responses from those listening to sacred music as part of a concert. The results from both surveys contained overlapping ideas: those claiming to have had a religious or spiritual experience were as evident in the concert audience survey as the church congregation survey. Thus, for example, a concert attendee commented:

> I find that I can experience the transcendent power that I call God through the unique beauty of unaccompanied song such as this: the finest music of its time, performed in the architectural context for which it was written, and with the highest quality of vocal refinement.[64]

Performance quality was a common factor to both surveys. Another respondent wrote:

> Overall, the experience was spiritually uplifting and the uplift was due partly to the performance. The quality of the choir and soloists was such that I felt confident in the performance. The sense of peace and awareness of having been in God's presence remained for some days after the concert.[65]

For others, the musical genre was also a factor in the quality of experience:

> Sacred music always brings me back to the knowledge that I have a spiritual dimension. It enables me to be grounded in my prayer and meditation. For me, sacred music ... is a bridge between our worldly existence and the wonder, power and awesomeness of God.[66]

Moreover, some respondents found that the venue was a contributory factor in their quality of experience:

---

63 *The Church of England, Cathedral Statistics, 2021* (London: Data Services, 2023), https://www.churchofengland.org/sites/default/files/2023-03/cathedral-statistics-2021.pdf
64 Jonathan Arnold, *Experience of Music*, 2018, www.experienceofmusic.org
65 Ibid.
66 Ibid.

> Sacred music and churches usually give me a space where I can be other than my quotidian self ... To walk into any place of worship and find sacred music being performed, usually makes me feel particularly blessed.[67]

Likewise, in the congregation survey, a consecrated venue and a liturgical context was significant for some respondents' experience:

> I have always loved evensong and will go to services and listen on the radio. I follow the psalm and make that a time for reflection. I appreciate the other music and often find it uplifting. I sing the hymns if there are any.[68]

Similarly, for this person, the liturgical and musical encounter helped to foster a sense of mental well-being and moral resolution: 'I find the weekly evensong spiritually enriching and feel it provides me with mental strength to realise my duties'.

Not everyone, however, had a spiritual or religious experience through music in a liturgical context: 'My reaction is entirely musical and not spiritual at all. I find that I may be overwhelmed by church music ... without having any spiritual or religious feeling at all'. However, the majority of responses, albeit from self-selecting participants of a largely middle-class and educated background, were positive towards the religious or spiritual aspect of the musical encounter. Moreover, for others, vocal participation is an important factor that is present in worship but not in a concert hall, even if the congregational participant is not of the Christian faith: 'I very much enjoy singing hymns, plainchant, etc., despite not connecting with (and actually opposing in some ways) what is said in the words and what it means, on account of practising Judaism and not Christianity'.

For some of those who are practising Christians, the liturgical and sacramental nature of a service is an essential difference from a concert performance, with regard to musical function: 'What a joy it is when music is in a church—doing its JOB! This was much, much, better than a concert—concerts don't include a Eucharist. With this, my soul could keep hovering, reaching in beauty to God'. Likewise, this respondent indicates why cathedral and chapel attendance at worship in England

---

67   Ibid.
68   Ibid.

might have increased so much over the last few years: 'I greatly value evensong and other liturgical offices in the public churches and cathedrals. It constitutes a real and valuable public service in offering a space of peace and meditation in the midst of life's routine and cares'. One interesting response to music within the liturgy involved a two-year old child:

> I had a two-year old with me. He is riveted by this experience every time. He is just still and calm and listens for minutes at a time. He is also clearly fascinated by the action and movement within the liturgy. In turn, I am moved and inspired by his response to this music, and it calms me too, drawing me, in a way I can only feel, and cannot articulate, closer to God.[69]

It must also be acknowledged that the participants of my own small survey were self-selecting and were not representative of the population as a whole. Indeed, there have been valid critiques concerning the exclusive nature of Anglican choral Evensong, particularly the gendered nature of the tradition, and in terms of ethnicity, class, disability, and vocal timbre.[70] However, the responses to sacred music recorded in my survey do align with Jeff. R. Warren's assessment of the ethical efficacy of music as relational, suggesting both the intrinsic value and the practical benefits of sacred music, at least to some people.[71] Sacred music had a positive effect on individuals, helping them to feel 'blessed', 'uplifted', and 'enriched', as well as providing a 'valuable public service' to the wider community.

Conclusion

King's ground-breaking research into choral Evensong in England, Rijken's mapping of the growth in popularity of choral Evensong in the Netherlands, and the results of my own 'Experience of Music' surveys all indicate that sacred music, and its ritual-sacral context, leads towards tranquillity, transcendence and sanctuary, re-enchanting both

---

69 Ibid.
70 Bertram J. Schirr, 'The Body We Sing: Reclaiming of the Queer Materiality of Vocal Bodies' in *Queering Freedom: Music, Identity and Spirituality*, ed. by Karin Hendricks and June Boyce-Tillman (Bern: Peter Lang), pp. 35-52.
71 Jeff R. Warren, *Music and Ethical Responsibility* (Cambridge: Cambridge University Press, 2014).

religion and the secular, and leading the listener or participant away from potentially destructive emotions of pride, anger, greed, or envy, towards more benevolent feelings of humility, patience, temperance, and generosity, to name but a few of the cardinal vices and virtues. The liminal space of Evensong, with its mystical overtones and transcendental properties, is not a consumerist distraction from the 'real' world of work, business, money, or other realities of the everyday that can give us anxiety and stress. It is a retreat into the numinous that can give strength, encouragement, and inspiration to face our problems, and look outwards from our own selfish desires. Both choral Evensong and semi-liturgical rituals bring us musical and sacral encounters which can increase our sense of empathy and galvanise us for action. Hearts and minds can be transformed by music and the word in combination, a transformation encouraged by a shared experience. Listening to sacred music in community, even as strangers, can also inspire a broader sense of cohesion and socially committed resolve. Now that the heritage of choral Evensong and its cousins in concert form are spreading once more, we should treasure it and support it, because those who take care of that ever 'fresh' expression of praise offer an enormous gift, not just to their local communities but to the wider society as a whole.

15. Listening to the Lived Experiences of Worshippers: A Study of Post-Pandemic Mixed Ecology Worship

Elspeth Manders

The COVID-19 pandemic—which temporarily restricted in-person worship but increased access to worship services online—has indelibly changed the profile of contemporary worship in the Church of England. According to worshipping and visitor data collected in 2021 from England's forty-two cathedrals and Westminster Abbey, 94% of cathedrals now offer online worship in addition to in-person services.[1] New practices, such as online worship, require time for reflection, as the Emeritus Dean of Chelmsford indicated in a monthly newsletter,

> ... where crises of one kind or another appear to be threatening, there is often more pressure to come up with urgent solutions to avert catastrophe and change direction ... The implications of this (the pandemic) for our theology and our ministerial practices and priorities ... will be something that it will take years or generations rather than mere months to explore.[2]

---

1   The Church of England, 'Church of England Cathedrals Showed Recovery in 2021 amid Covid-19 Measures', *The Church of England*, 24 March 2023, http://www.churchofengland.org/media-and-news/press-releases/church-england-cathedrals-showed-recovery-2021-amid-covid-19-measures
2   Nicholas Henshall, 'The Dean's Letter for 5th February', online video recording, *Chelmsford Cathedral*, 5 February 2022, https://www.chelmsfordcathedral.org.uk/media-clips/the-deans-letter-for-5th-february

Furthermore, worship leaders, musicians, and worshippers have different views about the purpose of worship in this new age, the faithfulness to scripture in an increasingly secular context, and the influence of online worship on religious narratives, to name just three areas of contention.

To contribute to a developing reflection on, and response to, post-pandemic worship, I conducted an empirical investigation for music in contemporary worship practice in 2023. While there have been several empirical studies exploring the status of worship following the pandemic;[3] a mixed-method survey conducted by Chelmsford Cathedral in 2021 formed the basis for my own research. The 2021 study uncovered some limitations: as one participant, for example, responded—'it is difficult to express opinions freely in this format'.[4] Recognising that lived Christian realities are highly complex, and difficult to capture via a questionnaire, I sought to unpack lived worshipper experiences using interviews. I thus thematically analysed five interviews with lay musicians from Anglican and Catholic denominations in the Diocese of Chelmsford to understand the experiences of churchgoers. My aim was to consider how qualitative research methodology—specifically, reflexive thematic analysis—can be used to inform the planning and implementation of mixed ecology worship following the pandemic. In this chapter, I introduce the contextual frameworks, qualitative methodology, and findings of my research on post-pandemic mixed ecology worship. In doing so, I outline the scope and limitations of this study, which used a controlled, purposive sample. Throughout the chapter, I use the term 'mixed ecology' to refer to worship that is receptive to new ways of accessing faith, specifically, online worship.[5] I

---

3   See, for example, Simon Dein and Fraser Watts, 'Religious Worship Online: A Qualitative Study of Two Sunday Virtual Services', *International Association for the Psychology of Religion* 45.2 (2023), 191–209. This study investigates the experiences of thirteen participants in two Sunday virtual services, with data drawn from interviews and analysed with thematic analysis.

4   Dean and Chapter of Chelmsford, 'Cathedral Survey Results: Pandemic 2020–2021' (unpublished empirical study, Chelmsford Cathedral, 2021). I am grateful to the Dean and Chapter for permission to use the survey here.

5   For a helpful summary of digital mixed ecology, see Ruth Perrin and Ed Olsworth-Peter, 'The Mixed Ecologists; Experiences of Mixed Ecology Ministry in the Church of England' (The Church of England, May 2021), https://www.churchofengland.org/sites/default/files/2021-05/focussed-study-2-the-mixed-ecologists.pdf: 'The rise of hybrid church, where physically gathered and digital church combine. This

use the term 'post-pandemic' to refer to the cultural landscape shaped by the COVID-19 pandemic (encompassing various belief systems and non-belief orientations).

I. The Post-Pandemic Landscape

(a) Theological Considerations

Post-pandemic worship, specifically online worship, raised several theological implications for the practice of religious ritual online. Much Christian worship is based on incarnational theology, which stresses corporeality: '…and the Word became flesh and lived among us' (John 1:1–14). However, online worship challenges the constitution of Christ's real presence in the Eucharist, rendering the sacramental viability of online worship unclear. The legitimacy of online worship, specifically the extent to which it upholds orthodox Christian values, requires examination. Coming together in worship is also a central part of the Christian ethos. As theologian Andrew Louth suggests:

> To be a Christian is not simply to believe something, to learn something, but to be something, to experience something. The role of the church then, is not simply as the contingent vehicle—in history—of the Christian message, but as the community, through belonging to which we come into touch with the Christian mystery.[6]

St Paul builds on this insight in his teaching: 'For as in one body we have many members, and not all the members have the same function, so we, who are many, are one body in Christ, and individually we are members

---

represents a new form of local mixed ecology in its own right. A digital mixed ecology has begun to emerge, with some fostering "church online," livestreaming what happens in the physical space of church, whilst others have experimented with "online church" where they have sought to form community and worship in the digital space'. See, also, Barry Hill, 'Why a Mixed Ecology Matters', *Church Times*, 12 November 2021, http://www.churchtimes.co.uk/articles/2021/12-november/comment/opinion/why-a-mixed-ecology-matters: 'The mixed ecology cannot be either/or, or even both/and, but learn/with, where we encourage the best in those worshipping communities that are most different from how we would do things'.

6   Andrew Louth, 'Tradition and the Tacit', in Andrew Louth, *Discerning the Mystery: An Essay on the Nature of Theology* (Oxford: Oxford University Press, 1989), p. 74.

one of another' (Rom 12:4–8). However, online worship has changed how Christians come together by facilitating communities that worship and socialise together online.

Empirical studies show variation in how worshippers view the theological viability of online worship. Some participants in the 2021 Chelmsford Cathedral study found that online worship was not sufficient because 'we need each other in the flesh, not just on an interactive screen. We need social contact'.[7] Others, however, found online worship spiritually sustaining, based on the idea that God's revelation can occur in any physical space: 'we don't have to be physically present or together for worship to be meaningful, sometimes we just have to go with it'.[8] The positive outlook reflects theologies which stress that even when the sacrament is not consecrated, there is theological integrity because of Christ's presence in the ordinary. As Simon Podmore summarises, 'incarnational theology encompasses the notion that God is revealed in the material, the mundane, the everyday as well as in the sublime and transcendent which seems to point beyond what is immediate'.[9] The suitability of online worship can therefore depend on the theological conviction of the worshipper.

(b) Musical Considerations

Theological considerations also arose for how to implement music in online worship. Congregational song has historically been celebrated as a means of active participation with the music,[10] which aligns with theological narratives that stress singing together as a theological imperative.[11] In the Chelmsford Cathedral study, the important role of

---

7   Dean and Chapter of Chelmsford, 'Cathedral Survey Results'.
8   Ibid.
9   Simon D. Podmore, 'Introduction Transforming Presence: Incarnation between Transcendence and Immanence', in *Christian Mysticism and Incarnational Theology: Between Transcendence and Immanence*, ed. by Louise Nelstrop and Simon D. Podmore (Farnham: Ashgate Publishing Limited, 2013), pp. 1-12 (at p. 3).
10 Martin Luther argued that psalms, and especially hymns, should have a place in church life and the education of young people: see Gesa Thiessen, *Theological Aesthetics: A Reader* (London: SCM Press, 2004), pp. 144–45.
11 See Joseph Ratzinger, 'On the Theological Basis of Church Music', in *Collected Works Theology of the Liturgy Volume II*, ed. by Michael J. Miller, trans. by John Saward, Kenneth Baker, S. J. Henry Taylor, et al. (San Francisco, CA: Ignatius Press, 2014), pp. 421–42.

active participation in the music was highlighted by several participants: when asked what they missed about being part of a church community since the pandemic, they mentioned singing (see Figure 15.1). However, the parameters for active participation in music have changed by inviting online worshippers to sing online. Singing online raises further implications, therefore, for evangelism as well as for the construction of religious identity.

> Question: What have you missed about being part of a church community (not just church) since the pandemic?
> - Singing!
> - Joining in with the music.
> - Singing praises together.
> - Fellowship, singing, involvement in the service and cathedral activities.
> - Professional choral singing and singing hymns together in church.
> - Singing oneself and listening to quality singing.
> - Singing hymns.
> - Singing and face to face contact.

Fig. 15.1 Participant responses about singing.[12] Created by author (2024), CC BY-NC 4.0

The rhetorical profile for music in worship has also been impacted by worshipping online, as the expectations for worship practices upheld before the pandemic change in the new post-pandemic conditions. Such expectations regard, for example, the appropriateness of style (including the desired balance between traditional styles of music and contemporary worship music),[13] presentation (including the balance of

---

12   Dean and Chapter of Chelmsford, 'Cathedral Survey Results'.
13   Some participants reflected on rhetorical variety, preferring modern styles of music such as contemporary worship music: 'We think there could be more variety in services and liturgy and especially the music. We love what we do

sung and spoken aspects of the liturgy, and who sings them),[14] and the quantity and quality of music in worship.

II. Building a Methodology

Whilst empirical data from questionnaires offers important insights into statistical findings, I sought to generate further insights by considering lived narratives. I chose reflexive thematic analysis (RTA)—which necessitates considering the relationship between the researcher, the research topic, and the design of the research process—as a fruitful qualitative research methodology, and I interweave a phenomenological approach throughout.

(a) Limiting Qualitative Research

To justify qualitative research methodology as a viable research method for listening to and analysing contemporary worshipper realities, it is critical to examine the relationship between researcher and participant. There is a phenomenological dialectical relationship between participant and researcher, which, because of respective contextual milieus, impacts the validity of the data-gathering process. As Martin Heidegger underlines, 'interpretation is never a pre-suppositionless apprehending of something to us'; individuals are 'always already in an environing world'.[15] Qualitative research methodologies therefore consider interactions between researcher and participant data, semantic literacies regarding the participant and their data (for instance, does the

---

but miss more modern styles of worship and would also doubt how accessible the services are for those who grew up in different or without tradition' (ibid.). John Frame defends Contemporary Worship Music on the basis that it edifies old and new, noting that 'to accent either pole of this dialectic without the other is to lose them both' (John Frame, 'Tradition and Contemporaneity', in John Frame, *Contemporary Worship Music: A Biblical Defence* (Phillipsburg, NJ: P and R Publishing, 1997), p. 130).

14 Participants in the Chelmsford Cathedral study commented on the balance of music they could partake in with music sung by the choir: 'I am finding current Sunday eucharists very choir heavy—more like attending a concert than a service' (Chelmsford Cathedral, 'Cathedral Survey Results').

15 Martin Heidegger, *Sein und Zeit* (London: SCM Press, 1962); Martin Heidegger, 'Traditional Language and Technological Language', *Journal of Philosophical Research* 23 (1998), 129–45.

researcher understand the words in the same way as participant?), and attempts to understand the contextual milieu from both perspectives.¹⁶ Understanding that the researcher is the central analytic instrument and their research uncovers dual perspectives from the phenomenon and researcher is central to qualitative research. Prior to undertaking qualitative research by interviews, I therefore engaged in consistent hermeneutic reflexivity to explore critically my own assumptions from different angles. I engaged in informal presuppositional interviews, the aim of which was to leaf 'through the language, ambiguities, contradictions, certainties and interconnections with the phenomena in questions, [...] to unfurl the layers of [the researcher's] own story [...] to probe into [the researcher's] relationship with the research and its purpose'.¹⁷ This enables the researcher 'to move beyond [their] familiar way of Being to identify other perspectives as well as re-examine [their] well-trodden and comfortable paths of knowing'.¹⁸ Considering this, I actively engaged in conversations with colleagues and acquaintances within the Diocese of Chelmsford, inviting input regarding my research questions.

I carefully considered the location, timing, frequency, and candidates for interviews. Two participants chose to interview online. Following the suggestions of Hilary Engward *et al.* for conducting remote qualitative interviews, my aim was to offer a safe space which could enable communication.¹⁹ I asked colloquial questions to facilitate a natural sense of space, checked if the participant was comfortable, if they had any questions, and invited questions about the research itself. Two participants chose to interview online, for which I actively accounted in the interview process. In determining the interview questions, I followed Kathryn Roulston's suggestion to use core and open-ended questions to provide an outline structure to steer the interview, with probing and

---

16   Ibid.
17   Lewis Barrett-Rodger, Sally Goldspink, and Hilary Engward, 'Being in the Wood: Using a Presuppositional Interview in Hermeneutic Phenomenological Research', *Qualitative Research* 23.4 (2022), 1062–77 (at 1076).
18   Ibid., 1066.
19   Hilary Engward, Sally Goldspink, Maria Iancu, Thomas Kersey, and Abigail Wood, 'Togetherness in Separation: Practical Considerations for Doing Remote Qualitative Interviews Ethically', *International Journal of Qualitative Methods* 21 (2002), 1-9.

supplementary questions used to add greater detail to the description.[20] I adopted a loose framework of questions to contextualise the phenomena regarding the research question, with the aim of generating directive but not limiting prompts.

Finally, I used purposive sampling to invite five lay musicians and employees who worshipped and worked in Catholic and Anglican contexts in the Diocese of Chelmsford to participate. In limiting my sample size, my goal was to implement RTA effectively. I recognised, of course, the potential limitations of a reduced sample, which did not include young people under the age of eighteen due to ethical considerations pertaining to consent. Clergy were not invited to participate, in order to manage the quantity of narratives for analysis. Moreover, insights into spiritual experiences from the perspective of ethnicity were not accounted for in the sample. Further considerations included my position as an employee within the Diocese of Chelmsford with a background in the Christian faith tradition, and my dialogic presence with the interviewees. I also recognised that participants undertook insider roles within the Diocese as staff or organisational leaders, in addition to worshipping. These role frameworks offer specific positionalities, which must be distinguished from worshipper narratives more generally and which may have limited the findings.

Table 15.1 Participant biographies. Created by author (2024), CC BY-NC 4.0

Role	Length of interview (minutes)	Location
Church music practitioner	57	Online
Church music practitioner	26	In-person
Pastoral officer	40	In-person
Communications operator	69	Online
Church music practitioner	49	In-person

---

20 Kathryn Roulston, *Interviews in Qualitative Research* (London: John and Wiley Sons, 2012).

(b) Reflexive Thematic Analysis

After the interview methodology had been systematically applied, I used RTA to interpret the findings. Virginia Braun and Victoria Clarke describe RTA as 'a theoretically flexible method' for 'developing, analysing and interpreting patterns across a qualitative dataset'.[21] A central component of RTA is that the researcher's position is unavoidable; the process involves 'critically interrogating' the researcher's influence and explicitly bringing forth these values in analysis.[22] Furthermore, Braun and Clarke suggest that RTA 'identifies, analyses and reports patterns (themes) within data. It minimally organises and scores your data in (rich) detail. However, frequently it goes further than this, and interprets various aspects of the research topic'.[23] This approach suited a key goal of my research: namely, to listen to worshipper narratives. Thus, using RTA allowed me to form outcomes using inductive generation of subjective codes and themes, driven entirely by the data.[24]

The RTA approach is characterised by six steps. The first step requires familiarisation with the data, which involved detailed review of the interview transcripts. Second, the data is coded by looking for recurring words, key patterns, and emergent themes. Third, the coded data is then re-organised into these emergent themes. Fourth, the arising themes are developed and grouped according to character or meaning (such as past/present/future narratives, or conceptual ideas/opinions/experiences). Fifth, the grouped themes are further refined and developed. Table 15.2 indicates the themes and sub-themes that emerged from my research. Finally, the sixth step is to produce the report using compelling examples to illustrate the findings. In the next section, I examine the interpretations and findings which arose in accordance with this sixth step, and I have structured the participant narratives according to the key themes in Table 15.2 below.

---

21 Virginia Braun and Victoria Clarke, *Thematic Analysis: A Practical Guide* (London: SAGE Publications, 2022), p. 4.
22 Ibid., p. 5.
23 Ibid., p. 79.
24 Ibid.

Table 15.2 Themes and sub-themes pertaining to step five of RTA. Created by author (2024), CC BY-NC 4.0

Theme	Sub-themes
The post-pandemic situation	Ideological tensions
	Literacy and understanding
Online worship	Access
	Music
	Active Participation
	Outreach
The philosophy of music in mixed ecology worship	Tradition
	Outreach
	Aesthetic
The choral musician's lifestyle	Lifestyle and Family
	Relationships
Music in practice in mixed ecology worship	Tensions regarding music and liturgy
	Rhetoric
	Communication

III. Key Findings from RTA

(a) The Post-Pandemic Situation

Participants noted ideological tensions pertaining to religious ideas in the contemporary world. This included tensions regarding the relevancy of church in contemporary lifestyles, such as 'now we're competing against loads of stuff. In my childhood, on Sunday mornings there was church or you stayed at home', and 'another challenge is to make the church relevant in busy people's lifestyles, and to show them that it's attractive and that children are welcome'.[25] Furthermore, 'as in lots of

---

25 Anonymous participant, 'Listening to the Lived Experiences of Worshippers: Planning and Implementing a Mixed Ecology Worship following the Covid-19

things, people got out of the habit of going'. Ideological incongruency and change, including the de-prioritisation of worship in lifestyles because of busyness, competition with other opportunities, and lack of habit formation are aspects of the post-pandemic religious situation. Participants also acknowledged that religious, musical, and digital literacy is problematising access to the church and sacred music. This is particularly an issue for 'children and families who have no experience or understanding of the church' which leads to 'anxiety about even going through the doors'. Regarding online worship access, one participant noted that it needs to be as simple to use as possible:

> So they haven't got to battle the technology and find Facebook and then see where they can search for it and find it streaming, which if you're used to doing it, is very easy, but if you're not used to the technology and you're one of these people, that kind of slow motion stops their finger on a button.

Participants recognised that intuitive online mechanisms are important for those who struggle to access and navigate online platforms. This is relevant given that 36.4% of the Church of England's worshipping community, as of 2021, are over seventy.[26]

(b) Online Worship

Overall, participants celebrated online worship; as one participant said, 'huge fan. I don't see a downside'. Several commented on its cultural relevance and, particularly, its congruency with modern lifestyles. For example, one participant engaged with different styles of worship at different times of day, and globally:

> I watch Morning Prayers at the Cathedral. I watch Evensong, mostly somewhere else if I see some music come up that I particularly want to listen to. I'm linked to Saint Hippo at Leytonstone, St Martin-in-the-Fields, St Thomas's Fifth Avenue and St. James in Australia... Absolutely love it, being able to access a tradition so far away from me.

Pandemic', interviews by Elspeth Manders, January–March 2023, audio. All subsequent interview quotations are as above.

26 Church of England and Ken Eames, *Statistics for Mission 2021* (London: Data Services, 2022), https://www.churchofengland.org/sites/default/files/2023-01/2021-statistics-for-mission.pdf

This reflects the greater dissemination of religious ideas, transcending geographical barriers. Participants also identified rhetorical and financial concerns that have emerged for musicians because of online worship. Philosophically-minded participants considered the impact of livestreaming on the ontology of worship, noting that the length of time music is shared online (and whether it is accessed in real time or after the event) affects the distinction between service and performance. One participant said: 'once you go into something that's permanently there, that's not a service. It's a performance'. Another participant noted:

> If it's something that's going to have your name attached to it and be out on the internet forever, you could say it was a performance, and it will be paid for differently. I think that the principle of taking it down after 24/48 hours really ought to be there to protect musicians.

Whilst participants shared an appreciation for music online, there were concerns regarding the safe implementation of online practice. Participants wished to establish parameters for sharing music online to ensure musicians are paid fairly.

Several participants commented on online worship and active participation. Some liturgical devices were praised; as one participant said, 'I thought the Church of England did cover it quite well in the sense of offerings, prayers of spiritual communion'. However, some found Eucharistic liturgies online more problematic, theologically speaking: 'I think my problem would be a mass because you can't make your communion. You're not fully engaging in it, and that's the central point of the mass'. As with previous empirical studies, there was disparity between the theological virtue of Eucharistic and non-Eucharist liturgies online. Participants also suggested that script planning—including of camera angles and microphone placements according to liturgical moments—prior to streaming can be used to 'make you feel you are part of the service', encouraging active participation.

In addition, participants commented on the outreach potential of online worship. This included the acknowledgement that musical offerings tended to be the most popular items shared online, with comments such as 'music always brings in the most views and the most positive comments, and it speaks to people even online. It speaks to people who don't have to be in the building'. However, whilst social media channels such as Facebook and YouTube are positive marketing resources for the church, participants suggested they ought to be used strategically and for specific functions. One participant found that softer church initiatives were popular, but 'in the pandemic, Facebook became our broadcast channel, and they all switched off. They unsubscribed'. There needs to be consideration of how often worship is shared online and which platforms it is shared on, as well as how to balance sharing worship online with softer church initiatives.

(c) The Philosophy of Music in Worship

The context for worship has shifted according to societal changes, with implications for the purpose and function of music. Specifically, participants commented on the sustainability of the choral music tradition and the imperative for outreach among church music spheres. This outcome reflects recent reports demonstrating that the sacred music tradition faces a long-term sustainability crisis.[27] A recurring theme was the unsustainability in contemporary practice of the traditional chorister timetable of numerous rehearsals and services a week. It was noted that the chorister timetable 'needs to move several decades ahead. We haven't moved as quickly as we ought to, we need to be much more flexible'. In addition, expanding demographic resources to incorporate 'combining boys with our girls, that kind of close cooperation', was desired. Whilst more ministries incorporate mixed gender choirs in their musical offering, a more diverse pool of resources including equal commitment for boys and girls is recommended.

Music was celebrated as a central facet of church outreach. It was noted that extra-curricular and networking opportunities are important in the chorister timetable and should 'be much, much higher priority'.

---

27 In 2022, a report commissioned by the Cathedral Music Trust found three areas requiring urgent attention: widening participation, sustaining excellence, and improving affordability. Eighty-one per cent said that widening access for participation in cathedral music—especially for young people—was a critical issue for the future, and that progress has been slow and inconsistent towards ensuring choirs reflect the diversity of the communities around them. See Peter Allwood, 'UK's World-Renowned Sacred Music Tradition Faces Long-Term Sustainability Crisis, New Report Shows', *Cathedral Music Trust*, 2 October 2022, https://www.cathedralmusictrust.org.uk/CMT/CMT/News/Articles/UK%E2%80%99s-world-renowned-sacred-music-tradition-faces-sustainability-crisis-new-report-shows.aspx

Regarding music in worship, participants noted the standard of musicianship in a cathedral as opposed to parish ministry is 'what's different and that's what attracts people to a cathedral'. Participants also shared in a plea to integrate children into church music at an early age, 'get them early, when they are seven, eight or nine, and present them with Palestrina as though this is completely normal'. However, participants also noted an incongruency between the desires of the musicians to perform and the imperative to communicate:

> I think there is an interest in making music and making beautiful high-quality music, but I don't think some people care whether anyone hears it or not. It's the process of making the music that is important, not how many people it reaches.

Whilst all participants celebrated music in worship, they disagreed on the extent to which music programming should consider its accessibility, shareability, and popularity.

Participants highlighted music's capacity to touch on the subjective human condition as an important gateway to the church. Beautiful music is 'fundamental to the worship, in the same way as if people can go into a church and they can be moved by looking at the stained glass or in places where they have them at the wall paintings'. It can also transcend barriers pertaining to church music literacy, because 'the vast majority of the people in congregations probably won't understand music in the way that a trained musician will understand it, but that doesn't matter, because they're being moved by that experience'. Whilst aesthetic experience is a key part of the participant feedback, it is important to acknowledge that the sample centralised musicians and, therefore, their responses to music may not be representative of worshippers in general.

(d) The Choral Musician's Lifestyle

Choirs are a key aspect of musical life in the Church of England. Several participants focused on parameters which impact the church musician's lifestyle and how this affects musical provision in worship. Participants acknowledged the difficulty in sustaining chorister life in the contemporary age. Singing in a choir as a young person is a commitment which includes the whole family, and demands compromise as a family unit:

> It's an extraordinary commitment, and it's one that I've never played down when I've had a chance to talk to prospective choir parents. It is an absolute lifestyle decision and it impacts on everybody... it's not that the chorister is put first, but all of that timetabling has to come together per family, because there are still hockey games for somebody else or rugby games.

Furthermore, participants identified a disconnect between the commitment of the children and the parents, noting many parents do not engage in the worship but 'just drop their kid off and pick them back up again'. Parents are not fully integrated in church worship, an indication that church worship does not fulfil an ideological or spiritual function for them.

Relationship building with families, schools, and peers was regarded as an imperative for choral musicianship. Participants argued that churches must invest more time into communicating with other organisations to secure a future for church musicianship. For instance, participants celebrated building relationships with schools. Specifically, a specialised communications strategy, implemented either as a distinct role or as a facet within music leadership, should prioritise fostering relations with schools because of the positive implications for recruitment:

> If you had relationships where your music staff had already contacted schools and had relationships, and were going in, for example, to support GCSE music students, or your seventh-grade music students, or going into an assembly, or to help with a summer concert, that's how you build relationships. Other things come from that, it might be recruitment, it might not.

It was also noted that fostering relationships between chorister parents at school institutions is important to manage the practical demands of chorister life, for example, lift sharing. However, this is difficult for parents with children from isolated or individual schools who 'found communication very, very difficult, because we went to school where nobody else attended the Cathedral'. Encouraging parents to communicate online can help to make chorister life more practically viable for families with children attending schools with fewer connections to a cathedral. One participant suggested WhatsApp groups should be used, because 'that kind of communication that means that one person goes to a sports field and picks up four choristers makes everybody's life so much easier'.

(e) Music in Practice in Mixed Ecology Settings

Belief is central to many accounts of musicianship in the church. Whilst it was recognised that belief is not necessary, having a spiritual calling helped participants when performing music underpinned by faith: 'it is up to me to respond to that and to, to worship God through music to the best of my ability'. For those working with children's choirs, belief was a central part of musical pedagogy. However, in some organisations, there are differing opinions between musicians and clergy regarding how often music should be used in church services. One participant said:

> I would like the clergy to acknowledge, accept and welcome the place of good music in worship, and to see it as a powerful tool of evangelism, rather than seeing it as a threat. There are far too many clergy still who see music as a threat.

Musical rhetoric was also a central concern. Several participants had strong views regarding the type of music that should be used in church worship: '"Shine Jesus shine" makes my toes curl'. Others offered a diplomatic approach to rhetoric, endorsing rhetorical compromise in musical timetabling:

> One needs to be aware that people have different likes and dislikes. So you try and programme as wide a repertoire as possible. Of course, you can't please all the people all the time. You just have to bear in mind that not everyone is going to like what you do. But you can please some of the people some of the time, that famous adage.

Participants worshipping at the Diocesan Cathedral spoke about recent polemics regarding musical devices in liturgy, including arguable compromises on taste. Whilst it was noted that a variety of musical offerings can help worship appeal to more people, clarity on distinguishing features in services ought to be used so that 'everybody (can) have an opportunity to hear what they like'. In this case, the participant liked 'the idea of a service that doesn't have a choral offering, because that clearly appealed to a congregation who wants to worship without a choir'. On the other hand, participants noted that for people 'that are not potentially regular worshippers', the presence of music is an incentive to worship because 'a lot of the time they will see the music of the day and be sort of pulled along by that'. Part of the conversation regarding the implementation of music in worship therefore involves how often to include a choral offering.

Participants discussed the theological parameters associated with musical rhetoric. A congregational emphasis in the Diocesan Cathedral's Eucharistic service on a Sunday included a 'congregational setting that is known universally and a lot of them can sing off by heart. Also, a nice selection of hymns, a rhetorical psalm with a response line that they can sing along to in between verses'. This was noted as 'a nice way of making sure everyone is involved'. Certainly, active participation in the music was important, reflecting the findings of the 2021 Cathedral questionnaire: 'I like singing. I'm not great singer, but I like joining in with things. So to me, if I've been to a service where I've only stood up once and sung it doesn't feel like worshipping'. However, whilst music can help to make worship more inclusive and accessible, it can also be divisive, because 'the musicians sometimes obstruct in the attempt to making it outward facing, just simple things like not being prepared to take a softer version of music out there'. The choice of musical style, and specifically the balance of traditional and modern music, is directly tied to incentives regarding outreach.

Participants suggested that developing strong relationships between music and communication departments are essential to the church and to the successful implementation of strategic outreach initiatives. It was noted that all church staff, including musicians, 'should be offering a high level of communications'. How music is programmed, and subsequently communicated in marketing and distribution, seems to be essential for integrating and retaining church worshippers in contemporary spheres.

IV. Future Directions

Having examined key themes from participant narratives through the six steps of RTA, I now respond specifically to participant reactions to the question 'what would you like to see in church worship in five years' time?'. For a sustainable church model in this post-pandemic praxis, I suggest the development of strategies for the implementation of music in mixed ecology in four areas: (a) online worship; (b) communication; (c) rhetoric around musical styles; and (d) chorister recruitment and retention. Although I centre my own qualitative research, I acknowledge that further qualitative study is required to develop outcomes.

(a) Online Worship Strategy

Online or digital worship practice requires standardising. Specifically, strategies are required for hybrid worship including the following points:

1. The frequency of worship made available online.
2. The length of time online worship is kept online.
3. The balance of worship offerings that are accessible online or in person only.
4. The angle, duration, and diversity of camera work.
5. How to efficiently use staff resources.
6. Financial sustainability.
7. Ideological and financial protection for musicians.
8. The outreach potential of online worship.
9. The different parameters for parish and cathedral contexts.
10. The theological considerations for accessing worship online.

Fig. 15.2 Online worship strategy. Created by author (2024), CC BY-NC 4.0

These ten concerns reflect the important role of online worship in worshipper narratives and show the broad scope of the task of implementation. While online worship is, it appears, a beneficial addition, there are significant limitations in terms of participation and the kind of religious experience engendered, and this is particularly relevant for Eucharistic liturgies. Furthermore, participants found the lack of clarity regarding the role of online worship in the church's mission led to disagreements between musicians and church leaders, negatively impacting music in both in-person and online worship contexts. Regarding the further implementation of music in mixed ecology worship, empirical research teaches us that a transparent strategy is required to use each component effectively.

(b) Communication Strategy

Developing systems of communication should include consideration of communication challenges within music departments and worship organisations. Specifically, participants would like to see the following:

1. More communication with chorister parents using online platforms such as WhatsApp.

2. More in-person extra-curricular activities and networking which include parents, such as chorister meetings or social events, to engage choristers from non-church schools.

3. Strategic relationship building with schools to navigate the increased demands of the schooling timetable, and a willingness from sacred organisations to recognise the increased demands upon young people and their education and to respond accordingly.

4. Centralising communications in strategic planning because good communication is a facet of every role in worship planning and implementation, including music-making.

5. The strategies of music and communications to align more closely. This might require additional staff roles which can take on the communication, blue-sky thinking, and administrative aspects of outreach-focused music work.

Fig. 15.3 Communication strategy. Created by author (2024), CC BY-NC 4.0

Participants sought to systematise how churches and musicians communicate with each other and with external secular organisations; to enhance internal communication systems; and to foster a culture which treats communications as a central aspect of all church roles. Asynchronous technology could be useful here for collaborations across remote spheres, increasing access to information, enabling flexible timetabling, and broadening social groups.

(c) Rhetorical Strategy

Tensions regarding the style and quantity of music in worship were cited as issues following the pandemic. Several participants spoke about their experience of rhetorical change concerning specifically the place of worship in the Diocese of Chelmsford, citing rhetorical consistency as an issue. A strategy for development might consider the following:

> 1. Leaders need to actively encourage an openness to compromise on taste.
>
> 2. Strategic use of esoteric music along with music that is more accessible. Whilst accommodating traditional music values are integral to the musical life of a sacred organisation, consideration of the non-commercial viability of sacred music on online platforms, including the use of music from other traditions, aligned with a strategy which retains the integrity of the foundation and protects musicians, including their ideological and financial interests, requires greater attention.
>
> 3. Recognition that successful implementation of musical rhetoric ties in directly with communication and administration strategies, which in coming together to offer a transparent and systematised programme, enables people to take their worship taste and consequent practice into their own hands.

Fig. 15.4 Rhetorical strategy. Created by author (2024), CC BY-NC 4.0

(d) Chorister Recruitment Strategy

The last observation from participant narratives pertains directly to the resources available to implement music in worship: church choirs and choristers. Participants stressed that the pandemic calls for a revised recruitment and retainment strategy, including:

1. A chorister timetable that accounts for increasing pressures on young people in education and reflects increasingly demanding lifestyles. This might include, as one participant suggested, devising a more flexible and reduced timetable with no/fewer morning rehearsals.
2. A recruitment strategy directly integrated with local schools.
3. A strategy for retaining choristers which includes actively engaging parents in the musical and worshipping life of the church.
4. Continuing to examine the impact the pandemic has had on the behaviour and executive functioning of younger choristers, and to use peer modelling as a method to improve such aspects.

Fig. 15.5 Chorister Strategy. Created by author (2024), CC BY-NC 4.0

Conclusion

The data generated from this small focus group located in the worshipping community of the Diocese of Chelmsford demonstrates that qualitative research methodology may offer important insights into the lived experiences of worshippers engaged in contemporary mixed ecology worship. The flexibility and inductive data-driven approach of RTA places lived realities at the forefront of conclusions. Examining these lived realities and experiences highlighted participants' passion for the church and their roles within it. Acknowledging the inevitable shifts in praxis following the COVID-19 pandemic, participants recognised that the musical and spiritual realities of their worshipping life, including access to worship online, were worth sustaining and developing. Furthermore, it is essential in future ecclesial music-making to strategise music in online worship as a theological and cultural imperative. Listening to worshippers' experiences indicates that churches have work to do to ensure the continued viability of traditional choral music-making in the post-pandemic praxis. On the basis of the data taken from interviews using RTA, I have thus suggested, in this chapter, four areas to consider in implementing mixed ecology worship following the pandemic.

16. An Abductive Study of Digital Worship through the Lenses of Netnography and Digital Ecclesiology

Tihomir Lazić

The rapid rise of digital technologies has dramatically transformed religious practices and communities, altering how people worship and experience spiritual realities, both individually and together. A notable shift has been the emergence of digital worship, often referred to as 'online' or 'virtual' worship. The COVID-19 pandemic significantly accelerated this transformation, solidifying the creation and dissemination of online worship songs as a new norm in religious circles. These initiatives sought to enrich communal worship experiences, bridging the gap between offline and online realms. In this evolving landscape, virtual worship choirs became increasingly popular, as they allowed musicians and vocalists to collaborate, producing music that nurtured a sense of shared worship despite the challenges of physical distance. The widespread practice of worship on social media, exemplified by platforms like YouTube, has become a rich reservoir of data, with a proliferation of virtual choirs presenting their multi-screen worship renditions.

This trove of abundant and readily accessible data offers an invaluable resource for researchers across diverse fields who are keen to untangle the intricate interplay between music, spirituality, and technology. Such inquiries are underpinned by pressing questions: what is the perceived impact of these online worship songs on people's spiritual growth and receptiveness to the deeper, unseen layers of our existence? What motivations lie behind individuals' gravitation towards digital worship? How do these virtual religious engagements shape people's daily spiritual interactions with the divine and their community? Can online music facilitate and shape a genuine expression of the church's communal adoration and, if so, to what extent? And, delving into the heart of the matter, can we truly classify digital worship as genuine worship? It is as an ecclesiologist, musician, and worship leader that I venture into the discourse surrounding online music's potential to nurture deep spiritual connections among digital worshippers. Drawing from an interdisciplinary perspective, my study seeks to unveil the profound relational dynamics underpinning the Holy Spirit's community-forming actions in digital spaces, particularly as evident in the responses to the music videos created by virtual worship choirs in times of physical distancing.

I. An Abductive Method

In this study, our methodological approach draws upon the emergent and promising fields of netnography and digital ecclesiology. To glean a deeper insight into the Spirit's role in community formation in the context of digital worship, it is imperative that research strategies adeptly integrate theory and empirical data. Traditional ecclesiological research typically relies on a deductive approach, beginning with theoretical foundations. Conversely, netnographic research, employing ethnographic principles to study digital communities, emphasises an inductive approach, examining empirical data derived from the stories and lived experiences within these online spaces.[1] However, employing an abductive approach presents an opportunity to bridge the gap between theory and lived experiences. Through this abductive lens, characterised by a dialectical method, one can oscillate between theory and data, creating a dialogue that enriches both domains.[2] This dynamic

---

1 Daniela Abrants Ferreira and Paula Castro Pires de Souza Chimenti, 'Netnography: Unveiling Human Narratives in a Digital World', *Brazilian Journal of Marketing* 21.4 (2022), 1433–55.
2 Kirstine Helboe Johansen, 'Analytical Strategies', in *The Wiley Blackwell Companion to Theology and Qualitative Research*, ed. by Knut Tveitereid and Pete Ward

process enables us to engage with the complexities of human experience in tandem with theological concepts.

Identifying the three critical domains—within, through, and around us— where the Spirit's community-generating activity is most evident, lays the groundwork for formulating relevant empirical queries. Leveraging the potency of an abductive approach, the research can yield nuanced understandings of the Spirit's dynamic community-building movements, as manifested in online worship responses facilitated through digitally-mediated music.[3] Within the realm of contemporary ecclesiological studies, the task of integrating an abductive method— merging netnography and digital ecclesiology—into the study of digital worship is still in its nascent stages. This study seeks to address this void, laying foundational groundwork for this innovative methodological approach and setting the stage for a more in-depth future exploration.

The spotlight on a multi-screen virtual choir video, 'The UK Blessing', serves not just as a case study but as a tangible testament to the efficacy of our abductive method. This well-known worship video—featuring a collective rendition of the song 'The Blessing'—garnered substantial attention upon its release on YouTube on 3 May 2020.[4] Penned by Chris Brown, Cody Carnes, Kari Jobe, and Steven Furtick, the song was originally introduced on Elevation Worship's YouTube channel in early March 2020, its debut coinciding with the initial surge of the global pandemic.[5] The 3 May video showcases a conglomerate of over sixty-five churches from the United Kingdom, harmonising to send a message of unity and hope during challenging times. The song draws inspiration from a well-known biblical text, Numbers 6:24–26, and has

---

(Hoboken, NJ: Wiley-Blackwell, 2022), pp. 396–98.

3 The tangible and historical manifestations of the faith community's participation in God call for interdisciplinary scholarly collaboration. Such collaboration should encompass theology, sociology, ethnography, history, anthropology, demography, cultural studies, and more. The incorporation of pneumatological insights with qualitative methodologies such as netnography, virtual ethnography, and grounded theory is especially promising, with regard to the burgeoning digital arenas where faith communities thrive. The confluence of online and offline ecclesiastical expressions in mediating divine presence constitutes an intriguing frontier ripe for exploration.

4 The UK Blessing, 'The UK Blessing—Churches Sing "The Blessing" over the UK', online video recording, *YouTube*, 3 May 2020, https://youtu.be/PUtll3mNj5U

5 Elevation Worship, 'The Blessing with Kari Jobe & Cody Carnes', online video recording, *YouTube*, 6 March 2020, https://youtu.be/Zp6aygmvzM4

amassed a considerable following, with over 5.3 million views and 6,276 comments on YouTube.[6] Surprisingly elaborate and extensive comments offer a treasure trove of insights into the spiritual impact and communal aspects of this phenomenon of digital worship. While the extensive engagement with this video illustrates the profound communal and spiritual impact of digital worship, our primary emphasis lies in establishing the abductive method's viability as a ground-breaking and academically rigorous avenue for subsequent research.

II. Digital Worship Through an Ecclesiological Lens

What might be the most fruitful ecclesiological approach for studying community formation in the context of digital worship? I posit that communion ecclesiology, with its focus on relational dynamics, offers the most insightful perspective for understanding the church's communal essence.[7] Within contemporary ecclesiological discourse, this relational approach has garnered endorsement from many theologians spanning diverse Christian traditions, primarily for its capacity to foster enriched ecumenical, inter-church, and inter-faith dialogues.[8] Yet, notwithstanding its broad acceptance, only of late has it been acknowledged as a salient methodology for examining the digital

---

6   For lyrics, see the video's accompanying script: 'The UK Blessing', *YouTube*. Verse: 'The Lord bless you / And keep you / Make His face shine upon you / And be gracious to you / The Lord turn His / Face toward you / And give you peace / As we receive, we agree, amen.' Chorus: 'Amen, amen, amen.' Bridge: 'May His favor be upon you / And a thousand generations / And your family and your children / And their children, and their children. / May His presence go before you / And behind you, and beside you / All around you, and within you / He is with you, He is with you'.

7   Dennis M. Doyle, *Communion Ecclesiology: Vision and Versions* (Maryknoll, NY: Orbis Books, 2000), p. 12.

8   World Council of Churches, *The Church: Towards a Common Vision*, Faith and Order Paper 214 (Geneva: World Council of Churches Publications, 2013). See also World Council of Churches, 'Towards Koinonia in Faith, Life, and Witness: A Discussion Paper', *Proceedings of the Fifth World Conference on Faith and Order in Santiago de Compostela*, ed. by Thomas Best and Gunther Gassmann (Geneva: World Council of Churches Publications, 1993).

manifestations of faith communities.⁹ This approach, rooted in the conviction that the church, at its core, is a communion of believers united with God in Christ through the Holy Spirit, adds breadth and depth to the sociological definitions of the term 'community' (communion or *koinonia*).¹⁰ It explores the ways in which the human community reflects and participates in trinitarian communion.¹¹

Two major approaches, *imitatio Trinitatis* and *participatio Trinitatis*, are prominent in clarifying the relationship between the Trinity and the church. The *participatio Trinitatis* approach offers a dynamic and theologically sound vision by emphasising the believer's participation in the divine life as revealed in history. It focuses on personal interaction, indwelling, and sharing among believers and with God. Rather than speculating about the inner being of the Trinity as a blueprint for human community (as in the case of *imitatio Trinitatis*), *participatio Trinitatis* grounds the church's being in aspects of divine life accessible through the event of Christ in which believers participate through the Spirit.¹²

Accordingly, I propose that this approach is at its best when it starts with a rich account of the movement of the Spirit among believers and then explores the ways in which the Spirit transforms and gathers believers around Christ, making them an essential part of God's triune

---

9   Heidi A. Campbell, *Ecclesiology for a Digital Church: Theological Reflections on a New Normal*, ed. by Heidi A. Campbell and John Dyer (London: SCM Press, 2022), pp. 65–66.
10 Ferreira and Chimenti, 'Netnography', 1433–55.
11 Tihomir Lazić, *Towards an Adventist Version of Communio Ecclesiology: Remnant in Koinonia*, ed. by Gerard Mannion and Mark Chapman, Pathways for Ecumenical and Interreligious Dialogue (Basingstoke: Palgrave Macmillan, 2019), pp. 146–53.
12 Within Catholic, Orthodox, and Protestant theological circles, the most coherent, creative, and profound theological attempts to define a vision of the church according to the image of a triune God have arguably been made by Metropolitan John D. Zizioulas (Eastern Orthodox tradition), Cardinal Joseph Ratzinger (Pope Benedict XVI), and Miroslav Volf (Protestant/Evangelical and 'Free Church' tradition). See John D. Zizioulas, *Being as Communion: Studies in Personhood and the Church* (Crestwood, NY: St Vladimir's Seminary Press, 1985); Joseph Ratzinger, *Called to Communion: Understanding the Church Today* (San Francisco, CA: Ignatius Press, 1996); and Miroslav Volf, *After Our Likeness: The Church as the Image of the Trinity* (Grand Rapids, MI: William B. Eerdmans, 1998). For a more detailed critical assessment of these dominant approaches, see Tihomir Lazić, '*Ecclesia Semper Migranda*: Towards a Vision of a Migrant Church for Migrants', in *The Church, Migration, and Global (In)Difference*, ed. by Darren J. Dias et al. (New York, NY: Palgrave Macmillan, 2021), pp. 241–61.

life.[13] To deepen this exploration, we can identify three principal domains where the community-making activity of the Spirit is most vividly and richly experienced: within us, through us, and around us.[14] A recognition of these realms is crucial for articulating a holistic trinitarian perspective of the church as *koinonia*. While leading digital ecclesiologists, such as Heidi A. Campbell, John Dyer, and others, have recently recognised the heuristic potential of the concept of *koinonia* in deepening our comprehension of the evolving landscape of digital faith communities, there remains room to develop this concept further within the realm of digital ecclesiology.[15]

The following section will trace the practical effects of the Holy Spirit's constitutive work in fostering spiritual connection (*koinonia*) among participants of digital worship, as reflected in the comments section of the multi-screen music video, 'The UK Blessing'. The case study, as will be demonstrated, underscores the heuristic potential and applicability of a *koinonia*-based digital ecclesiology framework in interpreting the data derived from the netnographic analysis of online worshippers' insights and narratives.

(a) Spirit within Us

The Spirit's movement within believers manifests in three distinct yet intertwined ways: transformation, enlightenment, and connectedness (*koinonia*). The first aspect, transformation, encompasses a comprehensive change in one's character, attitudes, and heart's

---

13 Gregory J. Liston, *The Anointed Church: Toward a Third Article Ecclesiology* (Minneapolis, MN: Fortress Press, 2015), pp. 12–14; Karl Barth, *The Humanity of God* (Richmond, VA: John Knox, 1972), pp. 24–25; D. Lyle Dabney, 'Starting with the Spirit: Why the Last Should Now Be First', in *Starting with the Spirit*, ed. by Stephen K. Pickard and Gordon R. Preece (Hindmarsh: Australian Theological Forum, 2001), pp. 3–27. This approach—recently gaining traction among theologians across Christian denominations—presents significant potential for fresh theological discoveries. These include authors writing from the perspective of Roman Catholicism (Yves Congar, Ralph Del Colle, David Coffey), Protestant denominations (Lyle Dabney, Myk Habets, Gary Badcock, Clark Pinnock), and ecumenical traditions (Veli-Matti Kärkkäinen, Amos Yong, Miroslav Volf, Steven Studebaker). Liston, *The Anointed Church*, p. 14.

14 For a more comprehensive exposition of this tripartite pneumatological framework, see Lazić, *Towards an Adventist Version of Communio Ecclesiology*, pp. 193–201.

15 Campbell, *Ecclesiology for a Digital Church*, pp. 65–66.

dispositions, shaping their overall demeanour. Often referred to as sanctification, this inner metamorphosis culminates in what the apostle Paul describes as 'the fruit of the Spirit'. Foremost among these fruits is love, which encompasses other facets such as joy, peace, patience, kindness, goodness, faithfulness, gentleness, and self-control.[16] In the Christian view, these attributes characterise the Spirit-filled existence of devoted followers of Jesus Christ.

Continuing to the second facet, enlightenment, it is crucial to recognise the Spirit's role in making divine knowledge accessible to believers via revelation, inspiration, and illumination.[17] The intertwining journey of knowledge and love is evident: deepening love fosters a more profound understanding of God, and in turn, an enriched comprehension of God amplifies love for Him and compassion for others.[18] The Spirit's dual roles—sanctification and enlightenment—cast discernible imprints on God's community, most notably in their interpersonal bonds. Jesus emphasised that selfless, loving connections stand as the most compelling testament to a community's divine affiliation.[19] For believers, the paramount aim is to embody and express the divine love epitomised by Jesus Christ in all their interactions.[20]

This leads to the third dimension, connectedness: through the Spirit's intervention, believers become profoundly attuned to God, strengthening their bonds with Him and with one another. This metamorphic journey moves individuals beyond a self-centric and insulated mode of being, ushering them into a more expansive, other-centric realm. Here, the solitary 'I' evolves into a communal 'We', without being suppressed or fused in the process. As a result of this relational evolution, believers become profoundly immersed in connections steeped in love, acceptance, forgiveness, commitment, and intimacy, forming the foundation of a thriving communal existence.[21] And so, by attuning themselves to the Spirit's inner movement with a posture of openness, their bond with the

---

16   Gal 5:22–23
17   John 14:26; 1 Cor 2:10–13.
18   2 Peter 1:3–8.
19   'By this all people will know that you are my disciples, if you have love for one another' (John 13:35, English Standard Version).
20   Richard Rice, 'The Trinitarian Basis of Christian Community', in *Biblical and Theological Studies on the Trinity*, ed. by Paul Petersen and Rob McIver (Adelaide: Avondale Academic Press, 2014), pp. 101–12.
21   Doyle, *Communion Ecclesiology*, p. 13.

divine deepens. This draws them further into a vast web of interwoven relationships that echo God's communal essence, encompassing not only humanity but the entirety of creation.

Through the transformative, enlightening, and connecting work of the Spirit within them, individuals find themselves oriented Godward in a profound manner. This deep transformation—encompassing mind, emotions, and actions—gives rise to the holistic and relational response of creatures to their Creator, a resonance known as worship. Within this act, all these aspects of human nature harmoniously align, responding with all that we are to all that God is. This whole-life response, in essence, captures the very heart of worship.

(b) Spirit through Us

The movement of the Spirit through believers is evident in the manifestation of spiritual gifts, or charisms, distributed by the Spirit for the edification and growth of the community.[22] These gifts unify and diversify the ecclesial community, creating a pneuma-dynamic communal life. Guided by the Spirit and sharing their unique gifts through various modes of communal service (ministries), believers shape the flow and rhythm of the community, fostering an organic connection and deep sense of rootedness in the mysterious realm of the body of Christ.[23]

The Spirit's movement through believers creates a space where the people of God can harness their talents, gifts, and experiences, progressing towards their full potential. In this setting, collective worship becomes an avenue where each person's unique contributions coalesce to bring glory to God. This highly connected and interdependent mode of relationships allows each individual not only to contribute to the well-being of others but also to experience the fullness of Christ through the gifts exercised by their peers.[24] Through the work of the Spirit, the community of believers becomes a welcoming and just community, offering a spiritual home to the uprooted, marginalised, rejected, and hurt. In this Spirit-forged haven, individuals can find their place,

---

22 1 Cor 12:7.
23 1 Cor 12:27; Volf, *After Our Likeness*, pp. 228–33.
24 Eph 4:11–13; Hans Küng, *The Church* (New York: Sheed and Ward, 1968), pp. 173–91.

healing, acceptance, and true belonging.²⁵ It is within this transformative community that human beings can truly flourish and experience the fullness of life and joy.²⁶

(c) Spirit around Us

The movement of the Spirit around the believers expands their community's sphere of interest to include all aspects of life and the world. It invites them to become aware of God's work in various domains of life and join forces with him.²⁷ This holistic outlook requires the Christian community to listen to and learn from those outside their religious boundaries, discerning the Spirit's action in the challenges and wisdom found there. Humility and openness are essential for the faith community to be true to its essence.²⁸ The Spirit's work extends beyond the church, drawing believers closer to others and making them sensitive to their needs. By participating in the mission of God, they engage in the movement of restoration of the broken world.²⁹

---

25 Lazić, 'Ecclesia Semper Migranda', pp. 256–57.
26 1 John 1:1–4
27 Lesslie Newbigin, *The Open Secret: An Introduction to the Theology of Mission* (Grand Rapids, MI: Eerdmans, 1995), p. 18.
28 Acts 10:34, 35.
29 Jürgen Moltmann is one of many modern authors who affirm a close connection between the political and economic event of liberation and the experience of the Holy Spirit. See, for instance, Veli-Matti Kärkkäinen, *Pneumatology: The Holy Spirit in Ecumenical, International, and Contextual Perspective* (Grand Rapids, MI: Baker Academic, 2002), p. 154; Jürgen Moltmann, *The Spirit of Life: A Universal Affirmation* (Minneapolis, MN: Fortress Press, 1992). In view of this recent re-discovery of the extra-ecclesial work of the Spirit, it is not accidental that one finds so many different types of liberationist movements and initiatives that insist on opening up the church to the world and engaging actively in its struggle to reach the ideals of justice, mutual solidarity, tolerance, and socio-economic, racial and gender equality. See Michael Welker, *God the Spirit* (Minneapolis, MN: Fortress Press, 1994), pp. 16–17; Jurgen Moltmann, *God in Creation : A New Theology of Creation and the Spirit of God* (San Francisco, CA: Harper San Francisco, 1991). A Belgian theologian, long resident in Brazil, José Comblin, sees a modern reappearance of the experience of the Spirit manifested in the social realm in the heightened desire to engage in social action, in the experience of freedom, in the growing need to speak out for the poor and marginalised, in the experience of community, and in a new aspiration for life. See José Comblin, *The Holy Spirit and Liberation* (Maryknoll, NY: Orbis Books, 1989), p. xi. Similarly, Moltmann talks about the liberating work of the Spirit in three dimensions, associating them with three classical virtues: (1) liberating faith: freedom as subjectivity; (2) liberating love: freedom as sociality;

In summary, the Spirit not only moves within believers to transform them into Christ's likeness but also flows through them, incorporating them into his spiritual body. Beyond this, the Spirit works around them, drawing them into active participation in Christ's movement in the world and back to the Father.[30] In its whole-life response to these three-fold currents of the Spirit, the community of believers is oriented towards its ultimate purpose—Jesus Christ. In Christ, the entire universe and the community of faith are united in the triune life of God. Through this ongoing spirited *koinonia* with Christ and the Father, the community of believers stands as a truthful witness, a foretaste, and a prophetic sign of the coming kingdom of God. As the imperfect church moves forward, it embodies the kingdom of God, offering hope for a better future in anticipation of its ultimate fulfilment.

As it navigates the complexities of the twenty-first century, this dynamic community of believers with God takes on diverse shapes, forms, and contexts. Yet, its dynamic communal essence remains unchanged. When the Spirit-generated *koinonia* takes tangible form, notably through open communal worship in both online and offline spaces, it deeply resonates with the contemporary generation. This manifestation captivates their imagination, serving as a powerful reminder of what it means to be fully and truly human—person-in-relation. Moved by this realisation, they are prompted to respond to the Spirit's community-making movements by becoming:

> ...a community of justice in a world of economic and ecological injustice; a community of generosity and simplicity (of being able to say 'enough') in a world of consumer satiation; a community of selfless giving in a world of selfishness; a community of truth [=humility and boldness] in a world of relativism; a community of hope in a world of disillusionment; a community of joy and thanksgiving in a world of entitlement; a community that experiences God's supernatural presence in a secular world where all days are the same, and nothing is exceptional or supernatural...[31]

---

        and (3) liberating hope: freedom as future. For more details, see Moltmann, *The Spirit of Life*, pp. 114–20.

30 John 1:18; Paul S. Fiddes, *Participating in God : A Pastoral Doctrine of the Trinity* (Louisville, KY: Westminster John Knox Press, 2001), p. 256.

31 Daniel Duda, 'Adventist Identity—A Never-Ending Quest', paper presented at TED Bible Conference, Newbold College, Bracknell, 18 June 2019,

III. Digital Worship through a Netnographic Lens

After examining ecclesiological perspectives on the internal dynamics of the Spirit-driven, community-generative movement, especially visible in the act of Christian worship, we now pivot to an empirically grounded inquiry facilitated by netnography. The central question arises: can these profound relational dynamics be discerned within the context of digital worship, specifically as facilitated by the YouTube video 'The UK Blessing'? I contend that an analysis of over 6,200 comments yields a resounding 'yes'. While numerous possible angles and inquiries could be pursued to substantiate this case, within the scope of this chapter, I will provide a summary complemented by an impressionistic overview of the predominant themes, trends, and sentiments emerging from the data. I will spotlight select comments that provide a helpful glimpse into the experiences and narratives of the online worshipper community interacting with the choir's multi-screen video.

(a) Worship as a Godward Response

To begin, an analysis of the comment section's word frequency and trends uncovers a remarkable spiritual resonance within the community, reflecting a Godward orientation.[32] The most recurrent nouns include 'God' (1,558 mentions), 'Lord' (626), 'Jesus' (562), the personal pronoun 'He' used to signify the divine (515), 'Christ' (274), and 'Spirit' (156). These word frequencies signify a deeply ingrained theocentric framework that permeates the community's experience and commentary on the song. This linguistic prevalence underscores the guiding influence of the Spirit, showing how individuals, even in a digital space, may pivot towards God, embodying the essence of worship as a God-centred response.

The theological perspective of these worshippers becomes more apparent upon closer examination of their comments. While the

---

https://ted.adventist.org/images/departments/Adventist_Identity_Bible_Conference-Duda.pdf

32 Analysis conducted on comments gathered until 8 September 2023; the video remains active and continues to attract new responses.

audience is wide-ranging, encompassing individuals from various monotheistic religions, a prevailing Christian influence is evident in their remarks. This Christian inclination is underscored by the frequent references to 'Jesus' and 'Christ' within the context of the Old Testament Aaronic blessing, even though these specific terms are not explicitly mentioned in this ancient text. These references strongly imply that viewers predominantly interpret the text through the lens of the New Testament, giving us clues about their likely identity and worldview.

Furthermore, the extensive repertoire of terms, names, adjectives, and phrases used to depict the nature and attributes of the Ultimate Being they hold in reverence reveals a multifaceted theological landscape. Expressions—such as YHWH, Almighty God, God the Father, Son, Spirit, Holy God, God of Israel, the Messiah, Comforter, God of all the nations, Triune God, Healer, Real God, Living God, Most High God, Lord Most High, the Saviour, Lord God Almighty, King Papa, Sovereign God, Our King, Light, Salvation, Compassionate Lord of all—emphasise a multifaceted understanding of God. This portrayal highlights their belief in a transcendent God who governs the ever-changing events of the world while also embodying an immanent presence—a God who is a close companion, co-sufferer, comforter, and intimate friend. This dual perspective of the divine—marked by intimate closeness and compassion, on the one hand, and transcendence and control, on the other—may offer profound comfort, hope, and insight to individuals navigating a world marred by pain, evil, and suffering, especially in the context of a global pandemic. It allows worshippers to find solace in a compassionate God while trusting in a higher, controlling power when facing adversity and uncertainty.

As individuals eloquently express their profound praises, adoration, and a sense of awe, a recurring and poignant theme often arises in the comments: the personal experience of God's tangible presence, with commenters recounting how it has brought them joy, love, fulfilment, transformation, peace, healing, comfort, and hope. However, these expressions are more than just uplifting, taking on additional significance when viewed against the grim backdrop of a global pandemic. Many of these commenters have faced the agonising loss of loved ones. In the face of adversity and personal tragedy, these worshippers seek solace and inspiration in God, turning to worship and adoration as a holistic response to the divine presence and self-disclosure they encounter in their faith journey.

(b) Worship as a Holistic Response

In the act of communal worship, the comments capture a spectrum of human experiences: from exhilaration to despair, from moments of joy to instances of sorrow. They serve as heartfelt testimonies of God's revelation in the lives of the commenters, depicting His interventions in their personal journeys, especially in these challenging times. The depth of emotion in these reflections is palpable. Moreover, the breadth of supportive, empathetic, and affirming responses they receive from other participants underscores a shared emotional resonance within the community.

Throughout the digital worship platform, the comments weave a vivid narrative that illuminates the transformative interplay between music and individual spirituality. One participant, highlighting their transformative journey, shared, 'Thank you Jesus for healing me, I'm 23 and finally met Christ after years of addiction, anxiety and pain'. This deep emotional connection is further mirrored by another: 'I was so depressed, then when I heard this song, I literally cried and cried. I heard the name of Jesus and it touched me'.

Music, in this setting, appears as a powerful medium, leading individuals to moments of introspection, solace, and fortitude. This sentiment is echoed by a commenter who shared, 'Today I woke up with hope again, and this song is helping me calm my heart'. Similarly, another expressed their personal struggle with profound loneliness, saying, 'I'm an only child to my parents and also very sensitive, the loneliness just eats me up sometimes, and I come here and listen to worship songs and cry my heart out, this gives me comfort on an unimaginable level'.

While the song serves as a catalyst, the underlying transformative experiences seem to suggest a greater spiritual movement at play. An individual confided, 'This song touched my soul in a way I can't explain. I found my way back to God'. Another individual poignantly described a spiritual metamorphosis, saying, 'I felt the darkness depart and light flood in, leading me to fall to the floor under the power of Jesus'. Many reported experiencing love, peace, joy, and comfort as they listened. For instance, one comment read, 'This song brought tears to my eyes. I felt God's love surrounding me'. One participant noted, 'Listening to songs like this touches my heart… Thank you, Jesus'. This sentiment is further echoed by others, with comments like, 'Love you, Jesus… this song helps me cry my heart out… Thank you for always being there for me' and 'This song moves me to tears and compels me to worship'.

Beyond personal emotional experiences, the song is a beacon of revelation and hope for many. One touching comment read, 'I found out I was pregnant after having a miscarriage… When hearing this song, I felt like it was God telling me and my family everything will be okay and to stay strong!' Such moments coalesce into a collective sense of worship and reverence, embodied in affirmations such as, 'I will praise you, Jesus, I will glorify your name! Jesus is the Lord!'

The song's continued relevance in the lives of the worshippers becomes apparent with remarks like, 'And again, I have come back to listen to this wonderful work and to drink in those beautiful faces and bask in the love that shines through'. The shared longing for divine intervention culminates in heartfelt prayers: 'This song brings me to tears every time I hear it. My prayer is, Lord Jesus, come soon; we truly need you. The earth is in turmoil; we long for your presence and intervention. Oh Lord, come soon! Amen'. These reflections not only capture the spectrum of human experience but also the deep emotional resonance the song evokes, further emphasising the song's role as a touchstone for many in their spiritual journey.

Such comments demonstrate the inward transformation, enlightenment, and connectedness arising from music-enabled worship. As previously discussed, this is emblematic of the Spirit's movement within, a movement that touches the entire breadth of the human experience, spanning cognitive, emotional, physical, and spiritual faculties. These worship reflections convey a profound spiritual experience that, while deeply personal, resonates widely. Moreover, they underscore the potency of music in eliciting an internal response and priming individuals for a deeper spiritual connection, both with the divine and with others.

(c) Worship as a Community-Forging Response

Data analysis reveals that the Godward orientation in digital worship, engaging every facet of human existence—mind, heart, body, and spirit—goes beyond mere individual experiences. This orientation culminates in a pronounced communal bond, engendering a palpable sense of togetherness. Intriguingly, a netnographic examination shows that the term 'together' is the second most commonly used word, following 'God'. Terms like 'unity', 'union', 'united', 'one', 'belonging', 'being with', 'community', 'we', 'fellowship', and 'togetherness' trail closely behind. Such linguistic patterns highlight not just a communion with the divine but also a profound bond with fellow worshippers.

The digital worship experience, with its synergetic combination of music and faith, has unarguably emerged as a salient force, for some breaking down denominational, racial, and other barriers and amplifying the sense of unity and shared spiritual journey. A participant passionately captured this sentiment, stating, 'We are all one in Jesus Christ regardless of colour, religion and race. Just Christ shining within us, radiating our unity and pure joy of serving and sharing him! The devil messed up when he thought closing churches would shut us up! More churches have opened, more people are coming together, and so many more have received Jesus as their Lord and Saviour!' Another viewer commented: 'I love this song and the unity between the churches. We may be in different churches, but we are all one family. I feel so encouraged by this song at these difficult times and know I have a big family out there and an amazing God'.

This strong spirit of unity, transcending boundaries, is a recurring theme throughout. 'So powerful and united. Long may this spirit of unity continue across the churches and the people of the UK', one viewer noted. This sentiment is echoed by another who jubilantly exclaimed, 'We loved being a part of this! Thanks to all who worked so hard to pull it together! What a beautiful time to come together as the Church to sing this blessing over our land!' Building on this theme of collaboration and inclusivity, another shared, 'Fantastic to see so many churches come together. Uplifting to see so many men, women and young people getting involved'. Amidst these comments, one particularly impassioned viewer revealed, 'I don't usually comment on YouTube videos, but I have to on this one because this is one of the most powerful things I have seen in a long time. The unity and the presence of God displayed here brought me to tears!!!! Wow wow wow!! This is so beautiful, this's what Jesus has been waiting for in the Body of Christ. The time has come for the true worshippers to come together in the Spirit of Unity. It's so Awesome!!!'

The adversity of lockdown only seemed to strengthen the resolve of the community. 'Love this. I can sense the power and love that happens when God's church comes together in unity. If there is anything we have learned from the Covid-19 pandemic, it is that when important things happen, we lose the things that divide and come together in unity'. The strength of this sentiment was mirrored by another: 'Awesome unity in worship. Hallelujah! We may be in lockdown but the body of Christ is waxing stronger from behind closed doors! No denominational or racial barriers whatsoever! The church is marching on!'

Expanding on this feeling of collective strength, one viewer mused, 'Sometimes as the church in the UK we seem so small, yet this has shown just how BIG we are'. Many were moved by the solidarity on display during this challenging time: 'This was absolutely beautiful... uplifting especially now with the chaos and coronavirus...seeing the church come together as one...the body of Christ...God is with us... He is for us...my children...their children...their children to a thousand generations...amen'. 'This almost brought me to tears. It's what heaven will be like!' remarked one individual, while another conveyed the depth of the impact of this shared worship initiative: 'On my knees as I am overwhelmed by the Holy Spirit. Beautiful unity'.

The assortment of comments accentuates a distinctive unity in diversity within the Christian community, showcasing a rich mosaic of beliefs, traditions, and voices. One viewer's statement stands out as especially reflective: 'A simple coming together of different flavours of the Church, singing from the same song sheet, with a heart and mouth of blessing over the nation. This is not just a collective of people singing words to music, it is a communication of God's heart over the nation. This is THE Church'. Such a plethora of comments is a testament to the unifying power of music and faith. Together, they craft a vivid image of unity within the body of Christ, illustrating how shared worship experiences can bridge divides, foster harmony, and create an overwhelming sense of togetherness.

(d) Worship as an Expansive and Transformative Response

Data analysis reveals that worship extends beyond the confines of the event. It is a highly dynamic and expansive response, deepening inwardly in spiritual richness and radiating outwardly into broader life realms. Internally, as worshippers bond, their shared experiences become more profound, enriched, and transformative. This heightened intimacy amplifies the collective allure, reminiscent of the early church, attracting others into their circle of unity.[33] The magnetism of this genuine worshipful response is evident in comments from those outside this religious tradition. An unaffiliated individual, touched by this unity, remarked: 'I'm not even religious, but this song is beautiful because it unites people through the faith of Christ, and even I can appreciate that'.

Externally, authentic worship reverberates beyond the confines of the collective moment, permeating daily lives, guiding interpersonal relationships, and shaping engagements with the broader world. As worshippers are uplifted, they are also compelled to interact with, support, and stand in solidarity with the wider humanity. This dual orientation, both inward for spiritual growth and outward for worldly engagement, positions worship as a resonant and transformative force in all aspects of human existence.

The sheer volume of comments vividly illustrates how the music became a catalyst for individuals to extend love, grace, and support to others using their spiritual gifts. In a sense, worshippers increasingly feel the pull to 'worship beyond worship'. For example, one commenter noted, 'This song has encouraged me to reach out to my neighbours and start a prayer group'. Echoing this sentiment, another stated, 'Feeling blessed to be part of a community that shows love and compassion, even in times of crisis'. There is a clear sentiment in many remarks pointing to a conscious alignment with the global Christian community, coupled with an invigorated drive for service and outreach. A notable comment read, 'This song reminds me that we are all part of a larger family across the world. We need to stand together and serve'.

---

33 Acts 2:47, 5:42.

To outsiders, the intricate, Spirit-fuelled dynamics at play within the faith community may seem elusive. Yet, the tangible outcomes of such dynamics are unmistakably evident. This is not just a community that proclaims hope; it embodies it. As illustrated by this case study, the community of believers does not merely sing about a blessing; they actively strive to be a blessing in their everyday lives. As indicated in the video description, many of the churches featured in this song have assisted with supplying over 400,000 meals to the most vulnerable and isolated since the onset of the COVID-19 lockdown.[34] Their outreach further extends to phone calls for the isolated, pharmacy delivery drops, and serving hot meals to frontline NHS hospital staff. These acts spotlight the profound resonance of spiritual unity—showing that it not only touches hearts through music but also drives real-world compassionate actions.

IV. Digital Ecclesiology Meets Netnography

In this section, we merge insights from digital ecclesiology and netnography, presenting preliminary conclusions regarding the Holy Spirit's role in shaping worship communities in digital spaces, especially as highlighted by the virtual worship choirs in times of physical distancing. Our focus is on the methodological prospects, potentials, and limitations of using these two closely interrelated disciplines. I argue that the marriage of these disciplines, when holistically pursued, could forge an invaluable interdisciplinary perspective, illuminating the intricate nexus of music, technology, and spirituality with clarity and depth. Together, they provide a richer portrayal of this emergent spiritual phenomenon of digital worship, each highlighting unique and critical facets of its manifestation and impact.

Digital ecclesiology, with its theological roots, reveals a deeper spiritual dimension of the observed phenomena. It provides a heuristic framework that serves as a reference point for interpreting the vast spectrum of responses and experiences as indicators of profound spiritual forces at work 'behind the scenes'. These forces are perceived as guiding and directing individuals, as well as the broader

---

34 The UK Blessing, 'The UK Blessing', https://youtu.be/PUtll3mNj5U

creation, towards their Creator—the origin, foundation, and ultimate purpose of their existence. These spiritual movements, often eluding immediate human perception, reveal the Spirit's agency in generating the ever-evolving communion of worshippers. They unveil the life-awakening currents of the Spirit and their pivotal role in eliciting these reactions within the intricate divine-human relational dance. Without overshadowing or infringing upon human agency, the Spirit subtly and gently steers their paths, fostering growth, unity, and holistic flourishing. Through its theologically informed lens, this discipline grapples with the foundational questions of 'why' and 'how' this form of worship comes into existence. By articulating these theological underpinnings and elucidating the divine agency in the orchestration of community, it positions the human participant in relation to this overarching theocentric narrative. This discipline's emphasis is more theoretical, delineating the broader relational structures and the dynamics between divine and human factors foundational to the digital worship experience.

In contrast to this theoretical lens of digital ecclesiology, netnography harnesses an empirically grounded approach, delving deep into the lived experiences of digital worshippers. In undertaking a netnographic investigation, this study employs a dual analytical approach. On a macro-level, it examines prevalent linguistic patterns, trends, and sentiments. Simultaneously, on a micro-level, it scrutinises individual comments. This methodology provides a window into the relational patterns, theological perspectives, convictions, and the myriad of lived experiences that define this digital worship community—experiences that often defy simple categorisation. Here, worshippers are depicted in the thick of life's messiness, replete with its inherent imperfections, struggles, and limitations. This empirical study presents worshippers in their authentic contexts, navigating the complexities of their existence. Rooted in diverse historical, cultural, and religious backgrounds, their narratives vividly express the ebbs and flows characteristic of an evolving relationship with the divine. In this context, the digital worship experience is laid bare: candid, tangible, and profoundly intimate. It captures the raw, tumultuous, and often chaotic nature of human emotions and experiences. This netnographic portrayal uncovers the more dramatic horizon of a digital worship community—one that is historically contingent and imperfect but equally embraced and animated by the divine, shedding light on the unique complexities and challenges inherent in their spiritual journeys.[35]

And so, the comments derived from the netnographic study seem to ground and qualify experientially this ecclesiological framework by shedding light on the effects of the Spirit's influence on individual worshippers, sparking their inner transformation, enlightenment, and a sense of connectedness. This spiritual flow, evident in their feedback, accentuates the profound communal bond they experience while being integrated into the body of Christ through the movement of the Spirit within them and through them. Within this communion, worshippers harness their Spirit-bestowed gifts and competencies to enhance collective well-being and growth. Furthermore, mirroring the ecclesiological framework proposed, the netnographic analysis indicates that believers' actions, steeped in love, compassion, and service, transcend mere declarations of faith, seeking tangible betterment in the broader world while aligning and collaborating with the Spirit's restorative endeavours throughout creation. Although the intricate dynamics of the Spirit's movement within, through, and around worshippers might often remain subtly veiled, their tangible effects are discernible in the testimonies and experiences of worshippers. Such manifestation lends concrete support to this spiritual narrative, opening a portal into a more comprehensive, nuanced, and experientially informed theology.

When viewed in tandem, these disciplines converge to form a symbiotic academic partnership. Their combined insights sidestep potential reductionisms, ensuring balanced navigation between dualities such as the divine and human, perfect and flawed, immutable and evolving, and the ideal versus the actual lived reality. The pursuit of this abductive method yields an integrative vision—one where convergences and unique contributions of these two (and potentially more) distinct disciplines harmoniously coalesce, enriching and refining one another. While there may be inherent tensions between the two, they collectively

---

35 For further insights into the theodramatic horizon's capacity to encapsulate the complex, imperfect, and historically anchored vision of the church, see Nicholas M. Healy, *Church, World, and the Christian Life: Practical-Prophetic Ecclesiology* (Cambridge, UK: Cambridge University Press, 2000), pp. 25–76; Hans Urs von Balthasar, *Theo-Drama: Theological Dramatic Theory* (San Francisco, CA: Ignatius Press, 1988). The metaphor of drama is also used in Robert W. Jenson, *Systematic Theology I: The Triune God* (New York: Oxford University Press, 1997), p. 75.

paint a holistic picture of digital worship as a spiritual response that, despite its virtual medium, remains profoundly embodied—deeply anchored in the lived realities, imperfections, and transient nature of human experience. This nexus, elucidated by both disciplines, offers an unprecedented window into a faith community's dynamics, revealing a digital worship space where the divinity gracefully dances with humanity. Such an alliance also allows for a more comprehensive assessment of the nature and the extent of the impact that online music has in fostering authentic spiritual communion among those immersed in digital worship.

V. Moving beyond Binaries in Digital Worship Discourse

The concluding arc of this chapter aims to challenge some of the common misconceptions and false dichotomies that obscure contemporary conversations on the nature, purpose, and legitimacy of digital worship. By elucidating these divisive issues and offering tentative resolutions, we aim to accentuate the value, relevance, and applicability of the critical insights derived from the abductive method of inquiry.

To counteract the binary perspectives prevalent in contemporary discussions—those that artificially set embodied against disembodied, online-only against offline-only, and real against unreal—we draw on insights from our exploration of digital worship, shaped by the synergy of digital ecclesiology and netnography. First, rooted in pneumatologically-informed digital ecclesiology, we acknowledge the Spirit's omnipresence, transcending time and space. The Spirit engages with us through various mediums, including human-made technology. As imitators of God's creativity, the tools we devise, such as digital platforms, can also be channels for experiencing the Spirit's movement. Second, we highlight the holistic engagement of worshippers in the Spirit-fuelled *koinonia*, encompassing their spiritual, psychological, and physical dimensions. A Godward, holistic, community-forging, expansive, and transformative response, worship is not limited to formal gatherings but is integrated into our daily lives and relationships. Such an all-encompassing experience of worship is always, and without exception, inherently embodied, and through our bodies, the Spirit is manifested.

These insights may prompt us to rethink notions of enfleshment and embodiment in worship. Digital worship spaces can be a legitimate medium for genuine spiritual community, where the Spirit's presence is experienced through collective participation, transcending physical barriers.

(a) Embodied versus Disembodied

To clarify our language and challenge inaccurate distinctions, we should abandon the notion of 'embodied' versus 'disembodied' experiences, which wrongly equates offline with embodiment and online with disembodiment. Psychologist Margaret Mary Wilson has shown that humans are always embodied, regardless of whether they are interacting through screens or in physical spaces.[36] Yet, we must recognise the distinctive forms and experiences of embodiment that online and offline interactions offer and acknowledge the specific impact that they have on forming individuals, relationships, and religious communities.[37]

Different platforms curate distinct experiences in music-facilitated digital worship. For instance, on YouTube, one-way broadcasts elicit a different sense of embodiment and engagement compared to two-way or multi-way technologies, like Zoom, with their interactive features. Similarly, an in-person worship service can provide a distinct experience of embodiment and communality depending on whether it is being live-streamed or not. While unidirectional mediums offer scalability and broad reach, engaging their worshippers via comments and allowing them to watch and sing along worldwide, multi-directional platforms permit real-time communal singing and spontaneous worship, turning isolated spaces into cohesive congregations. However, as Zoom worship sessions during lockdown demonstrated, technical challenges, such as sound lags or interruptions, can detract from the experience, in

---

36 Margaret Wilson, 'Six Views of Embodied Cognition', *Psychodynamic Bulletin and Review* 9.4, 625–36.
37 The following section is based on the basic definitions in John Dryer, 'Exploring Mediated *Ekklesia*: How We Talk about Church in the Digital Age', in *Ecclesiology for a Digital Church: Theological Reflections on a New Normal*, ed. by Heidi A. Campbell and John Dyer (London: SCM Press, 2022), pp. 5–8.

stark contrast to the polished nature of pre-recorded music videos. Nonetheless, this interactive online worship amplifies a different embodied sense of being together, fostering intimacy, vulnerability, and active participation, often with a smaller and tighter-knit group of worshippers.

Shifting our attention to 'virtual church' platforms, these online spaces craft fully immersive worship environments, enabling communities to gather within a virtual domain. Harnessing advanced virtual reality (VR) technologies, such as Second Life, Roblox, and Facebook Metaverse, the experience accentuates our spatial awareness and sensory engagement. Participants are plunged deeply into a complex representation of reality, acknowledging and celebrating our creaturely limitations. Moreover, such immersive platforms offer those with mobility constraints a preview of a promised divine future, envisioning a moment of complete healing and rejuvenation.[38]

Finally, a hybrid worship model, combining the best of both digital and in-person experiences, holds great promise in bridging the offline and online spaces. By integrating the local and universal expressions of *koinonia*, this approach expands worship horizons. It encompasses a mixture of in-person and technology-mediated expressions of worship, leading to a rich and variegated experience that broadens inclusion and transcends traditional worship boundaries.[39]

Based on our ecclesiological and netnographic findings, it becomes evident that the matter of embodiment should not be approached with a simplistic either/or binary perspective. Both online and offline spaces offer genuine and embodied experiences of connectedness in worship, albeit in different ways. Each space allows for the expression of certain aspects of human relationality that the other may not. They overlap in some sense but also operate differently, presenting opportunities for innovative and fresh expressions of worshipping *koinonia* in a world where the boundaries between offline and online are increasingly blurred. A deeper exploration and refinement of our techno-theological language and categories will enable us to better understand these

---

38 Dryer, 'Exploring Mediated *Ekklesia*', p. 13.
39 Ibid., pp. 15–16; Heidi A. Campbell, *The Distanced Church: Reflections on Doing Church Online* (Texas: Digital Religion Publishing & OakTrust-TAMU Libraries, 2020).

diverse worship expressions, prompting critical reflection on their essence, purpose, and importance.[40]

(b) Online-Only versus Offline-Only

This introduces the question of where online-only or offline-only approaches to worship fit within the broader scholarly discourse on ecclesial practices. As evident from this study, technology can serve as an effective medium, connecting both universal and local worship expressions. An online-exclusive worship approach may perceive its realm as covering the full breadth of the digital landscape, utilising platforms like Facebook and sophisticated VR technology to connect with adjacent worshippers. Additionally, it might position itself as addressing the requirements of particular demographics unable to convene physically due to security concerns, health issues, or individual inclinations. In this framework, the online worship community stands as an indispensable adjunct to a broader faith community, providing spiritual sustenance, camaraderie, and connectivity, whilst endorsing engagement with local congregation when feasible.[41]

When evaluating the diverse online platforms that enable *koinonic* interactions in worship, it is pivotal not to perceive all digital church forms as providing homogenous experiences. Descriptors like broadcast, virtual, interactive, and hybrid aptly convey the essence and the values underpinning these worship mediums. Addressing the evolving needs of contemporary worshippers, who seamlessly navigate both physical and digital realms in their daily lives, necessitates a balanced integration of both approaches. Here, a discerning appraisal of the merits of these diverse digital and physical spaces, the influence of proximity and the nuances of embodiment on our communities, and their contributions to worshippers' collective spiritual voyage is essential.

Undoubtedly, the path forward involves integrating both online and offline worship forms, leveraging the advantages inherent to each to cater

---

40 Dryer, 'Exploring Mediated *Ekklesia*', pp. 11–16; for the recent definitions of concepts of the 'lived body', 'mediated immediacy', and 'embodied space', see Gesa Lindemann and David Schünemann, 'Presence in Digital Spaces: A Phenomenological Concept of Presence in Mediatized Communication', *Human Studies* 43 (2020), 627–51.
41 Dryer, 'Exploring Mediated *Ekklesia*', pp. 13–16.

to the worshippers' varied preferences and needs. Overemphasising the sufficiency of digital worship might overlook the genuine desire many have for physical gatherings. Conversely, an exclusive focus on in-person meetings could diminish the significance of digital outreach and prevent believers' immersion in the currents of the Spirit in digital spaces.[42] Recognising this, a holistic 'hybrid' strategy affirms the genuineness of digital interactions and appreciates the unparalleled depth of in-person connections. Such an approach not only expands the reach but also augments the depth of communal worship experiences, ensuring that the church evolves and remains inclusive in our swiftly changing world.

(c) Real versus Unreal

By challenging unhelpful dichotomies, we move away from debates that put the real/embodied against the virtual/disembodied, where the virtual is often perceived as less genuine and authentic. Instead, we affirm that our relationships and worship experiences are always real, albeit formed differently depending on the mode of mediation. It is important to recognise that humans are always embodied, whether they are perusing a book, engaging in a video chat, or sitting in the local church pews. Throughout the course of a day, we might seamlessly shift between online and offline environments, each influencing us differently. This helps us explain 'Zoom fatigue' not as a direct effect of Zoom causing disembodiment but rather as a manifestation of our body's differential response to screen interactions compared to face-to-face encounters.[43]

Worshippers' engagements, whether online or offline, are characterised by authentic worship responses elicited by the life-quickening currents of Spirit, unfettered by spatial and temporal constraints. Recognising this, it becomes imperative to consider digital tools as potent mediums. They present fresh avenues for believers to engage in worship response that extends beyond the conventional

---

42 Bala A. Musa and Boye-Nelson Kiamu, 'Digital Technology and Mediating the *Pneuma* in Church Outreach', in *Ecclesiology for a Digital Church: Theological Reflections on a New Normal*, ed. by Heidi A. Campbell and John Dyer (London: SCM Press, 2022), pp. 117–29.

43 Dryer, 'Exploring Mediated *Ekklesia*', pp. 14–15.

limits of physical locations or timed services. While traditional church gatherings hold value, true worship is not bound to brick and mortar. Whether digital or in-person, no single approach fully embodies the holistic Christian experience. Responding with all that we are to all that God is demands consistent engagements, not just in collective worship, but in nurturing community and manifesting love throughout the world.

Conclusion: A Way Forward

In conclusion, we return to a question that sparked our inquiry: can online music truly foster authentic spiritual communion among those immersed in digital worship, and, if so, to what extent? To this, I would confidently respond, 'YES'. Grounded in our ecclesiological and netnographic investigation, there is a compelling argument to be made that the same Spirit-generated relational dynamics present in offline worship are equally discernible within the emergent online spaces. This not only affirms digital worship as genuinely authentic but also elevates online music as a powerful medium for nurturing and amplifying communal worship in digital areas. To fully grasp the extent of online music's role in fostering spiritual communion, further research is vital. This study indicates a multitude of variables influencing divine–human community formation. While music enhances these variables, the exact mechanics remain intricate. The experience of digital communion varies and is influenced by factors like the technological medium or platform, spiritual currents, and the worshippers' historical, cultural, and socio-theological context. All these elements, among others, shape the depth to which music fosters genuine spiritual engagement.

Building on this understanding, this chapter has demonstrated that the integration of digital ecclesiology and netnography provides a robust methodology for understanding digital worship. By bridging theological perspective with the lived experiences of worshippers, it offers valuable insights into how digital music, as exemplified by the recent virtual choir multi-screen video produced during the global pandemic's onset, continues to revolutionise and enrich spiritual communion. Furthermore, this interdisciplinary abductive approach showcases that worship in digital realms retains the authenticity, depth, and embodiment inherent in traditional practices. This invites a reconsideration of entrenched dichotomies that have long defined our traditional perceptions of sacred space and community. These binaries must be challenged decisively and thoughtfully. Only then can we reframe effectively the digital worship discourse and imagine fresh possibilities ahead. Here, in the evolving worship landscape, intertwining these disciplines—and potentially others akin to them—paves the way for forward-looking research, ensuring that the study of digital spirituality remains grounded, nuanced, and profoundly relevant.

For the Christian worship community to harness fully the potential of the digital era and to navigate adeptly both offline and online spaces, it must mirror a microorganism—'capable of rapid mutation and adaptation in response to changing environments while still maintaining continuity with its earlier forms'.[44] By striking a balance between consistency and innovation, this community can undergo a profound transformation, all the while staying true to its relational core. As such, it can further its mission of glorifying God and expanding His kingdom in both offline and online realms by fostering a genuine *koinonia* where individuals can encounter Jesus Christ and be transformed by the Spirit, taking their rightful place in the grand narrative of God's cosmic redemption. The intention of this chapter is to provide a constructive framework, advancing the scholarly discourse and deepening our appreciation for the myriad ways the Spirit is active within, through, and around believers, drawing them into a dynamic communion with God and fellow worshippers. As Christians traverse both offline and online realms, they not only uncover the essence of worship but also embrace what it means to be fully and truly human—persons-in-relation. Enveloped in the love and wisdom of the Father, they are drawn into the body of Christ through the unifying and diversifying actions of the Spirit, becoming active participants in the triune life of God.[45]

---

44 Alister E. McGrath, *Christianity's Dangerous Idea: The Protestant Revolution—History from the Sixteenth Century to the Twenty-First* (New York: HarperOne, 2007), p. 4.
45 For a more comprehensive exploration of this Spirit-guided journey of believers toward deeper communion with God and fellow believers, see Tihomir Lazić, *Towards an Adventist Version of Communio Ecclesiology*, pp. 141–306.

17. Choral Singers and Spiritual Realities: A Perspective from St Mary's Catholic Cathedral

Michael Ferguson

Since the foundation of the Roman Catholic Church, music-making has had an important role in Catholic worship and spirituality.[1] The Mass, which the Church understands as the source and summit of Christian life, is often characterised as an 'inherently musical' mode of worship.[2] The centrality of music within the Church's liturgical life has meant that throughout the history of Catholicism, music-making has shaped,

---

1   At the Last Supper, Christ and the apostles sang a hymn before going out to the Mount of Olives (Mt 26:30; Mk 26:3). Scripture does not tell us what was sung, but the Passover tradition suggests it was the Jewish Hallel (Ps 113–18). For good accounts of the centrality of music in the early Christian Church, see Christopher Page, *The Christian West and Its Singers: The First Thousand Years* (New Haven, CT: Yale University Press, 2010); and John Arthur Smith, 'Music in Early Christianity, 1: The First to the Early Third Centuries', in Arthur Smith, *Music in Ancient Judaism and Early Christianity* (London: Routledge, 2016), pp. 167–87. For discussion of the changing scholarly assumptions about the relationship between Jewish and early Christian liturgical practices, see also James W. McKinnon, 'Christian Church, Music of the Early', in *Grove Music Online*, rev. Martin V. Clarke (2001), https://doi.org/10.1093/gmo/9781561592630.article.05705

2   See, for example, United States Conference of Catholic Bishops, 'Liturgical Music Today (1982)', in *The Liturgy Documents: A Parish Resource*, ed. by David Lysik et al., 2 vols, 4th ed. (Chicago, IL: Liturgy Training Publications, 2004), I, 367–84 (at 370), which uses the 'inherently musical' phrase. See also Second Vatican Council, 'Sacrosanctum Concilium', *Vatican.va*, 4 December 1963, https://www.vatican.va/archive/hist_councils/ii_vatican_council/documents/vat-ii_const_19631204_sacrosanctum-concilium_en.html, art. 112, in Lysik, *The Liturgy Documents*, I, 26, which states that music 'forms a necessary or integral part of the solemn liturgy'.

and has been shaped by, Catholic spiritual realities. What, however, do we mean when we talk about spiritual realities in a Catholic context? Today, 1.3 billion Catholics worldwide share a collective spiritual life as members of the Catholic Church, worshipping and believing within a single, global institution, under the doctrinal and spiritual leadership of the Holy See. For all of these Catholics, regardless of their location or circumstances, the contemporary Catholic experience is defined to some extent by the official statement of doctrine and beliefs outlined in the *Catechism of the Catholic Church*, the official liturgy of the Mass as defined in the *Third Typical Edition of the Roman Missal*, the Rite of Christian Initiation (RCIA) adult catechesis programme for new Catholics, and more generally, the centralisation of doctrinal and spiritual authority in the Vatican under the headship of Pope Francis.[3] These shared doctrinal and liturgical truths reflect a kind of shared spiritual reality for Catholics, where the boundaries of the faith are defined by the institutional Church, albeit Catholics in their different territories live out their religious lives in many different ways.

This fundamental role of the institutional Church in defining the spiritual realities of Catholics sets Roman Catholicism apart from Protestantism, which in broad terms rejects the *Magisterium* of the Church as the primary source of spiritual authority, in favour of spiritual realities defined principally by the personal faith of the individual, and rooted primarily in the authority of the Bible.[4] Nevertheless, Catholicism

---

3   The Congregation for the Doctrine of the Faith (CDF), for example, is responsible for promulgating and defending Catholic doctrine throughout the Church worldwide. For a centralised, official source of information about the Catholic Church, including an online version of the *Catechism of the Catholic Church* and a central repository of Church documents, see the website of The Holy See: https://www.vatican.va/content/vatican/en.html. For a printed version of the *Catechism*, see *Catechism of the Catholic Church*, 2nd ed. (Vatican City: Libreria Editrice Vaticana, 2019).

4   See, for example, Mark A. Noll, 'Chaotic Coherence: *Sola Scriptura* and the Twentieth-Century Spread of Christianity', in *Protestantism after 500 Years*, ed. by Thomas Albert Howard and Mark A. Noll (Oxford: Oxford University Press, 2016), pp. 258–80. As Noll points out, 'from the very beginning of the Reformation, Protestants proclaimed *sola scriptura* ["the Bible alone"] as their foundational principle of God-given authority' (p. 258); 'They [Protestants after Martin Luther] would follow the Bible before all authorities [...] "my conscience"; or the individual Bible reader, aware of standing before God, would be the principal guide for interpreting the supremely authoritative scripture' (p. 263). See also Mark A. Noll, *Protestantism: A Very Short Introduction* (Oxford: Oxford

has sometimes been described as a union of contraries: it tends towards *both/and* paradoxes in its nature and beliefs, rather than *either/or* binary alternatives.[5] In this way, the Catholic faith is *both* institutional *and* personal in its nature. Catholics are called to a personal relationship with Jesus Christ, sustained in private prayer, personal devotion, and communal worship, and yet Catholics are also called to live out this personal relationship as a member of 'Christ's body on earth', i.e., the Church, in a way that integrates human persons into the whole without erasing their individual uniqueness. In a 'both/and' Catholicism, where opposites can co-exist stably, the spiritual realities of Catholics are potentially characterised both by a shared, collective spiritual reality, and by a uniquely personal spiritual reality, in a way that is complex, and yet that is stably integrated.[6]

This chapter explores the connection between music and spiritual realities in relation to one group of Catholics with a particularly important role to play in the Mass: namely, Catholic choir singers. In the first part, I underline the embodied nature of Catholic worship and music, which is anchored in a basic tenet of the Catholic faith: the Church's rejection of a dualistic anthropology, in favour of the complete integration of matter and spirit in the human person, which is understood as a body–soul composite.[7] Catholic spirituality is, in other words, by definition embodied, such that one cannot talk about spiritual realities as separate or as distinct from material, bodily realities. In fact, the body can, and should, represent an important starting point in our attempt to understand the spiritual realities of Catholics in relation to

---

University Press, 2011), where Noll remarks that 'it is challenging to write a coherent history [of Protestantism] because of the sheer multiplicity of Protestant and Protestant-like churches in the world today' (p. 9) but, nevertheless, that 'the authoritative importance of the Bible for all Protestants ... is probably the best reason why it is still possible to speak, in admittedly very general terms, about a common Protestant history' (p. 6).

5   For more discussion, see, for example, Robert Barron, *Vibrant Paradoxes: The Both/And of Catholicism*, 2nd ed. (Des Plaines, IL: Word on Fire, 2017). Barron points out Chesterton's assertion that Catholicism keeps its beliefs, 'side by side like two strong colours, red and white ... It has always had a healthy hatred of pink' (cited in Barron, *Vibrant Paradoxes*, p. xiii; see also G. K. Chesterton, 'The Paradoxes of Christianity', in G. K. Chesterton, *Orthodoxy* (Mineola, NY: Dover, 2004), pp. 74–94 (at 90).

6   See *Catechism of the Catholic Church*, arts. 787–96.

7   For a fuller discussion, see Robert Barron, *The Strangest Way: Walking the Christian Path* (New York: Orbis Books, 2002), pp. 13–30.

music-making. In light of this, I turn, in the second part of the chapter, to my own first-hand experience of directing choirs at St Mary's Catholic Cathedral in Edinburgh. I point to three specific areas—bodily positioning in the liturgical space, clothing and robes, and the individual vis-à-vis the ensemble—which, in my view, are worthy of further, more systematic investigation. Whilst my role as Director of Music involves managing many practical resources, the end is ultimately spiritual.[8] In seeking to carry out this role as effectively as possible, I am thus motivated to understand more fully how the Cathedral's musical life might best serve the spiritual realities of the musicians, singers, congregations, and clergy with whom I work.

I. The Embodied Nature of Catholic Worship and Music

Before considering the musical life of St Mary's Cathedral in more detail, it is worth reflecting on how body and spirit might actually come together to shape the realities of Catholic music-makers. The official documents of the Catholic Church present an unambiguous concept of the human person: essentially, 'though made of body and soul, man is one'.[9] Catholicism rejects any kind of dualistic understanding

---

8   As Director of Music, I help to shape the musical life of a busy city-centre cathedral, the Mother Church of the Roman Catholic Archdiocese of St Andrews and Edinburgh. I do this by working with the cathedral clergy to plan and realise an overarching strategy for music, managing resources including voluntary and paid musicians, choosing repertoire for services, acquiring new music, and working in a hands-on way each week to direct the different choirs and ensembles. Alongside the cultural and social benefits of this musical activity, the primary aim of the music-making is spiritual. Indeed, there is a basic assumption at St Mary's Cathedral that its musical life will have a positive effect on the spiritual realities of the community, in a way that makes music-making essential to the life of the cathedral. Thus, music has been part of its liturgical and spiritual life since it became the pro-cathedral of the new Archdiocese of St Andrews and Edinburgh at the restoration of the Scottish Catholic hierarchy in 1876. For a history the life of St Mary's Cathedral, including its music, see Darren Tierney, *St Mary's Metropolitan Cathedral, Edinburgh: A History 1814–2014* (Edinburgh: Scottish Catholic Historical Association, 2018). I am a life-long believing and practising Catholic and I have been in the role of Director of Music at St Mary's Cathedral since 2018.

9   Second Vatican Council, 'Gaudium et spes', *Vatican.va*, 7 December, 1965, art. 14, https://www.vatican.va/archive/hist_councils/ii_vatican_council/documents/vat-ii_const_19651207_gaudium-et-spes_en.html

of the human being, which might seek to separate body and soul, or to divide matter and spirit within the person. Rather, body and soul form an inseparable union in a way that, in the words of the *Catechism*, 'is so profound that one has to consider the soul to be the "form" of the body...i.e. it is because of its spiritual soul that the body made of matter becomes a living, human body; spirit and matter, in man, are not two natures united, but rather their union forms a single nature'.[10] This Catholic understanding of body and soul has important implications. The body is not somehow an afterthought, superfluous, or antagonistic to the spiritual life. Rather, it is an integral, necessary, and fundamental part of the human person's spiritual reality. Not least, this renders the body worthy of respect, to the extent that if one harms or abuses the body, one also harms and abuses the soul; body and spirit are intertwined and inseparable, and the dignity and infinite value of the human person encompasses their soul and their body on equal, composite terms.[11] It is reasonable to assume, then, that the body might allow one access to, or knowledge of, the spiritual domain in a fellow human person.

It is worth considering too that Christianity is often characterised as 'The Way' (Acts 9:2). Rather than primarily being a system of philosophical ideas, or a theological lens through which Catholics interpret the world, Catholic Christianity is, in its purest sense, a 'path that one walks'[12]: Catholicism is principally a way of acting in the world, physically, materially, and bodily. This essential reality of Catholicism forms the backdrop, for example, to theologian Hans von Balthasar's call for a 'kneeling theology', which is rooted in the embodied practices and devotions of Catholic life, as distinct from a more abstract, intellectually determined 'sitting theology'.[13] In particular, the embodied practice of Catholic spiritual life is centred on the sacraments. The seven sacraments of the Church—Baptism, Confirmation, Eucharist, Penance, Anointing of the Sick, Holy Orders, and Matrimony—are efficacious signs of God's

---

10 *Catechism of the Catholic Church*, art. 365. See also Thomas Aquinas, *Summa Theologiae*, Ia, q. 52, art. 1.
11 See, for example, 'Gaudium et spes', art. 14: '...man may not be allowed to despise his bodily life, rather he is obliged to regard his body as good and honourable...'.
12 Barron, *The Strangest Way*, p. 13.
13 See especially Hans Urs von Balthasar, 'Theology and Sanctity', in *Explorations in Theology, Vol. 1: Word Made Flesh*, trans. by A.V. Littledale and Alexandre Dru (San Francisco, CA: Ignatius Press, 1989), pp. 181–209.

grace, instituted by Jesus Christ and entrusted to the Church, whereby visible, physical signs, symbols and rites make present the invisible, spiritual reality that they symbolise.[14] The sacramental expression of Catholicism par excellence is the Sacrament of the Eucharist. As Jesus said at the Last Supper, 'This is my body… This is my blood… Do this in memory of me', so in the Mass Christ becomes physically present in the bread and wine, and the worshipping congregation physically unites with Christ, body to body, when they receive Holy Communion. This material coming together of Christ in the Eucharist and the Catholic faithful at Mass is the very pinnacle of Catholic spirituality, and it is the end to which the whole sacramental and spiritual life of the Church is orientated.[15]

In Scotland, the essentiality of this bodily dimension of Catholic spiritual life was brought to stark attention following the COVID-19 lockdowns. In early 2021, the Catholic Church in Scotland, alongside other church denominations, took the Scottish Government to court over the forced closure of church buildings during the early stages of the pandemic. The key argument from a legal perspective was that the Scottish Government had overstepped its powers to infringe upon the freedom of religion in Scotland that is enshrined in the European Convention on Human Rights. The collective case brought by the Scottish churches was successful, with the judge Lord Braid ruling that the Government's policies had indeed infringed these rights.[16] What is arguably more interesting, though, is that when spelling out its case in the public realm, the Scottish Catholic Church foregrounded the essential bodily dimension of Catholicism, underlining that Catholics coming together in a physical way at Mass is essential to the Catholic faith, that the bodily celebration of the Eucharist is indispensable for the spiritual well-being of Catholics, and that, crucially, this cannot adequately be supplanted by remote, online streamed services.[17] This

---

14 *Catechism of the Catholic Church*, arts. 1084, 1113, 1114–30.
15 *Catechism of the Catholic Church*, art. 1324
16 See the judgement summary on the *Judiciary of Scotland* website: 'Judgement Summaries: Success of Churches in Court of Session Action', *Judiciary of Scotland*, 24 March 2021, https://judiciary.scot/home/sentences-judgments/judgments/2021/03/24/success-of-churches-in-court-of-session-action
17 For example in Lucinda Cameron, 'Churches Reopen for Communal Worship after Legal Victory', *Evening Standard*, 25 March 2021, https://www.standard.co.uk/news/uk/

was not the case with streamed Evensong services in the Anglican Church, for example, or morning worship services in the Church of Scotland. For these denominations, bodily presence in the liturgical space is, from a theological perspective at least, less essential.

Just as the body is inextricably bound up with Catholic spiritual life, so the body is inextricably linked with music. In the last fifty years, musicologists have moved away from the primary study of abstract, disembodied musical works, towards an understanding that the full meaning of music can only really be known in action or, as Christopher Small famously puts it, in 'musicking'.[18] Modern scholarship now acknowledges the fundamentally embodied nature of music, and demands that this be taken seriously. Nevertheless, the study of Catholic music has been quite slow to catch up. In the nineteenth and early twentieth centuries, the understanding of Catholic music was shaped by influential movements such as the plainchant revival, and the Caecilian reform movement. These movements were predicated on the idea that the spiritual value of music is embodied principally in its musical score, where the authenticity and the intrinsic sacredness of music is determined by the provenance of its printed sources, or by abstract notions of style represented by particular arrangements of notes on the page.[19] These ideas have continued to shape the scholarship around Catholic music since the Second Vatican Council, and particularly some attempts to address the perceived problems in post-conciliar music.[20] Studies have often centred on critiques or recommendations of musical repertoire, or of particular technical

---

churches-catholic-church-court-of-session-scotland-government-b926255.html; see also Pontifical Council for Social Communications, 'The Church and Internet', *Vatican.va*, 28 February 2002, https://www.vatican.va/roman_curia/pontifical_councils/pccs/documents/rc_pc_pccs_doc_20020228_church-internet_en.html

18 Christopher Small, *Musicking: The Meanings of Performing and Listening* (Middletown, CT: Wesleyan University Press, 1998). See also Lydia Goehr, *The Imaginary Museum of Musical Works: An Essay in the Philosophy of Music* (Oxford: Oxford University Press, 2007), for an insight into what Goehr calls 'the work concept'.

19 For discussion of both movements in this context, see Anthony Ruff, *Sacred Music and Liturgical Reform: Treasures and Transformations* (Chicago, IL: Hillenbrand, 2007), chapters 6 and 7.

20 See, for example, Edward Schaefer, *Catholic Music Through the Ages: Balancing the Needs of a Worshipping Church* (Chicago, IL: Hillenbrand, 2008); and Joseph Swain, *Sacred Treasure: Understanding Catholic Liturgical Music* (Collegeville, MN:

styles of musical composition. Authors have generally been less interested in who will realise the compositions, and how they might do so.[21] Arguably these approaches, which focus on the promotion of ideal repertoires in a very abstract way, have had limited success in actually achieving the type of reform or improvement they seek. In my own work, I have argued instead for the need to take as a first consideration those music-makers who must ultimately realise in a practical way liturgical music in order for it to exist at all.[22]

II. A Perspective from St Mary's Catholic Cathedral

Thus far, I have underlined that both the Catholic faith, and music(king), are fundamentally embodied practices, in which the body is essential for, and fundamental to, the meaning and reality of each. For music-makers in the Catholic liturgy, bodily reality is not something to get past in order to reach a spiritual reality that lies beyond. Rather, bodily reality is spiritual reality, or at least it is an integral part of a whole-story reality that integrates body and spirit. With this in mind, I shall now reflect on how the embodied nature of choral singing might shape the spiritual realities of choir singers at St Mary's Catholic Cathedral.

I will mention two choirs in my reflections: the Schola Cantorum of St Mary's Catholic Cathedral, and the cathedral's all-ability voluntary choir. Both ensembles were formed in 2018 and sing at the weekly Sunday 12 noon and 9 p.m. Masses, respectively. The Schola Cantorum comprises eight singers, and primarily sings the repertoire of the European sacred music tradition, from plainchant and Renaissance polyphony to newly composed works. The octet is 'professional', in that

---

Liturgical Press, 2012), both of which recommend the promotion of Gregorian chant repertoire as a solution.

21 For a notable exception to this trend, see Thomas Day, *Why Catholics Can't Sing: The Culture of Catholicism and the Triumph of Bad Taste*, rev. ed. (New York: Crossroad, 2013). Day deals with the human dimension of what he sees as the 'culture of bad taste' around Catholic music in the US after the Second Vatican Council.

22 Michael Ferguson, 'Sacred Art Music in the Catholic Liturgy: Perspectives from the Roman Catholic Church in Scotland', in *Annunciations: Sacred Music for the Twenty-First Century*, ed. by George Corbett (Cambridge, UK: Open Book Publishers, 2019), pp. 279–95.

the singers are paid for their singing, and they audition competitively for their roles in the choir. The eight singers are a mixture of university students and working people, all of whom engage in other employment and/or study outside of the cathedral. By contrast, the all-ability choir members sing on a voluntary basis each week, and membership of the ensemble is open to all, with no audition, and no limit to the number of voices in the ensemble. The repertoire sometimes overlaps with the Schola Cantorum, but in general the all-ability choir sings music that is less technically demanding, and more musically flexible (for example, in terms of voice parts needed) than the Schola Cantorum.

Until the early 2000s, the principal choir of St Mary's Cathedral consisted of men and boys, after which the choir was reformed to include adults only, with women singers admitted for the first time. The current Schola Cantorum retains this basic model — i.e., it is open to adults of any gender—and it is currently made up of four men (two singing tenor and two singing bass) and four women (two singing alto and two singing soprano). This make-up is shaped to some extent by the singing range demands of the choir's historical European sacred music repertoire (i.e., the pitch span of the different voice parts). It is important, though, to note that much of this music was composed for liturgical contexts where male-only ensembles were the norm. Therefore, the present make-up of the Schola Cantorum is culturally determined: choirs of adults of mixed genders are the norm in church and cathedral choirs in Edinburgh city today, and the musical ensembles at St Mary's Cathedral are influenced by, and also shape, this wider local trend.[23]

The make-up of the all-ability choir is much less determined by the need to fill roles with specific vocal ranges, but rather is determined by the singers who happen to proactively volunteer to join the group, where each singer gains automatic entry and is able to choose any voice part they wish. Since its formation in 2018, the majority of singers in the all-ability choir have been women (usually around ten to twelve singers), with men in the minority (around two or three singers). Whilst

---

23 Churches where adult choirs of any gender are the norm include St Giles Cathedral, Greyfriars Church, Old St Paul's Church, St Cuthbert's Church, Morningside Parish Church, The Robin Chapel, and many others. In contrast, the main choir of St Mary's Episcopal Cathedral comprises boy and girl choristers (aged 9–14) from St Mary's Music School, and adult lay clerks and choral scholars of any gender.

it lies outside the necessarily limited scope of the present chapter, the full implications of these gender differences between the two choirs are worthy of more systematic empirical study, particularly in the context of choral singing as a necessarily embodied phenomenon, and in light of the close connection between gender and the body.[24]

In terms of the ethnicity of the singers, the all-ability ensemble tends to be more international in its membership, though both choirs have a majority white British membership. It is worth mentioning that the Cathedral does not formally gather data about ethnicity of its musicians (nor its congregations), and when the singers audition or volunteer for the ensembles, it is not something that I routinely ask them about as musical director. Therefore, any in-depth exploration would rely upon the specific and systematic gathering of empirical data, which could potentially enhance the overall understanding of the spiritual realities of those involved.

For the purposes of this present chapter, however, I will draw upon my more direct, first-hand insights as Director of Music to suggest three areas that I think are particularly worthy of more systematic empirical research: bodily positioning of choir members in the liturgical space; clothing and robes; and the individual singer vis-à-vis the ensemble.

(a) Bodily Positioning of Choir Members in the Liturgical Space

As I noted above, the conversation about Catholic music after the Second Vatican Council has tended to focus on musical repertoires and styles, with less focussed consideration of who will sing and play this music.

---

24 See Jeremy Begbie, *Resounding Truth (Engaging Culture): Christian Wisdom in the World of Music* (Grand Rapids, MI: Baker Academic, 2007). Begbie's concept of 'sonic order' is particularly useful here, which Begbie sees as 'patterns of constraints that exist before any music is actually made' (p. 41). Begbie highlights that there is an intimate connection between the grounded reality of the body—which in the case of choirs are the materials that directly produce the sound—and the 'in the notes' dimension of the musical composition. For one reflection on the implications of gender and the body on spiritual experience of singers in light of Begbie's 'sonic order', see Bertram J. Schirr, 'The Body We Sing: Reclaiming of the Queer Materiality of Vocal Bodies', in *Queering Freedom: Music, Identity and Spirituality*, ed. by Karin Hendricks and June Boyce-Tilman (Lausanne: Peter Lang, 2018), pp. 35–52.

Glaringly, though, there has been almost no in-depth consideration of where—from an embodied, physical perspective—this music might be sung or played in the liturgy.

At St Mary's Cathedral, physical positioning is, nonetheless, an important consideration, with not only musical implications, but also implications that seem to resonate with music-makers' experiences of, and connections to, the liturgy and community. The communication of musical sound is an important consideration for a music director when thinking about positioning a choir within a liturgical space. In one sense, a choir is like a large musical 'instrument', and the positioning of this instrument needs to take into account the particular acoustics of the space, the sound projection possibilities in different parts of the building, architectural elements that might help or inhibit sound projection, and the need to maintain musical balance with other instruments, which may or not be moveable, for example pipe organs, pianos, and instrumental ensembles. One of St Mary's Cathedral's principal choirs, the Schola Cantorum octet, underwent a major change of singing location, first brought about by the COVID-19 pandemic. This change in physical location seems to have affected the realities of the choir members in ways that go beyond the purely musical, and which potentially touch upon the spiritual domain.

The Schola Cantorum was established in 2018, with the aim of singing liturgical music to the highest of standards in cathedral liturgies, and principally at the weekly 12 noon Sunday Mass. The ensemble began its life singing from a gallery in the organ loft, situated at the west end of the cathedral, raised some twenty feet above ground level. The eight singers occupied the space between two sides of the large organ case, facing eastwards towards the Sanctuary, and standing behind the cathedral organist and a large three-manual organ console. To direct the ensemble, I stood to one side of the organ console, facing the singers with my back to the east end. From a musical perspective, this positioning allowed excellent communication between singers, the organist, and me as musical director. Acoustically, the close proximity of the organ pipes caused some difficulties with accompanied repertoire played at very loud volumes, but most of the time the raised gallery singing position allowed the Schola Cantorum to fill the acoustic space of the cathedral effectively. However, in the organ loft, the singers were unable to see the congregation and clergy during the Mass and were similarly invisible to them. Because of the position of the organ console in front of them, the singers could see very little of the liturgical action going on in the Sanctuary. In this way, whilst the Schola Cantorum singers were sonically present in the worship space during the weekly 12 noon Mass, they were absent in a visible sense, existing instead in the cathedral space as apparently disembodied voices.

The COVID-19 pandemic resulted in severe restrictions to choral singing across Scotland. When choirs were eventually permitted to sing again in churches following a complete ban, firstly in small groups and then in larger ensembles, distancing requirements for singers meant that the Schola Cantorum's organ gallery position was unsuitable. The choir therefore moved to a new singing position in the nave of the cathedral at floor level, about half-way along its length, to the right-hand (south) side as one faces liturgical east. From a practical perspective, this new position allowed the necessary physical space for distancing between singers. Acoustically, any issues created by the increased distance between the choir, the organ, and the cathedral organist were solved using a camera pointing downwards from the loft to the new position in the nave, with a microphone system relaying the sound of the singers to the organist in the loft as if they were in much closer proximity. This new nave position is flanked on three sides by congregational seating, and so despite social distancing measures, the move put the Schola Cantorum in much closer physical vicinity of the worshipping congregation during the Mass than had previously been the case.

In the debates about post-conciliar liturgical music, close integration of musicians and the congregation has often been promoted as a desirable ideal, at least in an abstract sense: i.e., there is a sense that singers should be integrated members of the worshipping community (whatever that might mean), and the more separate or removed they are, the more problematic things become.[25] In the case of the Schola Cantorum's relocation to the nave of St Mary's, some of the singers began

---

25 See, for example, Second Vatican Council, 'Musicam Sacram: Instruction on Music in the Liturgy', *Vatican.va*, 5 March 1967, art. 23 (a), https://www.vatican.va/archive/hist_councils/ii_vatican_council/documents/vat-ii_instr_19670305_musicam-sacram_en.html, which states that the choir should be placed in such a way as to ensure 'that its nature should be clearly apparent—namely, that it is a part of the whole congregation, and that it fulfills a special role'.

to report feeling a better sense of connection with the congregation and the liturgy, and that this enhanced their own experiences of the Mass. Similarly, some members of the congregation reported feeling more connected to the singers, and expressed a positive reaction in particular to being able to see the singers, in addition to just hearing them.

In hindsight, the original organ loft position made it more difficult for the singers to partake in the bodily gestures and actions of the Mass. In particular, the gallery position did not lend itself well to the physical gestures that form part of the usual congregational experience of Mass, including kneeling, sitting, standing, offering members of the community the sign of peace, and bowing. Moving to the nave allowed the Schola Cantorum singers to see the actions of the community, and it has also encouraged bodily entrainment with this worshipping community. The positive effects of the move, which seem to have extended beyond the purely musical, towards potentially encompassing the more spiritual concerns of connectedness to worship and fellow worshippers have led us to retain the nave singing position as a permanent location for the choir. This is despite the lifting of all distancing restrictions, which would permit a return to the original organ gallery singing position.

(b) Clothing and Robes

The physical attire of musicians is an aspect of liturgical music-making that has largely been overlooked in the academic discussion about Catholic music after the Second Vatican Council. From my experiences at St Mary's Cathedral, however, the physical dress of choir members appears to play an important role in shaping the singers' realities during the Mass.

Since the octet was founded, the eight Schola Cantorum singers have worn royal blue cassocks and white surplices as their regular liturgical attire. As the ensemble has become better known within the Archdiocese of St Andrews and Edinburgh and beyond, these blue and white robes have become synonymous with the Schola Cantorum to the point that they have become a kind of visual trademark. Whilst the choir is made up of eight permanent members, singers are sometimes absent, and we have a pool of deputy singers who can take their place. As is inevitable, over time the make-up of the ensemble has also slowly changed as singers come and go, especially as some of the singers are university students, and might only be in Edinburgh for a few years. In the midst of this natural ebb and flow of singers, the blue and white choir robes have given the Schola Cantorum a constant physical identity at St Mary's Cathedral.

Members of the St Mary's Cathedral all-ability volunteer choir, on the other hand, do not routinely wear choir robes. The rationale is that this allows the ensemble to be open to limitless singers whereby participation is not restricted by the number or size of available robes. From the perspective of singing, the all-ability choir's music is more congregationally focussed than the Schola Cantorum: for example, each week the voluntary choir leads the congregation in singing a congregational Mass setting, whereas the Schola Cantorum usually sings a choir-only setting.[26] In this context, the all-ability choir members wearing their 'ordinary' clothes, just as the congregation around them do, encourages less physical distinction between choir and congregation than is the case with the Schola Cantorum.[27]

On some occasions in the Church's year, for example at the Archdiocesan Chrism Mass and the Christmas Eve early evening Vigil Mass, the Schola Cantorum and the all-ability choir are combined within a single service. In the years before COVID-19, all of the singers simply wore black. However, post-pandemic, we have dressed the two choirs differently. Due to the growing renown of the Schola Cantorum, and the expectation of clergy and congregation that the octet will be a visible part of these big celebrations, the robed Schola Cantorum have joined the unrobed volunteer singers for the majority of the repertoire during the Mass, while they have also sung some repertoire as a standalone octet.[28]

The effect of combining robed and unrobed singers seems to connect in an interesting way with the lived realities of some of the singers. For a small minority of those not wearing robes, performing alongside robed singers in the same liturgy seems to have an unhelpful impact on their

---

26 The congregational setting is very often Dan Schutte, *Mass of Christ the Saviour* (Portland, OR: Oregon Catholic Press, 2013). Mass settings sung by the Schola Cantorum typically include works by Palestrina, Victoria, Mozart, Haydn, Schubert, MacMillan, and others.
27 Since its founding in 2018, the all-ability choir has always sung from the floor-level nave position in the cathedral, as discussed in the section above.
28 This has usually been an Offertory motet.

perception of their integration within the Mass, and particularly on their perception of their own ministerial role as part of the choir. It is not hard to imagine that different modes of liturgical dress can set up distinctions between robed and unrobed singers. However, there is a sense from at least some of the singers that they also perceive the special spiritual purpose of the all-ability volunteer choir to be somehow undermined when placed side-by-side with singers for whom physical attire—in this case, the wearing of robes—seems to confer higher spiritual purpose.

(c) The Individual Singer vis-à-vis the Ensemble

Ideally, a liturgical choir is like a microcosm of the whole Church: singers are integrated into a unified whole, musically, spiritually, and socially, without erasing the uniqueness of the individual.[29] Nevertheless, the singers appear to experience an ongoing negotiation between being part of a musical ensemble, on the one hand, and their responsibilities in the Mass as individual singers, on the other.

There are opportunities in both the Schola Cantorum and the all-ability volunteer group for choir members to step out, musically and sometimes physically, from the ensemble to sing as a soloist. In both choirs, this includes the singing of the responsorial psalm each week, where the verses of the psalm are sung by a single cantor, and the rest of the choir and the congregation answer with an ensemble refrain. For the Schola Cantorum, individual singing also includes solo moments dictated by their repertoire, for example in Mozart Mass settings where whole choir 'tutti' moments are interspersed with material written for four soloists.[30]

When singing as an ensemble, members of both choirs are encouraged to stand near their fellow choir members for the sake of tuning and balance, and to facilitate the blending of voices. Conversely, those singing solos are often encouraged to move away from the ensemble, either moving in front of the rest of the choir, or going to the front of the cathedral, facing the congregation (which is the default position

---

29 See *Catechism of the Catholic Church*, arts. 813–22.
30 Such settings from the choir's repertoire include *Missa brevis in C 'Coronation Mass'*, K.317; *Missa brevis in C*, K.220; *Missa brevis in B♭*, K.275; *Missa brevis in D*, K.194; *Missa brevis in G*, K.140, and others.

for a cantor singing the Responsorial Psalm). This is partly for the sake of acoustics, where standing forward of the main body of singers can make a difference to sound projection. In my experience, however, there appears to be something deeper going on. When the soloist is moved apart from the ensemble, the limits and boundaries of the performance space are redrawn to some extent, with the solo singer potentially having a more obvious physical presence in the liturgical space.

Conclusion

The embodied nature of the Catholic faith, and of music(king), points to the body as being a crucial access point in the search to understand better how music-making can shape the spiritual realities of music-makers. Whilst the embodied dimension of Catholic music has often been overlooked in scholarly discussions since the Second Vatican Council, considerations of the body—in this case, bodily positioning in the liturgical space, clothing and robes, and the individual vis-à-vis the ensemble—seem to have a resonance, at least in my own experience, which goes beyond the purely musical or practical. Of course, my reflections are rooted in my first-hand experience of working with singers as the Director of Music at St Mary's Catholic Cathedral, and there are natural limitations to the conclusions one can draw from this type of personal observation. However, these reflections are offered primarily to suggest three potential starting points for a more systematic investigation into how bodily realities in Catholic liturgical music-making might shape spiritual realities. If we are serious about understanding the spiritual realities of Catholic music-makers, the body is a valid and potentially fruitful place to start. As a Director of Music, the connection between bodily and spiritual realities is also of pastoral importance: when one actively shapes the physical, bodily reality of singers and musicians in the liturgy (as I have done in the cases above), what is the impact on their spiritual realities? A greater understanding of this could be at the heart not just of fulfilling the musical and practical dimensions of the music director role, but also of fulfilling its spiritual ends most effectively.

18. Music and Spirituality in Communal Song: Methodists and Welsh Sporting Crowds

Martin V. Clarke

Two vignettes highlight the connections between music and spirituality that this chapter seeks to explore. The first is an account of a Methodist meeting in 1829, recorded in a letter from Benjamin Bangham to Mary Tooth:

> The Meeting was very eminently crowned with the Divine presence, we had fellowship with him, and with each other; so that in the concluding part of the Meeting we were constrain'd to sing: -
>
> > 'And if our fellowship below,
> > In Jesus be so sweet,
> > What height of rapture shall we know,
> > When round his throne we meet?'[1]

The second concerns the departure of the Welsh men's football (soccer) team from the 2022 FIFA World Cup in Qatar, recounted on Twitter by journalist Peter Gillibrand:

> Welsh fans belting out Hen Wlad Fy Nhadau in front of the Welsh team clapping them is the spirit of Wales.[2]

---

1 Letter from Benjamin Bangham in Coalbrookdale to Mary Tooth at Madeley, 20 August 1829, Manchester, Methodist Archive, Fletcher-Tooth Collection, GB 135 MAM/FL/1/2/3.
2 Peter Gillibrand (@GillibrandPeter), *Twitter*, 29 November 2022.

Though separated by nearly two hundred years and taking place in markedly different cultural contexts, these brief examples have a common focus on how the communal singing of untrained groups of people expresses their commitment not only to one another but also to something intangible and greater than themselves.

Both Methodists and Welsh sporting crowds have long had reputations for their vigorous and passionate singing. Since its eighteenth-century beginnings, Methodism has sought to employ congregational singing as a tool for theological communication and as a means of encouraging participation and belonging.[3] The Welsh crowd's reputation for singing is one manifestation of a broader ascription of musicality to the people of Wales that became especially prominent from the latter half of the nineteenth century. The powerful singing of massed voices has been a central trope in this association, and the particular link with sport has been firmly made since at least 1905, when the singing of the players and supporters was widely reported in the press after Wales's victory in rugby union against the touring New Zealand All Blacks.[4]

For both Methodists and Welsh people, the association with musicality, principally manifested in song, has been a marker of self-identity.[5] The opening words of the preface to *The Methodist Hymn Book* (1933) evocatively capture the centrality of hymn-singing in Methodist spirituality: 'Methodism was born in song'.[6] Two appellations are frequently used with reference to Welsh musicality. The first, describing Wales as the 'land of song', can be traced to the triumph of the South Wales Choral Union in a contest at the National Music Meeting held at

---

3   For a brief summary, see Erika K. R. Stalcup, 'The Wesleys: John and Charles', in *Hymns and Hymnody: Historical and Theological Introductions*, ed. by Mark A. Lamport, Benjamin K. Forrest, and Vernon M. Whaley, 3 vols (Eugene, OR: Wipf and Stock, 2019), II, 210–25. For a more detailed account of the practice of hymnody throughout the history of British Methodism, see Martin V. Clarke, *British Methodist Hymnody: Theology, Heritage, and Experience* (Abingdon: Routledge, 2018).

4   See Helen Barlow and Martin V. Clarke, 'Singing Welshness: Sport, Music and the Crowd', in *A History of Welsh Music*, ed. by Trevor Herbert, Martin V. Clarke, and Helen Barlow (Cambridge, UK: Cambridge University Press, 2022), pp. 332–54.

5   Both areas of focus in this chapter are inevitably informed by my personal experiences and identity. I was born into an English-speaking family in South Wales and brought up in the Methodist Church. Although no longer residing in Wales, I remain an active member of the Methodist Church of Great Britain and served as the musical editor for its most recent authorised hymnal.

6   *The Methodist Hymn Book* (London: Methodist Conference Office, 1933), p. iii.

London's Crystal Palace in 1872. The equivalent Welsh language phrase 'Gwlad y Gân' was used in a newspaper report of the event, from where its use seems to have burgeoned.[7] The other widely used description of Wales as a 'musical nation' is a partial quotation from Dylan Thomas's radio play *Under Milk Wood*, where its use is partly satirical.[8] The notion that singing is a central pillar of both Methodist and Welsh identity is to some extent self-perpetuating; the idea is inculcated through communal activity and thus rehearsed and repeated over generations, albeit with changing emphases and within differing contexts.

Popular accounts of both Methodist and Welsh singing frequently attest to a link between musicality and spirituality. The popularity of Welsh folk singer Dafydd Iwan's song 'Yma o Hyd' with the Welsh men's football team in the FIFA World Cup 2022 is but the latest manifestation of a long-standing trend. Following the team's qualification for the tournament, BBC journalist Nicola Bryan explored how 'the song has cemented its place in the nation's heart' and its omnipresence during the team's participation in the tournament was widely reported, alongside the intense singing of the national anthem.[9] The Methodist Church of Great Britain itself highlights the historic and continued importance of singing in Methodism, noting on its website in a section on Methodist distinctiveness that 'Methodists are well known as enthusiastic singers, in choirs and congregations. Singing is still an important means of learning about, sharing and celebrating our faith'.[10] Historical accounts of Methodism abound with reports of the spirituality brought about through song. W. M. Patterson's summary of an event celebrating the

---

7   See Trevor Herbert, 'Popular Nationalism: Griffith Rhys Jones ("Caradog") and the Welsh Choral Tradition', in *Music and British Culture 1785–1914: Essays in Honour of Cyril Ehrlich*, ed. by Christina Bashford and Leanne Langley (Oxford: Oxford University Press, 2000), pp. 255–74 (at 268-69).

8   See Helen Barlow, '"Praise the Lord! We are a Musical Nation": The Welsh Working Classes and Religious Singing', *Nineteenth-Century Music Review* 17 (2020), 445–72 (at 445–46).

9   Nicola Bryan, 'World Cup 2022: Wales' Qualification Revives Yma O Hyd Success', *BBC News*, 11 June 2022, https://www.bbc.co.uk/news/uk-wales-61757909; Seren Morris, 'Hen Wlad Fy Nhadau: What do the Welsh national anthem lyrics mean?', *Evening Standard,* 28 November 2022, https://www.standard.co.uk/news/uk/hen-wlad-fy-nhadau-welsh-national-anthem-lyrics-meaning-football-world-cup-sport-wales-vs-england-b1043125.html

10 The Methodist Church, 'Born in Song', *The Methodist Church* https://www.methodist.org.uk/about-us/the-methodist-church/what-is-distinctive-about-methodism/born-in-song

centenary of Primitive Methodism, one historic branch of the movement, serves as an example:

> A great united choir filled the orchestra stalls; 'but in point of fact', remarked a journal in surprise, 'the entire gathering was one gigantic choir. Not a single one in the multitude but could sing, and did sing. The hymns chosen needed no restraint on the part of the singers, no delicate tone painting; they were the old, full-bodied psalms of praises, resonant and triumphant. So this magnificent gathering threw restraint to the winds, and the deep swell of the great organ led them in such paeans of praise as it refreshed one to hear'.[11]

This chapter contends that these examples and the musical cultures and practices to which they relate highlight the importance and value of studying the ways in which relationships between music and spirituality have been and are articulated in the communal musical practices of groups that gather not primarily for musical purposes, but for whom musical participation functions as a key element in expressing personal affiliation and in bonding the community. It examines the sources and methods that underpin and enable such study and reflects on theoretical frameworks that can assist in the work of interpreting the significance of such musical practices. It seeks to emphasise the interrelation of words, music, and participatory performance cultures in understanding the high value accorded to music within the communities examined.

I. Lyrics

The textual content of the repertoires that have historically been widely sung in Methodist chapels and on the terraces of Welsh rugby and football stadia provide important insights that help to explain both the popularity of specific songs and, more generally, the practice of communal singing.

Charles Wesley's name and lyrical output loom large in any discussion of Methodist hymnody. He has been the most represented author in every authorised hymnal in British Methodist history, although the actual number of his hymns included has declined steadily and significantly since the late-eighteenth century.[12] A selection of Wesley's

---

11 W. M. Patterson, *Northern Primitive Methodism: A Record of the Rise and Progress of the Circuits in the Old Sunderland District* (London: E. Dalton, 1909), p. 8.

12 See Clarke, *British Methodist Hymnody*, pp. 190–95.

hymns nonetheless retains considerable popularity within British Methodism, but compared even to the total of seventy-nine of his texts in the denomination's current authorised hymnal, *Singing the Faith* (2011), this is only a small subset. Some of these have also long been widely used ecumenically, such as 'Love Divine, All Loves Excelling', 'Hark! The Herald Angels Sing' and 'O Thou Who Camest from Above'. Others, such as 'And Can It Be that I Should Gain', while found in some hymnals beyond Methodism, carry a stronger denominational association. These hymns, and several others by Wesley that remain popular, share textual traits, but also strong associations with specific tunes, which are key to their endurance and appeal, as considered below.

Thematically, this small subset of Wesley's hymns is diverse: the examples cited above respectively cover the nature of God's love, the incarnation, the Holy Spirit, and the salvific work of Jesus Christ. There are, however, common textual features among many of them, relating variously to theological emphasis, poetic structure, and phraseology. Wesley's characteristic emphasis on personal salvation is typically to the fore, through which his evangelical Arminianism tends to be cogently expressed. In some cases, this is primarily addressed by stressing the universal offer of God's grace through the birth, life, death, and resurrection of Jesus Christ. This interpretation of the incarnation is, unsurprisingly, found in 'Hark! The Herald Angels Sing', in lines such as 'God and sinners reconciled' and 'born to raise the sons of earth, / born to give them second birth', and through the characteristic use of 'all' ('Joyful, all ye nations rise'; 'Light and life to all he brings').[13] Elsewhere, the emphasis is more directly personal, such as in 'And can it be that I should gain…', where the first-person singular is consistently used. The relationship between the individual and the whole of humankind is expressly articulated in the third stanza: 'emptied himself of all but love, / and bled for Adam's helpless race. 'Tis mercy all, immense and free; / for, O my God, it found out me!'[14]

In terms of poetic structure, many of Wesley's hymns that have attained the greatest popularity employ lengthy metrical patterns, often with six- or eight-line stanzas, such as 8787D ('Love Divine, All Loves Excelling') and 888888 ('And Can It Be'). While Wesley also makes extensive use of more concise metres such as common metre and long

---

13   *Hymns & Psalms* (Peterborough: Methodist Publishing House, 1983), hymn 106.
14   Ibid., hymn 216.

metre, it is notable that some of his most enduring texts in these metres have, at least in Methodism, typically been associated with tunes that extend them through the repetition of one or more lines, such as 'O for a Thousand Tongues to Sing' (common metre) and 'Jesus—the Name High over All' (common metre). As a long metre text, 'O Thou, Who Camest from Above' stands as something of an exception in both regards, as neither of the tunes associated with it within and beyond Methodism extend the basic metrical pattern. Wesley used these longer forms to considerable effect, often building to a powerful climax in the final couplet of each stanza. 'And Can It Be' is a fine example of this, enhanced by its ABABCC rhyme scheme; the penultimate line of each of the first four stanzas opens with a bold acclamation: 'Amazing Love!'; ''Tis mercy all!' (twice), and 'my chains fell off'.[15] 'Hark! The Herald Angels Sing' reuses the opening couplet as a refrain at the end of each stanza, while the final line of each of the three stanzas in the commonly accepted version of 'Love Divine, All Loves Excelling' directs the singer inexorably towards a spiritual climax: 'enter every trembling heart'; 'glory in thy perfect love'; and, finally, 'lost in wonder, love, and praise!'[16]

These features highlight Wesley's poetical skill, while the latter also shows his rhetorical command. Memorable words, phrases and couplets abound in these popular texts, such as the startlingly polysyllabic 'inextinguishable' amidst a stanza otherwise composed entirely of one- and two-syllable words in 'O Thou Who Camest from Above'.[17] Such poetical and theological features have long attracted the attention of hymnologists, theologians, and devotional writers within and beyond Methodism. J. R. Watson's *The English Hymn: A Critical and Historical Study* contains a chapter on 'John and Charles Wesley' but also devotes a separate chapter to 'Charles Wesley and His Art'.[18] In the latter, Watson draws attention to Wesley's biblical knowledge and interpretative skill, his wider field of reference, and his poetical facility and creativity, writing of his verse: 'Its principal feature is the richness of reference, and the fullness of doctrine which is compacted into the stanzas, and

---

15 Ibid., hymn 216. For an extended analysis of this text, see Martin V. Clarke, '"And Can It Be": Analysing the Words, Music, and Contexts of an Iconic Methodist Hymn', *Yale Journal of Music & Religion* 2 (2016), 25–52 (at 26–29).
16 *Hymns & Psalms*, hymn 267.
17 Ibid., hymn 745.
18 J. R. Watson, *The English Hymn: A Critical and Historical Study* (Oxford: Clarendon Press, 1997), pp. 205–29, 230–64.

that is made possible not only by the use of other writers, but also by the way in which their words and phrases are so skilfully used, either entire or in altered form'.[19]

A recent collection of essays entitled *Amazing Love! How Can It Be: Studies on Hymns by Charles Wesley* examines twelve of his texts.[20] Though written by North American scholars, where the reception patterns of Wesley's hymns have been somewhat different from Britain, seven of those covered are among the small group of Wesley's texts that remain in widespread use in the United Kingdom. While the volume does include a separate chapter on music and an appendix containing a selection of tunes from eighteenth-century Methodist sources, the studies of the texts themselves confine their remarks to literary, theological, and doctrinal matters. Such textual study is illuminating; nonetheless, separating the literary from the musical limits the potential for insights into the spiritual significance of hymnody and into the popular acclaim of a subset of Charles Wesley's vast corpus of hymns, as will be explored further below.

Lyrical structures and themes are similarly important considerations when examining the songs of the Welsh sporting crowd, while language is an additional factor. Their repertoire includes a mixture of religious hymns and secular songs, ranging from patriotic songs such as the national anthem, 'Hen wlad fy nhadau,' and 'Men of Harlech' to hit songs by popular Welsh musicians, such as Tom Jones's 'Delilah' and Max Boyce's 'Hymns and Arias', as well as the more recently popularised 'Yma o Hyd'.[21] The two most widely sung hymns are 'Guide Me, O Thou Great Jehovah', a translation of a Welsh-language hymn by the great Welsh Methodist hymn-writer William Williams, Pantycelyn, set to the tune CWM RHONDDA by John Hughes (1873–1932) and 'Calon Lân',

---

19 Ibid., p. 255. Similar emphases can be found in S. T. Kimbrough, Jr, *The Lyrical Theology of Charles Wesley: A Reader* (Eugene, OR: Cascade, 2013) and numerous chapters in Kenneth G. C. Newport and Ted A. Campbell, eds, *Charles Wesley: Life, Literature and Legacy* (Peterborough: Epworth, 2007).

20 Chris Fenner and Brian G. Najapfour, eds, *Amazing Love! How Can It Be: Studies on Hymns by Charles Wesley* (Eugene, OR: Wipf and Stock, 2020).

21 The Welsh Rugby Union's decision to prohibit choirs booked to provide musical entertainment for the crowd from including 'Delilah' in their sets early in 2023 attracted considerable media attention and debate. See Andy Martin, 'Bye, Bye, Bye Delilah: Wales Rugby Choirs Banned from Singing Tom Jones Hit', *Guardian*, 1 February 2023, https://www.theguardian.com/sport/2023/feb/01/delilah-welsh-rugby-union-choirs-banned-from-singing-tom-jones-hit

by Daniel James, set to an eponymous tune by a different John Hughes (1872–1914).

The bilingual nature of the crowd's repertoire is significant. Though such songs and many others besides are sung by the crowds at rugby union and football matches at club level throughout Wales, home international fixtures in both sports are customarily played at stadia in the capital city, Cardiff, in south-east Wales, a region in which the Welsh language is less widely spoken than in parts of north and west Wales. Though the crowd sing in both Welsh and English, many will not be conversant in Welsh and will not otherwise use the language regularly or routinely. The importance of being able to participate in Welsh-language songs, however, and most notably in the national anthem, is palpable in the intensity with which they are sung and attested to by supporters and journalists alike on social media and in many newspaper articles that comment on the phenomenon.[22]

The lyrics of the hymns sung by the crowd are, naturally, overtly religious, yet Wales, in keeping with the rest of the United Kingdom, has experienced significant declines in religious belief and participation in recent decades. That the hymns continue to be sung owes much to the prominence of Wales's Protestant non-conformist heritage in the popular imagination. Chapels remain visibly prominent in many Welsh villages and towns, even if no longer used for their original purposes, and the cultural memory of the hymn-singing tradition they encouraged and supported persists and has been actively revitalised by the Welsh media and other organisations in the twenty-first century.[23] Both the hymns mentioned exhibit some linguistic and structural similarities to the hymns of Charles Wesley discussed above. 'Guide Me, O Thou Great Jehovah', of which only the first stanza is commonly sung by the crowd, employs a metrical structure that, like Wesley's six- and eight-line

---

22 A plethora of such articles appeared in November 2022 as the Welsh men's football team competed in the FIFA World Cup finals for the first time since 1958. Examples include Ian Mitchelmore, 'The Amazing Rendition of the Anthem Wales Fans Have Been Waiting to Sing for 64 Years', *Wales Online*, 21 November 2022, https://www.walesonline.co.uk/sport/football/football-news/amazing-rendition-anthem-wales-fans-25571439

23 On the role of BBC Wales, the Football Association of Wales, and the Welsh Rugby Union, see Barlow and Clarke, 'Singing Welshness'. The inclusion of hymns in the repertoire performed by a new generation of Welsh solo artists and ensembles, such as Katherine Jenkins and Only Men Aloud, are further examples.

patterns, draws attention to an emphatic declaration in the final couplet: 'Bread of heaven, bread of heaven, / feed me now and evermore' (alternatively ''til I want no more'). Such is the power of that couplet that the hymn is widely known as 'Bread of Heaven', and those lines are heard more frequently than the whole stanza. The text's yearning for spiritual food may be readily translated to the secular sporting context as supporters seek the nourishment of their team's victory, but it is also indicative of a spiritualised national identity. 'Calon Lân', by contrast, is essentially a prayer for spiritual purity (the title translates as 'a pure heart'). It is not until the third stanza that the directing of this prayer to God is made explicit, which may partly contribute to its secular appeal. Beyond this, though, the looser sense of it conveying something 'of the heart' is easily reconciled with national sporting pride. Pride in Wales's musical heritage, in which religious song is a significant strand, and fervent support of the national team combine to considerable effect on such occasions, when national pride is naturally foremost in supporters' minds.

Regarding Wales's musical heritage as the primary factor rather than religion also helps makes sense of the easy interchange between sacred and secular texts. Indeed, this is a feature to which Welsh singer-songwriter Max Boyce draws attention in 'Hymns and Arias', a song that celebrates the tradition of the singing crowd: 'We sang "Cwm Rhondda" and "Delilah", / damn, they sounded both the same'.[24] Like 'Calon Lân', 'Hymns and Arias' and 'Delilah' employ a verse and refrain structure, with the repeated words of the refrains assisting their familiarity. Like the Methodist hymns noted earlier, all the popular songs of the Welsh crowd rely on fixed combinations of words and music, as will be explored in the following section.

---

24 Max Boyce, *Hymns & Arias: The Selected Poems, Songs and Stories* (Cardigan: Parthian Books, 2021), p. 3. The song also refers by name to 'Calon Lân' and several other Welsh songs. An adaptation of this song sung at the opening ceremony of the Rugby World Cup in Wales referenced the interweaving of religion and sport explicitly. Referring to the Millennium Stadium's sliding roof, Boyce sang 'They'll slide it back when Wales attack / so God can watch us play'. Max Boyce, 'Rugby World Cup 1999, Max Boyce, Hymns and Arias, Opening Ceremony', online video recording, *YouTube*, 26 June 2014, https://www.youtube.com/watch?v=O-EKY7z_jeE

II. Music

As noted above, many of Charles Wesley's texts that remain in widespread use have strong associations with particular tunes. For some, these musical associations are particular to British Methodism, for others they are shared ecumenically and internationally, though there are also some distinct differences, for example, between Methodism and other denominations in Britain, and between British Methodism and Methodism in the United States. Almost all are musical associations that became established after Charles Wesley's death, and in some cases more than a century later.

Many of these tunes share musical features that have led them to be regarded as characteristically Methodist. They flourished in the early nineteenth century, were often composed by church musicians, and sometimes betray a lack of technical training on the composer's part, particularly in their harmonic language. Prototypes had emerged in the late eighteenth century, the best known of which is HELMSLEY, composed by Martin Madan, set to Charles Wesley's 'Lo! He Comes with Clouds Descending', which, alongside 'Christ the Lord is Risen Today' set to EASTER HYMN are the only Wesley texts still widely sung to tunes likely to have been known to the author himself. Nicholas Temperley labels this type of tune as 'Old Methodist'; his technical description is worth citing at length:

> The typical tune that emerged was melodious, even pretty, and in the major mode. It often had a second, equally tuneful subordinate part, moving mostly in parallel 3rds or 6ths, either of similar compass or in a treble-tenor relationship; the bass was inclined to be static. In other words, the texture was that of the 'galant' or early classic style, and for the most part the compositional rules of that style were well observed; but it long outlived the departure of galanterie in secular music. The melody was often ornate, with two or three notes to many of the syllables, and could easily take ornaments such as the turn, appoggiatura or trill. Uneven syllable lengths were normal, whether in triple time or by unequal division of common-time bars. Dynamic contrasts between phrases were sometimes a feature, probably implying sections for women alone …. Usually there would be repetition of some lines of the text, delaying or reconfirming a cadence or half-cadence. Sometimes fuging entries crept in, despite Wesley. But the most typical feature of all was the final

cadence, of a very definite, foursquare kind, consisting of three chords: tonic 6-4, dominant 7th, tonic.[25]

Not all such tunes had their origins in Methodism but were often borrowed from other collections of hymn tunes. SAGINA for 'And Can It Be' is arguably the archetype, but several of the hymns mentioned earlier are associated with tunes of this type. Within British Methodism, 'O for a Thousand Tongues to Sing' is widely sung to two such tunes: Thomas Phillips's LYDIA (first published 1844), and Thomas Jarman's LYNGHAM (first published c. 1803). Both conform to most of the properties identified by Temperley; LYDIA is more heavily focused on a single melody line and repeats only the final line of the text, whereas LYNGHAM employs extensive textual repetition and clear separation of high and low voices in its elaborate setting of the final line of each stanza.

The musical qualities of these tunes need to be recognised as playing an important part in the overall spiritual impact of the hymns with which they were associated and, by extension, in the spiritual value Methodists placed on hymns and hymn-singing as a whole. Measured by conventional musical standards for evaluating common-practice era composition, they may easily seem unremarkable or unsophisticated, yet their efficacy lies in their immediacy and accessibility. These are tunes designed to be picked up quickly by untrained singers, and to create both an instant and lasting impression on them. Despite the tendency towards extension and repetition, they are fundamentally and necessarily concise. As a result, they deliver their musical climax swiftly and obviously.

In LYDIA, the repetition of the final line of each stanza adds emphasis, underscored musically by the contrary motion of the ascending melody line and descending bass line to reach the tonic on the first strong beat of the final line, as shown in Figure 18.1.

---

25 Nicholas Temperley and Martin V. Clarke, "Methodist Church Music', in *Grove Music Online*, rev. Martin V. Clarke (2001), https://doi.org/10.1093/gmo/9781561592630.article.47533

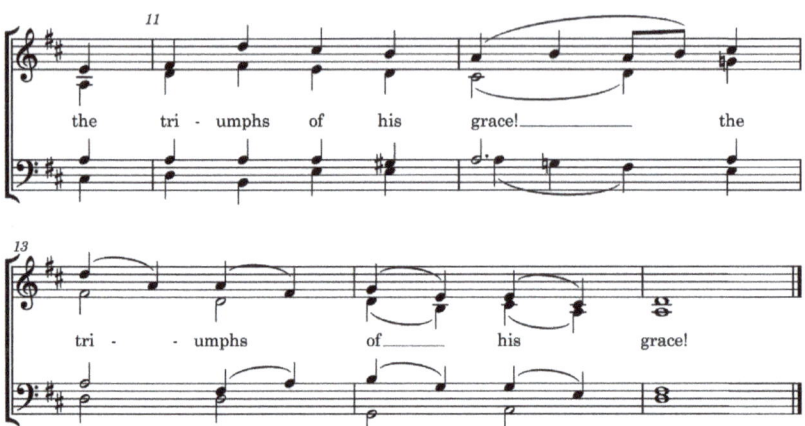

Fig. 18.1 Thomas Phillips, LYDIA, bars 10⁴–15. Transcription by author (2023), CC BY-NC 4.0

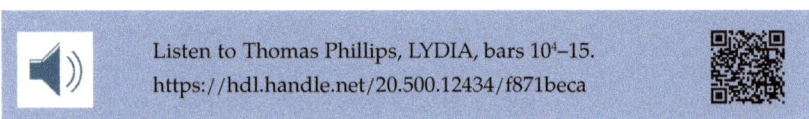

Listen to Thomas Phillips, LYDIA, bars 10⁴–15.
https://hdl.handle.net/20.500.12434/f871beca

In LYNGHAM, Jarman uses a combination of melody, text setting, and texture to bring the tune to a rousing conclusion in his extended setting of the final line, shown in Figure 18.2. With each textual repetition, the melody moves one step higher until it reaches its highest pitch on the first strong beat of the final repetition, at which point the four voice parts revert to homophony after a fuging section. The final repetition of 'triumphs' is extended over a full four beats, adding a last flourish.

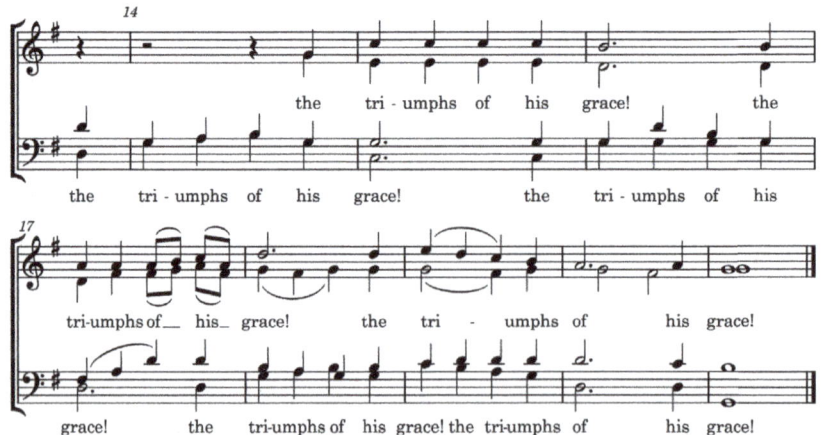

Fig. 18.2 Thomas Jarman, LYNGHAM, bars 13⁴–21. Transcription by author (2023), CC BY-NC 4.0

Listen to Thomas Jarman, LYNGHAM, bars 13^4–21.
https://hdl.handle.net/20.500.12434/180fa781

These tunes were designed to be sung vigorously. They highlight the evangelistic impulse of Wesley's text and accentuate the balance his words strive to achieve between personal piety and social holiness. They achieve their impact most readily when sung in large gatherings in which every individual participates in the singing.

Similar musical characteristics and contexts can also be found in the repertoire of Welsh sporting crowds. The widespread use of 'Bread of Heaven' as an alternative title for 'Guide Me, O Thou Great Jehovah' (set to the tune CWM RHONDDA) attests to the importance of the musical properties of that hymn tune in ensuring its popularity. The rising melodic sequence as 'Bread of heaven', followed by the declamatory 'Feed me 'til I want no more' and its surging echo are musically memorable and, like the examples of LYDIA and LYNGHAM, build to an obvious climax.

Fig. 18.3 John Hughes, CWM RHONDDA, bars 9–12. Transcription by author (2023), CC BY-NC 4.0

 Listen to John Hughes, CWM RHONDDA, bars 9–12
https://hdl.handle.net/20.500.12434/1bc53392

The eponymous tune to 'Calon Lân' reaches its high point at the beginning of the refrain, as the title words are sung, underscoring their verbal significance. Both 'Hymns and Arias' and 'Delilah', meanwhile, have marked melodic contrasts between their verses and refrains. The verses are confined to a narrow range and use simple, almost speech-like rhythms, while the refrains employ a wider range and more distinctive rhythms, notably using longer notes to emphasise key lyrical features.

The performance of 'Hen wlad fy nhadau' at Welsh rugby and football internationals has undergone a significant shift in the twenty-first century that seems to have intensified the experience for those singing it. The anthem's climax has traditionally been at its mid-point, with the words, 'Gwlad! Gwald!' (literally translated 'country', but understood as signifying Wales) that begin the refrain. Set to two long notes, first the dominant and then the upper tonic of the scale, it is a moment of textual and musical power that has few if any parallels in other national anthems. More recently, and seemingly following the lead of famous Welsh singers such as Bryn Terfel and Katherine Jenkins who have often been invited to lead the singing of the anthem at international matches, most of the final line of the refrain is customarily sung an octave higher than notated in the original melody. The words at this point, 'O bydded i'r hen iaith barhau' concern the ongoing preservation of the old language ('hen iaith', i.e., Welsh). The original melody has a descending contour to the final tonic, and while the now-customary modification disrupts the overall melodic balance of the anthem, its impact is undeniably significant, if unsubtle. Video footage of players and supporters confirm the near ubiquity of this modification; their strained facial expressions as they reach for the high notes symbolising their fervour and the intensity of the shared experience.

III. Context

The above analysis of popular Methodist hymns and songs of the Welsh sporting crowd indicates that textual and musical content are important factors in understanding the ways in which such repertoire is understood to enable or express spirituality, or to capture a perceived national spirit. Context, however, is also a vital element; the sharing of such experiences among people with common interests and commitments provides the environment in which the spiritual is perceived. Neither Methodist meetings nor sporting fixtures are primarily musical events or activities. While music has long played an important role in both, it does so in support of another purpose; it is not intended as an end in itself. This has implications for understanding music's role in articulating or conveying spirituality. While music in these contexts is not necessarily spiritualised in its own right, it is integral to the spiritualisation of the wider event for many participants.

Timothy Dudley-Smith published his reflections on hymn-writing in a volume entitled *A Functional Art*. Dudley-Smith's title, observations and arguments partly express this notion of hymns pointing beyond themselves. He defines the basic purpose of a hymn to be the praise of God, but also notes their benefit to the singers.[26] Drawing on the work of Erik Routley, Dudley-Smith highlights three ways in which hymns bring benefits to those who sing them: doxological, doctrinal, and communal.[27] Regarding the latter, he notes that 'It is something we do together, and everyone knows that a shared task is one of the key elements of "team building"'.[28] Throughout the volume, he makes frequent mention of Charles Wesley, and the human-focused aspects of hymn-singing he describes map clearly onto Methodist practice and repertoire. The singing of the Welsh sporting crowd is also obviously communal. While it is neither doxological nor doctrinal in the strictly religious sense that Dudley-Smith intends, there are nonetheless parallels. The act of singing, if not in praise of the team, serves both to celebrate it and encourage the players, while in different ways lyrics serve to express central tenets of national identity. In the case of 'Hen wlad fy nhadau', the lyrics directly refer to the nation, but in other Welsh language songs, such as 'Calon Lân', the language itself is the crucial factor, marking a distinctive cultural identity. As a renowned hymn-writer, Dudley-Smith's primary interest is unsurprisingly in the words of hymns. His description of the benefits to participants as 'side-effects' reflects this priority.[29] Contextual consideration of the spirituality of communal singing, however, places the emphasis on practice, in which the interaction of words and music is central. Indeed, if the songs of the congregation or the crowd are, in Dudley-Smith's term, 'functional' in that they point beyond themselves in enabling a spiritual experience, then investigating and interpreting practice is vital.

---

26 Timothy Dudley-Smith, *A Functional Art: Reflections of a Hymn Writer* (Oxford: Oxford University Press, 2017), pp. 1–3.
27 Ibid., p. 3.
28 Ibid., p. 5.
29 Ibid.

In a specifically religious context, Jeff Astley's concept of 'ordinary theology' offers a means of understanding the ways in which so-called ordinary believers, that is, those without formal theological training, learn and express their theology.[30] It is a useful theoretical framework for interpreting the spiritual value congregation members find in hymnody, as it is rooted in religious practice. Among the characteristics of ordinary theology identified by Astley are that it is meaningful, religious, and kneeling, or celebratory.[31] The opening vignette in this chapter highlights these in practice in a Methodist context: the sharing of a hymn helps make sense of the spiritual meaning of the meeting described, while the religious nature of the gathering is the spur for such reflection. The hymn also highlights how the belief is expressed in practice: it is manifested in the celebratory act of communal singing. In other ways, however, the singing of hymns departs from aspects of Astley's framework, most notably his observation that ordinary theology is typically tentative, or cautiously expressed.[32] The lyrics allow ideas to be expressed in words other than one's own, while the act of singing together, particularly in the vigorous manner commonly associated with Methodists and encouraged by such tunes as those discussed above, project a confident spirituality.

Astley's work is thoroughly contextual and points to the importance of understanding the relationship between practice and meaning. Though he focuses on theology, that is, people's beliefs, the emphasis on practice means that spirituality is thoroughly intertwined. Belief expressed through or learned via practice has a symbiotic relationship with spirituality. Setting aside the explicitly Christian focus of Astley's work, the concepts and characteristics he identifies have a wider applicability in relation to questions of belonging and identity. Rugby or football internationals are occasions on which national identity and pride are considerably heightened for supporters. Their commitment to team and nation, given voice through singing, is expressed in ways that stand apart from everyday life. If national identity takes on a spiritual

---

30 Jeff Astley, *Ordinary Theology: Looking, Listening and Learning in Theology* (Aldershot: Ashgate, 2002).
31 Astley, *Ordinary Theology*, pp. 68–76.
32 Ibid., pp. 61–62.

element on such occasions, communal singing of meaningful repertoire serves as both an enabler and expression of that identity.

Another practice-focused framework for interpreting the spiritual significance accorded to communal singing traditions such as those discussed here can be found in Ruth Finnegan's *The Hidden Musicians: Music-Making in an English Town*. Chiefly an ethnographic study of musical practices in 1980s Milton Keynes, Finnegan's study concludes with an analysis of its implications for understanding the meanings people accord to music. She highlights the importance of shared interests in members' sense of belonging to a musical group:

> People commonly did not know much about all their co-members in musical groups—but in the sense that mattered to them they knew *enough*. Individuals often joined because they knew one or more members already and their joint musical activity then reinforced and amplified that existing contact, if not through practicalities like sharing lifts or delivering messages then at least through supporting the same group and making music together.[33]

This illustrates Finnegan's argument that the meaningfulness of such activity, which could be very significant, emerged from engagement in shared practice with others about whom sufficient information was known in terms of this common interest. This has particular resonance with the sporting crowd, who gather solely for this purpose and whose collective voice is a temporary manifestation of what otherwise might be regarded as, in Benedict Anderson's term, an imagined community.[34] Making music together affirms a shared identity that becomes especially meaningful in that context. As Finnegan goes on to note, many of her research participants confirmed that 'their music-making was one of the habitual routes by which they identified themselves as worthwhile members of society and which they regarded as of somehow deep-seated importance to them as human beings'.[35] Observing that musical practices are bound up with other events, activities, and ideas. Finnegan

---

33 Ruth H. Finnegan, *The Hidden Musicians: Music-Making in an English Town* (Cambridge, UK: Cambridge University Press, 1989; repr. Middletown, CT: Wesleyan University Press, 2007), p. 303.

34 Benedict Anderson, *Imagined Communities: Reflections on the Origin and Spread of Nationalism* (London: Verso, 1983, revised and extended, 1991).

35 Finnegan, *Hidden Musicians*, p. 306

found that, despite this, many participants accorded music a different value from those other activities:

> What did seem unmistakable was an unspoken but shared assumption among the participants in local music that there was something *sui generis*, something unparalleled in quality and in kind about music which was not to be found in other activities of work or of play. This assessment was neither exactly measurable nor precisely definable, but was for all that itself part of the reality, one way in which music had indeed, as experienced by its local participants, its own inimitable meaning.[36]

As already noted, the musical practices considered in this chapter are intended to express meaning beyond themselves. However, in both cases, singing communally is one of the chief means by which the intense emotions or sense of spirituality associated with the occasion are created and perceived.

Finnegan and Astley both take seriously the lived experiences of those whom they variously term 'ordinary believers' and 'hidden musicians'. This allows them to theorise the ways in which values and meanings are learned and attributed through activities that have too often been overlooked because of their supposed lack of intellectual sophistication or aesthetic quality. Meaning and value emerge through participation and shared identity. Such perspectives, coupled with close engagement with musical and textual sources, offer a means of making sense of the perceived spirituality engendered by shared musical practices in Methodism and in Welsh football and rugby stadia. Textual meaning, structure, language, and imagery play an important role, as do musical settings that balance a simple directness with dramatic memorability. Paired, they thrive in contexts in which perceptions of common belief, meaning, identity, or value are already heightened, often reinforcing among participants and observers a sense of massed communal singing as an enabler and expression of spirituality.

---

36 Ibid., p. 332.

Afterword:
A Psychologist's Perspective

John Sloboda

I am grateful to the editors to have been placed in the position of 'participant-observer' to the workshop which allowed authors to try out first drafts of chapters destined for this book. I was a participant by virtue of reading a short paper and engaging in the cut and thrust of dialogue; but I was an observer in two senses. First, I am not currently professionally engaged in work on music and spirituality, and never really have been. I did write one chapter-length think piece a quarter a century ago,[1] which the editors were kind enough to consider raised some relevant questions and attempted sketches of answers. But this is a slender thread to link me to a group of experts who make this topic their professional daily bread and butter. Second, I was assigned the daunting task of constructing a brief response to the contributions as a whole in the conference's final session. Such a role inevitably forces one somewhat to the margins, standing outside and viewing the proceeding from a particular, and inevitably personal, vantage point. As is completely right and proper, and to be expected, the period between the workshop and the submission of final texts was a period of further reflection and maturation of ideas, both for the chapter authors and myself. Now, seeing the volume as a whole, and with some further distance from the event itself, I have refreshed and reframed my own observations shared with participants at the time. And so what is written here has some

---

1   John A. Sloboda, 'Music and Worship: A Psychologist's Perspective', in *Creative Chords: Studies in Music, Theology and Christian Formation*, ed. by Jeff Astley, Timothy Hone, and Micahel Savage (Leominster: Gracewing, 2000), pp. 110–25.

substantial overlaps with, but also some significant differences from, what I shared at the workshop.

The cumulative effect of these diverse and passionately engaged contributions has been to impress upon me ever more strongly that positionality is at the heart of the appreciation of the relationship of music to the spiritual. By positionality I simply mean what each individual brings to the table, and the lens through which that allows them to experience and understand the phenomenon in question, a phenomenon that was explicitly addressed by Maeve Louise Heaney (Chapter 11). Positionality has at least three distinct elements in this collection. We all bring different faith and worship orientations and histories which influence how we approach the spiritual. In my case, the history is of a post-Second Vatican Council English Roman Catholic. We all have a musical history which influences what forms of music we inhabit and engage with, and at what level. My musical history is primarily as someone trained in the European classical tradition and with a particular love for sacred choral music of the Anglican tradition. And finally we all have a professional practice, which involves a set of theoretical and methodological predispositions and resources, and which informs how we go about our investigations and our writing. My professional practice is neither musical nor faith based, but reflects the discipline of academic empirical psychology, conceived of as a science, and robustly materialist in its assumptions.

The brand of academic psychology which informed my stand-alone turn-of-the-century think piece was the dominant approach of the 1960s–90s, and might be described as cognitive universalism. It self-confidently assumed that, because the basic neural substrate of all humans is similar, universally valid conclusions about psychological mechanisms and outcomes could be arrived at by extrapolating or generalising from the experiences and actions of individuals occupying a specific time, place, and context. Indeed, the introspectionist tradition at the foundation of modern psychology was based on the belief that, with sufficient training and discernment, a sample of one—oneself—could be sufficient to draw universally relevant conclusions. As the twentieth century progressed, behaviourist approaches gained ascendancy, emphasising more the utility of collecting data from a range of individuals through various forms of measurement and quantitative analytic tools, often trading depth of meaning for formal rigour and statistical significance. In more recent decades, qualitative approaches have re-emerged to enrich the range of sources used to understand human response—recognising that people talking about themselves can offer as important insights as observing some quantitatively measurable aspect of their behaviour. That shift represented a renewed acknowledgement that interiority cannot be completely observed or understood from the outside, it has to be expressed and articulated by the person whose interiority it is. And, whatever commonalities might be discovered at more surface levels, interiority in its depth may be unique and unrepeatable, not only as between individuals, but even within the same individual at different times.

That observation brings us to the nub of one of the key issues with which the various authors of this volume grapple in different ways. Spirituality—however defined and articulated—is an interior and essentially private phenomenon, experienced by individuals, and not apprehensible from the outside by some reliable marker, whether an environment, a ritual, or a physiological event. From a theological standpoint, a spiritual experience might be taken to be an experience of encounter with the divine. A faith-based approach can situate the divine in specific human situations. So, for instance, the eucharistic theology of Catholicism asserts that God is present in a uniquely powerful and effective way when believers break bread together in memory of Christ's actions at the Last Supper. But even such a restricted lens doesn't lead to a reliable hermeneutic (or even correlatory) link between the external and the internal. It would be a mistake to identify the words or actions of the consecration themselves as the guarantor or sure predictor of the presence of a spiritual experience in a worshipper. The presence of God in the Eucharist might be a theological reality, given by faith, but that does not determine whether or how such reality presents itself in the spiritual experience of a worshipper. The individual concerned has to bear witness to this before we would know. And even such witness is problematic, because of the slipperiness of the term 'spiritual' as a marker for what we might be asking a person to report on.

C.M. Howell (Chapter 6) writes 'It is often noted that "spirituality" is inherently vague'. He goes on to outline half a dozen different ways in which it has been interpreted in the literature. Scanning through the rest of the chapters easily yields half a dozen more. Howells goes on to assert that 'despite this ambiguity, there is an ever-increasing use of the term spirituality. Indeed, the term's ambiguity, rather than being perceived as a deficiency, appears to be part of its strength and appeal'. But one could also argue that the ambiguity could also be a weakness when it comes to the task of making intellectual progress in understanding the spiritual, and its relationship to music. There is perhaps a danger that the very ambiguity and slipperiness of the term spiritual allows us to smuggle in unacknowledged premises and unnamed biases; or at least to be somewhat talking past each other as we deploy different understandings. Notwithstanding this, it was a pragmatic and fruitful idea for the editors to invite contributors to review a toolkit of methods to take us further in the exploration of the relationship between the music and the spiritual. And I would contend that one of the most useful elements of that toolkit would be a rigorous means of untangling this great web of ambiguity around the concept of spirituality in itself.

In this volume there are several chapters that highlight what can be learned from empirical social science methods, such as gathering survey, interview, or online responses from diverse groups of individuals. And just as there are a dozen or more different understandings of spirituality among the authorship of this volume, there is sure to be the same variety, and more, in the population at large. So that when we interrogate their experience with the blunt and ambiguous term 'spiritual' we may not really know what they have in mind when they engage in discourse using this term. One of the tools extensively used by psychologists is conceptual mapping.[2] In this process, one accumulates a set of related words and concepts and attempts to lay them out on some underlying dimensions which elucidate their relationship to each other. A scan through the texts of the various chapters easily generates a list of some recurrent descriptors:

Divine

Sacred

Religious

---

2   It has been extensively used, for example, to discern underlying conceptual structures among the plethora of words describing emotions (see Rick L. Morgan and David Heise, 'Structure of Emotions', Social Psychology Quarterly 51.1 (1988), 19–31).

Worshipful (praise / adoration)

Mystical contemplation

Immaterial

[Spiritual]

Transcendent

Ecstatic

Peak experience

Uplifting

Absorption

Transformative

Contemplative

Flow

Comforting

How can we make sense, constructively, and empirically, of such a ragbag? Psychology has provided a range of techniques through which we can ask people to compare these concepts, to rate each in some way (for example, their degree of similarity to the others), and then through statistical technique such as factor analysis or multidimensional scaling create a dimensionally organised visualisation of their closeness or distance in conceptual space.

The figure below is one personal and intuitive attempt at a conceptual map, constructed not as any kind of claim to truth, but as an example of how the ragbag might all be contained within a more comprehensible and coherent space that allows concepts to be seen as nearer or further to each other along bipolar dimensions. This space is two-dimensional (just for ease of display—three or more dimensions sometimes better represent the relationships present). From left to right we move from the incorporeal to the corporeal. From top to bottom we move from the active (or disruptive) to the passive (or accepting). Each concept can be placed on these two dimensions.

Fig. A.1 A conceptual map for descriptors pertaining to spirituality in this volume. Created by author (2024), CC BY-NC 4.0

The point here is not whether each is in the 'right' place, or even whether these are the most appropriate dimensions on which to compare the individual concepts collected here. The illustration is rather to demonstrate a possible empirical technique for distinguishing how different types of musical experience might map onto such a space. A person whose interpretation of 'spiritual' tends towards the 'passive' and the 'corporeal' may—for instance—react to different musics and in different ways, to a person whose interpretation of spiritual tends towards the 'active' and 'immaterial'.

This classificatory or dimensional approach offers a useful bridge between two equally unhelpful extremes. The one extreme is the view that everyone is essentially the same in their reactions to and predispositions towards a range of phenomena. The other extreme is that each individual is totally different from every other individual, and must be treated as a unique incomparable case. A dimensional approach allows the characterisation of types, the delineation of groups who have similar tendencies which can help predict and understand how they behave and respond in comparison to other groups. Personality psychology has flourished under the application of such approaches, and the use of such models as the Myers–Briggs Type Index has found its way into some approaches to spirituality and spiritual guidance.[3] Just as we should take care to understand what lies beneath a person's designation of an experience as spiritual, and thereby allow for and take account of distinct types of spiritual experience or engagement, so we should also take care to acknowledge that music is not one thing, but encompasses many styles, practices, contexts. We should be cautious of asserting 'Music is...', and rather opt for 'some types of music, when offered in certain contexts, may be...'.

In 'Music and Worship' (2000), I opined that music has characteristics conducive to a state of worship, and identified those affordances with ineffability, associative power, the power to unite or co-ordinate response.[4] To touch briefly on each of these three characteristics in turn, *ineffability* refers to the observation that no matter how much you can know about a piece of music, there is always an unknowable residue. The unknowability is both at a macro-level and a micro-level. These characteristics mean that engaging with music deeply is an act of constant and never-ending discovery—pointing us towards the never-ending ineffability of the divine. *Associative power* refers to music's huge power to evoke memories, sometimes deep memories, and so lift us from the present into recollections of times of great joy or sorrow, times with great personal or communal significance. Finally, music has *unifying characteristics* which allow responses which are shared or communal, and co-ordinated, not simply individualistic. This comes about because there are certain structural or communicative features of music which are perceived in similar ways by most people, regardless of their familiarity with the music or their degree of musical sophistication. In addition, I did argue, as has also been mentioned by authors of this volume, that these features offer affordances (or opportunities) for worshipful or spiritual experience, although they require an active response and do not guarantee such experiences. I would now be even more cautious, a caution which the range of musical and worship contexts covered in the current volume exemplifies and details. As a result of the work presented in this volume, we are now gaining a greater understanding

---

3   See, for example, Gill Hall, 'Applying Psychological-Type Theory to Faith: Spirituality, Prayer, Worship and Scripture', *Mental Health, Religion & Culture* 15.9 (2012), 849–62.
4   Sloboda, 'Music and Worship'.

of how *some* music, presented in *some* contexts *may* offer affordances for deeper worship to *some* people.

This understanding highlights why, in worship, the role of a liturgist or musical director is so important. This person is one who thoughtfully curates the relationship between the worshipping congregation on the one hand, and the compositions they engage with on the other. In some times and places the musical director and the composer have been the self-same person, writing music for a context and a congregation they know intimately and able to accompany through the liturgical year, and over the life cycle. In the current Western, consumer-oriented society this has in some cases been supplanted by opportunities to engage in something more akin to a type of musico-spiritual 'shopping'. Individuals can choose worship contexts where the music that is offered suits what they judge their spiritual requirements to be. In my tradition this can be a question of deciding whether to go to the guitar Mass or the High Sung Mass in a parish that offers both, or stepping down the road to a neighbouring church where the music is more to one's taste. It can also be a question of a discerning director of music adjusting the musical offering to the needs and capacities of the congregation. A hymn that he or she does not personally resonate with may be the exact one to stimulate fervent participation from a particular congregation, whereas his or her favourite (on aesthetic or theological grounds) may fall flat.

It is therefore good to see in the different chapters a fuller treatment of the range of ways in which music and spiritual experience may co-exist. Spiritual uplift is not the unique province of religious worship, and may be found in situations as diverse as American country music (Howell, Chapter 6), or singing on the football terraces of Wales (Clarke, Chapter 18). And even in worship, one's positionality within a worshipping congregation may significantly inflect the value one gains from musical engagement. Dimensions of interest are, for instance, whether one is or is not paid for one's musical engagement, or whether musical experience in worship is a daily (or several-times-per day) one, or an occasional one. This draws me to a framing and concluding point, which I hope will not be taken as pouring too much cold water on our joint enterprise. We probably do not yet have a sufficiently nuanced understanding of the situations in which music has no particularly positive effect on people, and may even have a negative effect. This is highlighted by Dilana Turan

(Chapter 8) when she discusses 'why some ritual settings promote the emergence of ASC [altered state of consciousness] experiences for some people, while the same music and setting might be meaningless, boring, or disturbing for others'. The same music that can afford worship and other profoundly positive effects may—for other people in other contexts and with other personal histories and orientations—become alienating, aversive, and in extreme but clearly documented cases amount to torture.[5] It is certainly the case that many people have definite music preferences, with clear categories of disliked music,[6] categories which are unlikely to offer a path to their spiritual uplift. In other cases it may just be that music is not particularly important to an individual. When people decide to write about music, or agree to be participants in research studies on music, it may be precisely because they fall into the category of people who are strongly drawn to music, and whose lives have been significantly and positively touched by their engagement with music. Of course, such people will rightly wish to assert and articulate its value.

There is one way of taking a body of perspectives on music such as is collected here, which is to see it as a collection of individual testimonies. In each case, the author is telling a story, constructing or curating a narrative which, when well-written, as all of these are, draws us into their worldview and persuades us of it by stimulating resonances, contrasts, and illuminations in the reader's thoughts and imaginations. When such testimonies are bent towards scholarly rather than literary endeavours, they are, of course, designed to shed light on something that has external reality, as opposed to being imaginative or fictional. But nonetheless, a scientific lens should not be held to have privileged access to the reality being explored—it is just one of the specific (and undoubtedly effective) lenses through which some of us can choose to curate our narrative, and sharpen our means of persuasion. Would someone with no affinity for either the spiritual or the musical be persuaded by the collective wisdom laid out so eloquently in this book?

---

5   See, for instance, Morag Josephine Grant, 'The Illogical Logic of Music Torture', *Torture* 23.2 (2013), 4–13, where the author explicitly warns against the assumption that such uses are some kind of extreme aberration from a universal positive norm.

6   Taren-Ida Ackermann and Julia Merrill, 'Rationales and Functions of Disliked Music: An In-Depth Interview Study', *PloS One* 17.2 (2022), e0263384.

Perhaps not! But for those who already resonate within their own hearts to the notion that music has a special role in shaping and bringing forth their deepest and most profound apprehensions, then this volume will undoubtedly bring into being new understandings and new sources of inspiration. For that we should be very thankful.

List of Figures and Tables

Figures

6.1	Transcription by author (2024), CC BY-NC 4.0	p. 125
6.2	Transcription by author (2024), CC BY-NC 4.0	p. 131
6.3	Transcription by author (2024), CC BY-NC 4.0	p. 133
8.1	Sampling methodology. Created by author (2017), CC BY-NC 4.0	p. 169
8.2	Number of examples by religion/belief system. Created by author (2017), CC BY-NC 4.0.	p. 171
8.3	Number of examples by ritual context. Created by author (2017), CC BY-NC 4.0.	p. 171
8.4	Number of examples by ritual function. Created by author (2017), CC BY-NC 4.0.	p. 172
8.5	Examples by social setting of ritual. Created by author (2017), CC BY-NC 4.0.	p. 172
8.6	Melody transcriptions of examples No. 5, 26, 35, and 49. Created by author (2024), CC BY-NC 4.0.	p. 174
15.1	Participant responses about singing. Created by author (2024), CC BY-NC 4.0	p. 304
15.2	Online worship strategy. Created by author (2024), CC BY-NC 4.0	p. 317
15.3	Communication strategy. Created by author (2024), CC BY-NC 4.0	p. 318
15.4	Rhetorical strategy. Created by author (2024), CC BY-NC 4.0	p. 319
15.5	Chorister Strategy. Created by author (2024), CC BY-NC 4.0	p. 320
18.1	Thomas Phillips, LYDIA, bars 10^4–15. Transcription by author (2023), CC BY-NC 4.0	p. 382
18.2	Thomas Jarman, LYNGHAM, bars 13^4–21. Transcription by author (2023), CC BY-NC 4.0	p. 382
18.3	John Hughes, CWM RHONDDA, bars 9–12. Transcription by author (2023), CC BY-NC 4.0	p. 383
A.1	A conceptual map for descriptors pertaining to spirituality in this volume. Created by author (2024), CC BY-NC 4.0	p. 394

Tables

15.1	Participant biographies. Created by author (2024), CC BY-NC 4.0	p. 307
15.2	Themes and sub-themes pertaining to step five of RTA. Created by author (2024), CC BY-NC 4.0	p. 309

Bibliography

Abbate, Caroline, 'Music—Drastic or Gnostic?', *Critical Inquiry* 30.3 (2004), 505–36, https://doi.org/10.1086/421160

Ackermann, Taren-Ida, and Julia Merrill, 'Rationales and Functions of Disliked Music: An In-Depth Interview Study', *PloS One* 17.2 (2022), e0263384, https://doi.org/10.1371/journal.pone.0263384

Adorno, Theodor W., 'On the Fetish-Character in Music and the Regression of Listening', in *The Culture Industry: Selected Essays on Mass Culture*, ed. by J. M. Bernstein (London and New York: Routledge, 1991), pp. 29–60.

—, 'On the Social Situation of Music', in *Essays on Music*, ed. by Richard Leppert (Berkeley and Los Angeles, CA: University of California Press, 2002), pp. 391–436.

Adnams, Gordan Alban, 'The Experience of Congregational Singing: An Ethno-Phenomenological Approach' (unpublished doctoral thesis, Concordia University of Edmonton, 2008).

al Faruqi, Lois Ibsen, 'What Makes 'Religious Music' Religious?' in *Sacred Sound: Music in Religious Thought and Practice*, ed. by Joyce Irwin (Chico, CA: Scholars Press, 1983), pp. 21–34.

Alcorta, Candace C., 'Music and the Miraculous: The Neurophysiology of Music's Emotive Meaning', in *Miracles: God, Science, and Psychology in the Paranormal*, ed. by J. Harold Ellens, 3 vols (Westport, CT, and London: Praeger, 2008), III, pp. 230–52.

Allwood, Peter, 'UK's World-Renowned Sacred Music Tradition Faces Long-Term Sustainability Crisis, New Report Shows', *Cathedral Music Trust*, 2 October 2022, https://www.cathedralmusictrust.org.uk/CMT/CMT/News/Articles/UK%E2%80%99s-world-renowned-sacred-music-tradition-faces-sustainability-crisis-new-report-shows.aspx

Alter, Andrew, 'Expressing Sonic Theology: Understanding Ritual Action in a Himalayan Festival', *Ethnomusicology Forum* 28.3 (2019), 321–37, https://doi.org/10.1080/17411912.2020.1770115

Anderson, Benedict, *Imagined Communities: Reflections on the Origin and Spread of Nationalism*, rev. ed. (London: Verso, 1991).

Anselm, 'Proslogion', in *Anselm of Canterbury: The Major Works*, ed. by Brian Davies and Gillian Evans (Oxford: Oxford University Press, 2008), pp. 82–104.

Ansermet, Ernest, *Les fondments de la musique dans la conscience humanie et autres écrits* (Paris: Robert Lafont, 1989).

Appelqvist, Hanne, 'Philosophy of Language', in *The Oxford Handbook of Western Music and Philosophy*, ed. by Tomás McAuley and others (Oxford: Oxford University Press, 2020), pp. 360–83, https://doi.org/10.1093/oxfordhb/9780199367313.013.18

Arhoolie Foundation, 'SACRED STEEL' [41:43], online video recording, *YouTube*, 6 April 2020, https://www.youtube.com/watch?v=yRZS86tmvDA&t=2501s&ab_channel=ArhoolieFoundation

Arnold, Jonathan, *Experience of Music*, 2018, www.experienceofmusic.org

Ashbrook Harvey, Susan, *Scenting Salvation: Ancient Christianity and the Olfactory Imagination*, Transformation of the Classical Heritage 42 (Berkeley, CA: University of California, 2006), https://doi.org/10.1525/9780520931015

Astley, Jeff, *Ordinary Theology: Looking, Listening and Learning in Theology* (Aldershot: Ashgate, 2002), https://doi.org/10.4324/9781315247595

—, ed., *Creative Chords: Studies in Music, Theology and Christian Formation* (Leominster: Gracewing, 2000).

—, Timothy Hone, and Mark Savage, eds, *Creative Chords: Studies in Music, Theology and Christian Formation* (Leominster: Gracewing, 2000).

Attali, Jacques, *Noise: The Political Economy of Music* (Minneapolis, MN: University of Minnesota Press, 1985).

Augustine, *Confessions*, in *Saint Augustine Confessions*, trans. by Henry Chadwick (Oxford: Oxford University Press, 1991).

—, *Confessions Books 9 to 13*, ed. and trans. by Carolyn J. B. Hammond (Harvard, MA: Loeb Classical Library, 2016).

—, 'Contra Faustum Manichaeum', ed. by Philip Schaff and trans. by Richard Stothert, http://www.documentacatholicaomnia.eu/03d/0354-0430,_Augustinus,_Contra_Faustum_Manichaeum_%5BSchaff%5D,_EN.pdf

—, *On Genesis: A Refutation of the Manichees, Unfinished Literal Commentary on Genesis, The Literal Meaning of Genesis*, ed. by Boniface Ramsey and trans. by O.P. Hill (Hyde Park, NY: New City, 2004).

—, *St Augustine on the Psalms*, trans. by Scholastica Hebgin and Felicitas Corrigan, 2 vols (Westminster, MD: Newman Press, 1961), II.

—, 'Tractate 2', in *Tractates on the First Epistle of John*, trans. by John W. Rettig, The Fathers of the Church 92 (Washington, DC: Catholic University of America Press, 1995).

Ayres, Lewis, *Augustine and the Trinity* (Cambridge, UK: Cambridge University Press, 2010), https://doi.org/10.1017/CBO9780511780301

—, 'The Fundamental Grammar of Augustine's Trinitarian Theology', in *Augustine and His Critics: Essays in Honour of Gerald Bonner*, ed. by Robert Dodaro and George Lawless (London and New York: Routledge, 2000), pp. 51–76.

Bachorik, Douglas Jr, *Emotion in Congregational Singing: Music-Evoked Affect in Filipino Churches* (Durham, NC: Durham University Press 2019).

Baker, Lynne Rudder, *Naturalism and the First-Person Perspective* (Oxford: Oxford University Press, 2013).

Balthasar, Hans Urs von, *Theo-Drama: Theological Dramatic Theory* (San Francisco, CA: Ignatius Press, 1988).

—, 'Theology and Sanctity', in *Explorations in Theology, Vol. 1: Word Made Flesh*, trans by A. V. Littledale and Alexandre Dru (San Francisco: Ignatius Press, 1989), pp. 181–209.

Bangham, Benjamin, 'Letter to [Mary Tooth at Madeley]', 20 August 1829, Manchester, Methodist Archive, Fletcher-Tooth Collection, GB 135 MAM/FL/1/2/3.

Bar-Tal, Daniel, 'Societal Beliefs in Times of Intractable Conflict: The Israeli Case', *International Journal of Conflict Management* 9.1 (1998), 22–50, https://doi.org/10.1108/eb022803

Barbour, Ian, *Religion in an Age of Science* (San Francisco, CA: Harper and Row, 1990).

—, *Science and Religion: Historical and Contemporary Issues* (London: SCM Press, 1998).

—, *When Science Meets Religion: Enemies, Strangers, or Partners?* (San Francisco: HarperCollins, 2000).

Barlow, Helen, 'Praise the Lord! We Are a Musical Nation": The Welsh Working Classes and Religious Singing', *Nineteenth-Century Music Review* 17 (2020), 445–72, https://doi.org/10.1017/S1479409819000570

—, and Martin V. Clarke, 'Singing Welshness: Sport, Music and the Crowd', in *A History of Welsh Music*, ed. by Trevor Herbert, Martin V. Clarke, and Helen Barlow (Cambridge, UK: Cambridge University Press, 2022), pp. 332–54, https://doi.org/10.1017/9781009036511.018

Barrett-Rodger, Lewis, Sally Goldspink, and Hilary Engward, 'Being in the Wood: Using a Presuppositional Interview in Hermeneutic Phenomenological Research', *Qualitative Research* 23.4 (2022), 1062–77, https://doi.org/10.1177/14687941211061055

Barron, Robert, *The Strangest Way: Walking the Christian Path* (New York: Orbis Books, 2002).

—, *Vibrant Paradoxes: The Both/And of Catholicism*, 2nd ed. (Des Plaines, IL: Word on Fire, 2017).

Barth, Karl, *The Humanity of God* (Richmond, VA: John Knox, 1972).

Bartleet, Brydie-Leigh, and Carolyn Ellis, *Music Autoethnographies: Making Autoethnography Sing/Making Music Personal* (Bowen Hills: Australian Academic Press, 2010).

Bauerschmidt, Frederick Christian, *The Love That Is God: An Invitation to Christian Faith* (Grand Rapids, MI: Eerdmans, 2020).

Baumberger, Christoph, 'Art and Understanding: In Defence of Aesthetic Cognitivism', in *Bilder Sehen. Perspektiven Der Bildwissenschaft*, ed. by Mark Greenlee et al. (Regensburg: Schnell & Steiner, 2013), pp. 41–67.

Beach, David W., 'The Submediant as Third Divider: Its Representation at Different Structural Levels', in *Music Theory in Concept and Practice*, ed. by James M. Baker, David W. Beach, and Jonathan W. Bernard (Rochester, NY: University of Rochester Press, 1997), pp. 309–35.

Beatrice, Pier Franco, *The Transmission of Sin: Augustine and the Pre-Augustinian Sources*, trans. by Adam Kamesar (Oxford: Oxford University Press, 2013), https://doi.org/10.1093/acprof:oso/9780199751419.001.0001

Beck, Guy L., ed., *Experiencing Music in World Religions* (Ontario: Wilfrid Laurier University Press, 2006).

—, *Musicology of Religion: Theories, Methods, and Directions* (New York: State University of New York Press, 2023).

—, *Sonic Theology: Hinduism and Sacred Sound* (Charleston, SC: University of South Carolina Press, 1993).

Becker, Judith, *Deep Listeners: Music, Emotion, and Trancing* (Bloomington and Indianapolis, IN: Indiana University Press, 2004).

Begbie, Jeremy, *Abundantly More: The Theological Promise of the Arts in a Reductionist World* (Grand Rapids, MI: Baker Academic, 2023).

—, *Music, Modernity, and God: Essays in Listening* (Oxford: Oxford University Press, 2013), https://doi.org/10.1093/acprof:oso/9780199292448.001.0001

—, *Redeeming Transcendence in the Arts: Bearing Witness to the Triune God* (London: SCM Press, 2018).

—, and Steven Guthrie, eds, *Resonant Witness: Conversations between Music and Theology* (Grand Rapids, MI: W. B. Eerdmans, 2011).

—, *Resounding Truth: Christian Wisdom in the World of Music* (London: SPCK, 2008).

—, *Sounding the Depths: Theology through the Arts* (London: SCM Press, 2002).

—, *Voicing Creation's Praise: Towards a Theology of the Arts* (London: T&T Clark, 1991).

Bell, Richard, *The Theology of Wagner's Ring Cycle i: The Genesis and Development of the Tetralogy and the Appropriation of Sources, Artists, Philosophers, and Theologians* (Eugene, OR: Cascade, 2020), https://doi.org/10.2307/j.ctv1trhssh

Benson, Bruce E., *Liturgy as a Way of Life: Embodying the Arts in Christian Worship* (Grand Rapids, MI: Baker Academic, 2013).

Besson, Mireille, and Daniele Schön, 'Comparison Between Language and Music', in *The Cognitive Neuroscience of Music*, ed. by Isabelle Peretz and Robert Zatorre (Oxford: Oxford University Press, 2003), pp. 269–93, https://doi.org/10.1093/acprof:oso/9780198525202.003.0018

Bivins, Jason C., *Spirits Rejoice! Jazz and American Religion* (Oxford: Oxford University Press, 2015), https://doi.org/10.1093/acprof:oso/9780190230913.001.0001

Björgvinsson, Thröstur, et al., 'Psychometric Properties of the CES-D-10 in a Psychiatric Sample', *Assessment* 20.4 (2013), 429–36, https://doi.org/10.1177/1073191113481998

Blacking, John, *How Music is Man?* (Seattle, WA: University of Washington Press, 1973; London: Faber, 1976).

Blascovich, Jim, et al., 'Immersive Virtual Environment Technology as a Methodological Tool for Social Psychology', *Psychological Inquiry* 13.2 (2002), 103–24, https://doi.org/10.1207/s15327965pli1302_01

Boersma, Gerald P., *Augustine's Early Theology of Image: A Study in the Development of Pro-Nicene Theology* (Oxford: Oxford University Press, 2016), https://doi.org/10.1093/acprof:oso/9780190251369.001.0001

Boeve, Lieven, *God Interrupts History: Theology in a Time of Upheaval* (New York: Continuum, 2007).

Bohlman, Philip V., 'Is All Music Religious?', *Black Sacred Music* 8.1 (1994), 3–12.

Böhme, Gernot, *The Aesthetics of Atmospheres* (London & New York: Routledge, 2017), https://doi.org/10.4324/9781315538181

—, *Atmosfere, estasi, messe in scena. L'estetica come teoria generale della percezione* (Milano: Marinotti, 2010).

—, *Atmosphäre, Essays zur neuen Ästhetik* (Berlin: Suhrkamp, 2013).

Bonds, Mark Evan, *Absolute Music: The History of an Idea* (New York: Oxford University Press, 2014), https://doi.org/10.1093/acprof:oso/9780199343638.001.0001

Born, Georgina, 'On Musical Mediation: Ontology, Technology and Creativity', *Twentieth Century Music*, 2.1 (2005), 7–36, https://doi.org/10.1017/s147857220500023x

Bouteneff, Peter C., *Arvo Pärt: Out of Silence* (Yonkers, NY: SVS Press, 2015).

—, 'Music as Translation: The Movement from Text to Reception in Arvo Pärt's Music', online video recording, *YouTube*, 26 March 2020, https://www.youtube.com/watch?v=xTLAvEWaR1M

—, 'The Sound—and Hearing—of Arvo Pärt', in *Arvo Pärt: Sounding the Sacred*, ed. by Peter Bouteneff, Jeffers Engelhardt and Robert Saler (New York: Fordham University Press, 2021), pp. 8–21, https://doi.org/10.5422/fordham/9780823289752.003.0002

—, 'Tacit Texts: Considerations on Pärt's Settings of the Word', *Res Musica* 14 (2022), 76–81, https://dspace.ut.ee/items/68756333-9407-4652-b7a8-0d5755aa2f42/full

Bowie, Andrew, 'Music, Transcendence, and Philosophy', in *Music and Transcendence*, ed. by Férdia J. Stone-Davis (Burlington: Ashgate, 2015), pp. 213–23, https://doi.org/10.4324/9781315596709

Bowlby, Ewan, 'From Beaune to "Breaking Bad": Using the Arts to Meet Cancer Patients' Need and Desire for Spiritual Care' (unpublished doctoral thesis, University of St Andrews, 2022), https://doi.org/10.17630/sta/243

Boyce, Max, *Hymns & Arias: The Selected Poems, Songs and Stories* (Cardigan: Parthian Books, 2021).

—, 'Rugby World Cup 1999, Max Boyce, Hymns and Arias, Opening Ceremony', online video recording, *YouTube*, 26 June 2014, https://www.youtube.com/watch?v=O-EKY7z_jeE

Boyce-Tillman, June, *Experiencing Music—Restoring the Spiritual: Music and Well-Being* (Oxford: Peter Lang, 2016), https://doi.org/10.3726/978-3-0353-0801-3

—, *Freedom Song: Faith, Abuse, Music and Spirituality: A Lived Experience of Celebration* (Oxford: Peter Lang, 2018).

—, *In Tune with Heaven or Not: Women in Christian Liturgical Music* (Oxford: Peter Lang, 2014).

—, and Karin S. Henricks, eds, *Living Song—Singing, Spirituality and Wellbeing* (Oxford: Peter Lang, 2021).

—, Stephen Roberts, and Jane Erricker, eds, *Enlivening Faith: Music, Spirituality and Christian Theology* (Oxford: Peter Lang, 2019).

—, Liesl Van der Merwe, and Janelize Morelli, eds, *Ritualised Belonging: Musicking and Spirituality in the South African Context* (Oxford: Peter Lang, 2021).

Brabec de Mori, Bernd, 'Musical Spirits and Powerful Voices: On the Origins of Song', *Yearbook for Traditional Music* 49 (2017), 114–28, https://doi.org/10.5921/yeartradmusi.49.2017.0114

Bradley, Margaret M., and Peter J. Lang, 'Measuring Emotion: Behaviour, Feeling, and Physiology', in *The Cognitive Neuroscience of Emotion*, ed. by R. D. Lane and Lynn Nadel (Cary, NC: Oxford University Press, 2002), pp. 242–76, https://doi.org/10.1093/oso/9780195118889.003.0011

Braun, Virginia, and Victoria Clarke, *Thematic Analysis: A Practical Guide* (London: SAGE Publications, 2022).

Brauneiss, Leopold, 'Musical Archetypes: The Basic Elements of the Tintinnabuli Style', in *The Cambridge Companion to Arvo Pärt*, ed. Andrew Shenton (Cambridge, UK: Cambridge University Press, 2012), pp. 49–75, https://doi.org/10.1017/ccol9781107009899.005

Brennan, Brian, 'Augustine's *De Musica*', *Vigiliae Christianae* 42.3 (1988), 267–81, https://doi.org/10.2307/1584121

Brooke, John Hedley, *Science and Religion: Some Historical Perspectives* (Cambridge, UK: Cambridge University Press, 2014), https://doi.org/10.1017/cbo9781107589018

—, 'Science, Religion, and Historical Complexity', *Historically Speaking* 8 (2007), 10–13, https://doi.org/10.1353/hsp.2007.0028

Brown, David, and Gavin Hopps, *The Extravagance of Music* (Cham: Palgrave Macmillan, 2018), https://doi.org/10.1007/978-3-319-91818-1

Brown, Julie, *Schoenberg and Redemption* (Oxford: Oxford University Press, 2014), https://doi.org/10.1017/cbo9781139048934

Brown, Steven, 'A Joint Prosodic Origin of Language and Music', *Frontiers in Psychology* 8 (2017), 1894, https://doi.org/10.3389/fpsyg.2017.01894

—, and Joseph Jordania, 'Universals in the World's Musics', *Psychology of Music* 41.2 (2011), 229–48, https://doi.org/10.1177/0305735611425896

Bryan, Nicola, 'World Cup 2022: Wales' Qualification Revives Yma O Hyd Success', *BBC News*, 11 June 2022, https://www.bbc.co.uk/news/uk-wales-61757909

Bull, Michael, *Sound Moves: iPod Culture and Urban Experience* (New York: Routledge, 2007).

Bullack, Antje, et al., 'Psychobiological Effects of Choral Singing on Affective State, Social Connectedness, and Stress: Influences of Singing Activity and Time Course', *Frontiers in Behavioral Neuroscience* 12 (2018), 223, https://doi.org/10.3389/fnbeh.2018.00223

Burnham, Andrew, *Heaven and Earth in Little Space: The Re-Enchantment of the Liturgy* (Norwich: Canterbury Press 2010).

Buss, David M., 'Selection, Evocation, and Manipulation', *Journal of Personality and Social Psychology* 53.6 (1987), 1214–21, https://doi.org/10.1037/0022-3514.53.6.1214

Butler, Melvin L, *Island Gospel: Pentecostal Music and Identity in Jamaica and the United States* (Urbana, IL: University of Illinois Press, 2019), https://doi.org/10.5622/illinois/9780252042904.001.0001

—, 'Musical Style and Experience in a Brooklyn Pentecostal Church: An "Insider's" Perspective', *Current Musicology*, 70 (2000), 33–60.

—, '"Nou Kwe nan Sentespri" (We Believe in the Holy Spirit): Music, Ecstasy, and Identity in Haitian Pentecostal Worship', *Black Music Research Journal* 22.1 (2002), 85–125, https://doi.org/10.2307/1519966

—, 'Performing Pannkotis Identity in Haiti,' in *The Oxford Handbook of Music and World Christianities*, ed. by Suzel Ana Reily and Jonathan M. Dueck (New York: Oxford University Press, 2016), pp. 606–28, https://doi.org/10.1093/oxfordhb/9780199859993.013.26

—, 'Researching Black Congregational Music from a Migratory Point of View: Methods, Challenges, and Strategies', in *Studying Congregational Music: Key Issues, Methods, and Theoretical Perspectives*, ed. by Andrew Mall, Jeffers Engelhardt, and Monique Ingalls (New York: Routledge, 2021), https://doi.org/10.4324/9780429492020-13

Cameron, D. J., Jocelyn Bentley, and Jessica A. Grahn, 'Cross-Cultural Influences on Rhythm Processing: Reproduction, Discrimination, and Beat Tapping', *Frontiers in Psychology* 6 (2015), 366, https://doi.org/10.3389/fpsyg.2015.00366

Cameron, Lucinda, 'Churches Reopen for Communal Worship after Legal Victory', *Evening Standard*, 25 March 2021, https://www.standard.co.uk/news/uk/churches-catholic-church-court-of-session-scotland-government-b926255.html

Campbell, Heidi A., *The Distanced Church: Reflections on Doing Church Online* (Texas: Digital Religion Publishing & OakTrust-TAMU Libraries, 2020), https://doi.org/10.21423/distancedchurch

—, *Ecclesiology for a Digital Church: Theological Reflections on a New Normal*, ed. by Heidi A. Campbell and John Dyer (London: SCM Press, 2022).

Campbell Brothers, The, *Can You Feel It?* (Ropeadope, 2005).

Campesato, Claudio, *Allegoria modale* (Vienna: LIT Verlag, 2021).

Capps, Michael, 'Warld in a Roar: The Music of James MacMillan', *Image* 54 (2007), 95–108, https://imagejournal.org/article/warld-in-a-roar-the-music-of-james-macmillan/

Caputo, John D., and Michael J. Scanlon, eds, *Transcendence and Beyond: A Postmodern Enquiry* (Bloomington, IN: Indiana University Press, 2007).

Carhart-Harris, R. L., et al., 'The Entropic Brain: A Theory of Conscious States Informed by Neuroimaging', *Frontiers in Human Neuroscience* 8 (2014), 20, https://doi.org/10.3389/fnhum.2014.00020

Catechism of the Catholic Church, 2nd ed. (Vatican City: Libreria Editrice Vaticana, 2019).

Caton-Greasley, Chris, 'A Mapping Between Musical Notes and Colours', *Stalybridge Music Academy*, 20 June 2020, https://www.stalybridgemusicacademy.com/post/colours-and-keys

Cerkovnik, Esma, '...*Et nos immutabimur*'—*Music and Conversion in Rome in the First Half of the 17th Century* (Kassel: Merseburger, 2020).

Chauvet, Louis-Marie, *The Sacraments: The Word of God at the Mercy of the Body* (Collegeville, MN: Liturgical Press, 2001).

Chesterton, G. K., *Orthodoxy* (Mineola, NY: Dover, 2004).

Chirico, Alice, et al., 'Effectiveness of Immersive Videos in Inducing Awe: An Experimental Study', *Scientific Reports* 7.1 (2017), 1218, https://doi.org/10.1038/s41598-017-01242-0

Choate, Tova Leigh, William T. Flynn, and Margot Fassler, 'Hearing the Heavenly Symphony: An Overview of Hildegard's Musical Oeuvre with Case Studies', in *A Companion to Hildegard of Bingen*, ed. by Beverly Kienzle, Debra L. Stoudt, and George Ferzoco (Leiden: Brill, 2014), pp. 163–92, https://doi.org/10.1163/9789004260719_009

Choir of Magdalen College, The, 'The Choir of Magdalen College Oxford Sing Choral Evensong on Thursday...', online video recording, *Facebook*, 29 April 2019, https://www.facebook.com/watch/?v=370168640373718

Chown, Marcus, 'Big Bang Sounded Like a Deep Hum', *New Scientist*, 30 Oct 2003, https://www.newscientist.com/article/dn4320-big-bang-sounded-like-a-deep-hum/

Christian, David, Cynthia Stokes Brown, and Craig Benjamin, *Big History: Between Nothing and Everything* (New York: McGraw-Hill Education, 2014).

—, *Maps of Time: An Introduction to Big History* (Berkeley, LA: University of California Press, 2005), https://doi.org/10.1525/9780520931923

—, *Origin Story: A Big History of Everything* (London: Penguin, 2019).

The Church of England, *Cathedral Statistics, 2021* (London: Data Services, 2023), https://www.churchofengland.org/sites/default/files/2023-03/cathedral-statistics-2021.pdf

—, 'Church of England Cathedrals Showed Recovery in 2021 amid Covid-19 Measures', *The Church of England*, 24 March 2023, http://www.churchofengland.org/media-and-news/press-releases/church-england-cathedrals-showed-recovery-2021-amid-covid-19-measures

—, and Ken Eames, *Statistics for Mission 2021* (London: Data Services, 2022), https://www.churchofengland.org/sites/default/files/2023-01/2021-statistics-for-mission.pdf

Claire, Jean, 'Évolution modale des antiennes provenant de la corde-mère DO', *Revue grégorienne*, 41 (1963), 49–62.

—, 'Évolution modale des antiennes provenant de la corde-mère MI', *Revue grégorienne*, 41 (1963), 77–102.

—, 'L'évolution modale dans les répertoires liturgiques occidentaux', *Revue grégorienne*, 40 (1962), 196–245.

Clark, Eric, Nicola Dibben, and Stephanie Pitts, *Music and Mind in Everyday Life* (Oxford: Oxford University Press, 2010), https://doi.org/10.1093/acprof:oso/9780198525578.001.0001

—, *Ways of Listening: An Ecological Approach to the Perception of Musical Meaning* (Oxford: Oxford University Press, 2005).

Clarke, Imogen N., and Katherine Harding, 'Psychosocial Outcomes of Active Singing Interventions for Therapeutic Purposes: A Systematic Review of the Literature', *Nordic Journal of Music Therapy* 21.1 (2012), 80–98, https://doi.org/10.1080/08098131.2010.545136

Clarke, Martin V., '"And can it be": Analysing the Words, Music, and Contexts of an Iconic Methodist Hymn', *Yale Journal of Music & Religion* 2.1 (2016), 25–52, https://doi.org/10.17132/2377-231X.1023

—, *British Methodist Hymnody: Theology, Heritage, and Experience* (Abingdon: Routledge, 2018), https://doi.org/10.4324/9781315570181

Clarkson, Michael, *A Secret Life of Glenn Gould* (Toronto: ECW Press, 2010).

Clift, Stephen, et al., 'Group Singing, Wellbeing and Health: A Systematic Mapping of Research Evidence', *Unesco Observatory* 2.1 (2010), 1–25.

Cloninger, C. Robert, et al., 'The Temperament and Character Inventory (TCI): A Guide to Its Development and Use', *The Psychology of Religion*, 73.3 (n.d.), 1176–78.

Colish, Marcia, *The Mirror of Language: A Study of the Medieval Theory of Knowledge* (Lincoln, NE: University of Nebraska Press, 193).

Coltrane, John, *A Love Supreme* (Van Gelder Studio, 1965).

Comblin, José, *The Holy Spirit and Liberation* (Maryknoll, NY: Orbis Books, 1989).

Cooke, Phillip A., *The Music of James MacMillan* (Woodbridge: Boydell and Brewer, 2019), https://doi.org/10.2307/j.ctvb6v59w

Cooper-White, Pamela, *Schoenberg and the God-Idea: The Opera 'Moses and Aron'* (Ann Arbor, MI: UMI Research, 1985).

Congar, Yves, *I Believe in the Holy Spirit II: Lord and Giver of Life* (London: Chapman, 1983).

Corbett, George, 'Introduction', in *Annunciations: Sacred Music for the Twenty-First Century*, ed. by George Corbett (Cambridge, UK: Open Book Publishers, 2019), pp. 1–6, https://doi.org/10.11647/OBP.0172

—, and Sarah Moerman, 'Call for Papers: Music and Spiritual Realities International Workshop: EuARe 19–21 June 2023 at St Andrews', *University of St Andrews*, https://music-spirituality.wp.st-andrews.ac.uk/call-for-papers/

—, and Sarah Moerman, 'A Toolkit to Measure the Spiritual', *University of St Andrews*, https://music-spirituality.wp.st-andrews.ac.uk/a-toolkit-to-measure-the-spiritual/

Correggia, Enrico, 'Inaudite banalità sul Canto Gregoriano: ovvero della necessità di osservare sempre le piccole ovvietà', in *VII Ciclo di Studi Medievali. Atti del Convegno 7–10 giugno 2021* (Florence: NUME, 2021), pp. 623–27.

Cottingham, John, *The Spiritual Dimension: Religion, Philosophy and Human Value* (Cambridge, UK: Cambridge University Press, 2005), https://doi.org/10.1017/cbo9780511614866

Couenhoven, Jesse, *Stricken by Sin, Cured by Christ: Agency, Necessity, and Culpability in Augustinian Theology* (Oxford: Oxford University Press, 2013), https://doi.org/10.1093/acprof:oso/9780199948697.001.0001

Cowen, Alan S., et al., 'What Music Makes Us Feel: At Least 13 Dimensions Organize Subjective Experiences Associated with Music across Different Cultures', *Proceedings of the National Academy of Sciences* 117.4 (2020), 1924–34, https://doi.org/10.1073/pnas.1910704117

Coyne, Jerry, 'Yes, There Is a War between Science and Religion', *The Conversation*, 21 December 2018, https://theconversation.com/yes-there-is-a-war-between-science-and-religion-108002

Crawley, Ashon T, *Blackpentecostal Breath: The Aesthetics of Possibility* (New York: Fordham University Press, 2016), https://doi.org/10.5422/fordham/9780823274543.001.0001

Cross, Ian, 'The Evolutionary Basis of Meaning in Music: Some Neurological and Neuroscientific Implications', in *The Neurology of Music*, ed. by Frank Clifford Rose (London: Imperial College Press, 2010), pp. 1–15, https://doi.org/10.1142/9781848162693_0001

Crowe, Frederick E., 'Rethinking God-with-Us: Categories from Lonergan', *Science et Esprit* XVI.2 (1989), 167–88.

Czepiel, Anna, et al., 'Synchrony in the Periphery: Inter-Subject Correlation of Physiological Responses during Live Music Concerts', *Scientific Reports* 11.1 (2021), 1–16, https://doi.org/10.1038/s41598-021-00492-3

Dabney, D. Lyle, 'Starting with the Spirit: Why the Last Should Now Be First', in *Starting with the Spirit*, ed. by Stephen K. Pickard and Gordon R. Preece (Adelaide: Australian Theological Forum, 2001), pp. 3–27.

Dalhaus, Carl, *The Idea of Absolute Music* (Chicago, IL: University of Chicago Press, 1991).

—, 'Schoenberg's Aesthetic Theology', in Carl Dalhaus, *Schoenberg and the New Music* (Cambridge, UK: Cambridge University Press, 1999), pp. 81–93.

Dannecker, Klaus Peter, and Melanie Wald-Fuhrmann, 'Wirkungsästhetik: Ein neuer Ansatz für eine transdisziplinäre empirische Liturgieforschung', *Liturgisches Jahrbuch. Vierteljahreshefte für Fragen des Gottesdienstes* 68.2 (2018), 83–108.

Davies, Peter Maxwell, 'A Composer's Point of View (I): On Music, Mathematics and Magic Squares', in *Peter Maxwell Davies, Selected Writings*, ed. by Nicholas Jones (Cambridge, UK: Cambridge University Press, 2017), pp. 211–18, https://doi.org/10.1017/9781316662519.058

—, 'Correspondence with Roderic Dunnett', currently uncatalogued (British Library, London).

—, 'Davies to Dunnett', 16 August 1974 (British Library, London).

—, *Journal 21* (1955–56), *Journal 35* (1974), *Journal 2010–11* (British Library, London).

—, 'Letters to Gerard McBurney', Ms Mus 1779, October 1991 (British Library, London).

—, Personal communication with the author from McBurney, 17 March 1995 (British Library, London).

Davis, Ellen S., 'The Multi-Faceted Phenomenon of Congregational Song: An Interdisciplinary Exploration of Interpretive Influences' (unpublished doctoral thesis, Claremont Graduate University, Claremont, CA 1997).

Dawkins, Richard, *The God Delusion* (Boston, MA, and New York: Houghton Mifflin, 2008).

Day, Thomas, *Why Catholics Can't Sing: The Culture of Catholicism and the Triumph of Bad Taste*, rev. ed. (New York: Crossroad, 2013).

Dein, Simon, and Fraser Watts, 'Religious Worship Online: A Qualitative Study of Two Sunday Virtual Services', *International Association for the Psychology of Religion* 45.2 (2023), 191–209, https://doi.org/10.1177/008467242211453

De Vaus, David, et al., *Surveys in Social Research* (London: Taylor & Francis Group, 2013), https://doi.org/10.4324/9780203519196

de Villiers, Pieter G. R., 'Re-Enchanted by Beauty: On Aesthetics and Mysticism', *HTS Teologiese Studies/Theological Studies* 72.4 (2016), 1–7, https://doi.org/10.4102/hts.v72i4.3462

Dean and Chapter of Chelmsford, 'Cathedral Survey Results: Pandemic 2020–2021' (unpublished empirical study, Chelmsford Cathedral, 2021).

Del Grace, 'Gospel of Sacred Steel—the Campbell Brothers 2020' [16:24], online video recording, *YouTube*, 25 February 2020, https://www.youtube.com/watch?v=SGqaWjw1wyI&t=984s&ab_channel=DelGrace

DeNora, Tia, *Music Asylums: Wellbeing through Music in Everyday Life* (Burlington: Ashgate, 2013; Aldershot: Ashgate, 2015), https://doi.org/10.4324/9781315596730

—, 'Music as a Technology of the Self', *Poetics* 27.1 (1999), 31–56, https://doi.org/10.1016/s0304-422x(99)00017-0

—, *Music in Everyday Life* (Cambridge, UK: Cambridge University Press, 2000), https://doi.org/10.1017/cbo9780511489433

Derkse, Wil, 'Nice Work: Beauty and Transcendence as Factors in Scientific Practice', in *The Concept of Nature in Science and Theology, Part II*, ed. by Niels Henrik Gregersen, Michael W. S. Parsons and Christoph Wassermann (Geneva: Labor et Fides, S.A., 1996), pp. 47–55.

DeSalvo, Karen B., et al., 'Assessing Measurement Properties of Two Single-Item General Health Measures', *Quality of Life Research* 15.2 (2006), 191–201, https://doi.org/10.1007/s11136-005-0887-2

Desmond, William, *Being and the Between* (Albany, NY: State University of New York Press, 1995).

—, *Ethics and the Between* (New York: State University of New York Press, 2001).

—, *God and the Between* (Hoboken, NJ: Willey-Blackwell, 2008), https://doi.org/10.1002/9780470692509

Deutsch, Diana, 'Grouping Mechanisms in Music', in *The Psychology of Music*, ed. by Diana Deutsch (San Diego, CA: Elsevier, 2013), 299–348, https://doi.org/10.1016/b978-0-12-381460-9.00006-7

Devito, C., *Coltrane on Coltrane: The John Coltrane Interviews* (Chicago, IL: Chicago Review Press, 2012).

Dingle, Genevieve A., et al., 'An Agenda for Best Practice Research on Group Singing, Health, and Well-Being', *Music and Science* 2 (2019), 1–15, https://doi.org/10.1177/2059204319861719

Doherty, Seán, 'The Mass "Transubstantiated" into Music: Quotation and Allusion in James MacMillan's Fourth Symphony', *Music and Letters* 99.4 (2018), 635–671, https://doi.org/10.1093/ml/gcy072

Doody, John, Adam Goldstein, and Kim Paffenroth, eds, *Augustine and Science* (Lanham, MD: Lexington Books, 2012).

Dowling, W. Jay, and Dane L. Harwood, *Music Cognition* (Orlando, FL: Academic Press, 1986).

Doyle, Dennis M., *Communion Ecclesiology: Vision and Versions* (Maryknoll, NY: Orbis Books, 2000).

Draper, John William, *A History of the Conflict between Religion and Science* (New York: D. Appleton and Company, 1875).

Dryer, John, 'Exploring Mediated *Ekklesia*: How We Talk about Church in the Digital Age', in *Ecclesiology for a Digital Church: Theological Reflections on a New Normal*, ed. by Heidi A. Campbell and Dyer (London: SCM Press, 2022), pp. 3–16.

Dubay, Thomas, *The Evidential Power of Beauty: Science and Theology Meet* (San Francisco, CA: Ignatius Press, 1999).

Duby, Steven J., *Divine Simplicity: A Dogmatic Account* (London: Bloomsbury, 2015), https://doi.org/10.5040/9780567665706

Duda, Daniel, 'Adventist Identity—A Never-Ending Quest', paper presented at TED Bible Conference, Newbold College, Bracknell, 18 June 2019, https://ted.adventist.org/images/departments/Adventist_Identity_Bible_Conference-Duda.pdf

Dudley-Smith, Timothy, *A Functional Art: Reflections of a Hymn Writer* (Oxford: Oxford University Press, 2017).

Dueck, Jonathan, and Suzel Ana Reily, eds, *The Oxford Handbook of Music and World Christianities* (Oxford: Oxford University Press, 2013).

Dumbreck, Geoff, 'Head and Heart in Christian Theology', in *Head and Heart: Perspectives from Religion and Psychology*, ed. by Fraser N. Watts and Geoff Dumbreck (West Conshohocken, PN: Templeton Press, 2013), pp. 19–48.

Dunham, Scott A., *The Trinity and Creation in Augustine: An Ecological Analysis* (Albany, NY: State University of New York Press, 2008).

Dupuis, Darcy R, Roni Porat, and Michael J A Wohl, 'Collective Angst in Intractable Conflicts: How Concern for the Ingroup's Future Vitality Shapes Adversarial Intergroup Relations', in *The Social Psychology of Intractable Conflicts, Celebrating the Legacy of Daniel Bar-Tal, Volume I*, ed. by Eran Halperin and Keren Scharvit, Peace Psychology Book Series 27 (Cham: Springer, 2015), pp. 131–42, https://doi.org/10.1007/978-3-319-17861-5_10

Edelman, Joshua, Alana Vincent, et al., 'British Ritual Innovation under Covid-19' (Manchester Metropolitan University, 2021), https://www.mmu.ac.uk/research/projects/bric-19#:~:text=The%20project%20Social%20Distance%2C%20Digital,came%20together%20for%20ritual%20worship

Edwards, Denis, 'Story of a Theologian of the Natural World', in *God and the Natural World: Theological Explorations in Appreciation of Denis Edwards*, ed. by Ted Peters and Marie Turner (Adelaide: ATF Press, 2020), pp. 21–30, https://doi.org/10.2307/j.ctv19rs0rs.5

Elevation Worship, 'The Blessing with Kari Jobe & Cody Carnes', online video recording, *YouTube*, 6 March 2020, https://youtu.be/Zp6aygmvzM4

Elgin, Catherine Z., *Considered Judgment* (Princeton, NJ: Princeton University Press, 1996), https://doi.org/10.1515/9781400822294

Eliade, Mircea, *The Sacred and the Profane: The Nature of Religion* (New York: Harcourt Brace Jovanovich, 1987).

Endō, Shūsaku, *Silence*, trans. by William Johnston (London: Peter Owen, 1976).

Engward, Hilary, Sally Goldspink, Maria Iancu, Thomas Kersey and Abigail Wood, 'Togetherness in Separation: Practical Considerations for Doing Remote Qualitative Interviews Ethically,' *International Journal of Qualitative Methods*, 21 (2022). https://doi.org/10.1177/16094069211073212.

Epstein, Heidi, *Melting the Venusburg: A Feminist Theology of Music* (New York: Continuum, 2005).

Estonian World, 'Video: Björk Interviews Arvo Pärt', *Estonian World*, 16 July 2020, https://estonianworld.com/culture/video-bjork-interviews-arvo-part/

Etheridge, J. W., trans., *The Targums Onkelos and Jonathan Ben Uzziel*, 2 vols (London: Longman, Green, Longman, Roberts, 1862).

Fachner, Jörg, 'Time Is the Key: Music and Altered States of Consciousness', in *Altering Consciousness: A multidisciplinary Perspective*, ed. by Etzel Cardeña and Michael Winkelman, 2 vols (Santa Barbara: Praeger, 2011), I, pp. 355–76.

Fancourt, D., and R. Perkins, 'Effect of Singing Interventions on Symptoms of Postnatal Depression: Three-Arm Randomised Controlled Trial', *The British Journal of Psychiatry* 212.2 (2018), 119–21, https://doi.org/10.1192/bjp.2017.29

Fassler, Margot, 'Angels and Ideas: Hildegard's Musical Hermeneutic as Found in *Scivias* and Reflected in *O splendidissima gemma*', in *Unversehrt und Unverletzt: Hildegards von Bingen Menschenbild und Kirchenverständnis Heute*, ed. by Rainer Berndt and Maura Zátonyi (Münster: Aschendorff, 2015), pp. 189–212.

Faul, F., et al., 'Statistical Power Analyses Using G*Power 3.1: Tests for Correlation and Regression Analyses', *Behavior Research Methods* 41 (2009), 1149–60, https://doi.org/10.3758/brm.41.4.1149

Felski, Rita, *Hooked: Art and Attachment* (Chicago, IL: The University of Chicago Press, 2020), https://doi.org/10.7208/chicago/9780226729770.001.0001

—, *The Limits of Critique* (Chicago, IL: University of Chicago Press, 2015), https://doi.org/10.7208/chicago/9780226294179.001.0001

Fenner, Chris, and Brian G. Najapfour, eds, *Amazing Love! How can it be: Studies on Hymns by Charles Wesley* (Eugene, OR: Wipf and Stock, 2020).

Ferguson, Michael, 'Sacred Art Music in the Catholic Liturgy: Perspectives from the Roman Catholic Church in Scotland', in *Annunciations: Sacred Music for the Twenty-First Century*, ed. by George Corbett (Cambridge: Open Book Publishers, 2019), pp. 279–95, https://doi.org/10.11647/obp.0172.25

Ferreira, Daniela Abrants, and Paula Castro Pires de Souza Chimenti, 'Netnography: Unveiling Human Narratives in a Digital World', *Brazilian Journal of Marketing* 21.4 (2022), 1433–55, https://doi.org/10.5585/remark.v21i4.22726

Festinger, Leon, *A Theory of Cognitive Dissonance* (Stanford, CA: Stanford University Press, 1957), https://doi.org/10.1515/9781503620766

Fiddes, Paul S., *Participating in God: A Pastoral Doctrine of the Trinity* (Louisville, KY: Westminster John Knox Press, 2001).

Filippo, Chet, 'Willie Nelson: Holy Man of the Honky Tonks. The Saga of the King of Texas, from the Night Life to the Good Life', *Rolling Stone*, 13 July 1978, p. 66.

Finnegan, Ruth H., *The Hidden Musicians: Music-Making in an English Town* (Cambridge, UK: Cambridge University Press, 1989; Middletown, CT: Wesleyan University Press, 2007).

Fischer-Lichte, Erika, *The Transformative Power of Performance: A New Aesthetics*, trans. by Saskya I. Jain (London, New York: Routledge, 2008), https://doi.org/10.4324/9780203894989

Flynn, William T., 'Liturgical Music', in *The Oxford History of Christian Worship*, ed. by Geoffrey Wainwright and Karen B. Westerfield Tucker (Oxford: Oxford University Press, 2006), pp. 769–92.

—, 'Singing with the Angels: Hildegard of Bingen's Representations of Celestial Music', in *Conversations with Angels: Essays Towards a History of Spiritual Communication, 1100–1700*, ed. by Joad Raymond (London: Palgrave Macmillan, 2011), pp. 203–29, https://doi.org/10.1057/9780230316973_9

—, '"The Soul is Symphonic": Meditation on Luke 15:25 and Hildegard of Bingen's Letter 23', in *Music and Theology: Essays in Honor of Robin A. Leaver*, ed. by Daniel Zager (Lanham, MD: Scarecrow, 2007), pp. 1–8.

Fogleman, Alex, 'Becoming the Song of Christ: Musical Theology and Transforming Grace in Augustine's *Enarratio in Psalmum 32'*, *Augustinian Studies* 50.2 (2019), 93–116, https://doi.org/10.5840/augstudies201943051

Frame, John, *Contemporary Worship Music: A Biblical Defence* (Phillipsburg, NJ: P and R Publishing, 1997).

Kai R. Fricke, David M. Greenberg, Peter J. Rentfrow, and Philipp Y. Herzberg, 'Measuring Musical Preferences from Listening Behavior: Data from One Million People and 200,000 Songs', *Psychology of Music* 49.3 (2019), 371–81 https://doi.org/10.1177/0305735619868280

Fricke, Kai R., et al., 'Computer-Based Music Feature Analysis Mirrors Human Perception and can be Used to Measure Individual Music Preference', *Journal of Research in Personality* 75 (2018), 98–102, https://doi.org/10.1016/j.jrp.2018.06.004

Friedson, Steven M., *Remains of Ritual: Northern Gods in a Southern Land* (Chicago, IL: University of Chicago Press, 2009), https://doi.org/10.7208/chicago/9780226265063.001.0001

Gabrielsson, Alf, 'Emotions in Strong Experiences with Music' in *Handbook of Music and Emotion: Theory and Research*, ed. by Patrik N. Juslin and John A. Sloboda (Oxford: Oxford University Press, 2010), pp. 547–604, https://doi.org/10.1093/oso/9780192631886.003.0019

—, *Strong Experiences with Music: Music Is Much More than Just Music* (Oxford: Oxford University Press, 2011), https://doi.org/10.1093/acprof:oso/9780199695225.001.0001

—, and Wik, S. L., 'Strong Experiences Related to Music: A Descriptive System', *Musicae Scientiae* 7 (2003), 157–217, https://doi.org/10.1177/102986490300700201

Gadamer, Hans-Georg, 'Ästhetik und Hermeneutik (1964)', in Hans-Georg Gadamer, *Kunst Als Aussage* (Tübingen: J. C. B. Mohr (Paul Siebeck), 1993).

—, 'The Relevance of the Beautiful', in *The Relevance of the Beautiful and Other Essays*, ed. by Robert Bernasconi and trans. by Nicholas Walker (Cambridge, UK: Cambridge University Press, 1986), pp. 1–56.

—, *Truth and Method*, trans. by Joel Weinsheimer and Donald G. Marshall, 2nd rev. ed. (London: Sheed & Ward, 1989).

Gallope, M., *Deep Refrains: Music, Philosophy and the Ineffable* (Chicago, IL: Chicago University Press, 2017), https://doi.org/10.7208/chicago/9780226483726.001.0001

Gao, Junling, et al., 'The Neurophysiological Correlates of Religious Chanting' *Scientific Reports* 9.1 (2019), 4262, https://doi.org/10.1038/s41598-019-40200-w

—, et al., 'Repetitive Religious Chanting Invokes Positive Emotional Schema to Counterbalance Fear: A Multi-Modal Functional and Structural MRI Study', *Frontiers in Behavioral Neuroscience* 14 (2020), 548856, https://doi.org/10.3389/fnbeh.2020.548856

—, et al., 'Repetitive Religious Chanting Modulates the Late-Stage Brain Response to Fear- and Stress-Provoking Pictures', *Frontiers in Psychology* 7 (2017), 2055, https://doi.org/10.3389/fpsyg.2016.02055

Ghisalberti, Giosuè, 'Listening to Hymns and Tears of Mourning in Augustine's *Confessions*, Book 9', *Early Music* 43.2 (2015), 247–53, https://doi.org/10.1093/em/cav014

Gibson, James J., 'Theory of Affordances', in *The People, Place, and Space Reader*, ed. by Jen Jack Gieseking et al. (London: Routledge 2014), pp. 56–60.

Girardi, Luigi, ed., *Liturgia e emozione* (Rome: Studi di Liturgia, 2015).

Glattfelder, James B., *Information—Consciousness—Reality: How a New Understanding of the Universe Can help Answer Ago-Old Questions of Existence*, The Frontiers Collection (Cham: Springer Open, 2019), https://doi.org/10.1007/978-3-030-03633-1

Godøy, Rolf Inge, 'Intermittent Motor Control in Volitional Musical Imagery', in *Music and Mental Imagery*, ed. by Mats B. Küssner, Liila Taruffi, and Georgia A. Floridou (Abingdon: Routledge, 2023), pp. 42–53, https://doi.org/10.4324/9780429330070-5

Godwin, Joscelyn, *Harmonies of Heaven and Earth: Mysticism in Music from Antiquity to the Avant-Garde* (Rochester, VM: Inner Traditions International, 1987).

—, *The Harmony of the Spheres: A Sourcebook of the Pythagorean Tradition in Music* (Rochester, NY: VM, Inner Traditions International, 1993).

Goehr, Lydia, *The Imaginary Museum of Musical Works: An Essay in the Philosophy of Music* (Oxford: Oxford University Press, 2007), https://doi.org/10.1093/oso/9780195324785.001.0001

Goetz, Stewart, and Charles Taliaferro, *Naturalism* (Grand Rapids, MI: Eerdmans, 2008).

Gomart, Emilie, and Antoine Hennion, 'A Sociology of Attachment: Music Amateurs, Drug Users', *The Sociological Review*, 47.1 suppl. (1999), 220–47, https://doi.org/10.1111/j.1467-954x.1999.tb03490.x

Good, Arla, and Frank A. Russo, 'Singing Promotes Cooperation in a Diverse Group of Children', *Social Psychology*, 47.6 (2016), 340–44, https://doi.org/10.1027/1864-9335/a000282

Gorsuch, Richard L., and Sam G. McFarland, 'Single vs. Multiple-Item Scales for Measuring Religious Values', *Journal for the Scientific Study of Religion* 11.1 (1972), 53–64, https://doi.org/10.2307/1384298

Gosling, Samuel D., et al., 'A Room with a Cue: Personality Judgments Based on Offices and Bedrooms', *Journal of Personality and Social Psychology* 82.3 (2002), 379–98, https://doi.org/10.1037/0022-3514.82.3.379

Gould, Stephen Jay, 'Nonoverlapping Magisteria', *Natural History* 106 (1997), 16–22.

Graham, Nancy L., 'Spirituality by Heart', in *Living Song—Singing, Spirituality and Wellbeing*, ed. by June Boyce-Tillman and Karin S. Henricks (Oxford: Peter Lang, 2021), pp. 67–82.

—, *They Bear Acquaintance: African American Spirituals and the Camp Meetings* (Oxford: Peter Lang, 2017).

Grant, Morag J., 'The Illogical Logic of Music Torture', *Torture* 23.2 (2013), 4–13.

—, and Férdia J. Stone-Davis, *The Soundtrack of Conflict: The Role of Music in Radio Broadcasting in Wartime and in Conflict Situations* (Hildesheim: Olms Verlag, 2013), https://doi.org/10.5771/9783487423708

Greenberg, David M., 'How Music Can Break Social Barriers | Dr. David Greenberg | TEDxRamatAviv', online video recording, *YouTube*, 3 December 2021, https://www.youtube.com/watch?v=evVRxrOo5iw

—, and Peter J. Rentfrow, 'Music and Big Data: A New Frontier', *Current Opinion in Behavioral Sciences* 18 (2017), 50–56, https://doi.org/10.1016/j.cobeha.2017.07.007

—, and Peter J. Rentfrow, 'Rules of Engagement: The Structure of Musical Engagement and Its Personality Underpinnings', in *Proceedings of the Ninth Triennial Conference of the European Society for the Cognitive Sciences of Music*, ed. by J. Ginsborg, Alexandra Lamont, and Stephanie Bramley (Manchester: Royal Northern College of Music, 2015), pp. 408–11.

—, J. Decety, and I. Gordon, 'The Social Neuroscience of Music: Understanding the Social Brain through Human Song', *American Psychologist* 76.7 (2021), 1172–85, https://doi.org/10.1037/amp0000819

—, et al., 'The Self-Congruity Effect of Music', *Journal of Personality and Social Psychology* 121.1 (2020), 137–50, https://doi.org/10.1037/pspp0000293

—, et al., 'The Song Is You', *Social Psychological and Personality Science*, 7.6 (2016), 597–605, https://doi.org/10.1177/1948550616641473

—, et al., 'Universals and Variations in Musical Preferences: A Study of Preferential Reactions to Western Music in 53 Countries', *Journal of Personality and Social Psychology* 122.2 (2022), 286–309, https://doi.org/10.1037/pspp0000397

Greenhalgh, Trisha, et al., 'Ten Scientific Reasons in Support of Airborne Transmission of SARS-CoV-2', *The Lancet* 397.10285 (2021), 1603–05, https://doi.org/10.1016/S0140-6736(21)00869-2

Griffero, Tonino, *Atmosferologia. Estetica degli spazi emozionali* (Sesto San Giovanni, MI: Mimesis Edizioni, 2017).

Guest, Mathew, Sony Sharma, and Robert Song, *Gender and Career Progression in Theology and Religious Studies* (Durham: Durham University, 2013), https://www.durham.ac.uk/media/durham-university/departments-/theology-amp-religion/GenderCareerProgressioninTRS-ProjectReport.pdf

Gumbrecht, Hans Ulrich, *Atmosphere, Mood, Stimmung: On a Hidden Potential of Literature*, trans. by Erik Butler (Redwood City, CA: Stanford University Press, 2012), https://doi.org/10.1515/9780804783453

Gurd, Sean Alexander, *Dissonance: Auditory Aesthetics in Ancient Greece* (New York: Fordham University Press, 2016), https://doi.org/10.5422/fordham/9780823269655.001.0001

Guthrie, Steven R., 'Carmen Universitatis: A Theological Study of Music and Measure' (unpublished doctoral thesis, University of St Andrews, 2000).

Guthrie, Steve, and Bennett Zon, eds, *The Oxford Handbook of Music and Christian Theology*, 5 vols (Oxford: Oxford University Press, forthcoming)

Gutierrez, Katie, 'The Colors of Music', *Bright Star Musical*, 24 October 2022, https://web.archive.org/web/20221024225859/https://brightstarmusical.com/the-colors-of-music-do-musical-notes-have-color/

Hagedorn, Katherine J., *Divine Utterances: The Performance of Afro-Cuban Santería* (Washington, DC: Smithsonian Institution Press, 2001).

—, 'Toward a Theology of Sound', *Harvard Divinity Bulletin* 34.2 (2006), https://bulletin.hds.harvard.edu/toward-a-theology-of-sound/

—, '"Where the Transcendent Breaks into Time": Toward a Theology of Sound in Afro Cuban Regla de Ochá', in *Theorizing Sound Writing*, ed. by Deborah Kapchan (Middletown, CT: Wesleyan University Press, 2017).

Hagen, Edward H., and Gregory A. Bryant, 'Music and Dance as a Coalition Signaling System', *Human Nature* 14.1 (2003), 21–51, https://doi.org/10.1007/s12110-003-1015-z

Hall, Gill, 'Applying Psychological-Type Theory to Faith: Spirituality, Prayer, Worship and Scripture', *Mental Health, Religion & Culture* 15.9 (2012), 849–62.

Hallam, Susan, Ian Cross, and Michael Thaut, eds, *The Oxford Handbook of Music Psychology* (Oxford: Oxford University Press, 2008).

Halpern, Andrea R., 'Foreword', in *Music and Mental Imagery*, ed. by Matts B. Küssner, Liila Taruffi, and Georgia A. Floridou (London & New York: Routledge, 2023), https://doi.org/10.4324/9780429330070

Ham, Robert, 'Classic Album Review: Willie Nelson Turns Outlaw on the Seminal Red Headed Stranger', *Consequence*, 17 September 2019, https://consequence.net/2019/09/classic-album-review-willie-nelson-red-headed-stranger/

Hamel, P. Michael, *Through Music to the Self*, trans. by P. Lemesuer (Shaftesbury: Element Books, 1978).

Hamlin, Cynthia Lins, 'An Exchange between Gadamer and Glenn Gould on Hermeneutics and Music', *Theory, Culture & Society* 33.3 (2015), 103–22, https://doi.org/10.1177/0263276415576218

Hanby, Michael, *No God, No Science?: Theology, Cosmology, Biology* (Oxford: Wiley-Blackwell, 2013).

Hanslick, Eduard, *Vom Musikalisch-Schönen. Ein Beitrag zur Revision der Aesthetik der Kunst* (Leipzig: Rudolph Weigel, 1865).

Harnoncourt, Philipp, 'Gesang und Musik im Gottesdienst', in *Die Messe: Ein Kirchenmusikalisches Handbuch*, ed. by Harold Schützeichel (Düsseldorf: Patmos, 1991), pp. 9–25.

Harrison, Carol, 'Augustine and the Art of Music', in *Resonant Witness: Conversations between Music and Theology*, ed. by Jeremy Begbie and Steven Guthrie (Grand Rapids, MI: W. B. Eerdmans, 2011), pp. 27–45.

—, 'Getting Carried Away: Why Did Augustine Sing?', *Augustinian Studies* 46.1 (2015), 1–22, https://doi.org/10.5840/augstudies20154911

—, *On Music, Sense, Affect, and Voice* (New York: T&T Clark, 2019), https://doi.org/10.5040/9781501326295

Harrison, Peter, and Jon H. Roberts, *Science without God?: Rethinking the History of Scientific Naturalism* (Oxford: Oxford University Press, 2019), https://doi.org/10.1093/oso/9780198834588.001.0001

Harvey, Alan, *Music, Evolution, and the Harmony of Souls* (Oxford: Oxford University Press, 2017), https://doi.org/10.1093/acprof:oso/9780198786856.001.0001

Healy, Nicholas M., *Church, World, and the Christian Life: Practical-Prophetic Ecclesiology* (Cambridge, UK: Cambridge University Press, 2000), https://doi.org/10.1017/cbo9780511605857

Heaney, Maeve Louise, *Music as Theology: What Music Says About the Word* (Eugene, OR: Pickwick, 2012).

—, *Suspended God: Music and a Theology of Doubt* (London: Bloomsbury T&T Clark, 2022), https://doi.org/10.5040/9780567695642

Heelas, Paul, and Linda Woodhead, *The Spiritual Revolution: Why Religion Is Giving Way to Spirituality* (Malden, MA: Blackwell Publishing, 2005).

Heidegger, Martin, *Being and Time*, trans. by Joan Stambaugh, ed. and rev. by Dennis J. Schmidt (Albany, NY: State University of New York Press, 2010).

—, *Poetry, Language, Thought* (New York: Harper & Row, 1971).

—, *Sein und Zeit* (London: SCM Press, 1962).

—, and Wanda Torres Gregory, 'Traditional Language and Technological Language', *Journal of Philosophical Research*, 23 (1998), 129–145, https://doi.org/10.5840/jpr_1998_16

Heidenreich, Achim, and Wolfgang Rihm, '"Größtmögliche unschörfe": Wolfgang Rihm über das Komponieren, das Politische in der Musik und sein neues Bühnenstück *Das Gehege*: ein Gesprach mit Achim Heidenreich', *Neue Zeitschrift für Musik* 168.1 (2007), 10–13.

Heisenberg, Werner, *Physics and Philosophy: The Revolution in Modern Science* (New York: Harper, 1958).

Helboe Johansen, Kirstine, 'Analytical Strategies', in *The Wiley Blackwell Companion to Theology and Qualitative Research*, ed. by Knut Tveitereid and Pete Ward (Hoboken, NJ: Wiley-Blackwell, 2022), pp. 393–402, https://doi.org/10.1002/9781119756927.ch38

Hendricks, Karin, and June Boyce-Tillman, eds, *Queering Freedom: Music, Identity and Spirituality (Anthology with Perspectives from Over Ten Countries)* (Oxford: Peter Lang, 2018).

Henshall, Nicholas, 'The Dean's Letter for 5th February', online video recording, *Chelmsford Cathedral*, 5 February 2022, https://www.chelmsfordcathedral.org.uk/media-clips/the-deans-letter-for-5th-february

Herbert, Trevor, 'Popular Nationalism: Griffith Rhys Jones ("Caradog") and the Welsh Choral Tradition', in *Music and British Culture 1785–1914: Essays in Honour of Cyril Ehrlich*, ed. by Christina Bashford and Leanne

Langley (Oxford: Oxford University Press, 2000), pp. 255–74, https://doi.org/10.1093/oso/9780198167303.003.0012

Herder, Johann Gottfried, 'Kritische Wälder, oder Betrachtungen, die Wissenschaft und Kunst des Schönen Betreffend, Erstes Kritisches Wäldchen', in *Schriften zu Ästhetik und Literatur 1767–1781*, ed. by Gunter E. Grimm (Frankfurt am Main: Detscher Klassiker Verlag, 1993), pp.

Hesketh, Ian, 'The Story of Big History', *History of the Present* 4.2 (2014), 171–202, https://doi.org/10.5406/historypresent.4.2.0171

Hicks, Andrew, *Composing the World: Harmony in the Medieval Platonic Cosmos* (Oxford: Oxford University Press, 2017), https://doi.org/10.1093/acprof:oso/9780190658205.001.0001

Highland, Jim, 'Transformation to Eternity: Augustine's Conversion to Mindfulness', *Buddhist-Christian Studies* 25 (2005), 91–108, https://doi.org/10.1353/bcs.2005.0054

Higman, Anita, and Hillary McMullan, *Daily Grace for Daily Life: Encouragement for Women* (Uhrichsville, OH: Barbour, 2013).

Hildegard von Bingen, *The Personal Correspondence of Hildegard of Bingen*, ed. by Joseph L. Baird (Oxford: Oxford University Press, 2006), https://doi.org/10.1093/0195308220.001.0001

—, *Symphonia: A Critical Edition of the "Symphonia Armonie Celestium Revelationum" (Symphony of the Harmony of Celestial Revelations)*, ed. and trans. by Barbara Newman, second edition (Ithaca, NY: Cornell University Press, 1998), https://doi.org/10.7591/9781501711879

Hill, Barry, 'Why a Mixed Ecology Matters', *Church Times*, 12 November 2021, http://www.churchtimes.co.uk/articles/2021/12-november/comment/opinion/why-a-mixed-ecology-matters

Hillier, Paul, *Arvo Pärt* (Oxford: Oxford University Press, 1987).

Hogan, Patrick Colm, *Cognitive Science, Literature, and the Arts: A Guide for Humanists* (New York: Routledge, 2003), https://doi.org/10.4324/9780203475881

Holmes, Peter R., 'Spirituality: Some Disciplinary Perspectives', in *A Sociology of Spirituality*, ed. by Kieran Flanagan and Peter C. Jupp (Surrey: Ashgate, 2007), pp. 23–42.

Holy See, The, 'Francis', *Vatican.va*, https://www.vatican.va/content/vatican/en.html

Hölzel, Britta K., et al., 'How Does Mindfulness Meditation Work? Proposing Mechanisms of Action from a Conceptual and Neural Perspective', *Perspectives on Psychological Science* 6.6 (2011), 537–59, https://doi.org/10.1177/1745691611419671

Hood, Ralph W., and Leslie J. Francis, 'Mystical Experience: Conceptualizations, Measurement, and Correlates', in *APA Handbook of Psychology, Religion, and Spirituality i: Context, Theory, and Research*', ed. by Kenneth I. Pargament, Julie I. Exline, and James W. Jones (Washington, DC: American Psychological Assoc., 2013), pp. 391–405, https://doi.org/10.1037/14045-021

Horgan, John, 'What Thomas Kuhn Really Thought about Scientific "Truth"', *Scientific American*, 23 May 2012, https://blogs.scientificamerican.com/cross-check/what-thomas-kuhn-really-thought-about-scientific-truth/

Huang, Tina L., and Christine Charyton, 'A Comprehensive Review of the Psychological Effects of Brainwave Entrainment', *Alternative Therapies* 14.5 (2008), 38–50.

Hughes III, Robert Davis, 'Catching the Divine Breath in the Paschal Mystery: An Essay on the (Im)passibility of God, in Honor of Elizabeth Johnson', *Anglican Theological Review* 94.3 (2011), 527–39.

Hutto, Daniel D., 'Getting into Predictive Processing's Great Guessing Game: Bootstrap Heaven or Hell?', *Synthese* 195 (2018), 2445–58, https://doi.org/10.1007/s11229-017-1385-0

Hymns & Psalms (Peterborough: Methodist Publishing House, 1983).

Idler, Ellen L., et al., 'Looking Inside the Black Box of "Attendance at Services": New Measures for Exploring an Old Dimension in Religion and Health Research', *The International Journal for the Psychology of Religion* 19.1 (2009), 1–20, https://doi.org/10.1080/10508610802471096

IMG Artists, 'Yuanchan Lim', *IMG Artists*, https://imgartists.com/roster/yunchan-lim/

Ingalls, Monique M., *Singing the Congregation: How Contemporary Worship Music Forms Evangelical Community* (Oxford: Oxford University Press, 2018), https://doi.org/10.1093/oso/9780190499631.001.0001

—, Carolyn Landau, and Tom Wagner, eds, *Christian Congregational Music: Performance, Identity and Experience* (Abingdon: Routledge, 2013).

Ingarden, Roman, *The Work of Music and the Problem of Its Identity* (Berkeley, CA: University of California Press, 1986), https://doi.org/10.1007/978-1-349-09254-3

Irwin, Joyce, ed., *Sacred Sound: Music in Religious Thought and Practice* (Chico, CA: Scholars Press, 1983).

Iwaszkiewicz, Jarosław, 'Barkarola Chopina', in Jarosław Iwaszkiewicz, *Pisma muzyczne* (Warsaw: Czytelnik, 1958), pp. 522–27.

Jacobsson, Martin, and Lukas J. Dorfbauer, 'Introduction', in *Augustinus, De Musica*, ed. by Martin Jacobsson, Corpus Scriptorum Ecclesiasticorum Latinorum 102 (Berlin and Boston, MA: de Gruyter, 2017), pp. 1–10, https://doi.org/10.1515/9783110471465

Jacoby, Nori, et al., 'Universal and Non-Universal Features of Musical Pitch Perception Revealed by Singing', *Current Biology* 29.19 (2019), 3229–43.e12, https://doi.org/10.1016/j.cub.2019.08.020

James, Dylan, 'Wales Players and Fans Stay Behind to Sing National Anthem in Stunning Moment', *Wales Online*, 29 November 2022, https://www.walesonline.co.uk/sport/football/football-news/wales-players-fans-stay-behind-25635832

James, Jamie, *The Music of the Spheres: Music, Science, and the Natural Order of the Universe* (New York: Copernicus, 1993).

James, William, *Varieties of Religious Experience: A Study in Human Nature* (New York: Longmans, Green & Co, 1902; repr. London and New York: Routledge, 2002), https://doi.org/10.1037/10004-000

Jankélévitch, Vladimir, *Music and the Ineffable*, trans. by Carolyn Abbate (Princeton, NJ: Princeton University Press, 2003).

Jankowsky, Richard C., 'Music, Spirit Possession and the In-between: Ethnomusicological Inquiry and the Challenge of Trance', *Ethnomusicology Forum* 16.2 (2007), 185–208, https://doi.org/10.1080/17411910701554021

Jenkins, Eric L., *Free to Say No?: Free Will in Augustine's Evolving Doctrines of Grace and Election* (Eugene, OR: Wipf & Stock, 2012), https://doi.org/10.2307/j.ctt1cgf3nb

Jennings, Willie, *Acts* (Louisville, KY: Westminster John Knox, 2017).

Jenson, Robert W., 'Joining the Eternal Conversation: John's Prologue & the Language of Worship', *Touchstone Magazine*, November 2001, http://www.touchstonemag.com/archives/article.php?id=14-09-032-f

—, *Systematic Theology I: The Triune God* (New York: Oxford University Press, 1997).

Jeserich, Philipp, Michael J. Curley, and Steven Rendall, *Musica Naturalis: Speculative Music Theory and Poetics from Saint Augustine to the Late Middle Ages in France* (Baltimore, MD: Johns Hopkins University Press, 2013), https://doi.org/10.56021/9781421411248

Jirtle, James V., 'Using Music Well: Reassessing Perception in Augustine's *De Musica*', *Augustiniana* 60.3–4 (2010), 263–81.

John Templeton Foundation, 'Sir John Templeton 1912–2008', *John Templeton Foundation*, https://www.templeton.org/about/sir-john

Johnson, Julian, *After Debussy: Music, Language, and the Margins of Philosophy* (Oxford: Oxford University Press, 2020), https://doi.org/10.1093/oso/9780190066826.001.0001

Johnson, Mark, *The Meaning of the Body: Aesthetics of Human Understanding* (Chicago, IL: Chicago University Press, 2007).

Jokela, Markus, et al., 'Geographically Varying Associations between Personality and Life Satisfaction in the London Metropolitan Area', *Proceedings of the National Academy of Sciences* 112.3 (2015), 725–30, https://doi.org/10.1073/pnas.1415800112

Joncas, Jan Michael, *From Sacred Song to Ritual Music: Twentieth-Century Understandings of Roman Catholic Worship Music* (Collegeville, MN: The Liturgical Press, 1997).

Jones, Alisha Lola, *Flaming? The Peculiar Theopolitics of Fire and Desire in Black Male Gospel Performance* (Oxford: Oxford University Press, 2020).

Jones, Cheslyn, Geoffrey Wainwright, and Edward Yarnold, eds, *The Study of Spirituality* (London: SPCK, 1986).

Jones, Jaime, 'Music, History, and the Sacred in South Asia', in *The Cambridge History of World Music*, ed. by Philip V. Bohlman (Cambridge, UK: Cambridge University Press, 2013), pp. 202–22, https://doi.org/10.1017/cho9781139029476.012

Jones, Nicholas, 'Analytical Perspectives on the Third Symphony of Peter Maxwell Davies' (unpublished doctoral thesis, Cardiff University, 1999).

Judiciary of Scotland, 'Judgement Summaries: Success of Churches in Court of Session Action', *Judiciary of Scotland*, 24 March 2021, https://judiciary.scot/home/sentences-judgments/judgments/2021/03/24/success-of-churches-in-court-of-session-action

Jüngel, Eberhard, '»Auch das schöne Muß Sterben«—Schönenheit im Lichte der Wahrheit. Theologische Bermerkungen zum Ästhetischen Verhältnis', in Eberhard Jüngel, *Wertlose Wahrheit: zur Identität und Relevanz des Christlichen Glaubens*, Theologische Erörterungen 3 (Tübingen: J. C. B. Mohr (Paul Siebeck), 2003).

Juslin, Patrick N., 'Emotional Responses to Music', in *The Oxford Handbook of Music Psychology*, ed. by Susan Hallam et al. (Oxford: Oxford University Press, 2008), pp. 131–40, https://doi.org/10.1093/oxfordhb/9780199298457.013.0012

—, 'From Everyday Emotions to Aesthetic Emotions: Towards a Unified Theory of Musical Emotions', *Physics of Life Review*, 10.3 (2013), 235–66, https://doi.org/10.1016/j.plrev.2013.05.008

Kaiser, Jochen, *Singen in Gemeinschaft als ästhetische Kommunikation: Eine ethnographische Studie* (Berlin: Springer, 2017), https://doi.org/10.1007/978-3-658-17711-9

Kang, Jing, et al., 'Review of the Physiological Effects and Mechanisms of Singing', *Journal of Voice* 32.4 (2017), 390–95, https://doi.org/10.1016/j.jvoice.2017.07.008

Kant, Immanuel, *Critique of the Power of Judgment*, ed. by Paul Guyer and trans. by Eric Matthews, The Cambridge Edition of the Works of Immanuel Kant (Cambridge, UK: Cambridge University Press, 2000), https://doi.org/10.1017/cbo9780511804656

Kaplan, Grant, *Faith and Reasons throughout Christian History: A Theological Essay* (Washington, DC: The Catholic University of America Press, 2022), https://doi.org/10.2307/j.ctv3006zqb

Kärkkäinen, Veli-Matti, *Pneumatology: The Holy Spirit in Ecumenical, International, and Contextual Perspective* (Grand Rapids, MI: Baker Academic, 2002).

Kearney, Richard, and Jens Zimmerman, eds, *Reimagining the Sacred: Richard Kearney Debates God* (New York: Columbia University Press, 2013), https://doi.org/10.7312/columbia/9780231161039.001.0001

Keeler, Jason R., et al., 'The Neurochemistry and Social Flow of Singing: Bonding and Oxytocin', *Frontiers in Human Neuroscience* 9 (2015), 518, https://doi.org/10.3389/fnhum.2015.00518

Keltner, Dacher, and Jonathan Haidt, 'Approaching Awe, a Moral, Spiritual, and Aesthetic Emotion', *Cognition & Emotion* 17.2 (2003), 297–314, https://doi.org/10.1080/02699930302297

Kerner, Hanns, *Die Kirchenmusik: Wahrnehmungen aus zwei neuen empirischen Untersuchungen unter evangelisch Getauften in Bayern* (Nürnberg: Gottesdienst-Institut der Evangelisch-Lutherischen Kirche in Bayern, 2008).

Kerr, Fergus, *Immortal Longings: Versions of Transcending Humanity* (London: SPCK, 1997).

Khan, Hazrat Inayat, *Mysticism of Sound* (London: Pilgrims Publishing, 1923).

Kilmartin, Edward, *Christian Liturgy: Theology and Practice i: Systematic Theology of Liturgy* (Kansas City, MO: Sheed and Ward, 1988).

Kimbrough, Jr, S. T., *The Lyrical Theology of Charles Wesley: A Reader* (Eugene, OR: Cascade, 2013), https://doi.org/10.2307/j.ctt1cgdz67

King, Kathryn, 'Tranquility, Transcendence, and Retreat: The Transformative Practice of Listening at Evensong' (unpublished doctoral thesis, University of Oxford, 2021), https://ora.ox.ac.uk/objects/uuid:0772a6ce-d68e-4356-af39-dfab545ee108

Koch, Anne, 'Epistemology', in *The Bloomsbury Handbook of the Cultural and Cognitive Aesthetics of Religion*, ed. by Koch and Katharina Wilkens (London: Bloomsbury Academic, 2020), pp. 23–32, https://doi.org/10.5040/9781350066748.ch-003

Korsyn, Kevin Ernest, 'The Aging of the New Musicology', in *Approaches to Music Research: Between Practice and Epistemology*, ed. by Leon Stefanija and Nico Schüler (Frankfurt am Main: Peter Lang, 2011), pp. 9–23.

—, *Decentering Music: A Critique of Contemporary Musical Research* (Oxford, UK: Oxford University Press, 2003), https://doi.org/10.1093/acprof:oso/9780195104547.001.0001

Kotzé, Annemaré, 'Structure and Genre of the Confessions', in *The Cambridge Companion to Augustine's 'Confessions'*, ed. by Tarmo Toom (Cambridge,

UK: Cambridge University Press, 2020), pp. 28–45, https://doi.org/10.1017/9781108672405.004

Kramer, Lawrence, *Expression and Truth: On the Music of Knowledge* (Berkeley, CA: University of California Press, 2012).

—, *Music as Cultural Practice, 1800–1900* (Berkeley, CA: University of California Press, 1990), https://doi.org/10.1525/9780520354555

—, *Musical Meaning: Towards a Critical History* (Berkeley, CA: University of California Press, 2002), https://doi.org/10.1525/9780520928329

Kreutz, Gunter, 'Does Singing Facilitate Social Bonding?', *Music and Medicine* 6.2 (2014), 51–60, https://doi.org/10.47513/mmd.v6i2.180

Kropf, Marlene, and Kenneth James Nafziger, *Singing: A Mennonite Voice* (Scottdale, PA: Herald Press, 2011).

Kuang, Lanlan, '(Un)consciousness? Music in the Daoist Context of Nonbeing', *Music and Consciousness 2: Worlds, Practices, Modalities*, ed. by Ruth Herbert, David Clarke, and Eric Clarke (New York: Oxford University Press, 2019), pp. 306–23, https://doi.org/10.1093/oso/9780198804352.003.0018

Küng, Hans, *The Church* (New York: Sheed and Ward, 1968).

Kunst, Jaap, *Musicologica: A Study of the Nature of Ethnomusicology, Its Problems, Methods, and Representative Personalities* (Amsterdam: Indisch Instituut, 1950).

Labriola, Christina, 'Recalling the Original Harmony of Paradise: The Nexus of Music, Ethics, and Spirituality in Hildegard of Bingen's "Ordo Virtutum"', in *Music, Theology, and Justice*, ed. by Michael O'Connor, Hyun-Ah Kim, and Christina Labriola (Lanham, MD: Rowman and Littlefield, 2017), pp. 163–79.

Ladinig, Olivia, et al., 'Enjoying Sad Music: A Test of the Prolactin Theory', *Musicae Scientiae*, 25 (2021), 429–48, https://doi.org/10.1177/1029864919890900

Ladouceur, Paul, 'Old Testament Prefigurations of the Mother of God', *St Vladimir's Theological Quarterly* 50.1–2 (2006), 5–57.

Lamont, Alexandra, 'Emotion, Engagement and Meaning in Strong Experiences of Music Performance', *Psychology of Music* 40.5 (2012), 574–94, https://doi.org/10.1177/0305735612448510

—, 'University Students' Strong Experiences of Music: Pleasure, Engagement, and Meaning' *Musicae Scientiae*, 15.2 (2011), 229–49, https://doi.org/10.1177/1029864911403368

Lane, Belden C., 'Writing in Spirituality as a Self-Implicating Act: Reflections on Authorial Disclosure and the Hiddenness of the Self,' in *Exploring Christian Spirituality: Essays in Honor of Sandra M. Schneiders*, ed. by Bruce H. Lescher and Elizabeth Liebert (New York: Paulist Press, 2006), pp. 53–69.

Lang, Martin, Panagiotis Mitkidis, Radek Kundt, Aaron Nichols, Len Krajčiková, and Dimitris Xygalatas, 'Music As a Sacred Cue?: Effects of Religious Music on Moral Behavior', *Frontiers in Psychology* 7 (2016), 814, https://www.frontiersin.org/articles/10.3389/fpsyg.2016.00814/full

Lawrence, Frederick G., 'Grace and Friendship: Postmodern Political Theology and God as Conversational', *Gregorianum* 85.4 (2004), 795–820.

Lawson, Hilary, '21st Century Metaphysics: Leaving Fantasy Behind', *Institute of Art and Ideas News*, 23 January 2023, https://iai.tv/articles/21st-century-metaphysics-leaving-fantasy-behind-auid-2367

Lazic, Tihomir, '*Ecclesia Semper Migranda*: Towards a Vision of a Migrant Church for Migrants', in *The Church, Migration, and Global (In)Difference*, ed. by Darren J. Dias et al. (New York: Palgrave Macmillan, 2021), pp. 241–61, https://doi.org/10.1007/978-3-030-54226-9_14

—, *Towards an Adventist Version of Communio Ecclesiology: Remnant in Koinonia*, ed. by Gerard Mannion and Mark Chapman, Pathways for Ecumenical and Interreligious Dialogue (Basingstoke: Palgrave Macmillan, 2019), https://doi.org/10.1007/978-3-030-25181-9

Le Guin, Elisabeth, *Boccherini's Body: An Essay in Carnal Musicology* (Berkeley, CA: University of California Press, 2005), https://doi.org/10.1525/9780520930629

Leibniz, Gottfried Wilhelm, 'Principles of Nature and of Grace, Founded on Reason', in Gottfried Wilhelm Leibniz, *Monadology and Other Philosophical Writings* (London: Oxford University Press, 1925), pp. 405–24.

Leonard, Neil, *Jazz: Myth and Religion* (Oxford: Oxford University Press, 1987).

Levitin, Daniel, *This Is Your Brain on Music: Understanding a Human Obsession* (London: Atlantic Books, 2007).

Levy, Jonathan, et al., 'Adolescents Growing up amidst Intractable Conflict Attenuate Brain Response to Pain of Outgroup', *Proceedings of the National Academy of Sciences* 113.48 (2016), 13696–701, https://doi.org/10.1073/pnas.1612903113

Lightman, Bernard, 'Introduction', in *Rethinking History, Science and Religion: An Exploration of Conflict and the Complexity Principle*, ed. by Bernard Lightman (Pittsburgh, PA: University of Pittsburgh Press, 2019), pp. 3–16, https://doi.org/10.2307/j.ctvqc6h4s

Lindberg, David C., 'The Medieval Church Encounters the Classical Tradition: Saint Augustine, Roger Bacon, and the Handmaiden Metaphor', in *When Christianity & Science Meet*, ed. by David C. Lindberg and Ronald L. Numbers (Chicago, IL: University of Chicago Press, 2003), pp. 7–32.

Lindemann, Gesa, and David Schünemann, 'Presence in Digital Spaces: A Phenomenological Concept of Presence in Mediatized Communication', *Human Studies*, 43 (2020), 627–51, https://doi.org/10.1007/s10746-020-09567-y

Liston, Gregory J., *The Anointed Church: Toward a Third Article Ecclesiology* (Minneapolis, MN: Fortress Press, 2015), https://doi.org/10.2307/j.ctt13wwwxb

Lonergan, Bernard J. F., *Insight*, ed. by F. E. Crowe and R. M. Doran, Collected Works of Bernard Lonergan 3 (Toronto: University of Toronto Press, 1957).

—, *Method in Theology* (New York: The Seabury Press, 1972).

—, 'Mission and the Spirit', in *Collected Works of Bernard Lonergan: A Third Collection*, ed. by Robert M. Doran and John D. Dadosky (Toronto: University of Toronto Press, 1985), pp. 21–33.

—, 'Theology in Its New Context', in *A Second Collection. Papers by Bernard J. F. Lonergan S.J.*, ed. by F. J. Ryan and B. J. Tyrell (London: Darton, Longman and Todd, 1974), pp. 55–68, https://doi.org/10.3138/9781442623231-007

Louth, Andrew, *Discerning the Mystery: An Essay on the Nature of Theology* (Oxford: Oxford University Press, 1989), https://doi.org/10.1093/acprof:oso/9780198261964.001.0001

Ludwig, Arnold M., 'Altered States of Consciousness', *Archives of General Psychiatry* 15.3 (1966), 225–34, https://doi.org/10.1001/archpsyc.1966.01730150001001

Lysik, David, et al., eds, *The Liturgy Documents: A Parish Resource*, 4th ed. (Chicago, IL: Liturgy Training Publications, 2004).

MacLachlan, Heather, 'Burmese Buddhist Monks, the Seventh Precept, and Cognitive Dissonance', *Asian Music* 53.1 (2022), 34–55, https://doi.org/10.1353/amu.2022.0002

James MacMillan, 'Divine Accompaniment', *Guardian*, 18 July 2003, https://www.theguardian.com/music/2003/jul/19/classicalmusicandopera.artsfeatures

—, 'The Most Spiritual of the Arts: Music, Modernity, and the Search for the Sacred', in *Annunciations: Sacred Music for the Twenty-First Century*, ed. by George Corbett (Cambridge, UK: Open Book Publishers, 2019), pp. 9–16, https://doi.org/10.11647/obp.0172.01

—, *Symphony No. 3: 'Silence'* (London: Boosey & Hawkes, 2002).

—, *Symphony No.5: 'Le grand Inconnu' (The Great Unknown)* (London: Boosey & Hawkes, 2018), https://www.boosey.com/cr/music/James-MacMillan-Symphony-No-5-Le-grand-Inconnu/102048

Mall, Andrew, Jeffers Engelhardt, and Monique M. Ingalls, eds, *Studying Congregational Music: Key Issues, Methods, and Theoretical Perspectives* (Abingdon: Routledge, 2021).

Malloch, Stephen, and Colyen Trevarthen, 'The Human Nature of Music', *Frontiers of Psychology* 9 (2018), 1680, https://doi.org/10.3389/fpsyg.2018.01680

Manders, Elspeth, and Anonymous Participants, 'Listening to the Lived Experiences of Worshippers: Planning and Implementing a Mixed Ecology Worship following the Covid-19 Pandemic' (January–March 2023), audio.

Mann, Thomas, *Doctor Faustus*, trans. by John E. Wood (New York: Vintage Books, 1999).

Manning, Russell Re, 'Unwritten Theology: Notes Towards a Natural Theology of Music', in *Music and Transcendence*, ed. by Férdia J. Stone-Davis (Burlington: Ashgate, 2015), pp. 65–73.

Margry, Peter Jan, and Daniel Wojcik, 'A Saxophone Divine: Experiencing the Transformative Power of Saint John Coltrane's Jazz Music in San Francisco's Fillmore District', in *Spiritualizing the City: Agency and Resilience of the Urban and Urbanesque Habitat*, ed. by Victoria Hegner and Margry (London: Routledge, 2017), pp. 169–94, https://doi.org/10.4324/9781315680279-20

Margulis, Elizabeth Hellmuth, *On Repeat: How Music Plays the Mind* (New York: Oxford University Press, 2014), https://doi.org/10.1093/acprof:oso/9780199990825.001.0001

Martin, Andy, 'Bye, Bye, Bye Delilah: Wales Rugby Choirs Banned from Singing Tom Jones Hit', *Guardian*, 1 February 2023, https://www.theguardian.com/sport/2023/feb/01/delilah-welsh-rugby-union-choirs-banned-from-singing-tom-jones-hit

Martin, Luther H., et al., eds, *Technologies of the Self: A Seminar with Michel Foucault* (London: Tavistock, 1988).

Mashek, Debra, Lisa W. Cannaday, and June P. Tangney, 'Inclusion of Community in Self Scale: A Single-Item Pictorial Measure of Community Connectedness', *Journal of Community Psychology* 35.2 (2007), 257–75, https://doi.org/10.1002/jcop.20146

Maslow, A. H., *The Farther Reaches of Human Nature* (New York: Viking Press, 1971).

—, *Religions, Values, and Peak-Experiences* (n.p.: Rare Treasure Editions, 1964).

Mathiesen, Thomas J., 'Harmonia and Ethos in Ancient Greek Music', *The Journal of Musicology* 3.3 (1984), 264–79, https://doi.org/10.2307/763816

Matthews, Aidan, 'The Arts and Spirituality', speech given at the Manresa Jesuit Retreat Centre, Dublin, August 2007.

Matz, S. C., et al., 'Psychological Targeting as an Effective Approach to Digital Mass Persuasion', *Proceedings of the National Academy of Sciences* 114.48 (2007), 12714–19, https://doi.org/10.1073/pnas.1710966114

Maxfield, Melinda C., 'Effects of Rhythmic Drumming on EEG and Subjective Experience' (unpublished doctoral thesis, Institute of Transpersonal Psychology, 1990), https://www.proquest.com/dissertations-theses/effects-rhythmic-drumming-on-eeg-subjective/docview/303885457/se-2

McAllester, David P., *Enemy Way Music: A Study of Social and Esthetic Values as Seen in Navaho Music* (Cambridge, MA: Peabody Museum of American Archaeology and Ethnology, 1954).

McCabe, Herbert, *God Matters* (London: Chapman, 1987), https://doi.org/10.5040/9781472965967

McClendon, James Wm., Jr, *Biography as Theology: How Life Stories Can Remake Today's Theology* (Nashville, TN: Abingdon Press, 1974).

McCord Adams, Marilyn, 'Anselm on Faith and Reason', in *The Cambridge Companion to Anselm*, ed. by Brian Davies and Brian Leftow (Cambridge, UK: Cambridge University Press, 2004), pp. 32–60, https://doi.org/10.1017/ccol0521807468.003

McCrae, Robert R., and Oliver P. John. 'An Introduction to the Five-Factor Model and Its Applications', *Journal of Personality* 60.2 (1992), 175–215, https://doi.org/10.1111/j.1467-6494.1992.tb00970.x

McDermott, Josh H., et al., 'Indifference to Dissonance in Native Amazonians Reveals Cultural Variation in Music Perception', *Nature* 535.7613 (2016), 547–50, https://doi.org/10.1038/nature18635

McGann, Mary E., 'Interpreting the Ritual Role of Music in Christian Liturgical Practice' (unpublished doctoral thesis, Graduate Theological Union, Berkeley, CA, 1996).

McGilchrist, Iain, *The Master and His Emissary: The Divided Brain and the Making of the Western World* (New Haven, CT: Yale University Press, 2012).

McGrath, Alister, *The Territories of Human Reason: Science and Theology in an Age of Multiple Rationalities* (Oxford: Oxford University Press, 2009), https://doi.org/10.2307/j.ctvcb5c0t

McGregor, Richard, 'Hunting and Forms: An interview with Wolfgang Rihm' in *Contemporary Music: Theoretical and Philosophical Perspectives*, ed. by Max Paddison and Irène Deliège (Farnham: Ashgate Publishing Limited, 2010), pp. 349–60, https://doi.org/10.4324/9781315573885-28

—, 'James MacMillan's *O Bone Jesu*', *Scottish Music Review* 2.1 (2011), 88–114.

—, '"Laus Deo?" On Composers' Expression of their Spirituality', *Spirituality and Health International* 6.4 (2005), 238–45, https://doi.org/10.1002/shi.22

—, '"Songs That Seem to Come from Nowhere": Composition: Inspiration and Spirituality May Share a Common Root, but Can We Talk about Them in the Same Breath?' (unpublished keynote lecture, Music and Spirituality conference, Middlesex University, 20 May 2022).

—, 'Transubstantiated into the Musical: A Critical Exegesis on James MacMillan's "Veni Veni Emmanuel"', in *A Companion to Recent Scottish Music: 1950 to the Present*, ed. by Graham Hair (Glasgow: The Musica Scotica Trust, 2007), pp. 21–42.

McGuire, Meredith B., 'Mapping Contemporary American Spirituality: A Sociological Perspective', *Christian Spirituality Bulletin* 5 (1997), 175–82.

McKinnon, James W., 'Christian Church, Music of the Early', in *Grove Music Online*, rev. Martin V. Clarke (2001), https://doi.org/10.1093/gmo/9781561592630.article.05705

McLeish, Tom, *The Poetry and Music of Science* (Oxford: Oxford University Press, 2019), https://doi.org/10.1093/oso/9780198797999.001.0001

Mehr, Samuel A., et al., 'Form and Function in Human Song', *Current Biology* 28.3 (2018), 356–68.e5, https://doi.org/10.1016/j.cub.2017.12.042

—, et al., 'Origins of Music in Credible Signaling', *Behavioral and Brain Sciences*, 44 (2020), e60, https://doi.org/10.1017/s0140525x20000345

—, et al., 'Universality and Diversity in Human Song', *Science* 366.6468 (2019), eaax0868, https://doi.org/10.1126/science.aax0868

Merriam, Alan P., *The Anthropology of Music* (Evanston, IL: Northwestern University Press, 1964).

Merrill, Julia, et al., 'The Aesthetic Experience of Live Concerts: Self-Reports and Psychophysiology', *Psychology of Aesthetics, Creativity, and the Arts* 17.2 (2021), 134–51, https://doi.org/10.1037/aca0000390

Methodist Church, The, 'Born in Song', *The Methodist Church*https://www.methodist.org.uk/about-us/the-methodist-church/what-is-distinctive-about-methodism/born-in-song

The Methodist Hymn Book (London: Methodist Conference Office, 1933).

Metz, Johann Baptist, *Faith in History and Society: Toward a Practical Fundamental Theology*, ed. and trans. by Norman David Smith (London: Burns and Oates, 1980).

Midgley, Mary, *Heart & Mind: The Varieties of Moral Experience* (London: Methuen, 1983).

Miller, Mandi M., and Kenneth T. Strongman, 'The Emotional Effects of Music on Religious Experience: A Study of the Pentecostal-Charismatic Style of Music and Worship', *Psychology of Music* 30.1 (2002), 8–27, https://doi.org/10.1177/0305735602301004

Mitchelmore, Ian, 'The Amazing Rendition of the Anthem Wales Fans Have Been Waiting to Sing for 64 Years', *Wales Online*, 21 November 2022, https://www.walesonline.co.uk/sport/football/football-news/amazing-rendition-anthem-wales-fans-25571439

Mithen, Steven J., *The Singing Neanderthals: The Origins of Music, Language, Mind and Body* (London: Phoenix, 2006).

Moltmann, Jürgen, *God in Creation: A New Theology of Creation and the Spirit of God* (San Francisco, CA: Harper San Francisco, 1991).

—, *The Spirit of Life: A Universal Affirmation* (Minneapolis, MN: Fortress Press, 1992).

Montague, Michael J., *The Science of Music and the Music of Science: How Music Reveals Our Brain, Our Humanity and the Cosmos* (St Louis, MO: Cosmic Music, 2019).

Morgan, Rick L., and David Heise, 'Structure of Emotions', *Social Psychology Quarterly* 51.1 (1988), 19–31.

Morley, Iain, *The Prehistory of Music: Evolutionary Origins and Archaeology of Human Musicality* (Oxford: Oxford University Press, 2013), https://doi.org/10.1093/acprof:osobl/9780199234080.001.0001

Morris, Seren, 'Hen Wlad Fy Nhadau: What do the Welsh national anthem lyrics mean?', *Evening Standard*, 28 November 2022, https://www.standard.co.uk/news/uk/hen-wlad-fy-nhadau-welsh-national-anthem-lyrics-meaning-football-world-cup-sport-wales-vs-england-b1043125.html

Mosch, Ulrich, ed., *Ausgesprochen Schriften und Gespräche*, 2 vols (Winterthur: Schott 1997).

Murdoch, Iris, *Sovereignty of the Good* (London: Routledge, 1970).

Musa, Bala A., and Boye-Nelson Kiamu, 'Digital Technology and Mediating the Pneuma in Church Outreach', in *Ecclesiology for a Digital Church: Theological Reflections on a New Normal*, ed. by Heidi A. Campbell and John Dyer (London: SCM Press, 2022), pp. 117–29.

Nadal, Amber R. C., Sam A. Hardy, and Carolyn McNamara Barry, 'Understanding the Roles of Religiosity and Spirituality in Emerging Adults in the United States', *Psychology of Religion and Spirituality* 10.1 (2018), 30–43, https://doi.org/10.1037/rel0000104

Nave, Gideon et al., 'Musical Preferences Predict Personality: Evidence From Active Listening and Facebook Likes', *Psychological Science* 29.7 (2018), 1145–58 https://doi.org/10.1177/0956797618761659

Nash, Graham, 'Wild Tiles', *And So It Goes* (Atlantic Records, 1974).

Nattiez, Jean-Jacques, *Music and Discourse. Toward a Semiology of Music* (Princeton, NJ: Princeton University Press, 1990).

Needham, Rodney, 'Percussion and Transition', *Man* 2.4 (1967), 606–14, https://doi.org/10.2307/2799343

Neher, Andrew, 'Auditory Driving Observed with Scalp Electrodes in Normal Subjects', *Electroencephalography and Clinical Neurophysiology* 13.3 (1961), 449–51, https://doi.org/10.1016/0013-4694(61)90014-1

Nelson, Kristina, *The Art of Reciting the Qur'an* (Cairo: American University in Cairo Press, 1985), https://doi.org/10.7560/703674

Nelson, Paul, 'Hemingway, Who Perfected', *Rolling Stone*, 28 August 1975.

Nelson, Willie, and Bud Shrake, *Willie: An Autobiography* (New York: Cooper Square Press, 1988).

Nettl, Bruno, Ruth M. Stone, James Porter, and Timothy Rice, eds, *Garland Encyclopedia of World Music*, 10 vols (New York: Routledge, 1998–2002).

Neusner, Jacob, *Judaism's Theological Voice: The Melody of the Talmud* (Chicago, IL: University of Chicago Press, 1995).

Newbigin, Lesslie, *The Open Secret: An Introduction to the Theology of Mission* (Grand Rapids, MI: Eerdmans, 1995).

Newport, Kenneth G. C., and Ted A. Campbell, eds, *Charles Wesley: Life, Literature and Legacy* (Peterborough: Epworth, 2007).

Noll, Mark A., *Protestantism: A Very Short Introduction* (Oxford: Oxford University Press, 2011), https://doi.org/10.1093/actrade/9780199560974.001.0001

—, 'Chaotic Coherence: *Sola Scriptura* and the Twentieth-Century Spread of Christianity', in *Protestantism after 500 Years,* ed. by Thomas Albert Howard and Mark A. Noll (Oxford: Oxford University Press, 2016), pp. 258–80.

Norris, John, 'Augustine and Sign in Tractatus in Iohannis Evangelium', in *Augustine: Biblical Exegete*, ed. by Frederick Van Fleteren and Joseph C. Schnaubelt (New York: Peter Lang, 2004), pp. 215–32.

Norwid, Cyprian K., 'Chopin's Grand Piano', trans. by Teresa Bałuk, *Visegrad Literature,* https://www.visegradliterature.net/works/pl/Norwid%2C_Cyprian_Kamil-1821/Fortepian_Szopena/en/1593-Chopin_s_Grand_Piano

Nussbaum, Martha C., 'Love's Knowledge', in Martha C. Nussbaum, *Love's Knowledge: Essays on Philosophy and Literature* (New York: Oxford University Press, 1990), pp. 261–85.

—, *Upheavals of Thought: The Intelligence of Emotions* (Cambridge: Cambridge University Press, 2001), https://doi.org/10.1017/cbo9780511840715

Ockelford, Adam, *Comparing Notes: How We Make Sense of Music* (London: Profile, 2017).

Oermann, Robert, *Behind the Grand Ole Opry Curtain: Tales of Romance and Tragedy* (New York: Center Street, 2008).

Olsen, Dale A., 'Shamanism, Music and Healing in Two Contrasting South American Cultural Areas', in *The Oxford Handbook of Medical Ethnomusicology*, ed. by Benjamin D. Koen (Oxford: Oxford University Press, 2008), pp. 331–60, https://doi.org/10.1093/oxfordhb/9780199756261.013.0014

Ondas, Riku, *Honeybees and Distant Thunder* (New York: Doubleday, 2023).

Ortiz, John M., *The Tao of Music: Sound Psychology Using Music to Change Your Life* (Boston, MA: Weiser Books, 1987).

Owens, Peter, 'Revelation and Fallacy: Observations on Compositional Technique in the Music of Peter Maxwell Davies', *Music Analysis* 13 (1994), 161–202, https://doi.org/10.2307/854258

Page, Christopher, *The Christian West and Its Singers: The First Thousand Years* (New Haven, CT: Yale University Press, 2010).

Parsons, Thomas D., 'Virtual Reality for Enhanced Ecological Validity and Experimental Control in the Clinical, Affective and Social Neurosciences', *Frontiers in Human Neuroscience* 9 (2015), 600, https://doi.org/10.3389/fnhum.2015.00660

Pat-Horenczyk, Ruth, et al., 'Posttraumatic Symptoms, Functional Impairment, and Coping among Adolescents on Both Sides of the Israeli–Palestinian Conflict: A Cross-Cultural Approach', *Applied Psychology* 58.4 (2009), 688–708, https://doi.org/10.1111/j.1464-0597.2008.00372.x

Patterson, W. M., *Northern Primitive Methodism: A Record of the Rise and Progress of the Circuits in the Old Sunderland District* (London: E. Dalton, 1909).

Pearce, Eiluned, et al., 'The Ice-Breaker Effect: Singing Mediates Fast Social Bonding', *Royal Society Open Science* 2.10 (2015), 150221, https://doi.org/10.1098/rsos.150221

Peltola, Henna-Riikka, and Tuomas Eerola, 'Fifty Shades of Blue: Classification of Music-Evoked Sadness', *Musicae Scientiae* 20 (2016), 84–102, https://doi.org/10.1177/1029864915611206

Pérès, Marcel, and Jacques Cheyronnaud, *Les voix du plain-chant* (Paris: Desclé de Brouwer, 2001).

Peretz, Isabelle, and Robert Zatorre, eds, *The Cognitive Neuroscience of Music* (Oxford: Oxford University Press, 2003).

Perrin, Ruth, and Ed Olsworth-Peter, 'The Mixed Ecologists; Experiences of Mixed Ecology Ministry in the Church of England' (The Church of England, May 2021), https://www.churchofengland.org/sites/default/files/2021-05/focussed-study-2-the-mixed-ecologists.pdf

Pfleiderer, Martin, 'Sound Und Rhythmus in Populär Musik. Analysemethoden, Darstellungsmöglichkeiten, Interpretationsansätze', in *Die Bedeutung Populärer Musik in Audiovissuellen Formaten*, ed. by Christofer Jost et al. (Baden-Baden: Nomos Verlagsgesellschaft, 2009), pp. 175–95, https://doi.org/10.5771/9783845220604-175

Piedmont, Ralph L., 'Does Spirituality Represent the Sixth Factor of Personality? Spiritual Transcendence and the Five-Factor Model', *Journal of Personality* 67.6 (1999), 985–1013, https://doi.org/10.1111/1467-6494.00080

Pinker, Steven, *How the Mind Works* (New York: Norton, 2009).

Pinson, DovBer, *Inner Rhythms: The Kabbalah of Music* (Northvale, NJ: Jason Aronson, 2000).

Pirsig, Robert M., *Lila: An Inquiry into Morals* (New York: Bantam Books, 1991).

—, *On Quality: An Inquiry into Excellence: Unpublished and Selected Writings*, ed. by Wendy K. Pirsig (New York: HarperCollins, 2022).

—, *Zen and the Art of Motorcycle Maintenance: An Inquiry into Values* (London: Vintage, 1974).

Plantinga, Alvin, 'Science: Augustinian or Duhemian?', *Faith and Philosophy* 13.3 (1996), 368–94, https://doi.org/10.5840/faithphil19961335

Podmore, Simon D., 'Introduction Transforming Presence: Incarnation between Transcendence and Immanence', in *Christian Mysticism and Incarnational Theology: Between Transcendence and Immanence*, ed. by Louise Nelstrop and Podmore (Farnham: Ashgate Publishing Limited, 2013), https://doi.org/10.4324/9781315571898

Polkinghorne, John, *Science and Theology: An Introduction* (London and Minneapolis, MN: SPCK/Fortress Press, 1998).

Pontifical Council for Social Communications, 'The Church and Internet', *Vatican.va*, 28 February 2002, https://www.vatican.va/roman_curia/pontifical_councils/pccs/documents/rc_pc_pccs_doc_20020228_church-internet_en.html

Post, P. G. J., 'From Identity to Accent: The Ritual Studies Perspective of Fields of the Sacred', *Pastoraltheologische Informationen* 33.1 (2013), 149–58.

Powers, Ann, 'God, Drugs and Lizard Aliens: Yep, It's Country Music', *The Record*, 17 April 2014, https://www.npr.org/sections/therecord/2014/04/17/304075384/god-drugs-and-lizard-aliens-yep-its-country-music

Preston, Geoffrey, *Faces of the Church: Meditations on a Mystery and its Images* (Edinburgh: T&T Clark, 1997).

Prins, Jacomien, and Maude Vanhaelen, *Sing Aloud Harmonious Spheres: Renaissance Conceptions of Cosmic Harmony* (Routledge: Abingdon and New York, 2019), https://doi.org/10.4324/9781315161037

Pritchett, James, *The Music of John Cage* (Cambridge, UK: Cambridge University Press, 1993).

Proust, Marcel, *In Search of Lost Time*, trans. by C.K. Scott Moncrieff (New York: Modern Library Edition, 1992).

Quinn, Barbara, 'Leading to the Edge of Mystery: The Gift and the Challenge', *Spiritus: A Journal of Christian Spirituality* 22 (2022), 3–19, https://doi.org/10.1353/scs.2022.0001

Qureshi, Regula Burckhardt, *Sufi Music of India and Pakistan: Sound, Context and Meaning in Qawwali* (Cambridge, UK: Cambridge University Press, 1986).

Rahner, Karl, 'Anonymous and Explicit Faith', in *Theological Investigations*, ed. and trans. by David Morland, 23 vols (London: Darton, Longman and Todd, 1979), XVI, 52–59.

—, *Hearers of the Word* (London: Herder and Herder, 1969).

—, 'Prayer for Creative Thinkers', in *Theological Investigations*, ed. and trans. by D. Bourke, 23 vols (London: Darton, Longman and Todd, 1971), VIII, 130–31.

—, 'Reflections on the Experience of Grace', in *Theological Investigations*, ed. and trans. by Karl H. Kruger and Boniface Kruger, 23 vols (London: Darton, Longman & Todd, 1967), III, 86–90.

—, *Spirit in the World*, trans. William Dych (London: Sheed & Ward, 1968).

Raichle, Marcus E., and Abraham Z. Snyder, 'A Default Mode of Brain Function: A Brief History of an Evolving Idea', *NeuroImage* 37 (2007), 1083–90, https://doi.org/10.1016/j.neuroimage.2007.02.041

Rampi, Fulvio, and Alessandro De Lillo, *Nella mente del notatore. Semiologia gregoriana a ritrorso* (Rome: Città del Vaticano, Libreria Editrice Vaticana, 2019).

Ratzinger, Joseph, *Called to Communion: Understanding the Church Today* (San Francisco, CA: Ignatius Press, 1996).

—, 'On the Theological Basis of Church Music', in *Collected Works: Theology of the Liturgy Volume 11*, ed. by Michael J. Miller and trans. by John Saward et al. (San Francisco, CA: Ignatius Press, 2014), pp. 421–42.

Reeves, Josh A., 'Science and Christianity: The Three Big Questions', *Journal of Biblical and Theological Studies* 2.2 (2017), 157–69.

Rehding, Alexander, and Suzannah Clark, *Music Theory and Natural Order from the Renaissance to the Early Twentieth Century* (Cambridge, UK: Cambridge University Press, 2001).

Rentfrow, Peter J., and Samuel D. Gosling, 'The Do Re Mi's of Everyday Life: The Structure and Personality Correlates of Music Preferences', *Journal of Personality and Social Psychology* 84.6 (2003), 1236–56, https://doi.org/10.1037/0022-3514.84.6.1236

—, 'The Role of Music in Everyday Life: Current Directions in the Social Psychology of Music', *Social and Personality Psychology Compass* 6 (2012), 402–16, https://doi.org/10.1111/j.1751-9004.2012.00434.x

Rice, Richard, 'The Trinitarian Basis of Christian Community', in *Biblical and Theological Studies on the Trinity*, ed. by Paul Petersen and Rob McIver (Adelaide: Avondale Academic Press, 2014), pp. 101–12, https://doi.org/10.2307/j.ctt163t9hn.11

Richards, Chris, 'Sturgill Simpson: A Country Voice of, and out of, This World', *The Washington Post*, 17 March 2014, https://www.washingtonpost.com/lifestyle/style/sturgill-simpson-a-country-voice-of-and-out-of-this-world/2014/03/31/46277cce-b8f9-11e3-899e-bb708e3539dd_story.html

Rihm, Wolfgang, 'De Profundis', *Universal Edition*, 2015, https://www.universaledition.com/wolfgang-rihm-599/works/de-profundis-16963

Rijken, Hanna, et al., 'The "Anglican Virus:" The Emergence of Anglican Music in the Netherlands', *Jahrbuch für Liturgik und Hymnologie* 54 (2015), 131–52, https://doi.org/10.13109/9783666572258.131

—, *My Soul Doth Magnify: The Appropriation of Anglican Choral Evensong in the Netherlands* (Amsterdam: Vu Press, 2020).

Ringer, Alexander L., *Arnold Schoenberg: The Composer as Jew* (Oxford: Clarendon, 1990), https://doi.org/10.2307/947439

Riva, Giuseppe, et al., 'Affective Interactions Using Virtual Reality: The Link between Presence and Emotions', *Cyberpsychology & Behavior* 10.1 (2007), 45–56, https://doi.org/10.1089/cpb.2006.9993

Robins, Richard W., Holly M. Hendin, and Kali H. Trzesniewski, 'Measuring Global Self-Esteem: Construct Validation of a Single-Item Measure and the Rosenberg Self-Esteem Scale', *Personality and Social Psychology Bulletin* 27.2 (2001), 151–61, https://doi.org/10.1177/0146167201272002

Rommen, Timothy, *Mek Some Noise: Gospel Music and the Ethics of Style in Trinidad* (Berkeley, CA: University of California Press, 2007), https://doi.org/10.1525/9780520940543

Roof, Wade Clark, *Spiritual Marketplace* (Princeton, NJ: Princeton University Press, 1999), https://doi.org/10.1515/9781400823086

Rosa, Hartmut, *Resonance: A Sociology of the Relationship to the World* (Medford, MA: Polity Press, 2019).

—, *The Uncontrollability of the World*, trans. by James C. Wagner (Cambridge, UK: Polity Press, 2020).

Ross, Alex, 'Consolations: Arvo Pärt', *The New Yorker*, 2 December 2002, https://www.therestisnoise.com/2004/04/arvo_prt_1.html

Rouget, Gilbert, *Music and Trance: A Theory of the Relations between Music and Possession*, trans. by B. Biebuyck (Chicago, IL: University of Chicago Press, 1985).

Roulston, Kathryn, *Interviews in Qualitative Research* (London: John and Wiley Sons, 2012).

Ruff, Anthony, *Sacred Music and Liturgical Reform: Treasures and Transformations* (Chicago, IL: Hillenbrand, 2007).

Sachs, Curt, *The Rise of Music in the Ancient World: East and West* (New York: Dent, 1943).

Sarbadhikary, Sukanya, 'Hearing the Transcendental Place: Sound, Spirituality and Sensuality in the Musical Practices of an Indian Devotional Order', in *Music and Transcendence*, ed. by Férdia J. Stone-Davis (Burlington: Ashgate, 2015), pp. 23–34.

Saulnier, Daniel, *Les modes grégoriens* (Solesmes: Éditions de Solesmes, 1997).

Savage, Patrick E., et al., 'Music as a Coevolved System for Social Bonding', *Behavioral and Brain Sciences* 44 (2020), e59, https://doi.org/10.1017/s0140525x20000333

Sawicki, Bernard, 'Chorał gregoriański—dziedzictwo coraz bardziej ... problematyczne?', *Teofil* 1.41 (2024), 81–105

—, *W chorale jest wszystko* (Kraków: Tyniec Wydawnictwo Benedyktynów, 2014).

—, 'Music and Spiritual Realities International Workshop (University of St Andrews, 19th-21st June 2023) The Main Topics and Outlook: the Perspective of New Horizon of the Sacre Music', *Ecclesia orans*, 41 (2024), 155-77.

Scarnati, Blase S., 'Religious Doctrine in the Mid-1970s to 1980s Country Music Concept Albums of Willie Nelson', in *Walking the Line: Country Music Lyricists and American Culture*, ed. by Thomas Alan Holmes and Roxanne Harde (Lanham, MD: Lexington Books, 2013), pp. 65–76.

Schaefer, Edward, *Catholic Music Through the Ages: Balancing the Needs of a Worshipping Church* (Chicago, IL: Hillenbrand, 2008).

Schafer, R. Murray, *Soundscape: Our Sonic Environment and the Tuning of the World* (Rochester, VT: Destiny Books, 1977).

Schiller, Friedrich, 'Über die Ästhetische Erziehung des Menschen', in Friedrich Schiller, *Briefen Werke* (Stuttgart and Tübingen: Gottaschen Buchhandlung, 1959).

Schirr, Bertram J., 'The Body We Sing: Reclaiming of the Queer Materiality of Vocal Bodies', in *Queering Freedom: Music, Identity and Spirituality (Anthology with Perspectives from Over Ten Countries)*, ed. by Karin Hendricks and June Boyce-Tillman (Oxford: Peter Long, 2018), pp. 35–52.

Schleiermacher, Friedrich, *Christmas Eve: Dialogue on the Incarnation*, trans. by Terrence N. Tice (Lewiston, NY: John Knox Press, 1990).

Schmitz, Hermann, *Atmosphären* (Freiburg and Munich: Karl Alber, 2014), https://doi.org/10.5771/9783495860441

Schneiders, Sandra M., 'Approaches to the Study of Christian Spirituality', in *The Blackwell Companion to Christian Spirituality*, ed. by Arthur Holder (Malden, MA: Blackwell, 2005), pp. 15–34, https://doi.org/10.1002/9780470996713.ch2

—, 'The Study of Christian Spirituality: Contours and Dynamics of a Discipline', *Studies in Spirituality* 8 (1998), 38–57, https://doi.org/10.2143/sis.8.0.2004088

Schoenberg, Arnold, *Style and Idea: Selected Writings of Arnold Schoenberg*, trans. by Leo Black (New York: St Martin's Press, 1975).

—, *Theory of Harmony*, trans. by Roy E. Carter (London: Faber and Faber, 1978).

Schubert, Emery, 'Affective, Evaluative and Collative Responses to Hated and Loved Music', *Psychology of Aesthetics, Creativity, and the Arts* 4.1 (2010), 36–46, https://doi.org/10.1037/a0016316

Schultz, Anna, *Singing a Hindu Nation: Marathi Devotional Performance and Nationalism* (New York: Oxford University Press, 2013).

Schutte, Dan, *Mass of Christ the Savior* (Portland, OR: Oregon Catholic Press, 2013).

Schwartz, Shalom H., and Sipke Huismans, 'Value Priorities and Religiosity in Four Western Religions', *Social Psychology Quarterly* 58.2 (1995), 88–107, https://doi.org/10.2307/2787148

Science of Colour, 'Tonality of Colors in Painting', *Science of Colour*, https://sites.google.com/site/scienceofcolour/tonality-of-colors-in-painting

Scruton, Roger, 'Music and the Transcendental', in *Music and Transcendence*, ed. by Férdia J. Stone-Davis (Burlington: Ashgate, 2015), pp. 75–84.

—, *The Soul of the World* (Princeton, NJ: Princeton University Press, 2014), https://doi.org/10.1515/9781400850006

—, 'Sounds as Secondary Objects and Pure Events', in *Sounds & Perception: New Philosophical Essays*, ed. by Matthew Nudds and Casey O'Callaghan (Oxford: Oxford University Press, 2009), pp. 50–69, https://doi.org/10.1093/acprof:oso/9780199282968.003.0003

—, *Understanding Music: Philosophy and Interpretation* (London: Continuum, 2009), https://doi.org/10.5040/9781474270199

Second Vatican Council, 'Dei Verbum', *Vatican.va*, 18 November 1965, https://www.vatican.va/archive/hist_councils/ii_vatican_council/documents/vat-ii_const_19651118_dei-verbum_en.html

—, 'Gaudium et spes', *Vatican.va*, 7 December, 1965, https://www.vatican.va/archive/hist_councils/ii_vatican_council/documents/vat-ii_const_19651207_gaudium-et-spes_en.html

—, 'Institutio Generalis Missalis Romani', *Vatican.va*, 13 November 2002, https://www.vatican.va/roman_curia/congregations/ccdds/documents/rc_con_ccdds_doc_20030317_ordinamento-messale_en.html

—, 'Musicam Sacram: Instruction on Music in the Liturgy', *Vatican.va*, 5 March 1967, https://www.vatican.va/archive/hist_councils/ii_vatican_council/documents/vat-ii_instr_19670305_musicam-sacram_en.html

—, 'Sacrosanctum Concilium', *Vatican.va*, 4 December 1963, https://www.vatican.va/archive/hist_councils/ii_vatican_council/documents/vat-ii_const_19631204_sacrosanctum-concilium_en.html

Senn, Frank, *Embodied Liturgy: Lessons in Christian Ritual* (Augsburg, MN: Fortress, 2016), https://doi.org/10.2307/j.ctt19qggc3

Shapin, Steven, *The Scientific Revolution* (Chicago, IL: University of Chicago Press, 1996).

Sheldrake, Philip, 'A Spiritual City: Urban Vision and the Christian Tradition', in *Theology in Built Environments: Exploring Religion, Architecture, and Design*, ed. by Sigurd Bergmann (London: Routledge, 2009), pp. 151–72, https://doi.org/10.4324/9781315135502-9

—, *Spirituality and Theology: Christian Living and the Doctrine of God* (London: Darton, Longman, and Todd, 1998).

Shelley, Braxton D., *Healing for the Soul: Richard Smallwood, the Vamp, and the Gospel Imagination* (New York: Oxford University Press, 2021), https://doi.org/10.1093/oso/9780197566466.001.0001

Shenton, Andrew, ed., *Messiaen the Theologian* (Abingdon: Routledge, 2010).

Sherman, Jacob Holsinger, *Partakers of the Divine: Contemplation and the Practice of Philosophy* (Minneapolis, MN: Fortress Press, 2014), https://doi.org/10.2307/j.ctt22h6rss

—, *Singing the Faith* (London: Hymns Ancient & Modern, 2011).

Silence, dir. by Martin Scorsese (Paramount Pictures, 2016).

Simpson, James Young, *Landmarks in the Struggle between Science and Religion* (London: Hodder and Stoughton, 1925).

Sircello, Guy, 'How is a Theory of the Sublime Possible?', *The Journal of Aesthetics and Art Criticism* 51.4 (1993), 541–50, https://doi.org/10.1111/1540_6245.jaac51.4.0541

Sirvent, Roberto, and Duncan Reyburn, 'Inside Out and Philosophy: What Does it Mean to be Okay?', *And Philosophy*, 7 November 2015, https://andphilosophy.com/2015/11/07/inside-out-and-philosophy-what-does-it-mean-to-be-okay

Sloboda, John A., 'Music and Worship: A Psychologist's Perspective', in *Creative Chords: Studies in Music, Theology and Christian Formation*, ed. by Jeff Astley, Timothy Hone, and Micahel Savage (Leominster: Gracewing, 2000), pp. 110–25.

Slough, Rebecca J., '"Let Every Tongue, by Art Refined, Mingle Its Softest Notes with Mine": An Exploration of Hymn-Singing Events and Dimensions of Knowing', in *Religious and Social Ritual: Interdisciplinary Explorations*, ed. by Michael B. Aune and Valerie DeMarinis (Albany, NY: State University of New York Press, 1996), pp. 175–206.

Small, Christopher, *Musicking: The Meanings of Performance and Listening* (Middletown, CT: Wesleyan University Press, 1998; Hanover, NH: University Press of New England 1998).

Smith, John Arthur, 'Music in Early Christianity, i: The First to the Early Third Centuries', in *Music in Ancient Judaism and Early Christianity* (London: Routledge, 2016), pp. 167–87.

Smith, Kit, 'The Singing Assembly: How Does Music Affect the Faith Life of a Worshipping Community?', *The Australasian Catholic Record* 87.3 (2010), 284–95.

Snyder, Bob, *Music and Memory: An Introduction* (Cambridge, MA: The MIT Press, 2001).

Sontag, Susan, 'Against Interpretation', in Susan Sontag, *Against Interpretation and Other Essays* (Harmondsworth: Penguin, 2009), pp. 3–14.

Spaethling, Robert, ed., *Mozart's Letters: Mozart's Life* (London: Faber and Faber 2000).

Speelman, Willem Marie, *The Generation of Meaning in Liturgical Songs* (Kampen: Kok Pharos Publishing House, 1995).

—, 'Music and the Word: Two Pillars of the Liturgy', *GIA Quarterly* 19.4 (2008), 14–45.

Spencer, Jon Michael, *Theological Music: Introduction to Theomusicology* (Westport, CT: Greenwood Press, 1991).

Spitzer, Michael, *Metaphor and Musical Thought* (Chicago, IL: University of Chicago Press, 2004), https://doi.org/10.7208/chicago/9780226279435.001.0001

—, *The Musical Human: A History of Life on Earth* (London: Bloomsbury, 2022).

Sprecher, Susan, and Beverley Fehr, 'Compassionate Love for Close Others and Humanity', *Journal of Social and Personal Relationships* 22.5 (2005), 629–51, https://doi.org/10.1177/0265407505056439

Stahl, Bob, and Elisha Goldstein, *A Mindfulness-Based Stress Reduction Workbook* (Oakland, CA: New Harbinger, 2010).

Stalcup, Erika K. R., 'The Wesleys: John and Charles', in *Hymns and Hymnody: Historical and Theological Introductions*, ed. by Mark A. Lamport, Benjamin K. Forrest, and Vernon M. Whaley, 3 vols (Eugene, OR: Wipf and Stock, 2019), II, 210–25, https://doi.org/10.2307/j.ctv14gpjf9.21

Stapert, Calvin R., *A New Song for an Old World: Musical Thought in the Early Church* (Grand Rapids, MI, and Cambridge, UK: Eerdmans, 2007).

Starkloff, Carl F., *A Theology of the In-Between: The Value of Syncretic Process* (Milwaukee, WI: Marquette University Press 2002).

Stearns, Chelle L., *Handling Dissonance: A Musical Theological Aesthetic of Unity* (Eugene, OR: Pickwick Publications, 2019).

Steger, Michael F., et al., 'The Meaning in Life Questionnaire: Assessing the Presence of and Search for Meaning in Life', *Journal of Counseling Psychology* 53.1 (2006), 80–93, https://doi.org/10.1037/0022-0167.53.1.80

Steiner, George, *Errata: An Examined Life* (London: Phoenix, 1997).

—, *Real Presences: Is There Anything in What We Say?* (London: Faber & Faber, 1989).

Steinmetz, David C., 'The Superiority of Pre-Critical Exegesis', *Theology Today* 36 (1980), 27–38, reprinted in *The Theological Interpretation of Scripture*, ed. by Stephen E. Fowl (Oxford: Oxford University Press, 1997), pp. 26–38.

Stone, Robert, *Sacred Steel: Inside an African American Steel Guitar Tradition* (Urbana, IL: University of Illinois Press, 2010).

Stone, Robert L., 'Interview with Chuck Campbell', *Arhoolie Foundation*, 13 June 1996, https://arhoolie.org/sacred-steel-archive-chuck-campbell-interview/

Stone-Davis, Férdia J., 'Making an Anthropological Case: Cognitive Dualism and the Acousmatic', *Philosophy: The Journal of the Royal Institute of Philosophy* 90.352 (2015), 263–76, https://doi.org/10.1017/s0031819115000017

—, ed., *Music and Transcendence* (Burlington: Ashgate, 2015).

Strassman, Rick, *DMT: The Spirit Molecule: A Doctor's Revolutionary Research into the Biology of New-Death and Mystical Experiences* (Rochester, VT: Parker Street Press, 2001).

Stravinsky, Igor, *Poetics of Music*, trans. by Arthur Knodel and Ingolf Dahl (Cambridge, MA: Harvard University Press, 1942).

Streib, Heinz, et al., 'The Mysticism Scale as a Measure for Subjective Spirituality: New Results with Hood's M-Scale and the Development of a Short From', in *Assessing Spirituality in a Diverse World*, ed. by Amy L. Ai et al. (Cham: Springer, 2021), pp. 467–91, https://doi.org/10.1007/978-3-030-52140-0_19

Streissguth, Michael, *Outlaw: Waylon, Willie, Kris, and the Renegades of Nashville* (New York: itbooks, 2013).

Stump, Eleonore, *Aquinas* (London: Routledge, 2003).

Suchla, Beate Regina, 'Gadamer', in *Music in German Philosophy: An Introduction*, ed. by Stefan Lorenz Sorgner, Oliver Furbeth, and Susan H. Gillespie (Chicago, IL: University of Chicago Press, 2011), pp. 211–32, https://doi.org/10.7208/chicago/9780226768397.003.0010

Swain, Joseph, *Sacred Treasure: Understanding Catholic Liturgical Music* (Collegeville, MN: Liturgical Press, 2012).

Swinton, John, *Spirituality and Mental Health Care: Rediscovering a 'Forgotten' Dimension* (London: Jessica Kingsley Publishers, 2001).

Sykes, Jim, *The Musical Gift: Sonic Generosity in Post-War Sri Lanka* (New York: Oxford University Press, 2018), https://doi.org/10.1093/oso/9780190912024.001.0001

Sylvan, Robin, *Traces of the Spirit: The Religious Dimensions of Popular Music* (New York: New York University Press, 2002), https://doi.org/10.18574/nyu/9781479875238.001.0001

Stalker, dir. by Andrei Tarkovsky (Goskino, 1979).

Tan, Siu-Lan, Peter Pfordresher, and Rom Harré, *Psychology of Music: From Sound to Significance* (London & New York: Routledge, 2018), https://doi.org/10.4324/9781315648026

Tanner, Norman P., ed., *Decrees of the Ecumenical Councils*, 2 vols (Washington, DC, Georgetown University Press, 1990).

Taylor, Charles, *The Language Animal: The Full Shape of the Human Linguistic Capacity* (Cambridge, MA: The Belknap Press of Harvard University Press, 2016), https://doi.org/10.4159/9780674970250

—, *A Secular Age* (Cambridge, MA: Harvard University Press, 2007).

Tedlock, Barbara, 'From Participant Observation to the Observation of Participation: The Emergence of Narrative Ethnography', *Journal of Anthropological Research* 47.1 (1991), 69–94, https://doi.org/10.1086/jar.47.1.3630581

Templeton Religion Trust, 'Music as a Bridge to Spirituality', online video recording, *YouTube*, 16 March 2023, https://www.youtube.com/watch?v=ei0mPuJBnUI&t=8s

Templeton Religion Trust, 'Request for Proposals', *Art Seeking Understanding*, March 2021, https://templetonreligiontrust.org/wp-content/uploads/2021/03/TRT_Art_Seeking_Understanding_RFP2_Mar2021-1.pdf

Temperley, Nicholas, 'Methodist Church Music', in *Grove Music Online*, rev. Martin V. Clarke (2001), https://doi.org/10.1093/gmo/9781561592630.article.47533

Tenney, James, *A History of 'Consonance' and 'Dissonance'* (New York: Excelsior Music, 1988).

Tenzer, Michael, 'A Cross-Cultural Topology of Musical Time: Afterword to the Present Book and to Analytical Studies in World Music (2006)', in *Analytical and Cross-Cultural Studies in World Music*, ed. by Michael Tenzer, and John Roeder (Oxford: Oxford University Press, 2011), https://doi.org/10.1093/acprof:oso/9780195384581.003.0012

Thibault, Paul, *Brain, Mind, and the Signifying Body* (New York: Continuum, 2004).

Thiessen, Gesa, *Theological Aesthetics: A Reader* (London: SCM Press, 2004).

Thompson, William Forde, and Kirk N. Olsen, eds, *The Science and Psychology of Music: From Beethoven at the Office to Beyoncé at the Gym* (Santa Barbara, CA, and Denver, CO: Greenwood, 2021), https://doi.org/10.5040/9798216011538

Tierney, Darren, *St Mary's Metropolitan Cathedral, Edinburgh: A History 1814–2014* (Edinburgh: Scottish Catholic Historical Association, 2018).

Tillich, Paul, *Dynamics of Faith* (New York: HarperCollins, 1957).

—, *Systematic Theology: Volume I: Reason and Revelation, Being and God* (Chicago, IL: University of Chicago Press, 1951).

—, *Systematic Theology: Volume II: Existence and the Christ* (Chicago, IL: University of Chicago Press, 1957).

—, *Systematic Theology: Volume III: Life and the Spirit, History and the Kingdom of God* (Chicago, IL: University of Chicago Press, 1963).

Titon, Jeff Todd, 'Ethnography in the Study of Congregational Music', in *Studying Congregational Music: Key Issues, Methods, and Theoretical Perspectives*, ed. by Andrew Mall, Jeffers Engelhardt, and Monique Ingalls (New York: Routledge, 2021), pp. 64–80, https://doi.org/10.4324/9780429492020-6

—, *Powerhouse for God: Speech, Chant, and Song in an Appalachian Baptist Church*, second edition (Knoxville, TN: University of Tennessee Press, 2018).

—, 'Reflexivity and the Study of Religious Folklife', revised response delivered at the Annual Meeting of the American Folklore Society, 1989 (unpublished manuscript, 1991).

—, 'A Song from the Holy Spirit', *Ethnomusicology* 24.2 (1980), 223–31, https://doi.org/10.2307/851113

—, 'Stance, Role, and Identity in Fieldwork among Folk and Pentecostals', *American Music* 3.1 (1985), 16–24, https://doi.org/10.2307/3052114

—, '"Tuned Up with the Grace of God': Music and Experience among Old Regular Baptists', in *Music in American Religious Experience*, ed. by Philip V. Bohlman, Edith L. Blumhofer, and Maria M. Chow (New York: Oxford University Press, 2006), pp. 311–34, https://doi.org/10.1093/acprof:oso/9780195173048.003.0019

—, ed., *Worlds of Music: An Introduction to the Music of the World's Peoples*, 2nd ed. (New York: Schirmer Books, 1992).

Tomlinson, Gary, *A Million Years of Music: The Emergence of Human Modernity* (Princeton, NJ: Princeton University Press, 2015; New York: Zone Books, 2018), https://doi.org/10.2307/j.ctt17kk95h

Torrance, Thomas F., 'The Mind of Christ in Worship: The Problem of Apollinarianism in the Liturgy', in Thomas F. Torrance, *Theology in Reconciliation: Essays towards Evangelical and Catholic Unity in East and West* (London: Geoffrey Chapman, 1975), pp. 139–214.

—, *Reality and Scientific Theology* (Eugene, OR: Wipf and Stock Publishers, 2001).

Townsend, Peter, *The Evolution of Music through Culture and Science* (Oxford: Oxford University Press, 2020), https://doi.org/10.1093/oso/9780198848400.001.0001

Tschacher, Wolfgang, et al., 'Audience Synchronies in Live Concerts Illustrate the Embodiment of Music Experience', *Scientific Reports*, 13 (2023), 14843, https://doi.org/10.1038/s41598-023-41960-2

Turco, Alberto, *Il canto gregoriano. Toni e modi* (Rome: Edizioni Torre d'Orfeo, 1996).

Turner, Bryan S., 'Post-Secular Society: Consumerism and the Democratization of Religion', in *The Post-Secular Question: Religion in Contemporary Society*, ed. by Philip S. Gorski et al. (New York: Social Science Research Council and New York University Press, 2012), pp. 135–58.

UK Blessing, The, 'The UK Blessing—Churches Sing "The Blessing" over the UK', online video recording, *YouTube*, 3 May 2020, https://youtu.be/PUtll3mNj5U

United States Conference of Catholic Bishops, 'Liturgical Music Today (1982)', in *The Liturgy Documents: A Parish Resource*, ed. by David Lysik et al., 2 vols, 4th ed. (Chicago, IL: Liturgy Training Publications, 2004), I, 367–84.

—, *The Roman Missal* (Washington, DC: USCCB, 2011).

University of St Andrews, 'Music and Spiritual Realities: International Workshop', online video recording, *YouTube*, 16 November 2023, https://www.youtube.com/watch?v=uWfXQGYYPO0&t=10s

Vallee, Mickey, *Sounding Bodies Sounding Worlds: An Exploration of Embodiments in Sound* (Singapore: Palgrave Macmillan, 2019), https://doi.org/10.1007/978-981-32-9327-4

van de Donk, W. B. H. J., et al., *Geloven in het publieke domein: verkenningen van een dubbele transformatie* (Amsterdam: Amsterdam University Press, 2006).

van den Tol, Annemieke J. M., Jane Edwards, and Nathan A. Heflick, 'Sad Music as a Means for Acceptance-Based Coping', *Musicae Scientiae* 20 (2016), 68–83, https://doi.org/10.1177/1029864915627844

van der Leeuw, Gerardus, *Sacred and Profane Beauty: The Holy in Art*, ed. by Mark Csikszentmihalyi, American Academy of Religion Texts and Translation Series (New York: Oxford University Press, 2006), https://doi.org/10.1093/oso/9780195223804.001.0001

van Harskamp, Anton, *Het nieuw-religieuze verlangen* (Kampen: Kok, 2000).

Vandenberghe, L., and F. Costa Prado, 'Law and Grace in Saint Augustine: A Fresh Perspective on Mindfulness and Spirituality in Behaviour Therapy', *Mental Health, Religion & Culture* 12.6 (2009), 587–600, https://doi.org/10.1080/13674670902911872

Vanhoozer, Kevin J., *Is There a Meaning in This Text? The Bible, the Reader, and the Morality of Literary Knowledge* (Leicester: Apollos, 1998).

Various, *Songs of the Old Regular Baptists, Vol. 2* (Smithsonian Folkways, 2003).

Varwig, Bettina, *Music in the Flesh: An Early Modern Musical Physiology* (Chicago, IL: Chicago University Press, 2023).

Vetö, Etienne, *The Breath of God: An Essay on the Holy Spirit in the Trinity* (Eugene, OR: Cascade, 2019).

Volf, Miroslav, *After Our Likeness: The Church as the Image of the Trinity* (Grand Rapids, MI: William B. Eerdmans, 1998).

Waaijman, Kees, *Spirituality: Forms, Foundations, Methods*, trans. by John Vriend (Leuven: Peeters Publishers, 2002).

Wainwright, Geoffrey, 'Psalm 33', in Geoffrey Wainwright, *Embracing Purpose: Essays on God, the World, and the Church* (Eugene, OR: Wipf and Stock, 2012), pp. 105–25.

—, 'Psalm 33 Interpreted of the Triune God', *Ex Auditu* 16 (2000), 101–20.

Wald-Fuhrmann, Melanie, 'Liturgische Aufführungsbestimmungen zwischen Semiotik und Ästhetik: Ein Durchgang durch die "Allgemeine Einführung in das Römische Meßbuch"', in *Wirkungsästhetik der Liturgie: Transdisziplinäre Perspektiven* ed. by Wald-Fuhrmann, Klaus-Peter Dannecker, and Sven Boenneke (Regensburg: Pustet, 2020), pp. 143–64.

—, 'Positive Aspekte des gemeinschaftlichen Singens: Ein Forschungsüberblick', in *Wirkungsästhetik der Liturgie: Transdisziplinäre Perspektiven* ed. by Wald-Fuhrmann, Klaus-Peter Dannecker, and Sven Boenneke (Regensburg: Pustet, 2020), pp. 191–214.

—, et al., '"He Who Sings, Prays Twice"? Singing in Roman Catholic Mass Leads to Spiritual and Social Experiences that are Predicted by Religious and Musical Attitudes', *Frontiers in Psychology* 11, 570189 (2020), https://doi.org/10.3389/fpsyg.2020.570189

—, et al., 'Music Listening in Classical Concerts: Theory, Literature Review, and Research Program', *Frontiers in Psychology*, 12 (2021), 638783, https://doi.org/10.3389/fpsyg.2021.638783

—, 'Verführung zur Konversion: Händel, Scarlatti und das römische Oratorium um 1700', in *Jahrbuch des Staatlichen Instituts für Musikforschung 2010*, ed. by Simone Hohmaier (Mainz: Schott, 2010), pp. 99–122.

Wallace, Maurice O., *King's Vibrato: Modernism, Blackness, and the Sonic Life of Martin Luther King Jr.* (Durham, NC: Duke University Press, 2022).

Wanous, John P., and Arnon E. Reichers, 'Estimating the Reliability of a Single-Item Measure', *Psychological Reports* 78.2 (1996), 631–34, https://doi.org/10.2466/pr0.1996.78.2.631

—, Arnon E Reichers, and Michael J Hudy, 'Overall Job Satisfaction: How Good Are Single-Item Measures?', *Journal of Applied Psychology*, 82.2 (1997), 247–52, https://doi.org/10.1037//0021-9010.82.2.247

—, and Michael J. Hudy, 'Single-Item Reliability: A Replication and Extension', *Organizational Research Methods* 4.4 (2001), 361–75, https://doi.org/10.1177/109442810144003

Ward, Keith, *The Big Questions in Science and Religion* (West Conshohocken, PA: Templeton Foundation Press, 2008).

Ward, Peter, *Liquid Church* (Eugene, OR: Wipf and Stock, 2002).

Warren, Jeff R., *Music and Ethical Responsibility* (Cambridge, UK: Cambridge University Press, 2014), https://doi.org/10.1017/cbo9781107358287

Watson, J. R., *The English Hymn: A Critical and Historical Study* (Oxford: Clarendon Press, 1997), https://doi.org/10.1093/019827002x.001.0001

Welker, Michael, *God the Spirit* (Minneapolis, MN: Fortress Press, 1994).

White, Andrew Dickson, *A History of the Warfare of Science with Theology in Christendom* (New York: D. Appleton and Company, 1896).

Wilke, Annette, 'Sonality', in *The Bloomsbury Handbook of the Cultural and Cognitive Aesthetics of Religion*, ed. by Anne Koch and Katharina Wilkens (London: Bloomsbury Academic, 2020), pp. 107–16, https://doi.org/10.5040/9781350066748.ch-010

Williams, Rowan, 'Keeping in Time', in Rowan Williams, *Open to Judgment: Sermons and Addresses* (London: Darton, Longman & Todd, 1994), p. 249.

—, 'Nick Cave: My Son's Death Brought Me Back to Church', *The Times*, 4 March 2023, https://www.thetimes.co.uk/article/nick-cave-my-sons-death-brought-me-back-to-church-qdskjx277

—, *Wrestling with Angels: Conversations in Modern Theology* (Grand Rapids, MI: Eerdmans, 2007).

Williams, Sean, 'Buddhism and Music', in *Experiencing Music in World Religions*, ed. by Guy. L. Beck (Ontario: Wilfrid Laurier University Press, 2006), pp. 169–89.

Wilson, Margaret, 'Six Views of Embodied Cognition', *Psychodynamic Bulletin and Review* 9.4 (2002), 625–36, https://doi.org/10.3758/bf03196322

Winkelman, Michael, 'Shamanism as a Biogenetic Structural Paradigm for Humans' Evolved Social Psychology', *Psychology of Religion and Spirituality* 7.4 (2015), 267–77, https://doi.org/10.1037/rel0000034

Winkett, Lucy, *Our Sound is Our Wound* (London: Continuum, 2010).

'Wolfgang Rihm in Conversation with Kirk Noreen and Joshua Cody', *Sospeso*, 2006, http://web.archive.org/web/20060525100029/http://www.sospeso.com:80/contents/articles/rihm_p1.html

Wolterstorff, Nicholas, *Art in Action: Towards a Christian Aesthetic* (Grand Rapids, MI: Eerdmans Publishing Company, 1980).

World Council of Churches, *The Church: Towards a Common Vision*, Faith and Order Paper 214 (Geneva: World Council of Churches Publications, 2013), https://www.oikoumene.org/sites/default/files/Document/The_Church_Towards_a_common_vision.pdf

—, *Towards Koinonia in Faith, Life, and Witness: A Discussion Paper. Proceedings of the Fifth World Conference on Faith and Order in Santiago de Compostela*, ed. by

Thomas Best and Gunther Gassmann (Geneva: World Council of Churches Publications, 1993).

World Economic Forum (WEF), *The Global Risks Report 2020 Insight Report* (Geneva: WEF, 2010), https://www3.weforum.org/docs/WEF_Global_Risk_Report_2020.pdf

Yaden, David B., et al., 'The Development of the Awe Experience Scale (AWE-S): A Multifactorial Measure for a Complex Emotion', *The Journal of Positive Psychology*, 14.4 (2019), 474–88, https://doi.org/10.1080/17439760.2018.1484940

—, et al., 'The Varieties of Self-Transcendent Experience', *Review of General Psychology*, 21.2 (2017), 143–60, https://doi.org/10.1037/gpr0000102

Yogananda, Paramhansa, *Cosmic Chants* (Los Angeles, CA: Self-Realization Fellowship Publishers, 1974).

Zizioulas, John D., *Being as Communion: Studies in Personhood and the Church* (Crestwood, NY: St Vladimir's Seminary Press, 1985).

Zon, Bennett, 'Elgar *as* Theology', in *The Oxford Handbook of Music and Christian Theology*, ed. by Steve Guthrie and Zon, 5 vols (Oxford: Oxford University Press, forthcoming), III.

—, 'Evolution', in *Edinburgh Critical History of Nineteenth-Century Theology*, ed. by Daniel Whistler (Edinburgh: Edinburgh University Press, 2018), pp. 124–42, https://doi.org/10.1515/9781474405874-009

—, *Evolution and Victorian Musical Culture* (Cambridge, UK: Cambridge University Press, 2017), https://doi.org/10.1017/9781139103985

—, 'Evolution: Music in the Autobiologies of Darwin and Spencer', in *The Oxford Handbook of Music and Life Writing*, ed. by Paul Watt and Michael Allis (Oxford: Oxford University Press, forthcoming).

—, 'Music', in *Handbook of Religious Culture in Nineteenth-Century Europe*, ed. by Anthony J. Steinhoff and Jeffrey T. Zalar (Berlin: De Gruyter, forthcoming).

—, 'Music', in *The Oxford Handbook of Nineteenth-Century Christian Thought*, ed. by Joel D. S. Rasmussen, Judith Wolfe, and Johannes Zachhuber (Oxford: Oxford University Press, 2017), pp. 459–70, https://doi.org/10.1093/oxfordhb/9780198718406.013.40

—, 'Music Theology as the Mouthpiece of Science: Proving it through Congregational Music Studies', in *Studying Congregational Music: Key Issues, Methods, and Theoretical Perspectives*, ed. by Andrew Mall, Jeffers Engelhardt, and Monique Ingalls (New York and London: Routledge, 2021), pp. 103–20, https://doi.org/10.4324/9780429492020-8

—, 'Religion and Science', in *The Oxford Handbook of Music and Intellectual Culture*, ed. by Michael Allis, Sarah Collins, and Paul Watt (Oxford: Oxford University Press, 2020), pp. 387–408, https://doi.org/10.1093/oxfordhb/9780190616922.013.21

Index

absolute music 26, 228
abuse. *See* trauma 7, 99
Adorno, Theodor 293
aesthetics 9, 74, 76, 91, 109, 112–114, 116, 126, 195, 199, 210, 213, 244, 273, 282, 287, 299, 308
affective cognition 97, 101, 105
affordance 4, 75, 395–396
agnosticism 140, 197, 200–202, 204–205, 207
angels 8, 37, 57–58, 63, 266, 375–376
annunciation 1–3, 65–66, 69, 362
Anselm of Canterbury 73, 82, 84–85
anthropology 30, 196–197, 329, 357
anticipation 174, 178, 336
anxiety 100, 123, 132–133, 155, 223, 269, 303, 315, 339
art music 362
arts 1–3, 5, 8, 22–23, 25, 42–44, 54, 59, 70, 75, 91, 98, 110, 113–114, 182, 185, 230, 233, 237–238, 250, 282, 287, 298, 357, 360, 369
ascension 59, 237
Astley, Jeff 3, 11, 386, 388–389
atheism 299
atmosphere 10, 130, 157, 177, 194, 196, 209–217, 219, 221–222, 224–231, 250
Attali, Jacques 293
attendance (church) 153, 288, 294, 299, 301
attunement 96, 117, 127
audience 45, 114, 121, 194–195, 198, 273, 282, 297, 300, 338
Augustine 9, 28, 39–40, 46, 87, 94–107, 200, 221, 238–239
authenticity 353, 361
awareness 35–36, 45, 56, 77, 80, 113, 121–122, 162, 219, 235, 241–242, 245–247, 249, 251–252, 295, 300, 349

awe 145–146, 152, 226, 288, 294, 338

Bach, Johann Sebastian 45, 49, 92, 225, 262
Balthasar, Hans Von 346, 359
beauty 16, 106, 111, 113, 298–301
Beethoven, Ludwig van 15, 53, 93, 226
Begbie, Jeremy 2–3, 8, 21, 23, 25, 28, 32, 34–35, 39, 46, 75, 103, 114, 364
behaviour 31, 106, 139, 156, 165, 169–170, 172, 198, 201, 216, 230, 288, 290, 295, 325, 391
belief 6, 16, 23, 27, 37, 91–92, 106, 117, 124, 132–134, 140, 155, 164, 170–171, 200–205, 237, 245, 275, 281, 291, 307, 320, 338, 342, 356–357, 378, 386, 388, 390
belonging 7, 203, 212, 214, 250, 293, 307, 335, 341, 372, 386–387
Bible. *See* scripture 35, 37, 58, 129, 297, 336, 337, 356, 357
biography 217, 226, 233, 235, 242–243, 245, 248, 254
blessing 225, 249, 329–330, 332, 337–338, 341–342, 344
Böhme, Gernot 209–214, 216
Book of Common Prayer 292, 294
boundaries 111, 134, 178, 230, 291, 298, 335, 341, 349, 356, 370
Boyce-Tillman, June 5–7, 111, 302
Brahms, Johannes 227
breath 4, 55, 57–65, 67, 69–71, 139, 195, 202, 255
Brown, David 2–3, 30, 93, 95, 110, 168, 261, 329
Buddhism 128, 139–141, 178
Butler, Melvin 193, 200–201, 203–206, 208, 210

chant 10, 46, 98, 141, 144, 148, 156–157, 177–178, 183–184, 188–189, 218–219, 275, 280–282, 292, 362
choir
   amateur 276
   church 325
   liturgical 369
Chopin, Frédéric 27, 222–223, 226, 228–229
choral music 299, 314, 317–319, 326, 390
choral tradition 285, 296
chorister 317–319, 322–323, 325
chorus. *See* choir 67, 84, 124, 129, 140, 155, 156, 330
Christian, Christianity 1–8, 10, 13, 22–23, 29, 34–36, 38–39, 42, 46, 52–53, 56–58, 60–62, 68–70, 75, 82, 85, 93–95, 97, 101–102, 106, 110–111, 114, 128, 132, 134, 139–141, 184–185, 199, 201, 204, 206, 235–241, 244–247, 250, 253, 273–277, 279–283, 299, 301, 306–308, 312, 330, 332–333, 335, 337–338, 342–343, 346, 352–353, 355–357, 359, 364, 386, 389
   Anglican/Episcopal 5, 7, 10, 59, 285, 292, 296–299, 302, 306, 312, 361, 363, 390
   Baptist 200–202
   Church of Scotland 361
   Evangelical 59, 93, 331
   Lutheran 296
   Methodism 372–376, 380–381, 388
   Orthodox 5, 16, 142, 206, 331
   Pentecostal 5, 7, 193–196, 200–201, 203–205, 276
   Protestant 28, 249, 276, 297, 331–332, 353, 357, 378
   Reformed 28, 296
   Roman Catholic 56–57, 234, 236, 261, 273–276, 355, 358, 362, 390
classical music. *See also* art music 79, 285
clergy 296, 312, 320, 358, 366, 368
cognition 32, 97, 101, 105, 109, 112–114, 116–117, 139, 141, 146, 164–165, 174, 181, 209, 348

cognitive science. *See* cognition 113, 126, 152
coherence 220, 356
Coltrane, John 45–46, 111, 147, 157–158
community 55, 60, 69, 80, 93, 142, 148, 155, 178, 203, 206, 223, 236–237, 245, 253, 273, 276, 292, 302–303, 307, 309, 315, 325, 328–337, 339, 341–345, 347–348, 350, 352–353, 358, 365–367, 374, 387
   religious 69, 236–237, 273, 309, 315, 325, 329, 333–337, 342–345, 347, 350, 353, 366–367
   spiritual 328–329, 336, 348
concert 26, 62, 71, 142, 227, 280, 282, 294, 297, 300–301, 303, 310, 319
connection 2, 23, 51, 56, 73, 82, 114, 157, 159, 163, 193, 197–200, 207–208, 216, 221, 233, 235, 238, 240, 244, 246–249, 254, 261, 266–267, 273, 289, 298, 320, 328, 332–335, 339–340, 351, 357, 364–365, 367, 370–371
consciousness 8, 10, 32, 57, 106, 125, 129, 145, 160, 164–167, 169, 172–173, 175, 178, 180, 207, 228, 243, 397
contemplation 73, 82, 112, 166, 293, 393
context, sacred and/or secular 306
conversion 98, 106, 134, 140, 210, 221, 235, 245–247, 249, 275
COVID-19 10, 56–57, 71, 148, 305, 307, 325, 327, 344, 360, 365–366, 368
creativity 143, 222, 244, 253, 258, 261, 266, 282, 287, 292, 347, 376
culture 2, 6, 14, 24, 27, 42, 64, 67, 87, 93–94, 106, 110, 117, 122, 129, 141, 146, 149–150, 153–155, 161, 166–167, 169–170, 174, 201–202, 206, 219, 228, 230, 235, 237, 241, 248, 281, 285, 293, 295, 298, 324, 362, 364, 374, 395

Dawkins, Richard 88, 95
DeNora, Tia 4, 74, 110, 290, 292, 294
devotion 10, 46, 50, 148, 169–170, 178, 183, 206, 251, 274, 357, 376
digital technology 351
digital worship 322, 327–330, 332, 337, 339, 341, 344–345, 347–348, 351–353

diversity 5, 141, 153, 166, 317, 322, 342
divine, divinity 1–2, 16, 25, 29, 34–35, 37–39, 43, 52, 55, 59–63, 66, 70, 82, 84–85, 99–100, 103, 105, 107, 111, 131, 139, 141, 156, 196–199, 203, 207, 230, 234, 236–240, 251, 273, 289, 291, 296, 328–329, 331, 333–334, 337–341, 345–347, 349, 352, 371, 375–376, 391–392, 395
doctrine 37, 107, 111, 122–123, 213, 253, 276, 336, 356, 376
drone (musical) 173, 176–177, 179

ecclesiology
  digital 327–329, 332, 344–345, 347, 352
ecological approaches 75
ecstatic 148, 195, 212, 393
Eliade, Mercea 111
embodiment 65, 69, 76, 174, 282, 348–350, 353
emotion 4, 28, 30–32, 48, 50, 80, 82, 97, 101–103, 105, 113–114, 116, 146, 149–150, 152, 156, 164–167, 170–171, 177–178, 195, 204, 211–212, 214–215, 217, 219, 221, 224, 226, 229, 234, 269, 275–277, 280, 282, 286–289, 291–292, 298, 303, 334, 339–340, 345, 388, 392
empathy 32, 47, 240, 303
empirical/empiricism 3–5, 8–11, 59, 71, 76, 80–81, 101, 106, 109, 118, 139, 141, 143–145, 147, 159–161, 163, 247, 251, 273–277, 279, 281, 283, 285–286, 297, 306, 308, 310, 316, 323, 328–329, 337, 345, 364, 390, 392–394
England 6, 10, 30, 235, 285–286, 299–302, 305–306, 315–316, 318
ensemble (musical). *See also* choir 11, 182, 183, 185, 268, 280, 358, 362, 363, 364, 365, 366, 367, 368, 369, 370, 378
epistemology 113, 200, 204–205, 244–245, 247
eternity 61, 106
ethics 97, 206, 211, 245
ethnography 201, 203, 205, 329
ethnomusicology 2–3, 10, 92–93, 165, 174, 187, 189, 193, 196–208, 240

Eucharist 55, 68, 253, 301, 307, 316, 359–360, 391
Evensong 10, 285–298, 302–303, 315, 361
event 13, 27, 71, 78, 109, 114–116, 119–121, 140, 142, 164, 171, 173–174, 177, 179, 217, 229, 254, 276, 282, 287, 295, 316, 323, 331, 335, 338, 343, 373, 384–385, 387, 389, 391
experience
  lived 46, 54, 236, 305, 314, 325, 328, 345, 352, 388
  musical 22–23, 79, 97, 139, 150–152, 179, 195, 209, 217, 224–225, 227–228, 252, 286, 294, 298, 394, 396
  mystical 129, 145, 159
  religious 129, 159, 200–203, 240, 243, 276, 301, 323
  spiritual 1, 6, 8–11, 117, 131–132, 142, 149–152, 159–160, 163–164, 166, 175, 181, 204, 209, 230, 278–282, 285, 291, 300, 312, 340, 364, 385, 391, 395–396
expression
  artistic 114
  religious 111
  spiritual 11, 147

faith. *See also* spirituality 5, 6, 7, 11, 29, 36, 49, 50, 53, 61, 70, 73, 74, 76, 77, 82, 83, 84, 85, 86, 101, 115, 118, 140, 147, 148, 204, 205, 206, 234, 237, 238, 239, 240, 242, 243, 245, 248, 251, 262, 264, 276, 288, 291, 294, 299, 301, 306, 312, 320, 329, 330, 331, 332, 335, 336, 339, 341, 342, 343, 344, 346, 347, 350, 356, 357, 360, 362, 370, 373, 375, 390, 391, 395
familiarity 166, 281–282, 379, 395
fantasy 47, 161, 255
Fassler, Margot 56–57, 63
feeling. *See* emotion 10, 13, 45, 48, 58, 59, 77, 145, 209, 210, 212, 214, 215, 216, 222, 265, 267, 273, 274, 277, 278, 279, 280, 286, 287, 288, 289, 294, 298, 301, 303, 342, 343, 367
flow 40, 44, 65, 149, 174–175, 179–180, 256, 291, 334, 346, 368, 393
folk music. *See* music: folk 188, 191, 202

football 11, 371, 373–374, 378, 384, 386, 388, 396
formation 3, 112, 118, 134, 230, 253, 315, 328, 330, 352, 363, 389
form (musical) 6, 9, 16, 21, 24, 27, 31, 33, 36, 40, 43, 47, 52–53, 63, 66, 69, 75–76, 78–79, 83, 86, 93, 96–98, 105, 111–113, 116–117, 119–122, 125, 128–130, 132–134, 141–142, 147–148, 153, 160, 168, 170, 173, 177, 195, 201, 212, 214–215, 219, 230–231, 243, 249, 252–253, 255–257, 259, 262–263, 265, 267, 270, 278–280, 297–298, 303, 307, 313, 336, 345–346, 348, 350, 353, 355, 359, 367, 376–377, 390
freedom 7, 29, 75, 81, 110, 116, 174, 221, 246, 270, 302, 335–336, 360, 364

Gadamer, Hans-Georg 115–117
gender 6–7, 242, 250, 278, 302, 317, 335, 363–364
genre. *See also* music 6, 45, 49, 97, 110, 122, 123, 125, 130, 148, 151, 199, 280, 300
Germany 10, 126
God
    experience of 249, 338
    revelation of 254
    silence of 13
gospel music. *See* music: gospel 193, 196, 206
Gould, Glenn 95, 117, 227
grace 44, 84, 100, 102–103, 106, 113, 194, 202, 237–239, 343, 360, 375
Gregorian chant. *See* chant 141, 218, 281, 282, 362
Griffero, Tonino 209
Gubaidulina, Sofia 263
Guthrie, Steven R. 2–3, 93, 103–104, 235

harmony 9, 41, 44, 49, 59, 63, 66, 70, 92, 94, 96, 104–105, 112, 120, 125, 144, 211, 221, 225, 241, 254, 342
Harrison, Carol 39–40, 97, 100–105
Haydn, Joseph 262, 368

healing 7, 50, 103, 107, 141, 152, 154, 171, 174–175, 189, 191, 195, 247, 335, 338–339, 349
Heaney, Maeve Louise 3, 7, 10, 93, 116, 120, 233, 238, 246, 390
heaven 6, 16–17, 29, 55, 66–67, 94, 204, 228, 298–299, 342, 379, 383
Heidegger, Martin 79, 114, 212, 310
hermeneutics 113–115, 117, 120, 240–242
Hinduism 6, 139–141, 199
Holy Spirit 9, 38, 59–60, 64–67, 69–70, 97, 107, 194, 200–206, 236, 239, 328, 331–332, 335, 342, 344, 375
Hopps, Gavin 2–3, 110
humanity 14, 37, 75, 91, 94, 102, 114, 147, 153, 238, 240, 332, 334, 343, 347
hybrid worship. *See* mixed-ecology worship, digital worship 322, 349
hymns, hymnody 28, 57, 61, 100, 103, 194–195, 249, 269, 280–281, 301, 308–309, 321, 355, 372, 374–379, 381, 383–386, 396

icon 16–17, 44, 67
identity
    cultural 216, 385
    national 379, 385–386
imagination 2, 16, 25, 42, 163, 167, 195, 217, 220, 222–225, 231, 267–268, 336, 378
improvisation 5, 227, 238, 264
incarnation 29, 56, 59, 65, 102, 105, 210, 237, 240, 308, 375
ineffability. *See* mystery 23, 28, 35, 74, 291, 395
inspiration (artistic) 10, 13, 129, 255–257, 262, 264, 270, 303, 329, 333, 339, 398
instruments
    drum 144, 175, 207
    guitar 125–126, 131, 134, 193–195, 207, 396
    instruments 43, 63–64, 70, 114, 145, 148, 167, 175, 199, 365
    organ 264, 365–367, 374
    piano 224–227, 229, 264, 266

intention 3, 34, 45, 48, 80, 98, 144, 165, 170, 180, 199, 280–281, 292, 353
interdisciplinary 1–2, 4–5, 57, 92, 94, 234–235, 240, 276, 328–329, 344, 352
interpretation
 musical 253
 Islam 141, 155, 188, 199

jazz. *See* music: jazz 43, 111, 238
Jennings, Willie 69–70, 110
Jesus 16, 36, 53, 58, 66–70, 123, 127, 229, 236–240, 320, 333, 336–342, 353, 357, 360, 371, 375–376
Judaism 6, 139–140, 142, 147–148, 155, 199, 301, 355

Kant, Immanuel 113, 160
King, Kathryn 195, 285–298, 302
knowledge 3–4, 9, 23, 37, 76, 80, 82–84, 98, 101, 113, 117, 147, 160–161, 163, 172, 197–198, 200, 206, 208, 228, 239, 245, 295, 300, 333, 359, 376

Last Supper. *See* Eucharist 355, 360, 391
listening, listeners 2, 4, 14, 16–17, 25–26, 30, 38, 49–52, 75, 79–81, 91, 97, 100, 103, 113–114, 121–122, 142, 150–152, 155, 157, 166–167, 176, 178, 194–197, 199, 202, 217, 222–224, 227, 235, 259, 265, 270, 273, 275–277, 280–282, 285–286, 288, 292–294, 300, 303, 305, 309–310, 314, 326, 340, 361, 386
literature 5–6, 24, 27, 30, 48, 83, 90, 110, 113, 139, 147, 152, 164, 209–210, 222, 225, 229, 277, 282, 377, 391
liturgical space. *See* context 11, 358, 361, 364, 365, 370
lived experience. *See* experience 7, 46, 54, 236, 305, 314, 325, 328, 345, 352, 388
lockdown 288, 293, 295, 342, 344, 348, 360
loneliness 339
Lonergan, Bernard 234–235, 239, 242, 244–247
lyrics 43, 120–121, 123, 129, 195, 238, 240–241, 330, 373–374, 378, 385–386

MacMillan, James 1–2, 11, 13, 43–44, 108, 255–256, 262–266, 269, 368
Maslow, Abraham 150, 269
Mass. *See either* worship, service or Eucharist 45, 55, 68, 69, 146, 264, 265, 275, 277, 278, 279, 293, 355, 356, 357, 360, 365, 366, 367, 368, 369, 396
material 8–9, 21–22, 58, 70–71, 74, 76, 82, 86, 100–101, 109, 111, 119, 125, 127, 133, 160–161, 181, 194–195, 199, 207, 218, 226, 235–236, 238–239, 257, 261, 266–268, 298, 308, 357, 360, 369
Maxwell Davies, Peter 255, 257–263, 266, 268–269
McLeish, Tom 91–92
meaning
 meaning-making 181, 236, 247
 musical 75–76, 109
 spiritual 74, 386
media 7, 28, 89, 180, 305, 316, 327, 377–378
medieval 56–57, 62, 84, 94, 98, 101, 221
melody 6, 39–40, 46, 51–52, 63, 79, 131, 144, 148, 174, 194, 199, 202, 220, 240–241, 380–382, 384
Messiaen, Olivier 3, 262
metaphor 33, 60, 64, 66, 70, 100–101, 112, 202, 209, 214, 221, 258, 298, 346
methodology 8, 95, 118, 169, 200, 202–203, 206–207, 265, 286, 306, 310, 313, 325, 330, 345, 352
mind 14, 23–24, 31, 35, 40, 60, 63, 73, 79, 83, 98, 100–101, 103, 105, 114, 117, 128, 132, 143, 145, 158, 165, 181, 206, 211–212, 226, 257, 260, 264, 287, 295, 320, 334, 341, 362, 392
mindfulness. *See* wellbeing 106, 107, 157, 253, 257, 289
mixed-ecology worship. *See also* digital worship 11
modality. *See* tonality 217, 218
modern, modernism 5, 15, 22, 24, 37, 62, 82, 87, 101, 105, 108, 112, 117–120, 123, 128, 139–141, 147, 160–161, 195, 224, 282, 309–310, 315, 321, 335, 361, 390

mood. *See* emotion 10, 31, 134, 209, 210, 211, 212, 214, 217, 225, 226
motivation 129, 132, 157, 170, 248, 263, 277, 279, 288, 290, 294–295, 328
Mozart, Amadeus 226, 270, 368–369
music
  chamber 296
  choral 11, 71, 277, 285–292, 294, 296–299, 302–303, 309, 314, 317–319, 321, 326, 355, 362–364, 366, 372, 390
  folk 188, 191, 202
  gospel 193, 206
  jazz 43, 111, 238
  listening to 142, 275, 281, 293
  outlaw country 9, 109–110, 116, 119, 123–124, 134
  popular 110, 194
  power of 35, 41, 44–46, 48, 342
  sacred 6, 9, 44–45, 49, 273, 275, 280, 285, 300–303, 315, 317, 324, 362–363
  trance 179
musical semiotics 240
musical time 175–176
music analysis 164, 269
musicking 3–4, 7, 30–32, 64, 91, 114, 163, 196, 200, 202, 205, 233, 235–236, 240–242, 244, 247–248, 250–252, 254, 274, 279–280, 361
musicology 2–4, 92–93, 141, 195, 200, 218, 240, 247, 257
music theory 94, 199, 240, 251–252
mystery 36, 44, 59–60, 66, 70, 83, 111, 249, 251–252, 266, 292, 307
mysticism 94, 141, 145, 152, 163, 230–231, 242, 251, 299, 308
myth 43, 119, 128–129, 218, 259

narrative 43, 118, 132, 152, 154, 186, 203, 235, 242–243, 254, 306, 308, 310, 312–313, 322–323, 325, 332, 337, 339, 345–346, 353, 397
national identity 379
natural theology 29, 57, 89
Nelson, Willie 110, 116, 119, 122–128, 130, 132–133, 194–195, 198, 351
Netherlands, The 10, 285, 292, 295–298, 302

netnography 11, 327–329, 331, 337, 344–345, 347, 352
neuroscience. *See also* cognition, psychology 1, 2, 4, 30, 91, 149, 156, 157, 165, 277, 288
Newman, John Henry 254
Nussbaum, Martha 83–84, 102

objective 10, 17, 95, 116, 161–162, 169, 171, 210–211, 213–214, 234, 242–243, 290, 294–295
online worship. *See* digital worship 11, 56, 305, 306, 307, 308, 309, 314, 315, 316, 322, 323, 326, 327, 329, 332, 349, 350
ontology 67, 113, 161, 204, 207, 292, 316
order 37, 43, 69, 78–79, 84, 94, 100, 103, 117–118, 125, 145, 170, 177–178, 217, 222, 230, 237–239, 243, 248, 256, 258, 270, 275, 289–290, 292–294, 296–297, 312, 330, 362, 364
outlaw country. *See* music: outlaw country 9, 109, 110, 116, 119, 123, 124, 134

Pärt, Arvo 9, 35, 42, 46, 49–54, 262
participation 62, 80, 99, 116, 174, 203, 209, 216, 250, 277, 279, 281, 291, 295, 301, 308–309, 314, 316–317, 321, 323, 329, 331, 336, 348–349, 368, 372–374, 378, 388, 396
pastor/pastoral 2, 251, 312, 336, 370
perception
  pitch 31, 153
performance practice 288
performance. *See* music 4, 7, 76, 104, 114, 148, 150, 168, 183, 193, 194, 195, 196, 204, 205, 206, 207, 208, 217, 222, 226, 228, 235, 257, 280, 288, 299, 300, 301, 316, 370, 374, 384
philosophy 22, 24, 30, 32, 36, 47, 74–75, 78–79, 82–83, 101, 116, 160–161, 212, 244, 247, 314, 317, 361
physical. *See* material 9, 22, 23, 25, 50, 59, 70, 76, 77, 78, 98, 102, 104, 143, 145, 171, 210, 211, 212, 213, 277, 306, 307, 308, 327, 328, 340, 344, 347, 348, 350, 351, 352, 359, 360, 365, 366, 367, 368, 369, 370

Pirsig, Robert 161–163
plainchant. *See* chant 49, 261, 301, 361, 362
Plato 46, 49
poetry 43–44, 92, 113–114, 261
popular music. *See* music, popular 110, 194
postmodernism 15
post-pandemic 305–307, 309, 314–315, 322, 326, 368
power
  of music 35, 41, 44–46, 48, 342
practices 5–6, 21, 42, 57, 86, 139, 141–142, 159, 170–171, 178, 193, 205, 207, 249, 258, 273, 278, 283, 288, 292, 295, 305, 309, 327, 350, 353, 355, 359, 362, 374, 387–388, 395
prayer 6, 15–16, 46, 50, 55, 62, 64, 67–69, 82, 84, 88, 145, 157, 195, 238, 275, 278–280, 282, 292–294, 297, 299–300, 316, 340, 343, 357, 379, 395
psalm/psalmody 39–40, 45, 53, 62–63, 200, 292, 301, 321, 369–370, 374–376
psychology 1–2, 4, 30, 85, 91–93, 106, 129, 139, 143, 145–150, 152–156, 164, 167–168, 173–174, 176, 178–179, 217, 275–276, 282, 287, 290, 306, 390, 392–394
Pythagoras 43

race 7, 224, 341, 375
Rahner, Karl 237–238, 242–243
reality 8, 22–23, 26–27, 34–35, 38, 41, 53–54, 74–75, 92, 96, 102, 104, 106–107, 114–115, 117–118, 143, 160–163, 205, 207–209, 213, 216–217, 223, 228, 231, 233–234, 236, 238, 245–247, 251, 285, 287–288, 346, 349, 356–357, 359–360, 362, 364, 370, 388, 391, 397
reason, rationality 32, 39, 56–57, 59, 70, 73–74, 81–85, 97–99, 101, 103, 112–114, 116–117, 120, 122, 133–134, 163, 196, 230, 234, 244, 262, 264, 281, 289–290, 294, 357
reductionism 21, 23–25, 34, 346
re-enchantment 298–299
reflexive thematic analysis 306, 310, 313

religion 1–2, 4–7, 9, 11, 49, 83, 85, 87–96, 106–108, 110–111, 119, 123, 125–126, 128, 132–134, 139–143, 145–146, 150, 153–156, 163, 170–171, 178, 193, 195–201, 203, 205, 230, 234, 239, 253, 265, 273, 283, 295, 297–298, 303, 306, 338, 341, 349, 360, 376, 379, 395
religious experience. *See* experience: religious 129, 159, 200, 201, 202, 203, 240, 243, 276, 301, 323
repertoire 199, 280–281, 320, 338, 358, 361–365, 368–369, 374, 377–378, 383–385, 387
resonance 21, 33, 156, 211, 215, 231, 249, 266, 268, 270, 299, 334, 337, 339–340, 344, 370, 387, 397
revelation 65–67, 81, 114, 222, 236, 238–240, 243, 250, 254, 269, 308, 333, 339–340
rhythm 31–33, 38, 43–44, 46, 92, 98, 100, 104, 134, 141–142, 144, 148, 165, 176, 180, 195, 207, 225, 241, 262, 334, 384
Rihm, Wolfgang 255–256, 263–268
Rijken, Hanna 285, 292, 296–299, 302
ritual. *See also* liturgy 58, 64, 69, 141, 142, 146, 160, 163, 164, 165, 166, 167, 168, 169, 170, 171, 172, 174, 175, 178, 180, 181, 184, 186, 187, 188, 189, 190, 191, 197, 198, 199, 253, 273, 275, 276, 296, 297, 298, 302, 303, 307, 391, 397
romanticism 199
Routley, Erik 385
rugby 11, 319, 372, 374, 377–379, 384, 386, 388

sacrament 55–56, 64–65, 68–69, 73, 123, 132–134, 236, 238, 250, 253, 301, 307–308, 359–360
sacred 1–2, 5–6, 9, 16, 29, 37, 42, 44–46, 49–50, 91, 111, 139, 141–142, 147, 149, 175, 193–197, 199–201, 206–207, 253, 269, 273, 275, 280, 285, 298–303, 315, 317, 323–324, 353, 361–363, 379, 390, 392
Schafer, R. Murray 216
Schmitz, Hermann 209, 214–215

science 4, 9, 23–24, 48, 56, 77, 87–96, 99–101, 105–108, 111, 113, 126, 139, 141, 143, 145–146, 149, 151–153, 155–157, 160–161, 201, 219, 234, 239, 248, 277, 390, 392
Scotland 360–362, 366
scripture 28, 36–37, 40, 49–50, 57, 68, 101, 236, 239, 306, 355–356, 395
Scruton, Roger 77–81
secular 6, 10, 111–113, 117, 124, 129, 133, 155, 157, 193, 197–201, 203–208, 279, 299, 303, 306, 324, 336, 377, 379–380
self 33, 35, 45, 61–62, 74–75, 80, 82, 98, 102, 106, 115–116, 125, 133, 139, 145–147, 149, 156, 165–166, 178, 180, 220, 236–237, 245–246, 282, 286, 289–295, 301–302, 333, 339, 372–373, 390, 396
sensation 160, 222, 224, 226, 230
sense 9, 21–23, 27, 29, 31–32, 34–36, 38, 42, 47, 60, 69, 74–75, 77–81, 83–85, 87, 94, 96, 98, 100–101, 103–104, 107, 112–113, 115–119, 122, 129, 131–132, 139, 141, 145, 148–149, 155–156, 161–163, 165–166, 174, 178, 180, 194, 198–199, 202, 208, 210, 212–214, 217–218, 221, 223, 225–226, 229, 231, 239, 242–243, 248–249, 253, 289, 292–295, 300–301, 303, 311, 316, 327, 334, 338, 340–343, 346, 348–349, 359, 365–367, 369, 379, 385–389, 393
sense-making 27, 32, 35, 75
sexuality 7, 252, 258
silence 13–17, 44, 46, 49, 61, 167
sin 36, 102–103
singing. *See also* choir, choral 5, 9, 29, 30, 40, 55, 56, 57, 60, 61, 63, 64, 69, 70, 71, 93, 96, 102, 142, 145, 148, 149, 153, 156, 178, 195, 202, 203, 206, 216, 229, 249, 264, 270, 274, 275, 276, 277, 278, 279, 280, 281, 282, 296, 301, 308, 309, 318, 321, 342, 348, 362, 363, 364, 365, 366, 367, 368, 369, 370, 372, 373, 374, 375, 377, 378, 379, 381, 383, 384, 385, 386, 387, 388, 396
Sloboda, John 4, 7, 11, 150, 269, 389, 395
Small, Christopher 3–4, 30, 91, 114, 233, 235, 247, 361

social media 316, 327, 378
social psychology/sociology 33, 110, 146–147, 149, 153–155, 287, 290, 292, 329, 392
sonic 6, 16–17, 126, 139, 164, 166–168, 173–175, 177–181, 195–199, 207–208, 216, 222, 364
soundscape 215–216, 291
Spirit. *See* Holy Spirit 9, 35, 38, 40, 55, 57, 58, 59, 60, 62, 63, 64, 65, 66, 67, 68, 69, 70, 71, 97, 107, 110, 111, 116, 117, 129, 189, 190, 191, 194, 199, 200, 201, 202, 203, 204, 205, 206, 208, 230, 236, 238, 239, 240, 246, 328, 329, 331, 332, 333, 334, 335, 336, 337, 338, 340, 342, 344, 345, 346, 347, 348, 351, 352, 353, 375
spirituality, spiritualities
  definitions of 45
sporting 11, 371–372, 377, 379, 383–385, 387
Stearns, Chelle 93, 112, 121
Steiner, George 26, 35, 115
Stimmung 117, 131, 210–212, 215
subjective 45–46, 109, 145, 152–153, 160, 162–164, 167, 173, 205, 213–214, 222, 234, 243, 276, 290, 313, 318
Sufism 140–141, 155
supernatural. *See* transcendence 9, 54, 91, 118, 124, 165, 336
Swinton, John 8
symbol/symbolism 69, 91, 112, 115–117, 119–120, 123, 126, 134, 154, 209, 212, 221, 228, 247, 249, 254, 260–261, 266, 360
synesthesia 212

Tavener, John 16
Taylor, Charles 27, 33, 109, 112–113, 117–119, 123–125, 129, 132, 289, 299, 308
tempo 10, 126, 173, 177, 194–195
temporality 173, 177, 181, 212
text. *See also* lyrics 9, 28, 29, 34, 35, 37, 40, 45, 46, 49, 50, 53, 57, 58, 63, 64, 66, 68, 83, 162, 222, 225, 253, 268,

275, 278, 282, 292, 329, 338, 375, 376, 377, 379, 380, 381, 382, 383, 389, 392
theology 2–3, 6–8, 22, 29, 34–38, 55–57, 59–60, 62–63, 66, 70, 75, 85, 88–90, 92–95, 99–103, 105–107, 110–112, 114, 116–117, 120, 128, 140–141, 163, 170, 178, 196–197, 199, 201, 207, 210–211, 221, 230, 234–239, 241–248, 250–252, 299, 305, 307–308, 328–329, 335, 346, 359, 372, 377, 386, 389, 391
theomusicology 92
tintinnabuli 50–52
Titon, Jeff Todd 193, 200–203, 206
tonality 48, 92, 121, 215, 217–219, 241
tradition 2–3, 5–6, 16, 22–23, 25–26, 29, 36, 39, 51, 53, 58, 63–64, 71, 77, 79, 83–84, 89, 94, 101, 109–113, 117–120, 122–123, 125, 128–129, 132–134, 141, 148, 160, 162–163, 167, 169–170, 182, 186, 189, 193–194, 197, 199–200, 206, 212, 218, 221, 229–230, 239, 241, 247, 253, 277–278, 280, 285, 296, 302, 307, 309–310, 312, 314–315, 317, 321, 324, 326, 330–332, 342–343, 349, 352–353, 355, 362, 378–379, 387, 390, 396
trance 5, 10, 159–160, 164–181, 199, 204
trance music. *See* music, trance 179
transcendence 3, 29, 35, 45, 74–77, 81, 86, 97, 106, 111, 117, 124, 133, 139, 143, 145–146, 152, 178, 204–205, 236, 269, 286–295, 299, 302, 308, 338
transformation 42, 83–85, 106, 210, 245, 257–258, 267, 286, 290–291, 293–295, 297, 303, 327, 332, 334, 338, 340, 346, 353, 361

transience 229, 291
trauma 7, 223, 250
Trinity 60–62, 87, 97, 99–100, 103, 105, 107, 237, 266, 331, 333, 336
truth 2–3, 27–28, 33, 35–37, 46, 60, 67, 71, 83, 85, 96, 115, 117, 121, 161–162, 202, 220, 234, 236, 238, 242–245, 247, 253, 259, 336, 364, 393
Turkey 5, 184

United Kingdom 150, 263, 329, 377–378

Vatican II 250
Von Bingen, Hildegard 57

Wales 371–373, 377–379, 384, 396
wellbeing 5–7, 75, 110–111, 215, 276–277, 289, 293, 295, 301, 334, 346, 360
Wesley, Charles 374–378, 380, 383, 385
Williams, Rowan 37, 40, 44, 61, 178
worship 1, 5, 8, 10–11, 35, 55–57, 59, 61–62, 68–71, 93, 140–141, 157, 194–196, 204–205, 207, 229, 249, 253, 271, 273–283, 285, 290, 293, 295, 299, 301, 305–310, 312–330, 332, 334, 336–353, 355, 357–358, 360–361, 366–367, 389–391, 393, 395–397
worship service 1, 71, 205, 249, 280, 282, 305, 348, 361

YouTube 1, 50, 149, 182–186, 194, 316, 327, 329–330, 337, 341, 348, 379

About the Team

Alessandra Tosi was the managing editor for this book.

This manuscript was proof-read by Adèle Kreager and indexed by Anja Pritchard.

The authors created the Alt-text.

Jeevanjot Kaur Nagpal designed the cover. The cover was produced in InDesign using the Fontin font.

Cameron Craig typeset the book in InDesign and produced the paperback and hardback editions. The main text font is Tex Gyre Pagella. The heading font is Californian FB.

Cameron also produced the PDF and HTML editions. The conversion was performed with open-source software and other tools freely available on our GitHub page at https://github.com/OpenBookPublishers.

Jeremy Bowman created the EPUB.

This book was peer-reviewed by Professor Bettina Schmidt and an anonymous referee. Experts in their field, these readers give their time freely to help ensure the academic rigour of our books. We are grateful for their generous and invaluable contributions.

This book need not end here...

Share

All our books — including the one you have just read — are free to access online so that students, researchers and members of the public who can't afford a printed edition will have access to the same ideas. This title will be accessed online by hundreds of readers each month across the globe: why not share the link so that someone you know is one of them?

This book and additional content is available at:
https://doi.org/10.11647/OBP.0403

Donate

Open Book Publishers is an award-winning, scholar-led, not-for-profit press making knowledge freely available one book at a time. We don't charge authors to publish with us: instead, our work is supported by our library members and by donations from people who believe that research shouldn't be locked behind paywalls.

Why not join them in freeing knowledge by supporting us:
https://www.openbookpublishers.com/support-us

Follow @OpenBookPublish

Read more at the Open Book Publishers BLOG

You may also be interested in:

Annunciations
Sacred Music for the Twenty-First Century
George Corbett

https://doi.org/10.11647/obp.0172

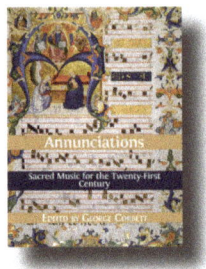

Classical Music
Contemporary Perspectives and Challenges
Michael Beckerman and Paul Boghossian

https://doi.org/10.11647/obp.0242

The Power of Music
An Exploration of the Evidence
Susan Hallam and Evangelos Himonides

https://doi.org/10.11647/obp.0292

www.ingramcontent.com/pod-product-compliance
Lightning Source LLC
Chambersburg PA
CBHW062025290426
44108CB00025B/2777